the book of family therapy

〜〜〜〜〜〜〜〜〜〜〜〜〜〜〜〜〜〜〜〜〜〜〜〜〜〜〜〜

the book
of
family therapy

~~~~~~

Andrew Ferber
Marilyn Mendelsohn
Augustus Napier

Science House

1972

We got here through the grace of our parents.
We get by with the help of our friends.
We go on for the future of our children.

contributors ⋀⋀⋀⋀⋀⋀⋀⋀⋀⋀⋀⋀⋀⋀⋀⋀⋀⋀⋀⋀⋀⋀⋀⋀⋀⋀⋀⋀⋀⋀⋀

Carolyn Attneave, Ph.D.

Assistant Professor Tufts University
School of Medicine
88 Marion Street
Brookline, Massachusetts 02146

Edgar (Dick) Auerswald, M.D.

Director of Clinical Services
Jewish Family Service
33 West 60th Street
New York, New York 10023

C. Christian Beels, M.D.

Supervisor, Family Studies Section
Bronx State Hospital *
Assistant Professor of Psychiatry
Albert Einstein College of Medicine **

Arthur Bodin, Ph.D.

Research Associate
Mental Research Institute ***

Ivan Boszormenyi-Nagy, M.D.

Eastern Pennsylvania Psychiatric
Institute
Henry Avenue and Abbottsford Road
Philadelphia, Pennsylvania 19129

Andrew Ferber, M.D.

Director, Family Studies Section
Bronx State Hospital *
Assistant Professor of Psychiatry
Albert Einstein College of Medicine **

Richard Fisch, M.D.

Director of the Brief Therapy Center
Mental Research Institute ***

Thomas Fogarty, M.D.

Supervisor, Family Studies Section
Bronx State Hospital *
Associate Professor
St. John's University Graduate School
Clinical Instructor in Psychiatry
Albert Einstein College of Medicine **

Laurence Greenhill, M.D.

Resident in Psychiatry
Albert Einstein College of Medicine
Russo Building
1165 Morris Park Avenue
Bronx, New York 10461

Philip J. Guerin, Jr., M.D.

Family Studies Section
Bronx State Hospital *
Albert Einstein College of Medicine **
Consultant in Family and College
Psychiatry
Student Counseling Center
Fordham University

Jay Haley, M.A.

Philadelphia Child Guidance Clinic
1700 Bainbridge Street
Philadelphia, Pennsylvania 19141
Past Editor, *Family Process*
Palo Alto, California

Adam Kendon, D. Phil. (Oxon)

Research Scientist
Project on Human Communication
Bronx State Hospital *

H. Peter Laqueur, M.D.

Associate Professor of Clinical
Psychiatry
University of Vermont Medical
College

	Director, Family Study and Treatment Unit
	Vermont State Hospital
	Waterbury, Vermont 05676

Harry Mendelsohn, M.D.   Supervisor, Family Studies Section
                          Bronx State Hospital *
                          Assistant Clinical Professor of
                          Psychiatry
                          Albert Einstein College of Medicine **

Marilyn Mendelsohn, M.S.W.   Supervisor, Family Studies Section
                              Bronx State Hospital *
                              Assistant Clinical Professor of
                              Psychiatry (Social Work)
                              Albert Einstein College of Medicine **

Augustus Napier, Ph.D.   Director, Family Therapy Training
                          Wisconsin Children's Treatment
                          Center
                          3418 Harper Road
                          Madison, Wisconsin 53704

Richard Rabkin, M.D.   234 East 68th Street
                        New York, New York 10021

Jules M. Ranz, M.D.   Acting Medical Director
                       Tremont Crisis Center
                       Albert Einstein College of Medicine
                       Residency Training Program
                       Supervisor, Family Studies Section
                       Bronx State Hospital *

Fred M. Sander, M.D.   Supervisor, Family Studies Section
                        Bronx State Hospital *
                        Assistant Professor of Psychiatry
                        Albert Einstein College of Medicine **

Albert Scheflen, M.D.   Director, Project on Human
                         Communication
                         Bronx State Hospital *
                         Jewish Family Service
                         Professor of Psychiatry
                         Albert Einstein College of Medicine **

Ross V. Speck, M.D.   Fellow, Center for the Study of Social
                       Change
                       New York City
                       221 Delancey Street
                       Philadelphia, Pennsylvania 19106

Paul Watzlawick, Ph.D.   Research Associate
                          Mental Research Institute ***
                          Clinical Assistant Professor
                          Department of Psychiatry
                          Stanford University

John Weakland, Ch.E.   Associate Director,
                        Brief Therapy Center
                        Mental Research Institute ***

Carl Whitaker, M.D.   Professor of Psychiatry
                       University of Wisconsin Medical
                       School
                       1300 University Avenue
                       Madison, Wisconsin

*   1500 Waters Place, Bronx, New York 10461
**   1300 Morris Park Avenue, Bronx, New York 10461
*** 555 Middlefield Road, Palo Alto, California 94301

~~~~~~ *acknowledgments*

Chapter four: Edited transcript of the American Orthopsychiatric Meeting, New York City, Spring, 1969.

Chapter five: This paper was given at a divisional meeting
of the American Psychiatric Association in New York on
November 17, 1967.

Chapter six: This work was begun under the sponsorship
of the Adult Psychiatry Branch, NIMH, Bethesda. We
wish to thank Dr. Lyman Wynne and Dr. Israel Zwerling
for their help and encouragement, and Donald Bloch,
M.D., Editor of *Family Process,* in which the original
version of this chapter appeared under the title "Family
Therapy: A View," September, 1969, Vol. 8, No. 2.

Chapter nine: Adapted from *Studies in Self-Cognition:
Techniques of Video-Tape Self-Observation in the
Behavioral Sciences,* Ed. Robert H. Geertsma. Originally
printed in *J. of Nervous and Mental Disease,* Vol. 148,
No. 3, pp. 251-261. 1969.

Chapter ten: We wish to thank Donald Bloch, M.D., Editor,
Family Process, in which the original version of this
chapter appeared under the title "A Didactic Course for
Family Therapy," December, 1970, Vol. 9, No. 4.

Chapter eighteen: We especially acknowledge the helpful
additions suggested by Barbara Lewis, M.S.W., Rodman
Hill, Ph. D., and Albert Scheflen, M.D.

Chapter twenty: The authors are indebted to Andy Ferber
who manipulated them into writing this paper. Most of
all, they are indebted to Milton H. Erickson, M.D., whose
creative work over 35 years has opened up new pathways
in humane manipulation.

Chapter twenty-two: By special arrangement this article
will also appear in *Changing Families,* Jay Haley, Editor,
Grune and Stratton, 1971.

Chapter twenty-three: We would like to thank Adele
Gottlieb, Judith Lessinger, Myrna Rubin, Dorothy
Kitchell, Dr. Julia Lichenstein, and Ray Pitt for their
excellent comments and library research on these issues.

please read this preface
〰〰〰〰〰〰〰〰〰〰〰〰〰〰〰〰〰〰〰〰〰〰〰〰〰〰〰〰〰〰〰

The Book of Family Therapy is for: people who are becoming family therapists; teachers of family therapy; experienced family therapists; prospective patients for family therapy; friends and relations of the authors; and do-it-yourself family therapists. It is for those of you who are interested in psychotherapy as part of the growing edge of western culture.

The book presents what and where I think family therapy is today. Most chapters are collaborative products by two or more of the authors. Those chapters not collaboratively written were circulated amongst the several authors while they were being written. Furthermore, most of the authors are familiar with the work of most of the other authors. They visit with one another, gossip, and trade notes regularly. It is a personal book, rather than a handbook. Whereas some writers of textbooks and handbooks assign specific topics to authors, I chose authors and said, "Write about what you are interested in now."

WHO IS RESPONSIBLE FOR THIS BOOK?

I decided to do this book in the spring of 1969 when I realized I was becoming more interested in research on natural family processes than in training family therapists. If I could collect and present my experience of the past six years as a teacher, I would feel free to become a researcher. And I wanted the status in the field that a good book might bring. I asked Chris Beels to edit it with me, but he begged off on the grounds of being too busy with other things. Marilyn Mendelsohn gave me a cautious o.k., depending on what the outline looked like. We called and wrote to the prospective authors in November, 1969. The outline of the book was accepted by Science House in the winter of 1970. We had hoped to have the book in press by the spring of 1971, but it took one year longer than that.

The rest of this preface is a portrait of the relationships between the people who made this book possible and me.

ISRAEL ZWERLING AND NATHAN ACKERMAN

Israel Zwerling is director of the Bronx State Hospital and a professor of psychiatry at the Albert Einstein College of Medicine. When I was a first-year resident (1960) I went to Iz and asked him how I could become a family therapist. He said that I should learn individual therapy first, and then come back and talk to him. I immediately started treating families and asked him for supervision. When I finished my fellowship in social psychiatry (1964), I asked him for a

job. He said, "You be head of the Family Studies Section."
I said, "Thank you. Who will my boss be?" He said, "You
are the boss." I said, "That's a grown-up's job." He said,
"There are only three or four grown-ups in the country
better than you, and none of them want the job." Since
then he has been my sponsor and protector. My job is to
develop innovative teaching and service programs based on
family and other natural social systems. We have a fight
every year that is both a difference of opinion over where
and how to introduce family therapy, and a father-son battle.
This book and the Family Studies Section could not exist
without the continued support and protection of Israel and
Florence Zwerling.

Nathan Ackerman was Iz Zwerling's training analyst,
friend, and teacher. Nat spent one day a month with the
Family Studies Section from 1963 through 1967. During
that time he gave me the courage to do things my other
teachers had taught me should not be done. He told me he
would like to put a finger up my ass and shake it hard to
loosen me up. He succeeded beyond his wildest dreams. A
three-year scrap followed, which he perceived as my being
rebellious and I perceived as my establishing my own autonomy. We were able to reconcile most of our differences the
week before he died, and I miss what I believe might have
come from a continued relationship with Nat. He read an
early draft of this book and found it messy, sprawling, and
too reflective of the diverse trends in the family field. It did
not represent his point of view enough, he said, and he
refused to write a preface.

HOME: THE FAMILY STUDIES SECTION, BRONX STATE
HOSPITAL

When the Family Studies Section started I had one
colleague, Marilyn Mendelsohn. She had been co-therapist,
co-teacher, co-author, constant companion, family advisor,
and close personal friend since that time. She is my closest
woman friend.

27

Chris Beels and I became friendly when he married Margaret Beels, who had gone out with several of my medical school buddies. He was a resident at Einstein, one year behind me. During his three years at NIMH we worked collaboratively on *Family Therapy: A View* and developed a deepening friendship between our two families. Iz Zwerling liked Chris, too, and as soon as Chris grew restive in Washington, Iz and I offered him a job at the Family Studies Section. Since then, he and I have run the Family Studies Section with Marilyn, who dropped out for a few years to have and raise her children. Chris and I function as a brother team, where I am his yes-man and he is my no-man. We are best friends, and it is hard to imagine life without him. Over the past two years we have both moved into designing and developing a new psychiatric training program based on family level intervention in natural systems. These are now being tried at the Tremont Crisis Center, Bronx State Hospital Residency Track, and on the family ward at Bronx State Hospital. Simultaneously we have also become deeply involved in natural history method analyses of films of family therapy and family life. Chris works very closely in his research with Jane Ferber, my wife, and I am doing co-therapy with Margaret Beels, Chris' wife.

Fred Sander was a medical student taking an elective at the day hospital when I was a third-year resident there (1963). We were neighbors for three years, and our families have become increasingly close. We have worked together closely for several years, but have followed somewhat different paths since he entered psychoanalytic training. Fred's forte, to my mind, is his ability to take a position outside a social system and see its historical continuities and strains.

Harry Mendelsohn is Marilyn's husband. We worked together in a seminar on how to supervise, and developed an enormous respect for each other's work. He is also very close to Jane and myself personally and is one of our chief counselors when we get into hang-ups with our extended families. This year, Harry, Marilyn, Jane, and myself are in a couples group made up of couples treating families. Harry is one of the first people I refer my relatives to when they ask for a therapist.

Larry Greenhill worked with me as a medical-student research assistant, and then asked me to supervise him when he was doing family therapy as an intern. It was our work together that was longitudinally watched by the seminar that Harry and I wrote up. He is now back at Einstein.

Julie Ranz was a fellow in social psychiatry (1969-71). We worked together as co-therapists and then wrote the "How to Succeed in Family Therapy" chapter. We also play recorder duets together. Julie now works full time at the Tremont Crisis Center.

Richard Rabkin worked with us for one year. His intellectual pyrotechnics were much appreciated, but we could not achieve a satisfactory working arrangement.

Norman Ackerman, Lawrence Grolnick, Marvin Nierenber, Rod Hill, Barbara Lewis, Ernest Kovacs, and Peter Caffentzis are other member affiliates of the Family Studies Section who participate in the development of our ideas, read and comment on drafts of papers, and make work a pleasure instead of a chore.

Peter Laqueur saved me and a group of other people at a workshop from a very embarrassing bad scene, by coming in out of the hall and taking over the leadership of the meeting when I got caught in a power struggle. Marilyn and I have watched him operate in groups, heard him present his own personal experiences as a double agent in Holland during World War II, and heard about his work which produces results with persons most family therapists write off as impossible. I feel Peter is one of the few old men of family therapy I can trust for leadership and guidance without repression.

BEING AND BECOMING A FAMILY THERAPIST

Chuck Cramer brought together Carl Whitaker, Art

29

Leader, Murray Bowen, Ivan Nagy, and me for a workshop at the Chicago Ortho meetings in 1968. It was terrific. The magic of this group has lasted for four years, with Art Leader and Murray Bowen dropping out and Fred and Bunny Duhl joining in. Chuck and I, after the power struggle in the 1969 conference, have become close colleagues and good friends. We have moved to the point where we agree on almost everything, after being at polar loggerheads on so many issues two years ago. We do not understand it, but are happy with it. Our wives dig each other too.

CARL, GUS, MURIEL, AND MARGARET

At the 1968 Ortho meetings, Carl and I role-played a family in which he was the therapist and I was the psychotic child. I fell in love with his oak-like solidity of character and I think he became enchanted by my ability to be three places at the same time and to move social groups out of their accustomed format. Carl, Jane, and I talked for hours that night at Chuck Cramer's house. Late that evening there was an informal meeting that Nat Ackerman called to try to discuss the formation of a national organization of family therapists. Carl, Norman Paul, and Murray Bowen led a crazy deterrent move that successfully scuttled the issue for another year. Leaving the meeting, Carl said, "First you become a judo master and learn to destroy your opponent with your own strength; then you become a jujitsu master and learn to destroy your opponent with his strength; then you become a kedo master and learn to dodge your opponent until he falls exhausted into your arms and becomes your friend." Jane and I both fell in love with Carl and his wife Muriel. After three years of this hysterical transference on our part Carl and Muriel announced to us that they didn't want to be our parents, but might try us as friends. When I got up off the floor two days later, I realized one didn't have to be in therapy to be in analysis, and that it was probably nicer to be a grown-up than a kid, anyhow. I still think Carl

Whitaker is the greatest therapist in America. He couldn't do it without Muriel.

We met Gus and Margaret Napier when we were visiting the University of Wisconsin Department of Psychiatry in January of 1969. Gus is a colleague, co-therapist, ex-student, and friend of Carl's. When he is not trying to disentangle himself from that complicated relationship, he is a beautiful therapist and an exquisite writer. When he thought he was going to leave Wisconsin he came by the Bronx for job interviews, and we offered him a job. He refused, but we got to like each other better. Marilyn and I brought him in on the book because we wanted at least one of us to be a good writer and we needed an eye from outside our own social system to comment on the proceedings. Gus did both of these things, and became a good friend on the side. Jane and I repair to Wisconsin yearly to get our heads together and try out new ideas. I suspect that Wisconsin likes us because we bring some new information to their somewhat ultra-stable social system.

MURRAY BOWEN, PHIL GUERIN, TOM FOGARTY

Murray Bowen and Iz Zwerling knew each other through the GAP Committee on the Family. Marilyn invited Murray to visit us in 1966. He handled every situation magnificently, and preached his usual sermon about getting to know your own family on a *personal* basis rather than the same old two-step. It took me three years to start to practice what Murray preached. I see Murray as the foxy grandpa in family therapy and its best strategic thinker. I don't know what he thinks of me, but I'm going to find out.

In 1967 Murray sent us Phil Guerin, who had been a student (disciple) of his at Georgetown. Phil brought the powerhouse to the Family Studies Section. Now that Phil is running our training program, much to Beels' and Ferber's relief, it is finally being well-administered. He will be a great department chairman someday. He would be pope,

31

if the church were only smart enough and changed a few rules. I think he sees me as an uncle of some sort who helps counteract the religious indoctrination he gets from his daddy Murray Bowen. Tom Fogarty is Phil's big brother. Phil brought Tom around for a job in 1968 and we took an immediate shine to each other. Tom's great sense of humor, absolutely independent position on every issue, and intolerance for bullshit make him invaluable at the Family Section. He refuses to take seriously the mass hysteria that occasionally sweeps over me and the rest of the group.

JAY HALEY, ART BODIN, JOHN WEAKLAND,
PAUL WATZLAWICK, DICK FISCH

Jay Haley and I first met when he was a guest at the day hospital, coming as an old friend of Iz Zwerling. Marilyn and I asked him for a consultation on a family we had been stagnating with for two years. He said that he would be glad to pass the time of day with them, although he didn't think it would be of much use. He saw them in what was a standard consultation interview. For five years I have found Jay irritating, fascinating, always helpful, always right, and always not quite complete. He has been a persistent gadfly, generous with criticism, stingy with praise, fun at the right distance, but opaque up close. He introduced me to Art Bodin, John Weakland, Paul Watzlawick, and Dick Fisch, his erstwhile colleagues at the brief therapy center of MRI. Though I find each of these men, none of whom I know very well, different persons, when they are working or talking professionally I feel the presence of Don Jackson hovering above them and Gregory Bateson off in the distance. I value this group's irreverence, irony, and intellectual rodomontade. Talking with them sometimes reminds me of what we would look like to the Martians.

AL SCHEFLEN, ADAM KENDON

Al Scheflen was brought to Bronx State by Iz Zwerling

in 1969. At that time my experience in family research and family therapy had led me to feel acutely dissatisfied with psychoanalytic, experimental, psychological, and social science descriptions and explanations for the processes I had been part of. Al has been a great teacher to me. He taught me the natural history method of thinking about and analyzing human behavior. He is also a fantastic gossip, and has stories that help destroy my myths about much of psychiatry and America. On a clear day with Al you can see fifty years into the future. I am his disciple, audience, apostle, and skeptical little brother. We are each other's occasional psychotherapist, and I do some of the administrative work that he loathes. Al Scheflen, Adam Kendon, and the Family Studies Section have offices on the same floor at Bronx State.

Adam Kendon was brought to Bronx State by Al Scheflen. We have worked together several times a week for two and a half years, looking at films and videotapes of human behavior and mapping in detail some of the territory that Al Scheflen, Greg Bateson, and Ray Birdwhistell have mapped in general and broad strokes. We are a complementary fox and hedgehog team who share a fascination for describing things as they really are. I have enjoyed my work with Adam more than any other job in the past three years.

EDGAR (DICK) AUERSWALD, FRED DUHL,
ROSS SPECK, CAROLYN ATTNEAVE

Dick Auerswald has been my colleague at the Family Council, my mother-in-law's colleague at Gouverneur Hospital in New York, my wife's boss and sponsor at Jewish Family Service in New York, a co-leader of workshops, and a friend. He introduced me to Fred Duhl.

Fred and Bunny Duhl quickly became friends with Jane and me. Fred and I form a producer-director team for family extravaganzas. He promised a piece on role-playing and psychodrama for the book but could not find time in his overcommitted schedule to do it. I hope he (we) slow down a little.

33

Fred and Dick and Al Scheflen helped me understand the perilous and interdependent condition of the species as it now exists. Each time any two or more of us would get together in 1969-70, we would hold agonizing discourses on the probably forthcoming apocalypse, and leave ourselves feeling depressed and hopeless. We now share the strange world view that it is quite possible that a few of us may form a sense of community and personal understanding just in time to participate in the accidental destruction of civilization as we now know it. And then again, we may survive. This urgency about the future of the species makes many of the concerns we were raised to be worried about seem less pressing, and is a liberation in that respect. This group introduced me to Ross Speck, and he to Carolyn Attneave. These two messengers of hope share a vision of a tribal and yet global society that is personal rather than bureaucratic. If the people in the Family Studies Section are my brothers and sisters, Dick, Fred, and Al are my kissing cousins.

SCIENCE HOUSE

Richard Rabkin referred me to Jason Aronson, his friend, who is the owner and publisher of Science House. Jason understood the idea behind this book, accepted it, encouraged it, and gave his support to breaks with prior traditions in order to get the idea across. The rest of his staff were also very kind to us. Jennifer Mellen, the managing editor at Science House, especially adored the book. Her enthusiasm and incredible dedication to helping us bring it out in the form we wanted brought me along at a time when enthusiasm might have flagged.

DOROTHY KITCHELL, MYRNA RUBIN, ADELE HERMAN, ELMETA PHILLIPS, IRENE PISACANO, JOHN SCHOONBECK

These are people who have done so much of the hard work that goes unacknowledged in a book like this. Dorothy, Myrna, and Adele formed a team who organized correspondence, typed, read, and edited manuscripts and provided enthusiastic and critical support as the book began to take shape. They were the first readers, and it was their reactions more than anyone else's that helped reshape both the structure and the details as the drafts began to come through.

Dorothy found me through a friend and came to the Section to learn family therapy three years ago. She offered free work in return for training. She has become a co-therapist, colleague, and co-researcher since then.

Myrna first met Jane when they both had children in the same nursery school class and had to sit with them during the first months. She then became a research assistant in the Section and has since gone on to social work school. We have become co-therapists and our families have become fast friends.

Adele came to the Section as a research assistant, referred by an ex-teacher and colleague of mine, and stayed to become a co-therapist, neighbor, and friend. She has just married Julie Ranz's brother-in-law.

Elmeta Phillips is a neighbor and friend. She is the administrative secretary of the Family Studies Section and the gatekeeper between the rest of the world and me in my personal life. She organizes my life and the life of the Section so that we may appear casual and disorganized in our everyday function. She and Irene Pisacano have done much of the typing, mimeographing, mailing, and other secretarial work involved in the book. In addition to secretarial work they have made coffee, held hands, been cheerful, and generally kept the climate pleasant so that the Family Studies Section could grow.

After Myrna left for social work school, John Schoonbeck came to work for us as a research assistant. He was Jane's colleague and friend at the West Side Crisis Unit of Jewish Family Service. John specifically brought his brilliant literary and critical faculties to bear on the later portions of the book. He has helped Jane and me understand what has happened to people under thirty in the last ten years, and incorporate some of the changes into our own life-style. I

35

think we have increased his options.

JANE, JOSHUA, AND ELIZABETH

Joshua, my son, is now seven. I told him I was writing a book about family therapy and he said, "Tell them that parents should be nice to children, shouldn't fight together too much, and shouldn't leave one another."

It is impossible for any of us to be in a bad mood for more than fifteen minutes when Elizabeth (age four) is around. She simply instructs us to stop fighting as she will not tolerate it. If we do not listen to her she raises a rumpus, then cries until we realize how ridiculously we are behaving.

Jane is the most important person in my life in these last fourteen years. Everything that I have contributed to this book either came from her, developed with her, or was experienced by us before I realized it. Almost everyone I know, she knows. She corrects many of my faults in judgment and makes up for most of my bad conduct with the other people in my network. My marriage is my greatest source of strength, comfort, and joy.

A. Ferber
October, 1971

What Is a Family Therapist?

one
the primary task

A. Napier

First, we are a generation, creatures of our time, and only then of our own histories. And the time, whatever else it is, is alive.

The time is open: the compulsion to confess has seized a people and the interior person is emerging. Emotions and acts that have been covert since history began are being worn like vivid, new cloth. The time is charged with the energy of people in confrontation: black and white, women and men, old and young, radical and conservative. The sexual revolution, largely accomplished, at least in behavior, may be mere practice for the anger revolution that is in process. The time is confused: authority, and its verbal dress, orthodoxy, are in disarray. It would be difficult to find an area where there is an accepted order, where multiple ideologies do not compete angrily and anxiously. The time is now: history is in disrepute, the future is untrustworthy, We largely acknowledge that life is an emergent process, that our era is unique and nothing human ever fully repeatable, and that the outcome for man may be tragic. There has probably never been a more existential moment. The time cries aloud: myself, now; the demand, not appeal, for equality is insistent, powerful, sometimes childish, hopeful, and is a final revulsion against the Christian ideal of self-denial, taking at last the idea of human democracy with tenacity.

And the time is getting it all together, all the parts, somehow. Personally: anger and sex and tenderness and illusionment and disillusionment crowd toward the center; people want to be all they are, and not in moderation, but cyclically — fully angry, fully tender, each in its time and turn. As a people: we are sensing at last the unit, the whole, the world. We have fallen hard on the realization of our ultimate dependence on our environment; if it is to nurture us, we must live within its systems. Going is the illusion that the rugged individual, or the tight nuclear family, or the aggressive corporation, or the powerful country, times n, could cut its swath forever with solitary purpose and impunity. Our purposes are joint, juxtaposed, shared — all people, all creatures. Our having to face our relatedness to the physical systems of the planet may provide a model for confronting the complexity of the social environment, its massive interdependence.

We probably get the courage to face the idea of the whole, of oneness, and its component, separateness, because we have to, and soon. But we may also be willing to risk greater intimacy and closeness because we have never been more free.

The emergence of family therapy is fractional to these larger changes. It is part of the movement toward greater

39

openness: people are less content to merely talk to therapists about their loves and hatreds, and therapists are less willing to sit and listen to histories and rehearsals of life. What is demanding in the consulting room is life itself, and the emergence of family therapy is testimony of a quantum jump in courage on all parts: therapists taking heart to face their own involvement with people, and facing the power of families' involvement with each other, the bitterness and the love; therapists facing their more honest place, not as substitutes but as catalysts to the growth efforts of more permanent units; and courage of the families to face each other and be open with what is, never mind what should be.

We are, families and therapists, in pursuit of the moment, in pursuit of confrontation and embrace and dialog in the clarion, crisp now. We suspect the unseen, the unseeable: psychoanalysis' reverence for the past, and for the metaphysics of internal dialog, fades; families and therapists meet together and discover hopefulness in understanding and experiencing the present. We are caught in the instant flicker of glances and gestures, in the eddy and flow of struggles for power, in the microseasons, circular and predictable, of family patterns, their climate of despair and joy; and in the search for warmer climates.

This faith in the present — perhaps it is not faith, but the realization that it is all we have — may have occurred because we have less faith in understanding or more interest in experience, or because we realized that the examination of the past was a form of mysticism because it was forever hypothetical and also lifeless. But this grouping, this confrontation may be appealing because we realize that experience cannot be mediated by words and ideas. It must simply occur, and if it is to be reshaped it must be a collective effort, and the reshaping must have all the will and emotion and power that we can muster. Perhaps you cannot tell someone to stop a destructive pattern; you must actively intervene, and you must model new alternatives.

And we are part of the confusion, the disorder of authority: a therapeutic unorthodoxy still, with its own

40

ideology and system of values, but fracturing into a cacophony of component unorthodoxies as it develops, family therapy has a certain commitment to instability. We are confused with, and confuse ourselves with, the religious tradition. The symbolism of a secular priesthood hovers around our centrality to values and our struggles with moralities. As a group, we tend to cluster around some values that are not professional, but personal. We are anti-authoritarian in large measure, tend to resent imposed struc-ture and rigidity. Our equalitarian bias searches for the per-sonal rather than the role-defined. Children in the families are seen and heard; co-workers are valued for their person and their competence, rather than their degree.

Our insistence on visibility and openness — family therapists tend to work together, to let others observe, insist on families meeting together instead of in separate cliques and fractions — may be instrumental to a search for equality and for common purpose among people; for the tyrannies of groups over individuals, and the conspiracies of individuals against themselves, and even the maintenance of incom-petence and inaction, are dependent on secrecy. So in addition to faith in the present, there is faith in the open group. As yet we are a mere cluster in the professional community.

We are part of the getting it all together, and most of us, eventually, endorse the revolutionary idea. The idea is at present a gauntlet: a challenge to face the whole, the "inter-ness" of being. As Jay Haley concludes in his chapter in this section, experienced family therapists are not practicing one method of treatment; they have a new way of viewing people and their activities. They struggle to see the gestalt, the pattern, the process, and to turn it. They see all indi-viduals in the family as *jointly* participating in the group process, and they see the family process as the superordinate pathology. The therapist relates to the family as a living organism, a synergism of systems, rather than a machine in which one component or part can be damaged without

41

affecting the others. Rather than seeing one member as sick, or one relationship as symbiotic or pathological, the therapist thinks configurally: mother's focus on daughter is a response to father's affair with his business, and both their involvements outside the marriage are easily seen as growing out of their fear of intimacy with each other.

The devotion to the individual patient out of which family therapy grew has its legitimate roots; it comes out of a history of social Darwinism, where the individual, independent and surviving, was supreme. As nuclear families were in the process of disentangling themselves from their families of origin, they formed tight, single fists of determination to move upward. The psychotherapist's work with the individual patient may have been a response to rescue, to extricate the individual from these tightly grasping units. It is a well-meaning strategy, but it has the disadvantage of splitting a family if it works, of being useless if it doesn't. The most successful individual therapy may result when the therapist is powerful enough to steal the patient from his family, and to help the patient change the family. Individual psychotherapy also has some of the implicit hostility of social Darwinism — it ignores the natural context, the environment of the individual. Family therapy, like the ecological movement, is responsible to the natural order, to the pattern and flow of growth, to the social nurturance within which people live. It contains in part a relinquishing of the omnipotence of conscious, deliberate design, of professional artificiality; it has an element of humility before the structures of families which will persist long after the therapeutic relationship has ended.

And only then of our own histories: "We" are at least three generations. There are the advance trappers and scouts, men like Nathan Ackerman and John Bell who founded this movement; the pioneers, people like Carl Whitaker, Murray Bowen, Virginia Satir, Don Jackson, who were trained in other traditions, but moved to this area and developed large tracts of it; and the rest of us, settlers, who moved deliberately to an existing community. We all came

42

from different places. In this section we asked a number of family therapists to trace their steps in print.

Some became family therapists because they felt individual psychotherapy was not effective enough. It was a relinquishing of old tools, a professional impetus for competence that forced the trial of new method. They stayed because it worked. Others stress the personal satisfaction, the joy of being involved and in seeing change take place before them, the fun of learning from observing directly. Some find roots in their families of origin for their taking the role of family therapist, and find rewards and stresses accruing to their present families as a result of their job. All have a quality of being drawn, of being curious and intrigued, as if somehow implicated in the drama of family life, seduced by its vitality. Several mention being pushed, stressed, challenged — the demands of being a family therapist are demands that we grow. It may be these very demands that are the greatest appeal, because becoming a family therapist seems to be not so much a deliberate choice, but a result of a growth process in the life of the therapist. We grow bored with the low-key tenor of the individual hour, we grow impatient for more change in the patient, we grow anxious to know more, to see the origins of the problems, we grow eager for more power, more intensity, more involvement.

So it is not just the needs of patients for more competent treatment, or the needs of therapists for more stimulation and more challenge, but a joint migration of a whole society: the time is open, it is intense, it is confused, it is now; it is getting things together.

We begin the next chapter with perhaps the most authentic and authoritative comment on our work: the statements of families who have been in family therapy. In large measure they are enthusiastic, though their comments may not be typical of the families of therapists who submitted statements. It seems fairly clear, however, that client families are usually more convinced of the worth of family therapy than most of the professional community. We proceed to comments by family therapists about how they became such. We found these comments intriguing and readable.

We looked forward to reading the autobiographical comments of both patients and therapists as they arrived in the mail, for they had an immediacy that much professional writing lacks. How much personal communication is there in the professional literature we all read? we ask ourselves. Not much. We have made an effort in this book to free the authors to speak straight, assuming that the real dishonesty is in a convention of writing and reporting, a prose straight jacket that is unnecessary.

two
~~~~~~
we're in family therapy

Early in the planning of this book we wrote the various contributors, asking each of them to "solicit one-page descriptions from two families: one family that you are currently treating and one family that you treated in the past. Have them describe their most valuable and least valuable experiences in family therapy. Leave the format in their control and allow them to decide who will prepare the summary. Have them include one sentence explaining how they arrived at this arrangement. Stress that the statements should be roughly four hundred words. All patients

45

will be identified by therapist. Each family that participates will receive a copy of the book. We may not use all descriptions, but we will use at least half."

wwwwwwwwwwwwwwwwwwwwwwwwwwwww *By a Patient of C. Whitaker*

We decided to go into family therapy, after many years of various individual work, because we were up against it. Our marriage was falling apart, we constantly fought, and the children were unhappy as we constantly and perpetually put them in the middle, as a ball, to be kicked between us.

My fatherhood and husbanding reflected my detachment, efforts to appease, and general failure to take a stand in the family. This was particularly complicated by an aggressive, satisfying administrative job and an active fantasy life, particularly sexual, to compensate for the lack in this area in the family.

Bab's motherhood and wifing were caught up in the web of being unable to do anything with which I was satisfied, and trying to compensate, with the children, for all the pangs of outrageous fortune they were experiencing. Her guilt about their plight was great.

We feel three valuable things came out of the therapy. First was the opening of the problems and discussion of divorce, separation, etc., with the children, out of corners and into the light where it could be seen, as well as their role in the process.

Second was my (Ralph) getting in touch with detachment, silence, withholding, and need to be the husband and father.

Third was Bab's willingness to accept me and herself, as we were, without having some impossible image to attempt to fulfill.

The least valuable was when you (Carl) and I (Ralph) tried to *convince* Bab we aimed to stay away from that area, but after Mike (co-therapist) left, particularly your

46

co-therapists were not as involved, and I felt you and I too easily got on Bab to do the changing, only.

This happened with Mike, but he was able to get after me, too, much better than you.

I feel very good about us now, as does Bab. We hope we can keep it going.

Feel free to use any and all of our letters as you see fit. The children wanted to put in their own and they are attached. We hope they are helpful to you.

Thanks again for your great help and for being yourself.

Bab and Ralph

Dear Dr. Whitaker, The most unpleasant time was when you said, "If you get a divorse, you get a divorse." The best time was when you told me to say, "Mindreader, mindreader, Nah, Nah, Nah." *Jennie*.

Dear Doctor Whitiker, The best experience in therapy (family) was when I almost spilled tea all over everyone when you said, "Your parents never fight." My worst experience in family therapy was when you said, "Let them get divorced" to my parents. And your a very good doctor. Your patient, *Bryn*.

Dear Doctor Whitker, You are helpful although at times it seems the way you go about it is pretty silly. I remember the time when you took out a lot on Mom. That helped us all to realize what a spot she was really in. That was real helpful I thought.

And there was the time when you told Mom she should get away for awhile. Then she did go away and that was the saddest day of my life (almost). She went away for three days. (Although she called us every night.) I cried all the time. Then she returned. All was well. Yours truly, *Julie*.

47

The repercussions, the echoes — o.k., I'll do it with music — the jarring, the surprises, the sudden blending, the weaving and then again tearing of the notes; the intertwining of one melody and then the playing of two against each other.

Relationships in a large family (we are eight) seem as complicated a symphony. There have been so many turns and twists in our five months of rehearsing therapy that I am not prepared to describe the whole of our experience. Ask me again in five years.

Each person in our family has a different feel of where we are and where we are going. We had more problems than we knew.

We're still learning to speak to each other. I can mis-speak and you can mis-hear, and vice versa. We're learning to hear the feeling behind the words now.

We're making an effort to flow with it more and not to "try" so hard. We're learning that one cannot see a situation clearly. The harder we work it over, the more understanding eludes us.

Important to the process of untangling us is the patience of the doctors, and their kindly good will towards each of us. The idea they urge upon us, young and old, to feel a "sense of yourself" can be comprehended as a life preserver in the storm of events and pressures in this crazy world. If a feeling is genuine and comes from within you, it's all right — it's safe — it's honest. Acting from the feeling of self can be exhilarating — even if at times frightening. Joy increases as you experience a new freedom.

It is my hope that each of us will be able to accept better the human predicament and continue to see that as we suffer we grow, as we bend we toughen, as we give in we conquer — ourselves, that is.

Nothing will ever be quite the same again in our family. Some sessions we all walk away from feeling utterly devastated and with knotted stomachs. No one speaks for several

48

minutes. Everyone feels drained. The bedrock footings are shaken. The superstructure grossly altered.

Time passes.

Then one realizes that though there are no philistines left in the entire tribe, the process is actually unifying. That truth is better than illusions. The re-weaving of the relation ships within the family makes them tighter and all the more secure. I cannot say how the process works. If no man is a hero to his valet, neither are any members of the family heroes to any other after family therapy. But need they be? Our common humanity, our idiocratic weaknesses, are probed, plumbed, and aired repeatedly. Yet, strangely, we are all closer to one another than ever before.

In our case the process was initially approached by my wife and myself from entirely antipodal viewpoints. She desired to sever the matrimonial bonds as painlessly as possible. I desired to renew and strengthen them. By some strange alchemy we are now both pulling the same way, both trying to renew and strengthen the marriage — to find each other again. The result is still unknown; progress still uncertain.

I will simply say that in the circumstances we found ourselves in at the beginning nothing else would have worked. The best endorsement the process can have is that we are all eager to continue, look forward to the sessions and have such enormous confidence in the wisdom and guidance of Drs. Whitaker and Napier that we all feel prepared to accept the results — whatever they may be.

They seem capable of blending the immiscible.

⁓⁓⁓⁓⁓⁓⁓⁓⁓⁓⁓ *By a Patient of C. Whitaker & A. Napier*

Wife: Although wary and on the defensive some of the time, along with each member of the family I joined the effort to discover ourselves. I struggled and then relaxed more into the game of being myself. I enjoyed a freer feeling of letting go in more self-expression and opening up to others. I'm not sure how much I changed, for I had been going through a slow process of feeling more sure of myself anyway — which is one of the reasons we originally came to the doctors. I had come to feel that I could not tolerate or understand my mate of twenty-six years. As a person I now have more confidence in my new assertiveness, and I'm still enjoying it. I have continued to feel that I could and do trust my feelings and judgment. Perhaps that is the gift I received from the therapy.

The family as a whole. The therapy was invaluable. Each child benefitted in a very personal way. To me it is terribly precious to feel that each person has acquired an individual sense of freedom in pursuing his own essence as a human being. Alice is floating with this and so are all the others. Without the therapy I think my leaving my husband might have done more damage to the children. With the therapy they have each matured with a sensitive tolerance to other's needs — including their mother's. (Even I notice here that I have not mentioned Don in particular. I can't get a grasp on him to this day, you see.)

Two complications. There are two things that complicate my view of the therapy at this point: One is that, as fate would have it, a very fine man started "courting" me last June, and I am wildly in love with him with all the breathlessness associated with such a condition. To me he brings all the love, understanding, spirituality, tenderness, humor, and intelligence that any woman could ask for. I wish I could pin a sign on him that says "world's greatest lover" because he looks like what he is: an aging professor. I delight in everything about him and am dumbfounded to learn how I crave what he provides. He's at the peak of his profession and I have exciting things to look forward to: living with a mature, wonderful human being and traveling all over the world. At this point I will try to restrain myself from raving further. Second, there's another factor in this whole thing — it might have been handled differently from your standpoint as well as mine. I don't know. Many months ago my husband (Don) told me that you had given him a book to read on the "psychopathic personality." He went into it in some detail, identifying his brother very definitely as such a person. Don concluded that he himself was not in this category, but too many bells rang for me. I read about it in a medical book, and some statements sound as if they were taken out of my mouth. At the risk of being self-righteous and arrogant, I find too much in my experience of the past and the present not to come to a conclusion on this. Since Don never brought it up himself in the sessions, I never did either — but it explains an awful lot to me. The pieces of the puzzle fit together.

I'm glad Don told me about it. As it has turned out, it seems that unless Don himself had alluded to it, it wouldn't have helped for you to have done so. So you are both very wise and restrained, I realize. It's sad but, to put it crudely, I spent as many years struggling with it as I could. And that's that. I had no idea what I was dealing with. I may be mistaken now, but with my new confidence and assertiveness — not to say brashness — I think much is explained by the fact that to some degree or other the man I married was and is a psychopath.

The role of the psychiatrists. As for Carl and Gus, your restraint was admirable and wise. Human interactions are so complicated that the doctor who barges in with answers is probably overstepping and he himself, being only human, cannot be sure. Restraint is his wisest policy. There are cases, I suppose, where a doctor can diagnose with much certainty. But acting on the side of caution is wise and encourages the patients to plumb their own depths before coming to conclusions. It was our desire for answers which made some of us wish you gave more direction. In a way it seems that the children have been helped to cope with what is a common plaint of today's world: that there are no answers and yet you have to go on. In other times humans were given satisfying reasons for living.

Closing. And so, with too many words, I close. Alice is becoming the glorious woman she can be. Sonja is living with a man she wants to get away from because he's too

51

revolutionary. John is fulfilling himself editing a "radical" publication. Paul is consumed by way-out experimental theater. Molly is bubbling like a fountain in art, the high school revolution, and women's lib. Janie (not quite so enigmatic now) has a *white* boyfriend for a change and pursues much the same activities as Molly but in her own way. I think Don is getting out socially and I hope so. For me, how incredible to be in such a state of happiness! In this mixed-up world what more can you ask? The adventure goes on.

Thank you for what you have given us.

Husband: In thinking back over the thirty-some-odd two-hour sessions we have had — attended for the most part by *ten* — count 'em — ten people (namely, Drs. Whitaker and Napier, mother and father and six children), I am struck first of all by a basic interior conflict, assuming the objective was to "disentangle" (whatever that means). We had two entities involved: One was the "marriage;" the second was the "family." To some degree they are antithetical. We didn't intend to dismember the family, but we *did* mean (most people in attendance meant to, anyway) to disengage the two parties involved in the marriage. It is possible the aims were mutually exclusive.

There was much *help* from the family in the "marriage" effort; there was much *hindrance,* too. Considering what is involved in a marriage, the presence of the entire family imposed some inhibiting restrictions on what might have been said about the marriage. A hell of a lot of things couldn't get said, weren't said, because there were six children of the marriage there. I felt somewhat inhibited myself, and I'm sure it was an immensely inhibitory thing to Hatheway — to whom it is so important that she stay on the pedestal. To some degree, it may have "cooled" the kids, too. And each parent, with an audience of all one's children, not only tends to be circumspect about one's own self, but also to be a little protective of one's mate. It would be my guess that we might have made some more progress had we had an occasional (perhaps every third or fourth) session with mother and father alone.

Obviously, the reciprocal is not necessarily true — mother and father, being members of the "family," are more or less necessary to integrate it. Even here, though, one or two sessions with the children alone might have yielded some new insights.

Considering the enormous "power" of the two therapists, I had some feelings more than once that they could have structured the sessions — "controlled the chit-chat" — somewhat more than they did. After the first four or five sessions, I felt they did not maintain direction. I do not mean by doing most of the talking themselves, but by getting us back on the track when we were way wide of the mark. I know they would say, "That's not the way it works. We're here to resonate, reflect, reverberate, and echo — not to originate." But the subjects, after all, regard them with awe — they have an almost hieratic relationship, the *deus ex machina* of the Greek drama's third act. Whether or not the subjects should endow the therapists with such powers is beside the point — they *do*; and the power should be utilized more, I think, than it was.

Probably that is why I got in the way so often. I wanted to stick to themes relevant to the objective — to carry it forward. The chit-chat was all right, but I had some pretty specific things I wanted examined, and some insights gained — maybe even a few conclusions reached. Of course, I wanted to get my wife back — if that was possible. But even more important, I wanted what anyone who loves and cares about someone else deserves and *should* get — the kind of interchange and examination of their lives together to learn what actually took place. The effort cannot be unilateral; the effort must come from both sides in a spirit of inquiry — not impersonal, but as objective as anything so intimately shared can be, without accusations and recriminations. This takes "trying" — hard effort by both; indeed, by *all* the parties concerned. After the first few months it was apparent Hatheway was not interested in making this kind of effort — "and all the king's horses and all the king's men couldn't get her to try it again."

Of course, this bumps into the "Zen" approach. But if "trying" is self-defeating by Zen definition, then it is at odds with the whole approach of family therapy, which must involve digging, and digging hard. Perhaps it is good to practice Zen with oneself — to cool the effort for a while. But you can't very well practice it at a session.

I think, too, if *all* the children had been younger, the family effort might have been greater. But they were, for the most part, starting to live their own lives, and the compelling need for "family" wasn't there any more. And the persistent push to get "at" the marriage — mainly by me — just plain bored them much of the time (maybe it bored everyone else, too). It seems it was just too late to get back into the "family bag." In other words, the same approach might have worked if we'd gone at this seven or eight years ago, say, when the twins were eight, and our oldest was eighteen. But I think it is a matter for the doctors to note: older kids are less involved in family, and still less in the marriage.

Borges said, in one of his "conversations:" "The exchange of thoughts is a condition necessary for all love, all friendship, and all real dialog. Two men who can speak together can enrich and broaden themselves indefinitely. What comes forth from me does not surprise me as much as what I receive from the other. I know there are people in the world who have a curious desire to know me better. For some seventy years without too much effort I've been working toward the same end. Walt Whitman has already said it: 'I think I know little or nothing of my real life.' "

The sessions gave us a matchless opportunity to get to know ourselves, to understand ourselves better. Like all human endeavors, they were only partially successful. But that may have been exactly what the majority of the participants wanted. It was a limited success. And that limited success, it just might be, is what everybody wanted.

In looking back over six months of family therapy, certain realizations are evident. I am aware of definable changes in myself and my wife, some reason to the therapeutic methodology, and, most significantly, a marked difference, over time, in my reasons for continuing therapy.

My wife and I are engaged in family therapy specifically geared to helping us re-establish our individual identities and deal with each other on new, more open and honest terms. For myself, this movement would be indicated by my being free, open, and more confident with my wife. I often find myself looking forward to our sessions as being opportunities to exert myself. I find our sessions to be particularly helpful when they result in clarification or definition of problem areas, and when I have been able to project myself in terms of what we have defined as the "big I position." Other sessions have resulted in a personal feeling of confusion, distress, and inertia.

Having always been very reluctant to seek psychiatric help, and having entered therapy only after my marriage had practically disintegrated and with strong urging from my wife, I can now state that I have gained much from our efforts. At first, I saw therapy as a means of solving our marriage problems. I tended to see help for my wife as being the real reason for being in therapy and was all too willing not to invest myself to any great degree. I have since accepted the fact that I have no need to negate my own problems, and, more important, that I am capable of working on myself. Therapy has helped me to view myself as a more effective person and I have become more willing to deal with my problems. My ability and willingness to sustain my involvement have been nurtured and sustained by the therapist's focus. We deal with personal and social movement, resultant perceptions and reaction, and potential individual change, rather than getting deeply involved with feelings and personal historical causations. This focus clearly puts the responsibility for change directly on us. We are not led to new positions, but are free to move based upon new awarenesses and understandings. We make great use of visually presenting our behavior patterns in terms of a conceptual framework. What we learn about ourselves and each other is based upon theory of social systems and our specific roles and actions.

Therapy has helped me move from a sense of dependency on my wife's growth and development to a greater reliance on myself. I have begun to accept our therapeutic roles as dealing with our individual problems, rather than struggling to revitalize our marriage. While separation has contributed to these changes, it has taken therapy to help us use that marital condition in a functional manner.

I now understand therapy as a potentially strengthening, instructive, and formative experience. I do not feel that I have been "molded," but, rather, that I have been shown new alternatives and have been encouraged to risk myself — with some satisfying results. I have learned that often you cannot simply sit back and wait for situations to resolve themselves, but that positive change takes strong, decisive action.

I plan to continue therapy for as long as I feel that it can help me grow and become an effective individual.

wwwwwwwwwwwwwwwwwwwwwwwwww *By a Patient of M. Mendelsohn*

Daughter: For many years, since I was a teen-ager, communication with my parents had been very strained. We did not express feelings of anger and resentment to each other or make any effort to resolve our differences. The last fights I can recall having with them occurred before I was sixteen. I left for college when I was seventeen and never really lived at home again. However, many deep resentments still remained as well as many warm feelings. None of us, however, dared to risk any confrontation or even any normal feelings of involvement. After I had two nervous breakdowns within a two-year period, and was divorced, my parents and

I were thrown into situations where I became dependent upon them financially, and they took care of my children when I was in the hospital. Many feelings of extreme resentment and dependence were re-awakened which were not brought out into the open. Communications became even more guarded, contributing to, at least on my part, my depression.

Family therapy was an occasion for the hostility both sides felt, as well as the involvement both positive and negative, to be brought out and discussed. Mrs. Mendelsohn, the social worker, was objective and this was of great value to me particularly when I got support for many of my feelings which I didn't believe would ever be supported. Much of the guilt I felt toward my parents was alleviated when I quite clearly saw that they had problems themselves which had contributed to the lack of communication. The most painful part of getting this realization that they had problems was to realize that they were unhappy. This was something that was hard for me to take.

I was disappointed that some of the openness which we obtained in the presence of the social worker was so difficult to continue outside of the sessions. We became quite guarded again as soon as we stepped onto the elevator to leave. We do not discuss any of the issues raised when alone. However, family therapy was extremely helpful as far as inner changes and viewing my relationship with them are concerned.

Though family gatherings are somewhat more relaxed, it is difficult to discuss issues and express feelings openly without the presence of the social worker who serves to keep the exchanges in perspective, arbitrate, and interpret.

Father: For me the most helpful aspect of family therapy was the effective way in which it broke down the communication barriers that existed between myself and my wife and daughter. I always knew that we had this problem but we were unable to overcome it without the family therapist who helped us see *in vivo* how we unwittingly cut off

57

communication when we thought we were aiding it. My own way of doing this was by asking questions of them, putting them on the defensive, and by being too "rational" — holding back my own emotions and feelings. Letting the feelings emerge and being more open was an excruciatingly painful but change-promoting experience.

I've always had a tendency to put on a facade of strength and to hide my own dependency needs and desires as well as my real needs for affection and closeness. The most painful aspect was to bare my weakness — human needs and underlying dependency revealed in front of my family. Though painful I found that it tended to improve the relationships rather than the opposite — that they *wanted* to be needed. I found that I didn't have to be a pillar of strength — that they really didn't know me — the side of me I had hidden from them because of my stereotyped conception of the father role. *They were stronger than I thought and I was weaker than I thought.*

My previous individual therapy and psychoanalysis and group experience helped me understand myself better, to grow vocationally, and to be maximally productive in work and social relationships. However, I had trouble implementing my insights in intimate, involved relationships with those closest to me, especially my daughter and my wife. Family therapy is aiding me to apply my knowledge of myself and others in my *personal,* intimate life in an emotionally charged context.

What I found least useful thus far was in dealing with what I see as my wife's difficulties in presenting events within the family as they really happened. I find it frustrating when I feel she is distorting. I find myself slipping into the role of trying to correct her instead of letting her express herself and discharge feelings. I see it as a short-coming of family therapy, for example, when one parent or both are unable to or cannot honestly present what happened. I hesitate to expose inaccuracies in front of the children — making my wife feel embarrassed, defensive, and angry.

58

Mother: The greatest value of family therapy to me is the creation of an atmosphere in which the patient's true thoughts are expressed to the rest of the family and the family is in communication with one another. Many things which I have been afraid to say to my family for fear of the reactions I would have to face, I have been able to say in the therapy session or I have found that my real feelings come out very often in spite of myself. In a situation where these feelings are expressed, it is much easier to understand one another's reactions. Many times we have completely misunderstood one another's feelings or avoided facing them. In the family therapy session this becomes impossible. I feel this is very helpful so that instead of keeping things to ourselves and building up hostility, we express ourselves more freely.

There is one thing that bothers me about having such free discussions on the part of parents and children, and that is that the dignity of a parent is lost in having both working on the same level. The respect one should show for a parent, even though it may be a surface one, is lost.

〰〰〰〰〰〰〰〰〰〰〰〰 *By a Patient of M. Mendelsohn*

Family therapy was for me good up to the point where I found myself helping the other members of the family more often than getting help for my own personal problems. I could see the other problems of the family very clearly and point them out. When anyone of the family would say something to me on my problems, it was hard to take their words or advice. If the family has one common problem that all the members share it is going to come out in different ways, which is a good way of looking at the main problem, but it can also hinder some members who wish to try to solve the problem and are being held back by others who won't go ahead. It seemed to get to the point where every session was a repeat performance of the last.

Being objective is hard to do when you are so involved

with every member emotionally every day of your life.

I think group or private therapy would be better for some people because they are freer in expressing what is on their minds and don't have to worry about the reaction to what they are saying is going to be afterwards.

It is hard to say if we outgrew family therapy or we just didn't care to work together as a family anymore.

I have a basic knowledge of what my problems are, and I think so do the other members of the family.

This is the main thing I got from family therapy.

ᴡᴡᴡᴡᴡᴡᴡᴡᴡᴡᴡᴡᴡᴡᴡᴡᴡᴡ *By a Patient of M. Mendelsohn*

I decided to see a marriage counselor because it seemed to be the only way remaining to try to make our marriage work. We are now living together, so something happened after all those torturous sessions of turning ourselves inside out — that part is hard to take. The most negative aspect is that it seemed to take so long to get anywhere — but impatience, it turns out, is one of my hang-ups. I feel that so many of our friends are divorcing without giving their relationship a second chance. In spite of what seemed to be insurmountable problems we can now talk things out, laugh at ourselves a little, think as a family unit, and hope that we can try to build on all of this to a point where our marriage is really solid. There is no question in my mind that this is due to marriage counseling — more specifically to our counselor, because she seemed to reach both of us in the way we each needed to be reached. I'm sure that compatible personalities is a big factor — favorable here to us, but it could be negative with the wrong counselor.

ᴡᴡᴡᴡᴡᴡᴡᴡᴡᴡᴡ *By a Patient of C. Attneave and R. Taber*

This tape was made by the Mr. and Mrs. S. in their car on the return trip from taking a child to camp, a year after terminating family therapy. The family household consists of five people plus pets during the time of therapy. The index patient was the younger sibling, Jerry. An older sister was away at college.

The parents were asked to reflect upon their experience in therapy, to discuss its good and bad points, and to make any comments they cared to make. Except for changing names to preserve their privacy, it has been transcribed essentially unexpurgated.

Mrs. S: I'm recording now . . .

Mr. S: Let's just stop and make sure it is before we talk for three or four hours and find we weren't . . .

Mrs. S: *(overlapping)* THREE OR FOUR HOURS! . . .

Mr. S: Hello . . . Yes, one, two, three, testing . . .

Mrs. S: O.K. . . . Let's start off at the beginning. First of all, Carolyn asked us how we felt about the uh experience at the clinic . . . the way things were run . . .

Mr. S: Well. . .

Mrs. S: What do you think, Jim?

Mr. S: Well as I've said before . . . I said it then, and I'll say it now . . . I never really was clear on what was going on. I know they sort of got us to talk quite a bit . . . to express ourselves in many ways, but . . . and after we got all done, it did seem to have a direction as to how we should act as a family. We could see how each individual fitted into the family, but I, myself, never really clearly understood what we were doing. So maybe I'm saying the results seemed to be there, but how we got them I guess maybe I'll never know. . .

Mrs. S: Well I think the whole trick to the thing was "we." I think the first time I went it was just my daughter and myself . . .

Mr. S: You mean the first time with the old method? Five years ago?

Mrs. S: Ten years ago. Yes.

61

Mr. S: Yeah, that's right, it was ten years before we went for help about Jerry.

Mrs. S: When I first went to a clinic — my first experience with my daughter, I was given very good advice. I knew what I was doing wrong, and the advice fit to a "T," but I didn't know how to apply it . . . it was very difficult. It was impossible to apply, and I feel that if I had gone with you, Jim, you could have helped me solve one of these problems. But then it was just she and I, and it wasn't the family unit, even though it was a family problem. I think anybody in a family, with a problem, it is a family problem! . . . Because I think the family basically is a unit and I think what we were doing there was working as a unit. I think the whole trick is "we" rather than one or two or dividing the the family. And I think then this way you work as a group to get at the root of the problem. After all the child is a product . . . of . . . the mother and the . . . father. You don't beget a child without two people. Therefore, the problem would be one of the family, and it would be both parents.

Mr. S: So . . . So, really . . . O.K., that's the case, and that's how it would work. Do you feel that it worked?

Mrs. S: Oh yes, I definitely feel it worked . . . yeah . . . it worked . . . because the first time when I went with just my daughter and myself, I didn't feel part of a unit. I felt . . . rather . . . since I was singled out . . . that . . . maybe it, uh . . . my fault, and my responsibility. And it really wasn't . . . it was a family problem. So this way, I think that the problem created within the family, no matter whether it's a school problem, or any other thing, it's still created in the family, therefore, I think it should be *both* parents . . . sharing equal responsibility trying to find, uh . . . the method of correcting it.

Mr. S: All right. Well, maybe it did work. Well, it did work! We know it did. But it certainly . . . well I felt it was sort of embarrassing to bring problems that I thought were maybe my own, or maybe mine and yours, and talk about them in front of the kids. In fact, some of those I didn't really need to talk about in front of the kids. If you'll recall, we sort of split up and one week just you and I would go and the kids would just not be there. But then it would be brought up again later when the kids were there and bring them into it. The whole thing was a sort of a harrowing experience. I didn't like it for this. . . . I didn't like it at all!

Mrs. S: Oh, I don't think anybody liked it. . . . Well, I don't think anybody likes to complain, and I think that a lot of times when you have problems, you don't know you have problems . . . until you talk about them, then maybe they get to be bigger . . . if you don't continue to talk about them. I think when you continue to talk about them they get smaller because you've got more people helping with the problem. Once you first open that can of worms, man, that's a big can! But then . . . you know, it sorts of gets in focus when you talk about a problem over and over again.

Mr. S: Well, yes, that's true. I . . . I don't know. . . . It's quite an experience. . . . Well, I don't know how the whole thing works. All I know is that Jerry was having troubles. He was having troubles in school. He was fighting with the other kids and he was just having trouble at school . . . behavior problems. And so we went to a clinic because we'd been to one before. We didn't know what to do, so we went. And I was very much surprised when . . . I won't say they made light of Jerry's behavior problems, but they seemed to keep asking us about family problems, and how the family worked. Really for the whole thing I was just there for them

63

to give me the answer. You know, the answer to what we should do with Jerry, or how we should handle Jerry. Whether if we should pull his left ear and twitch his right ear at the same time, then he'd act good. He won't have these problems. That's all I wanted. I just wanted the mechanics of what to do with Jerry. I didn't want to get into all this monkey business of how did this one fit into the family? or what you thought about this? or how this one reacted when this happened? . . . and was this one happy? and all that kind of stuff. I was just there for Jerry.

Mrs. S: But that's the whole point. The whole point is the fact that the family is the unit. In other words, Jerry's problem was not Jerry's problem. Jerry's problem is a family problem. Because he isn't a little uh . . . turnip. He is in the family. Basically if he has problems, the problem has got to be in the family, whether it's his older sister or his brother, or whatever. His problem comes from the family attitudes. And this is why it's a family problem. It's everybody's problem. Now you felt that you didn't have any problems until you went, and then you had problems! *(shared laughter)*

Mr. S: Well that *was* my problem — going! Although everyone seemed to think that maybe I had others. *(more shared chuckles)* All right, but I don't know, it seemed to go a long way around just to straighten Jerry out. I will admit though that the problem straightened out. I really don't know how . . . or why. . . . I'm sure the experts could say how we did that, we did this or why . . . I guess that's so, but we certainly didn't seem to zero in on his problem all the time.

Mrs. S: We didn't or we did?

Mr. S: We did NOT! We talked about something else. All in all, I don't know how rapidly these things should be solved. Being an architect, myself, and

64

sort of working with known factors, it would seem that for every problem there should be a time limit to solve it, and a method to do it. This working with human beings and taking these kinds of factors into account is beyond me. I don't understand it. I had thought at the time that there was an easier way to do it. They should have applied a certain formula and in a certain length of time I figured it would be solved. But I didn't know the formula so it went on . . . and all they did was to keep talking about everything except Jerry. . . . Although, after it was all said and done, he is, and right now seems to be, in much better shape. He doesn't have the problems he had. . . . I guess everybody has problems through their life at one time or another, and I guess he's got his share but they don't seem to be insurmountable right now anyway. . . . I guess maybe it works. . . .

Mrs. S: My criticism was that it took so long. I don't know whether there could have been a faster method with maybe a two-hour period . . . if maybe the sessions were longer, the time might have been cut in half. Maybe this is the way it's supposed to work, I don't know, but it seemed to me that every time we got started, it took us almost forty minutes to get to a plateau we could work from. Then maybe we had ten more minutes to work. Now if we had had two hours or an hour and a half, we wouldn't have been wasting the first forty minutes getting started again, so that the months involved would maybe be shortened.* But maybe this was

---

A check of clinic records shows that the family therapy totaled thirty-four hours over a nine-month period, including school and home visits, and subgroup sessions, intake and termination included. In 1958-59 the same family received thirty hours of individual therapy for the mother, thirty-three hours of individual child therapy, three hours of "brief service" at intake, and three hours follow-up one year after termination. The main body of therapy was administered over a period of eighteen months.

the way it was supposed to work. Maybe we were just supposed to be stimulated enough to think so that we could come home and do our own thinking. I don't know.

Mr. S: You're saying that maybe this was our problem, that we needed too much time to warm us up.

Mrs. S: That could be too . . .

Mr. S: Well, you're right! You're quite right, because . . .

Mrs. S: *(cutting in)* Yes, if we'd had forty minutes to get warmed up and forty minutes to get our teeth in it — that forty minutes would amount to about four weeks' time. That's what I'm saying.

Mr. S: Well, you're right. From a practical approach — from the breadwinner's side of the family this gets very expensive. This is not an efficient way to do it. Actually I don't know how people can financially afford this luxury of getting straightened out. . . . It never entered into my thinking, but if I hadn't had the resources that I had, it might have. You can't afford to spend three quarters of the working time warming up and then take the remaining quarter of the hour and divide that by the amount of the fee for each visit and boy — that was real money . . . quite a rate!

Mrs. S: Well, this could be us, too. Maybe in the beginning an hour was right, but after we got the point of what we were supposed to be doing . . . maybe at that point it should have been increased to an hour and a half. Then maybe you could have cut down on the weeks involved. But I go back again to the same thing — everybody's problems belong to the family — to a certain point. I mean after a certain age our older ones are still part of the family but it's different — basically I think if all people could work as a family unit there would be a lot less chaos and unhappiness, and maybe social and moral situations wouldn't be what they are today . . . according to the news media . . . but, I don't know . . .

Mr. S: Well, I guess you're right. . . . I can't argue that. . . . So all in all we're saying that it seemed to . . . uh . . . Well you're quite positive in your statement that you think it's great. That it works. That it's the right thing.

Mrs. S: *(laughing)* I'm not neutral about anything!

Mr. S: That I know! . . . I guess in summary I could say it works, too, but I don't know why. *(shared chuckles)* I guess that's it. . . . Do you have anymore to say?

Mrs. S: Nope. . . . Over and out!

Both: "Goodbye! . . . for now."

ᴧᴧᴧᴧᴧᴧᴧᴧᴧᴧᴧᴧᴧᴧᴧᴧᴧᴧᴧᴧᴧᴧᴧᴧᴧ *By a Patient of H. Mendelsohn*

Wife: My best experience in therapy was finding out that my husband was really a man. I remember when I first started in therapy, by myself, I had a dream and in the dream was a mayonnaise jar with waxed paper sticking out from under the lid. The effect of the waxed paper made me think of a tutu. I associated the jar with my husband. It wasn't until I left the session that day that I realized the significance of the dream — that I thought that my husband was unmanly. This was the worst possible thing I could think about him. Through therapy my feelings about my husband changed and I knew that he was very much a man. This has been one of the happiest experiences of my life.

My worst experience in therapy was going to a session at the hospital with our doctor and another doctor present and loads of others behind a one-way glass. I remember that our doctor said that he thought that this session would be of benefit to us. He said that it might be possible to have films taken of the occasion and to have a tape recorder catching our every word. We vetoed the films and didn't have it taped. I was extremely angry about the whole thing because I thought of it as being a Hollywood extravaganza produced to enhance the reputation of our doctor. I didn't tell the doctor how I felt because I mistakenly thought that he could do no wrong and that if he thought we should go, then that's what we had to do. I didn't like the other therapist who was present and I remember wanting to shout and tell him that he was full of shit and that he was a prick. I get angry every time I think about my not telling everybody off.

Husband: The worst experience in conjoint therapy was being able to see the active and responsible role that I had as relates to my wife's affair. It became a painful realization that I had actually contributed to the development and continuation of the affair.

It is difficult to label "best experience" but probably one with much meaning to me was the overt cessation of my premature ejaculation.

By a Patient of P. Guerin

Last summer, our family moved to a new community. By fall, it was apparent that our seven-year-old son was experiencing problems beyond those normally present during such an adjustment period. He was having trouble at home, in school, and with friends.

At that point, we discussed his school behavior with his teacher and she agreed it might be wise to have him tested by the school psychologist. This was done and those tests indicated he should be examined by a psychiatrist. This was done, and the psychiatrist advised that it was his procedure to work with the parents as well as the child, through regular weekly family sessions. As we understand it, this is done to determine the emotional interaction taking place within the whole family at the time. Following examination, the psychiatrist suggested our son be checked by a learning specialist and also by a neurologist. This was also done.

The learning specialist recommended the immediate

engagement of a tutor, advising that marginal instruction during his first two years of school might be a partial answer. This was done. The neurologist conducted a thorough examination which revealed no apparent physical disability.

Although I don't think I fully comprehended the situation at the time, all signs obviously pointed to an intra-family emotional problem, which suggested the need for further family counseling.

Seven months have passed since the start of our weekly session with the psychiatrist, and during this time we have learned certain things. First of all, we came to recognize that each of us handles anxiety differently. I tend to withdraw within myself; my wife tends to reach out toward me. Because I withdraw, while she is reaching out, she finds it necessary to move toward others. The net result of this stand-off, among other things, is regressive behavior on the part of our son. The fact that we finally became aware of these things, acknowledged that real problems exist, was a big breakthrough on the road toward the resolution. Beyond this, however, we realize that if we are ever going to be able to cope with the situation, in a satisfactory manner, we must learn how to develop and execute plans of action to deal with different situations. Toward the end we have been trying the following: 1. First of all, we have agreed to let one another know when we sense a condition of withdrawal or overreach. 2. We have agreed that we must learn to be able to express our feelings of anxiety, and accept such expression from each other, at such times, without either party feeling he or she must immediately dispel the other's anxiety, or feel guilty about it, with the ultimate objective being to help each other handle the overall anxiety problem.

An example of a situation that seems to cause anxiety in each other has to do with the maintenance and repair of the house. I move away from it and feel pushed. My wife becomes discouraged by my lack of interest and becomes anxious, which can easily lead to a serious period of drift and anxiety for both. Another example is housekeeping. If

I find the house in a sloppy state (despite my understanding of what these children can do), I tend to become uncomfortable and begin to drift. My wife first reaches out, wondering, and if I don't tell her, we can easily create another stand-off situation. There are probably better examples, but these are the petty day-to-day incidents that can mushroom into real problems.

One thing we now know better than before, however, is that we must really love one another deeply, for we are working hard at trying to preserve our marriage and make it as happy as possible rather than let ourselves fall into despair, separation, or divorce.

With the simple acknowledgment that there are failings and shortcomings on both sides, freely but not bitterly expressed, and open to constant assessment and improvement, we have been better able to communicate, understand, tolerate, recognize, cope, and generally live a much happier life than in recent years. There's probably some new-found recognition of each other as individuals rather than as "wife" or "husband" that has regenerated an element of respect for (and enjoyment of) each other that was missing.

Another insight we have had is that we can fall from these heights rapidly, and must really spend time developing the plans of action mentioned above if we don't want to fall into the same bad habits and stupid mistakes.

We are also slowly coming to understand that although it may take years, literally, to achieve a relatively well-balanced relationship between ourselves and with members of our family, this fact, though discouraging, is not overwhelming or devastating — but simply a fact.

As an additional result of all of this (and what led us to seek help in the first place) our son's emotional state is vastly improved. His school work picked up, and his relationships with friends and family have improved markedly.

In summary, we seem to have begun to live together — parents and children — in mind, as well as in body.

Father: The best part of our two-year family therapy sessions was the occasional realization that some of the tensions in our family were not unusual and were curable if tackled understandingly. The assurance that we were normal despite the fact that we didn't love all our children all the time was comforting.

The worst part of the sessions was the very long intervals between those that seemed to make progress. In brief, a lot of input for modest output.

There is a question in my mind as to whether we could not have made as much progress in shorter time by a series of individual sessions. Six people, in large measure reluctant to state their emotions, can spend a lot of time looking at the ceiling. Perhaps one or two people that the therapist has identified as having particular problems could have had separate sessions and come to grips with their solution quicker than in six-person sessions.

Mother: Best was that I gradually began to understand what a family could really be like. I started to enjoy the children instead of being exhausted by them and felt that this was mutual. I realized I hadn't been a very good wife or mother (more of an activities director, and underhanded in my methods, too) and emerged much more competent to discern actual problems in the family. Then we could face the real problem — not just some single manifestation. I don't think family therapy alone would have been enough, though; the combination of individual and family was excellent. I feel released from a prison, and constantly grateful.

Worst was that I (or we) didn't understand that we were supposed to be doing the digging ourselves. Perhaps we should have had some direction, such as "Talk about something you are bothered about, and see what the others think about it." Then the doctor might have us tell what we really meant. This might have taken a year off the therapy.

Daughter (Now age 17, then 12-14) : Best : I enjoyed having the opportunity to speak out my mind exactly as it was without feeling self-conscious or hesitant.

Worst : I sometimes resented the long silences. I felt that it was supposed to be your (the therapist's) job to keep us on the right track, and it seemed that you weren't holding up your end.

My single worst experience was the time I saw Dad act very upset during one of the sessions. I can't remember what the circumstances were, but it made me feel horrible to see him on what appeared to be the verge of breaking down.

Son (Now age 19, then 14-16) : Best were the times when I felt myself an equally important member of the family, not a subordinate, and when I felt a family togetherness on the basis of mutual feelings.

Worst were the times when I felt that we were doing nothing in the sessions, and I was most uncomfortable and resentful of my parents.

Son (Now age 15, then 10-12) : Well, you asked for the best and the worst. So the best was being saved from being totally picked upon. My only vivid memory is one night in which I was being picked at by my brother and sister and you rose to my defense. This was the only time anyone had really protected me in my early memories of these years. The worst was the boredom. Your office had some sort of poster in an adjoining room and I used to look at it. These endless hours of not saying anything used to just bore me to death. Yet I think that they were necessary to get us to talk of our own free will. To me it still seems so far away. Seeing as I don't remember much it must have been valuable as we don't fight as much anymore. Perhaps it was only a family stage. However, those are my memories. I think that boredom will be the worst experience of my brothers and sister also.

Son (Age 13, then 8-10) : I really can't remember too much

72

about our sessions. All I can remember is the complete boredom. I guess an eight-year-old kid is too restless to sit in a chair for an hour. I even said that there was a T.V. program that I had to watch so I wouldn't have to go.

~~~~~~~~~~~~~~~~~~~~~~~~~~~~~~~~~~~~~~ *By a Patient of A. Ferber*

Father: We found very few disadvantages to family therapy. Without the presence of the children we felt freer to discuss some of our problems. The presence of too many people sometimes seems to interfere with the progress of a session. Sometimes the working out of a pressing issue at the given moment has to be postponed because there just isn't enough time for each individual to be heard.

We now believe that one member of a family unit cannot be treated effectively without involving the others. One of our children was in individual therapy and the channels of communication between therapist and family were almost non-existent. As a result there was a pulling apart of the family.

In family therapy the conflicts are resolved in a more realistic fashion. The very presence of those who are involved brings about a greater awareness and insight. There is a more honest appraisal of the situation with more points of view. The therapist has a better picture of the individuals by studying their actions and reactions within the family.

Family therapy is a lesson in cooperative living. There is better understanding of ourselves and of those who share this most intimate relationship. With the guidance of the therapist, avenues of communication are forced open which would have remained closed. Innermost feelings and thoughts of the members of the family are revealed and, with opportunities for such expressions, tensions seem to disappear. There is less of a chance for members of a family to be pitted one against the other when family therapy sessions provide open discussion. With individual therapy

73

only one side of the story is presented. Therefore, family therapy aids in promoting greater family harmony.

The solutions to problems are easier because more people can participate and each can make a contribution to resolve the difficulty. Everyone's role in a conflict can be worked through, whereas in individual therapy only one person learns to cope with an issue. The changes can be more rapid when more than one person works toward that change.

The emotional growth of an individual is developed by and within the family. Family relationships are enriched by teaching the members to understand the feelings of others. The satisfaction and joy of observing changes taking place in the behavior of our children as a result of our changes are most gratifying.

The meeting of the family seemed unreal and contrived during a session. I like the results.

Mother: I found it very difficult to relate freely in front of the children. I felt their regard for me as their mother was being destroyed. I felt belittled.

I like this type of therapy because it gives everyone in the family the chance to participate in working out a problem.

Son (Age 8): Family therapy helped us get better. I didn't like to see you burst into tears. The first time I went, I had to tell lies and I hated it.

Son (Age 13): The family seems better and closer. There seem to be fewer arguments. I didn't like family therapy because sometimes it was boring because I couldn't understand. It was over my head.

Daughter (Age 20): I really wasn't involved. I didn't like to go because I was always being attacked.

When Dr. Ferber asked me to contribute an essay to this book, he told me that it was rare to have had — and thus had a chance to compare — three different forms of psychotherapy: psychoanalysis, group therapy, and family therapy. This is an expensive distinction, and one that I feel genuinely ambivalent about: glad to have gone through the experiences, but glad, too, to have it over with. It is with some misgivings, then, that I compare the three experiences.

I undertook psychoanalysis first, nine years ago. I had been recently married, had one child, and was completing work on a Ph.D. in English literature. I was never given a formal diagnosis, but to me the problem seemed to be one of a pretty low tolerance for anxiety, exacerbated by a precipitate marriage (our daughter came six months later) and the pressures of Ph.D. orals. Analysis was five days a week, for about two and a half years. Upon its completion, I felt that it was eminently successful. The damage in self-esteem was repaired, the marriage stuck together, I got my degree — largely by winning over a professor who had flunked me the summer of our marriage — and a good job. Although with the benefit of hindsight I can see that the experience introduced certain distortions in the marriage, at the time, and for four or five years afterward, it seemed a crucial and a central experience. I was able to function professionally; a marriage that might easily have broken up was saved; an incipient estrangement from my parents — especially my father — was averted, and generally I felt more confident of my powers and of my selfhood. I found the experience particularly illuminating as it dovetailed with teaching and writing about literature and literary meaning. The obviously freer and more plastic process of symbolization in dreams loosened up — freed up — my own powers of associative thought, and I found this invaluable in the classroom. As a learning experience — a source of insight and awareness, it seemed — and still seems — unique, all the more so in that it realized for me the traditional claims of literature and literary analysis in a way that literature itself had not. It put me in touch with my feelings and gave me a more lively and active sense of how feelings work, how they are expressed, and how important they are.

As therapy, it seems — again in retrospect — less uniquely successful. First of all, it was probably too short to be considered fully complete (I gather that six to eight years or more is the canonical period), and, as I found out later, it had not indeed gotten to the bottom of the problem. I wanted to stop because it seemed to me to have done as much — gone as far — as I wanted or needed at the time. Second, it was essentially self-directed and non-directive. The first enabled me to solve some of my problems in the marriage, but it did a good deal less in solving the problems of the marriage itself. My wife was intensely jealous of the whole process, and she took my turning to analysis as a direct criticism of her. Secondly, because of its non-directive nature, it was possible to misuse, or abuse, the experience within the marriage itself. Still — so far as I was concerned — it was successful; had I felt otherwise, I would not have stuck it out, or been willing to go back for additional psychotherapy when the occasion arose.

That came about upon my leaving one job for another, having been let go by my department — ostensibly for non-publication, but essentially because of having alienated my chairman. I spent the summer between jobs away from home doing research, had a brief but intense affair, and came back to find my wife had all but had a similar — indeed symmetrical — experience with a former colleague and close friend, and cast about for some way of repairing the damage and resuscitating the marriage. We were referred to a family therapist, who, in turn, recommended that family therapy (twice weekly) be supplemented with group therapy (once a week). I hesitated about the latter, but consented after three weeks or so. Both went on for about five months, and were by any standard spectacularly successful. The family therapist concentrated on defining the relationship and why it had become unstable: basically, it had become — perhaps always was — a question of my wife feeling obliged to give too much within the relationship and I too little, of her feeling victimized and aggrieved, and, as a result, withdrawing, and of myself demanding too much and of being hurt and feeling bereft at her withdrawal. The therapist was able to define for us the interlocking nature of our individual problems — how they related to our experiences within our own families, and how they governed the relationship and eventually had caused it to become unstuck. Because it treated a marriage and not an individual, it was able to show us how we fitted together into an entity that was separate and distinct from, though related to, the constituent elements — our individual selves, just as sodium and chlorine are each distinct from each other, and from their compound, salt.

Though I was initially skeptical (i.e. afraid) of the group, I found it the most intense and therefore the most "successful" and illuminating phase. For the first time, the major locus of the problem surfaced — the traumatic effects of having been left by my nurse of four years (who was essentially my mother) at the age of seven, when I went off to school. The unresolved oedipal conflicts that this left emerged as the root cause of a fear of closeness evident in my role in the marriage, the difficulty in giving, the rage at not being given enough "in return," the emotional vulnerability to another woman (who, it would appear, was acting out her oedipal wishes by trying to break up my marriage). I had been intellectually aware of Edie's leaving; I had been told that as a young boy the effects were not unlike those of an adult "nervous breakdown," but I had never really felt the anguish and hurt of that loss before, and I had never, as a consequence, really been able to cope with the anger and rage that sprang from it. This is the kind of thing that psychoanalysis, pursued long enough, might well have uncovered. But it took an affair that threatened a marriage I was proud of to provide the occasion and the motivation for being able finally to confront it.

77

I'm not sure I can very usefully discriminate among the three forms of treatment as abstract entities. Family therapy and group therapy were undertaken concurrently and are hence linked in this way, though, as experienced, they seem more distinct from one another than analysis is from either. Part of this is the differing styles and personalities of the therapists in each case. The family therapist, a woman trained as a social worker, was more detached, more judgmental, more reserved and clinical in her manner. The group therapist (analytically trained and also a family therapist) was more of a charismatic figure, who reached out more directly and more pointedly to individuals within the group when their turn had come. The analyst, orthodox and avuncular, had close to the ideal amount of "detached warmth" that a therapist needs, and I revered him for it. Thus, both family therapy and group therapy seem in my mind each more attached to that prior experience of analysis than to each other. Yet undeniably each went beyond analysis and was more successful — group in eliciting crucial trauma, family in defining wherein the marriage was unstable. Perhaps the fact is that analysis was simply more appealing — though not necessarily more successful — because it was so quintessentially verbal. Hence its congeniality to someone who is professionally verbal is an attraction that limits its effectiveness.

‿‿‿‿‿‿‿‿‿‿‿‿‿‿‿‿‿‿‿‿‿‿‿‿‿‿‿‿‿‿‿‿ *By a Patient of A. Bodin*

Since we could not come to an agreement as a family, we decided to each do our own thing and then assemble them to comprise the total.

Wife: The most valuable experience I have had in family therapy with Dr. Bodin is that I am able to talk to my husband and tell him my feelings. Now I can talk things over with him and tell him when I don't like how things are going, as before family therapy I would never talk anything over with him, and I was always disgusted with him. There was

78

very little communication between us. The technique that brought this about was, in my opinion, our open discussions, with Dr. Bodin injecting his observations of what was really going on. Another thing I found extremely valuable was psychodrama. This was an easy method of gaining insight to our relationship and my own personality. The one thing we did that had little value to me was having a group session with the trainees, who had been observing us. The main reason for this is that I am basically uncomfortable in larger group situations.

Husband: I blamed most of the family problems on my wife, but on going to Dr. Bodin with my wife and consulting with him I found I was as much to blame. The help I received was in the form of my listening to what my wife wants and needs and talking things over with her, rather than just thinking of how I feel and what I want. I find it has helped in our personal relations also, as we are a lot closer than we have been for a couple of years. Earlier we had almost lost contact. The thing that helped me most was the encounter with the group of trainees, which took place after a session with Dr. Bodin. The reason I feel this way is because the manner in which they questioned us, and presented back to us their observations, pointed out things that were wrong with us that were going unnoticed. I find it hard to say what was the least valuable because I feel I obtained some good out of each session. This was due to close observation and pointed remarks that made the guidelines for each session.

Daughter: I feel I was helped most by being removed from my home, by court order, and placed in an institution far from home. The shock of this demanded a lot of careful thought on my own contributions to our family disaster. In the beginning it was still hard to talk to my parents, but joint sessions with Dr. Bodin eased the strain. Now we talk often and we have a lot to share. I feel that communication, which was non-existent before, has improved not only between my parents, but between our family as a whole.

The most helpful experiences we have had in family therapy with Dr. Arthur Bodin have been in connection with his identification of less and more constructive patterns of behavior in our family. Both the style and insights of Dr. Bodin have been supportive. Part of the support comes, we believe, by his having been very direct either in identifying unconstructive behavior himself or in confirming our identification of such behavior. The discussion of alternative forms of behavior immediately following identification of problems enabled us to get over helpless feelings more quickly. For example, one child had encopresis. Dr. Bodin was very blunt in pointing out the difficulty of curing this problem. However, his identification of the behavior patterns in the whole family which contributed to the problem and specific suggestions or critiques of our suggestions about what to do have enabled real progress to take place.

Another illustration of Dr. Bodin's help through identification was his working through with us the way in which contrived confusion was used in the family. His emphasis upon the ways in which I, as father, could enjoy the rights and freedom of that role while fulfilling the responsibilities more effectively was most helpful. Enabling us to see alternatives after the analysis of what was going on scored high with us again. Dr. Bodin's emphasis on balance and on the ways in which our balance could be maintained is also illustrated with this problem exercising appropriate controls. My wife and I have both had previous marriages. We both brought children to this new marriage. I tended to lose control or hide behind confusion. Dr. Bodin first worked with us to the end of my gaining and actually enjoying wherever possible the authority I had as a father which the children badly needed. But later he also worked with us to the end of enabling both of us to see the importance of not carrying control too far.

Strengths often cover weaknesses, and weaknesses often hide strengths. Dr. Bodin frequently pointed this out in one

80

way or another. What seemed least helpful to us was that occasionally his gifts of insight came through as brilliant but premature. That is to say, sometimes he seemed to jump to a conclusion without sufficient time or exploration of the particular problem with us. This seemed to be the case in discussions we had about David and Martha. In pointing out some of the strengths they contributed to the family he neglected to some extent the depth of the problem we were having with these children. But even in these instances his method and style enabled us to identify things more clearly and more quickly consider alternative actions.

My wife and I talked about our experiences, and we decided that I would write down what we agreed upon and then we'd edit these paragraphs together.

ᠰᠰᠰᠰᠰᠰᠰᠰᠰᠰᠰᠰᠰᠰᠰᠰᠰᠰᠰᠰᠰᠰᠰᠰ *By a Patient of A. Bodin*

In reviewing sixteen months of therapy to cure a marriage that had gone as far toward dissolution as the filing of suit for divorce, we would single out as the most outstanding success the recognition that we are two distinct individuals with unique ways of looking at ourselves and others. The most valuable experiences we had in the course of family therapy were those that demonstrated this fact and taught us how to manage our relationship in full realization of it.

Since we are individuals bound together, one of the most valuable initial techniques shown us to assist in harmonizing our needs and interests was the *quid pro quo* — trading favors and concessions. This was enormously helpful in the early part of the sixteen months since it provided a means of succeeding in negotiating differences and, therefore, buoyed our hopes for reversing the discouraging trend of our previous experience.

Therapy was a boon in that it provided us with someone to whom we might take seemingly insoluble difficulties ("having someone take my side who was more articulate than me"). A very great deal depended on the unusual talent

81

of our therapist; he was able to not only spell out our respective feelings, but able to suggest what might be done to channel them usefully.

In retrospect, we marvel at the fact that two rather well-educated persons, equipped with elaborate and precise vocabularies, could manage to discover so many instances of misunderstood expressions and meanings despite a decade of intimacy. The therapist was alert to this at all times, and augmented his own comments with audio and videotape recordings to show us vividly how we "came across" — indeed, were bound to come across — to each other. Out of this instruction we have learned to take pains to assure ourselves that we really understand the other's point and, consequently, have had increasing success in reacting to each other at the appropriate level of annoyance, irritation, or anger without rapid escalation.

A major feature of our therapy was the focusing, from time to time, on the job situation of one and then the other. Since one of us is a practitioner of psychotherapy, the other at times became impatient when therapist and spouse permitted themselves ruminations of an academic or theoretical sort. More generally, each of us discovered that, despite considerable concern for our partner's happiness on his/her job, our interest in lengthy explorations of what was going on at the other's place of work had distinct limits. Each of us would say that attention to the other's career problems was of little value to us individually, but since those problems did make trouble — and, potentially, always will — for the two of us at home, we find it difficult to criticize that attention.

This summary was composed by the husband because he writes professionally but is based on notes from joint conversation and has been reviewed by the wife.

three

‸‸

we became family therapists

We wrote the contributors to this book, asking each of them to contribute a four-hundred word statement about "how and why you became and remain a family therapist . . . these statements will not be anonymous. We would appreciate it if you feature the personal rather than the ideological development."

We present here all of the responses we received. Most of them are considerably longer than four-hundred words, and we arbitrarily arranged them so that the shorter ones are first and longer ones later.

There must be several overt and covert reasons why I ended up doing family therapy fourteen years after I had started my work as an individual psychotherapist. I could list a number of pertinent reasons as they come to my mind.

If I make a more focused effort to answer the question, however, it appears to me that it was a genuine conviction about doing more relevant and hopeful work which caused my initial conversion.

Whatever my deeper personality reasons may be for choosing the approach to psychotherapy through family relations, ultimately I could not have made the complete switch without a *conviction about the effectiveness* of the approach. As professionals, our group could not have survived without a commitment to the principles of causal or rational treatment as it evolves from scientific medicine.

My conviction about doing a more causally relevant and therefore a better job of treatment through the family even as far as the designated patient is concerned pre-dated my subsequently growing conviction about the treatment needs of all other family members. Today I do relationship-based treatment whenever it is feasible because I consider it "scientifically" the most rational treatment for the "patient" as well as for all others involved in his important relationships.

It is difficult for me to make a comparative evaluation of my personal qualities and family experiences as distinguished from those of other people. On a somewhat deeper level, I must have wanted to fight the dark forces which captivate us in pathological relationship patterns. It was a challenge to meet with and fight these forces in what seemed to be an open battlefield.

As to changes in myself, I think as a result of family therapy work I have become more secure in human relationships — but also more demanding, I am afraid. Many things that I would have accepted in the past as satisfactory responses appear now to me as phony or lacking openness.

In my practice I have greatly lost my valuation of

secrecy and confidentiality as important therapeutic factors. I also have, I believe, a better understanding of what an individual is: patterns of action rather than patterns of conceptualization or reflections on experience.

I have experienced a greater separation from colleagues who have not made the transition to the relational approach. Their concepts are painfully incomplete for explaining the phenomena I am dealing with.

I believe I cannot help but apply my learning of relational patterns to my own family relationships in my everyday living. I have sharper frustrations and deeper satisfactions as a result.

〰〰〰〰〰〰〰〰〰〰〰〰〰〰〰〰〰〰〰〰〰〰〰〰 *By C. Beels*

As I think back on the turns in my career which led to the teaching and practice of family therapy they line up this way:

1. I was an only child, and perhaps for that reason I had plenty of time to brood upon the politics of my family's triangle. More important, we were an excessively mobile family, and I was always on the outside of a group of children in which I was the newest arrival. I developed a habit of observing and comparing, since I was a sojourner in a strange land.

2. From adolescence on, since my family was usually moving or abroad, I spent vacations from boarding school, college, and medical school with other families as a guest for weeks at a time. I became convinced there was a distinctive atmosphere in every house — that families literally lived in different worlds. I wanted to know more about that.

3. For two years, I was a teacher at a boarding school. I saw boys and their parents, boys in trouble with the school and their families in ways that made some sort of sense to me. I dimly suspected that the sense of that trouble was not inside the boys, but rather had something to do with the school and the parents as well. I decided to go into psychiatry.

4. I had an amateur craze for the theater and directed plays when I was a teacher. I learned that when a scene came to life it was because I had really understood the deliberate timing and movement of it. The idea that emotional truth can be produced by action, if you know how to choose the action, goes back to that time.

5. I have read Freud and anthropology together over the years from age seventeen to the present, and most of the papers I wrote along the way were arguments about inner vs. outer structure; drives vs. culture. The point is that by the time I got to studying psychiatry the psychoanalysts had already gone a few rounds with Margaret Mead and H. S. Sullivan, and from what I had seen of the preliminaries, I decided not to make any bets on the outcome.

6. I learned psychiatry at one of the most psychoanalytic residencies in New York, where I loved doing "formulations" and "interpretations," extracting literary insights from dreams, histories, interviews, and Russian novels. I loved it, but it was too much like school, and I had been getting good marks at school for a long time. I went to Israel Zwerling's Day Hospital at Westchester Square because the idea of a day hospital made sense to me, and I found people of all sorts hustling around seeing families. I found it hard, confusing work, but it was the stuff of life, or at least of the life I had been looking for and looking at. I have been a family therapist since then.

~~~~~~ *By E. Auerswald*

I am not sure it makes much sense these days to talk about "becoming a family therapist" — for two reasons. One is that I am not sure that one "becomes" anything. Rather, it seems more relevant to say one "enters" a given life arena, one participates and/or observes, and one learns. Also, the notion of "family therapist" as one who "does family therapy" seems to stem from a frame of reference that lays

86

out a spectrum of therapeutic modalities from which to choose in the "treatment of disorder" which is perilously close to the anachronistic idea that what "therapists" do is treat "pathology." Additionally, the ecological events that bring anyone into a room with families for the purpose of producing change are so complex that it would take a fair amount of time and an as yet undetermined methodology to study them sufficiently to make their description useful. Nevertheless, since I have been asked, I guess I can report some of the subjective events that led to my entry into that room and my participation in that arena populated by those who wish to produce change in family systems.

Like everyone else, my subjective interest in families began when I was born into one. That interest was enhanced under circumstances in which my parents' view of their mutual functions differed. During most of my first seven years, I was assigned the role of helping them stay together. Despite the intensity and clarity of that experience, the western myth of individual autonomy I had learned well obscured the nature of that early experiential data for many years after I got off the hook at seven with the birth of my brother. From that time until shortly after I acquired a certificate of autonomy from a psychoanalytic institute I continued to define myself by that myth.

Very shortly after having acquired my plastic card as a psychoanalyst, however, while I was attempting to learn something about children so that I, as a "therapist" for children, could help them achieve autonomy, I took a job at Wiltwyck School for Boys. Armed with the paraphernalia of a "child therapist" — family dolls, dart guns, etc. — I found myself in various rooms with various black ghetto children doing "play therapy." I discovered at that time that I had a problem. Nothing I did changed much of anything. The kids I was trying to "treat" were delighted to shoot mother "symbolically" *ad infinitum*. They were supposed to respond to my interpretations by entering into a process. They didn't. They just shot mother. Furthermore, they shot father, brother, sister and Jesus Christ with the same glee, depending on which stimulus I placed before them. Frequently, they shot me.

About the same time, following the model of success-oriented behavior I had learned well in my middle-West upbringing, I accepted a promotion to the job of medical director of the institution, at which point I contracted to design a program for these kids. As I look back, that acceptance strikes me as the height of arrogance, but in a typical "autonomous" way, I set about the task. One of the first things I had to do was recruit some staff. One of the people I recruited mentioned a word that I had by that time largely relegated to my personal, "non-professional" life (I was impressed by "professionalism" in those days, so I could make that separation). The speaker was Sal Minuchin and the word was "family." This was in 1960. Without going into all the details, the result of that encounter was that I began to "see" families and discovered the degree to which I had been working *in vitro*. I need not elaborate on the sense of emergence I felt in the process, since it has been described in many places by many individual therapists who became family therapists.

I thought for a while I had solved my problem. I did not know at the time, or for a few years thereafter, that I had only expanded the boundaries of the target of my work, and that I had not really made many fundamental changes in the conceptual frame in which I was operating. That realization only occurred when I began to understand that the reason I could not treat "delinquent" ghetto kids with play therapy was to be found in their general cognitive organization *vis-à-vis* my own and the frame of reference I was using, and not in the structure of psychodynamic defense systems which, in that particular group of kids, existed at best in only rudimentary ways.

One cannot study cognition without concerning oneself with information environments, which are, of course, the data of ecology; so for me the next step was to look at the total environment of a growing child, informational as well as affective. This added some other words to my vocabulary: community, for example.

So, since the family turns out to be only one ecological system in the human environment at this time, albeit perhaps the most influential, I have had to abandon the notion of working only within the boundaries of the family. I find myself defining my participation in various systems in different ways. I suppose if I dip into someone else's family system, during the time span of that piece of participation I could call myself a "family therapist," although the connotations of the words are disquieting. I am not sure that I can define family anymore. There is a new civilization aborning which is redefining the word. I also suspect that the word "therapist" will be anachronistic in that new civilization.

Like many of us, I suspect that the time of my life falls into a transitional period that will determine the viability of our species. That viability may very well depend on what kind of socialized beings our society produces. I believe that some sort of "family" will always play a major part in the process of socializing our young. It follows for me that there is a moral imperative for behavioral scientists to participate in efforts to understand and help with that process, so I expect to find myself in many places with many "families" in the years to come. However, I doubt that I shall be there as a "therapist," unless the connotations of that term change.

〰〰〰〰〰〰〰〰〰〰〰〰〰〰〰〰〰〰〰〰〰〰〰〰〰 *By A. Ferber*

I am a religious person. There is no god and Alfred North Whitehead is his prophet. I believe in the need for leadership of human groups, and that the leadership is usually corrupted by its power. I believe in brotherhood and communion amongst fellow men, and that schism and mistrust develop in all these groups. I believe in truth, and see lies in every social system.

I was the first son and grandchild in my own family of origin. My parents are second generation, upwardly mobile Jewish Americans. My father is a physician. So were my mother's father and brother. I felt that I was raised in a loving, guiding, and educative family. They especially encouraged my curiosity, and allowed me to try anything I fancied.

I am told that three nursemaids cared for me each of my first three years (one each from different cultures), while my mother taught grammar school. We moved when I was two, five, seven, eight, nine, ten, twelve, and fifteen. The trauma of reacculturation to novel conditions became a taste, and I learned to be a chameleon on the outside and myself on the inside.

My father is an only child. He has a good time with his friends, and is deeply caring towards his family. He is the most socially upwardly mobile of his clan. My father has felt a lifelong sense of domination by strong women, and desertion by his nice but ineffectual father. His adaptation to this situation was to keep distant from his family. He nurtures a lifelong sense of weakness and inadequacy that he tries to hide from me and conveys strongly. He named me after his father and implicitly asked me to be father to him. He raised me with minimal controls, and thwarted efforts by others to control me.

My mother is the eldest of three children. She was the drudge and surrogate mother. Her younger sister was "the star" and her younger brother "the bad boy." Her family is riven with selfishness, intrigues, and blaming of others. Their attractive features are a lively interest in the arts and a conviction that life be fun. My mother harbors a deep sense of hurt, resentment, and exploitation that she refuses to acknowledge. She is dutiful, loyal, and often depressed.

Betty, my sister, is five years my junior. Although an attractive and intelligent child, she was the family scapegoat. She was neglected and rejected. I was originally her torturer, then her hero and protector. My father would form an alliance with me against my mother, who was represented as dull and stupid. My mother formed an alliance with me against my father, who was called self-indulgent and neglectful. I served as a bridge between my mother and father and my sister. I was raised as a star and a show-off and reveled in it. I was a charming monster. We were all too self-centered, isolated from each other and from both extended families.

All these things were obvious in our behavior, and we never talked about any of them. I believe this discrepancy fed my desire to know what actually went on and then to tell it to anyone who would listen.

In all the aforementioned roles in my family, there was both a pleasure from fulfilling them and the sense of exploitation in their not being my proper position. I wanted out. I have both a desire to lead and an anarchist seed. Perhaps my current pleasure in steering families toward a family structure (the one I wish my own family would have had) is an active mastery of the forces I felt utterly controlled by as a child.

Jane is my wife. In the prolonged and painful confrontation of a four-year courtship, she led me to realize that I did what I did to gain favor and avoid disfavor with my intimates.

This was the major break in a fantasy of self-direction, and a denial of my connectedness to other persons. Jane constantly steers me toward rather than away from people, and toward being candid with myself.

Her family provided both a bosom for late adolescent growth and a laboratory for exploring alternate modes of family organization.

When we married I felt Jane was in charge of decisions in the family. A long struggle for equal power and more mutual trust has been of enormous importance in shaping my behavior as a therapist. This struggle is just about over. We sense an opening to new possibilities now. Through these ten years I have noticed how easily I could find the kinds of problems we had faced in the families I treated. It was easy to help them through ones we had solved, and very difficult to lead them past places where we were still hung-up.

I do not know how, but by the time I started my residency at Albert Einstein College of Medicine, I knew that I wanted to be a family therapist.

I sought Israel Zwerling, who told me that he would help me become one, but that I should not see families until I learned individual therapy. I started seeing families immediately, and was chewed up and spit out by the first eight families I worked with. Zwerling and I are still battling in a loving-rebellious embrace.

My earliest teacher and colleague was Marilyn Mendelsohn, who gently led me into allowing myself to be immersed in experiences I did not fully understand. The structure of the Westchester Square Day Hospital, where we worked, was that all families of patients were seen, and they were an integral part of, rather than a nuisance to, the operation.

Seeing many families both in their homes and the hospital was important. Nathan Ackerman, who consulted there, and I took special interest in each other. We grappled monthly for two years. It was moving to have someone more expert and more powerful than myself guiding my development.

Seven years of psychoanalysis with Ruth Loveland taught me to be utterly candid with myself, and trustful of subjective experience. This experience gave me a conviction of the possibility of growth and change in a psychotherapeutic relationship. I also learned how to be a patient, how therapists exert influence, and the limits of subjective experience.

In the last six years I have treated more than fifty families, and seen several hundred in consultation or teaching situations. A group of close colleagues have constantly shaped each other's work. Chris Beels and I reviewed the literature and visited many other therapists. Al Scheflen has led me to a behavioral systems theoretical orientation during a three-year dialectic. Carl Whitaker has become my hero-therapist and I repair to him for occasional major consultations.

I am still uncertain as to how much of the effort I use

with families is for their benefit, and how much for my own ends. Similarly, do I cling to families to still my loneliness? I am just starting to return to my parents and "get to know them" *à la* Murray Bowen. I do not know how well family therapy works, and mistrust some of my provocative and self-serving evangelism. I enjoy the work, the money, and the colleagues, and perhaps over-justify the outcome. My curiosity is currently in natural history research on human behavior, the results of therapy, and the results of training.

P.S. Two years later: 1971. Above the clouds. Jane and I enjoy living more, and care less about making it.

\text{~~~~~~~~~~~~~~~~~~~~~~~~~~~~~~~~~~~~} *By A. Napier*

I came at being a family therapist stepwise, sideways, and cautiously. And I don't think I really qualify yet — I tend to think "family therapist" should be used carefully, as Robert Frost said "poetry" should, as a praise-word.

I went into individual therapy as a beginning, and it just happened to be at a time when my family was deep in crisis. My father had lost a coveted job, my sister was unhappy about her choice of a college, and I was in the middle of a classical identity crisis. I can be flip about it now, but it wasn't at all amusing then. My therapist saw me with my family for two sessions; then we launched into individual therapy for four years. It was quite a journey — changed my life, turned me on, opened up a world of feelings which seem to be expanding indefinitely, helped me find the guts to get married and fight it out to a good marriage. But it didn't get me over being pretty dependent, and it didn't change my family for a long time.

My father died while I was in the middle of therapy. He had a coronary as he and I were in the early stages of reaching out to each other. I am still, eight years later, deeply saddened, not only by his death, but by the things unsaid. After his death, my sister went to individual therapy, and my mother was left alone, really alone. She had a good general practitioner who was both tough and supportive and was her "social therapist." My sister and I fought with her to change, gave up, and she did it on her own. Now my sister and mother and I love each other deeply and openly, and we concur: what a shame we didn't have family therapy. Dad might have lived a lot longer. Even if he hadn't, the unsaid things would have been said, the loving and hating open and clean. By the time I finished therapy, my therapist had, too late for us, become a full-time family therapist.

So part of me is always back with the only family I know intimately, trying to straighten it out, open it up. I don't really like that realization, but my transference gets me involved initially, gives me an investment, and gives me an incentive to be more mature if I am going to be helpful to the family in my office.

I think initially out of emulation of my own, I decided to become a psychotherapist. I went bounding off to graduate school at the University of North Carolina, where I soon found myself on a practicum assignment at a state hospital, in a bare, windowless room that I shared with a succession of suffering people. I mostly listened and sympathized and felt progressively bored and then enraged at my impotence. I remember vividly a prominent alcoholic lady whose fantasies about her family I entertained regularly between her fantastic acting-out sessions in the real world. I was trying so hard to be helpful, and I remember the pangs of regret when her latest lover sneaked into the hospital and ran away with her. I finally decided that I was her diary, and the windowless room began to seem like Plato's cave, with mere shadows from the outside.

Carolina is a good, liberal graduate school, and supportive. They let me move later to a community mental health center, where I went on seeing families. At least I wanted to *see* all the protagonists. Initially, that was all I did. I felt outgunned, outnumbered, outfoxed again. Half the family wouldn't show, the couple would speak in code, the children would tear up the office. There was not enough

94

staff to bring in a co-therapist. So to reduce the variance, I saw only the married couples. And that went fairly well. I became a marital psychotherapist. My own marriage had been through a series of clashes and had burst into flower.

Then I hit the research year. I continued seeing couples and began obsessing about a project. I hesitated at the edge, and my sponsor, Doug Schoeninger, urged me on. I began studying four married couples and the families of each partner. What an adventure that was. I fell into a web of intricacy that still makes me spin as I think about it. Whole family systems were at war with each other. Marital fights in a college-age couple seemed to have roots that went back three generations. There seemed to be an uncanny choice of partner that included his whole family. One of the families was a healthy one, and being admitted to its interior was a rare experience. I developed almost an awe at the evolving quality of the family patterns, and I watched these couples spontaneously using my structured interviews as a way of changing themselves. That did it. Families were really at work for themselves. What they needed was help at the process, not my blood.

I went to the University of Wisconsin as a psychology intern in the Psychiatry Department because Carl Whitaker was there. I went to his seminar; then we began seeing families together. I got my degree, stayed on as a postdoc, and it looks as if we could go on and on working together. Carl is a great therapist, and I feel privileged to have worked as an apprentice beside him. With him I have seen families go from being tragic prisons to becoming really loving communities. I have some notions of how it happened. I was curious, now feel convinced; what remains is developing more of myself in the process.

I have become convinced that the family group is the most powerful therapist anybody can ever have, at least in our present social structure. I am convinced that therapists need to work in pairs or teams to make it happen with real power. I find intensive family therapy fascinating to learn from. I find that it pushes me hard to grow: one is exposed, free to turn on (or off), on call for real intervention, exposed to the press and push of real drama, real tragedy, real triumph. It is not "out there" somewhere, but surrounds you, involves you, pushes you away, pulls you back, screams at you to do something.

My work is changing me, and changing my family. I become less predictable, but better organized. I become more active when I am active, more passive when I am passive; more angry, and more loving. I have gotten over being ironical. I have gotten tougher and more independent, but I think I love at least two whole families and would be very hurt if they quit. I need at least an hour's decompression to get out of the maze of families I have seen during the day. Margaret gets really angry if I play family therapist with our family.

That is the basic shape of the hill, though what's under it I hardly know. Some outcroppings are visible:

I was from a super-involved and somewhat isolated family in a little southern town, and I may be trying to find out what other families are like inside.

I know I am a voyeurist, and I enjoy it.

I am sometimes a critical teen-ager, telling parents how to run things better, my way.

I hate the establishment, and orthodoxy, and family therapy is now a convenient rebellion.

I probably want to anticipate pitfalls in life and avoid them by seeing what people do.

I want to do some co-therapy with my wife.

I think the best therapist in the future may be a small community of families committed long-term to building a therapeutic social system in micro.

〰〰〰〰〰〰〰〰〰〰〰〰〰〰〰〰〰〰〰〰〰〰〰〰〰〰〰〰 *By C. Whitaker*

One basic ingredient in making me a family therapist was my sneaky tendency to drift. I was a GYN resident, and I

96

drifted into a psychiatric hospital for one year. But intrigued by the problem of schizophrenia, I decided to go into child psychiatry, and after three years there drifted on into delinquency for two more. I went back to the one-to-one treatment of schizophrenics, got discouraged by doing it myself, and joined up as a team with first Dr. John Warkentin and then Dr. Thomas Malone. I began to treat groups; dissatisfied with each of these as a method of understanding or treating schizophrenia, we moved on to treating couples and then entire families.

I'm sure that part of the freedom to drift came from a tendency to go with my impulses and a persistent devotion to confusion. Then I discovered the values of multiple therapy where I could be supported, encouraged, and released by teaming up with another therapist. It's clear also that my own treatment by a two-therapist team also tended to make me move toward three-person processes rather than stay with the one-to-one. My third experience as a patient included my wife and son, so that I experienced the inner pressures of family treatment as well as the professional aspects of it. Part of my drifting had to do with my becoming bored with the one-to-one therapy. It seemed repetitive. It seemed more and more sterile, and I was more and more constrained by the symbolic role pressure.

Much more important than boredom with individual treatment as a work setting was my gradual drift into preoccupation with the state of stress emerging in my colleague Cuddle group. This professional family was itself obviously under stress, and the maturity of the individuals in it was not sufficient to resolve without divorce.

As I was untwisted by my six children growing up, I became enmeshed in my family as a large unit. The dynamics of each of us as individuals seemed only part of the picture. The dynamics of the triangles, of the couples and the generations, were more and more obviously a central problem in the growth of my own family.

Also, I began increasingly feeling the cuddling and the jobs at home were pushing me to work with other family

97

systems. I had become depressed by the relative isolation of my successful ex-patients, both lay and professional. Their individuation seemed grossly crippled by lack of unity with a significant other, usually their spouse, and with their social others. To see these patients who had done well in individual therapy thoroughly screw up their group living made the value of individual therapy seem very limited. Watching the process of change and no change in the families of friends, neighbors, and patients whose families I knew well seemed to evidence that individual therapy was often a feeble instrument.

Maybe it's because I run scared. When I was in my obstetrics residency I did a voluntary operation for painful menstruation on a woman with two kids. In the middle of the operation the anesthesia machine exploded and the next day the patient died. Maybe I gave up obstetrics because I was horrified at being partially responsible for this woman's death. I was scared when I moved into a psychiatric residency, presumably for one year. I discovered that the grossly psychotic patients were impossible to understand, in terrible pain, and I couldn't turn away — that was me there. In the child psychiatry residency that followed, I discovered it was fun working with those little kids. It was fascinating to be helpful, but the families didn't change. Maybe it was because when I worked with delinquents I gradually realized that my craziness, my childishness and even my delinquency were deeply involved in what I did. I'll never know how many delinquents stole cars because I got such a kick out of hearing the story.

Maybe I moved out of that because I was scared. Was I making it worse instead of better? Or because I discovered that some delinquents with psychotic and murderous parents loved those parents just as much as those parents I could see were lovable? Did I run from there to the treatment of psychotics in intensive therapy and discover that my guts in the therapeutic situation were not enough? That boy from Harvard whom I agonized with for three years didn't get better. He just got quieter. The boy from Menninger's got much better in the three years I worked with him, but

98

he was thrown back into a full-blown psychosis when his parents lured him back home by that new red Chevy convertible. He did keep calling every six months to tell us how well he was and how things were going so nicely with Mother and Dad, except that between times he would be in that distant hospital again. Was I running from that? Did the ten years of teaching medical students and being endlessly goosed by them during the two-year group therapy marathons do it? Did that get us desperate enough to tackle the whole family? Or did I just run scared from the teaching? Our private clinic with the same trusted group gave me courage, and the multiple therapy system helped us get more involved with patients' social problems. In private practice those patients are so insistent that it's helping. You feel more and more desperate to do something.

Did I move into family therapy because of those precious ones who didn't make it? I got more and more desperate to do something different. That homosexual salad cook who got more comfortable but stayed homosexual. The isolate schizoid CPA who told me six months later that he hadn't lied. He never called his mother. She, of course, called him every Saturday night. Or the old-maid biologist whom I thought would grow up and get married, but I didn't have enough of what it took. Or the physician whose schizophrenia I cured and then he couldn't leave me — he had to get himself addicted to Dexamyl and get in a psychiatric hospital in order to get rid of me. Or the other failures — the fantastic money-making woman psychopath who when I finally broke through her psychopathology got cancer. Or maybe it was the great divorce. When I finally decided, after twenty years of working and suffering with a group of colleagues whom I loved and leaned on profoundly, that it didn't seem to be enough, I decided I had to move out and try it on my own.

Maybe the only reason I finally got into family therapy was because my own family was fading into time and geography and my wife and I could think again of new families — like a marathon couple's group or a friendship network and the possibility of the individuals in it changing when we forced them to unite in this synthetic family.

Somehow through all this I developed a conviction that the group was more powerful than the therapist. Or maybe that was just because I was dependent upon the group. Since I grew up isolated, I needed a group — so I believed that each individual needed a group and that the only way to change him or help him move was to help his group move.

Why did I stay in family therapy? What did I get out of it? I stayed in it because I was seduced by it. What I got out of it was being scared — the fun and the challenge of mixing it up in the family. As increasing stress produced increasing anxiety, it produced a change in me. There seemed less need for self-denial, and less need for withholding. In the family I was freer to use my remaining slivers of pathology, and thus try to resolve more of them. With more freedom to unleash my humor and my sarcasm, I experienced a creative letting go and turning on. It seems also important that in family work I got further free of the past. My day was more alive, more current, and more exciting. In family therapy there is greater homeostasis to depend upon. The therapist need not be worried about using himself. He need not worry about harming the patient. There is a greater chance for him to be dependent, to discard his impulse control, or to regress at will. I was free to turn on a higher interpersonal temperature than was tolerable in the one-to-one, in the couples' treatment, in group treatment, or in any group of social squares. Furthermore, there is a greater diversification of experience working with families. One can move within the hour from cuddling the baby to fighting with the father or to straight talk with an adolescent. It seems to me, also, that greater experimental flavor and the more interpersonal poetic license that families offer opens me to more and more of my living. I become part of the joy of their wallowing in the ecstasy of self-love and the joyful despair of becoming people, and wade through the awesome despair of my being a self. Here I have the freedom to lose myself in endless new patterns of family interaction, to discover new ways of expanding both my union with the family and my individuation from it, to find myself again, and lose myself still again.

I find also I have less nostalgia for my own missing children, the loss of my own extended family, and the loss of the small-town heaven of my childhood. Family therapy then offers me a chance to tackle schizophrenia, tackle the complexities of the family dynamic patterns, to be mixed up in them myself, to struggle to get into the family, to struggle to create a therapeutic family, to regain my individual personhood after becoming lost in that new family, to re-live with excitement the growth of my own children and the infinite colors and tones of memory that are reactivated by being involved in reduplication of my original family. It's very hard to be bored with the kaleidoscope of family interactions and the relationship of the whole, its parts, and its individuals to the therapist and his co-therapist. The family resembles the old color organ, an infinite variety of shapes, movement, and color — framed in time and available for the plunging in and the jumping out. Treating the family has the quality of and the joys of general practice, in contrast with the specialist characteristics of one-to-one therapy with its tunnel vision, tremendous self-denial, and symbolic role pressures.

Some say he is still trying to get over the isolation of the farm and trying to learn how to make it with those city slickers. And it probably is important that he grew up with this feeling that mother nature always comes through although as I talked to him, I gather he still doesn't know whether mother nature is really a prostitute or just a Jewish mother who is never short of chicken soup even if she has to kill a well chicken to make soup for some sick chicken.

God protect my open synapses!

By P. Guerin

A personal statement as to one's evolution to the professional position of "family therapist" borders on the impossible. How does one portray an accurate, factual account of the numerous complex factors in any such evolution? The task, as issued by the editors, contained one simple and concise direction, that there be maximum "camp" and minimal "bull." The implicit difficulty with this lies in the fact that one man's "bull" is another's "camp," and vice versa. Another difficulty in this for me stems from my hereditary position in a long line of "Irish Bull."

The two most important determinants of my present professional position are my contact with Murray Bowen while in my residency training at Georgetown, and my part in the process of my own personal family system.

About three-quarters of the way through my first year of residency, while in the midst of working with my "prize schizophrenic," I first heard some of the ideas of family systems theory. These ideas seemed to make some sense when related to the context of my personal and professional experiences. However, the new concept of seeing peoples' problems as based in a dysfunctional family system rather than a dysfunctional ego state raised much confusion amongst my synapses and consequently in my verbal utterances.

My analytical supervisors became concerned. As time progressed, and the prognosis worsened, they became alarmed: was I heading down the road to *psychic degradation*?

As I experienced the concern of my supervisors, many of whom I still recall with a fond respect, I often felt like abandoning my heretical ways. Despite these feelings, I plodded on. In a sanctioned part-time evening clinic job, I began doing family work with three individual families, and four others in a multiple family model. I converted my "prize schizophrenic" into a research project called "An Attempt at Family-Social Network Therapy with a Schizophrenic Family." The supervision of this work also included the beginning of my research into the process of my own family system.

102

Part way into my second year of residency at Georgetown, I began having thoughts about shifting to another training facility. I believe my main reason had to do with the fact that I had also been a medical student at Georgetown and thought that perhaps moving to the public school system might be a broadening experience. When offered a position as chief resident at Albert Einstein College of Medicine of Yeshiva University in New York City, I went from one parochial system to another in the true spirit of ecumenism. I remember that my relieved supervisors thought I might regain my orthodoxy at Einstein.

My year as chief resident at Einstein was difficult. Once again I found myself surrounded by a group of superior caliber psychoanalysts. In addition, I had to teach the psychoanalytic model to the junior residents. I also didn't have much free time, and had to squeeze in a family case here and there. During this time my functioning as a family therapist declined and I had difficulty keeping my thinking clearly on either a psychoanalytic or family systems track. During this time I even considered once again the idea of embarking on a personal analysis. Somehow "resistance" prevailed. Once I was a few months past my year as chief resident, the ability to think clearly about family systems returned and I was on my way. During this difficult time, I think continuing to work on my own personal family system and seeing the theoretical concepts at work there, having a continuing relationship with Murray Bowen, as well as developing relationships with Tom Fogarty and Andy Ferber, sustained my commitment to the family movement.

Having seen some of the theoretical concepts of family systems theory at work in my clinical experience, it seemed reasonable to study myself in the context of my own personal family system using these concepts as basic assumptions. Prior to taking on this research project, I had tended to see myself and others in my family from a characterological point of view. Defense mechanisms, oral, anal, and genital fixation levels, were formulated in my mind as I observed the part of their behavior bothersome to me. As I began

103

this research project on self, the beginning of a new way of viewing life evolved. A personal vignette may serve to clarify. My wife and I, since our days as camp counselors together, have always enjoyed each other's company, and shared a certain number of common interests as well as a desire to laugh with life even in some of its most somber moments. Throughout our relationship I had desired a greater closeness, an increased mutual sharing of thoughts and feelings. Kathy's usual program of behavior is to create space between her and others, allowing others to move toward or pursue her. In a quiet, ladylike gentleness there is little open volunteering of thoughts or feelings. In face of stress or anxiety, she tends to frankly distance from others and further wall off her personal space of thoughts and feelings. The quiet gentleness can appear to turn to a confused helplessness. So it is not too surprising that as her mate I should be a spacefiller, or a mover toward people, an outpourer of personal thoughts and feelings. In times of stress and anxiety benevolent interest becomes over-concern, other-control, and a taking over of responsibility for the spacemaker. The closeness that I viewed myself as desiring was, in fact, operationally an attempt at other-control — to soothe my own anxiety.

In practical terms, the emotional process between Kathy and myself, as we attempted to deal with it, would take a form something like this: A stress would develop. In response Kathy would distance from me, and pull into herself. This would be accomplished by disappearance under the hair dryer, into a book, or if really pressed, into the land of dreams. Sensing the distance, I would barge forward, inquire as to what was going on with her. The predictable answer would be "nothing." In frustration and anger, I would attempt to pull back. However, the uneasy feelings involved were not a very comfortable cushion on which to sit. As a result I would do one of two things, move toward the telephone and subsequently other people, or, lodging in my bunker of hurt, I would lob out mortar shells of criticism. These of course would further add to the wall surrounding

104

Kathy's thoughts and feelings. Eventually tenderness and caring would break through and adaptation on one or the other's part would calm the waters of discontent; however, real growth, differentiation, or change failed to take place. The dysfunctional pattern would inevitably repeat itself. Over a period of time as a more objective awareness of this process developed, I decided to abandon my attempts at changing Kathy and begin to try to change myself. In doing this, I experienced the degree of anxiety and emotional pain that goes along with even *attempting* to change a program of behavior or a way of operating. By a series of experimental moves, I learned that if I could reverse the process with Kathy and create emotional space by my distancing from her, she would eventually have to move toward me. However, I found I could only hold the distance long enough if I had a planned series of moves. Also, initially Kathy's moves toward me would be to find out if I were bugged or upset. There still was little openness with her own thoughts and feelings. I eventually added another move to my plan and began airing my own personal thoughts and feelings without a fixed expectation of a reciprocal move by Kathy. Following my airing I would distance into a household project. Over a period of days, Kathy gradually began a process of sharing her thoughts and feelings with me. Kathy, being a perceptive girl (whom else would a perceptive person like me marry?), caught on quickly and very soon was doing her share of reversing the process. She would move toward and crowd me as a way of subtly letting me know I was off on a splurge of infantile and demanding behavior. The end result, I believe, has been an increase in separation and closeness on both our parts, an increase in each of our levels of emotional functioning and an increase in the functioning level of the nuclear part of our family system. At this point in time, I would view our relationship as a functional one, in which the potential for change on both our parts is possible. I believe that personal growth and maturity are best worked on and attained in the context of the marital relationship.

The emotional process between Kathy and me, described in preceding paragraphs, is at best oversimplified. It fails to speak sufficiently to the intricacy of the process itself and the way over the years it inevitably moved to involve both our children and our extended families. The corresponding increase in individuality and closeness in my relationship with my wife has provided part of the nidus for my continuing commitment to family as a way of thinking. The commitment entails an attempt at further developing a theory of family systems, as well as a continuing commitment to working on myself in this context, in order to become knowable to myself and others in my family. Hopefully, they also will come to be more knowable to themselves and to me.

At present, I am struggling to keep my professional belief system open and growing. I see family systems theory as a workable way to approach thinking about the problems of the human phenomenon. I see other theories (including psychoanalysis) as also being plausible explanations for human behavior.

Professionally, I now spend a portion of my time sharing with others (called trainees) some of my ideas about family systems. Another portion of my time is spent as a consultant to a large number of families in my private practice. The remainder of my time is committed to continuing work on my own family system, playing with three lovely little girls, mowing the lawn, and various and sundry other activities.

All in all, it's not a bad deal. I mean, in what other professional position could you look forward to the thirty-to-forty per cent bracket opportunity for dispensing pure "Irish Bull?"

⁓⁓⁓⁓⁓⁓⁓⁓⁓⁓⁓⁓⁓⁓⁓⁓⁓⁓⁓⁓⁓⁓⁓⁓⁓⁓⁓⁓⁓ *By T. Fogarty*

I can recall being eighteen, sitting in a dispensary as an enlisted man in the U.S. Army with my feet up on the desk, playing poker with the M.D. captain. I forget who was winning. The door opened and in strode a general, stopping by for an inspection while on a horseback ride. Honest to goodness, he was a real general. Both of us dropped our cards and had the grace to remove our feet from the table. It seemed like days went by while he glared at us and the dirty floor, before he shouted out "Attention!" I recall making myself as scarce as possible. The captain nearly got shipped out and my colonel swore that he would quit medicine the day a stupid klunk like me ever got into medical school. I figured he had already quit medicine and took this as a good omen for my future medical career. They could do very little else to me because I was already low man on the totem pole. Around about the same time, I went out and bought Karl Menninger's *The Human Mind*. I didn't understand it then and I still don't. Maybe I was trying to figure out what was in the colonel's head or my own or why a general couldn't just enjoy riding a horse and leave it at that.

Later on, I went to medical school (I assume the colonel retired) with the distinct goal of becoming a psychiatrist. I found the psychiatric department so inspiring that I ended up doing a three-year residency in internal medicine. Then I went out into private practice. Hospital medicine is interesting, stimulating, busy, and exciting. In private practice, after I developed my ritual for handling colds, diarrhea, arthritis, coronaries, diabetes, and vague aches and pains, I suddenly awoke to the fact that I was bored stiff. It was more interesting to talk to people about themselves than their colds. If they had six colds a year, why did they bring only this one to me? I saw "depressed" people who got a little better no matter what I said. After two years, I began to scout around for other professional possibilities. Perhaps those night calls at two, three, or four o'clock in the morning helped my resolve. My wife recalls answering the phone early one morning and my saying into the phone in a semi-stupor, "Tell them I'm not here." At any event, with the help of Uncle Sam, I put a closed sign on the front door and headed south to Washington, D.C. for a psychiatric residency. Finally, I was getting to my goal.

Psychiatric residency is a stimulating experience. I spent the first year working in a hospital. My supervisor had strange ideas. He believed in putting in a full day's work, if that is what you are paid for. Many others were spending minimal time at the hospital, preoccupied with their analysis or other important business. Because of this belief, my ward supervisor was called an "obsessive compulsive." Lesson number one. Psychiatric diagnosis has many uses not included in the handbook. It can be used for justification, judgment, explanation, cover, etc. Then there were those conferences. A person in one or many situations would be "presented." Then everybody around the table would give his personal "I feel such and such" explanation of what was going on. It didn't seem to matter that nobody agreed or that there was no movement toward agreement or that there was no evidence. This was a good conference because everybody was involved. Involved in what? The final "I feel" was usually rendered from the end of the table by the senior member present or a visiting dignitary. His "I feel" would have the singular honor of being entered on the chart. I would sit there and try to recall my medical days. If I ever dared to enter a conference and say "I feel this man has a myocardial infarction," I would be laughed out of the room and would not dare show up in the hospital for two years. They would want evidence. I would be pinned down. They would ask for the sed rate, the symptoms, the blood pressure, the Serum Transaminase, the EKG, etc. This was discouraging. It meant that I would have to wait any number of years before my "I feel" would ever carry any weight. Perhaps I would even have to become a colonel. Second lesson. Don't look for evidence. If you do, you are being intellectual, mechanistic, uninvolved, avoiding feelings, cold, and unfeeling.

In my first year of residency, a "patient" came in, hooked on drugs and wearing a patch over one eye from a childhood accident. He began to be known affectionately

108

as "ol' one eye." I did a masterful job with him. I talked to him, had him worked up by the eye men, sent him for an operation for a glass eye and, in due time, "presented" him. My cup overflowed with praise and glory and satisfaction at the conference. Two days later, "ol' one eye" went AWOL from the hospital, robbed someone, and was in jail. Lesson number three. Never do a follow-up. After you "present" a person, leave it alone. It is good enough that everybody feels better about it. Don't look for change.

In my second year, I met Murray Bowen, professor of psychiatry at Georgetown Medical Center and one of the leading figures in the field of family therapy. He, too, did strange things. He drew diagrams on the board, he interviewed families in front of us, he never went beyond the evidence. He actually looked for some evidence. He set up experiments between people in the family and wondered who was talking to whom and where the lines of communication lay. He let people talk about themselves and never tried to read their minds. He was impressive. I could feel the same degree of empathy for him as I did that M.D. captain in the army. Both were willing to play poker.

I continued to study with Murray Bowen and in my third year, I selected him for my elective. I ended working the student health program as their elective. Well, I suppose electives can be used just like diagnostic labels. After three years, I was ready to head north and try out my own wings. I decided to start out toward the top and secured a position as director of a community mental health clinic. My boss came in and said, "Tom, this is your clinic. Run it." Later he added, "And here's how to run it." I tried to understand this because I knew he was in analysis. I won't tell you how many years of analysis — beyond a decade that is. Now I went to directors' meetings. Now we would sit around a large table and discuss who was going to pick up the responsibility for what. As soon as this was fixed on someone, everybody seemed happy. But I wasn't. Somehow, I ended up responsible for over a hundred thousand people. I was responsible for Mount Vernon, Pelham, Tuchahoe, Eastchester, Bronxville, etc. I, who had so much difficulty assuming responsibility for myself, now had a hundred thousand more people to be responsible for. Needless to say, this caused some friction. My boss would tell me that, if I would just go into analysis and get some treatment, everything would be okay. Finally, he fired me. I retired to a back room where I sat down with families. This was a real good position. As a former director, the powers that be were reluctant to tell me what to do. I finally had a clear field. I started to see families. I opened a private practice. In the past six years, I have seen twelve to fourteen hundred families from one visit to three to four years. It was a long trip but a worthwhile one. For my start and my perseverance through it, I thank my family and Murray Bowen.

What I have said so far pretty much spells out the "how" of becoming a family therapist. Now for the "why." This is much more obscure. Let me try to say something about my family. My mother died about three weeks ago. She died peacefully in her sleep as was her ardent wish. It is a constant source of solace to me that I had planned making this type of statement before she died unexpectedly. I know, that wherever she is, she can hear me. My father died fifteen years ago. It is a constant source of discomfort to me that I was not able, willing, or wise enough to make such a statement to him before he died. I am not proud of that. I hope that, wherever he is, he can understand that too. Before proceeding, I would like to make a few general remarks. It has become fashionable to refer to one's parents in a somewhat patronizing, snide, pathologically oriented way. It is almost as if to say: "Look what I came from and see how far I have gone." My parents were not perfect. But then, neither am I. Nor is anything that I have ever known. I experience discomfort about things that I have done, thought, felt, and I assume that they did too. Basically, I think that I deserved them, that I deserve my wife and my children. I think that they deserve me too. Yet, at any given moment, I am perfectly capable of assuming the opposite posture. I am just as perfect-imperfect as anyone else.

My father and mother were both immigrants from Ireland, the only members of their large families who left the "old country." Later in life, my mother would often express her loneliness for members of her extended family, especially after the death of my father. He seemed more able to surround himself with friends. It is difficult to present a picture of a person because everybody sitting around that person will see him differently. I have spent some time talking to others and other members of the family about my parents. My father was a well-educated and cultured man. He believed in schooling and learning. He was strict, religious, but, above all, honest. I can recall traveling with him while he made out wills, etc., for poor people for nothing. These people adored him. They trusted him. I could always trust him. I knew he would be there. We had our disagreements and angry conflicts later. He taught me to be honest, to stand for something, to be impatient, often to be chronically irritated, and to have integrity. Some of these things I must change and some I must live up to. I wish that I had had a more personal relationship with him.

My mother was easygoing. So many people have said: "I could do no wrong whenever your mother was around." She was a gracious person who tended to be an overdoer. What someone would consider a burden, she would consider a snub if you didn't ask her to do it. She taught me compassion and how to "bend a rule" for a good reason. A good reason to her was that she cared about the person. She was not as clear in her beliefs as my father. Behind all this were some characteristics of the Irish family. These included pride and shame. It was the old philosophy of "Aunt Millie is in the nut house. Everybody knows it but ain't nobody going to mention it." Faith comes easily to the Irishman, openness only with a struggle.

I was the third of five children — four boys and then a girl. I loved to play ball and the only thing to this day that I would rather be than a family therapist is a professional ball player. The family considered me to be lazy, and even today they find it hard to believe that I actually work. I was considered a genius of some sort, though I knew this was untrue. I was a con artist from an early age. It still lingers on today. In a strange way, though I was impatient, I could wait indefinitely for certain things. I recall leading my class at college after the war, receiving the medal and saying nothing to the family. I knew they would hear about it. They did and, in predictable fashion, said "How about that, he gets the excellence medal and says nothing." It was generally acknowledged that everything that I touched turned to gold. I knew this was untrue. My friends said of me (I have checked since) that I was "independent and moody." That is a story in itself.

I am not sure what this all means. If I look at history, I realize that the Fogartys were pretty much the first of a generation. I think that we were lonely. Things didn't come easily, though they always came. I sometimes think that a family therapist is a lonely fellow. I know that in my extended family, I experienced trust, acceptance, but not as much closeness as I desired. I realize that I did not contribute to that closeness. In time I married a girl from Ireland, a girl who grew up within miles of where my mother was born. From the moment I met her, she has been the most important person in my life. She is a lady — gentle, proud, and a counterbalance to and for me. I have heard from friends, since the start of time, that I was fortunate to grow up in the family that I had. Earlier I did not know what they meant. I always thought that so and so had it so much easier. I have taken the trouble to check what this "easiness" has meant to many of them in their later life. Now I begin to know what they mean. I do think that I have been fortunate. I mean this for both the family I live in and the one I came from. As I said, they deserve me — and I deserve them too.

I would like to believe and do believe that something "good" occurred in my family. I also know it could be better. I would like to believe that my family can move a little beyond the family I came from. It gives me a kick and a sense of meaning in life to believe that I can contribute in some way to closeness in other families. I sincerely thank all those who have contributed to that. Perhaps someday I can really "become."

∿∿∿ *By J. Haley*

Not long ago a young man said to me, "A psychotic episode of an adolescent is a fluctuation in a family," and I found myself irritated that he could begin his career with an idea that took me so many years to grope toward. I began doing therapy in a more naïve period, the 1950's, with schizophrenic patients in a hospital setting and with private patients who had less bizarre disorders. Even though I was not properly trained, I was immersed in the traditional ideology of the individual, including the notion that helping a person become aware of what was behind his problem would cause him to change. My recovery from those ideas was slow.

At what part I began therapy with couples and families is obscure in memory, but the earliest tape recording I can find of myself interviewing a whole family is dated February, 1956. As part of Gregory Bateson's project on communication, I was doing therapy with schizophrenic patients in a Veterans Administration Hospital. One patient was unable to be with his parents on visiting day without collapsing into an anxiety state, and yet he could not conceive of going anywhere when he left the hospital except home to his parents. I asked his mother and father to come into a session with him to try to understand what was so upsetting to him, and I continued to see the family weekly. According to another recording, dated January, 1957, the Bateson project was conducting a program of formal treatment of the whole family of the schizophrenic with the focus upon changing the family as a unit. The steps leading up to this introduction of family therapy into the research project appear simple in restrospect, but were not.

Bateson received a grant to study the paradoxes of

113

communication in 1952, and John Weakland and I joined him at the beginning of 1953. It was not a clinical project and was housed in the Veterans Administration Hospital only because Bateson was ethnologist there. We examined a variety of kinds of animal and human communication. In 1953 we started to record the discourse of a schizophrenic patient and our interest in this type of communication grew as well as our interest in the therapy of schizophrenics. We visited and recorded John Rosen at work in 1954 and began to study a variety of therapists. Don Jackson joined us as a consultant and supervised the therapy we were doing with schizophrenics. He had written his paper on homeostasis in 1954 and was moving to the view that there was a balance in a family which was affected by therapeutic change.

In 1954 Bateson coined the term "double bind" and argued that it was etiologic to schizophrenia. This was deduced, not observed. Given the ways a schizophrenic confuses his levels of message, he must have been raised in a learning situation where his parents imposed conflicting messages. One might think that we would have brought in the families of schizophrenics at this time to examine double binds, but the theory was only etiological at this stage. We were apparently not assuming that schizophrenia was a current response to the family.

When we began to observe the schizophrenic talking with his parents, we shifted to the view that schizophrenia could be a way of adapting to a *current* family situation. Psychotic behavior could be thought of as an appropriate response to what was happening in the family (or the hospital) right then. This was a major step in our thinking and took time to clarify.

By 1957 we were not only accepting the idea that schizophrenia was a response of the patient to his family, but we had conceived of the idea of changing the family in order to change the schizophrenic. This, again, was a major shift in thinking about the cause and cure of that disorder. To think of the family as causal was one thing, and it could still follow logically that the patient could be "treated" without

114

changing the family. To think of his behavior as *responsive,* so that change in his family was necessary if he was not to be schizophrenic, was a new way of thinking. It coincided with our shift from trying to change the schizophrenic by individual therapy in the hospital setting to trying to move the patient out of the hospital into the real world where schizophrenic behavior was not as appropriate as it was in the hospital.

I believe it was in 1957 that we discovered other people who were doing family therapy. I don't mean therapists who were doing individual treatment while considering the importance of the family, or those doing diagnostic interviews. I mean therapists who were oriented to the idea of bringing about a change in the family by therapeutic interventions. As difficult as it was to re-define psychopathology into family terms, it seemed even more difficult to accept the idea that a new theory of therapeutic change must develop as a consequence.

In 1958 the Bateson project applied for a grant to study the family therapy of schizophrenics. We were treating quite a number of families, as well as supervising therapists who wished to learn how to do this. There were only three of us on the project, with Jackson part-time, and another psychiatrist, William F. Fry, who had joined us part-time. To increase our sample of families we exchanged training for the therapist if he would treat this type of family in our research setting.

Working with these families was changing our views about the cause of therapeutic change. We had carried over many of the ideas of the individual therapy of that time when we first began. We brought the family members together to help them understand themselves and each other. With understanding, lifting of repression, tracing problems to their historical roots, and clarifying communication, the families would change — or so we thought. After two or three years struggling with this approach, we found, as many others have found, that it was lively and dynamic but not effective. We sought more directive ways of working. We

115

also increasingly appreciated the impossibility of working with families where a member was plugged into a hospital. With each improvement and crisis there was re-hospitalization and stabilization, so that basic change could not occur.

As we were more able to think of psychosis as an adaptive response to a family, we began to view adolescent schizophrenia as a problem of disengaging from parents at the age when it is appropriate for the child to leave home. I have a recording of a conversation in 1958 with Milton H. Erickson in which John Weakland and I were talking with him about therapy as a procedure for successfully weaning child and parents from each other. Erickson had been working with couples and families for a number of years at that time. It was his view, and ours, that bringing about togetherness in these families was not a feasible goal at this point in the life cycle of the family. Yet insofar as the young person's behavior served a function in the family, it was also not wise to merely separate him from his parents and cut off contact. (Don Jackson became particularly skillful in keeping the schizophrenic involved with his parents while simultaneously setting him out on his own independent life.)

During this period when the project was working with families of schizophrenics, I was shifting to a family view in my private practice. I had begun a practice in the mid-1950's, specializing in brief treatment. My task was to get someone over a symptom as rapidly as possible. At that time there was not the variety of therapeutic approaches there is now. Long-term, insight therapy was about the only procedure available. Therefore it was necessary to innovate different procedures. This was particularly necessary with the patients who had been through long-term, insight therapy and still had their symptoms. There was an increasing population of psychoanalytic failures and they were seeking a different type of therapy. As I practiced symptom elimination, I found it was a psychiatric myth that if a patient recovered from a symptom he developed a worse one. But it became apparent to me that when a patient recovered there was difficulty in his marriage and family. As patients

116

improved, their spouses asked to see me. Although that seems an obvious response now, at that time I was slow to see that the appearance of a problem of the spouse was a response to the improvement I was bringing about. This led me to begin to anticipate this response by working with the spouse and other family members. The next step was to begin to view "symptoms" as a contract between two or more persons, and so change in the family became a logical therapeutic goal. This family orientation in my practice with non-schizophrenic problems came at the same time as the orientation developed in the research project studying therapy of families of schizophrenics. John Weakland and I also began teaching courses in hypnosis and brief therapy which became more family-oriented.

In about 1959 Don Jackson formed the Mental Research Institute, and Virginia Satir joined him. They began a training program in family therapy. Although the Bateson project and the Mental Research Institute have been confused in people's minds, there was actually no connection between them. Jackson participated in both enterprises, and our family experiment program shared a building with the MRI at one point. But the Bateson project continued its independent course and none of the personnel of the MRI were part of it. We also did not participate in the family therapy training there.

In 1962 the Bateson project ended after ten years. Bateson went off to study dolphins, Weakland returned to his interest in Chinese culture, and I joined the Mental Research Institute to continue an experimental program with families. Don Jackson and I founded *Family Process,* and as editor my obligation was to keep up with what was happening in the family field around the country. For a number of years I traveled and observed a variety of family therapists and lectured on what was happening. In each area people thought that what the local family therapist was doing was universal and did not know of the variety of treatment approaches developing quite independently in the different places.

In 1967 I joined the **Philadelphia Child Guidance** Clinic, where Salvador Minuchin was transforming a traditional child guidance clinic into a family-oriented treatment clinic. Since the staff could not learn family therapy in academia, they had to learn it on the job. A major problem, as in all training in family therapy, was the problem of the professional unlearning of much of what he had been taught if he was to be an effective therapist in the family approach. An additional problem was learning how to treat poor people when the clinic began to deal with that population. Although my job was research, I became more involved in teaching and supervision of family therapy.

In 1969 Minuchin received a grant to train poor and black people to treat families. They were to learn to treat a variety of types of families, but they would specialize in the low socioeconomic black family. This enterprise proved to be the most interesting family therapy training I have done. The faculty consisted of Minuchin, myself, Rae Weiner, Carter Umbarger, Jerry Ford, and Anna Wiggins. We faced the task of training eight people, who had never been acquainted with therapy, nor had had any professional education, to be fully responsible family therapists in two years. We had in mind the idea of training eight poor people; they in turn would train more who would train more so that we could multiply the number of therapists available to the neglected low socioeconomic community.

We selected four women and four men out of about sixty who appeared. Largely we selected on the basis of the person's competence in his personal life and what we could judge of his ability as a helper. Most of them were in their thirties and forties, and so had experienced marriage and childrearing. We preferred people with only high school education and wanted no knowledge of psychiatry or psychology.

The training program was intensive, particularly the first year. It was forty hours a week of activity. During the first two weeks we introduced them to the course and taught them to interview by simulating families. They began inter-

118

viewing a minimum of two people so they would begin with less of an individual orientation. After the second week we placed them in with families. The group of eight were housed in one large office and shared all observation and supervision so that each student therapist saw the families of others as well as his own. They were exposed to some didactic lectures, but there were no reading assignments and the teaching was largely built upon the active treatment of families. There were several aspects of this training which were, to me, innovative:

1. The problem was how to give the student full responsibility for his therapy while at the same time protecting the family from a novice therapist. We dealt with this by live supervision. The supervisor was behind the one-way mirror and could enter if need be, call in, or call the student out for consultation. Regularly the students left the family session to come out and consult. On home visits, the supervisor went along. He was defined as a consultant and not as a co-therapist, so the student had the responsibility for what happened, but the supervisor was there, in case of need. Although video- and audio-tape supervision was done, the live supervision allowed the student to be guided at a time when he and the family could use the guidance, not later when the moment had passed. We avoided co-therapy because the student tends to become an assistant and sits back; we wanted therapists who would intervene actively.

2. Students were not taught concepts and ideas first which they later applied in their work. Instead, they were taught only what was necessary in relation to a particular family. For example, when they dealt with a family with a retarded child, we would then teach about dealing with retardation. In this way the students' interest was aroused because they were introduced to ideas and generalizations only at the point when they needed them.

3. The students had no background in traditional psychological and psychiatric ideas, and so they did not have those notions to unlearn. They also had no roots outside the training, but knew only what was being taught. Professionals, in

119

contrast, are listening to a family therapy teacher with one ear tuned to what their teacher in academia would say about such ideas. The low socioeconomic students had a popular individual orientation, but they did not have the intensively trained individual ideas of a professional. They were also more free in their acceptance of ideas of what might cause change. For example, one of these therapists could conduct an interview without ever making an interpretation to help a mother discover how miserably she was treating her child. He had not been taught that such self-awareness caused change. Instead, he negotiated with mother and child to deal with each other differently, arousing none of the resistances that appear with insight interpretations.

4. We avoided as much as possible making interpretations to students which would focus them on their own motives and problems. We wanted therapists who would trust their impulses.

5. In order to teach in this style, the faculty had to clarify in their own minds, and with each other, their ideas about family problems and kinds of intervention, and to simplify these ideas so they could be easily grasped. Yet the goal was not to produce a student who could articulate and conceptualize his premises, but rather to produce a therapist who would do the right thing at the right time because it felt right for him to do it. Successful teaching was not indicated by how well a student talked about therapy, but by how well he did it.

Whether this training program will be successful cannot be determined at the time of this writing. However, the teaching of family therapy to this group in this way was a refreshing change. Once one accepts the idea that the family orientation is a discontinuous change from past ideas about therapy, it is a pleasure to teach a group of people who are not enmeshed in those past ideas. Both faculty and students could examine what kinds of intervention are effective, not what someone once said ought to be. Once the students learned to intervene to change real people with real problems in the real world, then it was possible to introduce them to the ideas of psychiatry and psychology so they could communicate with professionals.

For me, training professionals in family therapy with middle-class families was becoming a routine task with expectable difficulties. Training poor people to deal with the poor was a new experience with difficulties and rewards not easily anticipated. Let me give a vignette as an example. One of our students was dealing with a boy and his mother in a family where the father had died a few months before. The boy was possibly retarded and his mother hovered over him, keeping him at home. During the interview the mother said the boy had been seeing and talking to his deceased father upstairs, and this worried the mother. I began to anticipate the usual therapist reaction which would be an exploration of how psychotic was this boy. Instead, the student asked the boy what his father said to him when he talked to him. The boy said his father told him his mother should get him a bicycle. This led to a discussion with mother about her conflict with the boy over getting him a bicycle. (The mother was willing to buy him one but not willing to let him ride it.) The visitations of father upstairs disappeared and boy and mother worked out a different kind of relationship with more space for both of them.

One of the more interesting problems in family therapy training is how to persuade a professional who has been immersed in the diagnostic system and trained in mental hospital settings for a period of years to treat an apparently psychotic event as a transitory problem in human relations.

Looking back, it seems to me there are several ways to better understand the nature of therapy. One is to watch therapists at work rather than listen to what they say. Another is to do therapy oneself and be sufficiently experimental to try different procedures and examine the outcome to see what works and abandon what does not. A third is to train others, because then one can see a variety of responses to a variety of approaches. Over the years, therapists have moved from a unit of one person to a dyad to a triad and they are now trying to think in larger units. The most important unit is the one which includes the therapist, and often this is the most difficult one to think about. It was a step forward to discover that a person was resistant to change because of his family context. A more important step was to discover that a family can be resistant to change because of the ways the therapist is dealing with the family. When parents react unfortunately as a child improves, it is a comfort to theorize about homeostasis and the stability of systems. Yet seeing the parental reaction as a possible response to the ways the therapist is intervening can lead one nearer to Buddhahood, which is, after all, the goal of all therapy, is it not?

〜〜〜〜〜〜〜〜〜〜〜〜〜〜〜〜〜〜〜〜〜〜〜〜〜〜〜〜〜 *By C. Attneave*

How did I become a family therapist and a network intervenor? Maybe the question startles me because suddenly it makes me aware that I have a label and an identity that makes sense, and the recognition of it by others tells me things I didn't even know about myself. Certainly I began working with families in therapy because it seemed the only sensible thing to do, and not because I had any idea that anybody else ever had, or hadn't — or even that the idea was the least bit more unusual than trying to relieve distress and mobilize people's strengths in any other way.

For the major part of the 1960's I was involved in a setting rather isolated from the professional mainstream in the central rural counties of Oklahoma. It was an hour's drive to Oklahoma City, where the medical school orientation was largely analytic and individual-patient-oriented. However, Povl Tousing inspired and opened doors into many fields of consultation. Roger and Nancy Leinke kept me in tune on family medicine, and John Ramana and Pumpian Mindlin kept resonating family and community themes. It was two hours to drive to Tulsa where James Proctor shared with me a view of in-patient and group-oriented treatment. Ellidee Thomas and James Caldwell

122

kept me solidly grounded in pediatric neurology as a balance for my own socially oriented propensities.

In a sense, I was one of Szasz's gatekeepers for an area a hundred miles square, with a population of approximately eighty thousand people, with our clinic acting like a valve sorting out who got what kind of help where. I had undertaken the task as consulting psychologist and coordinator of health department community guidance services to see if the webs of dreams spun in the ivory tower of academia were strong enough to snare and repair real life problems. The job was to establish a beachhead for the development of comprehensive mental health services. The model was the preventive and early treatment one of public health, which emphasized childhood, medical team work, and practical politics, with some bows toward epidemiology.

Building on this we developed the theme of forming a team around each child referred. Such a model of necessity included the physician, the public health nurse, and any other institution or agency or individual involved in the case. By taking the coordination of other agencies (as well as my own) as an activity justifying fifty percent of my time, I filled a vacuum in the social network of caretakers, and began developing competencies and plans for each child and family out of the context of available skills and roles. Within the first year the case load jumped from forty-five or fifty referrals to about three hundred and fifty, and from then on leveled off to about five hundred new referrals each year.

We described our function in two steps. First, our task was to define the problems: We developed a diagnosis that included school learning, developmental evaluation, medical history, status, internal medicine, orthopedics, pediatrics, neurology, etc., and described the social context of family, socioeconomic factors and subculture. This formulated the problem and what might relieve it in "operational" terms.

Second, we undertook to find out who could do the job. Referral to other resources was one answer, and sometimes appropriate — not only for psychiatric treatment, but for facilities such as special schools and classes for the retarded,

123

job and literacy training, social casework, financial assistance from the Welfare Department of BIA, medical treatment, legal controls from the juvenile, county, and district courts, etc. We literally built the team from each community's own resources by involving in the diagnostic and treatment process anyone and everyone who had a contact with the family. In addition to the obvious professionals mentioned above these might include pastors, scout leaders, clubwomen, neighbors, and friends.

If there was anyone else who could do the job, it was my task to give them the consultative back-up they needed and facilitate their doing it. This often resulted in amusing double plays, as for instance when I discovered that we could apply behavior therapy nicely because the neighbor of an autistic child was a retired trainer of hunting and seeing-eye dogs. Why should busy professionals have taken the clinic time to work out the reinforcement schedules when the depressed dog trainer got a therapeutic lift from being needed? In three months a mute but hyperactive four-year-old had a vocabulary of forty words. Furthermore, he was housebroken! This acquisition of socialization opened a world of human contacts neither his mother nor tough-minded professionals could have predicted (or achieved so quickly?).

Another schizophrenic child was on a three-year waiting list for the State Hospital. The team turned her village into a therapeutic community, which took advantage of days she was "in" to strengthen human bonds and protected her when her daze indicated she was in another personal world. When finally notified that a bed was available we all realized with shock that she didn't need it and nobody wanted to use it.

Naturally, from this context we had deep involvement with the total family, its social network, and its cultural matrix. Cultural factors were more than a little prominent, since approximately one third of the population was American Indian (seven tribes), and unless some interpretive adaptation to their context could be made, they eschewed the white man's medicines and services, especially those encroaching on the medicine man's territory. The fact that I, too, was one of The People bridged the initial gaps and made linkage between the red and white worlds possible on an effective rather than a manipulative basis. In addition, there were islands of Bohemian and Greek emigrants sufficient in size to sustain second languages and customs. There were pockets of "little Dixie" as well as sophisticated participants on the national and international levels of finance, politics, and technology. Adapting team approaches, and creating them out of the agency and social networks of each type of clientele, called for sensitive awareness of family styles, and sociocultural elements affecting behavior, symptoms, and therapy.

The time not spent in coordinating diagnostic and consultative activities was reserved for psychotherapy. Therapy cases selected themselves because there was literally nothing else to do with them. They were not referrable for financial, geographic, or personal reasons, or often because there simply weren't beds or slots available for months in a more appropriate facility. Sometimes the families in most desperate straits did not appear curable or suitable patients to any other clinical facilities. In other words, when one had coordinated, consulted about, and referred all possible cases, the community and they were stuck with whatever therapy could be devised. B. R. Warsham, M.D. (a Menninger-trained psychiatrist) and I expected and wanted to provide it.

At first we tried the traditional divisions, with the psychiatrist and psychologist dividing up the family. In the early days, Dr. Warsham and I wistfully wondered why we didn't have a social worker to take the family off our hands, but our agency couldn't provide one. The Indians retaught me that it isn't just parents, but grandmothers, aunts, and uncles who influence what goes on in the household. One day we just began doing the practical thing of seeing everybody together at once, and sorting things out from there. We were into and doing family therapy because nothing else made sense, although we had not heard of it as a separate field.

After several years somebody editing *Family Process* decided to send some sample copies along to promote subscriptions (I think), and the issues that landed on my desk happened to include Jay Haley's article on communications in a schizophrenic family and another by Sonne, Speck *et al.* on "absent members." Both rang bells about cases we were seeing right then. That made us take note of the fact that other people someplace were seeing whole families too. I also saw Charles Malone's articles in the Ortho Journal and read Minuchin there, too. Families in the slums sounded much like rural folk transplanted.

When by the end of five years the Oklahoma program was established, and its impact on the social and political structures had been sufficient to underwrite its permanence, I decided that if there were other people in the world who had had time to study, conceptualize, and think about this type of therapy, it was high time I met a few of them and found out what they could teach me. Having spent not quite two years in the nest of Minuchin-Haley-Malone, having rebounded with Paul Fine and Dick Taber, and having tussled and soared with Speck and his "network of networkers," I find suddenly that many of my earlier techniques and ideas are labeled and I am permitted to consider myself a full-fledged family therapist — meanwhile appropriating the "network interventionist" title as my own. I'm quite willing to concede that my techniques are probably idiosyncratic; after all, for a good length of time I thought I'd made them up. I'm still not sure sometimes what's stolen, borrowed, or original. The very thought of a formal training course in family therapy is enough to make me drool. Even though I realize that one can teach and learn this complex field, I'm still sorting out the context from the experience.

Not that I belittle my own advantages. Many of the training programs I have observed spend a good deal of time (both for trainers and trainees) getting rid of hangups that arise from a thorough indoctrination in the rightness of individual treatment and the mystique surrounding it. In comparing my own training and growth processes with those I

126

see around me, I find a number of advantages of coming into a field sideways and backwards.

For one thing, having started in professional work as an artist, theater technician, and journalist, the techniques of sociodrama and psychodrama were built in early. I was telling elementary teachers how to use role playing and creative dramatics to help their children over emotional growth hurdles before I was twenty. In fact, when the federal theaters were padlocked I got my first teaching job on the strength of doing play therapy with one school's problem children as well as being a classroom teacher.

I dragged my heels about getting into teaching, largely because of a resistance to the school teacher stereotype that was forced on me from all sides. The thing that made it suddenly worthwhile was the insight into children's potentials provided by a couple of clinical psychologists working with Maude Merril James, and the solid common sense of Jack Hilgard, Paul Hanna (out of Lincoln School to Stanford), I. J. Quillen, and Grayson Kefauver. They somehow showed that concerned, interested adults could make childhood an adventure in self-discovery and world understanding. That blossomed in many ways. All of that group went on to UNESCO, administration, and aerospace planning, but in those days we shared the survival of silver-shirted attacks on "progressive education" and a dream of teaching teachers to find out *who* each child was and *where* he functioned best. Nobody was shouting slogans about making education "relevant;" we were just busy making it meaningful.

I dreamed of a career as a professor of something like educational sociology, and gobbled up philosophy, anthropology, child psychology, learning theory, cybernetics, and anything else that looked pertinent, all the while earning my living and tuition. Somewhere along the line it seemed practical to switch to the clinical counseling field as an insurance policy against the scarcity of academic jobs. Nobody had heard of elementary school counselors, but I liked the idea and hammered out a final degree including both the clinical child psychology and the secondary school and rehabilitation

127

counseling sequences. Prophetically my internship was with an agency called "Consultants to Parents."

Anchorman through the whole graduate performance was Lawrence Thomas, who as a philosopher could see the logic of my plans and who communicated faith in me as a person when all else would abandon it — including me. I began in a golden era at Stanford, when faculty/student relationships challenged one to participate in democratic peer status. Interest in the psychological and social factors affecting human development were given team attention and respect across disciplines and departments. By the time I finished, ten years later, the times had changed, and so had the staff in many ways. Of course, so had I — but for me that particular spirit of inquiry into social foundations of behavior was never extinguished. Finding it again in the family network field gives me a revival of youth and a sense of coming home. . . .

One of my personal changes was to get married and acquire children of my own — which shifted career emphases and locales to Mississippi and Texas. I had a seven-year furlough to be just a woman, wife, mother, and all-around citizen, which gave me time to catch up with some of my own developmental tasks, and to experience first-hand some of the problems and crises of living that show up in the lives of any clinic population. Later I did teach at universities, training clinical psychologists and rehabilitation counselors as the practical solution to supporting a family and raising it, too.

Marriage and motherhood were adventures I undertook only after being convinced that there were other and better ways of modeling them than those I had grown up with. My parents, bless them, probably were and are as confused about what to do with me as I was with them. My mother and I are still finding ways of learning how to get along with one another. Whatever else I got from them, though, they certainly provided the experience and models for learning about cultural differences and adaptations to different social contexts.

128

Up to the Stanford era I had never lived anywhere more than two years in my life, and when anyone asked where I was from, I used to mentally toss a die and decide whether to name Miami, Washington D.C., San Francisco, El Paso, or Esparto. (Never heard of that one? It is a California valley town that rejoiced because our family enabled them to count one hundred souls in the census.) If my father's work didn't force a migration, mother's and his restlessness did, so that even if we stayed in some city, we moved from one community and neighborhood to another. Upwardly mobile, I spent my infancy in a tent in the oil fields of New Mexico, and have vivid memories of the lovely patterns oil heaters made on ceilings, as well as light through the leaves of shrubs against screens in basement apartments, and the delicious fear of wasps' nests in outhouses.

I still blush remembering walking over a mile to a library with a stamp to pay a fine. And I can hear voices and feel kinetically the contrasting times of playing with tough kids mother didn't approve of and rich kids she did. I recall tea with "ladies" and teaching border Mexican chums to swear in English if they'd teach me to swear in Spanish.

In his leisure time my father was librarian for a symphony and later for the Bohemian Club, and I found out thirty years too late that mother, who never touched a piano in my sight, had given up a Carnegie Hall debut to marry him. Dad's mother was a Swedish immigrant who was deaf and his father a Texan whom one never queried about his antecedents. His motto was, "Live every day so you can look every damned man in the eye and tell him to go to Hell." Grandfather did just that, but with finesse. Dad didn't tell people off, but moved from roustabout to truck driver to sales and eventually to executive.

Mother's folks were Delaware Indians of stature and status. In the white community they "passed" as did "Uncle Will" Rogers, but my brother and I knew we were different. We knew too that it was not just because we were from somewhere else, or might move again any time.

In order to survive we had to learn to size up the ways of each new group we encountered, and to learn their languages, thought patterns, values and pet peeves. We also hung on, somehow, to a core of self that separated us from being mere shadows and chameleons. We learned to keep the internal identity that we often dared not expose externally — even at home — lest we offend and cut ourselves off from human contact.

Home had its rules against knowing that there were rules against . . . in the classic Laingian sense. Some of it was the bind of parents who had been raised by and in "foreign" cultures but educated in Anglo-American schools. Brainwashing via inducing guilt and shame about differences from the Victorian norm got through to their conscious levels, but when I find myself among the Indians or Europeans, I find the basic tonalities and harmonies are familiar. It's easy to join in the variations on themes absorbed through childhood's non-verbal antennae. Oriental, black, and Latin themes have their sympathetic vibrations too.

My brother, seven years younger, had less moving to do and learned to put down roots — but by the time I was fifteen I was off to earn and learn at whatever work I could manage from whoever would teach me. I'd already managed to graduate from high school in three years, and had attended five of them. One college registrar bet me I couldn't make five colleges in five years, but I collected that one too. . . .

A lot of the knitting back together of my own family network has come along in the past ten years, as I had the opportunity to find my own people (the Delaware), their close kin the Sac and Fox tribes, and nephews: the Seminole, Pueblo, Kickapoo, Cheyenne, and Pottowatomie and on into the intertribal world of the contemporary American Indian. Even more literally, I was able to rediscover kinfolk with my mother, who had left Oklahoma in 1911 and for many years repressed or rejected her beginning.

As my own youngsters faced some of their own crises I also grew. I remember the day, about a month into first grade, when I discovered my son in tears because he was the only child he knew who had been in several states (Tennessee, California, Texas), and on trains, airplanes, and camping trips. He was devastated because he hadn't lived all his life in one town and one house. It was fun to hear him at seventeen expound on the advantages of having learned that there are different social systems and that one can't recognize this until one has tried on a few for size. He was very aware that one can manage to understand any social system and see how it works. Somehow it makes more realistic his ideas on how he'd like to invent or reform a few aspects of contemporary living.

There was also a clap of insight when I heard my daughter at age ten describing the people in a new city as "Mrs. B is just like Mrs. S back in Texas, and Mrs. Chap is just like half of Miss Lottie and half of Mrs. Pat! Isn't it fun? We don't have to be lonesome because the same kind of people are everywhere and we just look around for the ones we like and look out for the kinds we don't. . . ." Someday maybe she will join me in an article on how one replicates one's own network as one moves through time and space.

I managed to provide my children with about five-year stable periods between moves, sometimes punctuated by a couple of hops before lighting again. They seem to have learned most of what I knew and they have also integrated fairly well the divided identities of divorced parents. Now they are teaching me about the worldwide peer networks of youth — and we have fun bumping into one another and one another's friends in all sorts of odd corners.

This sounds like the development of an opportunist that may fit a family myth: I was often allowed to overhear my Indian grandfather tell that I swallowed a jumping bean as a baby and was thereafter fated to jump about the world, so I might as well learn what I could from anyone, anywhere. I still have lots to learn but it's good to be making real his dream that I become a member of the family of mankind. If somehow this all adds up to the making of a family and network therapist, I'm happy to have somebody label it — in fact it's a little more flattering than a lot of things I've been called.

〜〜〜〜〜〜〜〜〜〜〜〜〜〜〜〜〜〜〜〜〜〜〜〜〜〜〜〜〜〜 *By J. Weakland*

I didn't become enmeshed in family therapy by the usual route — if indeed there is any such — because I began seeing families in the late 1950's when such work was just beginning, and because I am an anthropologist rather than a member of one of the usual clinical or helping professions. And correspondingly, not for the usual motives — except for the basic motive of reviewing and reworking my own family relationships in the course of working with other families, which all of us in this field probably share. In spite of my long involvement and interest in therapy, I have always considered myself as primarily a research worker.

It happened this way: In about 1957, Gregory Bateson's broad research on human communication had led our group to a particular interest in the peculiar communication of schizophrenics. In turn, this led, logically but fatefully, to interest in the communication of schizophrenics in their natural habitat — that is, together with their families. We had already been attempting to help as well as study the individual schizophrenics we had been interviewing. This developed partly from our human concern for these patients, but also because we saw this too as important for the research. Our communicational conception of schizophrenia challenged the prevailing view that this was an isolable and unalterable syndrome. Much is learned about any system only when change is attempted, and good research requires involvement as well as objectivity. As an extension of this stance, and to promote our patients' parents' participation in joint interviews, we said that in addition to our research on communication, we would use such meetings to try to help the patient — as far as possible.

At this time there was very little family treatment any-

132

where (and what there was seldom was mentioned publicly), although Don Jackson was sharing his early approaches with us. When we actually began to interview these families, the task of making any change in their system of interaction initially seemed immense. But we soon found that we could not safely withdraw from our perhaps rash offer of treatment, and become objective observers. The family members — both parents and patients, in different ways — exerted great pressure on us to become involved in their schizophrenic system, on their terms; our only recourse was to increase and improve our efforts to change them instead.

In short, as one thing led to another, I became a family therapist by one part good intentions, two parts scientific curiosity, three parts response to challenge, and four parts self-defense.

four

being and becoming a family therapist

Charles Kramer convened a workshop at the American Orthopsychiatric Association meeting, March 23, 1968 in Chicago, consisting of himself, Murray Bowen, Andrew Ferber, Arthur Leader, Ivan Boszormenyi-Nagy, and Carl Whitaker.

This group had such a good time together in 1968 that Chuck decided to meet a second time in 1969. The following is an edited transcript made from a videotape of that meeting. The five panelists sat in a semicircle in the middle of a large room all but surrounded by the audience. The meeting dealt especially with the tensions produced when therapists try to move from being individual therapists to being family therapists.

Panelists: Charles H. Kramer, M.D., Chairman; Murray Bowen, M.D., Andrew S. Ferber, M.D.; Arthur Leader; Ivan Boszormenyi-Nagy, M.D.; Carl A. Whitaker, M.D.

CK: We have no agenda, but we sent some questions to the panel to think about which we thought might kick off the interaction between the panel and the audience. Here are the questions:

1. Can you spell out what the factors are that made you make the choice of becoming a family therapist?
2. How do you think your personal qualities and your family experiences influenced this choice?
3. What changes have occurred as the result of your becoming a family therapist?
   a. in yourself?
   b. in your practice?
   c. with your colleagues?
   d. in your family of origin?
   e. in your present family relationships?
4. How have these changes influenced the evolution of your work both technically and theoretically?
5. How have your experiences as a family therapist influenced your supervision of the treatment of others?
6. What are some reflections which you might share with someone who plans to become or is becoming a family therapist?

CW: In our breakfast conference we decided that we were going to toss all these out and start off with the problems we're currently facing. And the biggest problem I'm currently facing is how can I operate, except as an individual, in the middle of a staff setting whose organization is basically on a one-to-one level?

Am:* Have you ever included your co-workers sufficiently so that they feel the fire of the direction you're going in?

CW: I've been doing multiple therapy** with them for four years, but don't know how to move beyond this point.

Am: I feel that this discussion is quite irrelevant because family therapy is an internal issue. You can't demonstrate family therapy and then expect your staff to take over because you can't do family therapy until you've worked out some of your own problems of being in a family and handling a family.

Am: Is there anything against family therapy?

CW: No, I don't think so. Therapists aren't quite willing to admit how bored they are with the one-to-one.

Am: When you feel competent as a one-to-one therapist, and you're asked to take on a whole new field, you feel like a novice. Then you're faced with the whole dichotomy of half expert/half novice. And there are very few people who can stand this dichotomy — particularly when you're at a high staff level.

Am: While in residency, I noticed that family conferences and seminars were a hell of a lot more interesting and fun than individual ones. And I wonder if the difference with family therapists is that they like to have fun and expose themselves in groups more than in one-to-one relationships?

CW: At my place the staff are beginning to do family therapy with each other — seeing families together, so that they can develop their expertise without me looking over their shoulders. This may work to solve my problem — I don't know.

---

*Am= Male participant from the audience.
 Af= Female participant from the audience.
**Whitaker and other staff members treat families simultaneously.

AL: Nobody knows in advance what he's capable of in a group or how much fun it can or can't be. We keep shifting through training and experience. For a long time I wasn't comfortable in groups.

Am: It's control!

CW: If you're interested in power, you're interested in groups?

Am: No — in family work you're moving away from the role of the doctor.

CW: If you like insecurity then you can go on in family work.

AL: *(to Whitaker)* I'm with you on the power. I think there's both more insecurity and more opportunity for power in family work.

AF: Do you really have a problem that you think we could tell you something about, or are you just trying to get the ball rolling?

CW: How I can establish a family therapy unit is a problem that sort of haunts me. But I don't know whether you can give me the answer.

AF: Do you have any money?

CW: There's money, but I don't control it. Maybe I should get a grant.

AF: Get a piece of the department.

Further suggestions come from the audience to Dr. Whitaker, but Mr. Leader finally suggests that, since most of the audience is probably sold on family therapy and a lot are doing therapy, the meeting move on to consider some technical problems.

AL: I think that one of my problems with a family, particularly in the beginning, is a tendency to go too fast and be a little too direct. The result is that the family gets more anxious and then they can't hear me or each other.

MB: I find myself in disagreement with a lot of the postures that have been taken this morning, particularly this notion of selling family therapy. I've taken the position that I'm not going to sell it — if it's any good, others will hear about it. If it's no good, it will wither on the vine all by itself.

IN: If you continue doing family therapy, you cannot isolate yourself from having to change your family members. And probably this is one of the reasons why people resist it more.

CK: Murray, do you want to tell us about that family of yours that you've been changing?

MB: I didn't say I'd changed my family. I have spent years and years on my own family. This is kind of a disciplined effort, not because I want to do it, but because I believe in it. It's for my own growth and development within me — not to change my family. I'm trying as hard as I can to be me and permit them to be themselves.

Af: What Dr. Bowen said really hit home with me. I've been in a psychiatric clinic for a long time, in individual work and seeing parents. But I've been interested in family therapy and how we can use it in the clinic, because we need it. However, the feeling I've gotten this morning is that it's one or the other, and I'd like to hear more about whether you really feel that you want the psychiatric clinics all to become family therapy clinics.

MB: I believe that one fine day all psychiatry will move into a direction which is being set in families. I think it will probably take a generation or two or three or four.

IN: I don't think that the aim is for family therapy as a method to conquer the field. I think the main point is to understand relationships, whether it's family or individual therapy. And I think a move towards families will be a natural process of growth in the field.

Am: I'm very concerned that my techniques as a therapist have deteriorated since I've been doing family

138

therapy. And I wonder about some of the safeties and repressions that are opened up in doing the work. Where is this going to leave me? What are the dangers?

CW: I'm very clear that this is one of the big detractions in doing family therapy. That's probably the only place that none of us have had any therapy, because we got our therapeutic experience in the one-to-one relationship, and we're now trying to resolve some of those things that weren't resolved in a live family setting. This, to me, is what makes it necessary to have a multiple therapist in learning family therapy. I want someone there to tackle me at that moment when the slivers of my own psychopathology of my own family relationships are interfering.

Af: I'd like to get some practical answers to some real problems. In one of my families I have a mother and father and an eleven-year-old boy. And every time they come there's a big hassle over the seating arrangement. Now do I move in right away, do I get at their feelings, do they need insight? This kind of situation raises real questions for me.

CW: It depends upon how you feel. There's only one way that's right, and that's your way.

Am: No, no, no!! Not your way, your way *and* their way together — otherwise it's too fast or too slow and nothing happens.

AF: *(points to a man in the audience who has spoken once quite extensively)* He has the microphone again! *(Ferber moves over to the man and takes the microphone)* Give me my mike!

Man: No, you can't have it!

AF: It's mine, I want it!

A big tussle ensues. It ends with the man becoming the panelist with the mike and Ferber becoming a member of the audience.

139

Am: I used the tape from last year with my staff, where similar acting out took place as just happened, and I think it scared the hell out of them.*

Af: I do follow-ups on all of my cases and I've been interested in seeing how often families have terminated prior to the time when I felt they were ready.

CW: I think there's the possibility that family therapy can effectively end within three or five or ten interviews. But we continue holding on to the old one-to-one model and think that maybe it should go on for a year or two or more.

Am: I find that the most I can do for patients is to relieve their wall against pain so that they can feel close to somebody, and to somehow let them know that their pain makes sense to me.

Am: *(to Dr. Whitaker)* In reference to your statement about being able to accomplish goals in one, two, or three sessions, what do you see as some of these goals?

CW: That's impossible to answer, but I will say that I'm not interested in observing or diagnosing. I don't ever expect to understand the family. I have a hard enough time just getting into the middle of it and stirring it up so that the family can rearrange things in a way that is more successful for them.

Am: Without them necessarily understanding anything about it?

CW: Without either of us understanding it.

Am: We've heard what "being yourself" is like in family therapy for Carl. Now what about the rest of the panel. What is it like for some of you?

IN: Maybe the threatening part is that in family work we cannot escape experiencing the decay of social structures. And eventually, at some point, we get down to bare bone, which is like a contextual collision. And we can't help experiencing it.

*In March, 1968, this panel first convened in Chicago. They role-played family interviews, and included some wrestling and shouting amongst the family members.

140

Am: Something has happened in this family right here. Andy was a rebellious little boy, had a fight, and ran out of the family. How come he hasn't been brought back? What are you going to do about it — or do you want to do anything about it? He's pouting!

AF: Maybe you're pouting, I'm not!

Am: He's not as out of it as he looks.

Am: I'd like to get back to this question of what it's like being a family therapist. I've gotten a feeling from Carl, but what is it like for the rest of you?

MB: This is going way back to my early days in psychiatry when I was beginning to get some ideas about the family, and this was a deep one for me. I felt that if I was ever able to know exactly what I believed about psychiatry, and I ever had the courage to say it, I would be all alone in "no man's land." And this struggle went on for a long time. After I made the first presentation of "family" there was immediate applause. Then, within two days I began to get messages — one from the Analytic Institute saying, "This interest in family is your own neurosis." My thought was, "Well, it could be." So I spent another year looking at me. Eventually I went back again to the family, and at each presentation the applause was less and the attack greater. This happens in any family or any social system. The family attacks the one who sets out to be, or think, or act in a way that's different from the system. And it happens in three steps: (1) You're wrong; (2) Change back; (3) These are the consequences.

Am: If family therapy is a helpful tool, why do we run into such resistance? I don't think it's judgmental. There must be something deeper!

AL: In all honesty, I think the whole issue of "differences of opinion" is very difficult to deal with. Every time we take on a new family, there's a big fight to push us out. And I think that maintaining our own position, our own identity, and our own differences in the face of this pressure is one of the most difficult things in the world to do.

Am: I think that there's something very profound at the bottom of the resistance to family therapy that we're not getting at.

CW: Well, hold your hats, because I've listened to two very competent young therapists lately who deal with crisis intervention, and they don't give a damn about individual dynamics, or family dynamics. They're just interested in invading the social system and creating change. So we might just learn family therapy when it's outmoded too.

Am: Can you maintain yourself in family therapy before you've learned how to maintain yourself in your own family?

CW: A single woman asked me that same question the other day and I couldn't give her the true answer, which is that you have to fight it out with your own family first. And maybe that isn't really first. Maybe you sort of do it zigzag. It seems to me that the more I move with families, the more I move in my own family.

AL: You know that's sort of a cliché, that we have to work out our own problems first. Because we all know some crazy mixed-up therapists who can do a good job in individual therapy and in working with families.

Am: I don't see what's so strange in finding resistance to doing family therapy. There's a big difference between doing one-to-one therapy and doing family therapy. So in picking out those to whom I'm going to teach family therapy, I pick those who can risk the insecurity of staying in there until they find out what it's all about.

AF: Fred *(Fred Duhl, M.D. is director of training at Boston State Hospital)*, how would you go about judging whether someone from this audience is the type you could polish into becoming a family therapist?

142

Am: *(Fred)* I'd ask him if he'd ever rebelled. When? Was he successful? What did he learn from it? I want to determine what his capacity is for taking a risk on a new idea, and/or involving himself in it. I'm also interested in how he learns — from people, books, a friend? Is he acting any differently with his own family now from the way he acted when he was eighteen, and how?

IN: I agree. I too am interested in social change. I can see a generation coming that may know some of the answers to social structure that we don't know yet. When is the time when the pacifist and the enlightened liberal decides whether or not he will die for his country? When is the time when the black man decides whether he's loyal to this society or not? When is the time when the American Jew decides to go and fight for Israel? We don't understand these types of deep commitments yet. And yet we work with them every day in families.

INTERMISSION

(people mill around for fifteen minutes)

AF: Before I take my chair I have a proposal: I think a lot of the audience came here today to learn within the old standard format, where they ask the questions and we, as the experts, give the answers. Some of the greatest constraints on learning are the forms of social organization we habitually use. And one of the major things we can do in family therapy is to change these social structures — then new learning occurs. What I'd like to suggest is that we fill the panel seats with six people from the audience who have said nothing. Let the panel join the audience. Then it's up to the fifty of us to run the meeting

143

and see what opens up. *(sits on floor next to panel)*

Am: Whereas I think that this might be an interesting way of learning, this isn't what I came here for today. This is the only chance I have of hearing, even in the old didactic way, what some of the people who have had the most experience in the field do.

Af: *(black woman who comes in late takes AF's chair)* What do I do?

CK: Tell us about the hangups you have in doing family therapy.

Af: One of the biggest problems I have is with fathers. Most of them just aren't interested. They're there — but not emotionally involved.

CW: Isn't it because you're not interested in them? Because I don't find that any problem at all.

Am: Do you work with low- or middle- socioeconomic class families?

Af: Pretty low.

IN: How do you try to approach your problem?

Af: What I try to do is to visit them in their home when the father is there, and I haven't been successful with that either.

IN: That's what I try to do — visit them in their home.

Af: In fact, on Saturday I went to a little girl's birthday party to meet the father and when I got there, he disappeared into his bedroom and locked the door. But I don't know what the mother had told him before I got there.

CW: Is it because you're trying to produce change where we're trying to respond to a request for change?

Af: I'm not really trying to produce change, I'm just trying to get a better family group.

Am: Trying to just make a father change isn't going to do the trick. I think a man has to feel like a father first. You may just have to work with the family as it is without a father.

CK: I found that my work with fathers improved when I got straight with my own father.

144

Am: I think that Mrs. Richards is being a family therapist personified, because she's bringing about change. But like most of us, she's not quite aware of how she's doing it. Those that wanted the panel as is are satisfied and Andy should be satisfied because a member of the audience filled his seat on the panel.

AF: I'm not happy at all because I feel that this is a form of tokenism where you get one lady up here, ask her questions, and then give her all kinds of expert statements about how you would solve her problems.

Af: I've worked for eight years in North Carolina and the black father is absent both physically and psychologically. He has been demoralized by his society. Most of us here are white. I've had no experience treating black families. And I wonder if there isn't an element of difference that we're avoiding.

Af: In my work, I treat black families, but in my involvement in scouting and my church, I work mostly with white families. And when fathers don't care, color is no barrier; they just don't give a damn. I try to get them to feel needed and important.

Am: I don't see why some of you find this so astounding. If you come from a real low-class family and a low-low-class neighborhood, you know there ain't no damned father around. And they don't like anyone sniffing around either. They're not much of a father, but they want their own way anyway.

Af: Could we get back to the original format of the meeting?

Am: I resent Andy manipulating us this way and I don't see why we have to go along with it.

Am: I don't think Andy did it any more or any less than the rest of us. We've all contributed to it. I need to respond to this father issue. I'm not hung up on the father being present in the beginning. I'll work with whatever part of the family comes to me. If the therapy is any good, the father comes in.

Am: I see the father problem as how far you're willing to

145

go outside of your ordinary role of psychiatrist to make contact with the father. I think it's wrong to ask, "What's wrong with these fathers that they won't come into a relationship on our terms?"

Am: I'd like to ask you, Dr. Bowen, how important is it to you to make contact with all of the family members?

MB: Mostly I don't have the time to do it. But one thing that's very important about this whole father issue is that, if there's great distance between the mother and father, the mother plays a part in it. So I'd focus on this, because *she* can bring him in if she wants to. If the therapist brings him in, while she continues doing the things that keep him out, it's going to be a pretty hard job.

Am: Dr. Whitaker sees all the members of the family — little children, older children. He's touching every one. You often see couples. How are you making contact with the other individuals, or are you striving to?

MB: No, I want to make contact with the family or some-one who proposes to represent the family and then take it from there. I'll usually see children who are the symptomatic ones, but I don't include me in with the family very much.

Am: What is meant by contact?

MB: That's a good question. I don't exactly know what you mean either.

Am: Well, Dr. Whitaker talks about becoming part of the family. And I know by watching you that sometimes you're out of it, when you're observing, and some-times in it, especially when you get personal.

MB: What I attempt to do is to back-peddle myself out of the emotional arena sufficiently so that I can see the humor going on, and comment from out there. That's a different comment if you can be with somebody but not too hooked into the seriousness of the situa-tion.

146

CW: I'd like to vote for that. If we can help families to see some of the absurdities that they're up to, it's tremendously helpful.

Af: I try to see the absurdity, but when the switchblade comes out at every session and the mother beats up her son, you have to be a pretty rugged individual to tolerate all this murder and aggression.

CW: Let me put you straight about this rugged individualism stuff. I did a hell of a lot of that kind of work with someone sitting right next to me every minute, before I ever tried any of it by myself. And now, if it isn't going to be easy or fun, I still have someone with me. I'm not for this rugged individualism; I'm preserving my arteries.

Af: I don't think it's coincidental that we've gotten hooked into discussing fathers. I think it's very easy to see the panel as fathers, particularly the older members. But I don't think that family therapists make good lecturers; they're better at doing. I'd like to see them make some contact with the rest of us and *do* something.

Am: I agree. I'm angry and frustrated. Panel members who have accepted the role of panelists are here in a leadership capacity and I'd like to hear more about technique — how they handle things. I want more from them than I'm getting.

Panel: *(consensus)* This is not a panel on technique.

Am: Last year we had a tremendous meeting. This year I'm a little disappointed. I think technique does play some part, because some of us are trying family therapy for the first time and we're having problems that we'd like you to help us with.

AF: I'll respond to that because when we started this morning I felt an enormous expectation from you to us, and boy, it was a crusher! Part of what made last year a terrific meeting was that we all went someplace together. I don't think that we ought to

147

fall back into the same old "idiot-expert" format, so I've been trying my damnedest to create some kind of tension here and then see where we can go together.

Am: (*to Ferber*) Since you were on the panel, what do you have to say? Do you have anything to say? Maybe you don't have anything to say!

AF: I've tried, but I'll say it again briefly. The main oppositions that family therapists meet today are traditional forms of social organization. All the dirt hides in the forms of the organization. The family therapist is a perpetual revolutionary who asks, "What would happen if we altered our rules a little bit?" And what I've been trying to do today is to say, "Let's take some rule that we use to organize ourselves here, and change it a bit — then see what happens."

Am: I think you are philosophizing too much. I'd like to hear something more specific like some of Dr. Nagy's experiences in visiting families.

IN: Well, I've been spending about twenty hours a week in a Community Mental Health Center and seeing other families too. And I think that all of the problems I see are similar. They are basic struggles in relationships. But one thought I had during our discussion about "fathers" is to me very frightening. The birth of boys, in fatherless homes, goes on and on. How can I keep a balance between trying to be a good father model for them and a good therapist?

Am: Do you find more interaction when you see a family in their home than when you see them in your office?

IN: Well, that's not my main reason for seeing them in the home. One reason is that they're more likely to attend the session at home. The other reason is that in their own home they're stronger, and confrontation is more possible.

Af: I'd like to ask for suggestions about how to deal with this "father-image" problem if you're a female therapist and there's no co-therapist available.

Af: Although lacking a male co-therapist or a father figure is not ideal, it's really the mother who first communicates to her son the image of a male. So it's possible for a woman to convey to a man what a man is, from her own feelings.

AL: I don't think that providing a model is the most important thing. It's the intensity of our involvement that really matters. When the father is out of the family, or the adolescent has left the family, and the rest of the family says, "He just doesn't care," I don't buy that! I've found that that father or that adolescent cares a hell of a lot. So I think that getting a very active discussion going that will bring out these buried messages and feelings can really make some difference.

CW: I get a little disturbed by something I picked up in our discussion, which I call the "Missionary Motif." I wasn't sure, when we were talking originally, whether these were families who wanted to change or families we were going to convert to health.

(long pause)

AF: I have a problem that I want to take up with the rest of the panel. My biggest problem this year has been to choose between two courses of action. Should I train those people who come to me, do my research, and say the hell with the way they've set up the department, the medical school, and the city, or should I really try to go out and shape up my elders? Should I say to the kids, "Okay, I hear you — let's go work on 'the establishment' together." Or should I say, "I hear you, and I'll go try to shape up the old guys who still have the power."

CW: You have no idea of how hopeless we feel about what you're trying to do. I hope to hell you keep at it, but I can't get with it like you can.

AL: Why can't you listen to the kids and really tune in

149

to what they are saying without having to rebel against the parents? Why is it either/or? Why can't you understand both points of view?

Am: You think that maybe you could be the "middle man" between the young and the old. But I don't think that there is any middle ground. The kids want a revolution. Maybe they're right, but I'm hooked! I like what I have now. I'm with the old.

Am: I work in an agency which is family-therapy oriented. And I'm getting the feeling that the family comes in to *maintain* its system — not to change it!

CW: That's what we're talking about. I want to maintain the system I have because I'm hopeless about changing it. I tried, but I got my head knocked in and quit! And I feel that it's the same with every family. They're scared, but I'll be damned if they want to change.

MB: I'm deeply grieved about all the problems that the kids are having. But there's only one person in this world that you can change, and that's yourself. I'm not pessimistic about the human phenomenon. I think it's great and I think it has a future. Family study has moved from "relationship" thinking to "system" thinking, and I think that one day this whole field of psychiatry will be a science. I've continually encouraged Andy. I too have had my head knocked in, but I'm still not pessimistic.

Am: I'm not sure what Andy was talking about, but I was interested in some of the things he said and in the fact that he tried so hard to change the format. Maybe he could clarify his remarks a little.

AF: We've tried to mount maybe ten family therapy programs at Einstein, and we've met with resistance from every area of the power structure. Kids put you to the test today too. They want your expertise — not your authoritarianism. If you'll sit down and talk things over with them they'll listen, otherwise they won't. Then there are the community groups who are trying to take over, who call you a mother-fucker and tell you you're exploiting them. If you play the role of the liberal, you're washed out, and if you play the role of the authoritarian, you're washed out too. This year particularly, I've run into these confrontations all the time and I don't know what to do. I also have my own skin to think of. The kids want me to act as a channel to the powers, but if I don't handle these powers the right way, I won't get support for myself and my programs. (*to the panel*) There is a revolution taking place in some of the forms of social organization and you can't ignore it. Murray and Carl pretend that they have things all under control, but I don't believe it. They're hurting as much as I am.

MB: I'm not hurting!

AF: I don't believe you!

CW: I asked you about my problem the first thing this morning, why didn't you get on with it?

AF: Because I don't think you asked it in a way that encouraged us to get on with it, Carl. You sounded like "I really have things under control, but I'll just ask it to get things going."

Am: I don't know the answer to your other problems, Andy, except to keep trying, but I think that here your mistake was in assuming that you wouldn't be able to work with the structure or organization the way it was set up. And you waited until you got into the meeting to try to do something about it. I think that you should have made your suggestions about a different kind of format as soon as you received your letter from Dr. Kramer. Instead, you chose to bring your battle here and fight it out. I've learned a lot from feeling it and watching it take place, but I would have preferred that you handle it the other way.

AF: The letter in which Chuck sent us this agenda arrived Special Delivery Air Mail on Saturday. We had a

151

breakfast meeting this morning in which we tried to work it out some, but we came in here this morning not quite knowing where the other stood. So I did try to get moving on it right away and not spring a fast one.

Af: I think it is too bad to focus this discussion on one person and ask, "Why didn't you do this before?" We all have unexpected things come up in our work all the time that we can't completely handle and plan for ahead of time, because there just isn't any format.

Af: I'm going to pick up that word agenda because I think that it sort of symbolizes the methodology of the "establishment" trying to come into some kind of relative relationship with the "new order." The *struggle* is the important thing. And I think the role of the older group is to encourage the young people in their struggle because that has meaning in the life cycle. And I don't think the older group lacks the desire to be helpful, but we just get tired sometimes.

Am: One of the first things that attracted me to this panel was the vagueness of the title. It seemed to leave a lot of opportunity for flexibility. Like Dr. Ferber, I too am faced with the problem of training family therapists in a setting that is rather resistant to the whole family-therapy idea. But I've been very interested to see the resistance toward change here, too, even although it became obvious that several people sitting on stage, trying to answer a few questions, just wasn't going to work. Perhaps some of the dissatisfaction expressed here today shows the need to explore other possible formats for the future.

Af: Dr. Ferber, I just didn't like the way you talked to us before. I think you talked to us as if we were children. At first I wasn't convinced that you really wanted us to do what you were suggesting, but I guess you did. You just didn't do it respectfully.

Af: I think this is very typical of family therapy. When a

152

child acts up and acts disrespectful, the parents reach a tolerance point. Then they say, "I have a sick child here." And this is dangerous because the child isn't sick, he's just thrashing around and acting up and he and his parents aren't connected, and he gets the label pinned on him. The same thing is going on here. This guy isn't saying anything that many of us don't feel. We're just in different camps. But whether he's disrespectful or not doesn't change the fact that this is honest behavior.

Af: I'm not saying that he's sick.

Am: But you're saying that he's disrespectful, which is getting pretty close.

Am: How can you listen to a family if you can't hear what this guy had to say? And his use of the word "mother-fucker" points up a very real situation. Let's face it! Family therapy has to do with "the establishment." Every step of the road any one of us takes in our fight to establish family therapy has so many side issues, it's unbelievable. And family therapy is just made the scapegoat. But my dear woman, I'm utterly appalled that you should feel that somebody who presented to us a real-life problem is disrespectful simply because he uses the word "mother-fucker."

Af: That wasn't what bothered me!

AL: Maybe it bothered him!

Af: He didn't get anywhere!

AF: Chuck, I'd like you to let us be of some help to you; first, because you're the leader of the meeting and you've been uncomfortable most of the day; second, you have a problem which many of us share to a greater or lesser extent. You're torn between your loyalties to the Psychoanalytic Institute and your attempt to be the leader of the family therapy camp here in Chicago. Exactly where are *you* hurting now? Could we get you into the discussion and be of any use to you?

CK: Well, Andy, I've been listening and learning. And

if you go away from the meeting unhappy that won't bother me because I've learned something. Here in Chicago I've been fighting my battle for about twelve years, and last year we decided to make a break. We started our own institution with our own money. I don't know how it's going to work out, or where it's going to go. Whether you're all happy with today's meeting or whether you think that you saw a good play isn't important. What *is* important is that we got our minds stirred up and got some new perspectives. I think it has been a good meeting and I've been with you all the way.

Am: I think that when Andy sort of took over at the beginning of this meeting, it was reminiscent of last year's meeting.

And from then on, the issue of the meeting became that of whether Andy could do a "takeover" again. People took sides. Art Leader even asked Andy why he had to alienate so much. It ended almost the way it began. Nothing was resolved, but maybe there was a lot of learning in the process.

five

~~~~~~

beginning and experienced family therapists

J. Haley

The clinicians who began to do family therapy in the early days were primarily people who had been trained in the ideology and practice of individual therapy. Whatever their professions, their focus had been upon how to change a person. As they began to discover the new problem of how to change a family, each of them developed a unique approach. Often their approaches differed because the therapists were innovating on their own and did not know that other people were doing family therapy. As a result, a number of "schools" of family therapy have developed which have their students and their followers. New approaches continue to develop as clinicians take up family therapy in different parts of the country and develop unique ways of working.

Comparing different family therapists is difficult because they differ markedly in their techniques of intervening into families. However, as family therapists have gained experience they seem to have developed a shared body of premises about human problems and the nature of change, despite working with families in quite different ways. Some family therapists, particularly those imbedded in academic psychiatry or the tight professional organizations of a large city, do not seem to change their views with experience. Yet most family therapists have gone through a transitional process, sharing now a basic shift in their ideas which comes about from the *experience* of working with families. One can assume that the shift in ideas comes from exposure to families, since often family therapists shift to a common view even though they have not been exposed to the work of other family therapists. At about the time a family therapist passes his two-hundredth family, he usually changes his perspective markedly and finds himself in a different conceptual world from the one in which he was trained. One way to describe this shift in thinking about therapy is to describe where a family therapist begins and where he ends. Contrasting the premises of a beginning family therapist with those of a person who has had many years of experience can help clarify what is new in the family therapy field.

METHOD VS. ORIENTATION

The beginning family therapist tends to see family therapy as a method of treatment — one more procedure in a therapist's armentarium. As he gains experience, the therapist begins to view family therapy not as a method but as a new orientation to the arena of human problems. This conceptual difference has practical results. For example, when asked what the indications and contra-indications for family therapy are, the beginning family therapist will attempt to answer the question. The more experienced family therapist will appear puzzled, since he finds himself defining any kind of therapy as a way of intervening into a family. Having shifted his unit of diagnosis and treatment from the single person to the processes between people, he defines psychopathology as a relationship problem. He cannot say this person should receive individual therapy and this person family therapy, because he views individual therapy as one way of intervening into a family. The therapist who treats a wife may be dealing with the woman's fantasies, fears, hopes, and so on, but by seeing the wife and not seeing the husband the therapist is intervening into a marriage in a particular way. While the family therapist might interview only the wife, it would be with the assumption that her problem involves the context in which she lives, and that the treatment must change that context. Even if drugs are given to only one person, the family therapist does not see this as drug therapy in the usual sense; it is the introduction of a drug into a family system with consequent concern about who is being labelled as the patient, or as the one who is at fault.

Whether family therapy is seen as an orientation or a method is similar to the contrasting approaches in psychiatry forty years ago when psychodynamic theory developed. It was not a question of deciding whether the neurological method of treatment or the psychodynamic method of treatment was indicated; the issue was the difference in conceptual framework between the two approaches, because they each represented a different way of thinking about the psychiatric problem. Similarly, one cannot contrast individual and family therapy as two different methods; they are not comparable at that level.

COLOR THE PATIENT DARK

The beginning family therapist tends to emphasize the individual patient as the focus of treatment, seeing the

157

remainder of the family as a stress factor. He may even do a style of family treatment which is called interviewing the patient in the presence of his family. The more experienced family therapist gives family members more equal weight, and struggles to find a better term than "patient" for the family member who is chosen to be *it*. Terms are used such as "the identified patient," or "the supposed patient," or the "person in pain," or the "person expressing the symptom," and so on. While the beginner tends to see a particular individual as a container of psychopathology or a person with a low stress threshold, the more experienced therapist sees the family system as needing some individual to express the psychopathology of the system. For example, if a child is agitated and is quieted, the mother will become agitated, and if mother and child are quieted, then the father or a sibling will become agitated because the system is such that this is necessary.

In a similar way, the beginner tends to see the family as a collection of persons who are describable with the past language about individuals. He sees relationships as a product, a projection, of intrapsychic life. For example, he will emphasize how a wife is being mistreated by a sadistic husband: the husband is expressing his aggression and the wife is satisfying her masochistic needs. The more experienced family therapist sees intrapsychic process as a product of the relationship situation. He will describe such a couple as involved in a game in which they must both contribute behavior which keeps the distressing sequence going. In a similar manner the beginner often sees the child as a victim of the parents' strife or as a scapegoat, while the more experienced therapist will view the child as a contributor and an essential part of a continuing sequence of events among all the people involved. As a result of this difference, the beginning therapist tends to intervene to get a person to shift his ideas or behavior, while the more experienced therapist intervenes to change a sequence of behavior involving *several* people. For example, in an interview the father might interrogate the child, while the child weakly

158

protests. At a certain point the mother will come to the support of the child and attack the father. The father will back down and apologize. After a while, the sequence will begin again and repeat itself. The more experienced family therapist will see the sequence occur, and when it starts again he will intervene. He might do so while the father is interrogating the child, just before the mother comes in to attack the father, or just before the father backs down when the mother attacks. His goal is to give the sequence a different outcome, and he may or may not point out to the family the nature of the sequence. The beginning family therapist will tend to see the behavior in smaller units, and he will usually intervene to interpret to the father that he should not behave as he is doing, or to help him understand why. He will be thinking about the father's motivations and possibly his history with his own father, rather than about the current sequence that is happening in the family.

Where is History?

The beginner at work seems much more interested in history than is the experienced family therapist. The beginner tends to see the family as a collection of individuals who have introjected their pasts, and the therapeutic problem is lifting the weight of this "programming" out of their inner space. The more experienced family therapist learns to see the present situation as the major causal factor and the process which must be changed. He inquires about the past only when he cannot understand the present, and thinks the family can discuss the present more easily if it is framed as something from the past. Assuming that what is happening now has been happening for a long time, the therapeutic problem is what is happening now. At times a therapist may emphasize the past when he is trying to define a time when the family members were enjoying each other more; this is a way of labeling the current problem as a temporary upset as well as clarifying a goal of the therapy. In general, the more experienced the family therapist, the more he assumes that a current problem must be currently reinforced if it is continuing to exist.

WHAT IS DIAGNOSIS?

The beginner tends to put more emphasis upon diagnosing and evaluating the family problem. He prefers to gather information before intervening. He tends to use diagnostic ideas in an individual language, and tries to define, in as much detail as possible, the family dynamics. The more experienced family therapists frequently work with minimal information. Since they view the opening session as important to the ultimate therapeutic outcome, particularly when it is a time of family crisis, they wish to intervene as rapidly as possible to bring about change. Therefore they intervene as soon as they have some grasp of what is going on. Many think careful diagnosis helps the therapist more than the family. Such therapists spend much less time talking about differences in family dynamics than they do in talking about ways they have intervened to bring about changes. Generally they like to end the first therapy session with some therapeutic aim accomplished so that the family has gained something from the immediate encounter and knows what the therapeutic experience will be like. This more action-oriented point of view does not mean that family therapy is always brief therapy.

Whether treatment is short or long term, most experienced therapists share an awareness of how much can be accomplished with active intervention at a time a family is in crisis and unstable. Some experienced family therapists say that if adolescent schizophrenia is not resolved with family treatment, the case has been mishandled. However, they are referring to family treatment at the time of acute onset of the family crisis and not after the adolescent has been hospitalized and the family has been stabilized. When hospitalization is involved, family treatment can become interminable because each improvement leads to renewed hospitalization.

160

The more experienced therapist looks upon long-term therapy as necessary to accomplish particular ends, rather than as meritorious in itself. It is also typical of more experienced therapists to see change as occurring in discontinuous steps, and they "peg" a change when they get one so that the family continues to the next stage of develop ment and does not slip back. Instead of the desultory movement one sees in the beginner's family treatment, the more experienced therapists tend toward a developmental improvement in the family.

Is the Therapist Part of the Diagnosis?

A major difference between the beginner and the more advanced family therapist is the way the beginner tends to leave himself out of the diagnosis. He describes the family as a set of problems independent of him, much as the individual therapist used to describe the patient's production in therapy as if they were independent of the therapist. The more experienced therapist includes himself in the description of a family. For example, the beginner will say that the family members are hostile to each other; the more experienced therapist will say the family members *are showing me* how hostile they are to each other. This is not a minor distinction. As a consequence, the more experienced person does not think of the family as separate from the context of treatment, and he includes himself in that context. He will consider, for example, whether the particular difficulty he sees between a husband and wife is created by the way he is dealing with the couple. A vignette can illustrate this: An experienced therapist was supervising a beginner by listening to a tape recording, and after five minutes of the first session with a family the supervisor said that several minutes had passed and the therapist had not yet made a therapeutic intervention. The beginner replied that it was an evaluation interview and he was gathering information about the family problem. The experienced supervisor replied, "Evaluation of a family is how the family responds to your

161

therapeutic interventions." This example illustrates how much more rapidly the experienced person prefers to work, and how he sees the family problem in terms of how the family responds to *him*. With such a view there are not different diagnostic categories of families, but different families in different treatment contexts. An important aspect of this more contextual view is the realization by experienced therapists that they must take not only the family into account, including the extended kin who always influence a problem, but also the other helping professionals who might be involved. In some cases, a family has been divided, with each fragmented part being treated by some professional, often without knowledge of each other. The record might be a family in California which had fourteen professional helpers involved. To deal with the family unit, the experienced therapist finds he must also deal with the wider treatment morass, or the total ecological system. The beginner tends to see the other helpers as irrelevant until he gains experience.

In relation to diagnosis, a sharp difference between the beginner and the experienced therapist is the concern with using a diagnosis that defines a solvable problem. Unless the diagnosis indicates a program for bringing about change, it is considered irrelevant by the more experienced therapist. The usual psychiatric categories are seldom used — not only because they apply only to individuals but because they have nothing to do with therapy. The beginner tends to think of diagnosis as something that exists independent of him, and he must adapt *to* it. For example, a family therapist who was both a beginner and worked in the conservative network of a large city posed a question to a more experienced family therapist from the provinces. She said she was working with a family, and after three diagnostic sessions she concluded with the family that the problem was a symbiotic tie between the mother and her daughter that was unresolvable. She asked, "What would you do with this problem?" The experienced therapist replied that he would never let that be the problem, and she did not understand

162

what he meant. She saw the problem not as one which she defined but one which was independent of her and she must struggle with it even though she had defined it as unsolvable. Given the same family, the experienced therapist might have concluded with the family that when the daughter began to move toward independence the mother became upset and there was open conflict betwen mother and father. This diagnosis indicates ways of bringing about change, and by the third session an experienced therapist would already have begun a change.

THE POSITIVE VIEW

Beginning family therapists tend to feel that it is helpful to the family to bring out their underlying feelings and attitudes no matter how destructive these might be. He interprets to family members how they are responding to each other and expressing their hostility through body movement, and so on. The more experienced family therapist has less enthusiasm for the idea that interpreting feelings and attitudes brings about change. In particular, he does not feel it is helpful to confront family members with how much they hate one another. Instead, he tends to interpret destructive behavior in some positive way — as a *protective* act, for example. His premise is that the problem is not to make explicit underlying hostility, but to resolve the difficulties that are causing the hostility. Therefore, the more experienced therapist is less free with his interpretations, except when using them tactically to persuade family members to behave differently. At times the beginner can seem to be torturing a family by forcing them to concede their unsavory feelings about each other. The more experienced therapist feels this is a waste of time and not therapeutic. For example, a beginning family therapist working with the family of a schizophrenic saw the mother pat her son on the behind. He could not overlook this opportunity to help her by interpreting this behavior as the product of an incestuous desire, with the result that mother and son avoided each

163

other even more than previously. A more experienced family therapist would probably have congratulated the mother on being able to show some affection toward her son. Although more experienced family therapists do not emphasize negative aspects of family living, they are quite willing to bring out conflicts if they are necessary to break up a particular pattern.

THE PROBLEM IS THE METHOD

The beginning family therapist, like the beginner in any field, would like to have a method that fits everyone who comes in the door. Being uncertain, he would like to have a set of procedures to follow each time. The more experienced family therapist tends to feel that any set procedure is a handicap; each family is a special problem which might require any one of several different approaches. Instead of fitting the family to a method, the experienced therapist tries to devise a way of working that varies with the particular problem before him. In contrast, the beginning family therapist tends to set rules which include seeing the whole family for a set length of time at regular, set intervals. Most family therapists began by working with whole family groups, but as they gained experience they found this too restricting. With experience, they shifted to seeing the whole group sometimes to get a total portrait of the situation, but then they interviewed people singly, then the marital pair, or the siblings, or any combination that seemed appropriate for the problem involved. Some family therapists are now trying out multiple family as well as network therapy, where not only the family but friends and neighbors are brought into treatment sessions.

EQUAL PARTICIPATION

When the experienced family therapist interviews the whole family group together, he puts special emphasis upon getting all the members to participate. If a family member is not speaking, the therapist tries to involve him. Often the experienced family therapist will turn the family upon each other so they talk together rather than to him, and when he does this he likes them all to talk. The beginner often focuses upon one person at a time, and tends to have the family members talk largely to him rather than to each other.

THE FACTIONAL STRUGGLES

When a therapist intervenes into a family, whether he interviews one person or the whole family group, he is caught up in the struggle of family factions. The beginner tends to side with some part of the family — often he sides with the child against the victimizing parents, or, if he is older, he may side with the parents against the child. In marital struggles, the beginner is likely to find himself siding with one spouse against another. The more experienced family therapist assumes quite flatly that if he sides with one part of a family against another there will be a poor therapeutic outcome. This is particularly so if he joins one faction while denying he is doing so, which often happens if the therapist still responds to one person as the "patient" but is trying not to. When experienced therapists take sides, they state this explicitly and announce that they are doing so, usually defining it as temporary.

LIVE SUPERVISION

Since the vital part of bringing about change is the way the therapist behaves in a session, the experienced person wants to know what is happening when he is supervising a trainee. The beginner tends to think in terms of traditional supervision, where he makes notes about what happened and carries them to his supervisor for discussion. This kind of delayed, content-oriented conversation arouses little enthusiasm in the experienced family therapist. He prefers to watch the trainee in a session through a one-way mirror or on a videotape replay, so he can give instructions in the technique of interviewing, which is the essence of therapy. More commonly, the experienced family therapist does live supervision by watching a session and calling in on the phone to suggest changes, calling the trainee out to discuss what is happening, or entering himself to guide the session. In this way a trainee learns to do what should be done at the moment something happens, not when the opportunity to change his form of intervention is long passed.

EMPHASIS UPON OUTCOME

The beginning family therapist tends to emphasize what is going on in the family; the more experienced therapist emphasizes what therapeutic results are happening in terms of quite specific goals. Some beginners become so fascinated with family history, family dynamics, and the complex interchanges in the family that they lose sight of the goals of treatment. Often the beginner will seem to define the goal as proper behavior by the family — if the family members are expressing their feelings, revealing their attitudes, and the therapist is making sound interpretations, then therapy is successful. The more experienced family therapist emphasizes whether the family is changing, and he shifts his approach if it is not. This does not mean that family therapists scientifically evaluate the outcome of their therapy, but it does mean that outcome is a constant focus as well as a subject of conversation among experienced family therapists. They talk about family dynamics largely in relation to family change. The willingness of therapists to shift their approach if it is not working is one of the factors that makes family therapy difficult to describe as a method. Not only will a particular therapist's approach vary from family to family, but his way of working evolves into new innovations from year to year as he attempts to produce better results.

What family therapists most have in common they also share with a number of behavioral scientists in the world today: there is an increasing awareness that psychiatric problems are social problems which involve the total ecological system. There is a concern with, and an attempt to change, what happens with the family, its interlocking systems, and the social institutions in which it is imbedded. The fragmentation of the individual, or the family, into parts is being abandoned. There is a growing consensus that a new ecological framework defines problems in new ways, and calls for new ways in therapy.

six

what family therapists do

C. Beels and A. Ferber

This personal view of the practice and the literature of family therapy is written to inform those who, like
ourselves, are second-generation family therapists, entering
a field which began in the early 1950's, and has since developed rapidly. The field has its journals, its books, its GAP
committee, its training programs, its internal wars, its multi-
plying hundreds of practitioners, and, most important for
us, its pioneering teachers. In an attempt to bring coherence
out of the various teachings and practices of these leaders
of the field, we try here to evaluate them by imposing our

own order upon them, in the light of our own experience with teaching and practice.

APPROACHES TO FAMILY THERAPY

We have looked for systematic efforts to evaluate the *results,* the outcome, of family therapy, but evaluation has been neglected here as in other therapies. We know of only three reports of any substance on outcome:

1. The *multiple impact*[46] therapists report a favorable result in seventy-five percent of their sixty-two families of disturbed adolescents at one and one-half year follow-up. All their schizophrenics got better.

2. Murray Bowen,[12] looking back over twelve years of practice with five hundred families, feels that in four years' time he can change the dynamics of most families, providing they are not schizophrenics. He feels he has never changed the fundamental dynamics of a schizophrenic family.

3. Langsley in Colorado[41] has used a family approach to prevent hospitalization in over ninety percent of acute crises judged to require hospitalization in the emergency room.

The main deduction from this is that no one seems to be talking about the same kind of outcome or treatment.

Our second approach to family therapy has been to watch it. We have succeeded in getting some experience, other than reading, with most of the people mentioned in this chapter.* The nature and extent of this direct experience varies widely: listening to audio tapes, watching video-tapes and movies, directly observing "demonstration" inter-

---

*The following is a list of people with whom we had more than a reading acquaintance: Virginia Satir, Ivan Boszormeny-Nagy and Geraldine Lincoln, James Framo, Murray Bowen, Frank Pittman and Kalman Flomenhaft, Salvador Minuchin, Braulio Montalvo, Gerald Zuk, David Rubenstein, Nathan Ackerman, Norman Paul, Don Jackson, Jay Haley, Jerry Jungreis, Lyman Wynne, Hanna Kwiatkowska, Carl Whitaker, Israel Zwerling, Harold Searles, Roger Shapiro, John Zinner, Gentry Harris, Fred Ford, Ross Speck, Edgar Auerswald, Richard Rabkin, Augustus Napier, and Frederick Duhl.

views, consultations, and ongoing therapy, and observing continuous therapy for periods of months to years. Clearly, there are some crucial differences between a therapist's behavior during a visit with a strange family in a strange setting, and his behavior in a private session of a long-term therapy in his private practice, and we have often had to compare the observation of one with writing about the other. We have tried not to endanger by over-generalization the great advantage which direct observation has given us: the opportunity of seeing personal and perhaps unwitting styles of work.

Watching family therapy and talking with the therapists about the experience has led us to believe that there is no "right" way to do it. Each man made his own style of work, and from those we got to know best it was clear that each had forged it from a life-long fascination with families, beginning with his own. It was pointless to try to abstract "the technique" from these many approaches, since the personal stamp of the therapist was so clearly the first thing we had to understand.

Many reproductions of interviews are now available. Haley and Hoffman's *Techniques of Family Therapy*,[27] a detailed analysis of taped interviews by distinguished family therapists, with the therapists and Haley as discussants, is especially revealing. Murray Bowen[15] has video-taped some of his work and Ackerman[4] has made movies of his. The Eastern Pennsylvania Psychiatric Institute has films of Ackerman, Jackson, Whitaker, and Bowen, each interviewing the same family.[16] Minuchin's *Families of the Slums*,[44] Ackerman's *Treating the Troubled Family*,[2] and the Houston Group's *Multiple Impact Therapy With Families*[46] all contain extensive transcriptions of interviews, with discussion by the therapists. The spread of this practice would make a new and uniquely valuable kind of library.

The most important approach is to do family therapy oneself. This is the only way to integrate the literature with one's experience. Reading or talking about it from the perspective of other therapies is an empty exercise.

As teachers we have had to be explicit about our choice of tactics. We have each watched and discussed several hundred hours of family therapy interviews over the past six years.

We have abstracted from the literature certain themes on the family therapist's use of himself as an agent of influence in interaction with the family. In doing so, we did not discuss in any depth the subject of "family dynamics" or "theory of family pathology" — that is, the family's behavior as it is imagined in the absence of the therapist. That field has, of course, a much larger and older literature, well reviewed by Meissner,[43] by Mischler and Waxler,[45] by Zuk and Rubinstein,[80] and by Frank,[20] and which we put beyond our scope. Nor have we said much about "theories of family therapy."

We avoided the evaluation of theory because we believed that in many cases the theories advanced were a rationalization for the practice of the therapy and not what we thought a real theory in this area should be: an ordering of diverse clinical phenomena to a scheme that would organize their diversity and provide a reason for different therapeutic measures.

There are some outstanding exceptions: Wynne's *Some Indications and Contraindications for Exploratory Family Therapy*,[75] the *Multiple Impact Therapy* by MacGregor et al.,[46] which contains a four-part diagnostic scheme, Tharp's breakdown of types of family contract,[65] Minuchin and Montalvo's differential descriptions of family types and therapist styles,[44] and some parts of the work of Bowen[13] and of Ackerman.[5] Clearly, another paper could be written on systems of diagnosis and therapeutic strategy.

A DEFINITION OF FAMILY THERAPY

To define family therapy, let us begin by comparing it with individual therapy. Ford and Urban in *Systems of Psychotherapy*[18] abstract four common elements from all types of individual therapy that they surveyed: 1. There

171

are two people in confidential interaction; 2. the mode of interaction is usually verbal; 3. the interaction is relatively prolonged; and 4. the relationship has for its definite and agreed-upon purpose changes in the behavior of one of the participants.

Applying these considerations to family therapy:

1. There are *more* than two people, and the interaction between them is to that important extent *not* confidential. As we shall show later the change of technique in the jump from a dyadic to triadic (or more) interaction is a discontinuous one.
2. Nonverbal interaction assumes a primary importance along with the verbal; manipulation of membership, gesture, seating arrangement and posture, by any and all participants is significant.
3. It is often shorter than individual therapy, but this is enormously variable.
4. The relationship has for its definite and agreed-upon purpose changes in the family *system* of interaction, not changes in the behavior of individuals. Individual change occurs as a by-product of system change.

This goal of changing the family system of interaction is family therapy's most distinctive feature, its greatest advantage and, especially to those who come to it from other disciplines, its greatest stumbling block.

Critics from the tradition of individual therapy fear that family therapy must be damaging or frightening to the members if it is going to deal effectively with what is "really" going on between them. Handlon and Parloff,[29] comparing family therapy with conventional group therapy, point out that, in attacking the family system, family therapy dispenses with almost all the tactical advantages of group therapy in order to make "an heroic frontal assault on manifestly relevant but securely guarded relationships." The interlocking system of family relationships may be the nub of the problem, but to approach it directly in its natural state seems to group and individual therapists a venture too radical or risky. They prefer to work with individual patients in safer contexts where, they think, it is more possible to enlist the ego functions of the patient in the examination of behavior which is the shadow rather than the substance of family interaction.

In addition to these experiential reasons for avoiding the family system in interaction, there is for all of us a conceptual difficulty with labeling *systems*. Even if we were able to remove ourselves from it emotionally, which we are not, the problem of accounting intellectually for the interplay of events and sequences in a family session is one for which there is not yet a good language.

In spite of these difficulties, let us look more closely at the family therapist's concern with the system of relationships rather than with the individual. Almost every treatise on family therapy begins with the author's view on this. John E. Bell[9] states it most succinctly, and most radically:

> Family group treatment takes the family and by professional action tries to help itself into becoming a more perfectly functioning group. The contract with the family specifies this end. To work thus with a group is new in psychotherapy. When we have worked with groups before we have used them instrumentally, as a means to the cure of individuals. We have not sought the effective functioning of the group as an end goal. Even the professional specialist in social work who calls himself a group worker, and who knows more than most mental health workers about the theory and natural history of groups, has not seen himself working with a group first for its own sake but rather as a means to help the individuals who compose it.
>
> I draw this distinction sharply. Family group treatment is a consulting sociological or socio-psychological technique and as such is unlike psychological treatment methods that aim for the welfare of an individual. Let

173

it be recognized, however, that although family group treatment seeks the well-being of the family, secondarily it has important consequences for the status of the individuals who make up the family. This reminds us of the arbitrariness in our distinctions between the family group and individual members of the family. Both the group and the individual are correlated open systems. To look at one or the other as independent is only a professional choice that later requires us to allow for the limitations imposed by our selective starting position. It is easy to see this in electing to work with the family. What now has become more apparent is that a similar choice process has been in operation in our work with individuals. Culturally we are so biased in favor of the individual that we have tended to ignore the fact that the choice to deal with him could be arbitrary, and that we are prejudiced in favor of seeing him as a closed system. Carelessly we ignored that we had adopted a posture for thinking. We believed that there was some positive objective validity to the individual, and that as a consequence it was our primary obligation in treatment to concern ourselves with his personal progress.

We shall return in our conclusion to some of the consequences of this definition of the family therapist as a professional whose commitment is to make the family "a more perfectly functioning group." Although different therapists might disagree on how to recognize that more perfect function, or what its relation is to the "status of the individuals," the therapists reviewed here would agree that the first purpose of working with the family group is to improve its *function as a family*. This definition is especially inclusive if one remembers that family therapists regard as one of the family's most important functions the promotion of the differentiation, and in the case of the children, the ultimate separation, of the individual from what Bowen[13] calls the "undifferentiated family ego mass." The therapist does not simply try to make the family more "groupy," more cohesive, but on the contrary tries to promote its growth and differentiation.

THE RELATION OF THE THERAPIST TO THE FAMILY GROUP

The therapist is a new member of the family group. How does he present himself to them? We will take this question and apply it to each of the therapists in turn. In this way we will also be presenting the therapists to the reader as they present themselves to the family.

To organize this catalogue, we begin by dividing *conductors* from *reactors*. Since the family is a group with an organization of its own, the therapist can enter it either as its *conductor* in this special and unfamiliar activity of meeting for therapy, or as a *reactor* who responds to what the family presents to him. Obviously all therapists do some of both in keeping control of the meeting, but if one thinks of what appears to be their dominant mode of keeping control, then some generalizations might be made concerning a classification of conductors and reactors. In a general way, conductors remain on the dominant side of dominance-submission complementarities or on the senior side of a generation hierarchy. They maintain that position, staying in the group by staying on top of it and leading it. Reactors may shift out to the boundary of the group from time to time, such as when consulting with co-therapists, and they may join in symmetrical same-generation relationships with family members.

Many of the conductors are vigorous personalities who can hold audiences spellbound by their talks and demonstrations. They have a keen, explicit sense of their own values and goals which they, in one way or another, hope to get the families to adopt. Some of them are regarded by their critics as sadistic, manipulative, exhibitionistic, and insensitive.

The reactors have, on the whole, less compelling public personalities. They present themselves to the families not only as themselves but in various roles dictated by the tactics

175

or by the group dynamics of the family. They refer often in their writings to the danger of being swamped, confused, inveigled, or excluded by families. They have goals and values, but they are more likely to be, as Whitaker[68] says, a secret agenda in the therapy.

The reactors can be further divided into two groups, the *analysts* and the *system purists,* depending on what they observe and respond to. The analysts tend to see in the family interaction and in the therapist's behavior things that would be recognizable to the psychoanalytic tradition, and they call them by familiar names such as "transference," "counter-transference," "acting-out," etc. To a variable degree, they are concerned with the internal processes of individuals. The system purists see in the family a system of counter-vailing power — a network of influence governed by rules that shape and constrain it. They have a minimal "black box" model of the individual psyche and are not concerned about what is happening "inside." They ask few questions about the motives of the power struggle. They see themselves as scientifically parsimonious while their psychoanalytical critics see them as naïve.

THE CONDUCTORS

Let us begin with two of the conductors who might be called respectively the East and West coast charismatic leaders of the field, Nathan Ackerman and Virginia Satir. Both generally made more statements than any family member during the course of a session, and although the aim and effect was to promote interaction between family members, they did it by establishing a star-shaped verbal communication pattern with themselves as the center.

Ackerman mobilized family interaction, watching it for non-verbal gestures and interactional clues to the more primitive relations of sex, aggression, and helpless dependency in the group, and then "tickles" the defenses against these. He cut through denial, hypocrisy, and projection, forcing the members to be more open to him than they were to each

176

other. With his confident manner and his honesty he promised them for the moment a relationship to him in which the defenses could be dispensed with. He opened up a family that was frozen with the fear of aggression, or promoted a sexy interchange in a couple where sex was feared. He broke the family's rules about the unmentionable, because nothing was unmentionable to him, and he went after what people were trying to hide until he got it. When he brought it out, it was under his own sponsorship — he loaned the family his pleasure in life, jokes, good sex, and limited aggression.

Satir[53] presents herself to the family as a teacher and expert in communication. She says of the therapist, "He must concentrate on giving the family confidence, reducing their fears, and making them comfortable and hopeful about the therapy session. He must show that he has direction, that he is going somewhere. His patients come to him because he is an expert, so he must accept the label and be comfortable in his role. Above all, he must show patients that he can structure his questions in order to find out what both he and they need to know."[54] Satir is determined to teach the family a new language, with which they can resolve the communication problems that she sees as the root of their trouble. To do this, she makes herself the embodiment of clarity and perception in communication, using simple words, keeping up a running explanatory gloss on what she is doing, and arranging encounters between family members according to her rules. She does, of course, much more than this, and her work with family dynamics shows that she translates into her own language the concepts of many more traditional theorists, but basically she is a teacher of a method of communication. The treatment is accomplished when the family has learned it, and the deepening of their relationship is a by-product.

Murray Bowen and Salvador Minuchin, the next two conductors, have as a primary tactic a selective way of arranging the therapist-family interaction — a sort of stage direction which enforces differentiation within the confused relationships of the family. Bowen[13] retains absolute control of the process of the therapy meeting and refuses all other responsibilities. He even avoids calling himself a therapist and eschews the model of a doctor treating someone with an illness, since that model implies a dependence of one person on another that is part of the family pathology. He presents himself as a researcher teaching the family to be researchers. There, however, the open-endedness ends, and shortly after his initial reconnaissance with the family he begins to work toward his goal. The goal is the differentiation of individuals from what he has called the "undifferentiated family ego-mass." He chooses one parent or the other, usually the more mature one who is closest to differentiating to begin with, and through individual sessions or joint sessions works on the marital relation and the transference to himself. The emphasis is on the futility of trying to influence, change or depend on, the other. Bowen presents himself as uninfluence-able, unchangeable and not to be depended on in this situation — he says what he will do and what he will not do. When he succeeds in getting one spouse to take such an "I stand," the other is shortly motivated to move off in *his* own direction. The marriage, after a stormy period, reaches a new equilibrium between two more different people who are still relating to each other. The subtlety of the process consists in the fact that only the pathological bonds are broken, and Bowen's trenchant definition of these is his great art.

Minuchin[44] is more elaborate in his stage direction. He works with poor families who have little ability to delay impulse or examine processes which are pointed out to them verbally. His interventions are directed to giving the family what he calls an "enactive," or "iconic," rather than a verbal, experience of a new way of operating. For example, he selects a mother and daughter in whose relationship a grandmother cannot avoid interfering. He instructs the mother and daughter to continue their talk while he takes the grand-mother behind the one-way screen to observe and tell him her feelings about the other two. He thus gets the grand-mother to enact the separation. He talks to a silent child

178

about something unrelated to the family in order to give the family and child the experience of the child's talking. He silences an overbearing wife by talking to the husband about the effect of her tactics on the men in the room, and colludes with the husband to handle her. The emphasis is on breaking patterns of action to produce feelings, and the therapist uses himself as the explicit agent or intermediary in making the break. For both Bowen and Minuchin the pattern of present interaction is manipulated — the unconscious content for the individual. The psychoanalytic theme is secondary if it is noted at all.

The next group of conductors, Roland Tharp and the Multiple Impact group under the leadership of Robert MacGregor, are most explictly concerned with conventional family roles. Their therapies are brief and action-oriented.

Tharp[64] makes an acknowledged simplification of family dynamics by examining the functional roles that the family members take in one of four areas: solidarity, sexuality, external relations, and internal instrumentality. He diagnoses the division of responsibility as it is within each of these, picks the area where the most trouble exists, and requires a new contract between the members. They are to work out an explicit contract, which will sometimes take the form of a written budget, or a legal-looking document describing jobs and penalties. The family is taught a technique of negotiating on concrete issues, which they can generalize. It is a secondary by-product that enhanced self-esteem comes to members who are newly seen to have bargaining power and responsibilities, and with this legitimate source of self-regard available, the pathological forms of seeking (the symptoms) will become dysfunctional and disappear.

The next example of the leader approach is the group that practices what they have called Multiple Impact Therapy, or MIT, at the University of Texas in Galveston.[46] They treat families with a disturbed adolescent in crisis. The family comes to Galveston, checks into a motel, and at eight in the morning begins two days of kaleidoscopic interaction with a team at the clinic that includes doctors, a female social worker, psychologists, ministers, and others. The whole team meets with the whole family for an hour, and then they split up into different combinations of interviewers and family members according to a strategy that is worked out during the opening meeting. The team with its leaders and followers, its male and female members, is a model of role differentiation, flexibility, open criticism, and communication, at the same time that it is examining the family's difficulties in this area. During the course of the two days, the marital relationship is examined in individual and conjoint interviews, the appropriate areas of authority and autonomy of mother and father are confirmed, the child's expression of anxiety about the parental relationship is acknowledged, and by the time of the last plenary session at the end of the second day, the family knows that it can be under the leadership of a father whose wife has first place in his heart, and whose children know their place in their developing separateness from the family. They are then told to go out and try it until the first six-month follow-up visit in the home. This is a very intensive, powerful experience — historical, prescriptive, and future-oriented. The team brings to bear the power of their number, the solidarity and depth of their relationships to each other, and their experience with their own and other families. They are explicitly conveying the values of the culture, as well as the understanding of the idiosyncratic position from which the family starts.

Up to this point we have presented our catalogue of conductors in pairs that have implied a similarity, at least for didactic purposes, however different the members of the pair might be to all other intents. We come finally to two at the end of our list for whom no such bracketing is implied — Norman Paul and John Elderkin Bell.

Norman Paul's[48, 49, 50] undertaking with the family, like that of a shaman-healer, is to exorcize the ghost that dominates their lives. He conducts an inquiry, which is in style something like individual therapy, into the present and past of the family. The aim of the inquiry is to disclose the figure from the past, usually a parent of one of the parents, whose

180

influence as an unrelinquished object affects the present relations of the family members. In this inquiry, he is the center and organizer of the communication pattern, and does not spend much time with the analysis of open interaction between family members.

When the unmourned parent of, say, a husband is identified, Paul will interview the husband intensively, bringing out memories and fears, while the wife listens and Paul points out to her, in an aside, whose shoes she was being asked to fill. If the grandparents are still living, all three generations may come together for what is often a very tearful session of recognizing and relinquishing.

Paul tries to present himself, the therapist, as the transference substitute for the lost one, and encourage in the separation at the end of therapy a more open and benign recognition of the realities of parting. He also presents himself as the model of *empathy,* which is the second cornerstone of his method. When one family member is in the process of re-experiencing the misery of early loss, or another conflictual experience, Paul empathizes deeply and openly with his experience and invites another family member to do the same. One of his goals for the family is that through his example they can discover the rapport with one another that comes from the conscious exercise of empathy.

The point to carry forward is the central position Paul gives to unresolved internal object relations as the key to pathology. We will meet this again when we come to the analysts: Paul's theoretical background is very close to theirs, and indeed he would be classed with them in our scheme if he did not present himself so clearly as a conductor with the definite goal of freeing the family through mourning.

John E. Bell is a lone and original figure in family therapy. He was one of the people who independently began it as a technique in 1951, and he has continued to break new ground in his writing about it, as can be seen from the number of passages in this review where we have felt that the best way to make a point is to quote him. His Public Health

Monograph of 1960 is the first handbook of family therapy, and we have taken our picture of his style of leadership from the case report in that publication.[8]

The quality of Bell's leadership is rather gentle, sympathetic, and polite, but it is at the same time clear that he knows where the family ought to be going and how to get them there. He proceeds through an orderly and definite set of *phases*, each one laying the groundwork for the next, and by comparison with many other therapists he works quite rapidly — the treatment reported in the monograph took eleven sessions.

Working with families in which the symptomatic one is the child, he begins by seeing the parents alone in an initial interview. There (as Haley has noted) he makes a paradoxical contract with them: he hears their complaints about the child, thus seeming to accept for the moment the idea of the child as a patient, and then asks them to bring the child and siblings next time, and to agree beforehand to accept a suggestion the child may make in the second interview about a change in the family's way of doing things. This puts the parents in the position of control as co-strategists with the therapist, but paradoxically their first move is to agree to see what happens if the child is put in control of a limited aspect of the family's rules. We shall meet this kind of technique again, more explicitly tied to theory, in the paradoxical instructions of Jackson.

With this unsettling of the usual order, Bell enters a "child-centered phase" where the aim is to encourage the child to state his fears, grievances, and wishes, while the parents listen and react but do not dominate. The key to his phase is the therapist's supervision of the dialogue so that "everyone has a chance to speak." He thus establishes the rule that the family members will be equals in the task of self-expression, and in this way he gets himself benignly but solidly established as the rule-maker.

He next moves to a "parent-child interaction," where the major resistances, tensions, and often denials of difficulty by the whole family occur. The handling of this crisis by sympathetic urging, interpretation of parents' childhood experience, encouraging some resolution outside of sessions, or getting suggestions from the children, leads to a decision by the couple to do something differently.

From here, the therapy moves to a denouement of consideration of sibling relations, roles outside the family, and termination. During this phase, the family makes plans for how they are going to continue to manage their affairs by using the techniques they have learned — they discover new potentialities in each other for the resolution of difficulties and thus do not have to depend on the therapist. There is also an increased interest in the success of each member in his role outside the family, which goes with the release from the pathological function each was serving within the family — the differentiation from the family ego-mass of which Bowen speaks.

We have abstracted Bell at such length because in this first paper in the field he brings together so many of the subjects that other therapists have developed over the years. In addition to Jackson's paradoxical instruction, there are: the establishment of communications in the session as the focus of interest and of the therapist as communications expert (Satir, Zuk); the redefinition of the child problem as a parent-conflict problem (Satir most explicitly, but many others as well); the focus on positive interpretation (Haley, MIT); and planning for the future (MIT, Tharp); and phase-specific planning of tactics so that the therapy proceeds from one focus to another, from the family's definition of the problem to generation conflict to parental conflict (Framo).

Before we proceed, notice the abundant value-statements of the conductors: Ackerman's writing is replete with statements about what the good life is like. Satir has a remarkable summary where she says: "Everyone must manifest uniqueness in himself and validate it in others, settle differences according to what works rather than who is right, and treat all differentness as an opportunity for growth."[53] Bowen[13] has a scale of 100, designating degrees of mental

183

health on which he is confident that he can rate people within five points or so. MacGregor[47] makes no apology about reinforcing what he refers to as the "middle-class values" of his patients. Bell[10] speaks of establishing "a more perfectly functioning group," though he has in mind that "the value system that should be the family's own system rather than that of the therapist."

We would summarize this section by saying that the conductors conduct a meeting with a very definite end in view. They arrange for the family a new experience in the possibilities of relating to one another, and they are quite direct about setting that experience up.

REACTORS-ANALYSTS

The first group of reactors are Carl Whitaker,[70, 71, 72] whose co-authors in several papers include Warkentin,[66] Felder[42] and Malone,[42] Lyman Wynne and his colleagues at NIMH, and the group of family therapists in the Philadelphia Family Institute who are best known under the editorial leadership of Alfred Friedman,[21] Ivan Boszormenyi-Nagy, and James Framo.[75] The group is distinguished by a terminology and interest more or less similar to that of the psychoanalytic tradition of therapy. They believe that the individual carries within him a non-rational and unconscious truth that, when encountered meaningfully in the therapy, will help to set him free. They are also the leading exponents of the use of co-therapists. Sonne and Lincoln[61] of the Philadelphia group, for example, prescribe the use of male and female co-therapists for the working through of parental transferences in the family members, and they would agree with Whitaker that having two therapists is essential to the emotional equilibrium of either one. The following quotation from Whitaker[69] conveys the mood of the co-therapy team in the family:

We have been forced to admit that family psycho-therapy can be effectively undertaken only by a team of two therapists. A good surgeon can do a routine appendectomy, but even a good surgeon wouldn't attempt a major abdominal operation without a colleague of equal adequacy across the table. We believe family psychotherapy is a major operation. Moreover, we are convinced that no team is powerful enough to *"handle"* the family. Manipulative psychotherapy may be sufficient in minor operations, but it does not seem effective in major operations. Although we do manipulate transference feelings, it is impossible to gain "control" of what goes on in a family. Furthermore, it is not possible at this stage of our knowledge to *understand* the family. We do not know enough, we are not clever enough, and God knows we are not mature enough, to be subjectively involved in a family and still be objectively perceptive of our own subjective involvement and its relationships to the family process. By implication, then, our task in family psychotherapy is to be available as a team to move as participants in the psychological and social patterns of this family, and thereby to aid the family unit in its autopsychological reparative process.

The concern about the *dangers, pitfalls,* and *need for help* in the major abdominal operation is something that often seems to distinguish these therapists from the conductors.

Whitaker[68] describes as the heart of the therapeutic process the periodic *almost* acting-out by one therapist of the projected wishes of the family, such as their wish for a parent figure. Attention is called to this when he stops himself, or is rescued from it by his co-therapist, and the dynamics of the group that would have induced him to play this role are thus first illuminated and then frustrated. This is similar to a tactic described by Jungreis[36] in which he threatened to give in and have himself adopted by the family in the place of their schizophrenic son — he considered being taken care of by the father, seduced by the sister. It was too much for them, and they began to change.

Whitaker sees himself as functioning in the role of activator. His intent is to invade the family as a person either by usurping one or another family member's place or by forcing a new mobility of roles within the family. He may link with father to help him become dominant, be seductive of mother and make father jealous, or organize an overt war between the generations. His constant use of co-therapist helps this objective and helps maintain his freedom to deny his involvement and serve as prototype for each member by moving back out of the family at will. He demands an exciting experience for himself to give them the courage to raise the family thermostat.

Wynne's group has written little about treatment other than his excellent paper on "Indications and Contraindications" referred to above, in which he writes about the effort to tailor the approach precisely to the family's problem. This concern does not easily lead to "structured admonitions about method," as Wynne says. Schaffer, Wynne, Day, Ryckoff, and Halperin[56] described the inevitability of the therapist's becoming disturbingly involved in the family's confusion and distress, and noted that the involvement can be turned to therapeutic account. For the most part this group at the National Institute of Mental Health also prefers to work in co-therapist pairs. From what we have observed of Wynne and Harold Searles working together there, they count on each other very much for support as they register the confusion, blurring of focus, futility, anger, and so on, induced in them by the family system. Their struggle to be empathic with what is happening at the moment in the family, and to talk with family members about it with intuition. Candid self-revelation is followed, sometimes, by a demand that comes from the therapist's involvement: that the family clarify something to help him out of his confusion, for example, or fight openly because the therapist is oppressed by their deviousness.

For Nagy and Framo, the heart of the therapeutic undertaking, after the initial scuffling and settling down, is the uncovering of the distorted internal part-objects of the

186

family members, especially the internalizations and projections of the parents within the current family. This is analyzed by examination of distorted pseudo-involvements between family members and transference projections onto therapists, and especially by the identification of stereotyped *phasic interaction patterns.*[11] Thus, a mother repeatedly provokes her daughter to misbehave and her husband to punish her, so that the mother can then both identify with the punished daughter and attack her husband for being too strict. She later sees the connection between this and her own punishing father, for whom she has not mourned, and whom she revives to live again in the play between her husband and daughter. As we saw, this return to an arrested mourning for lost objects is also central in the method of Norman Paul.

One final note about the experience of the Philadelphia group: Jungreis[36] remarks that in the midst of all the interpretation, most of their therapies with schizophrenics moved forward after the therapists had insisted on a particular strategic change in the family's activity. For example, they insisted that the family have more contact with friends. This is a particularly obvious abandonment of the reactor and commentator role, and there are others of a subtler sort that Jungreis describes. The family therapist, he points out, must be active and insistent, or he will not have an effect.

SYSTEM PURISTS

This leads us to the final group of reactors, the system purists: Gerald Zuk, Jay Haley, and Don Jackson.* Jay Haley is a far-reaching student of other therapists' work.

---

*A note on our sources for Jackson. There are, unfortunately, only three descriptions written by himself of Don Jackson's work with families.[30, 33, 35] The rest of our acquaintance with him was through lectures in which he presented tape fragments and anecdotes, a movie of a demonstration interview, and the excellent interview in Haley and Hoffman's book.[27] He also discussed two tapes with us during a visit.

He does not call himself a "school" of family therapy, but we include him because his formulations about how family therapists behave have been very influential in the development of the field.

We group Zuk, Haley, and Jackson among the reactors, but they are also very conscious activists of a certain kind. They each have a wary regard for the power of the family to maneuver, exclude, and otherwise subdue the therapist, and each is for that very reason interested in devising a strategy by which he can emerge as a covert leader. In this search for the pivot point where the therapist's influence can be applied, they seem sometimes cynical or disingenuously artful, and it is this attitude that offends their critics. They do not think, for example, that the truth of the unconscious shall make the family free. The curative agent is the paradoxical manipulation of power, so that the therapist lets the family seem to define the situation, but in the end it follows his covert lead. There is something chilly about the idea of the therapist as trickster, as presented in their theory, and we have found it hard to recognize in their warm and concerned work with actual families. We shall pay attention to their theories as well, however, because there is a power struggle involved in all therapy, and these workers have made a perspicacious attempt to define what it is.

The general basis for these theories is the communication concept of behavior first described by the group working with Gregory Bateson[7] in California in the 1950's. It has been more recently elaborated in three texts: Jackson, Beavin, and Watzlawick's *The Pragmatics of Human Communication*,[67] Haley's *Strategies of Psychotherapy*,[24] and two papers by Jackson.[32] The reader should really look at these works to see the system in its logical elegance. We present some of it here because the method of therapy is impossible to appreciate without it.

The communication theorists assume that human interaction is like a chess game: although an historical explanation of the position of the pieces can be found by looking at the moves that have been made from the start of the game,

188

the crucial question is, nevertheless, what is the relationship of the pieces *at present,* what are the rules that govern the players, and what is the next move? They adopt a "black box" model of the mind, comparing it to an electronic instrument so complex that the investigator pragmatically leaves speculation about its inner workings to the psychoanalysts and concentrates instead on its input and output — what it is actually seen to do in response to certain stimuli.

Some axioms that govern the human communication game are, greatly abridged, as follows:

1. *All behavior is communicative.* It is impossible not to communicate, since even the refusal to send or receive messages is a comment on the *relationship* between people who are in contact.

2. *Messages have "report" and "command" functions.* Thus, "It's raining" is a report, but depending on the context, inflection, and relationship of speaker to hearer, it may also be a command to remember an umbrella.

3. *Command messages define relationships.* The command aspect of communication is the troublesome part, because it is the medium through which relationships are shaped, and in this process, ambiguity, misunderstanding, and duplicity are possible. Communicants are often unaware of commands they are giving, receiving, or obeying.

4. *In families, command messages are patterned as rules.* If two or more people are in relationship for a long time, the multiplicity of commands they exchange assumes a pattern from which rules for the relationship may be derived. These rules constrain and order the behavior of family members in patterns of mutual influence that have cybernetic properties. When anybody's behavior approaches the established limits (the governor, the setting of the homeostat) sanctions (negative feedback) are dealt out until the behavior is again within the acceptable range.

5. *Change and stability.* If a family wants to change the relationships, the regulating response of others that stabilizes the system by reducing change makes it appear that the "governor" or conservative element in the system

resides in the person or persons resisting change. Children, especially adolescents, are natural initiators of change in families, and mothers in the family literature have acquired a reputation as the guardians of homeostasis. Jackson and others present good evidence, however, that *all* members resist change by any of them.

6. *Inability to change rules is system pathology.* The system is considered pathological when the *rules* are set in such a way that there is no way of changing *them*. This happens when there are two rules that paradoxically negate each other: an operating rule and another rule-about-rules that denies it.

Thus, a family has an operating rule that says "Mother decides when we go to bed" and another that says "None of us believe that anyone sets the rule for bedtime — we need sleep for our health." In such a family it is impossible to negotiate about bedtime without breaking one or both rules. No one can take a position outside the communication (become *meta* to it) and talk *about* it with the intent of changing it. Jackson calls attention to the pernicious effect of the invocation of values ("health") to conceal operating rules.

7. *The family therapist must install himself as the meta-communicator, or change-maker of the family.* He can help them set the stuck family homeostat in a new way. The techniques for this are tricky, and some will be described below. The general form of the process is this: he is the third person to whom two (or more) others present themselves with their "stuck," endlessly cycling system. They are playing a "game without end," and he must intervene to change the rules because they cannot get out of it.

Zuk[78, 79] describes a particular kind of change-maker with the phrase, "the go-between." The go-between mediates between two people in conflict, trying to change the relationship by selecting issues for the two to struggle or negotiate about. He sides judiciously with first one and then the other, and finally insists that the conflict have new rules, with himself as the referee.

Zuk says the therapist must take over from "pathological go-betweens" in the family. A pathological go-between is a person who avoids being one of the principals in a conflict by deflecting it to an innocent third party and then assuming the stance of mediator. The therapist must capture this position of go-between, because in any triangle, it is the most powerful spot. The therapist must avoid being the judge, since he is then a principal in a conflict, and the rest of the family who bring him the victim for sentence become pathological go-betweens or mediators.

Haley[24] notes several strategies therapists use to establish themselves as the family's change-maker.

1. A therapist may engage in alternate siding to force a stalemated conflict to resolution.

2. He comments openly on the way he is being influenced, thus breaking the rule of silence that has maintained the paradoxical bind between the conflicting rules described above.

3. He presents a professional relationship to a conflicting pair, which is outside their rules, since they are unwilling to acknowledge any such complementary relationships between themselves.

4. He gives directives impossible to avoid, such as "express yourself."

5. He accents the positive aspect of otherwise conflictual relations, which presents the family with a paradoxical situation in which their efforts to fight are redefined.

6. He encourages and labels behavior that is already going on at the direction of the family's rule-keepers, thus making the momentary leadership of the group explicit and breaking its power.

A quotation from Haley[25] on marital therapy will illustrate some of these points.

As an example of a typical problem, a couple can be continually fighting, and if the therapist directs them to go home and keep the peace this will doubtfully happen. However, if he directs the couple to go home

191

and have a fight, the fight will be a different kind when it happens. This difference may reside only in the fact that they are now fighting at the direction of someone else, or the therapist may have relabeled their fighting in such a way that it is a different kind. For example, a husband might say that they fight continually because his wife constantly nags. The wife might say they fight because the husband does not understand her and never does what she asks. The therapist can relabel or redefine their fighting in a variety of ways: he might suggest that they are not fighting effectively because they are not expressing what is really on their minds; he can suggest that their fighting is a way of gaining an emotional response from each other and they both need that response; he might say that when they begin to feel closer to each other they panic and have a fight; or he can suggest that they fight because inside themselves is the feeling that they do not deserve a happy marriage. With a new label upon their fighting, and directed to go home and have a fight, the couple will find their conflict redefined in such a way that it is difficult for them to continue in their usual pattern. They are particularly tempted toward more peace at home if the therapist says they must fight, and that they must for certain reasons that they do not like. The couple can only disprove him by fighting less.

Note that in this view, the precision of the explanatory insight is unimportant; it is the precision of the *intervention* of relabeling the fighting and thus taking control of it that counts.

In the writing and work of Don Jackson, the *intervention* of the therapist in the family's communication system, its balance of power reached its most inventive heights. These prescriptions or tasks sometimes have the quality of magic rituals, the carrying out of which seem to deliver the family from a curse; in fact they are carefully tuned to a clinical picture of repetitive interaction patterns, which the

192

therapist sees but keeps to himself. "Our experience with this kind of repetitive pattern is that pointing it out does little good. However its meaning, intent, and focus can be shifted by the therapist's intervention."[34]

Before making his move, however, the therapist constructs his position with the family carefully. He starts with a frame of minimal ground rules that are optimistic, forward-looking, minimizing the "sickness" of the identified patient, and leaving the therapist free to make any response: "Free, to me, is not to give them so much direction that they know how to use it against you."[28] Jackson was particularly expert at increasing this freedom by remaining casually "one-down," avoiding struggles by changing the subject, and emphasizing the positive and appealing aspect of the most disturbing communications. Saying such things as "I can't get too upset about that," he showed himself proof against the family's attempts to bind him and each other with the threat of disaster.

In this context, the intervention is the one requirement he made of them, and it was delivered as a serious prescription that they must follow in order to improve. The instruction, like the pathology it counteracts, has two levels: the obvious one in which it appears to be something not very difficult to do, and the interpersonal one where it shifts the meaning of a symptom, or the balance of power. There is, of course, also the third "meta" feature of the intervention — that it comes from the therapist and therefore cannot be irresponsible or "crazy" like the symptoms.

Though they should be read in the original papers to be appreciated, we present here a few examples of Jackson's interventions.

1. The "well" sibling of a schizophrenic is instructed to be more of a problem to the family. This has the effect of revealing how much of a problem he already is, and changing the "sickness" image of the patient.[34]

2. The depressed widow of an alcoholic who has moved in on her married son is instructed to have a drink with him every evening, no matter how much she dislikes it.[30]

3. A family is told to have a fight before they go on vacation so that they can enjoy the trip.[31]

4. A delinquent stepson who will not mind his new stepmother is asked to agree that no matter how angry she gets he will pay no attention to her orders — indeed she is not to give any. He will be disciplined only by his father.[16]

Note that in each case the prescription is to continue or exaggerate something already going on — "prescribe the symptom" — so that it comes under therapeutic control. Often the symptom will disappear before the task is carried out — it seems to wilt under intention.

Looking back on the methods of the reactors, it appears that they gain entry and control in a way that is more indirect and complex than that of the conductors. They may, for example, impose the relationship between co-therapists on the family system, and that is a more difficult "foreign object" for the family system to deal with, since the co-therapist's relationship is part of the larger social system, and has some other "incorruptible" qualities, such as freedom to change, or a feedback loop of its own, etc. Or they may, like Jackson, impose their control in such a way that it is "unbeatable" because it is a paradoxical instruction. The point we want to make is that it is, in some crucial sense, control.

MOVES AND TACTICS

Having completed a survey of the various presentations of self with which therapists approach families, let us turn to what happens next — what the therapists attempt to deliver. We will select here some moves and tactics that are of special interest to us, since a comprehensive survey would be much too long.

MEMBERSHIP

As we said in the introduction, one of the most powerful moves the family therapist makes is to concern himself with the family as a group. This concern does not require, however, that everyone in the group participate equally. The extremes of membership policy may be seen by contrasting the work of Ross Speck with that of Murray Bowen.[63] Speck sees "networks" — the extended family and friends of the nuclear family that contained the original patient — about thirty or forty people in the same room. Bowen[12] may see one person at a time, but in this respect he is the exception among family therapists, and one which "proves the rule." Even when he is seeing an unmarried person living in a different city from his family, he starts by teaching about the operation of family systems. Then, he says, "time is devoted to the part this one plays in the family system and some fundamentals of 'differentiating an I' out of the 'we-ness' of the family system, and to changing the part that 'self' plays in the system. It is necessary that [he] arrange fairly frequent visits home with [his family] . . . these [sessions] are similar to supervisory hours with young family therapists. When this 'differentiating one' begins to change, the family will get negative or reject, at which time it is absolutely necessary that [he] keep in contact with the family in spite of the rejection."

The point we want to make is that family therapy's attention is devoted towards a family group, but the whole group does not need to be present at any one time. The *interest* and *allegiance* of the therapist is towards the whole family, and this interest and allegiance defines family therapy, not the number of people in the room, or the membership of the meeting. The membership of the meeting is, rather, something that the therapist manipulates for particular ends.

One approach to the problem of membership, prevalent in Philadelphia and in Wynne's group at NIMH, is to set up a fairly inclusive membership of the nuclear family and continue with it for some time. The practice is sometimes not to meet if one member is absent and to treat this as a resistance, called the "absent member phenomenon" by Sonne, Jungreis, and Speck.[62] This is a safe form of projection, resistances

195

being attributed by those present to the absent member. Such meetings of the whole family may represent the first time they have talked together in any healthy self-awareness of themselves as a bounded group with real relationships and responsibility for their feelings toward each other. Thus, the inclusiveness of the membership has a therapeutic value in itself, as well as supplying information to the therapists not obtainable otherwise.

Others, such as Satir and Bowen, deal with only the marital pair in the main part of the therapy, seeing the whole family mainly to get some information about how the children are expressing the marital conflict or attempting to mediate it. Bowen, Jackson, and others have observed that even when the family presents their very disturbed child as their symptom, if the therapist makes it clear that he is going to work with the parents, and the children should go on about their business, the symptoms of the child usually stop at an early stage of the treatment and the trouble in the family does shift to the marital relationship.

There are many rationales for focusing on the marriage, e.g., Bowen's three-generation hypothesis, Shapiro's delineation hypothesis, Bowen's idea of "the triadic one," Satir's child-as-a-messenger, and Tharp's role theories. They might be summarized by the idea that if the illness is in the family group, one should start with the group's leadership, and the parents are, in Satir's phrase, the architects of the family, the place where the main authority ought to be and where the lasting sexual and contractual bond should be cemented. Bowen[13] and Haley[26] carry this further in pointing out that the therapist-husband-wife group forms an essential triangle in which the therapist replaces the child or grandparent, and this puts the therapist in the position of the projected external others who have formed pathological triangles with these parents. The ideas of these authors about triangles seem to us of great theoretical importance and practical power, and are worth more attention than we can give them here.

196

In the remainder of this chapter we will compare various approaches to the problem of bringing the family to a new experience of their behavior. Framo describes this as the "middle phase" of family therapy, following the initial phase of confrontation and accommodation between family and therapist. It is the phase during which the essential work is done. For Framo, in the ideal case, that is the "understanding and working through . . . the introjects of the parents, so that the parents can see and experience how those difficulties manifested in the present family system have emerged from their unconscious attempts to perpetuate or master old conflicts arising from their families of origin."[19] This is often called "insight." We note at the outset, however, that there is an argument about what this means, which turns around some of the most fundamental attitudes in the field.

In its most superficial form, the question is, "Do the family members acquire what a classical psychoanalytic writer could call insight in such forms as, say, a resolution of the Oedipus complex?" In another form the question is the one posed by Ackerman[1] in answer to the challenge, "Is family therapy a 'deep' therapy or is it merely support, suggestion, and environmental manipulation?" He concluded that family therapy was as "deep" as any other because there are no issues or emotions with which the family therapist does not deal in as intense and decisive a way as a psychoanalyst does.

There is an exchange about this in the pages of *Family Process,* where Haley reviewed Nagy and Framo's book.[23] The book, the review, and Haley's reply to a letter of ours about the review[22] are worth reading, because they summarize a major division within the field. This is a conflict between the psychoanalytically oriented and the communication theory-oriented partisans, and although much of it is a mere conflict of loyalties, it reflects a genuine dilemma: What should one search for in working with a family? Should one just get them to change what they are doing, on the assumption that a stuck pattern of behavior is the cause of their trouble? Or should one seek a further cause in the subjective experiences of the individual members, which, unchanged, will re-establish the troubled patterns? Haley says the answer to this question lies not in argument but in experience, but there has been no evaluation of our experience that would tell us the answer.

Looking back on it, we think, on the one hand, that the argument was a trade union dispute about whether analysts or non-analysts do better family therapy, with the implied further question of whether classical individual psychodynamics is an important part of the training of family therapists. On the other hand, politics aside, the question is even more critical and more difficult to answer as we now see it: it is not a matter of the *family's* gaining insight but rather of the *therapist's* doing so. Understanding what is happening in the family, the therapist may interpret it, or arrange a task in the light of it, or reflect on it to himself in the hope that knowing it he will in some empathic way be more useful to the family. Now the question is, does an understanding of the individual motivations put him in a better position to do any of those things? We think so, but until someone does an outcome study of family therapy with that question in mind, our answer will have to be based on personal experience.

Let us proceed by examining several forms of insight or redefinition of experience as they appear in different schemes of therapy.

INSIGHT: PROJECTIVE IDENTIFICATION

Let us look first at one kind of insightful formulation that turns up so frequently and in so many forms in the writings of different authors that it is worth our particular attention. There is a whole group of phenomena that Klein[38, 39] in individual terms calls projective identification. By this is meant a splitting off of a disavowed part of the self and projecting it onto others. Lyman Wynne points out that in families this results in what he calls a "trading of dissociations . . . there is an intricate network of perceptions about others and disassociations about oneself in which each person 'locates' the totality of a particular quality of feeling in another family member. Each person receives one or more of the others in a starkly negative preambivalent light and experiences himself in a similar but reciprocal fashion, with the same abhorred quality in himself held dissociated out of his awareness. . . . The fixed view that each person has of the other is unconsciously exchanged for a fixed view of himself by the other. The interlocking result is similar to the system of reciprocal role expectations that sociologists have described in intrafamilial relationships. However, here I refer to a system or organization of deeply unconscious processes, an organization that provides a means for *each* individual to cope with otherwise intolerable ideas and feelings. . . ."[74]

Zinner and Shapiro[76] refer to a "defensive delineation" of the adolescent by his parents so that the adolescent is seen as having qualities that the parent denies in himself. The adolescent, allowing unconsciously for the parents' need to preserve their self-esteem through this denial, shapes his developing identity to fit the parents' delineation.

Nagy[11] locates the prototypes of many such defensively dissociated and projected part-objects in the parents' experience with their own parents, thus completing a three-generation picture of this phenomenon that often results in the illness of the developing adolescent of the third generation. He and Paul describe their versions of the therapeutic working-through of the parents' attachment to or denial of the grandparent objects as essential to the therapy. Other workers confront the families with these phenomena in other ways, but their importance is widely recognized. Bowen sends his patients on trips to visit their parents and grandparents and in-laws to "establish a person-to-person relationship" with each of them and to interview them about their family tree. We suspect that one of the effects he achieves is the realignment of fundamental-object relations in which those kinfolk serve as distorted part-object representations.

INSIGHT: THE ACTIVE EXPERIENCE

We next come to something we think is of central importance in family therapy, not only because it unites so many seemingly disparate practices, but because it is crucial to our own thinking about what we do. This is the idea that the altered perception of family relationships that is the therapeutic *sine qua non* results from an active or participatory or nonverbally immediate experience within the therapeutic hour.

First, as we have said before, the mere act of getting the family members together for treatment implies that something more immediate is going to happen than would be possible if they meet separately to talk about one another. They will have more an encounter than a discussion, more drama than narrative, more theater than literature, and the therapist, to keep himself clear about what is happening, will use more the juxtapositions of the stage director than the explications of the *literateur*. Kantor and Hoffman[37] have compared family therapy with Brechtian theater, emphasizing in each the liberating effect of seeing an interaction both as a participant and an observer. The whole subject of nonverbal communication in family therapy was also discussed in a symposium of Zwerling, Scheflen, Jackson, Ackerman, Nagy, and others,[81] which is well worth reading.

Having worked with this sort of medium for a while, some family therapists and people allied with them have carried this natural property of the family interview further into an interesting array of practices and conceptions. We will conclude our review by putting this array together before the reader. In several ways, these workers seem to be saying that the words people use — the verbal channel of

200

communication — is at best a recapitulation and affirmation of something primarily experienced in a nonverbal mode, and is at worst a means of disguising what is *happening* between people. Family therapy provides a means of getting at what is happening, not as in individual therapy, by explicating the contradictions, connotations, and hidden levels of the verbal channel, but by bringing the happening into awareness, manipulating or highlighting its features: seating arrangements, gestures, interruption patterns, tones of voice, laughter, and what Zuk calls "silencing strategies;"[77] and visual (symbolic) artifacts, whether natural (such as clothing and posture), or intentionally unfamiliar (such as pictures drawn by the family or the reviewing of videotapes of the interaction).

ARRANGING THE EXPERIENCE

We present next, in no particular order, examples of what therapists are doing that seem to come under this heading. These techniques are more fully described in chapters eight (see page 272) and nine (page 318).

THE USE OF TAPES

Norman Paul,[48] Alger and Hogan,[6] and many others have written of the practice of using audio or videotapes of the interaction to give families a chance to observe "from the outside" what is happening. The response to this is often a revelation to the family members because the things attended to are manners of influencing the interaction, especially tones of voice and facial expressions, which are extremely powerful, and of which the members are unaware. These experiences often have the force of an interpretation, without, as Alger points out, the accusatory mode, "Let me tell you what you are doing." Paul uses a videotape from *another* family to put the family before him in an empathic mood from which he wants them to proceed. This is, literally, the use of theater in therapy.[51]

201

Role-Playing

We have described the use of role-playing and role-reversal as a means of developing sympathy between family members, but further to our purpose, we notice that it has the effect of making people aware of their nonverbal influencing behavior, since they cannot play the part of another without noticing the discrepancy between what they say as the other person and how they say it.

Family Art Therapy

Gentry Harris and Hanna Yaxa-Kwiatkowska[40] successfully treated a family with a schizophrenic son by getting them to draw pictures at the beginning of sessions and in connection with impasses. The pictures avoided the level of *verbal* exchange and mystification that Harris says is the schizophrenic's weakest area, and produced enduring images that the therapists and other members could recognize and validate. In accounting for the importance of the visual iconic level, Harris uses an explanation that is similar to Minuchin's explanation of his own technique.

Tasks

The assignment of tasks, either within the hour or outside it, is a frequent practice in family therapy. We mentioned Jackson's "interventions" above. Any such intervention, if the members agree together to try it, even as an experiment, has the effect of putting them in a new behavior pattern with one another and of shaking up their present methods of mutual control. We mention here several kinds of tasks that seem to have a particular relevance to this.

Virginia Satir assigns tasks that make it impossible to continue the old forms of mutually disturbing action. She has a blaming couple sit for five minutes a day, holding hands, facing each other and talking only of their own feelings, or she has an adolescent daughter communicate with

202

her mother only in writing for a week.[55] Her insistence that the family adopt her own form of completely unambiguous clarity makes it difficult to shade communication with provocative inflection.

Bowen asks a husband to estimate with accuracy, *"What percent* of the time are you successful in getting your wife to blow up at you?" *"How many times* in the last *two* months have you succeeded in turning away when she starts trying to get you worked up? Is that getting better as compared with six months ago?" He carries on a cool, precise, interrogation in these terms, changing from one member of the family to another, asking the next, "What is *your* reaction to *that?*," thus keeping the whole communication system under his control. No family member responds directly to another in his interviews. The thing to note here is that it is impossible under these circumstances to perform any of the dramatic projective provocations on which family trouble depends — one is induced by the questions and the format to think of the problem as a rational one, full of percentages and frequencies.

We referred above to Bowen's techniques of sending family members on trips to visit parents and in-laws. He instructs them not to "do the same old two-step that you always did when you visited before, but try to get a real person-to-person relationship with them." He suggests settling disputes that have lain dormant for years, and often assigns the specific task of interviewing the relatives about their kin, to get an accurate family history, and find out what the ancestors were really like. The unaccustomed visit, the unusual task, and the emphasis on changing the old dance-step are all ingredients of an experience designed to put the "patient" in benevolent control of the interaction by which he felt victimized before. The taking of the family history is a task with a surprisingly powerful effect on the mutual understanding of both parties: it must be tried to be appreciated.

The authors[17] use an interview format that is the opposite of Bowen's but which has the same objective of

203

changing interaction patterns. We *ask* the family to interact directly while we observe, and wait until we see a sequence being repeated over again that we recognize clearly. We may play a tape back to demonstrate the general form of the sequence we are referring to. We then show them the gestures and postures they use to keep the sequence going. We ask them to try changing these monitoring signals to see if they can stop the sequence. The kind of sequence we are talking about is very similar to the *phasic interaction pattern* described by Nagy and we suspect it is what he is interfering with by interpreting that pattern to the family.

MINUCHIN

Salvador Minuchin's system of treatment is one of the most carefully described in the literature, and we think his description bears a remarkable similarity to what he actually does. He says, in *Families of the Slums,*[44] that his method is designed especially for lower-class families with an impaired ability to use abstraction and delay: the benefits of the verbal channel of communication. In the light of the comparisons we are making here, it seems to us that his method is not special to that group, but rather describes something of much more general importance.

Minuchin gets the family to talk briefly until he identifies a central theme of concern, and has an impression of who is most involved with it. He also makes a guess at what interrupting, silencing, or diverting maneuvers are keeping the discussion from going further. He then assigns the family the task of continuing with their work on this issue, but he gives them specific stage directions, as described above: he rearranges the seating, blocks an interruption pattern, or takes a family member behind the screen where they can observe but not interfere. He paces the family by adopting their mood and tempo at the beginning and then changes it through his example. His questions are in an *enactive* mode: not, "*Why* doesn't your mother talk to you?" but, "See if you can *get* your mother to talk to you."

204

Watching Nathan Ackerman interview a family was always a vivid experience, and sometimes a confusing one because of the strong feelings the observers had about what he does. Sometimes he seemed by turns intrusive, insulting, seductive, and autocratic. Families and therapists who consulted with him, however, generally found that he focused on important problems of theirs with speed and accuracy, and with liberating effect. If we examine what he did in terms of the comparisons we have been making, we may understand this discrepancy. Ackerman worked rapidly, paying careful attention from the beginning of the interview to the nonverbal relationship messages of the family members.[60] He engaged them directly with his own posture and gaze, and talked to them about the ways in which they were covering themselves from him with their behavior. He spent some time clearing away what he called "hypocrisy" in the verbal channel, and tried to read what the family was telling him directly. He offered himself directly also, not only in the above way, but sometimes as the interview proceeded, his hand, the seat next to him, his lap to the children, his handkerchief to the crying mother, a cigarette to a woman who said, "My husband won't let me smoke," his tie to a young man who felt he was not respectable enough.[3] He worked quite literally as a catalyst. By his availability and what he called "tickling the defenses," he opened interpersonal balances in the family members that then became available for interaction between them. Once that interaction was going, he interpreted it in terms of sex, aggression, dependency, and so on; a language that he then shared with the family.

In addition to the comparison with other forms of nonverbal work, it was almost impossible for an observer listening to the words to be in tune with what was going on in an interview with Ackerman. Later interpretations may sound just intrusive. It is hard to imagine that the family was prepared for it through any change of their defensive position.

We suspect also that one of the reasons Ackerman had so few successful imitators was that the personal use he made of the nonverbal material was almost impossible to teach.

CONCLUSION: NOT THE DANCER BUT THE DANCE

Looking back now, we are in a position to see some patterns that have been running through our explorations.

We saw first that the family therapist works with the family as a natural group whose members or acts are related to each other in a mutually responsive way so that we may describe them as a *system,* and that the conceptual difficulties of viewing them so come from our arbitrary (cultural) assumption that the individual is the "natural" unit, rather than the group or system. Once we are committed to the idea that the group is the unit to be addressed, we can ask the following questions:

Is there a way of viewing the individual-in-the-group that bridges the gap in terms of two different approaches? Norman Paul seeks to define a person in the family as suffering unexpressed grief in a way the others have not recognized, and his task is to get everyone to validate that unique experience through empathy, to see the person as a sufferer and not a manipulator of the others. This is the opposite of the position taken by Jay Haley, who would see the family as a group of people trying to influence one another by various means, including suffering.

The group's organization is one level in a hierarchy of open systems; the individual's organization is another. Seen this way, the dichotomy between the group and individual foci is a false one, and both are always true: *behavior that is expressive for the individual is communicative for the group.* For momentary tactical purposes, one may use the approach either of Haley or of Paul, but the richness of the practice of family therapy consists for us in seeing the interlocking of these systems.

The family maintains what Jackson and Haley call its homeostatic organization — and troubled or "stuck" families

206

seem to be particularly concerned with doing so. How does the therapist introduce himself as the new element in the system? *He must do so in such a way as to avoid becoming a regulated part of the system, or he will produce no change.* The therapists we have called conductors enter with their own values and rules of communication strongly in the fore, and in certain crucial respects they take charge. The reactors are more gradual and indirect, but they also eventually require that a key element in the system move the way they want it to.

How is this done? *Our review of the delivery or discovery of the altered sense of family relations suggests that it is somehow encoded in a level of communication or perception other than the verbal-abstract.* In fact, one of family therapy's reasons-for-being is the experience of some of the early workers that for some people "understanding" or "insight" did not "take;" it was not acted upon unless it was somehow brought forth in the midst of the family.

This suggests that both the family's regulatory system — benign and pathological — and the experience which is the key to change in that system are embodied in a communication system that is only fully developed and clear when the family are in each other's presence. When they are not present to one another, but represented by verbal or symbolic traces, the system is much more difficult to read, for both them and the therapist. In this way the "conjoint" and "nonverbal" aspects of family therapy are clearly related.

Let us conclude with one scientific and one clinical citation, each of which seems to make this point in a different way.

Albert Scheflen,[57, 58, 59] in examining motion pictures of family therapy and other groups, has worked out in some detail a description of repetitive patterns of body positions and shifts, gestures, gazes, paralanguage, etc. These patterns occur in relatively unvarying sequences, enacted over and over again. When the "meaning of these patterns is analyzed by careful recording of their *contexts* as beginning, ending, or changing other sequences, they reveal a rather simple grammar of command to, or comment on, relationships in the group." Scheflen suggests that this is how, often outside awareness, the relationships in a group are defined and controlled. Further, the sequences are themselves organized into larger sequences he calls "programs." These programs are participated in by several members, as if they were dances, and have a cyclic, automatic quality quite familiar to both family therapists and watchers of family therapy.

John Bell, in an address we have quoted before,[9] described his experience with trying to provide families with insight into their behavior. He began in the old way, relating history to motivation and thus "interpreting" the motives of family members. He also tried a sort of positive approach to family dynamics, saying they must have "good reasons" for the things they do. All this fell flat. He then turned to making rather neutral observations of nonverbal communications between family members. He found that at last they did not feel he was accusing or taking sides, and that, having noted what was going on, they provided their own "insight." This agrees with our experience.

Bell went on to suggest that his experience tells us something about "emotional insight." He said, "As a consequence of this technique and the reactions that occur, we have revised our theories about the relationship of insight to action. We have concluded that in part we have seen the sequence entirely the wrong way about. Whereas formerly we assumed that insight ultimately led to action by some unknown process, we have now concluded that action may be seen more fruitfully as coming before insight. Action has the primacy rather than insight. That is, insight and action do not take place in some parallel psychological processes, but insight is within the mainstream of action. What is even more important, we have concluded that the action that leads to insight takes place with, for, and because of others — that it is a process of, and in, a social group rather than of and especially within an isolated individual. Insight has the appearance of identity with an individual because it is abstracted from the social action, and, as all thinking, is seen from the point of view of a person who is acting. Thus, to call it intellectual insight is indeed appropriate. But we have traditionally overlooked the social matrix within which this occurs, forgetting that the individual is never independent, a fact that becomes especially obvious when the whole family group is before us."

What interests us is the way in which these observations again suggest that the action in a group is primary, the declarations of the members secondary. Especially in families, we are doing a dance, listening only rarely to what we say to one another. Family therapy is the bringing together of the family and the therapist in order to experience that pattern of action and change it.

DISCUSSION

*The preceding chapter was sent to the fifteen
family therapists mentioned in it with an invitation to comment. Four therapists chose to
respond, and their comments follow.*

COMMENTS BY JAMES L. FRAMO, PH.D.

Chris Beels and Andy Ferber, in my judgment, have
performed a valuable service for the family field, and I submit that this chapter will become required reading for the
student family therapist. It was absorbing reading for me. I
do not agree with those critics who claim that no one has the
right to characterize the work of others; one of the vital
aspects of the family movement that distinguishes it from
others is the free spirit of inquiry and cross-examination that
leads to self-questioning and further discovery. I recall with
pleasure Chris and Andy's visit to observe my work some
years ago, and I only wish that the visit were more recent so
they would have become acquainted with the development
and changes in my thinking and practice over the last few
years.

My chapter on "Rationale and Techniques" in *Intensive Family Therapy* was actually completed in 1963, even
though the book came out in 1965, and although I stand by
most of what I said then, there are some things I stated that
I no longer feel are true (e.g., that one should meet with the
whole family at all times, or that only long-term family
therapy is likely to lead to meaningful change). From my
point of view, the family approach is not a form of therapy
or a technique but a philosophy or way of viewing emotional
disturbance transactionally in its intimate context. It does
not so much matter who happens to be in the treatment room
at the time (although certain behaviors are exhibited in particular constellations of those present and not in others).
There are some people seeing family members conjointly,

210

doing "family therapy," who, in my judgment, do not have this necessary outlook; in other words, they don't get it. My approach has become more flexible (always a worthy adjective to apply to oneself), and more adaptive to the kind of family and particular difficulties of a given family. Accordingly, as I read this chapter I was surprised to find that at one time or other I use almost every technique mentioned — cutting through denial and hypocrisy and forcing members to be open to the therapist (Ackerman); promoting an "I" position and differentiation (Bowen); breaking patterns of action to produce feelings (Minuchin); exorcizing past ghosts and elucidating mourning experiences (Paul); negotiating on concrete issues (Tharp) and giving paradoxical instructions (Jackson, Haley). When I have observed other family therapists I have been impressed with how similarly *experienced* family therapists function in the actual therapy situation, despite differences in theoretical persuasion. Everyone feels uncomfortable when they see their work reduced to a few sentences that may seem pallid and misleading. While it is true that my own view of family dynamics centers around object-relations theory, and that I believe that the transactional use of this theory as a bridge between the personal and the social has more explanatory power for what we see in families we treat, in the actual treatment situation I work with introjects rarely, and only under special conditions (e.g., when a family has been well into treatment and when some inappropriate attitude or behavior is arrested and the person himself questions its appropriateness in time or questions the target — for instance, "I wonder why I have this unreasoning resentment toward my son."). Since most family therapy consists of the short-term crisis variety, I mostly use other techniques. In private practice you sort of feel more pressed to get results, and while on one level you are more careful with private patients, on another level you are more experimental. In the process of inducing change you try out many things and have to be concerned with such practical questions as how to deal with the referring professional who is not familiar with family therapy and sides with the family in not bringing the kids; what the timing of family therapy should be; what to do if one member of the family is in individual therapy with someone else; how to combine other forms of therapy with family therapy; what "the priorities of intervention" should be; whether to meet the request for a private session with one individual; and so forth.

I would agree with Beels and Ferber that the distinction between individual systems and family systems is a false dichotomy, and I do object to those who polarize this dichotomy and fractionate the family field into the "good" and "bad" family therapists in terms of their emphasis on intrapsychic vs. family system. These two systems are different levels of phenomena which interact at some times and not others. The mother who just *knows* her baby will turn out to be a schizophrenic by the look in his eyes is making an interpersonal resolution of intrapsychic material from the past, as well as current system factors: as Santayana put it, "He who forgets the past is condemned to repeat it." We know now that the family does not always function as a system. One cannot wipe out entirely the realm of inner experience as irrelevant to family system theory; inner experiences both mediate and are mediated by system phenomena. Yet there are those who claim that anyone who deals with intrapsychic phenomena in family sessions may be doing something interesting, but they are not doing family therapy.

This stance of declaring certain data off-limits occurred when behaviorism entered academic psychology and determined what the study of man should be; by reducing people to action tendencies and thought to sub-vocal speech they attempted to get rid of man's mystical soul, but somewhere along the line the individual as a person with feelings in a social context got lost. And since every psychologist has been trained as a methodological behaviorist since then, the individual has been artificially segmented, and whole rich areas of human functioning are considered bad form to be studied. My dander gets up whenever anyone attempts to set what the limits of investigation of a field should be, and

212

proclaims that to examine certain phenomena is out-of-date or unscientific. I myself prefer to work with the gut issues of family life because that's where I think the pay-dirt lies; it's damn difficult to work in this area — which is the main reason, I feel, for its avoidance by those who adopt a more mechanistic approach, and also probably accounts for the use of co-therapists. It is also my bias that if you deal with interlocking motive systems among intimates, with irrational role assignments derived from attempts to live out the inner conflicts through one's family, that the communication styles are more likely to change than if you change the communication patterns and let the motives remain unknown, to take care of themselves. Despite my bias, however, I feel the communication theorists and therapists, who have made a great contribution, have every right to proceed without having their work labeled as "bad" family therapy. Since no one knows what change in families is, what really leads to change, and whether indeed all change is desirable, family work should proceed at all levels.

It has become fashionable and "in" nowadays to attack psychoanalysis, often without making a distinction between psychoanalysis as a method of treatment and psychoanalytic theory. More to the point, words like "psychoanalytic," "psychodynamic," "unconscious," and "insight" have come to be bandied about like dirty words. One wonders, parenthetically, whether anyone can discuss any kind of dysfunctioning for five minutes without using some psychoanalytic concept or derivation thereof (e.g., defense mechanisms, concepts like narcissism or mourning, etc.). The concept of insight has become so grossly over-simplified and distorted that it's difficult to discuss anymore. Aside from the trite distinction between intellectual and emotional insight, every experienced clinician knows that when he uses the word he is communicating in short-hand fashion an extraordinarily complex blend of experience, understanding, action, relationship, etc. Any therapist worth his salt knows that just pointing out, confronting, or interpreting things to people cannot work by itself.

213

At any rate, I feel that Beels and Ferber have written a definitely worthwhile chapter that highlights some of the important issues in such a way as to lead to enrichment of the family field.

COMMENTS BY F. GENTRY HARRIS, M.D.

Doctors Beels and Ferber, in their review and careful analysis of family therapy, have rendered a significant and badly needed service that I feel will gain wide appreciation. I personally found it quite stimulating. There are many comments I would like to make and questions I am tempted to raise. These I will forgo, however, in order to devote the limited space to an issue of more direct concern to myself.

While at a disadvantage inasmuch as the paper I wrote with Kwiatkowska and Smith[40] has not yet been published, I may be able to add something of value to the comments that Beels and Ferber so kindly thought fitting to include about it. Since, in the paper, our work is directly compared to that of Minuchin and his colleagues (hereinafter referred to as Minuchin), it would seem fitting to use this as a reference point. They say, "In accounting for the importance of the visual iconic level, Harris uses an explanation that is similar to Minuchin's explanation of his own technique." But, as I read Minuchin, there are important differences between us. Before proceeding, a brief resumé of my orientation is necessary. In particular, my primary interest lies in the types of *signs* manifest or lacking in therapeutic contexts, and in their classification as both a research tool and a guide to formulating problems and evaluating the significance of conduct in therapeutic endeavors. For this purpose I have found Charles Sanders Peirce's theory of signs and ontological frames of reference* a constant source of inspiration

---

*Scattered in the Collected Papers of Charles Sanders Peirce, edited by C. Hawtshorne, P. Weiss, and A. W. Burks, 8 vols., Harvard Univ. Press, 1933-1958; and especially Charles S. Peirce's Letters to Lady Welby, edited by I. C. Lieb, Whitlocks, 1953. A good exposition of the relevant aspects of Peirce's work is J. J. Fitzgerald, Peirce's Theory

and insight. While too voluminous to present here in detail, here is a brief indication of essence and implications of Peirce's work.

Peirce speaks of three categories of phenomena that he calls simply firstness, secondness and thirdness, and alternately, in other contexts, of monadic, dyadic, and triadic structures. (These *do not* refer to one, two and three person relationships. Any one of these structures can predominate with respect to one or to any number of persons.) The signs of these are called respectively icons, indexes, and symbols, of which more presently.

Firstness he defines as a mode of being that is without reference or relation to anything else. *Secondness* is that which is such as it is by virtue of some relation to any second, but regardless of any third, phenomenon. *Thirdness* is a mode of being that relates a second to a third phenomenon. A predominant unchanging mood or feeling is an instance of firstness, essentially of monadic structure. Peirce speaks of it as a person in his inertness identified with a feeling state. An uncontrollable change from one feeling to another, *as change*, an emotional clash or conflict, an action on something else, are instances of secondness, essentially of dyadic structure. Peirce speaks of this as mere brute force or fact, of something simply happening. A thought or idea that relates certain contents and procedures in some intentional or lawful way, such as the phenomenon of giving (A gives B to C) is an instance of thirdness, essentially of irreducible triadic structure. If giving is reduced to A relinquishes B and C takes it up or merely comes into possession of it, it is no longer genuine giving, but a series of two dyadic structures. (It may, however, have the superficial appearance of giving and so be mistaken for it.)

The signs of the referents of these phenomena Peirce calls icons, indexes, and symbols. Icons are essentially things

of Signs as Foundation for Pragmatism, Mouton, 1966. I am also indebted to a little-known paper by Walker Percy (The Symbolic Structure of Interpersonal Process, Psychiatry 24 : 39-52, 1961) and to many personal exchanges with him.

in themselves; they have a direct, intimate "reference," or are direct substitutes. Indexes we are familiar with as symptoms or as *Freudian* "symbolic" phenomena. Symbols (not to be confused with Freudian "symbols") represent in general high-level phenomena uniquely characteristic of the human being. Full awareness, and conscious motivation, intention and responsibility are its marks. One can see there are thus many occasions for confusion and deception in the use of signs.

There are other important aspects to this theory of sign behavior, e.g., the nature of interpretants, but I can here only refer the reader to the original sources for additional elaboration. This much I hope will suffice for my subsequent comments.

What I am thus striving for is the delineation of a broad frame of reference encompassing all forms of experiencing and participation and of understanding and communication, and capable of analysis in terms of various types of signs — of icons, indexes, and symbols (or signs respectively of monadic, dyadic, and triadic structure). In the work of Kwiatkowska, Smith, and myself, on the use of free-hand pictorial productions in the family treatment of schizophrenia, I am concentrating on the monadic level, while I conceive Minuchin to be primarily concerned with the dyadic level. We are both, however, aiming for the achievement of a triadic level of functioning. Both of us are seeking ways to open up prospective, rather than merely retrospective (causative), channels to more efficient and satisfying functioning. Our means to this end differ, I think, because of the differences in our patient populations. There are nevertheless many points of contact in our separate concerns. In some passages, for instance, I believe Minuchin is alluding to phenomena of a monadic structure, perhaps used defensively by patients, in other cases as simply a manifestation of lack of development beyond a monadic level. He says, for example: "These families display a mono-affective quality in their interactions, generally adhering to a narrowly defined, restricted mood level, despite the content of the issues to which they might be attending" (p. 274).

216

For the most part, however, Minuchin classifies what he calls "communicational modalities" into the verbal and the actional. In my classification these correspond closely to triadic and dyadic structural levels. He is specially concerned with the latter, and has developed a method suitable for understanding and communicating in that mode. His actional or manipulative techniques seem to be admirably suited to his population. I, however, am specially concerned with still another modality (of monadic structure), and thus do not consider Minuchin's classification exhaustive. Minuchin, I take it, makes direct use of *action*, in connection with problems couched in strong tendencies to externalize. I make direct use of *feeling* (pictorialized), in connection with problems couched in strong tendencies to internalize (i.e., to withdraw, fail to express, to avoid commitment to some communicable form). Both of us freely apply what he calls "task-oriented family therapy." He is dealing with what I call second level or dyadic phenomena; I am dealing with first level (or monadic) phenomena. Again, both of us are concerned with the most suitable media for recognizing and communicating about these structures, and so have decided on the use of different media. I am more preoccupied with the "feeling modality" and a medium to handle it; Minuchin with the "actional modality" and a medium to handle it.

I consider my work as in essence directed to an expansion of media for participation, apprehension, understanding, and communication — in line with but supplementary or complementary to Minuchin's study. I am in full sympathy with his emphasis on techniques utilizing an expanded range of media as preludes to higher level functioning, typically characterized in verbal terms (which, if genuine and appropriate to the facts, is the triadic level).

Minuchin thus operates primarily in the action mode, offering paradigms of what is actually the case or conceivably possible. This is quite different from my own orientation in the work with Kwiatkowska and Smith, which is that of designing a setting and medium of communication to facilitate the development of feelings, of possible moods toward various matters, where they did not previously exist. An attempt is then made to relate these feelings to the contents that the pictures help to define. As I see it, I am operating on a sign level different from that of Minuchin, which I view as more appropriate to schizophrenic situations. I wish to spell out, to develop a language for the potential contribution of monadic phenomena to triadic structure, while Minuchin wishes to develop a sign modality for the potential contribution of dyadic phenomena to triadic structure. Thus Minuchin concentrates on dyadic structure (which he calls "tension") as the most plastic element in the organization of his families. He avoids, at least initially, tangling with the monadic and triadic structures, which he sees as constricted or degenerate in his families. I have concentrated on the monadic, and avoided the dyadic and triadic structures for similar reasons, primarily because I consider this a more appropriate approach to schizophrenic problems.

There may seem to be a certain paradox in the fact that Minuchin, in effect, maintains that activation (of conflict, tension, etc.) is the operation of choice in the treatment of acting-out patients. I think this is only apparent, however. What is at issue is the unfocused automatization or routinization of acting-out that is producing trouble. To break this up, to mobilize other action, then, is understandable under the circumstances. I take a similar view with respect to monadic structure (feeling, etc.), when I consider it absent, unfocused, automatic, or routinized. Minuchin, incidentally, puts his finger on a crucial aspect for both of us when he emphasizes his objective of stimulating an exploratory orientation and curiosity, rather than simply the development of competence, as the impetus of problem-solving endeavors. I would add that getting patients in a position to accept what is going on and what is happening to them (whatever the sources) as simply materials to be used in their own enterprises is also crucial in developing responsibility for one's effective being-in-the-world. For this tends to confer a new range of meaning and significance even to unmotivated (biological) levels of behavior, in contrast to the sense of having things, as it were, dropping on one's head out of the sky. Thus, even though one has uncontrollable impulses, there are still a number of different ways in which, and a number of different purposes for which, they can be used, and used responsibly.

COMMENTS BY LYMAN C. WYNNE, M.D.

Because of the apparent diversity of family therapists, it is perhaps inevitable that efforts should be made to find unifying dimensions or features along which comparisons and contrasts can be made. Beels and Ferber have made an interesting and useful attempt. However, their valuable comments have stimulated me to have the contrary thought that such characterizations of therapists may be inappropriate or misleading unless one *also* describes the kinds of persons the therapists see; we need to remind ourselves that the therapist meeting with the family (or other persons seen) constitutes a *new* transacting system. I am aware of not being the same therapist (a) when I am seeing an upper-middle-class urban Jewish couple, and (b) when I am meeting with a lowerclass Southern Protestant family with two hebephrenic children. The therapist-family *system* is different in these instances; even when the therapist does not let himself become a "regulated part of the system," as Beels and Ferber put it, the impact of the family upon him will differ and what he does in response to their impact will differ.

A decade ago a number of family therapists were concentrating on treating intact middleclass families with a schizophrenic offspring, often in a hospital setting. The form of the treatment relationship under those conditions was necessarily and appropriately different, indeed radically different, from that found, for example, when multiple, "broken" slum families are seen together in a community network. It is my impression that some therapists have shifted their recommendations about treatment "techniques" without specifying that the families in their practice have also changed.

219

Both the behavior of family therapists *and* the families with whom they work are becoming more diversified; if we discuss *only* the therapists, we implicitly fall into the trap of looking at them out of context, which no family therapist would do (I hope) when talking about family members! Our system precepts need to be followed consistently when we speak of therapists, as well as when we talk about families.

Beels and Ferber somewhat oversimplify the therapeutic endeavor when they emphasize that therapists "take a position against the system of the family." I feel we need to distinguish two therapeutic phases or tasks. The first, as Beels and Ferber recognize elsewhere in this chapter, is for the therapist to make entry into the family, to "introduce himself as the new element in the system." "Entry" means discovering and showing the family he knows how the family uses "language," verbal and nonverbal, and how the family regulates itself using various special rules and values. Genuine entry, especially with families that have idiosyncratic or unfamiliar rules and forms of language, may of course be very difficult.

One of the major reasons family therapists, both "conductors" and "reactors," must be more active than other psychotherapists is because the family has existed as a long-enduring system that tends either to resist entry or to absorb and dissolve those who enter. Therefore, if the therapist enters at all and remains reasonably intact, he has necessarily altered the family system. But the second and still more difficult phase of family therapy is to steer the family in the direction of more satisfactory rules, values, and ways of communicating and relating, which can survive as a new system in the therapist's absence. Here it is especially important for the therapist to recognize that taking "a position against the system of the family" has been a necessary first step that, however, has not completed the therapeutic task.

Beels and Ferber are probably correct when they suggest that the therapists they call "reactors" use more complex and indirect modes of entry into families. I share what I understand to be Carl Whitaker's view that a therapist can-

220

not be free to "react" unless he has first provided himself with a workable structure for the therapy — and it may require a good bit of "conducting" to set up such a structure. This structure may include specifying vigorously and definitively who is going to be present, when meetings are going to take place, what the ground rules are for, what is allowed and not allowed in the meetings, etc. Within a given framework the therapist can then "react" flexibly, be bored and quiet, or involved and talkative, be an emotional member of the family — *and* intermittently be free to *stop* "reacting," to step outside of the family, and to conduct the proceedings whenever he feels that he and the family are ready. The key aspect of "reacting" as I see it is for the therapist to allow himself to notice his own subjective, ongoing experience with the family. Only with inward observations can he grasp important features of the emotional impact and meaning of the interaction and "tune in" on what the family members are trying to do with him and each other. The therapist's difficult task is to intervene on the basis of *both* behavior and experience; this calls for an interplay of "conducting" and "reacting."

I believe that the problem of grasping immediate subjective experience is a more critical issue than what has been called "insight" — a term that has too many divergent meanings to be worthy of retention. As I pointed out to the authors, and as they have now stated, if the term is to be used at all, the gaining of "insight" about the family may be useful to the therapist, rarely to the family. "Insight" has lost its reputation as the primary agency of therapeutic change even in classical psychoanalysis; I suggest that this dead concept be left in peace.

COMMENTS BY GERALD H. ZUK, PH.D.

These cats are doing their own thing, all right; but baby, that ain't where it's at.

The main dialogue — one might say, struggle — in family therapy today has been between advocates of the

221

psychoanalytic model (once they discovered family therapy), with their special focus on exploration of the unconscious, their attempt to reconstruct the historical sequence of pathology, their attachment to such notions as transference and countertransference and oedipal situations, and attraction to the concept of therapeutic insight; and those advocates of what might be called — for want of a better term — the system approach, with their focus on comprehending sources of power and leverage in the immediate field of action, their preference for explanation not bound by linear cause-and-effect sequence but rather put in terms of negative and positive feedback, their attachment to the notion that insight is not a requirement for therapeutic change, but rather that change may be an outcome of the bargaining or negotiation that goes on between therapist and family members, and their attempt to catalog the different negotiations that take place in family therapy.

Essentially, the main struggle between the camps is over the definition of the basic unit of observation: is it to be the dyad, the two-person system, to which the psychoanalytic model can be adapted without great difficulty; or the triad (more accurately, triadic process), the three-person or more system, focused mainly on locating the sources of leverage in groups, and on the processes of mediation and coalition formation occurring between family members, between the therapist and family, and between the family and community agencies, such as the school or court system?

Of what possible relevance for family therapy is the Beels and Ferber distinction between conductors and reactors? Are conductors better or worse family therapists than reactors? Do conductors get one kind of result from families, reactors another? The authors steer clear of such inferences that, however premature or unwarranted, might at least have provided a legitimate rationale for this point of view. In my opinion, this chapter simply distracts from the main arena to which I have referred above, and which others have spelled out also in previously published work. Such distractions may sometimes provide moments of amuse-

222

ment through imparting a breezy, newsy flavor to a field —
a kind of "here's the latest dope" quality; but the paper has
not very many such moments.

I have wondered about the authors' tortured references
to and interpretation of insight: their enlargement of it to
a point at which it seems to me to lose shape and sense. I
can only ascribe this need to their at-all-costs commitment to
the psychoanalytic model.

I imagine other discussants will want to comment on
the flimsy, superficial characterization of persons and
positions. While this is a basic hazard of reviews and over-
views, it seems to me the authors might have made a more
serious effort to check it. The chapter seems to be addressed
mainly to newcomers in the field, whom I would urge to
check original sources.

Beels and Ferber have given birth to something that is
not just simply inadequate; it is also downright mischief-
making. It is pretentious to claim to make a major distinction between family therapists, when in reality the distinction
is irrelevant to the central issues in the field. It is mischief-
making in that it introduces side issues that divert attention
from those that are central.

If I may be permitted a more personal note, I would
like to draw attention to the authors' description of "the
system purists," the subdivision of reactors in which I am
included as a member. (Even now I can hear the authors'
protestation that the statement has been snatched from its
context; but I believe it does accurately convey their
"feeling tone.") The statement reads: "There is something
chilly about the idea of the therapist as a trickster, as
presented in their theory. . . ." This is an inaccurate, misleading assertion of the authors. On the other hand, it is
evidence of the extent to which their psychoanalytic bias has
colored their perception.

RESPONSE BY BEELS AND FERBER

The comments presented above, as well as the many

223

letters we had from others after we presented our first draft to them, have been gratifying in just the way we hoped. They have raised the discussion to some new levels and new questions. In this reply we would like to address ourselves to those, rather than to the customary mixture of bows and rebuttals.

We begin with the comment of Gerald Zuk, who, if he had not been so upset about what he sees as our hopeless thralldom to psychoanalysis, might have joined us in discussion of several points:

First, the chapter is, as Zuk says, "addressed to newcomers in the field," and its first purpose is to make an introduction to the original sources. The reason for classifying and subclassifying conductors and reactors is that the beginner is confused by such a variety of personalities and techniques, and we present one way of looking at them in groups. This presentation makes the point that the therapists' personal style *is* a large part of what is called "technique." Since, as we say and Zuk agrees, there is no evidence that one approach works better than another, the best advice to get across to the beginner is that many styles seem to lead to success. He should fashion his own synthesis from as many models as he can watch, together with whatever the strong points in his own character are.

Once that has been said, however, there is a further point, and here we are no longer talking only to beginners: *all* these therapists work to get *control* of some vital aspect of the meeting. That is the purpose of their entry into the family, whether they do it openly like the conductors, or, like the analyst reactors, come to it indirectly and not as a conscious goal until late in the game, or whether, like the system purists, they gain covert control through the exercise of a sort of benign guile. Zuk is offended that we refer to the latter as "the therapist as trickster." He has missed the point: we are agreeing with Haley's view that *control* is a fundamental issue in all psychotherapy, but it can rarely be gained by the therapist's simple assertion. It requires what Haley has called *strategy*.

224

The further question, which we addressed at the end of the paper, is "control over what?" We think the thing that most needs to come under the therapist's control is the process of communication in the new group of therapist plus family: he must set the rules for what goes on in the session. Such a conclusion is a long way from an "at all costs commitment to the psychoanalytic model." In fact no one, not even Jim Framo, is attached to the psychoanalytic *model* of doing therapy. In that connection, we would agree with Wynne and Framo and Zuk that it is time to stop talking of insight about introjects as a goal in its own right in family therapy. As we noted in the last quotation from Bell, such insight is a by-product of treatment, and not a necessary one, at that. Its name should probably not be given, as we have given it, to the "altered sense of family relations" which results from the therapist's control over communication, or power, or whatever it is. That should not be called "insight," but something else.

Now the question is, what is this thing that the therapist does? We have presented our ideas about it, here and elsewhere, as the changing of family behavior programs (Ferber and Beels, "Changing Family Behavior Programs," *International Psychiatric Clinics*, 1969) and we have tried in this chapter to present the views of others about what really happens in therapy. The debate is still wide open. It seems to us that Wynne in his comments about the problems of *entry* into the family makes an important further contribution.

Harris is apparently saying in his theory why his approach to the family of a schizophrenic would be different from that of Minuchin to the family of one of his "multiple-acting-out" youngsters. Clearly, however, Minuchin and Harris would have to watch each other at work to understand the distinctions he is talking about, and from what we have seen of each of them it would be very fruitful.

The next step in the field is to describe, as Wynne suggests, the specific moves a therapist makes when presented with a specific kind of family and social context. We took this up to point out that apart from that short list, nobody writes about the diagnostic specificity of their treatment tactics, although everyone talks about it. Perhaps this is because the talk would not bear public scrutiny.

The GAP report on family therapy (1970) made a first systematic attempt to relate therapist training, treatment settings, patient populations, practice, and theory to one another, but that was only a statistical look at the question. What is needed, and what is barely in sight, is a description of treatment approaches to different kinds of family problems. When we seriously set about that task, we will find our current notions of classification, theory, and tactics put to a real test.

Since we wrote this chapter, we have become deeply immersed in natural history method analyses of films of family therapy. It is clear to us that *all* prior descriptions of therapy, including our own, are exceedingly poetic and deductive metaphors about the behaviors of both therapists and families. We now see our review as a temporary guide into the field. We hope it will have some utility while a new antidisciplinary behavioral science develops a scientific language that can accurately describe what we are beginning to see. Until then we urge fellow family therapists to watch each other at work.

∿∿∿∿∿∿∿∿∿∿∿∿∿∿∿∿∿∿∿∿∿∿∿∿∿∿∿∿∿∿∿∿∿∿ *References*

1. ACKERMAN, N. (1965), The "depth" question in family psychotherapy. Paper read at the annual meeting of the American Orthopsychiatric Assoc.
2. ———— (1966), *Treating the Troubled Family in New York*. New York: Basic Books.
3. ———— . Direct observation.
4. ———— . Films available from The Family Institute, New York, N.Y.
5. ———— and BEHRENS, M. (1956), A study of family diagnosis. *Amer. J. Orthopsychiat.*, 26: 66-78.

6. ALGER, I. and HOGAN, P. (1968), Enduring effects of videotape playback experience on family and marital relationships. Paper read at the annual meeting of the American Orthopsychiatric Assoc.

7. BATESON, G. et al., *The Natural History of an Interview*, ed. N. McQuown. New York: Grune & Stratton. To be published.

8. BELL, J. (1961), *Family Group Therapy*, Pub. Health Mon. No. 64, U.S. Dept. Health, Education, and Welfare.

9. —— (1963), Promoting action through new insights: some theoretical revisions from family group therapy. Paper read at the meeting of the Amer. Psychol. Assoc.

10. —— . Personal communication.

11. BOSZORMENYI-NAGY, I. (1965), *Intensive Family Therapy*, ed. by I. Boszormenyi-Nagy and J. Framo, ch. 3. New York: Harper and Row.

12. BOWEN, M. Personal communication.

13. —— (1966), The use of family therapy in clinical practice. Comp. Psychiat., 7: 345-374.

14. —— . Available from Dept. of Psychiatry, Univ. of Virginia College of Medicine.

15. —— . Television tapes, Dept. of Psychiatry, Univ. of Virginia College of Medicine.

16. Films available from Hillcrest Family Series, Eastern Pennsylvania Psychiatric Institute, Philadelphia, Pa.

17. FERBER, A. and BEELS, C. (1970), Changing family behavior patterns. In *Family Therapy in Transition*, ed. N. Ackerman. Boston: Little, Brown.

18. FORD, D. and URBAN, H. (1963), *Systems of Psychotherapy*. New York: Wiley.

19. FRAMO, J. (1965), in *Intensive Family Therapy*, eds. I. Boszormenyi-Nagy and J. Framo, 167. New York: Harper and Row.

20. FRANK, G. (1965), The role of the family in the development of psychopathology. *Psychol. Bull.*, 64: 191-205.

227

21. FRIEDMAN, A. *et al.* (1965), *Psychotherapy for the Whole Family*. New York: Springer.
22. HALEY, J. (1967), in Comment. *Fam. Proc.*, 6: 121-124.
23. ———— (1966), review of *Intensive Family Therapy*, eds. I. Boszormenyi-Nagy and J. Framo. In *Fam. Proc.*, 5: 284-289.
24. ———— (1963), *Strategies of Psychotherapy*, chs. 6 and 7. New York: Grune & Stratton.
25. Ibid., 144.
26. ———— (1967), Toward a theory of pathological systems. In *Family Therapy and Disturbed Families*, eds. G. Zuk and I. Boszormenyi-Nagy. Palo Alto: Science and Behavior Books.
27. ———— and HOFFMAN, L. (1967), *Techniques of Family Therapy*, 188. New York: Basic Books.
28. Ibid., 184.
29. HANDLON, J. and PARLOFF, M. (1962), Comparisons between family treatment and group therapy. Unpublished monograph. See also: Treatment of patient and family as a group. *Int. J. Group Psychother.*, 12: 132-141, 1962.
30. JACKSON, D. (1962), In *Contemporary Psychotherapies*, ed. M. Stein. Glencoe: Free Press.
31. ———— (1967), Lecture before Washington Psych. Soc.
32. ———— (1965), The Marital quid pro quo. *Arch. Gen. Psychiat.*, 12:589. See also: The study of the family. *Fam. Proc.*, 4:1-20, 1965.
33. ———— and WEAKLAND, J. (1961), Conjoint family therapy: some considerations on theory, technique, and results. *Psychiatry*, 24:30-45.
34. Ibid., 39.
35. ———— and YALOM, I. (1963-64), An example of family homeostasis and patient change. *Current Psychiat. Therapies*, ed. J. Masserman, 4. New York: Grune & Stratton.
36. JUNGREIS, J. (1965), In *Psychotherapy for the Whole Family*, ed. A. Friedman. New York: Springer.
37. KANTOR, R. and HOFFMAN, L. (1966), Brechtian theater

as a model for conjoint therapy. *Fam. Proc.,* 5 : 218-229.

38. KLEIN, M. (1964), Notes on some schizoid mechanisms. *Intern. J. Psycho-Anal.,* 27 : 99-100.

39. _____ (1963), On identification. In *Our Adult World, and Other Essays.* New York: Basic Books.

40. KWIATKOWSKA, H., HARRIS, G., and SMITH, J. (1967), The use of drawing and painting as a primary medium for communication in the family therapy of schizophrenia. Presented at the Nat. Inst. of Ment. Health, Bethesda, Md.

41. LANGSLEY, D., PITTMAN, F., MACHOTKA, P., and FELDER, R. (1968), Family crisis therapy — results and implications. *Fam. Proc.,* 7 : 145-158.

42. MALONE, T., WHITAKER, C., and FELDER, R. (1961), Rational and nonrational psychotherapy: a reply. *Amer. J. Psychol.,* April : 212.

43. MEISSNER, W. (1964), Thinking about the family — psychiatric aspects. *Fam. Proc.,* 3 : 1-40.

44. MINUCHIN, S., MONTALVO, B., GUERNEY, B., ROSMAN, B., and SHUMER, F. (1967), *Families of the Slums.* New York: Basic Books.

45. MISCHLER, E. and WAXLER, N. (1966), Family interaction processes and schizophrenia. *Inter. J. Psychiat.,* 2 : 375-430.

46. MACGREGOR, R., *et al.* (1964), *Multiple Impact Therapy with Families.* New York: Grune & Stratton.

47. MACGREGOR, R. (1967), Communicating values in family therapy. In *Family Therapy and Disturbed Families,* eds. G. Zuk and I. Boszormenyi-Nagy. Palo Alto: Science and Behavior Books.

48. PAUL, N. (1966), Effects of playback on family members of their own previously recorded conjoint therapy material. *Psychiat. Res. Reports,* 20 : 175-187.

49. _____ (1967), The role of mourning and empathy in conjoint marital therapy. In *Family Therapy and Disturbed Families,* eds. G. Zuk and I. Boszormenyi-Nagy. Palo Alto: Science and Behavior Books.

50. —— and Grosser, G. (1965), Operational mourning and its role in conjoint family therapy. *Comm. Ment. Health J.,* 1: 339-345.
51. Paul, N. Personal communication.
52. Pittman, F. *et al.* (1966), Family therapy as an alternative to psychiatric hospitalization: family structure, dynamics, and therapy. In *Psychiat. Report of the A.P.A.,* Jan.: 188.
53. Satir, V. (1964), *Conjoint Family Therapy.* Palo Alto: Science and Behavior Books.
54. Ibid., 160.
55. —— (1967). Workshop in family therapy, Falls Church, Va.
56. Schaffer, L., Wynne, L., Day, J., Ryckoff, I., and Halperin, A. (1962), On the nature and sources of the psychiatrist's experience with the family of the schizophrenic. *Psychiatry,* 25: 23-45.
57. Scheflen, A. (1966), *Stream and Structure of Communicational Behavior,* Behavior Science Monograph, I. Philadelphia: Eastern Pennsylvania Psychiat. Assoc. Press.
58. —— (1964), The significance of posture in communications systems. *Psychiatry,* 27: 316-331.
59. —— (1968), Human communications: behavioral programs and their integration in interaction. *Behav. Science,* 13: 1.
60. Sherman, M., Ackerman, N., Sherman, S., and Mitchell, C. (1965), Nonverbal cues and reenactment of conflict in family therapy. *Fam. Proc.,* 4: 133-162.
61. Sonne, J. and Lincoln, G. (1965), In *Psychotherapy for the Whole Family,* ed. A. Friedman. New York: Springer.
62. ——, Speck, R., and Jungreis, J. (1965), In *Psychotherapy for the Whole Family,* ed. A. Friedman. New York: Springer.
63. Speck, R. and Bowen, M. (1966), Lecture at Georgetown Univ.

64. THARP, R. (1963), Dimensions of marriage roles. *Marr. Fam. Liv.*, 25 : 389-404.
65. ——— and OTIS, G. (1965), Toward a theory for therapeutic intervention in families. Paper read before the Western Psychol. Assoc., Honolulu.
66. WARKENTIN, J. and WHITAKER, C. (1966), Serial impasses in marriage. *Psychiat. Res. Report*, 20.
67. WATZLAWICK, P., BEAVIN, J., and JACKSON, D. (1967), *Pragmatics of Human Communication*. New York: Norton.
68. WHITAKER, C. (1965), Acting out in family psychotherapy. In *Acting Out: Theoretical and Clinical Aspects*. New York: Grune & Stratton.
69. Ibid., 191.
70. ——— (1958), Psychotherapy with couples. *Amer. J. Psychother.*, 12: 18-23.
71. ——— (1965), Psychotherapy of married couples, Lecture No. 2, Cleveland Institute of Gestalt Therapy.
72. ——— (1965), *op. cit.*
73. ——— and WARKENTIN, J. (1965), Countertransference in the family treatment of schizophrenia. In *Intensive Family Therapy*, eds. I. Boszormenyi-Nagy and J. Framo. New York: Harper and Row.
74. WYNNE, L. (1961), The study of intrafamilial alignments and splits in exploratory family therapy. In *Exploring the Base for Family Therapy*, eds. N. Ackerman, F. Beatman, and S. Sherman. New York: Family Service Assoc.
75. ——— (1965), Some indications and contraindications for exploratory family therapy. In *Intensive Family Therapy*, eds. I. Boszormenyi-Nagy and J. Framo. New York: Harper and Row.
76. ZINNER, J. and SHAPIRO, R., *The Operation of Projective Identification in Parental Delineations of Adolescents*, Section on Personality Development, Adult Psychiatry Branch, National Inst. Ment. Health, Bethesda, Md.

77. ZUK, G. (1965), On the pathology of silencing strategies. *Fam. Proc.*, 4: 32-49.

78. ────── (1966), The go-between process. *Fam. Proc.*, 5: 162-178.

79. ────── (1967), Family therapy: formulations of a technique and its theory. *Arch. Gen. Psychiat.*, 16: 71-79.

80. ────── and RUBINSTEIN, D. (1965), A review of concepts in the study and treatment of families of schizophrenics. In *Intensive Family Therapy*, eds. I. Boszormenyi-Nagy and J. Framo. New York: Harper and Row.

81. ZWERLING, I., SCHEFLEN, A., JACKSON, D., ACKERMAN, N., BOSZORMENYI-NAGY, I., *et al.* (1967). In *Expanding Theory and Practice in Family Therapy*, eds. N. Ackerman *et al.*, 83. New York: Family Service Assoc.

section two
Tools of the Trade

introduction
∿∿

A. Ferber

In the past, most people just started seeing families. Today, in becoming a family therapist, most people go through a training program. These programs typically are composed of four kinds of groups, which are interwoven. The first, a *family therapy group,* is composed of a family with some sort of problem and one or more therapists seeking to assist the family in solving these problems. The primary function of this group is to change the family; the secondary function is to train the therapists. The family therapy group is the keystone of this training. Without it,

235

training is an entertainment or a sterile academic exercise.

The other three varieties of groups — *supervisory groups, seminar groups,* and *peer groups* — share common functions: training therapists to do family therapy, shaping professional identity as a family therapist, monitoring and hopefully assisting the treatment occurring in the family therapy groups, and justifying the teachers' existences.

A *supervisory group* consists of one or more beginning therapists and one or more experienced therapists. It meets regularly, usually somewhat formally, and primarily focuses on records of meetings of family therapy groups. Depending on the allocation of responsibility for treatment of families, these are also called observation, co-therapy, or socializing groups. (If the beginners' family therapy groups are examined, it is called supervision. If the teachers' family therapy groups are examined, it is called observation. If they both sit in the room with families, it is called co-therapy.) If they meet formally, but without records of family therapies, it is called a tutorial or career guidance. No names are given if the same processes occur without formal appointments. *Supervisory groups are the special arena for the indoctrination and identity shaping of beginning therapists.*

Seminar groups are usually composed of a regular membership of several beginning therapists, one or several experienced therapists, and occasional guests or family therapy groups. Seminar groups usually meet formally. Subgroups usually develop within seminars, often from preexisting affiliations. In seminar groups, training therapists is the pre-eminent function. Interesting and entertaining seminars are therefore desirable. This demand of the seminar group may conflict with the interests of individuals, therapists, or families who often complain about being exploited. *Seminars are for exemplary behavior: How do therapists and families behave? What are good and bad examples of family therapy?* What happens in seminars maintains the working therapist's ideas of what he usually should and should not expect of himself and his patients in their day-to-day work.

236

The least formal groups are the *peer groups* of both beginning therapists and teachers. Peer meetings are often less formal and less regular than those of other groups in the training network. They meet when there are crises. Peer groups monitor each other's work and set group norms. Also, they introduce innovations to the program. *But the most important function of the peer group is to protect its members.* Beginning therapists protect each other from assault and mystification at the hands of the families and the teachers. Teachers protect each other not only from beginning therapists and families, but also from other networks of family therapists, other professional membership groups, the service facilities they work in, and their own families.

Training has an optimum range of commitment from trainer and trainee. The training program ideally should not be the most important network affiliation for any of the members of that network. (It can become so if patients, learners, or teachers become too serious; trouble usually develops around the "too serious" member.) The most important network affiliations for the families in treatment are their extended families, work groups, and communities. The most important networks for the therapists, both beginners and experts, are their families of procreation and origin. Their professional peer community — outside of their particular training program — and their friendship networks follow. The entire program is strongly defined by the bureaucratic structures, and/or network of treatment services, upon which or within which it exists. All of the individuals within the program are profoundly influenced by their ties to the broader society, their social class, and, to a lesser extent, their ethnic groups. (The relationships between the training network and its contexts are considered in sections three and four of this book, and will therefore not be dealt with at any length in this section.)

COMMUNICATION, INFORMATION, AND PROCESS

Therapy and training for therapy are both processes

where curious, inexperienced, naïve or pained people buy opportunities to communicate with persons whom they consider more expert than themselves. The buyers hope that during these opportunities to communicate with experts, they (the buyers) will acquire new information and modify their behaviors within a more satisfactory repertoire.

The chief stock-in-trade of family therapy and its training is the development and manipulation of information about persons' relationships with one another. Information is developed within each of the four groups (family therapy, supervisory, seminar, and peer groups) from the latent repertoire of the members. Information is conveyed from one group to another within the network. Information is carried back and forth to networks outside of the training program. Much of this book is a discussion of just what information should be *developed in* the groups, *transmitted among* groups, and *exchanged with networks* outside the training program. This section deals especially with *how information is developed and transmitted.*

This section can be thought of as a map or plan for a training network. Certain structures and processes will be described in greater detail than others. Most of the examples have been drawn from experiences at the AECOM-Bronx State Hospital over the past ten years. Comparisons with other programs have been made at some points; I urge the reader to look for the connections and repeating processes that shape the whole experience. To look at the parts and ignore the whole misses the point. No seminar exists without trainees who are seeing families, doing work, being supervised, involved in informal contacts with the training staff, etc. We are presenting a view here that one should not "take" a course in family therapy. Teachers must design programs that fit both the state of the art and the programs' local conditions. Trainees should have the option to choose paths through the program that suit their individual proclivities.

238

seven
∿∿
a training program

M. Mendelsohn and A. Ferber

We work in New York City, Borough of the Bronx. Our city moves too fast, and competitive tensions are very high. Few of our staff and trainees are in the Bronx, and we are not members of our patients' community. Our department staffs several psychiatric facilities which occupy different territories and are relatively independent of one another. These facilities develop different policies — policies shaped more by the desires of the higher echelon staff of the facility than by the people they serve or the students they train. None of the facilities have any significant degree of community control.

239

Our department has grown so large — several hundred faculty, a few thousand employees, a ten-million-dollar budget — that it is more a corporate bureaucracy than a community of scholars. Many members of the department do not even know of each other's existence.

The influence of psychoanalysts has been strong in our department. There is a continuous dialectic between them and us social psychiatrists. We seek to define ourselves outside of psychoanalysis, and to view it as having an interesting method for working with one person, as well as a theory derived from the analytic situation. They seek to define us as *within* applied psychoanalysis; sometimes supportive, sometimes wild. This ideological competition bewilders trainees who wish the psychoanalysts and social psychiatrists would fight to the death, so that the winner could tell the trainees the real truth.

Our trainees in family therapy come from almost all the clinical units affiliated with the psychiatry department of the AECOM and include staff psychiatrists, residents, staff social workers, student social workers, staff psychologists, psychology internes, art therapists, rehabilitation workers, nurses, and research workers. Our program has evolved and continuously changed over the past ten years. It has grown from a teaching staff of two with eight trainees to a teaching staff of thirteen to twenty-five for twelve to a hundred and fifty trainees. The count of trainees and trainers depends on whether one is looking at the entire network of training throughout the department in all levels of training, or at the small group of intensively trained family therapist specialists who are trained by our permanent staff in a several-year program. The Family Studies Section is currently constituted as a separate teaching unit and has no primary service responsibilities.

The Department of Psychiatry conducts training programs in a complex network of institutions in the Bronx of N.Y.C.: two Municipal Hospitals (one in a poverty area), two voluntary hospitals, a 1500-bed State Hospital, and a Community Mental Health Center. Family training began

240

in 1960 as an exploratory treatment modality in the then circumscribed and isolated Division of Social and Community Psychiatry. It is now a basic and legitimized portion of the training of all new psychiatrists and psychologists in the entire department. In 1961, the first seminar was begun for eight trainees on Dr. I. Zwerling's Day Hospital Service. Each year thereafter, increasing numbers of trainees from several other divisions in the department asked for family training and were added to the group of trainees who staffed the Day Hospital and other programs of the Division of Social Psychiatry. Residents who had family treatment experience in the Day Hospital brought new practices to other services in the Department. By 1965, we had trained forty people in Level I programs, some people were interested in becoming family therapy specialists, and our Level II program was begun. Each year requests for training increased rapidly. By 1968, our Level III program emerged when there was again a small group of people who had had two years training with us and were eager for another year of training in the practice of Family Therapy. Our Level IV program (the program for training the teachers) has been on the scene from the beginning. Some of our trainees have set up their own training programs on their own services and maintain ties with us in Level IV programs.

Families are drawn from the work contexts of the trainees (if the work context does not yield families for treatment, we make use of a variety of informal referral sources, mainly clinicians in the Einstein complex with families who need treatment but have no one to treat them). We now offer four levels of training. The first three levels each represent about one year of training toward becoming a family therapist. Level I is an orientation to the field of family therapy. Level II aims to immerse the trainee in treating families. Level III aims to produce an independent-practitioner family therapy. These three levels of training are usually sequential. The fourth level trains teachers of family therapy. Trainees' aims vary from wanting to learn family therapy to use in some part-time fashion in their work (i.e. as a

241

diagnostic aid), to wanting to become teachers of family therapy.

The overall format is that in each of the first three levels the trainees are required to see at least a specified number of families for whom they have some clinical responsibility; to have an hour's supervision on these families; and to attend a two-hour weekly seminar. On an informal basis, in any of the levels, the trainees on their own initiative elect a variety of other involvements: observing on-going therapy by instructors, treating more families than is required, joining on-going therapy as co-therapists with instructors, joining some on-going research, socializing in a variety of ways with each other and with instructors, and seeking out instructors as advisors.

Each seminar is created each year by the specific people involved in that seminar. The design of the seminar is usually influenced by variations in the following five areas:

1. *The Leaders.* Each seminar has two leaders. The teaching staff is an eclectic one and the main orientation of the teachers is nearly as broad as that of the field itself. The mix of the two leaders can vary enormously. They might differ or agree markedly on their theoretical orientation to family treatment, their preferred teaching methods, their personalities, their own personal experiences as therapists, and/or as teachers. In any given year a team of two teachers may be old hands at having worked together, or may be entirely new to each other. Two leaders may be teaching together because they enjoy teaching together, or one is training the other to be a teacher, or the two people want to learn from each other, or the particular student group interests both teachers. We can usually count on a good bit of change each year, in that we have regularly added new people as leaders and as the older ones become more experienced, their ideas change.

2. *Level of Experience of Trainees.* The trainees within each group vary: in how much training and experience they

have had in their profession; in how much personal therapy they've had; in how rich their own life experience has been; and how much family therapy they have done.

3. *The Work Context of the Trainee.* This becomes a crucial and extremely variable factor in the life of the seminar since all the case material is drawn from the work contexts of the trainees. For example, trainees may come from an outpatient clinic where family work is encouraged, where the trainees are given free rein to do their work, and where families are intact and fairly well-organized. Or trainees may come from a state hospital, where the trainees' family work may be seen as less important to the work with the individual patient, and families may be split and disorganized. The picture is seldom as one-sidedly positive or negative as exemplified here; instead there is often a mixture of influences deriving from the work context. A variety of types of families, attitudes toward trainees, and attitudes toward family therapy are inherent in the case material the trainees have available for study. Sometimes the work context is the same for all the trainees in a particular group, as in the case of first-year residents who are getting their training while on six-months' rotation on a state hospital ward. Here the work context has an overriding influence on the life of the seminar, in that the residents are new to the work, pressed to attend to patients as individuals, and preoccupied with the pressures of ward life.

4. *Shared Definitions of the Work.* There always has to be some negotiating about where a particular group of trainees is, where they want to get, and what experiences will take them there. For example, trainees may think they are better or less well-prepared for the level of work they want to do than teachers think they are; they may expect they can learn to do family therapy in one year; or they may expect they can learn to do family therapy by reading about it, or watching someone more experienced do it.

243

5. *Material Available for the Year.* Some of the clinical materials we consider useful for teaching are: 1. families in treatment; 2. the personal families of trainees; 3. the group's own group process; 4. audiovisual aids; 5. literature. Materials available vary from year to year and group to group. For example, one year we may not have good video-tapes or movies of family interviews, while in another year they might be available. Use of personal family histories may be more available in one group than in another because of the interest of leaders and trainees.

Prior to mapping out the levels, we want to discuss the basic assumptions underlying all levels of training, as well as some views on issues of group process and leadership.

SOME BASIC ASSUMPTIONS

These are the working hypotheses that guide our training program:

1. While there is a considerable body of data and observations about families, there is no single systematic and comprehensive theory of family process and of the relationship of family process to the development and sustenance of individual behavior.

The complex, relevant units of behavior in family interaction have yet to be adequately described or conceptualized. This also applies to family therapy.

2. The learning achieved by first-hand contact with family units, when the trainee has some defined responsibility *vis à vis* these family units, is far superior to that achieved by reading about, hearing, or seeing families for which the trainees have no responsibility. Furthermore, in view of our earlier point above, this first-hand contact is of paramount importance for adequate involvement in the complex phenomena involved in the study and treatment of families.

3. These first-hand contacts with families must be experienced within a framework of didactic and supervisory experiences. Contact without teaching is overwhelming, con-

244

fusing, and frightening to trainees. It usually leads to avoidance of further direct family work. Teaching about families without contact leads to preoccupation with, and slogans about, individual psychodynamics issues or abstract social issues, and is experienced as meaningless or trivial by the trainees.

The efficacy of training, in terms of both trainee learning and supervisor utilization, is markedly increased by mutual participation in family-therapy interviews. This requires tape-recorders, one-way screen rooms, and sitting in on either the supervisors' or the trainees' work.

4. This training is best done in small groups (five to fifteen) of relatively stable composition, which meet regularly over a fairly prolonged period of time (i.e. one year). Trainees should have approximately equal experience as therapists.

LEADERSHIP ISSUES

First and foremost, the seminar leader must know his field and be able to continue to learn as he teaches. The seminar leader must be a first-class therapist, and he must be able to lead a good meeting. The leader is in charge of the group process of the seminar. This entails setting the rules for time, place, etc.; initiating inquiry as to causes when the rules are broken; deciding when the discussion is relevant and when it is irrelevant; setting the example by his openness, candor, etc., for how the trainees are going to open themselves to the group; actively challenging and discouraging excessive formalism and the "student-teacher" games.

Coordinating these several functions is challenging work. Seminars do not run themselves, nor can they be programmed to happen by fiat. The leaders must continually monitor and integrate the current knowledge of the trainees, the family interview data they are dealing with, the aims of the course, and the group process phenomena that they are all enmeshed in.

We usually use two teachers, because this has several

245

advantages. While one teacher interviews a family behind the one-way screen, the other makes comments to the viewers. Trainees find this one of the best ways of learning to see the situations on which we build our labels and abstractions. Teachers usually err on the side of assuming the trainee understands what the teacher is seeing. Furthermore, a seminar can continue if one teacher is absent. There is less irrational attachment to and/or hatred of the leader than we find in one-teacher seminars. The trainees may respond to one teacher's style of work or teaching better than another's. A teacher feels freer to "get lost" in one aspect of a family, knowing that his colleague can bail him out if he gets irrelevant. A model for "helpful criticism" and "there is no one right way" is provided by the dialogue between teachers. It is an excellent way of training new teachers.

Some disadvantages of the two-teacher model are that relationship problems between the teachers can paralyze effective leadership; dissonant emphasis can confuse the trainees; and there is greater cost in staff time. Trainees can be intimidated, paralyzed, or allowed to remain apathetic and nonparticipant. This can occur with one or two teachers. The particular danger with two teachers is that they can protect each other from becoming aware of the impasse and carry on a dialogue that excludes trainees.

GROUP PROCESS ISSUES

The thrust of our teaching is experiential. We encourage — and most of us conduct seminars with conscious awareness of group process. We consider use of the group process in seminars as a powerful, immediately available teaching material. In all levels of the training program we try to maintain an atmosphere where there can be increasing openness on the part of the trainee to the emotional experience of understanding families. We expect the trainee to immerse himself in the puzzling human situation, and to conceptualize after feeling it. If we expect and encourage openness, then we are obligated to deal with the inevitable

246

tensions that impede openness: hostility, competitiveness, lack of friendliness, mistrust, lack of respect. In early sessions our aims are to promote group formation, set the rules for the seminar, and to explore trainee resistance to working with families.

We have tried many formats for the first few sessions and have found that starting immediately with a family interview or role-playing a mock family is best. These techniques are uniquely suited to accelerating group formation, presenting family as the system level of observation, and bringing resistances to working with families to the fore. Lectures and general discussions, for example, do not further these ends. The role-playing is especially exciting, as well as a superb arena for establishing the kind of relationship with and between members of the training group that we seek with the program as a whole. We ask for volunteers from the group, assign them age, sex, and relationship positions within a make-believe family, label one a problem, and then take it from there as though it were a real first diagnostic interview by a family therapist. We assign members of the spectator group to observe specified issues or to identify with family members. A common experience is that the players assert they were "too self-conscious and just putting it on," and yet they are unable to stop being the members of the "family" after the interview stops and the discussion starts. The watchers are equally gripped by the experience.

The built-in structure of using cases from the trainees' caseloads provides an important opportunity and challenge to the teacher. This type of training stimulates in both the trainees and teachers many phenomena that the teachers must deal with if the aims of the program are to be achieved via our format. Fear of exposure of one's actual work with patients is almost universal. This fear manifests itself through reluctance to bring families to be seen, or to tape-record sessions, accompanied by elaborate rationalizations of how difficult for and/or destructive to a particular family the experience would be.

Once the family is behind the screen or being taped,

the therapist and the family routinely conspire to having a stalemate, close-to-the-chest, nothing-happens type of session. Some of the sources of these fears are the therapists' exhibitionism, and inhibitions against it; excessive therapist self-criticism projected onto the group of peers and/or teachers; and high competitive tensions in the group leading to destructive mutual criticism. The teacher must be aware of these and several other potential sources of stalemate-producing behavior. It is possible by a combination of example, confrontation, and mutual airing to work through many of these problems. The initiative usually rests with the teacher. We generally encourage sharing of anxieties about these situations up to the point where the locus of the problem is experienced as being with the therapist himself. We do not go into why a particular therapist experiences his own particular anxieties except in the most general way. This is our boundary between teaching and therapy. (Incidentally, our impression is that once the trainee has interviewed behind the screen, he becomes more involved and behaves more as the expert.)

We try to maintain a constant alertness to signs of problems in the group. For example, if the trainees stop bringing material to seminar, if discussion is sterile or lags, if quiet prevails, then we initiate direct discussion about the causes, always aiming to achieve cohesive, cooperative, uninhibited groups.

In one group there was dissatisfaction because of the disparity in the amount of clinical experience of trainees. In another group there were competitive feelings among the different disciplines involved. Making these conflicts explicit allowed the group to deal with them, and to go on with the work in a more cohesive way. For example, in one group after three or four of the more self-confident members had presented a family behind the one-way screen, there was a sudden cessation in availability of families. We suspected tension within the group and we asked one of the leaders of the seven trainees who had not presented to explore the situation while the others who had presented were asked to leave the room, go behind the screen, and observe the discussion. When the less confident people began to talk about how increasingly anxious they had become for fear they wouldn't measure up and do as well as the previous ones had done, there was palpable relief in the entire group at "having it out," and the group was able to move ahead and continue to present families.

INEVITABLE TRAINEE CONCERNS

There are some typical issues and questions in early phases of family therapy training that impede the work. First, an anxious "What can we do to help this family?" (This is initially phrased as a demand on the teachers.) "What can you do for this family?" Later, self-righteous attacks on the teachers or the method occur, usually prefaced by, "Isn't it criminal to . . ." (a) have parents arguing and fighting with each other in front of the children; (b) have parents alluding to or discussing sexual material or hatred toward children in front of the children; (c) have children discussing sexual material or hatred toward parents in front of the parents; (d) have family secrets, such as illegitimacy, affairs, etc., opened up; (e) hold up the father and/or the mother to ridicule in front of the children (that is, make the parent look bad and undermine the authority structure of the family).

We usually answer these questions directly and emphasize whatever data and experience we have. Then we go to explore the latent concerns of the group.

Over-identification with one or more of the participants in the families that they have seen, as well as feeling overwhelmed and confused by the family interviews, are difficulties trainees commonly encounter in later phases of training. These experiences are often accompanied by complaints of not enough "intellectual" structure in the course. Our approach to these problems is to emphasize the systematic nature of what we see, and to request that someone act the part of the family member with whom he does not side in order to make clear how the family system defines and controls all its members.

Often in later phases of the training there is a resurgence of shyness in presenting in front of the screen. Exploration usually leads to feelings that at the more advanced level performance should be perfect.

Another late-phase phenomenon is that trainees like to raise issues about their own personal difficulties as therapists. For example, one trainee presented a problem with a family and said, "I think I'm having this trouble because of the trouble I have dealing with my father." Another trainee brought a problem to the seminar that dealt with her personal difficulty in getting to the "giving position" with a family that she (correctly) saw was therapeutically indicated. We think this occurs because the trainees have had the kind of experience with us and each other that allows them to get more personal. They have also had enough experience as family therapists to catch on to their own personal difficulties in doing the work.

We have only recently begun to introduce the study of the trainees' own family into the seminars at all levels. We find that this enormously intensifies the groups' experiences with each other. It tends to foster interest in each other, friendliness, and empathy.

THE LEVEL I PROGRAM

Our Level I program is geared toward teaching conceptualization about family process. It begins to acquaint the trainee with a new way of using himself in a family interview. When the trainee completes this program he should know how to interview and evalute many types of family groups with a variety of difficulties, and to manage referrals and minor interventions. Family interviews are done for many purposes other than effective family therapy, and we do *not* expect a person who completes our Level I program to be able to conduct family therapy. He should know *about* the family as a unit of study, transaction, and therapy. He should know what is a well, as well as a malfunctioning, family. He should know a good deal *about* the relationships between family process and the individual development. He should know what the indications for further family therapy or evaluation are. In addition, the Level I program encourages trainees to seek more family training.

In the early part of the training, the leaders both in supervision and in seminars need to do a good bit of "modeling" behavior. Frequent opportunities are provided for the trainees to observe the leaders interviewing. We do not expect a lot of the trainees in regard to performance with families. Some of us regard the main objective in this first phase of training as "putting on a good show." The main activity is interesting the trainee and enticing him into involvement in the work.

The trainees are required to see one family in treatment. We do not consider this optimum, so we would prefer to require that they see several families. Some of the trainees do indeed see more than one family, but many are unable to do so because of conflicting commitment to their service obligations. Their contact with families is usually brief, either because they tend not to hold families in treatment, or because they see families for purposes other than treatment (for example, for diagnostic purposes).

Our emphasis in starting people out in this field, in orienting them to family process, has always been "experience first, conceptualization later." It always seemed intuitively right to us that to understand the family as a system and oneself as an agent of change in that system it was more to the point to arrange involving experiences rather than to fill heads with new knowledge.

Early in our experience in teaching we thought it important to start by teaching the different languages of the conceptual frameworks that describe and categorize family phenomena. Even then we had the trainees observe families in treatment and apply the labels in the context of the experience — and encouraged personal involvement by

251

asking trainees to role-play, to identify with various family members and report on the experience. We came more and more to believe that teaching jargon had little to do with teaching about the family system to someone in the role of changing that system. We have come to rely increasingly on the use of common language; we push for trainees to drop or set aside prejudices; and we try to open the trainees emotionally to the experience of families.

Level I seminars are taught by one experienced instructor, usually in combination with a fairly new or beginning instructor. The trainees are paired for one hour's supervision with a different instructor, and we usually assign our newer and less-experienced teachers to this group. The format is somewhat different for first-year residents, who are taught together in small groups for six months while on a state hospital ward. The seminar teaching and supervision are combined. First-year residents are not expected to treat families, but only to see them for evaluation in connection with their treatment of individual patients.

These are the major variables and basic premises that go into designing a teaching experience for each new group. Following are two detailed descriptions of the experience of two different seminar groups in training during this past year in Level I.

Group A

The two male psychiatrists: Leader I was a senior, full-time member of the Family Studies Section. Leader II trained with us, and volunteered part-time service as supervisor in exchange for further training. Leader II was reluctant to "take hold," seemed uneasy in this more public teaching role, and in effect Leader I led the seminar by himself. The two leaders were on rather uneasy terms with each other, and had no explicit discussion between them about it.

Group B

Leader I was a male psychiatrist, full-time director of the Family Studies Section. Leader II was a female psychologist, who had had considerable training with us, and wanted to learn seminar teaching. Leader I had a high degree of interest in teaching her. Leader I also had some other special interests in this group. Two of the members were his research assistants, and he was personally interested in two other research people in the group. He also wanted to try out some new teaching techniques (working with the trainees' personal family histories and pressing for highly intense group process). He interested Leader II in this and they worked well together, although there were some moments of open anger from Leader II about being "pushed around" by Leader I.

Group A's Level of Experience

This group was composed of four youthful social workers, a young art therapist, and five middle-aged rehabilitation workers. All but one of the rehabilitation workers were female. Only one of the younger group was married. All of the middle-aged group had been married once or twice, and had children. This was the core group. In addition, a psychologist from the outside community attended irregularly, and a social worker dropped out early in the year. There was a very definite split in this group between the social worker and the rehabilitation workers. The rehabilitation workers were more settled in their personal lives, and more relaxed in the presence of families. The social workers were interested in men, trying to attract the attention of the male leaders, much more verbal about "dynamics," and, although uncertain in their therapeutic stance, they were more educated as therapists.

Group B's Level of Experience

This group consisted of three men, two of whom were

253

research assistants and Ph.D. candidates in psychology (the third was a third-year resident), and six women. Two of the women were research assistants to Leader I, and one of them was a Ph.D. candidate in educational psychology. The third woman was a rehabilitation worker, the fourth a chief nurse, and the last two were social workers. Three more social workers dropped out early in the seminar, and two more nurses about halfway into it. The nine survivors in this group all had had personal therapy. They were distinctly less experienced as clinicians than is usual in most seminar groups, but on the whole they had more life experience. None had done any family therapy. They were having no other training in doing therapy. There was a very high degree of voluntarism in the group. They were notably inattentive to their own professional labels.

GROUP A'S WORK CONTEXTS

The social workers with jobs in the out-patient clinics were in the most secure position with their caseloads. Social workers from the ward at the state hospital, as well as the rehabilitation people, were regarded as "helping out" on their jobs, and did not have a clear license to treat people. Because of this, a good bit of time was spent in the seminar discussing external constraints on the therapy, i.e. ward directors, other therapists of family members, etc.

GROUP B'S WORK CONTEXTS

All were in work situations that allowed them to seek families in a relatively neutral way, although they usually had to see the families outside of the work context.

GROUP A'S SHARED DEFINITIONS OF THE WORK

All wanted to learn to do family therapy. The social workers started with the conviction that they had to learn to elicit "real" feelings that were hidden, and the main

254

tool was empathy. The rehabilitation workers were also concerned with eliciting "real" feelings, and in addition wanted to be concretely helpful. The leader dealt with this by trying to field the approaches they came with and using gentle persuasion to get them to set aside their prejudices.

GROUP B'S SHARED DEFINITIONS OF THE WORK

All wanted to learn to do family therapy. Leader I had strong convictions about what experiences would take them there. He confronted, immediately and dramatically, all issues of whether they would follow his rules. In the first few minutes of the first meeting, he asked half the group to go in front of the one-way screen. His instructions were to "get to know each other and find out what each expects to get out of the seminar." The other half of the group stayed behind for the first ten minutes, and commented about posture and kinesics. He asked the observing group to make guesses about how the performing group was aligning itself in regard to leadership and sub-groups. The sound was then turned on, and after the group talked for a while, they exchanged with the other group. So immediately everyone had: 1. been behind the one-way screen; 2. had to take some active responsibility; and 3. was introduced to non-verbal material. Three people dropped out early in the seminar and it is not known if they refused this kind of experience, or other reasons caused them to leave.

GROUP A'S MATERIALS

Observation of families in treatment: 1. with the leaders; 2. with other experienced people on video-tape; 3. with the trainees. Active discussion was encouraged. Leader I lectured from time to time. Role-playing was used only occasionally to make a specific point. Group process issues were dealt with to some extent, but the split in the group was bypassed. Leader I felt he would have taken it up if he had been on better terms with Leader II or if there

255

had been more men in the group. He was concerned that the issue would become, "What do you think of us as women?" He was more inclined to deal with issues all had in common: fear of exposure, of being new at work. He managed the split in the group indirectly by asking over-talkative people to be quiet and quiet ones to talk more. In retrospect he wished he had paid more explicit attention to the differences between the leaders and the rehabilitation or social workers.

GROUP B's MATERIALS

Observation of the families in treatment: 1. with the leaders; 2. other experienced family therapists on film and video-tape; 3. with the trainees. Personal family history of leaders and trainees were presented and everyone was asked to do some project with his own family. Role-playing, sculpturing, and discussion about the group's own process was here emphasized throughout the year.

GROUP A's SEMINAR WORK

First Leader I interviewed a family for six sessions behind the screen. After that trainees began to bring in families they were treating for behind-screen interviews. In the first few months, however, there was heavy use of audio and videotapes (from our library) as well.

The emphasis in the seminar was on the beginning encounter between the family and the therapist. There focus was on:

1. evidence about what the family was willing to do;
2. willingness to do what the therapist asked;
3. willingness to answer questions;
4. their subtle forms of evasion;
5. how the therapists were "put down;"
6. the alignments and splits in the family toward the therapist, and the consequences of these splits.

Toward mid-year, as trainees were interviewing their own families, there was a shift to the process in the family. Observations were made on postural behavior — repetition of patterns of behavior in a session. The task became to abstract what the important repetitive patterns were, and what strategy might shift this pattern. The leader saw his job as teaching them that events in an interview and the patterning of those events had a validity in themselves, and that the business of the family therapist was to change those events. He wanted them to get some experience in picking a strategy to try to change a pattern and see what happened in making that change. His main message was:

1. find some way of being in charge of the process;
2. sit back and see what's going on;
3. think of the easiest way to change it;
4. see the effects of your attempts.

The leader relied primarily on the use of common language for discussion, and steered away from the use of jargon.

GROUP B's SEMINAR WORK

In the early months of the seminar the leaders presented live interviews of families they were treating as well as taped and filmed interviews. They expected active participation in discussion, expected all trainees to be prepared to re-enact sessions they saw, and to participate in sculpturing. The leaders also quite early presented work with their own personal families. About mid-year they applied more and more pressure for trainees to bring in their own material. The trainees did begin presenting families they were treating, but around this time two nurses dropped out, apparently feeling they could not treat a family. It was toward the end of the year that trainees presented their projects with their personal families, and the most intense and intimate process in the group occurred during this period. The leaders were interested in the trainees' learning about the family from

257

the role of someone having to change the family in some way. They were not interested in the group's learning facts, but in learning how to learn. They wanted them to learn something about conducting an investigation into a family and precipitating change in a social system from the vantage points of observing experienced therapists; taking some kind of therapeutic responsibility for a family; and going to their own family system. The leaders emphasized the use of common language in conceptualizing, although they also played with the jargon of several thought systems.

GROUP A'S SUPERVISION

This group was supervised by different supervisors. Three of them were quite new at supervising and were fairly cautious. The fourth supervisor was a very experienced man, but his general philosophy about training differed from most of the rest of us in that he believed in a long apprenticeship of observing before doing (the prevailing attitude is that learning is accelerated by doing). Altogether the supervisors were very concerned about how much trouble the trainees were having in working with families. They were urging them not to "do" anything, and pressing them into a position of observing. Meanwhile, the seminar leader was geared toward finding ways to activate them into doing. The rehabilitation workers were more inclined to ask for direction, and more distressed by this difference than the social workers, who were accustomed to being given differing instructions by supervising people.

GROUP B'S SUPERVISION

The leadership of the seminar was largely indifferent to the supervision arrangements made by the trainees, who were left to scratch on their own and whatever they wanted to do about supervision was licensed by the leadership.

Supervision was highly uneven, some of the more enterprising trainees picking up high-level supervision and the

258

others less satisfactory supervision. It was not possible to get a grasp of the supervision experience as a whole.

GROUP A'S PEER GROUPS

The rehabilitation workers and the social workers were free and easy in their own group, and on friendly terms within it. By the end of the year the group as a whole worked well with each other. Leaders I and II felt that this became a good working group. Probably all of the trainees knew a good deal about how to explore and conceptualize a family situation. About a third of the group could go further and begin some effective work with families. Seven of the group chose to go on to Level II.

GROUP B'S PEER GROUPS

There were several small sub-groups of two's and three's who had very close friendships with each other. Some of this developed in the seminar. Some of the trainees had very close tie-ins with Leader I and members of the Family Studies Section. Both leaders felt that there was an unusual degree of intense interest in this group. Negative features were that the group was too critical. Too many "interpretations" were made in too accusatory a context. Leader I felt that all but one person knew a good deal about how to explore and conceptualize a family situation. He felt that a third of the group could begin to take control of a therapy situation and move it. Four people elected to go on to Level II. Several others who wanted to do so were leaving the geographic area.

LEVEL II

The Level II program aims to involve trainees in the actual process of treating families. Trainees at this level are required to have had previous experience as psychotherapists and some familiarity with family process. Usually the

259

trainees have been through our Level I program or its equivalent. When the trainee completes the Level II program he should know how to conduct conjoint family therapy and marital therapy. He should know how to interview and evaluate all kinds of family situations. He should know a good deal about the functional inter-relationships between individual developments and family life — especially about the relationship between family processes and the precipitation and maintenance of behavior that is sometimes called disturbing or disturbed in the members of the family. We usually find that people who complete this program seek out further supervision or equivalent additional training.

In contrast to Level I, Level II demands a different and more threatening commitment from the trainee — the families he treats are his families. And we expect him to stick with each family long enough to pursue real changes, and to involve himself fully enough to try to effect this change. From the very beginning he is expected to bring his families to be interviewed before the one-way screen. This requires a deeper commitment from the trainers as well as a much closer working relationship with each trainee. Our motto in Level II is "give support."

Before we arrived at this concept we found that bringing their families to the seminar for an observed interview was a major crisis for the trainees, often with a negative outcome — even for the trainees who had already been well initiated into exposing their work before the one-way screen. The trainees were defensive — arguing that the seminar group didn't have all the information about the case or didn't appreciate the long-term course of treatment. This was accompanied by feeling attacked, outraged, discouraged. At worst the trainee was ready to leave the field; at best, he was reluctant to present his work again. We began to believe that the beginners' efforts needed to be encouraged by a close working relationship to his teachers. We therefore redesigned the Level II program so that each trainee would have one of the two co-leaders of his seminar for personal supervision.

The supervisor-seminar leader is in a position to attend much more closely to the trials of the trainee as he attempts to make contact with a family, start treatment, and then expose his work to his peers. He is in a position to share the impact of the group's reaction to the treatment and to follow through in supervision sessions on the inevitable confusion, questions, and anxiety that occur in the trainee as a result of the presenting of his work. The trainee is no longer alone.

A bonus is that the supervision can provide the trainee with a model for learning because, of course, the supervisor learns something new each time. Inevitably, there is a difference between viewing a case in live presentation before a group and hearing about it in supervision. In one of the seminars this phenomenon was made explicit by planning that the teacher who was not the supervisor on the case would lead the discussion for that particular presentation. In other words, the explicit expectation is that the supervisor and the trainee learn something new about their mutual work on the case. We believe that offering this kind of support enormously reduces the strain on the budding therapist.

The content of what we teach about family therapy varies considerably with the theoretical orientation of the leaders of the seminar. In family therapy the contract is between the therapist and the family, in contrast to individual therapy where the contract is between the therapist and the individual. The therapist's action must always be reactive to something in the family. They are there for their problems, not his. This necessitates profound knowledge and self-control on the part of the therapist. The therapist is in charge of the structure of the meeting and group process of the therapist/family group (Zuk's "Go-Between-Process"). When the therapist knows what seems important to pursue or change, he follows through and refuses to be inducted into the family (i.e. intimidated, silenced, squelched, etc.). The family is responsible for initiating moves toward change.

Here is a detailed presentation of one of the Level II seminars that took place during 1969-1970.

LEADERS

Leader I was a male psychiatrist, and a full-time member of the Family Studies Section. Leader II was a female social worker, and a senior part-time member of the family studies section. The two leaders chose to teach with each other because they liked each other, enjoyed teaching together, and had a special interest in trying the Level II program in its format of having the seminar leaders also supervise the trainees. They were extraordinarily compatible, and were fond of the group as toward a "favorite child." The trainees often described the seminar as a "happy home." Midway in the year, the trainees complained that although some differences in viewpoint between the leaders were apparent, these differences were often lost to the group because the leaders were "so nice" to each other. The leaders were both reserved personally and while they provided a safe, comfortable, affective atmosphere, they also did not deeply tap the enormous potential for interchange in this group.

LEVEL OF EXPERIENCE OF TRAINEES

The group consisted of seven men and three women, all in their late twenties, most married, and some with children. Five of the men were second- and third-year residents, and two were staff psychologists about two years out of training. Two of the women were staff psychologists a year or two out of training, and the third woman was a social worker. Almost all were, or had been, in individual therapy. All had arrived at some idea of what they wanted to do as individual therapists. All but one were quite adequate for their level of experience and some were exceptionally talented. (One of the male psychologists, who had primarily a research background, was significantly less

262

sophisticated as a clinician.) At least three of the pairs had close friendships or work relationships. There was a clearly shared social style among the group. There was a rather high degree of mutual respect and straightforwardness. The group seemed quite content to belong to each other and to the leaders. Work was produced very promptly by the seminar. Three of the most talented trainees volunteered immediately to present family sessions behind the screen. They were "model students," and the others clearly identified with them and wanted to do as good a job as they had done. The rest of the group, at first fearful that they wouldn't do as well, maintained an unusually high level of producing work for the seminar. All members picked up families for treatment early in the year and most kept their families throughout the year.

WORK CONTEXTS

Only the two people on state hospital wards had difficulty in getting or keeping families in treatment. They took considerable initiative but clung too long to the idea of getting the families on their own wards. The rest of the people were in settings that provided no difficulty.

SHARED DEFINITIONS OF THE WORK

Everyone wanted to learn how to do family therapy. There was an immediate positive interest in learning through studying their own case material. One of the people who emerged early as a leader in the group announced in the first sessions, "It's nice to be in a seminar where I approve of the official program."

MATERIALS USED

Observation and study of the families in treatment with the trainees was the main material used. With unusual regularity the families appeared for interviews as scheduled.

263

About half the sessions were on video-tape and half were live sessions. Almost all of the interviewing was done by the trainees themselves, and there was a minimum of "watching the expert." In the second half of the year — at the request of the trainees — it became the regular procedure for one of the leaders to come into a session, after a problem had become clear, to demonstrate how he or she would handle it.

Early in the year one of the trainees began presenting a continuous case every third week. The presenter was well-chosen in that he was clearly someone who sensed the competitive level of the group and knew he could survive it. This became the case the seminar was treating, and it provided a high focus of interest for the group.

In the latter third of the year the leaders introduced the idea of presenting personal family histories. There was time for only three presentations, but the group was intensely interested and if time had permitted, this material would have become the popular choice.

The leaders chose not to use the group's own process very much.

WORK IN THE SEMINAR

The main work was the constant assessment of the therapies presented behind the screen and on video-tape. They were regarded as projects in process that had or had not reached a certain point of development. There was a clear focus on how the therapist engaged with the family and how he became accepted into the family. The leaders assumed that everyone was heading toward some end-point in therapy, and that it was a developmental process. The trainees were taught to think in terms of what the next step would be. The end-point *per se*, or termination, was never defined or discussed explicitly. Some of the assumptions the leaders made were: 1. the therapist had to be moving the therapy in a clear direction; 2. the family members should be defining the direction in which they were going; 3. there should be some progressive, self-definition, and differentiation of family members; 4. family members should be progressively able to say what they want from each other (there should be some emotional as well as functional development in this).

Work in Supervision

The work in supervision was more continuous in seminars than when the supervisor and seminar leaders were two different people. In supervision, there was more discussion comparing family therapy with what the trainees had formulated for themselves about individual therapy. The trainees were supervised in dyads and three of the pairs who were friends or co-therapists were particularly successful, in that there was much give-and-take and learning from each other.

Work in Peer Groups

As indicated elsewhere, the potential for a close peer group was higher than we realized in this group. Twice during the year there was a move to have a party inviting spouses. This was unusual; it probably occurred because the group was so easily imaginable as a social network.

For comparative purposes we want to make brief mention of the other two Level II seminars that were held last year. Each had a distinctly different character because of one variable. In one of them the mix of the two leaders gave a special cast to the seminar. They were two strong leaders, male psychiatrists, who had quite different theoretical orientations and had never taught together before. There was a lively, active, debating quality to the seminar. There was a heavy emphasis on theoretical discussions, and the families observed were used largely as examples from which to outline a body of theory.

In the other of these two seminars the level of experience of the trainees largely determined the character of the seminar. There were highly varying levels of competence, but most of the members were on jobs in state hospital wards. They were psychologists and social workers, a number of whom seemed to have chosen the state hospital as a place to hide and get their thesis done. They were largely anti-psychotherapy. They did not seek the seminar expecting to do any work. They used the bureaucracy continuously as an excuse not to pick up families or to keep them in treatment. The tide was also against them in that family therapy is largely an outpatient enterprise, and their primary and only responsibility was for inpatients. The two leaders particularly enjoyed working together, and tried to make up for the lethargy of the group. They sat in on interviews almost every time, largely did the interviewing, showed films, and paid very careful attention to the group process. However, the group tended to little work, and little learning.

LEVEL III

The overall aim of this program is to train a person to manage a family therapy practice. The program is a continuation of Level II, and the aims are essentially the same. At Level II some people have tried family therapy and decided that this kind of therapy is not suited to them, or that our training program was not suited to them. In the Level III program we usually find that the trainees have enough experience with us as trainees to be quite serious and committed to the work. We rarely find any trainees who are still exploring the field or likely to drop out. While our theme in Level II is "offer support," our theme in Level III is "work hard."

We have conducted this program for two years now and have emphasized two areas: 1. promote group formation to facilitate the trainees' learning from each other; 2. encourage the trainees' independence for their own continuing education.

To promote group formation, we have used encounter techniques to increase intimacy in the group. We aim for greater openness and frankness, and encourage more discussion of trainees' personal problems as family therapists. Last year, we had two structured sessions to provide a frame for "opening up" the group. In the very first week of the seminar we asked the trainees to pair up. Each pair spent ten minutes before the one-way screen discussing how they felt about the seminar, the co-trainees, and the leaders. We followed this with group discussion of the entire experience. For the next six weeks there were a number of trainee presentations of therapy sessions.

In the eighth session we had the second structured meeting. We asked the original pairs to group into teams of four, and each team was asked to discuss, "How am I doing?" before the screen. The instructions were not more specific than this, and we found that people tended to discuss how they personally were doing as family therapists and how they felt others on the team were doing. These two structured sessions provided an impetus and a context for the group to talk more personally to each other. Both groups in the two years we've run this program enjoyed this emphasis, and in both groups quite close peer relationships developed. There was an atmosphere of support and taking care of each other. For example, in the eighth session during a team discussion one of the group confessed he had not been able to find a family to treat and was afraid he was out of his depth with the group since he was still afraid of treating families. The others encouraged him. One of the group immediately found a family for him to treat, and throughout the rest of the year, the group supported and encouraged this man. What might have been a very demoralizing situation for a trainee developed into a good learning experience.

Our location in a big city and a very large impersonal institution requires this special attention to promoting closeness and friendship in the peer group. (In smaller, more intimate locales, the peer relations may already exist and the problem may be to risk changing established relationships.)

The second area of emphasis in the program has been to encourage independence as a learner. This is usually the end of formal training for most, and we want the trainees to learn how to learn on their own. The third-year residents have been pupils for twenty-four years, and they usually comprise fifty percent of the group.

We ask the trainees to take turns on alternate weeks leading the post-discussion after viewing a family therapy session. Having to take this role presses the trainees for their best in terms of their ability to understand and formulate the clinical material. We found early on that the trainees were reluctant to take the task seriously. That is, they went through the motions of leading the group, but really waited for the leader to take over before serious discussion began. A tactic we devised to meet this problem was to have the leaders observe the discussion from behind the screen and come into the room only toward the end. The leaders rarely had a great deal to add, and the group felt very encouraged by how much they were able to do on their own. (Level II people are much less able to carry on a discussion without the help of the leaders.)

Last year we experimented with having the group take over the leadership of the seminar entirely at mid-year. We are inclined to believe this was not so successful, and would not do it again, although there were some positive features. The negative side of it was that the trainees almost entirely discontinued presenting their own case material. Instead they arranged presentations by other people, usually the leaders or other instructors on the staff. We believe this happened because the presentation of one's own work to peers is always difficult. Given the choice, people shy away from presenting. However, there was probably an important function they did innovate. We find that Level III people "try on" a lot. They seem to go through a phase of trying to imitate certain people, and usually reluctantly come to the conclusion that each person has to forge his own personal style. Their viewing of "the experts" at this stage probably helped this process. However, our general feeling is that this is too passive for this level.

More than any other group, Level III trainees typically say they learn most from the families they treat. The number of families the trainees are required to treat is less than ideal throughout our training programs. People in the Level III program are usually in a better position to find the time to treat more families, and we are now requiring that they treat a minimum of three families. While this prevented some people from joining the program for next year, we are convinced that the most important activity to enhance learning at this stage is to treat many families.

LEVEL IV

Our Level IV program is a continuous education for those of us who like to teach and supervise family therapy. We pick people we like and think we would enjoy working with and incorporate them into our teaching staff. We have a weekly supervisor conference, co-lead seminars with each other, supervise family therapists, run a seminar on how to supervise family therapy, do co-therapy and consultation with each other, and often become friends.

Premature hardening of theoretical position, refusal to show one's work, and reluctance in sharing responsibility are the cardinal symptoms of the immature leader syndrome. The major task of our Level IV program is to keep us open and growing. We demand of ourselves hard work, showing our actual teaching and practice to each other, and a modest level of good manners and high spirits. People who do not fit the group's norms leave or are fired, usually after a year of agonizing.

We are often dubious about supervision of our own therapy. We say, "I am too busy and don't have the time;" "I'm too advanced and do not really need it;" "There is no one available who knows more than I do." We are also reluctant to present the supervision work that we do. This is also characteristically excused from a one-up position: "The relationship between me and my supervisee is too private;" "It will suffer from that kind of intrusion;" "I don't have time and it's not that important;" "I know as much as any of you who can teach me about it."

A different variety of hesitation and foot-dragging is encountered when first assigning supervision or seminar leadership. This is usually excused from a subtler one-down or attack-on-content position: supervisory sessions do not occur and it is blamed on the supervisee; supervisees seem not to pick up families and therefore no supervision occurs; supervisions start and stop after a short period. In regard to beginning seminar teaching: pleas of not enough time or preparation are common; attacks on the content preparation of the seminar and the readiness to present such a seminar are given; sometimes attendance is poor and the seminar peters out.

These are difficult phenomena to deal with and understand in our training system. We won't discuss the inevitable individual and idiosyncratic psychodynamic factors that bedevil the best-laid plans of mice and men. However, some factors are common to each individual joining the staff group, and some factors are a common product of the group process of being a member of the staff group.

Becoming a staff person and a teacher is the final step in the transition from learner/student status to teacher status. While the transition from residency to practice or job carries a good deal of this, there is no experience that brings one more sharply up against the graduation that has occurred than confronting a group of people who have recently been one's peers and who now treat one with all the respect, derision, and open-mouthed eagerness that the teacher is given by the student. New staff (and old staff, too) frequently experience fear of responsibility, a feeling of not having the goods to deliver, of not knowing enough about family work, and of not knowing how to supervise or to run a seminar. We find ourselves irritated at "recalcitrant," or "resistant," or "stupid," or "irresponsible" trainees. We now level at ourselves the criticisms that we had leveled at our teachers when we were the students, when we made ourselves inadequate and over-idealized the teacher.

The joining of a small group of peers, one's true colleagues, is a significant event. We see each other as more able to judge one another's work than anyone else. Our standing

270

with one another has a significant influence on what happens with the rest of our lives, our salaries, our academic careers, our referrals, and our precious and tender feelings of self-worth or self-worthlessness.

All of the exercises that we find ourselves reluctant to participate in involve showing each other exactly what we do and do not have, and putting ourselves in positions where our competitive hostilities to one another can flare. These factors are fundamental to the situation. They cannot be ignored. It is to manage them that our efforts toward group cohesiveness and staff growth are especially directed.

Supervision of family therapy and our seminar for training supervisors are discussed by Dr. Harry Mendelsohn on page 431. Co-therapy and consultation are discussed by Whitaker and Napier on page 480, and by Ferber and Whitaker beginning on page 477.

IN SUMMARY

We have presented a description of a training program in family therapy that evolved over a ten-year period and grew to encompass the needs of a psychiatric department in a large medical school with several different institutional contexts and with large numbers of people of diverse professional backgrounds.

In the course of the years, three levels of trainees emerged as distinct groups: first, mental health professionals who had had virtually no systematic study of the family and needed a basic orientation; second, a group of trainees who had some kind of orientation to family work and were interested in becoming expert in the use of family treatment method; and third, a group of family therapists who wished to teach and do research in family studies.

In this relatively new field the teaching position is poised rather delicately. What we believe is now known must be clearly conveyed, and yet we must not embalm either the curricula or the learner's mind. We hope that we teach a method of learning, not a body of knowledge.

271

eight

how to go beyond the use of language

A. Bodin and A. Ferber

After a period of discord and agony within the household, a family member will seek advice from friends, a priest, or a physician. If this consultation fails to resolve the situation satisfactorily, and if the consulted person or the family member knows about family therapy, there is a chance that some member of the family will call a family therapist. Elaborate telephone negotiations usually ensue, and in some fraction of cases two or more members of the family will appear at the office of the family therapist. They will greet each other, sit down, and have an extended conversation about the family's difficulties and prospects. If this first meeting goes well a series of similar conversations will follow. These face-to-face conversations are the usual format for the experience of family therapy. The usual media of communication are spoken language and the kinesics that one can perform when seated and spaced between four and twelve feet from the other members of the conversation. The family therapist experiences the people who are having trouble with one another, because they have some of their trouble in his office. The therapist also hears them tell stories about things that have happened outside of that office. On the other hand, the individual psychotherapist has a more restricted presentation of experience to work with. His experience is a conversation with one person, and the stories that person tells about life outside the consulting room.

Family therapy has evolved from the traditions of individual therapy and has struggled to try new ways of presenting experience. Any variation in the form of the experience or the media of communication is immediately met with criticism from people who have never varied the form of therapy. The standard criticism is that doing anything different will destroy the hallowed traditions and the effectiveness of the therapy.

We have found this to be quite simply not true! When we tried new formats and new media for presenting experience, or representing life outside the office, we found that our work as family therapists and teachers of family therapy became more interesting, and, we think, more effective. So we are offering here an anecdotal collection of our experiences with many formats and many media in order to encourage therapists and teachers to go beyond conversation in their work.

The leader of the therapy or teaching meeting has the prerogative to choose what format people will communicate within, and which media they will communicate with. It is the responsibility of the therapist-teacher to keep the meeting lively, interesting, and relevant to the task at hand. The limitations of this situation are often the limitations of the

273

leadership. We have found too often that teachers follow the motto, "I could if I would, but I won't so I can't." It has been our experience that patients and students will try almost anything an enthusiastic and competent therapist-teacher requests.

GENERAL PRINCIPLES

LIVELINESS

Variations in format and media assist the therapist-teacher in keeping his meeting lively, interesting, novel, and pleasurable. This is a paramount consideration in teaching and therapy. A session need not be dull in order to be useful. People spend so much of their lives talking that they often pay no attention to messages or experiences that are solely talk. Skillful use of media impresses people enough to remember the experience, including the message that the therapist-teacher wishes to impart.

Avoid too long an exposure to any one medium during a single session, for boredom may be the result. Boredom also ensues from repeating the use of the therapist's favorite medium session after session. By the same token, although a variety of media may be useful in some instances, their application must be determined by patient-focused considerations rather than by any preconceived notions about some general utility or sequencing of media. Such patient-focused considerations may include the use of a medium already well-known to a patient, so as to draw out strength in a familiar activity, as well as the use of an unfamiliar medium as a means of fostering change through new experience and expressive activity.

TAILOR-MAKE THE EXPERIENCE

The therapist-teacher has the responsibility of structuring the experience to suit the situation at that moment. Since people vary enormously in their tastes, the palatability and

274

even the impact of the various experiences will differ according to the individual.

A couple are entangling each other in a tortured net of contradictory accusations. They have done so for several consecutive weeks. The therapist requests that they continue in pantomime. Both members clamp their bodies shut and refuse to move an inch in any direction, while poking fingers at each other. After five minutes all dissolve in ironic laughter. The husband asks the wife if she wants anything.

The therapist-teacher might best regard his therapies and teaching meetings as works of art. The formats and media are his materials. The more varied his experience, the better he will be able to choose the proper medium to make a moment come alive.

RE-STRUCTURING POWER RELATIONSHIPS

We recommend a shift away from the expert-layman format that characterizes high-hierarchy arrangements such as traditional doctor-patient or teacher-student meetings. The use of novel formats and media favors this shift, and changes the relative responsibility of the leaders and the followers. It allows a more nearly peer collaborative relationship between the therapist-teachers and the learner-patients. Therapist and patient alike should examine their behavior, or filmed records of it, and both make active abstractions and percepts about the records they are watching.

IMPORTING FEATURES OF THE OUTSIDE CONTEXT INTO THE MEETING

Information can be brought to the meeting in the form of recollections in the minds of the participants, as well as in the form of still or motion pictures, letters, or other old records of their behavior. People may be dispatched to various locations in their lives with cameras or recorders and asked to record the actual behavior in the home for review during meetings. With the advent of low-cost portable video-tape equipment in the next decade, it will become possible to have families video-tape their own home lives routinely and bring segments to sessions for therapists to review.

Regardless of the particular medium employed, the general principle is the same: barriers of time and space may be breeched. Thus, the home and vacation situations may be made more vivid to the therapist and, similarly, childhood, friends, relatives, and settings may be shared for their informational value and, in some instances, for the sake of rapport.

EXPORTING FEATURES OF THE MEETING TO AN OUTSIDE CONTEXT

Video-taped records of meetings are reviewed by one or several participants. Therapists often playback short segments during the session itself, and people then talk with each other about the feedback they have just received. Patients and therapists can listen to audio-tape recordings between sessions. Key sessions of perhaps a year prior can be reviewed to highlight progress or stasis.

Records of therapy or teaching meetings may also be used (with proper consent and release forms) for the education of persons other than participants in the meeting. This involves building libraries of sessions on various media or pictures, diagrams, etc., of families for training purposes. The use of media for consultation and supervision also falls into this category. The richness of the clinical and training situation may be better grasped if exported via suitable media to such outside contexts as conventions, research studies, and continuing education workshops.

DO NOT TAKE SIDES UNWITTINGLY

In marital therapy, for example, it is important to avoid the use of a medium which may delight one spouse but repulse the other. Circumventing such *faux pas* by

276

anticipating the differential reactions of spouses of differing backgrounds is worthwhile, since it is easier for the therapist to maintain a rapport with both spouses if he limits his departures from neutrality to short periods and spontaneously acknowledges the fact whenever he does take sides. Such acknowledgment requires that the therapist not take sides unknowingly, and it is particularly easy to stumble unwittingly from the path of neutrality when arranging experiences less familiar than conversations. Even in his use of language the therapist will be scanned by both partners for signs of natural affinity for one "side" or the other. For example, we sometimes encounter a couple with entrenched and differing ideologies about therapy due to long exposure to quite different types of therapy on the part of each spouse. Thus, if the wife has had years of psychoanalysis, while the husband has been frequenting the verbal and nonverbal encounter group scene, the therapist is likely to discover before long that any suggestion he makes in the direction of openness — particularly if he uses such words as "sharing" — will be greeted with alarm by the wife and triumph by the husband. Similarly, if one parent is crowding a teenager's sense of autonomy by continually probing for intimate self-disclosure, the therapist might well exert a favorable influence by commenting on the right to privacy about personal matters, but only if the prying parent is the one who has experienced psychoanalysis with all its privacy; the other parent is more likely to be persuaded by the observation that the teenager's reticence is a form of "doing his own thing," such as "finding out where his head is at" or trying to "get himself together." Talk about "monitoring for feedback" may put off an artist but not an electrical engineer, while the reverse is true if the therapist speaks about "watching your audience for signs of emotional response."

DON'T LET THE TAIL WAG THE DOG

With the plethora of procedures available other than just plain talking, it is tempting for some therapists to become enamored of particular methods in the media. People and their problems may be overshadowed by such enthusiasms. If too much emphasis is placed on a particular medium or on extra-linguistic media in general, then no matter how well the media have been chosen to fit the people, the people may not choose to accommodate the therapist by following the method.

The feedback is initially experienced as a bit of a shock by nearly every therapist and patient. Thus, with a particularly self-conscious patient or therapist it may be desirable to delay such feedback until greater confidence has been obtained. Another such factor is the attention the therapist may have to give to the apparatus if he is operating it without assistance; the resultant diversion of attention from his patients may interfere seriously with rapport, particularly at the opening of treatment. A third and related factor is the feeling of gimmickery that elaborate equipment imparts to the therapeutic atmosphere; and excessively equipment-laden milieu may over-impress the patients and leave them with a feeling of awe or fear, rather than with a feeling of warm personal interest.

MYRIAD MEDIA AND FANCIFUL FORMATS

LANGUAGE AND CONVERSATION

Language is the most familiar medium, and face-to-face conversation the most familiar format during psychotherapy sessions. Any of the uses that can be made of language in training and therapy can be tried with any other medium. People have turned to other media when conversation failed or became boring.

THE TELEPHONE

The telephone has a number of special uses in family therapy. Since the initial contact may be made by telephone, and since there is often a question about who should attend the first session, the conversation may include some discussion of this matter. Since one or more of the family members may be very reluctant to involve themselves in the therapy and since there is not, as yet, any strong rapport set up, the therapist may wish to express his preference regarding who comes, but it is wiser not to be rigid in insisting on the whole family's presence in this first interview if the concept meets with strong opposition. There will be time enough later to involve others if this proves desirable.

If, as is so often the case, a married woman appears alone for the first session and the therapist wishes to involve the husband, he may ask her simply whether the husband will be willing to come to the next session. If she says he will, her opinion should be taken at face value. If, on the other hand, she expresses doubt about his willingness to come in, the therapist should avoid sending her home with the message to try to get him to come in. The doubt expressed by the wife may very well be a reflection of her own reluctance to have him present. Consequently, she is likely to covertly sabotage the effort to get him in, for example, by issuing a crass demand rather than an earnest invitation. Family therapists of quite disparate ideological persuasions have encountered this phenomenon. One way to circumvent this difficulty, particularly if she offers explanations such as, "He doesn't believe in going outside the family for help, and, besides, he had his bellyful of shrinks in the army" is for the therapist to state that he would like to telephone the husband at work right then and there, during a therapy session. Although the wife will probably demur, saying it won't do any good, the therapist may express an interest in getting the feel of how the husband deals with him. Even if this telephone contact proves futile for its stated purpose, it serves to let the husband know that the therapist has wanted to count him in as an important member of the family. In fact, men reluctant to enter marital or family therapy are often reacting to a feeling that they have been excluded by the wife from significant participa-

279

tion in making important family decisions. The therapist, therefore, after introducing himself, might proceed something like this: "Your wife has consulted me about what *she* describes as marital problems, and she is sitting right here in the office with me now, hearing my end of the conversation. I can't help getting the feeling from what she has told me that there's more to this than meets the eye. Naturally, she has presented the picture from her point of view quite clearly, but I get the feeling that there's another point of view which only you could do justice to. I don't know whether it's that she doesn't know your side of things or simply isn't eager to present it as powerfully as her own point of view, but I have a suspicion that there are aspects of this situation that I would understand much better if you could talk with me directly yourself. Now, I must tell you that I'm making this phone call not at your wife's suggestion, but on my own initiative. In fact, she protested against the idea and warned me that it wouldn't do any good, since you have had your bellyful of shrinks in the army."

The question of whether the therapist, by this maneuver, had widened the schism between husband and wife is more apparent than real, since his comments have given overt recognition to what may have been only a covert prelude to open war, and the maneuver would not work unless the marital situation was quite tense, with both partners already in an adversary position and poised for battle. Such an approach usually results in the husband coming in for the next session and expressing gratitude for having been invited.

WRITING

Writing is conversation without kinesics or paralanguage. Since writing is slower than speaking, in the time between the initial thought and the written word there is a sporting chance for such rare elements as restraint and tact to emerge.

One of the authors was asked by a couple just before

280

their vacation time what they might do to avoid their usual pattern of spoiling the vacation. They would fight halfway through the vacation, then decide to come home, since each spouse said the other showed no sign of willingness to avoid spoiling the rest of the vacation. Very gravely the therapist instructed them to make sure to begin their fight during their first day out on the drive to Mexico. He imposed only one special condition, namely that from the opening bell to the end of the fight the parents desist completely from talking to each other and substitute writing messages. In the session after their vacation, the parents reported with pleasure that they had begun their fight on schedule and had continued it entirely in writing for three days, to the growing amusement of their children. Their mood changed to embarrassed laughter, and they abandoned the fight, resuming conversation with gusto for the remainder of the trip, which they thoroughly enjoyed. The pen is more cumbersome than the word, and writer's cramp is disarming.

Written records and reports are so familiar that they require little comment. Most family therapists make no written notes during sessions, write few notes after sessions, and avoid written records as a means of transmitting information to each other (at least compared to individual therapists). This may be because the experience of family therapy is so much less like the form of literary narrative than is the experience of individual therapy.

People have been asked to write autobiographies for their own benefit, to bring to the therapist, or to show each other. They may write summaries of their experience in family meetings for supervisors, other trainees, publications, etc. Autobiographies, letters, diaries, dreams, etc., as documents about a family and its history are useful to evoke distant contexts and relationships within the moment of the therapy.

Writing requires reflection and abstraction in a way that no other medium does. Therapists who wish to convey a cool, thoughtful, abstract posture may write notes during

281

sessions. Instructing patients to keep notes during sessions accomplishes the same end.

An additional application of writing in family therapy is as follows: having the family members record the details of any homework assignments given for implementation between sessions, so as to circumvent the excuse that they couldn't remember the assignment. Since they can still get around this by claiming that they have lost the assignment slip, it may be a good idea to point out casually that they can, of course, avoid getting their money's worth by simply misplacing the assignment slip.

Some tense situations in family therapy can be eased by informal written contracts, such as the details of children's work schedules in relation to their linked earning of money (a written assignment best carried out by the children as a committee of the younger generation making a recommendation to the parents), and details of visitation agreements going beyond what the court, in its wisdom, has elected to keep simple in the hope that flexibility will foster sufficient good will to avoid snags. Thus, in one instance, it proved useful to have the divorced parents sign an agreement that the husband would appear promptly for his visits to the children if the wife would desist from having her new boyfriend conspicuously present at precisely that time.

The assignment to make written lists of certain categories of events that occur between sessions is useful in stimulating greater attentiveness to other people in the family, as well as greater hope that others will notice the efforts each one is making to please. The very manner in which such an assignment is made, particularly at the beginning of therapy, is important. For example, if a couple provides a pyrotechnic display of unrelenting mutual criticism, the therapist might give a homework assignment as follows: "I'm going to ask you both to do something rather peculiar between this session and the next one, and although it will probably seem quite kooky to you, I think you'll discover something important about yourselves in carrying out this outlandish assignment. Furthermore, it won't be very

282

difficult for you since you are already so accomplished at the fundamental skill that is required. You are already in the habit of noticing all the big and little things the other one does that irk you, and you are already fairly good at making mental notes of these irritations, so that you can talk them out at some future date, such as you have been doing tonight. Nevertheless, I suspect you are missing some points, so I'll ask you simply to add one ingredient to your pattern: Don't trust your memory to keep score; do it in *writing*. Carefully keep a detailed list of all the affronts and grievances you can gather in the coming week. You're in the habit of stirring up such lists mentally, at least until the dam breaks, so it won't take much extra effort on your part to keep your list secret except for leaving it where your spouse can see it if desired, such as on your dresser at night. Since it may make you feel too guilty to keep such a one-sided list, I'll ask you also to keep in mind the possibility that your spouse might do something during the coming week which could please you. Just on the off-chance that this should happen by some quirk, make a note of any such unexpected events on a separate list, and this list you're to keep entirely secret. That's not asking very much of you, since you're both already so good at preventing your spouse from getting complacent about how much he or she is contributing to the marriage. Agreed?" Any protest offered by husband or wife at this point, though secretly welcomed by the therapist as a sign of self-recognition, should be parried with a poker-faced reiteration of the therapist's seriousness in wanting the assignment carried out as an adventure in self-discovery. When giving homework assignments that entail writing — or any other type for that matter — it is important to make a note of the assignment where it will remind the therapist to inquire about it sometime during the following session. The absence of such follow-up, of course, discourages the carrying out of future assignments.

A final note on the use of writing in family therapy concerns the process of its utilization by the therapist as a means of calling attention to particular highlights of either process or content which occur during the session. If the therapist is taking any notes of the session, and if he elects to note a particular piece of information provided by one of the patients, or observe their interaction process from his own point of view, he can make use of his note-taking activity as an aid to the therapeutic process rather than an interruption of it by speaking aloud as he writes each word, so as to give emphasis to what he is taking the trouble to write. This feature has the advantage of getting significant features of the session noted while not implying that the therapist is a sort of distant expert standing with both feet outside the family and coolly observing them. Also, by immediately demystifying the family regarding the therapist's note-taking, he is setting an example of letting others in on matters that concern them. By the same token, the request to have patients describe in writing what it was like to be in family therapy with the authors of this book amounted to a reversal of this demystification process, and a salutary one, not only because turnabout is fair play, but also because it re-emphasizes the therapist's belief in feedback and his willingness to continue learning while providing the family with an additional opportunity to consolidate their experience and take a bit of public credit for whatever gains were achieved.

BIBLIOTHERAPY

The influence that books can have is evidenced not only in the fact that patients spontaneously bring up various ideas they read about recently, but also in the fact that some patients are self-referred as a result of reading such books as *Mirages of Marriage* (Lederer and Jackson, 1968). Since the reactions of patients to particular books cannot be entirely predicted, and since the suggestion to read a particular book is not tantamount to asking the patients to consult an article, it is a good policy to accompany the assignment with a warning to take everything with a grain of salt and an invitation to read critically, so as to discriminate between

284

those portions which do not fit the individual and those which do. There are three books which, in addition to *Mirages of Marriage*, are often mentioned by patients as having been helpful to them before the start of therapy: *Psychocybernetics* (Maltz, 1960); *I'm OK, You're OK* (Harris, 1969), and *Your Inner Child of the Past* (Missildine, 1963). Three books likely to be particularly helpful in the course of family or marital therapy are: *Conjoint Family Therapy* (Satir, 1967), *Mirages of Marriage,* and *The Intimate Enemy* (Bach and Wyden, 1968). All three contain suggestions for communication exercises which may be undertaken between sessions and without the therapist. All three emphasize the importance of communication in marriage and family life, and all three have the virtue of siding with reality against any residual Hollywood expectations remaining after the honeymoon. *Conjoint Family Therapy* is particularly strong in dealing with the role of unmet expectations in the development of dissatisfaction, the relationship between communication and self-esteem, and the handling of differences so as to make room for oneself *and* the other person. *Mirages of Marriage* is good at exploding marital myths and at elucidating some of the "rules" which operate out of an awareness, but not necessarily in the interests of, a smooth functioning of a family system. *The Intimate Enemy,* because it is a detailed exposition of constructive family fighting, is especially reassuring to couples who argue vehemently but were brought up to the accompaniment of such mottoes as, "Don't argue at the table; it spoils the digestion;" "If you have nothing pleasant to say, don't say it at all;" or "There's no such thing as a *good* fight." If any additional bolstering for this point of view is needed, an article in *Family Process* entitled "Love and Hate in Marriage," by Charney, may prove helpful. In relation to sexual problems, one woman in her forties reported having her first orgasm after many years of marriage the week after she read *The Power of Sexual Surrender* (Robinson, 1959). Some patients are pleased by the light tone of *Everything You've*

285

Always Wanted to Know About Sex, But Were Afraid to Ask (Reuben, 1969), which they find a welcome relief to the heavy-handed best-selling marriage manuals that so often emphasize simultaneous orgasm as a goal and *hard work* by the male as a means to that end. It takes an athlete to resonate to their challenge of herculean labors. Perhaps the most useful book for most patients is the simplified condensation of their work approved by Masters and Johnson: *Understanding Human Sexual Inadequacy* by Belliveau and Richter (1970). Without being as dry and heavy as the original, this paperback covers the essentials. Another book which is occasionally useful — particularly for younger women having orgasmic difficulties without being exceedingly strait-laced in their attitudes, is *The Sensuous Woman,* by "J" (1970). Because of the chapters on extra-marital and group sex, it may be particularly important in suggesting this book to invite the patient to sort the wheat from the chaff.

For parents considering divorce but hesitating because of their fears of its impact on their children, it may be useful to read a book which illuminates the possible damage to the children from continued exposure to a bitter marriage, such as *Children of Divorce,* by Despert (1953). For divorcing parents who seem tempted to drift back toward a clinging, post-marital relationship that is keeping the situation confused, a book emphasizing the advantages of a more complete break can be helpful in divorce counseling, particularly with people a bit on the tender side who need special preparation, is *The World of the Formerly Married* (Hunt, 1966). A book helpful to children is *The Boys and Girls Book About Divorce* (Gardner, 1969).

In the area of child-rearing, there are several good books which come to mind. Benjamin Spock's *Baby and Child Care* (1946) remains the middle-class bible. There are two self-administering programmed instruction manuals for parents and professionals: *Child Management,* by Smith and Smith (1966), and *Living with Children,* by Patterson (1900). The first emphasizes using rules to provide consist-

286

ency and creating a comfortable environment, while the second, using a social-learning framework, emphasizes the reciprocity of reinforcement in parent-child interaction and the systematic application of reinforcement to a variety of problematic childhood behavior patterns. These books may be particularly helpful for parents lacking solid information about social learning, but they are not likely to produce much lasting change unless followed up by careful analysis and discussion with the help of the therapist. Though it is true that fortune favors the prepared mind, there is no substitute for moving beyond sound attitudes into the detailed nitty gritty of specific behaviors. Direct observation, particularly in the home, will be of special help to the therapist in deriving the greatest gains from these books. Despite the fact that both these books are worded simply, their orientation is a bit technical, and it is therefore probably unwise to use them to exclusion of other books in working with families who treat their children as objects rather than as people. A leavening influence in such situations is the rather humorous *Between Parent and Child* (Ginot, 1965), and its sequel, *Between Parent and Teenager* (1969).

War and Peace and *Anna Karenina* by Leo Tolstoy, and *Joseph and His Brothers* by Thomas Mann, have taught one of the authors more about family life in the context of its times than any professional literature. Families caught in the soup of their own ethnic group can often profit from reading autobiographical or semi-autobiographical novels and discussing them amongst themselves. *The Autobiography of Malcolm X* and *Portnoy's Complaint* are useful examples. If adolescents are having trouble convincing their parents that the future is a frightening place to go toward, a joint reading and discussion of Kurt Vonnegut's *Slaughterhouse Five* may prove depressing and illuminating.

A literate therapist enjoys the privilege and advantage of knowing where his culture is going several years before the scientific one. Also, the literate therapist is like a physician with a well-practiced pharmacy, who can prescribe the right book for the right situation.

287

The importance of poetry to some patients is attested to by their desire to show the therapist what they have composed. Some patients can be helped toward greater freedom and expressiveness by composing some poetry. (If the patient is somewhat rigid, however, the therapist should suggest free verse instead.) Occasionally it can be useful to quote from a poem as a way of touching deeply an otherwise walled-off patient. One of the authors was treating a couple who were struggling with their differences. The wife was a tender-minded lover of poetry, while the husband was a tough-minded military officer. The wife criticized the husband's lack of appreciation of poetry as symbolic of his steel armor. The therapist, knowing of the husband's German background, quoted the following lines from Goethe:

> *Vom Vater hab' ich die Statur,*
> *Des Lebens ernstes Führen,*
> *Vom Mütterchen die Frohnatur*
> *Und Lust zu fabulieren.*
> — From *Zahme Xenien.*

Because the husband's childhood German was very rusty, he did not fully grasp the meaning at first. The therapist translated the poem as follows:

From my father I have my stature,
my earnest bearing in life,
From my dear little mother I have my joyful nature,
my love of inventing stories.

While listening to this translation, the husband's eyes filled with tears, and then he sat sobbing softly while his wife moved closer physically and emotionally, expressing how moved she was to see him cry for the first time in their marriage.

STORIES, PARABLES, AND DREAMS

The use of stories in family therapy permits points to

288

be made about process as well as content, and allows the therapist to set an example regarding presentation of views and values without causing others to lose face. The sharing of personal experiences can also serve as a model of self-disclosure within the family.

Stories may be told by members of the family or by the therapist. They may be apocryphal, from literature, from personal experience with other families, or from personal experience with one's own family of origin or adult family. The range of sources permits the therapist to modulate the immediacy of the point being made, for instead of confronting blatantly, the therapist can make his point indirectly, using for example his own experience as a fellow human being. When the point is especially painful, he can make it more palatable by telling a story at his own expense. Doing so sets an example of humanity and humility which takes the sting out of probing the patient's smarting wounds. It should be noted that telling exemplary stories about himself may have precisely the opposite effect, stirring resentment at his smugness. The chances are that the person who may be most benefited by a humble story will be most put off by a self-satisfied story, since the moral one-upmanship adherent in such stories has probably been overused by the victim's spouse to keep him or her relentlessly reminded of events from the past, which are not permitted to die.

By telling a story from his own childhood, the therapist encourages parents to follow suit — sometimes to the surprise and delight of their children. If the children offer no response, the therapist can invite some expression of their reaction, particularly if it seems likely that what will emerge will have a positive reinforcing effect on the parental show of humanity. Telling a well-disguised story of some other family that has made progress with similar problems is a technique useful in stimulating hope. Murray Bowen is one of the advocates of this tactic based on the parables of Jesus.

Carl Whitaker was an early advocate of using the therapist's own associations to stories from his own life and experiences as part of the flow of therapy. Similarly, discussing your own dreams, jokes, or songs is often a useful way of getting information in the room while abdicating the "expert" position.

HUMOR

Comic relief, as valuable as it may be, is insignificant compared to the lubricating functions of humor in therapy. The discharge of tensions by the breakthrough of recognition through the ambiguity of conflicting elements placed in apposition to each other is particularly valuable if it brings forth a smile of recognition. Jokes, like dreams, can be artful in representing without quite revealing, disguising without quite concealing. The resultant subtlety makes the listener reach for latent meaning.

Each therapist must rely on his own judgment regarding what, if any, applications he will make of humor, and whether jokes will be used at all. For this reason, only one example will be offered here. One of the authors was working with a family in which the wife consistently took a stance that could be summarized by the following saying: "If you *really* loved me, you'd know what I want without my having to tell you." She thought her subtle hints were clear communications. The therapist told her the following story. A man seated himself in a Jewish restaurant and ordered a bowl of borscht with sour cream. The waiter brought the bowl and was returning to the kitchen when the man called him back and said to him, "Taste dis zup!" The shocked waiter queried, "What's the matter? Not enough sour cream? I'll bring you a bigger bowl." The customer persisted, "Never mind that. Just taste dis zup!" The waiter, now really puzzled, said, "If it's too cold, I'll take the chill off it for you." The customer, increasingly irate, said, "Plez, just taste dis zup!" The waiter, now insulted and irate, said, "Look, if it's too warm, I can put an ice cube in it for you." The customer, now throughly exasperated, retorted, "Plez! Do me a favah! JUST TASTE DIS ZUP!"

290

After the two men's eyes had met in mutual study for endless seconds, the waiter backed down, saying, *"All right.* (Long pause.) Where's your *spoon?"* "Ah *ha!"* shot back the customer instantly in overdue but total triumph.

After the laughter that followed this story, the husband told me he felt understood, and the wife proceeded to recall a number of routines in her childhood family life. For example, her mother would remark, "The door is open!" She would become annoyed if this were not construed as, "Please close the door." Similarly, she would announce, "It's five o'clock!" and become irate if this were not taken as tantamount to saying, "Please set the table." Finally, the wife recalled her mother exploding with anger one day after hours of riding silently in a car en route to the family vacation spot. The words with which the mother exploded were, "My God! What are you trying to do, kill us all?" Her husband simply kept puffing on his cigar, until his wife made it clear that the smoke was suffocating her. (It is perhaps interesting to note that the couple for whose benefit this story was told is the same couple who had never completed a vacation successfully until they accepted the challenge to program a fight and conduct it entirely in writing.) In the summer following the use of this story, this family vacationed abroad and wrote the therapist a letter which began as follows:

"As we have traveled these months, your name has come up almost daily. You really helped us to see that a lot of our family difficulties lay in poor communication. We now have a family saying, 'message sent is not necessarily message received.' Sometimes this took a really humorous turn when we would order breakfast and get something quite different from what we expected! After about four weeks of riding in the car, when fatigue had really set in, we found that our facial expressions were carrying more weight than our words. Then because of conflicting messages (between words and face), the receiver really didn't know which to believe. It was then that we really worked at applying what you taught us. We've also learned that usually there are more solutions available than appeared at first-hand."

AUDIO-TAPE RECORDINGS

Audio recordings, by comparison with video recordings, already have a venerable history as adjunctive media in psychotherapy (Baily and Sander, 1970; David, 1970; Paul, N., 1966). Before this tradition was established, however, it was conventional for traditional therapists of the day to object to audio recordings of therapy sessions on the basis that rapport would be disrupted by the intrusion of a machine that could raise doubts about the complete privacy of one-to-one self-disclosure, thus inhibiting the patient. Since family therapy entails self-disclosure in the presence of one or more family members — making the situation a transaction among members of a natural and ongoing group with a past and, perhaps, an anticipated future — the definition of privacy has already been recast to accommodate more than one family member with the therapist. Since family therapists are comfortable working in this situation, it is no accident that they have been in the vanguard of video-tape recording as an integral part of family therapy itself, as well as of family therapy training. To hear someone doing family therapy a decade ago talk with a traditional therapist was to hear two utterly disparate views of how patients would respond to a request for permission to tape-record a session. The traditional therapist claimed his patients were exceedingly reluctant to agree to the request for permission to record their sessions, whereas budding family therapists usually encountered eagerness to experience the taping. Detailed discussions with both types of therapists at the time suggested that their difference in experience rested on the different responses they evoked through distinctions in their personal approach. For example, the more traditional therapist reported approaching a subject as follows: "Although it's unusual procedure, and I don't *ordinarily* ask to use it, I'd be interested in

292

making an audio-tape recording of this session with you. I realize you may have some reluctance to do this, particularly inasmuch as the therapy relationship is, of course, so private and confidential. Since I don't want to inhibit you from saying anything at all, I do want to offer you a full opportunity to explore your feelings on this matter before you make a decision." Family therapists, on the other hand, reported approaching the matter as follows: "I usually find it useful — and so do the families I work with — if we tape-record a few of the sessions. During the session we may want to play back something that's just happened so that we can discuss it immediately and get a more detailed picture of how it happened, or you may want to borrow the tape to review it at home, or we may find it useful later in the therapy to play back part of an early session in comparison with part of a later session to take stock of progress. Everything's set to go, if it's all right with each of you. O.K.?" (The therapist then nods to each participant in turn, repeating the question, until each has given his reaction.) The predilections of the therapist are powerful self-fulfilling prophesies, probably quite sufficient to elicit the expected reactions to the request to tape-record.

One of the authors tape-records all family sessions and gives them to the family to listen to as homework between sessions. The instruction is that each member must listen alone, though each may also listen collectively if they wish. The purpose is to promote freedom during the session and reflection afterward, to make it clear that therapy is something that occurs outside the office as well as in it, and to give more responsibility to the patients for their therapy. Early reactions to the tape are usually horror and disgust at how silly, inaudible, and generally unflattering one sounds. This usually gives way to considerable recollection and reflection during the listening, the stimulation of memories and reveries in amazement of one's own redundancy and stupidity. Failure to listen to the tape is an early sign of resistance to the process of the therapy and may be analyzed as such.

Audio-tape does not travel as well as video-tape. Groups of people unfamiliar with the particular family whose tape they are listening to will often grow bored while listening to long segments or entire sessions of audio-tapes. On the other hand, short segments of it are infinitely preferable to straight narrative description in presenting a situation to strangers.

RECORDINGS

Occasionally some use may be made of a commercial recording in the family therapy situation. One recording which has proved useful in a specific type of situation is the telephone conversation between a rocket expert and his mother called "Mother and Son," on side two of Mercury's disc, *An Evening with Mike Nichols and Elaine May*. This six-and-a-half-minute masterpiece traces the degeneration of dialogue into drivel as an unsurpassed Jewish mother reduces her son from a rocket expert to a regressed infant in a matter of minutes. The situation in which one of the authors found this record useful is the one in which a young adult is painfully aware of awakening from the parentally induced trance state. This concept has probably been best described by Laing (1969) as follows:

> My hunch is that what is usually called hypnosis is an experimental model of a naturally occurring phenomenon in many families. In the family situation, however, the hypnotists (the parents) are already hypnotized (by their parents) and are carrying out their instructions, by bringing their children up to bring their children up . . . in such a way that includes not realizing that one is carrying out instructions: since one instruction is not to think that one is thus instructed. This is a state easily induced under hypnosis. . . . There are usually great resistances against the process of mapping the past onto the future coming to light in any circumstances. If anyone in a family begins to realize he is a shadow of a puppet, he will be wise to exercise

294

the greatest precautions as to whom he imparts this information.

It is not "normal" to realize such things. There are a number of psychiatric names, and a variety of treatments, for such realizations. I consider that the majority of adults (including myself) are or have been, more or less, in a post-hypnotic trance, induced in early infancy; we remain in this state until "when we dead awaken," as one of Ibsen's characters says, "we shall find that we have never lived."

Any attempt to wake up before our time is heavily punished, especially by those who love us most. Because they, bless them, are asleep. They think anyone who wakes up, or, who is still asleep, realizes that what is taken to be real is a "dream," is going crazy.

One of the authors had in therapy a twenty-three-year-old woman who, despite being married and a mother, felt like a little girl. This was so much the case that she deeply resented having to fill the mother role in relation to her own child, while being continually startled and terrified by the depth of this resentment. After playing her a tape of the Nichols and May conversation between mother and son, the therapist proceeded to discuss this interaction and the young woman's reaction to it, introducing Laing's trance analogy. The young woman was instantly struck by the aptness of Laing's notion that a parent stands in relation to his child much as a hypnotist stands in relation to his subject, except that the hypnotist knows what he is doing and how he is doing it. The young woman pleaded desperately for some help in coming out of her trance, but she was told that she would need no such help, since her excited recognition of the beautiful "fit" of Laing's trance analogy was proof that she was no longer in a hypnotic state of unawareness. So entranced by Laing's metaphor was this young woman that she took it quite literally, as the therapist learned at the following session, when the young woman reported having gone home and telephoned her mother to announce that she was coming out of the trance state she had always been in without realizing it. As might be expected, the mother launched a pyrotechnic display of desperate attempts to reinduce her daughter's trance state. If ever a sequence of events deserved the caption, "Family Homeostasis in Action," this was it. As she grappled vainly with her daughter's disenchantment, the mother descended through five stages of techniques for reinducing the trance. These stages proceeded in descending order of finesse and subtlety, the more blatant ones betraying greater risk-taking as a function of desperation. The mother's reactions proceeded as follows: 1. "I don't know what you mean, dear;" 2. "I know you don't mean that;" 3. "You don't know how much you hurt me;" 4. "You've made me very angry with you;" and 5. "Well, if that's the way you're going to be, then maybe we'd better not see each other at *all* anymore!"

This whole incident is remarkable, not only because of the clarity with which the young woman reported the techniques with which her mother sought to reinduce the trance, but also because her account of them had not been influenced directly by Laing's prediction of parental panic, since neither the young woman nor the therapist had read *The Politics of the Family* — the therapist having been impressed by its message as reported to him in a one-paragraph verbal summary. A final noteworthy feature of this incident is the fact that the several elements which converged in the therapist's mind as he devised an intervention had also been converging on our culture at approximately the same time, and, as is so often the case, the *Zeitgeist* was heralded by jesters, whose art anticipated science. And how science still must strive to contribute anything additional to the brilliant illumination Mike Nichols and Elaine May shed on the problems of parents and their children-in-perpetuity.

MUSIC

In these days of electronically augmented music it is

296

not unusual for a family therapist to hear the generation-gap theme echoed in discussions of the different vibes the children trip to and the way the power output really sends the parents — usually up the wall. Any energy source powerful enough to split the nuclear family may also have potential for facilitating fusion. Simply hearing a lot of music that other people were brought up to love just doesn't do it for everyone.

One of the authors once made a visit to a home that proved to have a living room with cathedral high ceilings and all walls painted deep elephant grey, illuminated by one lamp of low wattage. After dark-adapting, the therapist discovered an organ in a far corner of the room. Now it happened that both spouses were singularly unexpressive, and sexually inhibited, so this presented some interesting possibilities. The therapist could not help thinking of his seventh grade sex lecture, in which a visiting representative of Planned Parenthood had euphemistically told the boys about condoms, saying "You can put a cover over your organ," to which the class clown queried from the back of the room, "Can you also put a cover over your piano?" Unable to suppress such mischievous thoughts, the therapist ascertained that it was the wife who played the organ. He asked whether she played from music, by ear, or from extemporaneous impulse. As the reader may have guessed, she played by the book. The therapist then inquired how she had learned how to use the organ when she first had it. He was patiently informed that she had always played by the book. He proceeded then to suggest a series of simple homework exercises, after checking in each instance to learn whether she had perhaps already tried the action he was about to suggest. For example, he asked whether she had tried each of the stops, in turn, and was told that she had simply left them in the original configuration they had occupied when the organ first came. The therapist expressed surprise that a woman so concerned about doing things right would not have systematically explored the effects of each stop in turn and in various combinations. He suggested that to savor the experience, she make up for lost time by trying the various stops separately and together but with only a single note, so as to focus all her timbre, without diverting her efforts to produce any melody or harmony. She was asked to proceed with introducing these additional elements, in turn, but, in each instance, only after thoroughly enjoying the experience of letting her fingers massage the organ while savoring its tone in the simpler mode. A faint smile as the therapist spoke suggested that they were listening between the lines, hearing not so much the therapist's words as the music of their overtones. A number of sessions later, after the suggested assignments had been completed, the couple was seeing the therapist in his office shortly before Christmas. Continuing to explore expressiveness and abandon through the medium of music, all three sang Christmas carols. After singing the *Gloria in Excelsis Deo* section of "Angels We have Heard on High," a couple of times, the therapist asked the couple to sit up straight and breathe more deeply. Then he urged them on to stand, staying seated himself and coaching with such remarks as, "Open your mouths wide as if you wanted to give birth to robin's eggs!" As they became increasingly involved, abandoned, and enthused, he ceased even conducting and sat back and enjoyed their highly spirited singing with a bit of awe, tinged only by regret that Christmas comes but once a year and he had not thought of this except in the permissive context of an annual celebration.

BODY SCULPTURE

Body sculpture, like music, is a fairly intimate and expressive medium. What body sculpture consists of, as the name implies, is the positioning of the family members and the molding of their features — such as their facial expressions — by one of the family members. Each member of the family may be sculpted individually or the whole family may be sculpted into a group tableau, in which case the sculptor completes this phase of his work by "sculpting" himself into the tableau in some pose of his own choosing. It is usually a good idea to let each family member have a turn at being the sculptor.

The therapist sets the stage by instructing the sculptor to create his impression of the family, capturing some important characteristics of how the members appear as individuals and how they relate to one another. The therapist should then take a tour around the tableau and among its figures, commenting on what he sees and how he interprets and what he feels about what he sees. He may converse with the figures as he goes, and he may invite the sculptor to accompany him in this whole process.

Before turning the task over to a new sculptor, the therapist may ask the sculptor of the existing tableau to change it in any way he wishes. The inspection and interpretation tour is then repeated. This remodeled tableau often sheds additional light on what is bothering the sculptor about the family and on what changes he would like to see.

This technique has a number of interesting virtues. One is that it entails touching, a fact of great importance in families which have minimized this modality of communication. Another is that its non-verbal nature allows for the representation of some important family features which may otherwise elude expression — either because of reluctance to speak of them or difficulty in putting them into words. Finally, each family member has an opportunity to make a dramatic statement about how he sees and how he would like to see the family members individually in relation to one another; the rotation of the role of "sculptor" permits even the children to experience themselves as having the right to make powerful statements about the family. In some families the moments in which a child molds a parent are experienced first with anxiety and then with exhilaration, as the child discovers he is not utterly helpless and the parent discovers he does not have to do everything, since the child has perceptions and preferences of his own. Moreover, the way the child positions the parent is often so gentle that the parent is doubly moved to experience what his body is communicating.

The impact of body sculpture on families is sometimes very dramatic. For example, one child positioned everyone in the family close together at one end of the room and his mother way down at the other end of the room, with her right arm and index finger fully extended in a frozen scold. The implications for goal-setting often derive drama from their directness. For instance, one little girl sculpted a tableau in which the parents were staring blankly at the girl and her brother, who were between the parents, holding hands with each other but not with the parents. When asked to show what changes she would like to make, the little girl had the parents stand behind the children with the father's arm around the mother's shoulder and the mother's arm around the father's shoulder and each parent taking a child's free hand in his own free hand. In a sense body sculpture is like dancing, in that it involves the whole body. The time-lapse choreography bridges two frames: how things are, and how they could become. The combination of participation and observation often evokes strong emotions. Polaroid snapshots of the family sculpture provide a useful additional feedback loop. As the family dances and discusses the choreographer's dream, they may find themselves moved at two levels, with the metaphorical one often having the most meaning.

ROLE-PLAYING, THEATER GAMES, PSYCHODRAMA, AND SOCIODRAMA

We can be barely anecdotal in covering the vast repertoire of dramatic techniques at the therapist's disposal.

Most of the everyday life of pre-school children is a series of encounters that are more drama than conversation. It is only with age, inhibition, and abstraction, that our lives become that most precious form of drama — conversation — in their major communicative moments. We have yet to meet the family who could not enact a situation that they

300

were having difficulty describing. The chief stumbling blocks to the use of dramatic technique are the inhibition and lack of inventiveness on the part of the therapist/teacher/director, and the embarrassment of the participants before they start. Everyone knows that it is much harder to lie with drama than with words.

The two most consistently useful dramatic techniques one of the authors has used are non-verbal enactments to simplify complex and obscure situations, and playing each other's roles to accelerate the rate of change when a family pattern shows some signs of loosening up. At a recent national meeting of family therapists and their spouses, the instruction was given that each person hold a five-minute dialogue with his spouse about how their family life had been affected by their professional life. There were to be no words spoken. Twenty-four dramas took place simultaneously in the meeting room. People chased or dragged reluctant or fleeing spouses from one corner to another, couples stood fast glaring at each other, others tentatively reached out and were rebuffed, etc. During the ensuing conversation, at least three couples said they had learned things about their marriage in that five minutes that they had not known for twenty years.

The Corsini book on role-playing (1966) is a classic, brief, non-partisan description of the techniques of both role-playing and psychodrama and includes an annotated bibliography.

DRAWINGS

Drawings are the oldest medium and the one most familiar to everyone. Everyone draws, even people who can neither speak nor write nor read. Drawings are cheap and quick to make, present virtually no technical problems, and require only paper and crayons, pencil, or paints. Drawings are most often made during sessions and fed back into the process of the session. They are treated both as representations of experience outside the session, and communications generated within the stream of the session.

301

Many therapists give children crayon and paper during family therapy sessions, and encourage them to draw while listening to grown-ups talking. Often the children will present their drawings to the grown-ups. These may then be used as commentary upon the process of the session or regarded as expressions of the children's sentiments.

Many therapists encourage people to draw their family, and then start a dialogue around the drawings. Drawings are also used to make diagnostic impressions, as well as useful supplementary information when presenting a family to another group of colleagues.

People draw willingly if the therapist provides drawing instruments and interest. Give a general instruction at the beginning of therapy or training to the effect that talking sometimes is inadequate to communicate what one wishes, so that people should feel free to use drawings or any other media. This will elicit specific suggestions to use drawings or other media. Drawings are not so likely to be perceived as invasions of privacy, or as disturbing gadgetry, as are some of the other media.

A particularly interesting development is the use of drawing to aid in family assessment while engaging the family members in the tasks of family therapy on a non-intellectual plane. Kwiatkowska (1967a, 1967b) described a promising six-step procedure as follows: 1. individual free drawings ("Draw whatever comes to mind."); 2. individual drawings of the whole family; 3. abstract drawings of the whole family (like step 2 above, but without human figures); 4. individual free scribbles; 5. a joint scribble; and 6. another set of individual free drawings. The abstract family picture often taps deeper emotional meanings than the family picture that immediately precedes it, since the nonrepresentational "set" helps break free from sheer spontaneity, as well as attitudes about where others in the family stand in this respect. Freer members may comment about the hesitation of stiffer members to let their hair down. The joint scribble often elicits comments revealing awkwardness or uncertainty about how to coordinate a joint effort. Some

302

couples discuss whether to use one pen or two, whether to scribble independently or to make a single integrated scribble, whether to take turns or work simultaneously. The comments and how they are made provide material for assessment and therapy just as valuable as, if not more valuable than, the joint scribble itself. *Kinetic Family Drawings* (Burns and Kaufman, 1970) is another good book on the subject.

DIAGRAMS

Diagrams, unlike drawings, are symbolic or map-like rather than pictorial representations of the family. They may also assume a tabular or chart-like form, but in any case they constitute relatively abstract statements about the relations among persons in social systems and the interaction processes in which they participate. Because of the relatively structured nature of diagrams in comparison with drawings, they are more palatable to people who disclaim any artistic ability, but who are at home with visual structures such as blueprints or schematic diagrams. Thus, while some engineers are uncomfortable about drawing tasks, which they think they will perform clumsily while their spouses excel, they are not put off by diagramming tasks, and neither are their spouses, since the diagramming entails some drawing and is not of a type familiar to the engineer through specialized training.

In addition to comprising a fairly neutral task, diagrams allow enormous compression of time and space, so that generations and continents can be spanned in a single diagram.

Diagrams lend themselves to an enormous variety of uses, but because of their abstractness they run the danger of being confusing and misleading, rather than being clarifying and revealing. The essential factor is that there be some checking back to less abstract experiences among those who drew the diagrams. Otherwise the possibility exists that acknowledged speculations and unwitting assumptions will guide the formation of abstract categories about processes within the family, thus giving rise to considerable disagreement among those present. Allowed to drift, discussions of diagramming can degenerate into competition for possession of the chalk, and the right to attach labels to various parts of the diagram. Thus, diagrams of the family through time or the process of therapy, while apparently an attractive idea, have actually been little used in family therapy or the training of family therapists. Perhaps the arbitrariness of the variables or qualities abstracted has held back this development, since diagrams can become illusory visions or illuminating vistas, according to their application.

Some of the types of family diagram in current use are: 1. floor plans; 2. chronology scrolls; 3. genealogical charts; 4. notations depicting sibling order and age differences; 5. family tree diagrams; 6. the Marbles Test; and 7. Family Life Space Diagrams (Venn Diagrams).

The use of floor plans was suggested by Virginia Satir in her family therapy training courses. A comparison of floor plans drawn by each member of the family often reveals considerable discrepancy in the way they view the layout of their house, perhaps reflecting differences in the importance they attach to particular rooms. One of the authors has applied this technique with the additional feature of having each family member indicate — with upper-case initials — the room in which each member of the family spends most waking hours. Similarly, lower-case initials were used in these diagrams to show the room in which each family member spent the least time. In one instance the post-diagramming discussion revealed a misconception on the part of the older son, who thought his younger brother and sister were spending most of their waking time sitting in their parents' bedroom hearing stories, whereas they diagrammed themselves spending more time in their own respective rooms. Further discussion disclosed that the older son's misconception was a fantasy which would not have existed had he slept on the upstairs level with the others, rather than in the basement by himself. It can readily be seen that such floor plans may serve, in some limited sense, as vicarious home visits.

Family histories lend themselves to a variety of notational and graphic representational schemes. The three most commonly used schemes were identified in a letter to the authors by Eugene Watermann, through a survey of the literature and family therapy training centers. He pointed out that genealogies emphasize blood lines and allow for concise recording of limited data across several generations. A notational scheme, on the other hand, can depict the sex and birth order of siblings, and, if desired, their age differences. Finally, a family-tree diagram can be used to show sex, marriage, divorce, birth, birth order, and death. Complex marital situations with divorce, remarriage, and children by different marriages are also clearly shown, and chronological sequences can be noted by recording the dates of birth and death rather than mere ages. Such a scheme has the advantage of compressing onto a single page the data from various nuclear family units of a large extended family which would otherwise require several pages of writing. Toman (1969) gives detailed directions for the notational scheme.

The family tree diagrams developed by Murray Bowen resemble genetic charts, but to use them for recording family histories in either family therapy or family therapy training courses it is helpful to have a standard set of symbols and procedures. Such a standard scheme has been developed and proposed by Watermann (1970) as follows:

DIRECTIONS FOR A FAMILY HISTORY CHART

Symbols to be used are: circle for female, square for male. A person whose sex is not known is a triangle. Marriage is indicated by a vertical line from the circle and the square. The lower ends of the two vertical lines are connected by horizontal lines. Children are indicated by vertical lines extending below the horizontal lines. The oldest child is to the left and the youngest to the right.

Twins are indicated by a vertical line followed by a horizontal line from the lower end of the vertical line for a short distance followed by a vertical line from the ends of the horizontal line. This would then look like an upside-down Y or an inverted slingshot. A common-law marriage or a long-term affair may be indicated in the same way as a marriage except that the line is dotted rather than solid. This dotted line may also indicate a liaison resulting in a childbirth without the two being married. There are times when it is useful to indicate that one knows that a person is not married, in which case a horizontal line can be drawn underneath the circle or the square. If it is useful to indicate that the marriage has not produced children, then a horizontal line may be drawn underneath the horizontal line indicating the marriage. An interruption of a vertical line by a diagonal line indicates either separation or divorce. Dates are indicated as follows: a "d" followed by a date indicates the date of death. A "b" indicates the date of birth. An "m" indicates the marriage date. "Sep" gives the date of separation. One date followed by a dash and another date indicates the length of separation and the date reuniting. "Div" indicates the date of divorce. The following will serve as an illustration.

Jane married Bob. They have four children, including fraternal twin boys. The boys have an older sister and a younger sister. The younger sister died in infancy.

306

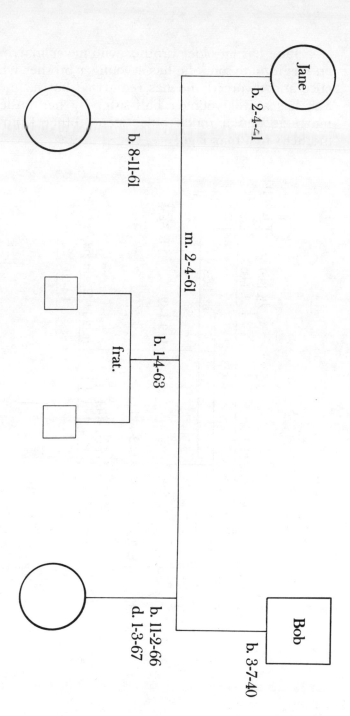

Figure 1

307

Jane has an older brother who never married, but has an illegitimate son. She has a younger brother who married once and divorced and has remarried but has no children. She has a still younger half-sister by her father's second marriage and a much older step-brother from her step-mother's first marriage.

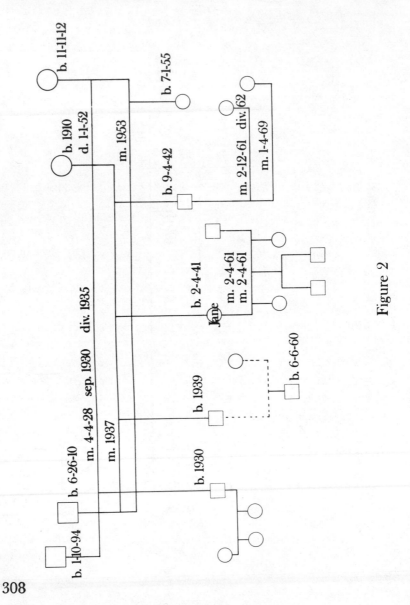

Figure 2

Although the directions for a family history chart presented above as written down by Watermann deviate slightly from the details of Bowen's procedure which Watermann was trying to follow, the Watermann version is presented here since it was the only one available in writing. Further examples of the use of this diagramming convention can be found in Guerin and Fogarty's chapter in this volume. Watermann (1970) mentions two main uses of family diagrams, as follows: "The family tree diagram facilitates the taking of a detailed multi-generational history of a family. There is a distinct difference between a history of a person and a history of a family system. . . . Diagrams (visual), analogies, and chalk-talks on the blackboard are ways of demonstrating the system concept of the ongoing cycles of behavior patterns, and homeostasis mechanisms are more easily seen if diagrams are used."

One of the cleverest and most intriguing developments in conjoint family representations amounts to jointly diagramming some salient features of the family's interaction processes. Called simply the "Marbles Test," it was originated in Argentina and reported by Usandivaras, Grimson, Hammond, Essaharoff, and Romanos (1967). It requires only a set of marbles and a board on which to set them. This test has been described by Bodin (1968a) as follows:

Though the test can be given by one person, it is easier to have two people conducting it: one to administer the test and one to record the details of its results. The test begins with the family members standing around a table on which there are opaque bags, each containing twenty marbles of one color. No two bags contain the same color, and there are just enough bags for each family member to choose one, which they do without knowing the identifying color of the set of marbles within it.

The board is square and has an arbitrary number of holes in which to place the marbles. The number of holes suggested for a family of three is two hundred and twenty-five (15 rows x 15 columns); for a couple, a hundred and forty-four (12 x 12); and for a family of four or five members, four hundred (20 x 20). The participants are asked only to put the marbles in the holes to make something, working together with the others. These vague instructions permit myriad possibilities for forming different patterns, either simultaneously or with some rotation of turns.

As is so often the case with psychological instruments, performances that represent departures from the instructions are those particularly likely to prove revealing. For example, a family seen by one of the authors had a mother and three teenaged children, but no father. The mother was extremely permissive most of the time — more through passivity than through patience. The middle child, a large boy, filled the power vacuum, playing clumsily at the father role with a rather heavy-handed personal interpretation of paternal style. The younger brother and older sister found this style obnoxious, but the mother, finding it useful, rarely objected. Occasionally, however, her tolerance would also be exhausted, and she would spring into uncharacteristic action with a jagged edge of harshness, not one smoothed by the firm and steady pressure she could have been applying whenever parental firmness was appropriate. Physical fights were common in this family and involved all possible combinations of its members. The favorite family recreation was watching wrestling or the roller derby, and all members of the family enjoyed actual participation in living-room wrestling matches. It is not surprising that when this family took the Marbles Test there was considerable shoving and elbowing as one or another of the family members would rearrange or even remove the pegs (pegs being used in this instance instead of marbles) which had been placed on the board by another family member. After the mother and younger son had withdrawn from the field, leaving the board to the daughter and middle son, the scene looked and sounded increasingly like the spectacle of some ancient arena. The situation had become a contest which was finally decided when the gladiators both grabbed their corners of the board between them and so shook up their little arena that all the men in it were catapulted from their holes.

310

Laughing sheepishly as this pandemonium of pegs settled into a random mess, the daughter remarked, "That's us! Our family exactly. We're a chaotic mess."

A new technique for representing family relationships in terms of set theory has been developed by Bodin (1968b). In essence, the Family Life Space Diagram technique consists of asking each member of the family to make a diagram in which each member of the family is shown not as a human figure but as a rectangle. These rectangles are then labeled (with names, initials, or family role symbols) so that they can be identified when the family compares and discusses diagrams. The technique is useful not only in getting family members to think about and clarify their own conceptualizations of the family relationships, but also in getting them to appreciate how others see the family situation, at least to the extent that they can represent it by such graphic configurations or discuss what they were not able to represent.

Still Pictures

Most people have many snapshots that record distant times and far away people. These images are wonderfully evocative during family therapy meetings. Pictures made during sessions, especially with new high-speed Polaroid equipment, offer splendid rapid feedback. People like pictures, will bring them easily or let them be taken relatively unself-consciously, and are interested in looking at them. The technical use of a Polaroid camera is easily learned by a therapist, and how to feed back the information to the group requires little practice.

Some family therapists ask families to bring in some or all of the family albums and pictures at the beginning of therapy, ostensibly so that the therapist may become more familiar with the family outside the office. The experience of looking through an album with a family often is a ritual admittance to its inner circle, a change from stranger to a friend. All kinds of conversations about character, etc., can

311

be easily stimulated when looking at pictures. Who is, and is not, with whom in these pictures is often very telling information. At later times when exploring a particular relationship and, hopefully, changing (e.g., between the mother and her father), it is useful to instruct people to go back and look at their pictures of kinfolk and muse upon them. These uses of pictures as evocative foci seem worth a try.

Pictures taken during meetings with Polaroid film are instant feedback of spacing, postures, facial displays, etc. This gets the therapist out of the "I-told-you-so" position and allows everybody to consider the information about themselves. Showing at least one picture of the office one works in and one of the family one is treating will supply an enormous amount of contextual information when presenting a family to trainees. Still, pictures have some of the liabilities of diagrams, in that they are arbitrary slices of time. People may argue about how representative of the entire relationship the behavior portrayed in the picture is.

MOTION PICTURES

Everyone loves the movies, but not many people know how to use them. Making movies is a difficult and expensive proposition. Showing them is technically simple, but demands everyone's focus of attention more than most other media. Movies, however, provide the highest fidelity sound and image available in any medium. Also, they may be shown more times than video-tape without wearing down. They are used more in training than in therapy.

A few persons have asked families to bring their home movies to therapy sessions and show them. They are used to familiarize the therapist with the family and to evoke certain memories, much in the way we described the use of still pictures in the prior section.

One of the authors has been intensively studying movies of his own family during the past several years. Most of the changes that he and his family have undergone from watching these movies and hearing their analyses have been

312

in the area of becoming aware of things that they did—but not necessarily changing their behavior very much as a result of this awareness. There have been some exceptions. The two grandfathers had a clear pattern of mutual avoidance so complete that they would frequently be seen standing back to back, or having only the most perfunctory of discourses with one another. When they both saw this at a showing of the movie at Christmas, they laughed loudly and said that they understood each other and their relationship very well. However, since then they have been exploring common ground, and spending more time talking with rather than standing apart from each other at family gatherings. One of the common grounds they discovered was that they shared the view that the youth today are lazy, not fond enough of work, too lawless, and not grateful enough to their country. The author sometimes, especially at Christmas and Thanksgiving, regrets having prodded this particular sleeping dog.

The major use of film has been to show people learning family therapy sessions of families being interviewed by other family therapists. To a lesser extent, films of families living their lives have been used to educate therapists about family life.

Naturalistic films of actual family life are perhaps the most directly provocative stimulus for discussion currently available.

A group of family therapists viewed a film of a family being treated. The post-film discussion was somewhat contentious, revolving around the treatment of the family and what one should or should not do in treatment. When films made in that same family's home were shown to the same group, the discussion became much more personal. People started comparing the memories of their own families with what they had seen on the screen. There was much less contentiousness and much more sharing of novel information. Most of us are still very ignorant of how others live, sharing only some rather extravagant myths about what a family life ought to be like at its best or worst. Naturalistic

313

films of family life in several subcultures and at different life stages will probably rectify some of this ignorance in the next few decades.

When viewing a film of a therapy session, persons who are not experienced therapists often become bored, restless, etc. Instructions from the leader/teacher ameliorate this: stop the film at various times and have brief discussions; give people assignments to discuss aspects of the film; ask individual viewers to identify with particular actors in the film, etc. Natural punctuation points in the therapy, such as shifts in body posture by the therapist, are good places to interrupt the showing of a movie for discussion. We have found film discussion to work best if all members of the viewing group are required to make at least some comments; if the comments are kept brief; and if discussion is focused by the teacher. The major error in the use of film, in our experience, has been for everybody to become too passive in the face of it.

Some excellent teaching films of family therapy are available, and a partial list appears at the end of this book. In both therapy and training, we expect an increased use of films made in families' homes and other natural contexts during the next decade.

‿‿ *References*

ALGER, I. and HOGAN, P. (1970), The use of video-tape recordings in conjoint marital therapy. In *Readings in General Psychology,* ed. W. Vinacke. 161-169. New York: Brunner/Mazel.

BAILEY, K. and SOWDER, W. (1970), Audiotape and video-tape self-confrontation in psychotherapy. *Psychol. Bull.* 74: 127-137.

BERGER, M. (1970), The use of video-tape in the integrated treatment of individuals, couples, families, and groups in private practice. In *Video-tape Techniques in Psychiatric Training and Treatment*, ed. M. Berger, 119-160. New York: Brunner/Mazel.

BODIN, A. (1966), Family interaction coalition, disagreement, and compromise in problem, normal, and synthetic family triads. Doctoral dissertation, State University of New York at Buffalo, Ann Arbor, Michigan: University Microfilms, No. 66-7960.

──── (1968a), Conjoint family assessment: an evolving field. In *Advances in Psychological Assessment*, ed. P. Mc Reynolds, 223-243. Palo Alto: Science and Behavior Books.

──── (1968b), How to square the family circle — and Venn: Family life space diagrams in therapy, assessment and research. Paper read at Western Psychological Association, San Diego.

──── (1969), Video-tape applications in training family therapists. *Journal of Nervous and Mental Disease,* 143, 251-261. Also in *Studies in Self Cognition: Techniques of Video-taping Self Observation in the Behavioral Sciences,* eds. R. H. Gaertsma and J. B. Mackie. Baltimore: Williams and Wilkins, 1969.

BURNS, C. and KAUFMAN, S. (1970), *Kinetic Family Drawings* (K-F-D). New York: Brunner/Mazel.

DAVID, A. (1970), Using audio-tape as an adjunct to family therapy: three case reports. *Psychotherapy: Theory, Research, and Practice,* 7: 28-32.

KWIATKOWSKA, H. (1967a), Family art therapy. *Family Process,* 6: 37-55.

──── (1967b), The use of families' art productions for psychiatric evaluation. *Bulletin of Art Therapy,* Jan.: 52-69.

LAING, R. (1969), *The Politics of the Family.* Toronto: CBC Publications.

NATHAN, P., STUART, S., and ROSSI, A. (1968), Experimental analysis of a brief psychotherapy relationship. *Amer. J. of Orthopsychiatry,* 38: 482-492.

PAUL, N. (1966), Effects of playback on family members of their own previously recorded conjoint therapy material. *Psychiat. Res. Reports,* 20: 175-187.

PERLMUTTER, M., LOEB, D., BUMPERT, G., O'HARA, F., and HIGBIE, I. (1967), Family diagnosis and therapy using

315

video-tape playback. *Amer. J. of Orthopsychiatry,* 37 : 900-905.

TOMAN, W. 1969, *Family Constellation,* 2nd ed. New York : Springer Publishing Co.

USANDIVARAS, R., GRIMSON, W., HAMMOND, H., ISSA-HAROFF, E., and ROMANOS, D. (1967), The marbles test. *Arch. Gen. Psychiat.,* 17 : 111-118.

〜〜〜〜〜〜〜〜〜〜〜〜〜〜〜〜〜〜〜〜〜〜〜〜〜〜〜〜〜 *Bibliotherapy*

1. HALEY, A., ed. (1965), *The Autobiography of Malcolm X.* New York : Grove Press.
2. BACH, G. and WYDEN, P. (1968), *The Intimate Enemy.* New York : William Morrow.
3. BELLIVEAU, F. and RICHTER, L. (1970), *Understanding Human Sexual Inadequacy.* Boston : Little, Brown.
4. CHARNEY, I. (1969), Marital love and hate. *Fam. Proc.,* 8 : 1.
4a. CHITTENDEN, G. (1944), *Living with Children.* New York : McMillan.
5. CORSINI, R. with CARDONE, S. (1966), *Roleplaying in Psychotherapy: A Manual.* Chicago : Aldine.
6. DESPERT, J. (1953), *Children of Divorce.* New York : Doubleday.
7. GARDNER, R. (1970), *The Boys and Girls Book About Divorce.* New York : Science House.
8. GINOT, H. (1965), *Between Parent and Child.* New York : Macmillan.
9. ——— (1969), *Between Parent and Teenager.* New York : Macmillan.
10. HARRIS, T. (1969), *I'm OK, You're OK.* New York : Harper and Row.
11. HUNT, M. (1966), *The World of the Formerly Married.* New York : McGraw-Hill.
12. "J." (1970), *The Sensuous Woman.* New York : Lyle Stuart.
13. LAING, R. (1967), *The Politics of the Family.* New York : Pantheon.

14. LEDERER, W. and JACKSON, D. (1968), *The Mirages of Marriage*. New York: Norton.
15. MALTZ, M. (1960), *Psychocybernetics*. New Jersey: Prentice-Hall.
16. MANN, T. (1948), *Joseph and His Brothers*. New York: Knopf.
17. MISSILDINE, W. (1963), *Your Inner Child of the Past*. New York: Simon & Schuster.
18. POTTER, S. (1962), *Three Upmanship*. New York: Holt, Rinehart & Winston.
19. REUBEN, D. (1969), *Everything You've Always Wanted to Know About Sex But Were Afraid to Ask*. New York: David McKay.
20. ROBINSON, M. (1959), *The Power of Sexual Surrender*. New York: Doubleday.
21. ROTH, P. (1969), *Portnoy's Complaint*. New York: Random House.
22. SATIR, V. (1967), *Conjoint Family Therapy,* rev. ed. Palo Alto: Science and Behavior Books.
23. SHAW, C. (1930), *The Jack Roller*. Philadelphia: Seifer Press.
24. SMITH, J. and SMITH, D. (1966), *Child Management*. Ann Arbor, Mich.: Ann Arbor Press.
25. SPOCK, B. (1946), *Common Sense Book of Baby and Child Care*. New York: Duell.
26. STEINZOR, B. (1969), *When Parents Divorce*. New York: Pantheon.
27. TOLSTOY, L. (1942), *War and Peace*. New York: Simon & Schuster.
28. ——— (1939), *Anna Karenina,* 2 vols. New York: Random House.
29. VONNEGUT, K. (1969), *Slaughterhouse Five*. New York: Delacorte.

nine

∿∿∿

the use of video-tapes

A. Bodin

The advent of video-tape has opened new avenues of development in therapy, training, and research, some of which I will describe as they have been evolving at the Mental Research Institute. This chapter relates in part to work supported by NIMH Training Grants, MH=10001 and MH=10829, but the views expressed are mine.

THE CONTEXT

Since the context is as important in using video-tape

techniques as it is in using other techniques in training and therapy, I want to describe some relevant features of the Mental Research Institute setting. The MRI is a multi-disciplinary, non-profit institute which, since its inception in 1959 under the leadership of Dr. Don D. Jackson, has focused its research efforts on the exploration of communication and the nature of interaction in families and other social systems. Paralleling these concern, a training program has evolved, focusing at first on conjoint family therapy, and continuing now, under the leadership of Dr. John E. Bell, to broaden its scope of communication and human systems.

THE SPECTRUM OF USES

The video-tape uses discussed here relate to training and therapy applications, but not necessarily to research applications. Training applications presented here are as follows: 1. taping prior to particular courses; 2. tape libraries; 3. splitting audio and visual channels; 4. "on line" feedback; 5. self-presentation exercises; and 6. comparative analysis of an individual's on- and off-stage performances in order to gain perspective on what constitutes authenticity.

Therapy applications presented are as follows: 1. early uses; 2. overt rather than covert use of the video controls; 3. temporal variations in the duration and timing of video-tape recording and replay in relation to certain purposes — such as recapturing previous moods and consolidating the participants' grasp of change and stability evidenced across the sweep of therapy; 4. some examples of what patients learn by watching post-session replays; and 5. some generalizations about what the therapist may learn from patients' reactions to themselves.

EQUIPMENT

THE MAN-MACHINE SYSTEM

Any discussion of video-tape equipment must take into

account the intimate relationships between the machine set-up and the people and the purposes connected with its use. These factors, inextricably linked, comprise a man-machine system. The optimal installation and operation of such a system requires attention to its human and non-human elements, as well as an understanding of the inevitably mutual effects they have on each other. The spectrum of desired applications must be defined; the machine best suited to the technical demands of the situation must be selected; and personnel must be trained adequately to make good use of the equipment. For instance, home-visit or field-work applications demand portability, and thus dictate selecting one of the lighter machines recording on half-inch tape. Gains through portability and both initial and subsequent economies are accompanied by some loss in resolving power, so that the finer features of facial expression are less faithfully rendered. Where "on line" feedback is desired, a monitor screen is needed in the same room with the camera along with relatively simple controls or else a skilled camera man who might even double as co-therapist (this technique is being explored at the Family Therapy Center in San Francisco by its directors, Ben Handelman and Dr. Alan Leveton, with Todd Bryant as camera man/co-therapist). The configuration of camera(s) in relation to the seating arrangement must be considered. The choice in height of the camera mounting(s), the focal length of the lens(es), and the availability of remote-controlled zoom, as well as pan and tilt capabilities, must all be weighed in relation to the room size, number of people to be squeezed on to the frame (or split-frame), the amount of money available, and the accessibility of patients and therapists who will not be paralyzed by visible and audible paraphernalia.

THE RECORDER

A significant new range of therapy training at the Mental Research Institute was opened up in 1963 by the acquisition of a video-tape recorder. The total set-up during the half-year period discussed in this report, consisted of a GE television camera equipped with a wide-angle as well as a standard lens, a TV monitor, and an Ampex VR-7000 tape recorder (which takes one-inch wide tapes lasting one hour and costing about $60 per tape).

We have several options available for improving our stationary one-camera video set-up. One option is to purchase a second video camera and install a corner shelf for it diagonally across from the one already in use. Another is to forgo the coverage afforded by two cameras in favor of the flexible focusing afforded by a remote-control zoom lens. This latter alternative would permit individual faces to be brought into sharp focus when particular facial expressions were apparently revealing for more than a few seconds at a time; and dyadic, triadic, and whole group kinesic patterns could be brought within the video frame when gross bodily movements or positions might be revealing. We opted for a third configuration: a fixed camera on a high mount, equipped with a wide-angle lens (12.5 mm) to take in the whole family and the therapist, plus a movable camera with a close-up lens (50 mm), mounted on a tripod at eye-level and equipped with remote-controlled pan and tilt functions. The therapist has an on/off switch at his elbow during the sessions, and in uses for training, the co-teacher in the observation room has another switch. A third "master" switch in the observation room determines which of the other two will work at any point in time.

DEVELOPING USES IN TRAINING

The developing uses in training fall into an order based on two factors: an historical or evolutionary sequence, and a continuum in terms of subtlety-complexity. Fortunately, these factors display considerable congruence.

An innovation designed for a ten-week intermediate course in family therapy at MRI consists of video-taping a family's initial therapy session about a month before the first class session, when the tape is played and discussed, to

321

provide a basis for noting changes which occur by the family's fifth session, which the trainees observe in their second class period as a "live" demonstration. This family's intervening sessions might be skipped, unless the sequence seemed particularly valuable. Subsequent demonstration sessions would continue to show what changes take place over the period of the course (though some assessment-focused sessions with other families might be interpolated for the sake of variety; this does not interfere with the trainees' ability to comprehend the sweep of therapy with their main demonstration family).

The pre-course taping of a demonstration family, an innovation conceived by Dr. Sheldon Starr, achieves an obvious advantage for the class. It permits a relatively short-term class to see family therapy changes over a longer time period than spanned by the course itself without "tying up" many valuable blank tapes which can be used for library development. This advantage is a particularly vital one for teaching in short courses, such as two-week family therapy summer workshops.

LIBRARY POSSIBILITIES AND PROBLEMS

An obvious extrapolation of the pre-course taping idea is the development of a library containing several families' therapy sessions video-taped at some appropriate intervals, such as every five weeks, from the initial session through termination, and even follow-up.

The value of such library materials will undoubtedly increase as we continue to accumulate, prune, and codify our library materials, and as publishing companies, professional associations, and other centers offer an increasing variety of such materials on a purchase, rental, or loan basis.

Though such library plans have considerable merit, they also have distinct drawbacks. One such drawback is their enormous expense. Because of the high cost of video-tape, it is extremely important to formulate an overall plan for deciding which material to discard. Perhaps the most

322

essential step is to take the time immediately after each recorded session to write down just what seems worth saving in terms of what points of theory or technique are highlighted, and approximately where these occur on the tape. If the recorder is in another room and a knowledgeable observer is on hand, the digital counter may be used to good advantage. The on/off switch permits a certain amount of "on line" editing.

Another drawback in video-tape library materials is that no matter how well used, they cannot give the trainees quite the same "feel" for family therapy that they can get by "live" observation, which can be rendered still more valuable by inviting the family in with the trainees for some post-session rehashes. We have found this procedure effective as an additional aspect of therapy for the family and as a powerful way of having trainees experience at first hand what it feels like to deal with the family system and how easy it is to overestimate and thus foster fragility of individuals and of families, while underestimating their strengths, including their ability to cope with therapists as fellow human beings. This procedure, by its structure, creates a context which often permits the families to give useful, growth-producing feedback to the therapist (the trainees, in our more advanced courses) which the families might not otherwise feel free to offer, particularly within the context of a demonstration session. Thus, for our purposes, we view the use of video-tape *library* materials an important but supplementary aspect of the training.

CHANNEL SPLITTING

A training application of our video-tape system which we plan to try soon is as follows: half the trainees will watch a family therapy session through a one-way mirror with the sound turned off while the other trainees listen to the same session in the other observation room with the curtain drawn across their one-way mirror. Each sub-group will be given a few minutes after the session to consolidate individual notes

323

into a group account of the highlights of what has happened and how. Then the whole class will get together again, each sub-group reporting its impressions to the other. After some discussion of the differences in sub-group impressions, which will probably include greater emphasis on process by the seeing-without-hearing group and greater emphasis on content by the hearing-without-seeing group, the video monitor will be used to present all the trainees with the full audio-visual replay of the session. In a subsequent meeting the two sub-groups may be asked to reverse roles.

Another way of achieving this reversal — though without the advantage of approaching the material "cold" — is to precede group reporting and combined channel audio-visual replay with the use of a standard audio recording of the first session to let the initial vision-only group hear without seeing, while in another room the original sound-only group views the video-tape with the sound turned off. This procedure has the advantage of letting each group experience each condition for the same therapy session. Following this reversal step, a second report based on the added cues might prove enlightening.

We shall need some experience with the various logistic possibilities of such audio-visual channel separation exercises before learning how best to use them, but we expect one or more variations will vividly demonstrate the importance of attending to non-verbal communication, *per se* and in relation to verbal communication, as a means of understanding the processes of family interaction and therapy.

In Situ Feedback to Patients, Therapists, and Supervisors

The phrase "*in situ* feedback" is used here to connote any feedback given within the context of the actual situation, whether or not it is genuine "on line" feedback. Thus, *in situ* feedback in the context of training is not limited to continuous or instantaneous feedback to those in the therapy room. Since the training situation extends beyond the

324

therapy hour, *in situ* feedback could consist of prompt post-session replay with participation of the family therapy trainee and perhaps even the patients in the viewing and discussion. This feedback process is well suited to aid in illuminating counter-transferences; and it can be enhanced by the exercise of good judgment in selecting segments of the tape to be viewed and in deciding when to stop for discussion or back-up for another look. These procedures often provide helpful learning experiences for the patients as well as the therapist. The use of such procedures in relation to observed interviews conducted by the trainees is designed to provide feedback *for* the supervisory process which follows immediately after each interview; however, this supervisory process *itself* is not video-taped. Video-tape utilization for feedback in relation to various supervisory roles would therefore be one of the interesting possibilities for further exploiting this equipment in our program. The co-teachers of the intensive course would not be the only ones to receive such feedback, inasmuch as the trainees are paired and each trainee gives feedback to his partner after observing him. Thus, this supervisory application of the video-tape would provide a rare opportunity for our family therapy trainees to receive direct audio-visual feedback as a feature of their supervised experience in the supervision of family therapy.

PRESENTATION OF THE SELF

Planned feedback demonstrations outside the context of therapy have several advantages. One is that such demonstrations have evolved here so as to usually focus on the full-face image of just one trainee at a time — an important feature of using this particular equipment, inasmuch as the resolving power of the monitor does not permit *detailed* observation of facial expressions of a whole group "taken" with the wide-angle lens. Secondly, the use of video-tape outside the therapeutic context permits the setting up of tailor-made situations to highlight the particular issues at hand, such as creating a self-disclosure task in order to have

325

the trainee see how he comes across in a context calling for openness.

A particularly interesting self-presentation use of the video equipment has been evolved by Dr. Frederick Ford, chief teacher of the MRI Intensive Course in Family Therapy. In this technique the teacher outlines to the class a number of salient features which they may wish to observe when they view themselves on the video monitor, and he widens the discussion to include features suggested by the class members themselves. Each trainee is advised to specify in advance which facets of feedback he will be most interested in receiving. Then the trainees go before the video camera one at a time for a five-minute individual self-presentation. The task is structured in such a way as to call for a certain amount of self-disclosure. For example, the trainees might be asked to cover several topics: "Where are you in your professional and personal life right now?" "Where do you expect to be in your professional and personal life six months from now?" In subsequently viewing themselves answering these questions, the trainees are asked to deal with such questions as the following: 1. "What did you see and hear?" 2. "What sense did you make out of what you saw and heard?" 3. "How did you feel about it?" and 4. "What are you going to do with the information provided by this exercise?" The value of this exercise may be enhanced by doing it once at the beginning of the course and again at the end of the course. The use made of the material at that time would then include enhancing the trainee's ability to see what growth he had made and how he presents himself to others. The material might also be useful in a research evaluation of training programs.

I have seen the training use of video-tape feedback just described as it was used with thirty-four individuals, including myself. Shifting now to a more personal point of view, since these were personal experiences, I noticed the anticipatory excitement and joking most individuals displayed before being video-taped. Some handled their anxiety by commenting on it immediately when they got "on camera," and these people later reported that their comment had put them at ease by removing the anxiety from the category of things unspeakable. My own moment of greatest anxiety was that immediately preceding the group feedback while watching the replay of my video-tape. I experienced relief and a little surprise at the consensus that I came across as calm and self-assured, particularly since I had been experiencing some anxiety while watching my replay. The others in the group seemed relieved when I expressed these feelings. They said it made them feel better to know that everyone participating had experienced anxiety in this situation.

A particularly common occurrence — quickly noted by the group members with mirthful self-recognition — was the opening self-introduction followed by licking the lips, gulping, clearing the throat, tilting the head, or some combination of these. Each expressed surprise at seeing himself perform one or more of these superfluous gestures. All three training groups in which this occurred (courses in communication and human systems for nurses and for male professionals who work with people) expressed strong feelings that these gestures were self-depreciatory and distracting. The group members felt that such gestures were an equivalent of saying something like, "I'm Joe Smith (though I don't expect any of you to have heard of me and I don't really know why you should listen to me . . .)" The trainees generally felt that becoming aware of this and other mannerisms was a helpful experience.

SEPARATING ACTING FROM AUTHENTIC BEING

In one course an incident occurred closely paralleling a development in our therapeutic application of video-tape feedback. One of the trainees handled her five-minute presentation of herself before the video camera by introducing herself with a string of fictitious names and past nicknames, adding, "I don't know who I am; you may call me anything." Inasmuch as this same trainee had created quite a stir several weeks earlier by screaming suddenly in appar-

327

ent panic during a stressful encounter group situation, I felt that her video-tape self-presentation afforded an opportunity to deal with her now familiar histrionics. Therefore, instead of letting the next trainee proceed, I entered the room with the video camera and asked the trainee who had just finished to take another turn before the camera, explaining that I felt she had presented herself in a manner that was at one and the same time somewhat poetic, self-consciously artistic, and exaggeratedly theatrical. Then I presented her with a paradoxical request; namely, that this time she exert every effort to *act* undramatic. She represented herself in a way which no longer prompted her teachers and fellow trainees to engage in clinical speculations about her. More specifically, she began by introducing herself with her real name — which she had totally omitted from her earlier string of aliases — and proceeded without further ado to describe some relevant feelings about herself before the course, during the course, and as she expected to feel after the course. The observers concurred in their post-replay discussion with the trainee that they had been far more comfortable during her second turn. They stuck to their guns even in the face of her protestation that she had been not only uncomfortable, but damned angry at having been double-bound into acting un-theatrical. The group, nevertheless, insisted that she had seemed far more natural although she maintained that her *apparent* unaffectedness had been achieved only by the greatest affectation. She soon became more popular in the group, and her supervisor began making more glowing reports from her field-work placement setting.

The general principle inherent in the above example can be put very simply. There is a special use of video-tape with people who are acting in a way which strikes others as somehow "unreal" or who are complaining that they themselves are troubled by not being able to distinguish clearly between when they are in some sense "on stage" and when they are "being themselves," if ever. The application consists of placing the person in a situation clearly calling for a "performance." When the person subsequently watches his own performance on the video monitor, the change of context imposes a powerful demand characteristic, "pulling" for authenticity, now that he has shifted his "set" from the role of the actor to the role of the critic viewing the actor.

EARLY THERAPEUTIC USES

Our use of the video-tape equipment as a treatment tool in the course of training family therapists has until recently been somewhat limited. Its main early application consisted of experimental use of therapeutic video-tape feedback, conceived and conducted by Dr. Robert Spitzer, formerly director of training at MRI. Realistic time limitations comprise one of the barriers to applying it further for this purpose on a routine basis in the intensive course in family therapy. Another factor discouraging the routine use of video-tape as a therapeutic modality in our training courses has been its relative rarity as a readily available tool to those who complete our courses. This situation, however, is changing at an apparently accelerating rate; there are now at least two other groups in our local area which own their own video-tape recorder setups and use them in combinations of practicing, studying, and teaching family therapy.

USE OF THE OBVIOUS: DON'T HIDE THE CONTROLS

Another technical question arises around the use of our on/off video-tape recording switch in the therapy room itself. From the start, we envisioned the use of this switch as an integral part of the therapy, since both ethical and rapport factors weighed against the use of any concealed switching device, such as a floor pedal. In deciding to keep the switch literally right out on the table in full view, we realized that its use would inevitably come to be interpreted by family members — "on" meaning "this interests the therapist," and "off" meaning "Oh, oh, why did he just tune

329

out?" Probably the families will learn that turning the recorder off is *not* the same as the therapist turning *himself* off. Bowing to the inevitable, we decided to try to make use of the therapy room switch as a therapeutic modality or at least adjunct, by self-consciously using its social reinforcing potential by doling out pre-coded signals of therapist approval or disapproval, according to whether the behavior seems to fall within some pre-specified category. We shall need much experience to learn how best to do this, but an example may convey the underlying concept. The father of an under-achieving junior high school student was given to long-winded sermonizing. Her poor school performance was due in part to tuning out the teacher, including during the giving of homework assignments. Had the therapist been able to literally tune out the father every time he went into one of his sermons, the point would have been made quite powerfully, particularly since this father demanded a *show* of attention.

The switched "on" position need not be limited to signalling interest or approval. Let us suppose there is a couple with this pattern: the wife constantly interrupts her husband, while the husband looks down and pauses as though inviting interruption. Each spouse has complained of the pattern as he sees it, and despite further discussion, it has not changed. The therapist might announce that he sees a particular interaction pattern he believes is dysfunctional or upsetting to both of them and which he's not sure they are able to be aware of — at least so far as their own individual contribution to it is concerned. Next, he could tell them that he was going to get that pattern down on the video-tape for them with many illustrations, so they could study them later. Each time the therapist pushed the switch to the "on" position, both husband and wife would soon be asking themselves what they had just done to deserve it. Perhaps, however, each would attribute the switching to the action of his spouse. The therapist could state that he was going to get a number of video shots which — whatever else they included — would definitely show what the husband was

330

doing that was lousing things up. After perhaps five or ten minutes of this or some appropriate behavior change on the husband's part, the therapist would announce a shift in his focus to the wife's behavior. Such a procedure may prove *less* distracting than a further interruption from the therapist to tell the wife when she is interrupting and to tell the husband that he has once again invited interruption. Moreover, the procedure places considerable pressure on the patients to become more actively engaged in the process of monitoring their own behavior rather than being told about it by the therapist each time. Of course, there are many other such signals which go on all the time in therapy without benefit of an electrical switch, but having such a switch at hand may help make the therapist more aware of how and when to use all such signals.

Another possibility for the use of such a switch became evident to the author when he heard how the participants in some marathon groups all get early practice in using the video camera — partly as a means of facilitating an attitudinal change in those who are timid about overtly calling attention to specific features of another person's behavior. The author was struck with the possibility of offering the use of the on/off switch to *any* member of the family after having each member practice it a couple of times. One form of usage expected to prove popular will be to call attention to some irritating habit of someone else in the family. In other words, a wife may turn on the machine as a way of saying, "Now my husband's doing that thing of his, only this time I'm going to get it recorded so you'll all be able to see how inconsiderate he is and even he will have to admit it this time!" If family members do experience such "between-the-lines" meaning in their own and one another's utilization of the on/off switch, the desire to deprive the others of self-incriminating evidence will constitute a powerful motive to desisting from annoying behaviors. Even struggles over who is to control the on/off switch may prove extremely productive to work with as interaction process material in therapy.

Duration of Taping and Replay

The applications just presented raise a pair of interesting technical questions: How long should the video-taping session last and how long should the replay segment last? These are related questions, of course, and probably in most instances they will have to be thought through together. Outlining some of the probable considerations may help. For example, if the session is to be limited to one hour, and there is to be immediate total replay and some discussion with the family, then twenty-five minutes would be about the upper limit of the video-taped session *per se,* assuming the equipment is all ready to go at the start of the session and there is to be little or no stopping and starting of the tape during the replay. A shorter segment should be selected or a longer total session arranged for if there is to be much opportunity to stop and start the tape and maybe even repeat some portions several times as various viewers express their reactions *during* the replay. Replaying a full fifty-minute session may be too taxing unless each viewer has some specific and active task, such as to note (perhaps even in writing) some type of interaction or to comment right away when feeling surprise or some other strong emotion. The therapist must come to terms with some compromise solution if the monitor he works with is not in the therapy room itself, since moving a family back and forth for immediate viewing of several brief segments is not feasible under these conditions.

Timing of Taping and Replay

Dr. Frederick Stoller, who developed the participating on/off technique previously described, manages not to compromise, since he uses highly portable equipment rather than a permanent two-room installation with the monitor outside the therapy room. Thus, in his marathon groups, he can immediately play back short segments at will, blending these into the flow of the total session. With the MRI set-up

332

already described, a possible solution may be to provide a monitor mounting in the therapy room, with a provision for turning it off at times when it might otherwise prove distracting.

RE-CREATING LOST OPPORTUNITIES

A third possible application of the replaying of video-tape from an earlier session has been suggested by Dr. Robert Spitzer. This somewhat more focused technique would entail showing the family a selected segment of a particularly meaningful moment of breakthrough. Dr. Spitzer's example was that of an over-controlled, tyrannical father who cried in one session for the first time in the memory of anyone else in the family. They responded with acceptance and even with relief at his belated show of humanness, and he himself spoke of the tremendous burden he had needlessly been carrying by fearing to show that he sometimes feels sorry for himself, is frightened, and needs to depend on others as well as have others lean on him. Despite some verbal priming in later session, however, the magic of that moment's mood was never quite recaptured. What if the therapist had had a video-tape of the father's "breakthrough" session and had replayed to the family the most moving moments? Might not that have recaptured the magic mood, thus catalyzing the arrested process of its consolidation by all as a new aspect of father, with which the family might move on to new and more comfortable ways of interacting?

The therapeutic gains of this technique will, of course, be associated with some corresponding costs in terms of the therapist's time; you cannot recreate the past without sacrificing something in the present.

RECOGNIZING GAINS AND GAPS

Extrapolating from Dr. Starr's idea of pre-course video-taping as an aid to trainees in noting changes over time

333

during family therapy, we realized that the families themselves might benefit directly from viewing earlier tapes of themselves. Though we have not yet made much use of these particular ideas, I mention them in order to share our current thinking about some likely areas for exploration. When families (or groups or individuals) feel at an impasse, or the therapist wishes to get moving again after a plateau seems to have lasted long enough for whatever consolidation was needed, it might prove helpful to replay and discuss with the family tapes made early in their therapy. Gains may be noticed which were not otherwise evident to the family or the therapist or both, thus heartening the family to make further progress, by demonstrating that they are capable of change and that they have already made some changes they feel good about without having fallen apart. In addition to the encouragement they may derive from their own pleasure at recognizing progress already made, they might also be spurred on by being reminded of old patterns which they still want to change.

Another use of early-session replay may be in the termination phase, as an aid to consolidating what has happened. Going backwards in time momentarily, so as to highlight changes, may increase the family members' sense of control and hence decrease their fear of undergoing spontaneous irreversible retrogressions.

REACTIONS TO REPLAY

WHAT IS LEARNED

A number of families, couples, and individuals in therapy with me have viewed and discussed one or more of their video-taped sessions. I asked that each person write down on a card immediately after viewing the session whatever he could to shed light on the following three questions: 1. What did you learn about yourself from watching the replay? 2. What did you learn about anyone else in the family? 3. What did you learn about how you interact or relate to one another in terms of the whole family functioning together?

Some examples of what people claimed to have learned from video-tape replay *prior to further discussion* may be helpful in appreciating some of the potential of even this crude technique for therapeutic video-tape application. A husband who had been complaining of his wife's aloofness and reluctance to express warmth wrote that he saw himself spending a good deal of his time leaning away from her, looking out of the window when she was talking. Another husband wrote that his wife " . . . was pretty much left out. I cursed a lot. She was not involved, smoked a lot. This shows my inattention." In other words, he saw that she lit up (he detests her smoking) as a signal to recapture his attention when he had been talking purely about himself. One daughter wrote that her father should be given a chance to talk about anything at length since he usually doesn't. She added: "Mother needs to gesture more and talk less. . . . [younger brother] should quit interrupting, even if it's for the truth that no one else will speak. . . . He just doesn't pay attention. Maybe we haven't paid attention to him when he talks about his interests, but when someone doesn't pay attention, he just goes deeper into the subject matter." In another family, a daughter who had been acting like her younger sister in order to draw attention (which the parents gave promptly though disapprovingly) wrote, "I learned that I sounded more sulky than I felt, and I looked and sounded like I was being real stubborn. Hm . . . come to think of it, I guess I was stubborn." With this family, the function of replay was largely to remind them how much they had enjoyed a three-phase role-taking sequence we had just completed. At first I took the daughter's role in such a way as to include rather than belittle her younger sister, then the father's role in such a way as to notice and appreciate the older sister's new behavior while she now took over her own new role — and finally, both father and the older daughter took their own roles, grinning with obvious relish

335

at having affected a transition, at least momentarily, to new and more mutually appreciative roles.

A related use is envisioned by the author and Dr. Stanley Clemes in connection with human-relations training at a local police academy. To train police in "keeping their cool," they may be asked to participate in a series of difficult confrontations in which blacks or radical students will take increasingly provocative roles, but only after viewing and discussing each confrontation scene with the police before proceeding to the next and more difficult confrontation.

SOME GENERALIZATIONS

In order to draw some generalizations from the collected feedback cards that patients had written about the experience of seeing themselves, I went over them. With the aid of summarized comments, I arrived at only two generalizations: 1. those people who had made the least progress in therapy were characterized by having written no comments to show they had learned anything about themselves, and they had written only something negative or else nothing at all about their spouses; 2. only these people were unable to take a more self-distanced position during the replay, evidenced by such running comments as, "Yeah! I said it before, and I'll say it again, 'cause I agree with every word I'm saying there!"

Two points emerge in connection with the generalizations drawn above. First, that one of the uses of video confrontation may be as a prognostic aid; second, that a particularly vital aspect to observe in such confrontation is each person's reaction to seeing himself in interaction with others.

IN CONCLUSION

A subtle, yet significant, feature implicit in the video-tape applications described is that the trainees themselves may be exposed to a wide variety of ways of using video-

336

tape. Increasingly, we are making *explicit* to the trainees, as part of their courses, our thinking thus far about the uses of video-tape in training and therapy. We feel that paying some attention to this area and opening it up as a worthy topic for discussion and demonstration will add to our own understanding of how to use video-tape and will better equip and encourage our trainees to use this powerful medium for therapy and training in their own work settings.

ten

~~~~~~

what to read

F. Sander and C. Beels

Family therapy training has been largely clinically oriented, due, in part, to the newness of the field and the consequent dearth of good literature. Bodin's paper on family therapy training literature in *Family Process* concluded that "surprisingly little has been written explicitly about the content of [clinical] family therapy courses." There is no mention in his review of *any* didactic course on the theory and practice of family therapy.

This contribution is an outline and brief description of a course which has evolved and been added to Ferber and

Mendelsohn's clinical training program at the AECOM. We offer this course to trainees who have generally had at least a full year of experience in conducting family therapy. This is in keeping with our view that the experience of working with families is the primary learning experience and ought to precede premature conceptualization, especially in a field where theories are in their infancy.

COURSE STRUCTURE

A. *Reading Material.* We presented the seminar members with a loose-leaf volume of reprints, especially those more difficult to find. This effort on our part was more than repaid by the care with which the works were read.

B. *Leadership.* The two of us taught the seminar together. Joint teaching has paid off in this as in most of our other [clinical] teaching, in the obvious sense that having two teachers insures against absence due to illness, and much other division of labor is possible. Beyond this, however, the dual leadership had some consequences for the character of the meetings themselves.

One of us, who felt most familiar with, interested in, or responsible for, the day's material, led the discussion. The other made notes and took the role of a silent but occasionally provocative student. Thus the leader could concentrate on leading the discussion to focus on certain questions, while the second one could look for difficulties the group was having with the material, and supply missing connections which the leader, because of his involvement, was overlooking. When it worked well, there was little for the co-leader to do, but the relationship supplied a model for the group.

Obviously, also, the criticism and re-planning of the course as it went along was much more fruitful than it could have been if we had worked alone. We kept each other's spirits up.

C. *Work Assignment.* We expected all the seminar members to read each article, and for each work assigned one member of the seminar to its criticism, and one to its defense. This made it possible to focus issues early in the discussion. The seminar met weekly for an hour and a half for a total of about forty sessions.

D. *Membership*. The course was open to anyone in the AECOM complex who had had experience in family therapy or research. It thus included a vertical range from professors of psychiatry to people still in training, and a broad lateral range of disciplines. This provided a forum for exchange of ideas that was unique in the institution. We have taught the seminar to twelve to fifteen participants at a time, and feel that fifteen is the upper limit for active involvement by everyone.

THE CURRICULUM

When we planned the seminar, the following areas emerged rather naturally. We shall describe them in turn, together with some of the issues raised in each of them.

A. *Scientific Basis*. Before plunging into the literature on family theory and therapy we thought we ought to ask a somewhat naïve preliminary question: "How much 'scientific evidence' was there that 'family factors,' in fact, could be viewed as 'etiological agents' in the production of 'mental illness'?" We chose what we felt were the better studies representing the clinical, epidemiological, field, and laboratory approaches to this knotty problem.

One of the most interesting clinical descriptions of a family is to be found in Freud's case of Dora. The correlation between family circumstances and Dora's symptoms is elegantly demonstrated. Historically the significance of this case is, of course, the discovery of the importance of infantile sexuality, the function of dreams, and intrapsychic factors in general. In fact, Freud's elucidation of Dora's complicity in the family system due to her oedipal and unconscious homosexual wishes reflects the present-day view of the necessary collusion of all the members of any system to keep it going. The case lent itself beautifully to the age-old question of, "Is it in ourselves or in our stars that we are

340

underlings?" The roles of constitution, infantile experiences, and current social forces in the etiology of mental illness (hysteria in this case) emerged in the discussion. (Incidentally, one might similarly start such a course with Freud's case of Little Hans.)

Other psychoanalytic writers (Maine, Johnson, and Szurek, for example) afforded a view of the additional theory required by the shift to working concurrently (though not conjointly) with the relatives of the identified patient.

With the work of Thomas, Birch, and Chess we returned to the interplay of temperament and environment in a more systematic — though still primarily clinical — study. Problems of sampling, clinical biases, and interpretation of results were explored in greater detail.

We turned from these clinical impressions to read some attempts at objective specification of the *experience* end of the temperament/experience interaction. We considered "hard" data such as family structure, father-absence, or maternal death, and "soft" data such as Cheek's characterization of the mothers and fathers of schizophrenics. Most of the studies could be seriously faulted for their methodology. Even the best, such as Wynne and Singer's studies of the parental contribution to thought-disorder in schizophrenia, were unsatisfying in the sense that they all seemed to represent such a small piece of the clinical picture. Wender's paper on "Necessary and Sufficient Conditions in Psychiatric Explanation" summed this problem up quite well: the examination of a single variable as the partial cause of an event which occurs rarely and has many causes, will yield a very low predictive grasp on the event, even though it has a high level of statistical significance. Wender's review of the genetic studies of schizophrenia, the best paper we could find on the *temperament* end of the formula, suffers from the same difficulty.

At this point, we abandoned the medical model of diagnosing a sick or deviant patient and then seeking the etiological cause in his family. We assembled several papers which could be read as descriptions of the activity of the family as a disordered or malfunctioning *group*: Ravich, Roman and Bauman, Haley, and Ferreira. We then looked back to the Wynne and Singer, Reiss, and Cheek papers, and viewed them in the same light. From this standpoint, the family can be seen as setting about a task (provided either by life or by the experimenter) and doing it well or badly. The trouble they are having with it appears in each study to be strikingly the same: they are spending time managing their relations with each other rather than thinking about the task. They are keeping cool rather than getting work done. (Parsons would say they are occupied with pattern maintenance at the expense of means/ends relations.)

Once that point of view was reached, we were ready to appreciate work such as Scheflen's on the ethology of the family as an interactive group. We were also ready to be open to theoretical contributions from a wide variety of disciplines, since conventional psychology and psychiatry, with their emphasis on mind and illness, have been of too little help to us.

Reactions to this material varied, depending upon the previous experiences and frames of reference of the participants. What emerged time after time was an appreciation of the conceptual and technical complexities involved in the testing of any etiological hypotheses.

We succeeded in establishing an attitude of scepticism towards single-factor etiological investigation, and in starting the seminar members on their progress towards their own formulations about the nature of normal and disturbed family process.

B. *Theory*. Aware that psychiatry has had little to offer in the way of a comprehensive theory of families, we included a brief survey of what other disciplines have described and theorized. We reviewed what some historians, anthropologists, sociologists, ethologists, and family psychiatrists have said in the way of theoretical observations of the family as a unit.

We took the family as a social entity, its history and

structure, rather than the individual as a family member, his biology and psychology. In fact, we studied the family as a collection of institutions, such as marriage; of values, such as constancy; and of motivational systems, such as sexuality. We began with Aries' *Centuries of Childhood* to study the historical development of the idea of "the family," especially of such values as intimacy, privacy, and the specialness of children. We contrasted the cultural anthropology of Levi-Strauss with the biology of Desmond Morris, for two different views of the family's universality, and of the extent to which some of its institutions, such as sex differences, childbearing, and incest-taboo, are biologically or socially obligatory. Readings in Parsons showed how one theory of the sociology of small groups would require these institutions to mesh together. We then read system theorists such as Haley and Jackson, who construct a theory of the family that dispenses with almost all the values, institutions, and motivations the others have required. At the end of such a quick tour of the field we were at least in a position to have a second look at the theoretical assumptions on which our clinical work is based. We could re-read such psychiatric theorists of family therapy as Boszormenyi-Nagy and Laing with the recognition that their task of building a bridge between the theories of individual and social function has only begun.

C. *Therapy.* Having surveyed the question of "scientific evidence" and available theories of the family, in the final section of the course we turned to the writings of the major family therapists, and viewed films or video-tapes of their work. In addition, we read individual papers considered "classic" on specific issues of "technique."

This final section occupied half of the time. We tried to understand what each of the therapists was trying to accomplish, and to identify the special techniques he used to get that result. In this way we concentrated on their unique characteristics — their philosophy, personality, and tactics — rather than on what they all have in common. We did this not only because it is difficult to abstract a

343

useful general theory or description of family therapy from the literature, but also because we believe that the most important thing that can be gotten from the literature of family therapy is a collection of models and scenarios from which the student chooses what best suits him and the problem presented by the family in front of him.

D. *Fiction*. Both as a relief from some of the weighty reading and as a source of further perspectives on our subject, we read classic works of world literature before each of the above three sections and at the end of the course. Much of our other reading had emphasized that the "modern nuclear family" we live in and treat is a special and unique structure when viewed historically. We included in the format works of fiction which illustrated the changing structure of the Occidental family from Biblical times to the present.

COURSE READING

Section A. The Family as Etiologic Agent in Psychopathology

1. Organization meeting and discussion of *Genesis,* chs. 1-10.
2. *Genesis,* chs. 11-50.
3. Freud, S. (1905), Fragment of an analysis of a case of hysteria. *Standard Edition,* 7: 15-63; 112-122. London: Hogarth.
4. Bell, N. and Vogel, E. (1960), The emotionally disturbed child as the family scapegoat. *Psychoanal. Review,* 47. Also in *A Modern Introduction to the Family,* eds. N. Bell and E. Vogel, 382-397. New York: Free Press.

   Johnson, A. and Szurek, S. (1952), The genesis of antisocial acting out in children and adults. *Psychoanal. Quart.,* 21: 323-343.

   Main, T. (1966), Mutual projection in marriage. *Comprehensive Psychiatry,* 7: 5, 432-449.

344

5. RUTTER, M., KORN, S., and BIRCH, H. (1963), Genetic and environmental factors in the development of "primary reaction patterns." *Brit. J. Clin. Psychol.*, 2: 161-173.

THOMAS, A., CHESS, S., and BIRCH, H. (1968), *Temperament and Behavior Disorder in Children.* New York: New York Univ. Press.

6. CHEEK, F. (1965), The father of the schizophrenic. *Arch. Gen. Psych.*, 13 (Oct.); 336-345.

———— (1964), Schizophrenic mothers in word and deed. *Fam. Proc.*, 3: 1, 155.

7. BARRY, H. and LINDEMANN, E. (1960), Critical ages for maternal bereavement in psychoneurosis. Psychosomatic Medicine, 22: 3, 166-181.

ANDERSON, R. (1968), Where's Dad. *Arch. Gen. Psych.*, 18 (June): 641-649.

FERBER, A. *et al.* (1967), Current family structure: psychiatric emergencies and patient fate. *Arch. Gen. Psych.*, 16 (June): 659-677.

BURTON, R. and WHITING, J. (1961), The absent father and cross sex identity. *Merrill Palmer Quart. of Behavior and Development*, 7: 2, 85-95.

8. WYNNE, L. and SINGER, M. (1963), Thought disorder and family relations of schizophrenics, I and II. *Arch. Gen. Psych.*, 9: 191-206.

———— (1965). In *Arch. Gen. Psych.*, 12: 187-212.

9. REISS, D. (1967), Individual thinking and family interaction, I. *Arch. Gen. Psych.*, 16: 80-93.

———— (1967), *J. Psychiat. Res.*, 5: 193-211.

FERREIRA, A. and WINTER, W. (1965), Family interaction and decision-making. *Arch. Gen. Psych.*, 13: 214-233.

10. WENDER, P. (1967), On necessary and sufficient conditions in psychiatric explanation. *Arch. Gen. Psych.*, 16: 41-47.

11. RAVICH, R. (1969), The use of the inter-personal game-test in conjoint marital psychotherapy. *Amer. J. Psychother.*, 23: 2 (April), 217-229.

345

BAUMAN, G. and ROMAN, M. (1966), Interaction testing in the study of marital dominance. *Fam. Proc.,* 5:2, 230-242.
12. SCHEFLEN, A. (1968), Explaining communicative behavior: three points of view. In *Expanding Theory & Practice in Family Therapy,* eds. N. Ackerman, F. Beatman, and S. Sherman, 93-98. New York: Family Service Assoc. of America.
——— (1968), Human communication: behavioral programs and their integration in interaction. *Behav. Science,* 13:1 (Jan.), 44-55.
13. Work of fiction: Aeschylus, *Oresteia Trilogy.*

SECTION B. THEORY

History

14. ARIES, P. (1962), *Centuries of Childhood: A Social History of Family Life,* 9-33, 339-419. New York: Vintage.
ERIKSON, E. (1969), *Gandhi's Truth,* 33-45. New York: Norton.

Anthropology

15. LEVI-STRAUSS, C. (1960), The family. In *Man, Culture, and Society,* ed. H. Shapiro. New York: Oxford University Press.
MEAD, M. (1967), *Sex and Temperament,* chs. 17-18. New York: Dell.

Primatology

16. MORRIS, D. (1969), *The Naked Ape,* chs. 1-3, 5. New York: Dell.
MEAD, M. (1963), Totem and taboo: reconsidered with respect. *Bull. of Menninger Clin.,* 27:4 (Jul.), 185-199.

346

Sociology

17. Burgess, E. (1926), The family as a unit of interacting personalities. In *The Family,* 7 (March): 3-9.
    Parsons, T, (1955), The American family — its relations to personality and to the social structure. Family structure and the socialization of the child. In *Family Socialization and Interaction Process,* eds. T. Parsons and R. Bales. Glencoe: Free Press.
18. ——— (1964), *Social Structure and Personality,* chs. 1-3. New York: Free Press of Macmillan.

Systems

19. Haley, J. (1967), Toward a theory of pathological families. In *Family Therapy and Disturbed Families,* eds. I. Boszormenyi-Nagy and G. Zuk. Palo Alto: Science and Behavior Books.
    Jackson, D. (1965), The study of the family. *Fam. Proc.,* 4:1.
    ——— (1965), Family rules: the marital quid pro quo. *Arch. Gen. Psych.,* 12:589.

Psychiatry

20. Boszormenyi-Nagy, I. and Framo, J., eds. (1965). *Intensive Family Therapy,* chs. 2-3. New York: Harper and Row.
21. Laing, R. (1967), Individual and family structure. In *The Predicament of the Family.* London: Hogarth.
    Mishler, E. and Waxler, N. (1966), Family interaction process and schizophrenia. *Intern. J. of Psychiat.,* 2:4 (Jul.).

Fiction

22. Austen, J., *Pride and Prejudice.*

23. BOWEN, M., video-tape. Available from Dr. Murray Bowen, Dept. of Psychiatry, Medical College of Virginia, Richmond, Va.

24. ——— (1966), The use of family theory in clinical practice. *Comp. Psych.*, 7:5, 345-374.

25. ACKERMAN, N., *Hillcrest Family*. Movie available from Psychological Cinema Register, Pennsylvania State Univ., University Park, Pa.

26. ——— (1966), *Treating the Troubled Family*, chs. containing interview transcripts. New York: Basic Books.

27. WHITAKER, C., *Hillcrest Family*. Movie available from Psychological Cinema Register, Pennsylvania State Univ., University Park, Pa.

28. ——— (1958), Psychotherapy with couples. *Amer. J. Psychother.*, 12: 18-23.

——— (1965), Acting out in family psychotherapy. In *Acting Out: Theoretical and Clinical Aspects*. New York: Grune & Stratton.

——— and WARKENTIN, J. (1965), Countertransference in family treatment of schizophrenia. In *Intensive Family Therapy*, eds. I. Boszormenyi-Nagy and J. Framo. New York: Harper and Row.

——— (1968), Interview. In *Techniques of Family Therapy*, eds. J. Haley and L. Hoffman, 265-360. New York: Basic Books.

29. JACKSON, D., *Hillcrest Family*. Movie available from Psychological Cinema Register, Pennsylvania State Univ., University Park, Pa.

30. ——— (1962). In *Contemporary Psychotherapies*, ed. M. Stein. Glencoe: Free Press.

——— and WEAKLAND, J. (1961), Conjoint family therapy: some considerations on theory, technique, and results. *Psychiatry*, 24: 30-45.

——— and YALOM, I. (1963-4), An example of family homeostasis and patient change. In *Current*

Psych. Therapies, ed. J. Masserman. New York:
Grune & Stratton.
31. SATIR, V. (1964), *Conjoint Family Therapy: A
Guide.* Palo Alto: Science and Behavior Books.
32. ZUK, G. (1967), Formations of a technique and its
theory. *Arch. Gen. Psych.,* 10 (Jan.). 71-79.
HALEY, J. (1963), *Strategies of Psychotherapy,* chs.
6-7. New York: Grune & Stratton.
33. PAUL, N. (1967), Role of mourning and empathy in
conjoint family therapy. In *Family Therapy and
Disturbed Families,* eds. I. Boszormenyi-Nagy
and G. Zuk. Palo Alto: Science and Behavior
Books.
———— and GROSSER, G. (1965), Operational mourning and its role in conjoint family therapy. *Comm.
Ment. Health J.,* 1:4, 339-345.
34. SCHAFFER, L., WYNNE., L., DAY, J., RYCBOFF, I., and
HALPERIN, A., (1962), On the nature and sources
of the psychiatrist's experience with the family of
the schizophrenic. *Psychiatry,* 25: 23-45.
WYNNE, L. (1961), The study of intrafamilial align-
ments and splits in exploratory family therapy. In
Exploring the Base for Family Therapy, eds. N.
Ackerman, F. Beatman, and S. Sherman. New
York: Family Service Assoc. Press.
———— (1965), Some indications and contra-
indications for exploratory family therapy. In
Intensive Family Therapy, eds. I. Boszormenyi-
Nagy and J. Framo. New York: Harper and Row.
35. MINUCHIN, S. (1968), *Families of the Slums.* New
York: Basic Books.
36. FRIEDMAN, A. *et al.* (1965), *Psychotherapy for the
Whole Family,* chs. 4-7, 11-12, 14, 16, 19, 23. New
York: Springer.

Fiction

37. ELIOT, T. S., *The Cocktail Party.*

In Conclusion

What function does a literature survey have in a primarily treatment-oriented training program? We wanted to emphasize the variety of treatment approaches in the field, and to prepare the trainees to search in their own experience for the combination of therapeutic philosophy, therapists' temperament and outlook, and type of family problem, that leads to effective treatment over the years of a therapist's development. In the absence of objective studies, the only criterion of success we have is this slow sorting-out of approaches. A literature survey, then, should both challenge whatever preconceptions the trainee brings with him into the field, and offset the parochialism which is bound to exist in any one training center.

To this end we wish to emphasize that the specific assigned readings could easily be substituted by other readings. The value of the seminar is the forum provided for the discussion of the underlying conceptual issues.

It is the confrontation of these issues that provides the less practical, but ultimately more important, reason for the variety of readings in the "etiology" and "theory" parts of the course. Some of the venerable individually centered theories have had a limited applicability. We are being challenged to come up with ideas of greater generality and deeper grasp about what occurs *between* people in a variety of situations. We hope that family therapy and the study of natural groups are staging areas for the next development in behavioral science. For this two things are needed. One is the maintenance of a common language by building concepts from the older and the developing disciplines. The second is the maximum openness to new theories and approaches.

350

eleven

how people interact

A. Kendon

When we are in the presence of others, in guiding
our conduct we rely a great deal upon the information we
can gather by vision. For instance, in any encounter it is
important for us to know the sex and age of the participants,
and this information is most readily and rapidly gained
from an individual's appearance. Appearances also provide
many indications of the individual's relative status, personality characteristics, sources of identity, and even, when
uniforms are worn, his role in the situation. In looking at
others, in addition, we can observe what they are doing and

351

where they are placed spatially within a setting, and this, too, provides us with much information which will be used in the guidance of our conduct. If we are talking with another, information available through vision is often of prime importance: we gauge who is attending to whom from where people are looking, and we gather, from changes in facial expression, and from particular gestures, how they are reacting, or how what they may be saying is to be understood.

This visible information is continuously available, and it cannot be concealed. And just as such information from others is available to us, so we make the same sort of information available to them. Thus it is that, just as we regulate our behavior in the presence of others in the light of what we can see of them, so we also must take into account what they can see of us. Each, then, can exercise a degree of control over the behavior of the other by what he may be seen to do, and indeed we generally find that when people are in one another's presence they display a subtle and continuous interdependence of behavior (Goffman, 1963). What each can see of another, then, plays a central role in the process of interaction. Yet, though this is generally acknowledged, it is only recently that the role of visible behavior in interaction has been studied systematically.

The functions of visible behavior in interaction are very diverse. Visual signaling of one sort or another plays a part in the initiation of social encounters, serves in the maintenance of the relationship between interactants, and signals emotional states, subtleties of attitude and expectations, as well as gestures and gesticulations, in the process of talking — the active sending of specific messages. It can also serve to supplement what a person is saying, or qualify it, or substitute for it. Instead of trying to review all of these functions, I shall concentrate mainly upon those features of visible behavior which appear to establish the context or condition within which talking takes place. Therefore, I discuss how explicit "communication channels" are established between people, but do not deal with what, as one might put it, the channel is used for. Thus, I discuss the posture and spatial relations of members of encounters, and the means by which people indicate whom they are talking with, and how they regulate one another's behavior so that time is properly shared to make talking possible, but I do not discuss gesture and gesticulation, which are very closely bound up with talking, nor facial displays. For work on facial displays see Darwin (1872), Woodworth and Schlosberg (1954), Ekman, Sorenson, and Friesen (1969), Izzard (1970), and Grant (1969). For work on gesticulation see Efron (1941), Kendon (1972), and references therein. For the best available general review of visible behavior in face-to-face communication see Vine (1970) and Duncan (1969).

Almost all my observations, whether they are original or taken from the work of others, have been made upon people who are Americans of North European extraction. This should be kept in mind, for there are considerable cultural differences in the way in which visible behavior functions in interaction.*

It seems likely that the *principles* by which visible behavior is employed in interaction are the same for all mankind. For instance, different kinds of encounters between people are systematically related to different spacing patterns of the participants. While the specific patterns adopted for specific types of encounter may vary from culture to culture, it seems unlikely that the significance of spacing *as such* for communication will differ from culture to culture.

THE CONCEPT OF COMMUNICATION

Before proceeding to deal exclusively with visible behavior and its communicative significance, I would like to say a few things about the concept of "communication"

---

*See Weston LaBarre (1964) for a comprehensive survey of cultural differences in visible behavior in interaction. An intelligent discussion of this question may be found in Ekman and Friesen (1969). Cultural differences in postural habit have been discussed by Hewes (1955).

353

in general, and also outline briefly other ways in which we communicate. For the purposes of the present discussion, the term "communication" is used in a very broad sense to refer to any patterned interdependency of behavior between people. As Birdwhistell (1970) said, "Communication is a cover term for the structured dynamic processes relating to the interconnectedness of living systems." Thus, when people are in one another's presence, if it can be shown that each adjusts his behavior in relation to the others, though they may not be gesturing or talking with one another, then we shall say that these individuals are in communication with one another.

For example, if you observe a reading room of a library, particularly at a time of day when there is ample choice of seats for anyone newly entering, it is not hard to observe regularities in how people sit in relation to one another. In one such study (Sommer, 1967) it was found that almost everyone entering the room in the morning would choose to sit at an empty table, if there were one, and where all the tables had a single occupant, additional newcomers would tend to sit several chairs away from those already at a table. It was exceedingly rare for newcomers to sit either right next to an occupant, or immediately opposite him. And when in an experimental study (Felipe and Sommer, 1966) instructed newcomers deliberately sat next to an occupant, or directly opposite him, the person already seated was much more likely to move away than he was if the newcomer sat several chairs away from him. Evidently, in a situation like a reading room which is defined as a place where people do not engage in focused interaction, people nonetheless cooperate to maintain, as far as they can, spacing arrangements whose principal features appear to be to minimize the chances of inadvertent social contact between people.

In more crowded situations this cannot be done by keeping apart from people, and here we see rather different strategies adopted. Everyone must have been faced with the problem, in a crowded elevator, of where to look. Here people are close — close enough for what, in another situation, would be a really quite intimate kind of interaction — and here it becomes of great importance not to catch the eye of another person. The meeting of the eyes is an important social event, a very common (and powerful) means by which we signal a mutual openness, and it is thus an important part of the process by which encounters are initiated. When there is some distance between people, accidental eye-catching does not matter — one can easily make it appear as if one did not see the other's eyes, or that one was not seen by the other. In an elevator, however, this is much more difficult, so elevator riders often adopt the strategy of studiously observing the floor indicator, as if they are afraid they will miss their stop. And this, incidentally, is quite a good solution, for it is important, in the presence of others, not to show *explicit* avoidance of them. Erving Goffman (1963) has pointed out how strangers in one another's presence commonly accord to one another what he has called "civil inattention" — whereby one at once does not *engage* with others, but at the same time one behaves in such a way as to indicate one is aware of the other's presence. In this way, one shows to others that one is not hostile to them or afraid of them, and that one is oneself, thus, a person to be trusted. This contrasts with what may be called *non-person* treatment, where an individual makes no adjustment in his behavior as he comes into the presence of others. And, of course, in doing so such an individual may be understood to be sending another kind of message to the others around him.

There are, of course, many other ways in which we adjust our behavior to the presence of others, and thereby engage in non-explicit or *unfocused interaction* with them. Each of us learns, more or less, to wear clothes that fit the setting we are in; to abide by the conventions of posture, movement, and emotional display; and how loudly to speak. In abiding by these conventions, or by deviating from them, often subtly, we show to others, whether intentionally or not, a great deal about who we are, what we are doing, and what we intend to do.

355

All this must be counted as communication, as well as our talk and our gestures. It has been said with justice that nobody, when in the presence of another, fails to communicate. By his mere appearance in a setting he makes available information about himself, some of which, at least, will be received and used by others. In approaching an analysis of communicational behavior, then, we must be prepared to deal with all that we can observe, and it is only after we have shown that some aspects of behavior make no difference to the behavior of others that we can know what does not count. Anything you do, as well as anything you say, then, is to be presumed communicative unless proved otherwise.

The necessity to begin by taking everything into account, to begin by suspending judgment on the significance of all behavior until it has been properly examined, means that the investigation of communicative behavior can be a very difficult undertaking. This difficulty is further compounded, for not only is communication at least potentially a continuous process, and one that makes use of several sensory channels at once, but in communicating we always exchange a multiplicity of messages. Furthermore, the communicative significance of any particular item of behavior is not something it carries around with it like a badge. Its significance is, instead, highly determined by how it is used by contexts in which it occurs. For example, suppose we know that somebody produced the lexical item "coffee." We have no idea about what might be meant by this until we know that this was all he said, that he said it with a low-falling intonation tune, that he said it just after he had sat on a stool at a counter in a coffee shop, and just after the waitress had stopped in front of him, pencil and order-pad raised at the ready. And only then — *after* we have observed the nature of the utterance, and the situational and behavioral contexts in which it occurred — can we state what the function of that utterance was. The *utterance* did not request a cup of coffee. The cup of coffee was requested by his total action — by entering the coffee shop and sitting at the counter in the particular fashion that he did, he conveyed to the waitress that here was a customer in need of the kind of service due to customers. The item "coffee" served only as a final specification of the request for service that he was making. This theoretical position owes most to the work of Birdwhistell (1970). Its methodological implications have also been stated in practical terms by Scheflen (1965). The interdependence of utterance and context and the importance of this for a theory of semantics is well stated by Rommetveit (1968) and Olson (1970).

Now of course we, as ordinary human beings, know all these things. We know them because we know how to interact with others, much as we know how to ride a bicycle or drive a car. As Edward Sapir (1927) once said, much of communicational behavior comprises a code that is "known by no one, but understood by all." As students of communicational behavior, our task is to produce a systematic account of what people do that is communicatively relevant. This means that we shall have to engage in meticulous and intricate descriptions of behavior, as it may be observed in a wide variety of situations. By careful comparison and contrast we may eventually arrive at an explicit statement of the functions of the various components of the behavioral flow.

It should be evident, then, that I am claiming that we shall only understand how behavior works communicatively if we can understand the structures of its total configurations. We cannot fully understand how language operates without a grasp of its total behavioral and situational contexts. The same is true of any other aspect of behavior we might start with. However, as a strategy of investigation we have to limit our attention — and here I limit it to visible behavior. Such a limitation is, I believe, an arbitrary one, but so long as this is clearly understood, and so long as we continually try to see the behavioral items we have chosen for study within their wider contexts, this limitation should not impede us.

357

It is convenient to classify behavior, from the point of view of its relevance in communication, according to the sensory channel by which it may be detected. The broad classes of behavior or communicative modes which are thus distinguished may then further be divided into "instrumentalities" (a term coined by Scheflen during a talk with me), according to the effector system providing the behavior. Thus it is that I have singled out "visible behavior" as a class for study, which, as we shall see, may be further subdivided into at least three instrumentalities.

We know least about the role of *taste* and *heat* in communication. If taste functions communicatively at all, it does so only in very obscure and intimate situations. Thermal stimuli likewise can function only when people are in or near bodily contact with one another. There is no doubt, however, that the detection of bodily heat can play a part in the regulation of behavior between people. One might speculate on how far the detection of differential distribution of bodily heat plays a part in lovemaking, and E. T. Hall (1963) has cited one case of a girl who could always tell, so she claimed, whether the man she was dancing with was interested in her or not, from changes in temperature she could detect in the region of his lower abdomen. Also, we are occasionally aware of how we detect the extreme proximity of another person by feeling the heat of their body.

Touch, of course, has been much elaborated. It is widely used, and very important, though it has received almost no systematic attention. It is of particular importance in courtship, where a good deal of what goes on may be conveyed by stroking, squeezing, and pressing. It is important, in courtship, to know when and where one may touch the other, and what this may signify about the progress of the relationship, and of the different ways in which touch may be responded to.

Touch is not only important in courtship, of course. It

occurs commonly in greeting and parting, as in the handshake, which is itself a highly complex event. Whether the grip is strong or weak, prolonged or perfunctory, or if the pressure is varied within the grip, can have significance. Touch is also used within an encounter to soothe, to remonstrate, to reassure, and to heighten the intensity of the other's attention. I have observed how, with my own children, I use several different sorts of touch: there is the head stroke; the arm hold and the hand hold; tapping with the fingers on the shoulder; putting the whole hand on the shoulder. There are doubtless variations in pressure. Though I have not studied these variations systematically, my incidental observations suggest that each variety has its typical context. Thus: the rapid tap with the tip of the fingers on the shoulder occurs in contexts in which I am attempting to discipline the child into *not* doing something; the head stroke occurs when the child has been hurt or offended, and one is trying to soothe him; the head pat typically occurs *en passant* — perhaps it serves as a kind of reminder, both to the child, and to myself, of my affection for him.

There appear to be only two systematic studies of touch in the literature. One, by Frank (1957), is a general essay on the subject in which he demonstrates its importance, some of its functions, and draws attention to how there are cultural differences in the use of touch. The other, by Jourard (1966), is an investigation of where, on the body, an individual is touched, and by whom, though no account is taken of the context in which touching occurs. Jourard's "touch targets" were male and female college students. He showed that there are substantial differences in where people are touched, according to whether the toucher was the subject's father or mother, sibling, or friend of the same or opposite sex. This study was conducted among white students in Florida. An extension of this study to compare people of different cultural groups would be highly interesting, but an attempt to survey the contexts of touching is of prime importance, if we are to progress in our understanding of its use in communication.

Olfaction has been explored to some extent in its communicational functions, but since we, at least, have a rather poorly developed sense of smell, and since olfactory signals do not fade rapidly, and cannot be given direction, we find that smell tends to function for us as a marker of the persistent characteristics of the individual. In American and North European culture, at least, natural body smells are suppressed as much as possible, though these are then replaced by perfumes, particularly by women, and this clearly has some sort of signal function. In some cultures, according to E. T. Hall (1966), it is important, if we are talking with one another, that we be close enough to be able to smell them. If we are able to smell them it means that we are sufficiently close to be in good rapport. It has also been claimed by some that one can tell something about the individual's prevailing emotional state from the way he smells.

Hearing is one of the two distance-receptor systems most highly developed in us, and it is not surprising that the auditory communicative modes are the most highly developed. There are three classes of auditory instrumentalities that can be distinguished, though with further work it may be necessary to make further distinctions. These three types of instrumentality may be referred to as *strepitus,* or nonvocal sound; *phasis,* or vocal sounds that are not part of language; and of course, *speech* itself. We will say a few things about each.

Strepitus, first suggested as a separate category by Roger Westcott (1966, 1967), has been the least studied. Some varieties of non-vocal sound, such as hand-clapping, finger-snapping, thigh-slapping, table-pounding, or foot-stamping, are well-known and highly codified. Other varieties are more specialized, like key-jingling in prison warders or mental-hospital attendants. Other examples are sounds which are the incidental consequences of other actions, such as the sound of footsteps, a chair scraping, or someone closing a door, which are nonetheless often highly informative and may, in some cases, be fully incorporated into a communicative system.

Phasis (a term also suggested by Westcott) refers to vocal sounds which are not regarded as part of the language. These phenomena are referred to by some authors as *para-linguistic* phenomena. We include here emotional cries, sighs, whistles, gasps, and laughter, as well as "tones of voice," loudness of voice, pitch, resonance, and so on. So far as those aspects of vocalizations closely associated with the production of speech are concerned, extensive work has been done in developing methods for their systematic transcription, while rather less has been done in the investigation of how these aspects of vocalization actually function (but see Crystal, 1969).

Language needs hardly any comment here, though this is, of course, the most fully developed of all communicative modes, and it is the one that has received the most attention.

It is worth remarking in passing, however, that though an immense amount is now known about the structure of language and about the mechanism of its production, very much less attention has been paid to the employment of language in face-to-face interaction. No definitive set of statements can be made, for instance, about how much people speak, or when and where they speak, and though writers such as Joos (1962) and Bernstein (1964) have pointed out how language is differently organized according to the kinds of communication tasks the speaker is faced with, this aspect of language, of central concern to us as students of communicational behavior, has been very little studied, comparatively speaking, at least until recently. Hymes (1967) discusses the most recent developments.

Behavior which can be *seen* is included here, and we may distinguish three aspects: *appearance, proximation,* and *kinesis.*

Appearance refers simply to the way people look, and an analysis of this would have to include not only the significance of the individual's physique and physiognomy, but also of his clothing, use of cosmetics, and how he grooms his hair. Appearance is of great importance for signaling such

361

things as sex differences, age differences, and also, of course, such differences as differences in situational role, as well as nuances in the person's overt identity. It is through appearance that much of our self-image finds overt expression. Representative studies of appearance include Roach and Eicher (1965), Stone (1962), and Pear (1957).

Proximation refers to the communicative aspects of how people arrange themselves in space. As we shall see in more detail later, when people engage together in talk there are always consistencies in the way they arrange themselves in space in relation to one another, which have significance for the kinds of relations prevailing in the gathering; and people, by assuming particular positions in respect to another, can thereby communicate much about their attitude toward them, and their expectations about the interaction that is to ensue.

Kinesis refers to body motion and posture. Of all the visual modes, those employing body motion and posture are the most fully elaborated, and also they have been more studied than any of the others.

Body movement serves a wide variety of communicative functions. In some circumstances it can even come to take on all of the functions of language.

Almost any movement that a person makes that can be detected by another can be of significance in communication. Whether it is or not, however, is not something that can always be settled easily. On the one hand, there is a good deal of movement that may be said to be highly specialized for communication, and if we observe this we can be certain that it is communicatively significant, though we cannot, of course, without further investigation, say what its significance might be. Here would be included facial expressions and those movements of the hands and arms called gesticulations and gestures. One of the characteristics of much communicatively specialized behavior is that it almost always occurs only in an interactional situation. On the other hand, there is much that a person does that does not appear to be communicatively specialized, so that communicative signi-

362

ficance is much more ambiguous. For example, stroking the hair, drawing on a cigarette, jiggling the foot, smoothing the clothes, shifting one's stance or posture, are clearly not like gestures and facial expressions. However, though they can occur when the individual is alone, unlike gestures and facial expressions, they also occur in the presence of others and when they do so we can by no means discount their significance for communication.

It should be clear that each of these communicative modes and instrumentalities does not function separately from the others. Messages that can be sent by body motion, for instance, can also be sent by speech, and vice versa. Furthermore, there is often a complex relationship between the modes, so that they may be used *together* to convey *one* message. Compare, thus, the difference between the remark, "You are a very bad boy," said by a father to his son, in the one case with a severe face, in the other case with a smile. Reinterpreting, to state what the father "said" in each case, would be quite different. Nevertheless we do tend to find that some modes are more suited to sending certain kinds of messages than are others. For example, postures, or sustained body positions, as we shall see, probably function to provide background or "setting" for more short-lived acts like speech or gestures. Persistent features of the individual, such as his clothing, function to provide information about his identity and his situational role which persists through the various things he may do, providing context for them. Similarly, body motion and facial expressions are used in accompaniment to speech, providing commentary upon it, modifying it, and signaling its "direction" — all of which could be accomplished with much less efficiency if only one mode was available. The classification of communicative behavior into modes, then, is to be seen as a device of convenience only. Perhaps, when much more is understood, another kind of classification, in terms of functional communicative systems, might be offered — a classification that would then have more than mere convenience as its basis.

363

In any conversation, the participants must signal their presence in the conversation, indicate that they are attentive, and be able to so organize their activity of talking that they do not interrupt one another. In addition, each must respect the working agreement by which the roles of the participants are defined and sustained. In other words, in having a conversation, the participants must cooperate together to maintain a system of relationships, an organization, within which the talking, whatever it may be concerned with, can be carried out (see Goffman, 1967).

When people engage together in a conversation, they typically arrange themselves in space, adopt certain orientations to one another, and adopt certain postures which remain relatively stable for as long as the conversation continues. These relatively static features of behavior may be seen as providing a setting or context within which the exchange of talk can take place. These aspects of conversational behavior will be dealt with first, so that we can then go on to look at some of the ways in which people manage utterance exchanges within the gathering — how they signal whom they are addressing, for example, and how they coordinate their behavior so that interruption is avoided. Finally, we will see how an individual organizes his behavior in conversation.

Spatial Arrangements. Participants in conversation arrange themselves in space in a characteristic way. This point has been made by Goffman (1963) when he says that in occasions of talk the participants tend to form themselves into a "huddle" in which they are physically close to one another, facially oriented to one another with their backs to those others who may be present but who are not participants. Conversational gatherings are as a rule, thus, immediately perceivable. Members of such gatherings stand or sit relatively closer to one another than they do to others who are not participants, and they tend to orient themselves to one another in such a way that each can turn his head to face another without any substantial change in the orientation of his upper body.

By such arrangements, the participants in a gathering signal to one another their joint engagement, and they also signal to others who may be nearby that they are busy together, and thus not accessible to new engagements. It is also important to observe that the particular shape that the gathering assumes which, once formed, tends to be stable for the duration of the encounter, and reflects aspects of the relationships between the gathering members. Thus where the participation rights of the members tend to be equal, as in informal conversations between friends, the gathering tends to assume a circular form. Where there is some differentiation in role in interaction, however, we tend to find some spatial differentiation among the gathering members. Thus a chairman or leader tends to assume a position, relative to the other members, from which he can most easily command the attention of all of them. If the gathering is sitting around a rectangular table, the most influential member is likely to be found at the table's "head." Several studies have confirmed this traditional observation, but have also shown that even in gatherings where the participants are initially equal in their participation rights, the individuals who occupy "head" positions from which they can attend easily to a larger number of the other members tend to emerge, in the course of interaction, as more influential than the others (see Sommer, 1961; Strodtbeck and Hook, 1961; Hare and Bales, 1963).

It also seems that the kinds of spatial arrangements individuals adopt in a conversation are related to the kind of task they are undertaking, or the kind of conversation they are going to have. In one study (Sommer, 1965) the spatial arrangements adopted by pairs were compared, when the pairs were either cooperating together, competing with one another, or working separately, each on his own task. It was found that for competitors, the strongest tendency was for people to sit opposite one another, whereas in cooperative pairs, as where they were having a discussion on some point

365

of mutual interest, the tendency was for participants to sit either side by side or, more characteristically, to sit at a diagonal to one another.

It has also been pointed out that the distance participants are likely to stand or sit from one another will vary according to the kind of interaction they are engaged in. As E. T. Hall (1964, 1966) has suggested, for intimate conversations, where the participants are engaged in a mutual sharing of feeling, with little exchange of external information, the distance adopted will rarely be greater than eighteen inches, and is usually much less. In conversations or discussions where much new and external information is being exchanged, however, the distances adopted will vary between five and ten feet, and where an individual is addressing a number of others in a formal fashion, distances of upward of ten feet will be adopted. Hall points out that at different distances the senses operate differently, and that this will have consequences for the kinds of communications channels that can be used. At intimate distances, for example, touch, smell, and heat sense can all be used in the transmission of information, and each may observe changes in breathing rate of the other, and changes in the state of the epidermal capillaries. At greater distances, only vision and hearing can be used, and with increasing distance these are less and less effective for fine detail. Thus it is that, with increasing distance, we find that language becomes more formal and that speakers come to rely less and less upon such listener behavior as head nods, changes in facial expression, and so on, which, in more intimate types of interchange, play such an important part.

It is important to remember that the distances adopted by conversationalists will also depend upon the settings in which they take place. For instance, people are likely to stand nearer one another in open or public settings (such as streets, or parks) than they are in closed or private ones (such as offices and living rooms) (Little, 1965, and Sommer, 1959). This may be because the distance adopted in conversation not only reflects the kind of interaction, but it also expresses

366

the relationship between the encounter, as a joint venture, and the other activities that may be going on round about. In a public setting, on the other hand, closer distances may be adopted for conversations because the participants must emphasize their "withness," in a way that is not necessary in a living room or office.

It will be evident from these hints and suggestions, that how an individual places himself in relation to the other members of a gathering he may be participating in, can be one of the ways in which he can express his position in it. He can choose a *distance,* and thus signal the degree of intimacy he hopes to maintain in the interaction. He can choose a *location* (such as a "head" position) to signal his claim to a particular kind of role in the gathering. Clearly, however, the particular location in a gathering an individual occupies depends upon the particular locations occupied by the other members. Hence, for an individual to maintain a location in a gathering, this means that all members have agreed to the spatial dispositions of one another. A gathering that is stable in its spatial arrangement, therefore, is a gathering that has a stable consensus about the current level of intimacy, relative dominance, and other role relationships of the members. Changes in the spatial arrangement will reflect changes in this consensus. An analysis of the process by which such stable arrangements are arrived at would constitute an analysis of that initial process of negotiation which characterizes the early stages of all encounters. Studies of the formation of the physical arrangements of gatherings remain to be done, however.

Orientation. In dealing with the spatial arrangements of gatherings, we have taken it for granted that the participants are all facing either directly toward one another, or at least in the same direction. It is highly unusual for people to converse with one another when they are back to back, and if they do so they are unlikely to do so for very long. However, within the limits of "facing inward," there are many possible variations.

In looking at how interactants are oriented to one

another, one may consider the degree to which they are directly facing one another, or the degree to which they are *vis-à-vis*. Scheflen (1964) has suggested that when people are fully *vis-à-vis* they are likely to be engaged in a direct interpersonal transaction. The less directly they are turned to one another, the more they are also sharing some focus of attention outside their direct relationship. Thus it is, for example, that we find that when people greet one another, which is a purely interpersonal event, they tend to do so *vis-à-vis*. Once the greeting is over, and they continue their reciprocal conversation on some joint topic, they tend to turn away from one another slightly, placing their bodies more or less at right angles and directly facing one another only at intervals by turning the head to each other. Similarly, in the more intense moments of courtship or fighting, the participants face one another directly. In conversation one may observe how a speaker may turn to full *vis-à-vis* with his addressee when he is talking with particular emphasis. To fully face another is to maximize the intensity of one's address to him, and it has the effect of maximizing his attention to oneself.

In considering how people in conversations orient to one another, it is useful to consider their bodies as divisible into three segments: the head, the torso, and the hips. The head is the most mobile of these, and varies in its orientation most often. The hips change their orientation least often, and when they change they change with them the segment of the environment to which the other two parts of the body may be oriented. In seated groups, especially where there are more than two, how people orient to one another becomes more complex. We may observe, for example, how people may face the different segments of their bodies in slightly different directions, and so signal that they are including in their attention more than just one other person. This is most clearly seen in groups of three, where each may orient his lower body to one participant and his upper body to the other, and he then will look from one to the other as he speaks.

368

The above notes on bodily orientation are based largely upon the observations of Scheflen. Mehrabian (1969) and Rosenfeld (1965) have reported experimental studies in which they find that a subject will vary the direction of his orientation to another in relation to his attitude to him, and Hall (1963) has included orientation in his system of proxemic notation.

However, most of the work that has been done on orientation in interaction has been concerned with the orientation of the head, or, as it is usually referred to, direction of the gaze. Here studies have been made in which the total amount of the time an individual spends looking at another is related to his attitude to the other and also to personality dynamics of the subject. This work has been well summarized in several recent articles. In general, it appears that in situations where the participants are equal in status, and where interaction is cooperative, people look at one another more, the more they like one another. However, the amount of "looking" the other will receive will be much less if he is of very low relative status (Hearn, 1957, and Efran, 1968). Where the subjects are low in "need affiliation" they look less than do subjects high in "need affiliation" in cooperative interaction. They look more than subjects high in "need affiliation" when the interaction is competitive (Exline, 1963). One study has examined patterns of gaze in a gathering of several persons. This was a seminar study of seven persons conducted by Rita Weisbrod (1965), where who looked at whom was systematically recorded over several sessions. She found that who looked at whom was closely related to patterns of power relations in the group. Thus the person who was looked at most when he spoke was perceived by the other group members, and by himself, to be the most influential in the group. It also emerged that sub-groupings of individuals, in terms of perceived mutual support, were marked by patterns of exchanged glances. In this situation, personal preferences among members were not marked by mutual looking, and whereas studies by others have reported relationships between amount of looking and such personality variables as "affiliativeness," in this study this was not found.

Weisbrod's findings point out clearly the need for more extended naturalistic studies of gaze behavior, before we can embark on generalizations about its significance, beyond the point that to "look at" another person is one of the most obvious ways in which one signals one's attention to him. The significance of this attention, and thus the significance of the act of looking, depends upon the context in which it takes place.

Posture. When people gather for conversation they hold their bodies in a particular arrangement. They may stand, sit, kneel, squat, or even lie down. Within these broad categories there are many variations in posture that are possible, though only some of these will be found. Some postures are not found because they are physically difficult to maintain for any length of time, but even within the range of easily maintainable postures, for any given gathering we usually see a considerable limitation in the variety of posture. In some situations — on the military parade ground or in religious ceremonies, for instance — the postures assumed by the participants are specified explicitly. More usually, participants in a gathering will unthinkingly assume postures that are appropriate to the occasion, but what these postures are — whether "relaxed" or "formal" for instance — will signal the atmosphere of the occasion. At conferences or seminars, for example, people do not usually sit on the floor or lie down, though they may do this at picnics. At least in some sections of society, there is a proper way to sit at the dinner table, and children are frequently corrected and trained in the postural style they should adopt.

Scheflen (1964) has pointed out that the relationship between the posture adopted by one participant and the posture adopted by another is likely to be consistent with other aspects of their relationship to one another in the interaction. Thus he suggests that where interactants sit in similar or congruent postures, they are sharing a common viewpoint or perspective. Thus people in parallel orientation, where

370

they are both attending to the same focus, are likely to show similar postures, whereas if they are attending to different foci they are likely to show different postures. Charny (1966) has investigated this suggestion in a study of a psychotherapy session in which he showed that when patient and therapist displayed similar postures they were much more *en rapport* than when they did not. Thus during periods of congruent posture, the patient talked objectively, whereas when their postures were dissimilar the patient was more withdrawn and tended to "act out" emotionally. Charny also noted that periods of postural congruency increased as the interview developed in time. Subsequent to completing the study Charny learned that the therapist used in the study, who was of Rogerian persuasion, deliberately sought to be posturally congruent with his patients as part of his technique of gaining rapport. What was not analyzed in this study was *which* postures it was that the therapist chose to try to "mirror." A viewing of the film suggested that the postures adopted by the patient when she was not congruent with the therapist were postures that are not usually seen in conversation. During non-congruent periods in the film she would sit with her shoulders hunched forward and her head hung forward. It would seem to be worth pursuing the idea that when somebody is trying to build "rapport" with another, there is only a limited range of postures in the other he may attempt to mirror, since there are only certain kinds of postural relations within which a jointly oriented exchange can take place.

Where there is marked incongruence in postures, this often reflects sharp differences in role relations within the gathering. This is most clearly seen in a lecture, where the lecturer stands while his audience sits. An individual may also adopt a posture dissimilar to that of another as a way of showing dissociation from him. Wherever, within a gathering, there are differences in status, this is likely to be marked in differences in posture. Higher status members are more likely to show greater postural relaxation than lower status members, for example.

371

In gatherings of more than two participants, people may often use their bodies as if they were divided into several separate parts. Just as we saw in the discussion of orientation, people may maintain some degree of postural congruence with several different participants at once. Or they may show congruence with some members at the same time that they show incongruence of posture with others. In this way each participant may, in how he relates his posture to the others present, express the multiple nature of his relationships to them.

Apart from the work of Charny, cited above, Scheflen has been the main source of observations on postural relations, though studies have also been reported by Machotka (1965) and Mehrabian (1969). Detailed systematic observations are still very much needed, however, before the significance of posture in interaction can be fully described.

The Regulation of Utterance Exchanges

So far we have considered those aspects of behavior in conversation that are maintained for the duration of the occasion. The spatial arrangement of a gathering and its associated postures and orientation may be considered as the setting for talking and listening, the activities with which the business of the conversation is carried forward. This setting provides the conditions within which conversational activity becomes possible.

When a person speaks in a gathering, or in some other way actively sends explicit messages, these messages, conveyed by a combination of utterances and gestures, are always addressed to some target, or addressee. We find that the addressee or recipient tends to organize his behavior in relation to that of the addressor. That is, we find that speaker and listener or listeners tend to exhibit a relatedness of behavior so that they may be said to perform together in what I call an *axis of interaction,* which may be considered to be the basic unit, at the social level of organization, of any gathering. In many gatherings we have an axis of interaction in which a speaker directly addresses one specific other member while the other members of the group give their attention to what is going on in varying degrees. In other situations, a speaker may so address another group member as to make the axis of interaction more exclusive. A speaker may also address more than one individual at a time — indeed, he may address the whole group. For the moment, however, let us consider simply the speaker/listener relationship in the case where this constitutes single individuals. What does such a relationship look like, in terms of what these individuals do?

First, the persons in an axis will be jointly oriented toward one another. Usually they will repeatedly scan one another visually, and from time to time their eyes will meet. This orientation toward another, with intermittent aiming of the eyes toward him, is one of the principal ways in which a person signals to whom his behavior is directed. In "aiming the eyes" what we characteristically observe is that the head is repeatedly returned to the same position (in the case of a speaker), where the head then pauses. When the speaker is not looking at his addressee he looks up, or down, or to the side, but not at another person. In the case where the speaker is addressing several others at once, his repeated positioning will be replaced by a repeated scanning of those who constitute the recipients of his address.

Looking at the addressee and looking away, so characteristic of a speaker, have been found to have a systematic relation to the structure of the speaker's utterances. Thus, in a study of this in two-person conversations (Kendon, 1967), it was found that the speaker tended to look away from his listener as he began an utterance, and in many cases somewhat in advance of its beginning; that he looked back at his listener as he approached the end of his utterance, usually during the last phrase of it; and that he then continued to look at him for some time after he finished speaking. During the course of the long utterance, the speaker would characteristically glance at his interlocutor as he came to the end of each phrase, but he would always look

373

away again just before he resumed speaking. Hesitations within an utterance were always accompanied by looking away.

It was suggested that this patterning of gaze in relation to speech, though it could clearly have important functions for the speaker, for instance in relation to his need, on the one hand, for information about his interlocutor, and his need, on the other, to cut out input as he worked out the details of his speech, it could also function communicationally. It was suggested that by looking away just in advance of speaking, the speaker could signal his intent to claim the floor. By looking at his listener, and sustaining this look, as he brought his utterance to an end, he could signal his intent to finish. This could thus be a cue to the listener to begin speaking.

Secondly, listener and speaker in a interactional axis are joined together in movement. As a speaker begins his address, often the listener will move in time with the speaker and in the same way as the speaker is moving. This commonly involves the listener's engaging in a postural shift, or head movement of the speaker as he begins his address, but in some instances it may include movements of the limbs as well. It is as if the listener momentarily dances the speaker's dance, before settling in to a more or less sustained "listening position." This rather gross sharing of movement that occurs at the beginning of a speech may have the effect of both enhancing the speaker's attention to the listener and of facilitating the listener's attention to the speaker, since by moving with him, the listener can "tune in" to the rhythm of the speaker. This dancing the other's dance is usually not maintained for very long, though it may reappear intermittently during the speaker's address if the speaker speaks for some time, but close analysis of films of speaker/listener pairs has shown that the minor or incidental movements of a listener — his eye blinks, minor changes in the position of his head or hands, and so forth — are performed in synchrony with the flow of speech of the speaker (Condon and Ogston, 1966, 1967, and Kendon, 1970).

374

In addition, listeners who are directly addressed, unlike those who are not, also exhibit a particular set of gestures, such as head nods, and also certain changes in facial expression, which are shown by those who are not as a rule directly part of the interactional axis.

When there is a change in the axis of interaction, this is marked by shifts in posture and orientation of the various participants. For each new axis, a new set of postural relations may be established, or there may be a period when there is considerable change in posture, in spatial position, and in orientation, and then the original arrangement is restored.

The coordination of movement between speaker and listener referred to above may serve to keep them mutually attuned to one another's behavior, and in this way facilitate the maintenance of their attention. Close observation also shows, however, that movement coordination may occur before the members of an interactional axis are explicitly engaged with one another. Instances where this occurs suggest that one of the ways that an individual can signal to another that he wants attention from him is by sharing his rhythm of movement. In one example described in more detail elsewhere (Kendon, 1972b), two members of a discussion group are observed to move into the joint orientation characteristic of an axis of interaction before either of them speaks and, furthermore, they orient to one another simultaneously. Prior to this, one member of the pair had begun to move with the other, as he leaned forward to pick up a cup of coffee on the table in front of him. It appeared that by doing so, the individual in question had signaled in a nonexplicit way that he was ready for attention from the other. Initiating an axis of interaction with another is always somewhat risky, since there is always the possibility that the other party does not wish to reciprocate. By simply picking up the rhythm of another person's movements one can establish a connection with him which at the same time does not commit one to a positive initiation. If, after having joined the rhythm of another, the other makes no move toward establishing an axis with one, one can continue as if one had made no attempt at initiation, and no one's face is thereby lost.

The Individual's Performance

Scheflen (1964) has proposed that an individual's performance in interaction may be seen as organized into a set of units, related hierarchically. These units are units of communication, and Scheflen's particular contribution has been to point out how these units are marked by contrasting bodily positions or postures, and how boundaries between them may be marked by shifts in bodily positions. At the highest level we may distinguish the *presentation,* which constitutes simply the individual's presence in a configuration. This unit is characterized by a relatively stable physical location in the individual, and it is bounded by changes in the individual's location.

Within an individual's presence in a gathering, or within his presentation, an individual may be said to take up or to enact one or more *positions*. Typically, each participant in a gathering tends to have a limited repertoire of such positions, which may be said to constitute the various sub-parts of his *role* in it. Each of these positions, Scheflen has observed, is marked by a different postural arrangement, and the change from one position to the next is marked by a shift in posture.

This may best be seen in an illustration. I observed a lecturer whose performance could be seen to be made up of four different major units, or positions, as follows: *lecturing position,* in which he talked continuously to the audience; a *question-asking position,* in which he invited people to ask questions; a *question-receiving position,* in which he listened as a specific question was being asked; and a *question-answering position,* in which he answered the question. Each of these different positions was distinguished from the other not only in the way he spoke, but also in the postural arrangement he adopted, and the change from one to another was

376

marked by, or might be said to be announced by, a change in his posture. For the whole of the time that he was in his role as lecturer, he sat on a table facing the group, with his legs swinging clear of the floor. During *lecturing,* he sat with his spine somewhat curved, his arms resting on his thighs, his hands loosely clasped together. When he finished lecturing, he put his hands under his thighs, palms down on the table, and raised his head somewhat, scanning the group with raised eyebrows, asking for questions. In the *question-asking* position, he merely scanned the group with raised eyebrows. As soon as someone began to ask a question he craned his neck forward, turned his head to one side, slightly "cocked" at the time, raised his brows maximally and looked at the questioner from the corners of his eyes. This was the *question-receiving* position. At the end of the question, the lecturer turned his head frontally again rapidly, pushed his neck forward, hunched his shoulders, straightened his arms, generally increased the level of tenseness in his posture, and maintained this posture for the duration of his answer: this posture change and position characterized his *question-answering* position.

Within each of these positions, further units can be discerned, which Scheflen has termed the "point." For instance, in lecturing, a lecturer will make a series of statements that comprise his total discourse. In continuous speech, as in the lecture, such segments would probably correspond to the series of "points" that a lecturer might be said to make as he talks. A psychotherapist, in interpreting, may first give a résumé of something the patient has said, before giving his interpretation of it.

Scheflen (1964) suggests that one of the ways in which each point is distinguished from another is by a change in the position of the head. He reports that interactants in psychotherapy show a repertoire of three to five different head positions which occur repeatedly. He gives an example of two "points" a therapist was observed to use repeatedly during interchanges with a patient during an "interpreting" position. While listening to him, her head was slightly lowered, cocked to the right, averting eyes from the patient. At the termination of this point she would raise her head up, then hold it erect and, looking directly at the patient, produce an interpretative remark. As she ended it, she turned her head to the far right, away from the patient. Likewise, in some recent work of my own (Kendon, 1972a) I have analyzed in detail the way in which movement associated with speech is organized, and how it is related to the accompanying speech. In this it became clear that associated with each unit of speech approximately equivalent to the sentence, there was a distinct movement of the head which always *began* from the same place, and always ended up at the same place.

To re-state what we have been saying, if we observe a participant in an interaction, we are likely to observe that he will arrange his body in a series of different postures, and that within each one of these postural arrangements he may be observed to "cycle" his head positions. These segments of body motion and position are found to correspond to segments in other aspects of his behavior, notably his speech. If we look in more detail at the flow of speech and how body motion is organized in relation to it, we find that successive units of speech are "set off" from one another by contrasting patterns of body movement, even to very low levels of speech organization. Thus, in the study referred to (Kendon, 1972a), a speaker who was speaking at length was studied. His discourse, which lasted for about two minutes, was analyzed into a number of different sets of speech units, at each of five levels of integration (very roughly, phrases, sentences, sub-paragraphs, paragraphs, and the whole discourse). For each level of organization of speech we were able to find contrasting patterns of body motion by which each unit at that level was made distinct from each other unit. Thus, for the whole *discourse,* the speaker held himself in a different posture from the one he held when listening before speaking. Associated with each "paragraph" of the discourse, the speaker gesticulated in a different fashion — over the first he used only his right hand, over the second he used only his

378

left, and over the third he used both. Then, each "sentence" was distinguished by a different pattern of gesticulation. Thus in the second "paragraph" the speaker used movements of the whole arm over the first "sentence," but movements only of the wrist and fingers over the second. Over the third, he lifted his hand up, then lowered it again, and so on. At a still lower level of organization it was found that each phrase was distinguished from each succeeding phrase again by a different pattern of movement. Over the first phrase, for instance, the speaker moved his arm out and then moved it in over the second phrase, and so on. Going below the phrase, to syllables and to the sound units within syllables, as Condon and Ogston (1966, 1967) have shown, we again find contrasting changes in body movement.

This finding raises many questions, many of them having to do with the role of movement in the production of speech. I shall not pursue these here. Presumably, however, the "marking" of speech units by movement does have some communicative function. Among other things, it probably facilitates the listener's attention to the speaker, though no work has been done to investigate this hypothesis.

In Conclusion

What I described, in outlining Scheflen's observations on posture and posture shifts in relation to units of communication, takes us as far as being able to say that one of the ways in which units of communication within an individual's performance are marked is in postural or body part shifts or changes. But we have not dealt with the question of *how* these different units are distinguished from one another. How are we led to label them as "questioning," "contending," "flirting," and so forth? Scheflen's hypothesis is that there are a limited set of modes of presenting to others, though neither he, nor anyone else, has given us a catalog of what these modes might be. Each mode of presenting, however, is characterized by a number of properties, though it is very doubtful that we could finally specify what these

379

properties are, since this would always have to be done in terms of the patterning of the behaviors involved and in terms of the relation of the unit to its larger context. However, I make the following suggestions.

We may distinguish a number of different postures, which appear to function as signals of "attitude." The thrust-forward trunk, combined with the raised head and eyebrows of the "question-asking" lecturer described earlier, possibly speaks for itself. An expanded chest and erect posture are, at least in males, "challenging." We perhaps know, too, what "seductive" postures are like, what "subordinate" postures are like, and what postures of "contempt" are like, and doubtless many others. What is needed is a criterion to distinguish "units" of posture, and careful observation to delimit the contexts of occurrence of such units, if we are to be able to make clear statements about postures.

Second, for a given presentation, there may be characteristic accompanying sets of displays. This is suggested by among other things the work of Rosenfeld (1966, 1967), who instructed subjects to act in such a way as to make another like them, or to dislike them, and he showed that there were consistent differences in the amount of smiling, in the amount of gesticulation used during speech, and so on.

Third, there are probably differences in the way in which a person relates to that of others, according to his prevailing position. Thus one of the characteristics of persons in superordinate status in a group, such as the doctor in a psychotherapy session, or a chairman in a seminar, at least in the initial stages of the interaction, is that he does *not* accommodate his pace of action to those around him. They, instead, accommodate their pacing to his.

Fourth, different positions are distinguished by distinct speech styles — for instance, in the type of vocal qualifiers used — and we also observe that different linguistic aspects may be associated with different positions. This, for example, was one of the implications of the early observations of Bales (1958) on the way in which people in different roles in discussion groups tend, in the things they say, to be differentiated from one another.

I have described some of the regularities in visible behavior that are associated with the activity of face-to-face interaction. In much of what I have said I have had to be content with describing these regularities and with merely saying that these postural and spatial patterns, and these patterns of movement, occur, and that they are thus at least *available* as a means of communication, though we do not have as yet the necessary evidence to say conclusively that they are so used. However, I make no apology for this, for it has been my intention to try to give an idea of how visible behavior might work in interaction, rather than merely survey only what has been firmly established.

I have stressed how visible behavior serves to organize people together into social encounters, how it appears to provide much of the necessary background and context that make speech possible. But, as I have tried to remind you, this is only part of the story. I have omitted much about gesture and gesticulation, and I have said nothing about facial displays. It should also be clear that many of the statements I have made are really of a most preliminary nature. I have attempted, instead, to provide a sketch. At the same time, I hope I have indicated how very much more in the way of purely descriptive research there is that needs to be done.

〰〰〰〰〰〰〰〰〰〰〰〰〰〰〰〰〰〰〰〰〰 *Bibliography*

ARGYLE, M. and KENDON, A. (1967), The experimental analysis of the social performance. In *Advances in Experimental Social Psychology*, 3, ed. L. Berkowitz. New York: Academic Press.

BALES, R. (1958), Task roles and social roles in problem solving groups. In *Readings in Social Psychology*, 3rd ed., eds. E. Macoby, T. Newcomb, and E. Hartley. New York: Holt.

381

BERNSTEIN, B. (1964), Elaborated and restricted codes: their social origins and some consequences. *Amer. Anthropologist*, 66:6 Part 2, 55-69.

BIRDWHISTELL, R. (1970), *Kinesics and context:* In *Essays on Body Motion Communication*. Philadelphia: University of Pennsylvania Press.

CHARNY, E. (1966), Psychosomatic manifestations of rapport in psychotherapy. *Psychosomatic Medicine*, 28: 305-315.

CONDON, W. and OGSTON, W. (1966), Sound film analysis of normal and pathological behavior patterns. *J. of Nerv. and Ment. Disease*, 143: 338-347.

—— (1967), A segmentation of behavior. *J. of Psychiat. Res.*, 5: 221-235.

CRYSTAL, D. (1969), *Prosodic Systems and Intonation in English*. Cambridge: Cambridge Univ. Press.

DARWIN, C. (1872), *The Expression of the Emotions in Man and Animals*. London: John Murray.

DIEBOLD, A. R., Jr. (1968), Anthropological perspectives: anthropology and the comparative psychology of communicative behavior. In *Animal Communication: Techniques of Study and Results of Research,* ed. T. Sebeok. Bloomington: Indiana University Press.

DUNCAN, S. (1969), Nonverbal communication. *Psychological Bulletin*, 72: 118-137.

EFRAN, J. (1968), Looking for approval; effects on visual behavior of approbation from persons differing in importance. *J. of Per. and Soc. Psychol.*, 10: 21-25.

EFRON, D. (1941), *Gesture and Environment,* New York: Kings Crown Press.

EKMAN, P. and FRIESEN, W. (1969), The repertoire of nonverbal behavior: categories, origins, usage and coding. *Semiotica*, 1:49-98.

——, SORENSON, E., and FRIESEN, W. (1969), Pancultural elements in facial displays of emotion. *Science*, 164: 86-88.

EXLINE, R. (1963), Explorations in the process of person perception: visual interaction in relation to competition, sex, and need for affiliation. *J. of Personality*, 31: 1-20.

FELIPE, N. and SOMMER, R. (1966), Invasions of personal space. *Social Problems*, 14: 206-214.

FRANK, L. (1957), Tactile communication, *Genetic Psychology Monographs*, 56: 209-255.

GLEASON, H. (1961), *An Introduction of Descriptive Linguistics*, New York. Holt, Rinehart and Winston.

GOFFMAN, E. (1963), *Behavior in Public Places*, New York: The Free Press.

———— (1967), *Interaction Ritual: Essays on Face-to-Face Behavior*, Chicago: Aldine.

GRANT, E. (1969), Human facial expression. *Man*, 4: 525-536.

GUMPERZ, J. and HYMES, D., eds. (1972), *Directions in Socio-Linguistics*. New York: Holt, Rinehart and Winston.

HALL, E. (1963), A system for the notation of proxemic behavior. *American Anthropologist*, 65: 1003-1026.

———— (1964), Silent assumptions in social communication. *Res. Pub. Assoc. Nerv. and Ment. Disease*, 42: 41-55.

———— (1966), *The Hidden Dimension*, New York: Doubleday.

HARE, A. and BALES, R. (1963), Seating position and small group interaction, *Sociometry*, 26: 480-486.

HEARN, G. (1957), Leadership and the spatial factor in small groups. *J. of Abnormal and Social Psychol.*, 54: 269-272.

HEWES, G. (1955), World distribution of certain postural habits, *Amer. Anthropol.*, 57: 231-244.

HOCKETT, C. (1958), *A Course in Modern Linguistics*, New York: Macmillan.

HYMES, D. (1967), Models of the interaction of language and social setting. *J. of Social Issues*, 23: 8-28.

IZZARD, C. (1971), *The Face of Emotion*, New York: Appleton-Century-Crofts.

JOOS, M. (1962), The five clocks. *Inter. J. of Amer. Linguistics*, 28: V.

JOURARD, S. (1966), An exploratory study of body-accessibility. *British J. of Soc. and Clin. Psychol.*, 5: 221-231.

383

KENDON, A. (1967), Some functions of gaze direction in social interaction. *Acta Psychologica,* 26: 22-63.

———— (1970), Movement coordination in social interaction: Some examples described. *Acta Psychologica,* 32: 1-25.

———— (1972a), Some relationships between body motion and speech: an analysis of an example. In *Studies in Dyadic Interaction: A Research Conference,* eds. A. Siegman and B. Pope. New York: Pergammon Press.

———— (1972b), The role of visible behavior in the organization of social interaction. In *Social Communication and Movement,* M. Von Cranach and I. Vine, eds. London: Academic Press.

LA BARRE, W. (1964), Paralinguistics, kinesics, and cultural anthropology. In *Approaches to Semiotics,* eds. T. Sebeok, A. Hayes, and M. C. Bateson. The Hague: Morton and Co.

LITTLE, K. (1965), Personal space. *J. of Exper. and Soc. Psychol.,* 1: 237-247.

LYONS, J. (1968), *Theoretical Linguistics.* Cambridge: Cambridge Univ. Press.

MACHOTKA, P. (1965), Body movement as communication. *Dialogues: Behavioral Science Research.* Boulder, Colorado: Western Interstate Commission for Higher Education.

MEHRABIAN, A. (1969), Significance of posture and position in the communication of attitude and status relationships. *Psychol. Bull.,* 71: 359-372.

OLSON, D. (1970), Language and thought: aspects of a cognitive theory of semantics. *Psychol. Review,* 77: 257-273.

PEAR, T. (1957), *Personality, Appearance, and Speech.* London: Allen and Unwin.

ROACH, M. and EICHER, J. (1965), *Dress, Adornment, and the Social Order.* New York: John Wiley.

ROMMETVEIT, R. (1968), *Words, Meanings, and Messages: Theory and Experiments in Psycholinguistics.* Oslo: Universitetsforlaget and New York: Academic Press.

384

ROSENFELD, H. (1965), Effect of an approval seeking induction on interpersonal proximity. *Psychol. Reports,* 17: 120-122.

────── (1966), Instrumental affiliative functions of facial and gestural expressions. *J. of Person. and Soc. Psychol.,* 4: 65-72.

────── (1967), Non-verbal reciprocation of approval: An experimental analysis. *J. of Exper. and Soc. Psychol.,* 3: 102-111.

SAPIR, E. (1927), The unconscious patterning of behavior in society. In *The Unconscious,* ed. E. Dummer. New York: Knopf.

SCHEFLEN, A. (1964), The significance of posture in communication systems. *Psychiatry,* 27: 316-321.

────── (1965), Natural history method of psychotherapy. In *Methods of Research in Psychotherapy,* eds. L. Gottschalk and A. Auerbach. New York: Appleton-Century-Crofts.

SOMMER, R. (1959), Studies in personal space, *Sociometry,* 22: 247-260.

────── (1961), Leadership and group geography. *Sociometry,* 24: 99-109.

────── (1965), Further studies of small group ecology. *Sociometry,* 28: 337-348.

────── (1967), Sociofugal space. *Amer. J. of Sociol.,* 72: 654-660.

STONE, G. (1962), Appearance and the self. In *Human Behavior and Social Processes: An Interactionist Approach,* ed. A. Rose. Boston: Houghton-Mifflin Co.

STRODTBECK, F. and HOOK, L. (1961), The social dimension of a twelve man jury table. *Sociometry,* 24: 397-415.

VON CRANACH, M. (In press), The role of orienting behavior in human interaction. In *The Use of Space by Animals and Men,* ed. A. Esser. New York: Plenum Press.

VINE, I. (1970), Communication by facial-visual signals: a review and analysis of their role in face-to-face encounters. In *Social Behavior in Animals and Man,* ed. J. Crook. London: Academic Press.

385

WEISBROD, R. (1965), Looking behavior in a discussion group. Term paper submitted for Psychology 546 under the direction of Professor Longabaugh, Cornell University, Ithaca, New York.

WESTCOTT, R. (1966), Introducing coenetics. *American Scholar,* 35 : 342-356.

—————— (1967), Strepital communication. *The Bulletin,* 12 : 30-34.

WOODWORTH, R. and SCHLOSBERG, H. (1954), *Experimental Psychology.* New York : Holt.

section three

<hr>

Teachers and Learners

introduction

A. Ferber

The process of family therapy is a complex system of behaviors. The therapist's contribution to this process includes much, but not all, of his behavioral repertoire. Transactions with his immediate group of colleagues, his family therapy training network, and the tribe of family therapists contribute to each therapy. The therapist's spouse is almost always an important part of the process, and to a lesser and more variable extent, so are his children, extended family, and friends.

In the shaping of family therapists, how do the teachers

389

and learners work upon each other? What happens to people as they become family therapists? What do they and their intimates endure? What sorts of experiences and characteristics seem to well-equip or ill-equip persons for becoming family therapists? These are the substantive issues in this section of the book.

The Tribe of Family Therapists

We use the word tribe because it seems to fit the degree and kind of organization that family therapists have. Tribes are more personal and less professional in their relations with one another than is common in America today. Family therapists form a tribe or reference group composed mostly of Americans, eighty percent of whom are forty-nine years of age or less. They come from varied backgrounds — forty percent are social workers, forty percent are psychiatrists and psychologists, and the remaining twenty percent are clergymen, nurses, physicians, child psychiatrists, etc. Men outnumber women by a ratio of 2:1. In addition, there is no uniform religious affiliation — virtually all faiths are represented, including those with no religious affiliation. No decisive set of circumstances is associated with initiating a therapist's interest in family therapy. However, there is unanimity among family therapists that their desire to treat people more effectively was a most important influence.* This tribe is determined to keep its boundaries to the rest of the society blurred and relatively open. The tribe refuses to organize formally and be clearly identified as different from many other tribes. Repeated attempts by a minority from the tribe to organize formally have been defeated. Its members retain significant professional identities and memberships other than that of "family therapist." Our tribe differs from some other evangelical tribes of this century

---

*Demographic data based on *The Field of Family Therapy: A Report of the Committee on the Family of the Group for the Advancement of Psychiatry,* pp. 7-11. New York : Science House, 1968.

(e.g. the psychoanalytic movement, the Communist Party in this country) in this and several other key dimensions.

The tribe is a comparatively open social system. There are indistinct gradations of membership. Actively doing family therapy is the only credential. There are no certificates that assure a permanent rank. Status hierarchies exist, but are fluid and carry somewhat fewer dominance and deference rituals than are common in other professional groups. This commitment to low hierarchical distance combines with an anti-bureaucratic posture. Existing bureaucratic institutions are viewed with considerable skepticism, and are considered to do at least as much harm as good.

A language for the tribe has been rapidly developing and changing, and continues to do so. The language is part argot* and part technical jargon.† The dual purposes of the language seem to be: to create a boundary between the members of the tribe and outsiders, so the tribal members may mystify outsiders and share a communion with each other; and second, to communicate relevant shared experiences for which little common language exists. The language is impenetrable to most people who have not shared the experiences of sitting with family groups while the families do serious business. There is both a rapid rate and a large amount of information flow among members, and among the networks that comprise the tribe. Members often visit each other and watch each other at work. Gossip circulates rapidly. Films, video-tapes, and audio-tapes of each other's work circulate within the networks of the tribe.

There is an exceptionally high degree of candid description of the behaviors of the members of the tribe. Most social systems have much behavior that is either not described,

*Argot: A special vocabulary and idiom used by a particular underworld group especially as a means of private communication; the language of a particular social group or class.
†Jargon: Technical terminology or characteristic idiom of a special activity or group.
Definitions from: *Webster's Seventh New Collegiate Dictionary*, pp. 47 and 454. G. and C. Merriam Co., Springfield, Massachusetts. 1965.

391

or systemically misrepresented in order to mask and mystify. The unusual candor of family therapists stems both from the larger amount of exposure to each other's actual work, and from a shared conviction that distortion or omission of accurate descriptions of behavior are bad things in families and other groups.

THE NETWORKS OF THE TRIBE

In the first stage there were a few pioneers, e.g. Ackerman and Bell. In the second stage there were groups of persons providing treatment services as the major nexi of the tribe, e.g. New York Jewish Family Service in the 1950's, Palo Alto's Mental Research Institute in the late 1950's, New York's Wiltwyck School in the late 1950's, the Denver, Colorado, Family Treatment Unit in the 1960's. Currently, the most organized networks within the tribe are the training program networks. This is a third stage in the development of the tribe. Most new locales experience accelerated and truncated stages one and two before moving into training network organization.

The organization may be understood if one keeps the models of the Mafia and of an unorganized evangelical religion in mind (the Mafia, because each territory has an informal hierarchy around a local leader, and this local leader exerts considerable power and influence with his followers — a loose confederation with almost no formal central powers. The evangelical religion, because each family therapist seems to feel an individual call and conviction such that he proselytizes others and carries on alone if he is outside a network.)

Each training program network inhabits a territory. This may be a city, medical school, or some other geographical or professional region. Each network develops its characteristic set of rules about how family therapists should behave to their patients, to their peers, and to their own families. Each network has its leaders and heroes, both local and national.

The rules of family therapist behavior in each network often prescribe and proscribe a wide variety of important activities: for instance, how much and in what way the prospective therapist should change his relationships with his wife and his parents; how to dress at work; where it is allowed and preferred to conduct family therapy; which furnishings should be in the place where therapy is done and how these furnishings should be used; which family members should attend meetings; how frequently, for how many minutes and for how many months or years, families are to be seen; how much to charge; whether to work alone or with someone; how close or distant a posture he should maintain *vis-à-vis* his colleagues and clientele. These, and many other "moral" judgments, are implicit in the structure of the family training network. If the beginning therapist does not conform to the rules of his network, he will suffer criticism, and occasionally non-acceptance or ostracism.

Local dialects of the tribal language develop. These dialects often are knit together to form a local family theory. The members of a network speak to each other in their own dialect. These dialect-theories often function as ideological banners at inter-network gatherings. People indicate their allegiances by which dialect they speak. While there is much claim to these theories, being scientific languages, they are used like common languages and evolve via fashions of shared usage; scientific languages evolve via refinements of the operations that define the terms. The authors know of no formal attempt to translate from one dialect to another. It is our impression that the dialects often put different labels on similar processes. Also, they borrow unsystematically from the four main streams of description of human behavior extant in this culture (common language, psychodynamic psychology, structure-function sociology and anthropology, and symbolic interactionist communications theory). The language will probably not become clearer until a unified science of human behavior emerges. The local dialects are worth studying, especially when directly observing the behavior of the people who speak the dialect. The dialects

393

stress both what one should especially notice, and what one should avoid noticing in that particular network's practice of family therapy.

The relations among networks are complicated and informal. Cooperation predominates in sending accurate information about persons, programs, etc. Competition occurs for training staff, support money, prospective trainees, institutional affiliations, and private practice referral sources. The territory goes to those who win these competitions. There are no franchises. Territory is not centrally distributed as in the Catholic Church. Therefore, relations among networks in the same city are much tenser than among those where territorial possession is not the issue.

THE TRAINEE AND THE TRAINING PROGRAM NETWORK

To benefit from a training program it is necessary to become a member of its community. A *we*-ness, a mutual shared definition of the situation, a mutual acceptance by trainee and trainers is a necessary condition for useful work.

Any relationship is defined by those behaviors that the participants do together.* There are some prescribed activities that they must do together, e.g. meet more or less regularly, establish dominance and deference relationships. There are some proscribed activities that they must not do together, e.g., have sexual intercourse during sessions, defame each other's character publicly. There is a large area of possible behaviors between the pre- and proscribed units. Networks vary considerably in the amount of conformity required, and in the degree to which the rules are explicit. A third assumption is that the rules of a training network and the groups within it shape the trainee, and give much form to the therapy that he will do. If a trainee cannot accommodate himself to the rules of a particular training network, he has little chance of success in that network,

---

*These working relationships are discussed under the rubric "working alliance" in the psychoanalytic literature. The general notion of the contract in any teaching, working, or psychotherapeutic situation covers much of the same territory.

though he may be accepted and learn in a different one.

While many of the differences among networks seem evanescent, local, and inconsequential, a polarity appears nationally, and has persisted for at least twenty years. We will describe it in some detail because it seems of great consequence that the prospective trainee should know of the varieties of networks and the consequences to himself from joining or attempting to join one or the other. We will call the two poles "the lone wolf position" and "the all-together-now position."*

THE LONE WOLF POSITION

Lone wolves state that the therapist's role in the therapist-family group is that of outside expert. They act as though one cannot trust anybody and must therefore always watch out for oneself. They prefer to be explicit about what trainees are or are not doing with the families they are seeing. The vocabulary stresses the power aspects of relations. They initially negotiate a circumscribed and explicit contract with their trainees. Thereafter, they prefer to be evasive in discussing the relationship between the trainee and the trainer. Further changes in relationships are implicitly defined and negotiated. Persons using this style keep the relationship rather formal with their trainees and patients. Much of the training involves teaching a person to become the most powerful member of any dyad or larger group by the use of complex refusals to become involved with the member of the group except on the therapist's terms. Awareness and relatively total comprehension of current transactions should be possessed by the therapist, and it is therefore incumbent to restrict, constrain, and slow down the flow of information and behavior so that the thera-

---

*The polarity is different from the A-Z family therapist spectrum described in the GAP report. It resembles Apollonian versus Dionysian positions in Western culture. The debate is also similar to the red *vs.* expert debate in developing socialist societies. Beels and Ferber's characterization of therapists seems to fit roughly as follows : Systems purists are almost all "lone wolves." Analysts are almost all "all-together-nows." Conductors go either way.

pist may understand what he is doing, make his moves consciously and deliberately, and not become enmeshed within the transacting system. They tend to prefer seeing couples or very small collections of persons where the dialogue can be controlled and verbal.

Lone wolves sit at consultative distances (five to twelve feet) from their patients and trainees, often behind or at desks. They rarely take off ties and jackets. They favor postures that exclude themselves from the family group. They often use sarcastic, sardonic, or other wry paralanguage along with the instructions or comments that they deliver. There is a gentle insistence that trainees and families see the paradoxes, irony, and absurdities in their lives. Some of the warmest moments are when the therapist and family share a joke upon their common predicament. The flow of speech is orderly, measured, and polite. The therapist tries vigorously to be on equal terms with all other persons in the room, acknowledging each as who he is while treating each as a willful, consenting adult. Little physical touch of family members by the therapist or among family members is encouraged. The hope is to get people to be reasonable adults by refusing to be anything else with them.

The lone wolf posture is that of an expert who promises accurate information, not emotional catharsis. It is important to keep your cool and not blow it. The training stresses that the therapist must understand a great deal but that the family need not.

The lone wolves prefer not to acknowledge the dependent gratifications the therapist receives during the therapy. They often are over-distant personally, and may refuse to discuss issues except on their own terms. They are often accused of not being friendly.

This Apollonian, intellectual, and distant position finds adherents among persons from psychoanalytic, anti-psychoanalytic, and non-psychodynamic traditions. It allows therapists a fairly wide range of hierarchical stances vis-à-vis the family, ranging from clearly a generation up to a big brother/little brother collegial stance. It is an adult or late adolescent rather than occasionally child-like posture that looks askance at much of what might be considered infantile or regressive. Other similar models in the culture are surgeons, preachers, technocrats, and diplomats. Persons who flower in these networks tend to be more formal than persons who do well in the "all-together-now" school. They tend more often to be North European Catholic or Protestant.

Philip Guerin, a self-proclaimed lone wolf, was asked to comment on the description of the lone wolf position from the inside. (The three authors of the book all consider themselves all-together-nows.)

Dr. Guerin's Description. The lone wolf serves as a consultant to the family by investigating, eliciting, and defining how emotional process in the family operates. He emphasizes defusing intensely emotional situations with clear questioning and forcible slowing down of reactivity. He believes trust develops in a relationship through experience and increased knowledge of how self and others feel and think and behave. He believes personal relationships develop by mutual increase in self-knowledge and knowledge of others. He places great emphasis on thinking, and holds one basic premise: people in emotional difficulty are operating on feelings with little rational thought between feeling and acting. The therapist's job is to prod thinking. A session will often be organized around an idea and its development.

The lone wolf may seem personally distant, closed off, cold; he may have difficulty handling feelings of anger and/or tenderness. Yet, when viewed as a reasonable person he freely opens up and discusses his own experiences with his own family. He tends to isolate a person or persons in the family viewed by him as possessing the most potential for change, and works with those persons. Most often he sees one or two members of the family. His training stresses that if he is able to remain emotionally free from the family process, this will allow a member of the family to accomplish this also, with an eventual domino effect. This will result in an increase in the level of family functioning.

397

The ATN position seems to have a basic assumption that most people can be trusted some of the time, and some people can be trusted most of the time. Furthermore, the therapist cannot trust himself to be correct much of the time, but can seek to form alliances with persons in and out of the therapy room whom he can trust to pick up his distress signals when things are going awry, and these trustworthy people will move in and help him out. The ATN school seeks to form an interdependent collectivity among its trainees, and between therapists and families that they treat. There is a much greater explicit reliance on total communication flow, as opposed to explicit, conscious, lexical speech, in both their training and their teaching. There is an encouragement toward a free-flowing type of process where everyone is bound to make many mistakes and show his worst aspects. Group therapy and psychodramatic formats rather than doctor/patient or consultant/client formats are much favored. Role-playing, family sculpture, and enactment of artistic and dramatic representations are favored. There is considerable call for "what we can share" and "what we can do together." There are often huggings, holdings, tusslings, and other existential and nonlexical contacts among participants. The relationships among the trainers and trainees, or therapists and patients, are considered as prime topics for negotiation and discussion within the training and therapy. Affection and "honesty" are featured. Discussions of power are difficult and embarrassing. They often sit in the same kind of chairs as the customers, and take off coats and ties — sometimes they don't even wear them. There is an aura of earnestness, personal dedication, and friendliness in these networks, and frequent over-promising of what they will do for each other. They often have difficulty in being explicit about what they will not do with and for each other. These people rely heavily on consultations and co-therapies, and prefer larger and more fluid memberships to their meetings. ATN people attract

Jews, Southern Europeans, persons who feature feeling over thinking, and being with someone over being alone. They prefer not to acknowledge the power gratifications in relationships. They tend to blaming, name-calling, and boozy clinging-together. Sentiment may substitute for science. They are often accused of not being professional enough.

The use of hierarchy is again complicated. Some of these networks have rather inflexible dominance and submission hierarchies. Others allow a somewhat more mutual and egalitarian definition of the intimacy. At times, childish behavior is allowed and even encouraged.

IMPLICATIONS OF THE DISTINCTION

The processes of training and therapy involve considerable indoctrination and behavior shaping. When one enters such a system one will be moved quite a bit, and the reverberations will resound through one's networks. The consequences of this discussion for a prospective trainee are that he had better find a training network that he likes and that likes him, because once he is in he will be moved. A personal sniffing-out by trainee and trainer seems an advisable process.

A paradox is that the therapist must forge a personal style and yet must become part of the we-ness of his training program. Those who are true believers and imitators do not seem to grow beyond their teachers and never fill the confines of the model in their network. Those who grow personally and forge a personal style either must leave a confining network, or change that network and broaden it by their own liberation.

The implications for those who teach family therapy are that the shop you have will determine who comes to you and how they turn out. It is a moot question as to how much deviance from the network norms any network can stand, and still keep the we-ness and cohesiveness necessary for a functioning network. We have no hard information as to which posture is more effective for training, or for therapy, though our preferences are obvious.

twelve
〜〜〜〜〜〜〜〜〜〜〜〜〜〜〜〜〜〜〜〜〜〜〜〜〜〜〜〜〜〜〜〜〜〜〜〜〜
the trainee speaks

A third collective effort that we asked, via letter, of all the authors of this book was to "solicit one-page statements from two trainees that each of you pick, either current or former, and ask them to write on their most and least valuable training experiences. We will try to publish all of these responses and to identify both the trainee and his mentor. All trainees will receive a copy of the book for their troubles."

Here then are all of the statements we received arranged in the order in which they arrived.

Who were you when you began? A greenhorn. I thought I knew something about interpersonal relations from having been a natural helper all my life. My head was filled with official New York street analysis: transference, interpretation, blank screens, symbolism, resistance, defenses. My heart was filled with angry rebellion against the anti-people cast from the official analytic doctrine of how to help people. But I was confused. I still thought of the Analytic Institute as the only legitimate path to being a legitimate helper, or at least to being a *profound* helper (as contrasted for example, with the kind of superficial helping that social workers do, or are supposed to do).

What happened then? I began watching families through a one-way screen. The family studies section has a seminar for first-year psychiatry residents which involved families of patients in treatment being interviewed for an hour, followed by an hour of discussion. I don't remember much of those discussions, but, watching those families was a breakthrough. I saw people in their natural habitats. I saw symptoms growing out of personality styles, and personality styles being shaped by family interaction.

So what? I found it impossible after that to see people isolated from their people-environments. God knows I tried, and I had the full support of most of the residency training program. I spent the rest of the first year with in-patients, and most of the second year with out-patients, doing my best to apply the one-to-one therapy model: interpret and don't get involved with relatives, or with the patient either, for that matter. But it didn't work, maybe because I didn't really believe it. Andy Ferber had said to me that being a good therapist was being a good friend. I believed that, and I found it hard to see why it wouldn't be better to be a good friend to husband, wife, and children, rather than just one of them. So I saw families where they existed, and where they existed I saw only families. Where they didn't exist, I encouraged people to make them, in the sense of forming more intimate bonds than they had before.

Sure, but that's what happens to all therapists as they mature — they become more human and less dogmatic! Maybe so, but it was nice to have found someone who talked straight to me from the very beginning. Schizophrenics get into a lot of trouble because they go through their formative years not having that someone. I took a seminar in my third year in the family studies section, where we all sat around and watched some families in treatment through the screen, and tried to act out the family patterns. My clearest memory of that whole seminar was trying to show how I would have dealt with a depressed, apathetic mother — after the girl playing the mother turned down a few of my approaches with downcast eyes and averted body, I moved my chair around in front of her, stuck my face into hers, and said my piece so she *couldn't* not listen. She listened. And I found insight. I had developed my repertoire during that exercise, by trying until something worked. I discovered that you can't teach someone about himself if he isn't listening. Why did it take me two and a half years of training to discover that? I suppose I never felt comfortable enough up till then to try out new behaviors and explore the problem. That was one thing about that seminar — it accepted a great deal of exploratory behavior.

Where are you at now? I'm more human and less dogmatic. I see people in therapy in any shape or form in which they present themselves. But I always try to keep in mind the background, the other people at home, the wife jealous of her husband's private relationship with a therapist, the kid flunking out of school and no one telling me about it, the scoutmaster/father paddling young asses while Mom worries about her son's homosexuality. Instead of insisting that the whole family see me right from the beginning, I see the negotiations over getting to know everyone as part of the process. I make home visits and many telephone calls. I try to become intimate, because I doubt that teaching about intimate matters can go on except within the context of an intimate relationship. I also keep thinking that I've progressed past my teachers, only to remember a line of Andy's that seems to come in just where I'm at.

wwwwwwwwwwwwwwwwwwww *By J. Krainin, a trainee of T. Fogarty*

I would like to preface this by stating that it is my belief that to write it now is premature: ask me again in ten years. At this time I am still involved in the training and struggling with the concepts and phenomena of family therapy. I have not yet reached any luxuriant point of perspective.

Nonetheless, I have of necessity reached certain conclusions. Foremost of these is the necessity of each therapist to work out his own style of doing therapy, consonant with his personality. Hence the most important experience for me, and I believe most important in any training program, is the actual treatment of families. Variety (types of families) and depth of treatment are important. As of this writing, I have seen about a dozen families for five to fifty sessions. Most have been couples; often families have included members of three generations. Ethnically, they have been Jewish, Negro, Catholic (mostly Italian), and Protestant. Some have included psychotic members and some have not.

Offerings of the family therapy department at Einstein vary greatly in the nature and depth of the learning experience. In looking at the weak points, one can see faults of omission as well as commission. Of the former, I think the most important is the lack of instruction of the residents during their emergency-room rotation in the first year. At this stage of my training I had not the courage to try to deal with acutely agitated patients with their (usually) similarly agitated relatives. I missed many opportunities for crisis intervention. Moreover, at this time, I have not been able to impel myself to brave the confusion of the emergency room to gain this experience.

The weakest of the formal offerings was a seminar in which for five months we watched a staff member treat a family in ongoing therapy. Since the residency did not allow time for us to treat families concurrently, the seminar dealt with problems remote from our contemporary experience. I began to find the seminar boring and irrelevant.

The teaching experience of greatest value to me has been the individual supervision. The consultation aspects of supervision have helped provide me with the ability to keep therapy moving and to backtrack from false steps. I have also begun to develop a theoretical model for myself which I think is necessary, at least for me, to do therapy. Watching video-tapes and reading transcripts of experienced therapists at work have been valuable in this regard. But, to repeat and summarize, what has been most valuable have been the experiences I can relate most directly to the therapy I do with families.

∿∿∿∿∿∿∿∿∿∿∿∿∿∿∿∿ *By J. Geller, a trainee of R. Rabkin*

As a practicing social caseworker, I have had experience mainly with casework and, on several occasions, family therapy. I had been taught, as have most of us in the mental health field, to proceed along fairly traditional lines, which includes letting clients proceed at their own pace, helping clients develop insight into their behavior, and the role of the therapist as a non-judgmental, non-suggesting clinician. Therefore, this is the way I had been proceeding — a slow and non-dynamic route.

Our consulting psychiatrist advocated what I considered a revolutionary approach to all therapy. Among other things, he advocated confrontation, directness, and watching the family in operation. After having discussed this approach and seeing it demonstrated, I thought it was a great idea, and I decided to incorporate these techniques into my practice. Trial and error at first resulted in disaster. I began to reconsider using "revolutionary" techniques. The first situation I tried resulted in a parent's demanding my removal from my position and calling me every condemning

405

name. I quickly realized a direct approach had not worked there. Undaunted, and with our psychiatrist's encouragement, I tried again, and this time I met with more success in a situation involving twin thirteen-year-old daughters, with a working mother. The parents separated in August, 1969. In the first family meeting, I asked the family to begin talking about the problem. All parties were able to be themselves, and as the interview proceeded the family dynamics became quite clear. I remained silent for about twenty minutes and simply, although actively, observed the family in operation ("revolutionary" idea number one). After observing the family for a while, I told the family that I had heard enough to know what the problem was, and with confrontation and directness, I explained the dynamics of their inter-actions ("revolutionary" idea number two). I told each member exactly what she was doing that was "bad," and suggested what each had to do in order to make things better ("revolutionary" idea number three). All members understood and agreed to try out my suggestions.

I feel that I have learned a great deal about effective therapy. Directness and confrontation work well when the timing is right and the analysis of the situation is accurate. In discussing this case with our psychiatrist, and the one mentioned earlier where the session was not successful, what became clear was that I handled both cases very differently. In the unsuccessful case, I used many of the techniques used in the second case, but the timing was off and I sided with the daughter. What I have learned is that the family must be watched in operation long enough to develop a picture of the family dynamics. Also, I believe that puts the therapist outside of the situation, rather than a part of it, and it clearly says that the therapist is here to help all members involved change the situation. Secondly, if confrontation is to be used, it has to be directed at everyone, rather than just some family members, or else it alienates the people against whom it is directed and chooses up sides, with the therapist on one side. Similarly, suggestions regarding change should be made to all members.

406

Some people might argue that there is no process — that phenomenon which allows people to gauge where they are at and when they are ready for the next step. (This was one of the questions that I raised, as I am a big believer in process.) It is not a matter of lack of process, but hastening the process — with the twins, for example, I could have seen the family many times, and *then* asked them what they thought was happening in their family. If they were still unaware of the dynamics, I could have helped them see it through various probing questions. The end result should have been that the family dynamics and the part each member played would become clear to them. In the approach used, we arrived at the same conclusion, but quicker. The family was able to hasten the process. In sum, I not only feel the techniques described above are effective, but I am personally delighted with them because the use of these various techniques allows me to play a more active role.

〰〰〰〰〰〰〰〰〰〰〰〰 *By J. Spikes, a trainee of P. Guerin*

This evaluation has been prepared after nine months of participation in the Level II Family Studies Program, which includes the seminar and supervision.

Supervision is conducted in tandem — i.e. with one supervisor and two supervisees. Our supervisor is Dr. Philip Guerin, who is also the co-leader of the seminar; and my co-supervisee is Mrs. Phyllis Ziegler, who is a psychiatric social worker in the Jacobi Hospital Out-Patient Clinic. Mrs. Ziegler and I worked together closely in preparing these evaluations. We had two formal discussions and numerous informal ones on this material, and we found these most helpful in clarifying the ways we viewed this experience. I will make frequent reference to her views, especially where they disagree with mine.

The supervision was set up from the beginning as free and open; each supervisee presents the families he is treating on alternate weeks. Each supervisee is working with only one family. From the beginning, it was agreed upon that both persons who were not presenting would serve as supervisors.

My background in family therapy dates from January to June of 1969, when I was a first-year resident on the training unit at Bronx State Hospital. I participated in the Level I Family Seminar, and for about four months I worked with the family of one of my individual patients, a twenty-year-old schizophrenic man. In this project I had a co-therapist, Miss Alma Wolber, who was the social worker on our ward. We were supervised by Dr. Lawrence Grolnick, who is a member of the Family Studies Section and one of the leaders of the Level I seminar. At the time, I was not very interested in family therapy, and it was really because of Miss Wolber's urging that I undertook this project. She had had six months' experience in family therapy and was very interested in it. Both she and Dr. Grolnick believed that we could help this young man and his family to learn to live together again through family therapy, although the family therapy was clearly seen as secondary in importance to his individual treatment with me. My interest increased as I observed that we were actually helping to effect some change, however minimal, in the family. Through our interventions, we were able to get the father to see that his hypercritical attitude was not helpful to his son. In addition, the mother achieved minor success in giving up her depressed and withdrawn stance in favor of a more open, assertive relationship with her husband and her son. I was quite pleased with such a good result in so short a time, and began to think seriously about exploring family therapy more thoroughly. As a result, I entered the Level II seminar.

Although I am now very interested in family theory and family therapy, my primary interests remain in psychoanalytic theory and practice. I have been undergoing a personal therapeutic analysis for the past year, and I plan to seek training at an analytic institute in the future. However, as an individual therapist, I am often too active, and I have found that the necessarily more active approach I use in family therapy has provided a much-needed contrast to my individual work.

I had asked Mrs. Ziegler to share supervision with me for three important reasons. First, I liked her and had a lot of respect for her ability. Second, I thought that her distinctly feminine, intuitive approach would complement my strategic and somewhat rigidly theoretical stance, thereby enabling us to learn a great deal from each other. Third, the fact that we got our training through different disciplines appealed to me and I was interested to see how this would affect our working together. As it turned out, we did, indeed, complement each other effectively in the manner mentioned above, and have continued to learn from each other. So far, I have discerned no obvious effects or differences in approach that I could attribute to our coming from different disciplines.

From the beginning, our supervisor, Dr. Philip Guerin, stuck pretty rigidly to a theoretical and technical approach based on the work of Murray Bowen. At first, this was seen as a disadvantage by both supervisees. We would have preferred to know what other theoreticians would have done and why they would have done it, although we did appreciate Dr. Guerin's openness about his bias.

Technically, I see Bowen's approach as mainly employing three devices: investigation, suggestion, and manipulation. These techniques are based on a theoretical conception that views difficulties in families as arising from the inability of the members to differentiate sufficiently from each other. Too much of the energy and time of each person is spent in concerning himself with his reactions to the other members and their reactions to him, so that he has difficulty functioning as an individual in his own right. Bowen seeks to break up this process. He does this by using the above technical devices to get each individual in the family to observe his part in the process and to change toward a more differentiated stance. Thus, although he sees all the family members together, he usually speaks with only one member at a time, tries to get him to see his part in the process, and makes suggestions as to how changes can be made. He specifically avoids direct confrontation and interpretation, reasoning that these interventions get the family members involved in an undifferentiated relationship with the therapist (as in psychoanalysis), thereby removing the therapist from his ideal position, that of a consultant.

People with different theoretical orientations, such as Beels, Ackerman, and Whitaker, are much more inclined to observe and interpret interaction between family members, and sometimes they will even become directly involved in the interaction, although in a strategic way. This latter approach appealed much more to both me and Mrs. Ziegler because of our psychoanalytic orientation, but our responses to Dr. Guerin's bias were quite different. Mrs. Ziegler continued with a predominately interpretive approach and integrated Dr. Guerin's suggestions where she thought they would aid this approach. In contrast, I switched to a stance pretty nearly identical to Dr. Guerin's. In retrospect, I have to admit that I did this mainly because I so often found myself floundering around in my sessions with the couple I was treating. I would interpret a piece of interaction after listening for several minutes, and right after this they would be back at it again, as if the interpretation had not taken place. This was both alarming and frustrating to me and I found the Bowen technique a steadying influence on which to lean. In fact, I bought the technique so completely that when I brought the couple before the one-way screen it was quite apparent, both to me and the observers, that I talked and acted like Bowen and made the same kinds of interventions.

Clearly, a rather strong identification had taken place. I should also mention that Dr. Guerin seems to be *very identified* with Bowen, because many of his comments, both in supervision and in the seminar, *sounded almost identical to statements found in Bowen's papers on family therapy.* However, he appears to be in the process of "differentiating" himself from Bowen at this time. My evidence for this can best be shown in my observations of their theoretical conceptions, as I am not yet able to see any significant differ-

410

ences in technical approach (this may be due to my own lack of sophistication). Bowen's main goal seems to be to help the individual to change and thereby to differentiate himself from dysfunctional relationships in the family. Guerin is more concerned with changing the entire dysfunctional system — the family — by getting individuals to change in one direction or another. Now it may be that these two statements are corollaries of each other, but I do not see it this way. Whether or not one is primarily interested in changing a system (family) or a person is of paramount importance to me. However, it may be that if the system is changed all the individuals are changed, and vice versa. At any rate, this is a theoretical question that I am incapable of answering now. Bowen's theory seems much more compatible with psychoanalysis, and I comment on this below.

Lately, I have also begun to differentiate. Although I still operate like Bowen and Guerin, in recent weeks I have been leaning back toward a more interpretive approach and have found this to be quite satisfactory. Where I will go from here I don't know, but it is clear to both me and the couple that they have benefited a great deal from our sessions.

I will now comment on what Mrs. Ziegler and I see as advantageous and disadvantageous in the supervision. First, we both think that the free and open discussion in the sessions is helpful. It gives each person ample opportunity to air his views and to hear what the others think. Dr. Guerin usually is not defensive about disagreement with his approach and is quite willing to discuss and observe the effects of other approaches. However, I found him a bit rigid and unable to listen to some of my examinations of Bowen's theory and technique in the light of psychoanalysis. Second, following two families simultaneously provides obvious advantages, and the fact that Dr. Guerin, myself, and Mrs. Ziegler are also in the family seminar gives us even more very useful material to work with. We think this is the most fruitful way to conduct supervision — that is, in intimate relation to the seminar — and cannot improve on the idea.

411

Third, we both think there is a good balance between theory and technique. However, I should mention that Mrs. Ziegler and I later came to disagree about Dr. Guerin's bias in favor of Bowen. She still thinks that she could get more from the supervision if other theoretical and technical stances were investigated. I believed this at first, too. But I now think that the examination of more theoretical and technical ideas would have taken too much time and would have made the supervision unnecessarily chaotic. I am pleased to have learned one theory and technique in depth, because it has provided me with a steady base from which I can now branch out. Our training in psychoanalytic theory in this residency does no more for us than this. Fourth, Mrs. Ziegler objected to Dr. Guerin's frequent pontifications on the subject of family therapy versus psychoanalysis. I have to admit that I rather enjoy this. Dr. Guerin and I have been fighting this battle in a friendly way ever since he was my chief resident at Bronx State Hospital last year. However, since Mrs. Ziegler was not aware of this little game of ours, I can see how it has made her uneasy.

Another important aspect of this experience was that of my being a psychoanalytically oriented therapist exposed to theoretical conceptions that claimed to be quite different. My first reaction to seeing Bowen on tape was that he practiced some kind of simple-minded family counseling that would best be left to preachers and ladies next door. After reading his papers on family theory and practice, I have changed my point of view radically. (I would encourage anyone who teaches Bowen's theory and technique to present his theory along with his tapes, because what he is doing just cannot be conceptualized in one or two tapes any more than the evolution of the sonata form can be derived from hearing one Beethoven sonata.) I found that after a little reflection I could easily integrate Bowen's theory with general psychoanalytic theory. What he talks about as the failure of a person to differentiate in his family is seen in psychoanalytic terms as the persistence of infantile attitudes, which are then projected onto, and acted out with, present

412

family members. Bowen even goes so far as to quantify the degree of differentiation (persistence of infantile attitudes in psychoanalytic terms) with percentages in describing the feelings, thoughts, and behavior of individuals. Thus, he seems to me to be clearly oriented toward the individual and will even go so far as to say that one person may have more difficulty than another.

The next question to answer is: if Bowen's theory does, indeed, fit within the framework of psychoanalysis, how could his treatment method be explained in psychoanalytic terms? What I think happens is this: instead of getting the patient to examine his relationship with the therapist and thereby exposing the infantile attitudes (undifferentiated-ness, in Bowen's terminology), he encourages the family members to do this with each other. In psychoanalytic terms, he gets the family members to examine their neurotic (or psychotic) "transference" to each other and encourages them to try to change it.

In my opinion, Guerin's approach is quite different from this. He sees the trouble as being in "the system" and would look upon attempts to quantify the degree of disturbance in one individual as useless and perhaps even detrimental. At present, I see no way of integrating this stance with psychoanalytic theory.

Thus, I have been able to synthesize some of my own thinking with Bowen's theory but not with Guerin's. I do not think that Guerin's theory is correct, but I have to admit that it appears to be more original than Bowen's. As I see it, Bowen's main contribution has been to introduce a unique and effective mode of therapy that is not basically different from psychoanalytic therapy. Guerin's theory, if correct, could radically change our way of looking at mental processes.

In conclusion, I have found family supervision and working with families to be a stimulating and thought-provoking experience. The interlocking structure of the seminar and supervision is largely responsible for my positive reaction, but most of the credit must go to Dr. Guerin and

413

Mrs. Ziegler for providing a consistent atmosphere of emotional and intellectual stimulation.

〰〰〰〰〰〰〰〰〰〰〰〰 *By P. Ziegler, a trainee of P. Guerin*

This evaluation of my experience in family supervision with Dr. Guerin was prepared after eight months of supervision by him along with attendance at the family seminar co-led by Dr. Guerin. Previous to this, I had had a limited exposure to family work. While I was a social work student at Psychiatric Institute, a psychoanalytically oriented training center, I saw the parents of in-patient adolescents frequently in couple therapy, although very little attention was given to the family process; the couple was viewed, for the most part, as individuals, each with his own psychopathology. Even though family therapy was an acceptable modality for the "right" case, very few cases were actually seen in this manner. However, several times throughout the year, I would have a session with the resident who was treating the adolescent with the entire family; this would usually focus upon a particular issue, such as visiting privileges. The following year (1968-69) I began seeing a family jointly with a second-year resident for about eight months. We were supervised by a psychologist who was trained in family systems theory. Our supervision initially focused a great deal on the relationship of the therapists, who in many ways seemed to mirror the interaction of the couple. As we became more comfortable in working together, the focus of the supervision stressed understanding the interaction of the family (verbal and non-verbal) and making comments (i.e. interpretation) on the process. For example, a suicide threat on the part of the wife clearly made other family members distance from her, rather than respond to her call for help.

It is of particular interest to consider the above experience (individual psychoanalytic and family process orientation) as a means of assessing my reaction to the present family experience with Dr. Guerin, which consists of bimonthly supervision on an on-going case with the participation of another supervisee, Dr. J. Spikes, a psychiatric resident, who would present his case the alternate week as well as aid in my supervision. This atmosphere tended to encourage an explorative approach to the family interaction and a consideration of various techniques which were initiated by us. This enabled me to begin formulating a strategy of my own rather than following the advice of Dr. Guerin.

Initially, I was aware of a great deal of confusion although I was not certain of its source, as Dr. Guerin seemed to approach working with the family very differently than my other supervisor. It seemed that he would often encourage me to explore issues in enabling the family to understand their position *vis-à-vis* other members. Gradually, I began to acknowledge that both approaches (family as unit *vs.* individuals) appeared suitable. However, seeing the family as a system of individuals seemed in such contrast to my past frames of reference that initially I had difficulty accepting the validity of this approach. Being supervised by Dr. Guerin after having had a previous supervisory experience made me more aware of alternatives in doing family work.

The opportunity for each supervisee to participate in the supervision of his teammate not only enhances the feedback during supervision, but enables each of us to have the opportunity to work through the difficulties with another case in a continuous way. It has become clear that it was easier to maintain an objective position with someone else's family. Dr. Spikes, my teammate, would often pick up on some area that had been overlooked, or suggest another possible approach in resolving a particular bind. For example, he would often note that the couple played "the good patients" as a way of masking threatening areas. The use of time was handled in an informal, no-structured manner so that the total family experience of the seminar and supervision was well integrated. Any points from the seminar that needed to be clarified were often dealt with in supervision.

In general, there was an excellent balance between discussion of theoretical material and technical approaches. Dr. Guerin primarily focused on the theoretical framework of Murray Bowen, i.e. family seen as working toward differentiating from other members. The technique of probing into each issue would then assist them in defining the on-going process in the family, i.e. the thinking and feeling systems of each member in relation to other members were clarified. Although he gave very little consideration to other frameworks, he was very direct about his bias. At times, I had the feeling that he was proselytizing; there seemed to be some pressure to make a total commitment to family therapy rather than to consider it as one of several acceptable modalities. Although this stance provided some tension, it forced me to begin to clarify meaningfully my own intellectual understanding of this modality.

Thus, this overall experience served to broaden my theoretical conception of family work; it also stimulated my interest in comparing individual with family therapy.

By A. Zelman, a trainee of M. Mendelsohn

In both Levels I and II, the family therapy course has without doubt been one of the most instructive experiences in residency for me. I can identify a few of the reasons for this.

First, it has introduced to me in a vital way the value of looking at individual behavior in terms of its context. Second, it has demonstrated a great variety of the options a therapist has in dealing with a family, and, by implication, other situations as well.

Third, the kind of open techniques used in teaching the course have done much to help me approach psychiatry and patients from the point of view of a "person" rather than a "professional." This approach, I believe, both helps one see clearly what is happening and ultimately gives one more therapeutic leverage.

Fourth, the informal and action-oriented approach enables the student to make discoveries, as well as mistakes,

416

for himself. As a result, in this course I have been much more willing and able to learn from supervisors, since their experience and knowledge have been demonstrated from example rather than by fiat.

I have but two suggestions for improvement, neither of which I'm sure can easily be included in the time allotted.

First, a more systematic attempt, at some time in Level II particularly, would make explicit the theoretical assumptions we are making in talking about our families.

Second, I'd like a little more attention to the stages, and in-depth analysis of a complete family therapy.

∿∿∿∿∿∿∿∿∿∿∿∿ *By J. Gordon, a trainee of H. Mendelsohn*

The fault, dear Harry, lies not in our stars, but in our supervisors. My general experience in training was that I valued people rather than specific programs, seminars, and such. I also tended to favor more organized over more open-ended seminars. The Ferber-led seminar I liked least because it struck me as being seen in too diffuse and egocentric a way, with too much attention to what struck me as irrelevant group process. I tend to like more didactic approaches (obiously personal feeling). I couldn't tell where I was going.

I thought personal supervision with Harry Mendelsohn my favorite part of the show mainly because of his personal qualities — those that I like in a supervisor — knowledgeable, friendly, willing to share personal experiences in an honest way. I clearly got the most from this.

I liked the Beels seminar, which had a sense of purpose and was well done, but in the end I think that seeing families with individual supervision and watching an experienced therapist with a continuous case are the best teaching methods (with, of course, good people seeing them).

∿∿∿∿∿∿∿∿∿∿∿ *By E. Weiss, a trainee of H. Mendelsohn*

To me the most interesting phenomenon of learning about family treatment is the way that the therapist insidiously

417

gets inducted into the family system. I found this sharply illustrated when I worked with a co-therapist with a schizophrenic boy and his mother for a period of seven months under weekly supervision. As we got into working we found that our co-therapy relationship was replicating the mother and son's relationship. The boy, G, had been hospitalized for about a year and a half for paranoid delusions and bizarre, ritualistic behavior. This behavior had the effect of paralyzing the family, and the mother and his two younger siblings withdrew from G in helplessness. It was as if G's tantrums put him in charge, and his mother felt she had to keep out of his way. At a deeper level, however, G was acting out his mother's unconscious wishes. She had been widowed for a number of years and was clearly terrified of G's growing up and leaving her. Her prohibitions about sex, friends, and adult activities hopelessly confused G and reduced him to the level of a child having tantrums. Thus, she was really in charge although she felt very much the victim.

It was fascinating how the family induced us into the mother/son roles. She worked on my co-therapist by looking to him as the supreme authority, seducing him, and letting him know she was completely helpless and dependent upon him. This made him feel as if he were the main therapist, which doubled his frustration when she refused to follow any of his directives. G worked on me by criticizing my manner, questioning my competence, and overtly rejecting what I said. As sessions progressed, however, it became clear that he felt attracted to me and controlled by me, and was acutely sensitive that I might be judging him. This surprised me as I felt rejected by him and impotent as a therapist. The co-therapy relationship became very much like this mother and son's interaction. Although my co-therapist directed the sessions, he felt ineffectual, and checked his perceptions with me constantly, like the son did with the mother. This surprised me each time because like the mother, I felt like a fifth wheel and was sure he was in control of the situation. It was quite interesting when we became aware of how we were acting out the family's problem.

418

One of my first encounters with the family orientation of a staff man came in the first year. One of the staff and I decided to act as co-therapists for an acutely paranoid young woman admitted as the identified patient. The struggles generated by multiple therapists became quickly evident. However, the most striking feature of this arrangement was the way the staff man could directly relate this woman's psychodynamics in individual sessions to the on-going family equilibrium. The family pressure to see the patient in the "sick" role became a stumbling block on her way toward a more solid integration in her individual work with us.

My experiences in staff/student co-therapy teams helped me learn to sit on my impatience for longer stretches of time, until the patients were ready to experience their own growth. The staff member was a direct buffer between the family and me, the sometimes over-eager junior partner. I also worked in peer co-therapist teams. This allowed pairing of trainees to supervise our own therapy. For some types of counter-transference problems it is a lot easier to have a peer confront you than to lose face with someone in the more traditional authoritarian role of teacher. You are more likely to be able to accept a direct criticism about something that you're *doing* wrong from a peer, but less likely to be able to take his advice about what *should* be done in any abstract sense. Also it's easier to talk about the ideal therapeutic situation with a more traditional teacher, but much easier to accept your own fumbling around when it's pointed out by a peer who does many of the same things.

In a similar vein, staff/staff co-therapy teams who allow the trainee to view their work directly have been a great help to me. To watch staff members pushing each other toward their own "growing edge" as therapists helped me realize that the old-timers in the business were struggling with conflicts in themselves similar to those I had been experiencing in my own life as a therapist.

Basic to my exposure to family work was the eagerness

419

with which Carl Whitaker, Milton Miller, and others of the staff shared their own private therapy families with us from behind the one-way mirror and/or sharing their co-therapy slots with student therapists with these private families. These seminars and the more formal reading and didactic seminar formats constituted our baptism in the family "faith." The importance of viewing the family as a system became more evident when I learned that various staff members (when dealing with their own personal problems) engaged in therapy as marital couples or with their entire families to aid in their personal growth. Also the realization that the attending staff from the community around the University had made similar use of the family modality for their personal lives also underscored the importance of the family system for me.

I'd also have to include in my training experience the fact that I've lived for thirty-two years in a complex, sometimes sick, tightly knit extended family system. Following the death of my grandmother, who was a very controlling but warm intrusive woman, I saw the breakup of three marriages at close hand. Her support had kept one of the marriages alive for over twenty-five years! This instilled in me a profound respect for the homeostatic balances within family groups, and it also taught me what devastation can occur in people's lives after just a single shift in a large family system. As a physician in the Navy, the experience of seeing what can happen to men in combat areas following good and bad news about family members four thousand miles away also underlined the importance of family dynamics in people's individual lives. To see what happened to wives and the dependents of Navy personnel who were on extended deployments was also enlightening. In that setting the importance of conceptualizing the depth of family involvement of all psychopathology (or health) became painfully obvious. Lastly my own personal individual therapy and family therapy showed me how screwed up family relationships can get and how extremely difficult it was for one to change habit patterns once they become established.

420

~~~~~~~~~~~~~~~~~~~~~~~ *By G. Coffee, a trainee of C. Whitaker*

I think family therapy learning for me has been a process of coming to know that the family may be uniquely different from other families, and that there may be different and personal ways of describing family phenomena (different, that is, from analytic and technical terminology). With this there goes the sense that things are possible within the family, and further that the family does not change by the energy of the therapist, but that being present with him briefly during the week they then go on and must find their own internal ways of arriving at the change they need. From my early encounters with Carl Whitaker during my first year I probably didn't get much because I couldn't understand the things that he said, but subsequently, of course, as I gained experience, things became clearer. The earlier part of the training that was valuable to me had to do with the accumulation of an amount of experience which allowed me to comprehend and to have a basis for formulating ideas of family interaction. Subsequently, what seemed to be most valuable and certainly exciting were the conferences through the one-way mirror where a family was interviewed. That gave me a chance to share ideas and to listen to ideas of others concerning the phenomena of family interaction and family therapy. I valued the chance to sit with Carl and Milt through about four months of therapy with a family that Carl had for quite a while. For instance, this contributed to a sense that the family does find their ways of changing and that the therapist does not really provide the energy for change. In other ways it provided a sense of that the long-term feeling of a family therapy was that change doesn't come about immediately, but that things are possible, and that time plays an important part. I guess the sense of possibility was an important derivative from the lack of clear structure to family therapy conceptualizations that each family may allow to some extent its own formulation, that things can happen within the context of family therapy seems to be a result of this less-than-structured approach. I also feel that, through the time that I've been around, Carl's willingness to have me or someone in has contributed to a sense that there is an inside, and further that I am not naughty for being on that inside within the family system.

〰〰〰〰〰〰〰〰〰 *By M. Zunitch, a trainee of H. P. Laqueur*

A. Ferber's Questions: 1. When did I stop being H.P.L.'s student and emulator and become "me" as a therapist? 2. What did I find valuable in my training and experience?

My thoughts: H.P.L. says that the day I became "me" was in elementary school when, while wearing my Girl Scout uniform, I challenged an offensive boy to a fight after school, and won. After giving some thought to the quick word-portrait my friend has painted of me, I wonder how much of "me" I bring to therapy in what has been termed as the therapist's style. I recall that I have been Peter's student since my senior year of school and cannot say when, in an association of mutual confidence such as ours, a learning process ceases. I cannot believe that it ever does.

Regarding when I became "me" as a therapist: I think the turning point was when I returned to work after what might be termed as several years of semi-retirement.

The research project was in full swing, with a need for therapists for the family therapy groups being formed.

At a team meeting I was informed by Carl Wells that I would be assigned to a group as their therapist. Being still in the throes of readjustment to professional activity, I timidly said, "Well, I'll do it if you really think I fill the bill." Carl replied in his inimitable way, "No, you don't, but you're all we've got!" I think at that moment the Girl Scout in my personality was activated. I requested that H.P.L. sit in on my first few sessions, but insisted that he should not aid me in any way nor act as my co-therapist in any way. I asked to be informed if, after several sessions of *silent supervision,* I did not "fill the bill."

422

Regarding what I found valuable or not valuable in my training and experience requires some explanation. Since I was not in a formalized training framework, my training took the course of personal involvement over a period of years. First, as an observer-recorder in my undergraduate days when H.P.L. was conducting family groups at a child guidance clinic and at the hospital, I learned the value of listening to what was *not* being said as well as what was. Added to this was appreciating the need to *see* gestures, the intentional but more important, the unintentional; facial expression, body movement, posture, etc. To put a valuable lesson simply, a would-be therapist does well to aim for highly developed skills in observation and sensitivity to his and others feelings before he or she decides to "unbutton the mouth."

In fact, the most valuable aid to my development as a therapist was and still is direct and personal involvement. In other words, "where the action is!"

The least valuable in my growth as a therapist in the past and present involves the competitive sessions in the guise of "scholarly exchange" in which the various schools, biases, approaches, etc., are attacked, defended, name-dropped, quoted, and generally run through the fifty-dollar wordmill, answering the oneupmanship needs of those participating. The results of such times, if they can be credited with results, to me are always quite sterile.

Perhaps the deficit in my training by H.P.L. can be found here, since he omits such experiences in his training approach.

By M. Woods, a trainee of A. Ferber

It was flattering to be asked to write something about why and how I got interested in family therapy, and I thought it would be fun. When I tried to get started, though, I found it was a rough assignment.

As with most family therapists, my interest sprang from

frustrations in practice. This is the easier part to write about. Frequently while working with one individual it became crystal clear that his distress was inseparable from the web of complicated relationships and experiences shared by members of his total family. If one person was agonized, others in the family were living in some kind of hell, too, whether they said so or not. So I was spurred on to read about family dynamics and systems, watch what others were doing, and try seeing some families myself.

My other motives are more personal and painful to explain. From childhood (I was motherless from age seven) it seemed like a matter of survival to appraise and become sensitive to the most subtle aspects of families who took an interest in me and to whom I became attached. These were families of all sizes, and economic and ethnic backgrounds; with very little awareness on my part, I developed a host of intuitions, attitudes, and techniques to cope with the various family systems. I concerned myself with the conflicts, moods, fears, and joys of the life of the families, and soon learned what I must do to make it with them. Thus, at an early age I began my "training" as a family diagnostician and, when I felt called upon, family "therapist," mediator, and appeaser. With each family I had to learn when intrusion was welcome or helpful and when I must lie low. I could not afford many mistakes, since I wanted to hold on to them. Once, when I was about ten, the father of a family I was close to was being asked to leave by his wife when I halted the move temporarily by pointing out to the woman that she had overlooked a significant peace overture her husband had just made. The position of outsider helped me to maintain perspective, however, and in retrospect I think saved me from induction into some of the more pathological aspects of the systems while I was being nourished by the genuine and loving qualities which prompted the family to care about me in the first place.

So, becoming a family therapist was a natural evolution of my professional concerns and my young life experience. But the process of training and growing into the work

424

brought on a whole new set of problems. Like most psycho-therapists, I was not used to having my work observed and picked apart by others. Talking and writing about it were much less scary, although considerably less useful. The open seminar, with one-way screens and live supervision, part and parcel of my training in family therapy, helped me to *begin* to have the courage to be wrong, to take risks, to make a fool of myself, and to face up to my own complacency and defensiveness — as a therapist and as a human being.

It wasn't easy. It was an intrusion to be scrutinized by teacher and colleague. I admired my teacher, but he made life difficult. He prodded, insulted, withdrew his interest when defied, scared off some of my fellow workers, and I had some pretty nervous and angry moments when I first began. Yet he also had the confidence to press me to stretch myself further, and perhaps this was crucial to my hanging in rather than indignantly retreating and saving face.

As a beginning family therapist, I found myself further pressured by the opposition of families and colleagues alike, skepticism ranging from patronizing tolerance to vigorous challenge of my judgment. Families determined to peg one member as sick, or individuals who did not want to share their therapy with others, formulated brilliant defenses or guilt-provoking pleas to sway me to change my treatment plan. Perhaps even more disturbing were the colleagues — often the most seasoned and successful psychotherapists — who implied with kindness or with anger that family treatment was a second-class approach, or at best applicable only to the most recalcitrant or hard-core patients. Only with time and repeated successful experiences could I be more measured in my responses to such attacks.

For me, then, becoming a family therapist demanded and continues to demand a great deal of hazardous work, complicated by the very nature of the task, and further requiring an ability to be open to scrutiny, and crust enough to take abuse. I suspect that learning how to learn family therapy will go on as long as I practice.

~~~~~~~~~~~~~~~~~~ *By G. Abelin, a trainee of M. Mendelsohn*

I have procrastinated for about three months and feel uncomfortable to say the least, about writing this. I have wondered why and guessed that my emotional involvement with the teachers at Bronx State has made the task of criticizing the program a difficult one for me. Besides, I feel by now part of the training staff and — let's get into business. I don't know other training programs in family therapy. I will therefore compare ours to an ideal one, and tell what I would try to imitate from it and what I would avoid or change.

I enjoyed the freedom of expression, the joy of being listened to respectfully (as if something sound could come out of me, a young fly therapist). I appreciated the lack of strict rules, the possibility of experiencing to learn, mostly through play-acting and the openness of leaders and their wish to learn from the students. In fact, one of the most important experiences for me, as an advanced student, was to be part of a group which in the course of the year lost its leaders. They were present but non-acting; they just watched us through the one-way mirror. Therefore, it was up to us to structure the discussion, to give a sense to our seminar, and to discover the wealth of knowledge that the other members, at our own level, could offer us.

I consider it an error to teach large groups. It should never go beyond six to eight for best results. The intimacy of small groups allows for more productive and intense work. I would make a "must" the participation in a reading seminar and would give more room to discussion of techniques used by different schools and the course treatment takes following each one of them. I would offer an ongoing treatment to watch through the years, *to the end*. One of the big problems of training has been how much we learned about diagnostic and dynamic aspects and how little about therapy itself. This unbalanced knowledge provokes a feeling of hopelessness in the trainee; he never sees the end of a treatment and wonders if it exists. I would be very clear

426

about the considerable length of family therapy, to avoid false expectations, and I would try to listen carefully to doubts, complaints, depression arising in the group (without escaping into "interpretation" but taking them to the word).

It would be useful to meet with the trainees a year or two after they leave the program and listen to their post graduation experiences.

~~~~~~~~~~~~~~~~~~~~~~~~~ *By C. Fowle, a trainee of A. Bodin*

I have been in two training sessions devoted to family therapy techniques with Dr. Bodin of the Mental Research Institute, in Palo Alto, California. As for my personal background, I am a licensed psychologist with a small private practice and also am a director of pupil personnel services in a medium-sized school district, supervising a number of school psychologists, counselors, and speech therapists.

I am very enthusiastic about the concept of conjoint family therapy. As a psychologist, I "cut my teeth" on psychological tests and previously spent a considerable amount of time in individual assessment of individual family members before beginning therapy. Through the training program I learned that much of this same information can be gained by simply observing the interaction of the family members when together in a session — and in much less time!

For me the most valuable experience in the training session was the demonstration of family therapy with "live families," and an opportunity to observe a real situation rather than reacting to a "canned" example in a textbook or manual. Most of us in the workshop had had a wealth of theory in our academic training; this was an opportunity for training in application of theory, an aspect that is too often minimized in professional training programs.

The training experiences were of great value to me, for I gained techniques and understandings that I can use not only with my own clients but also with school personnel who work with families.

There was only one concern that I experienced and I shall relate it for what it is worth. In observing the family identify and then work through their problems, it was difficult for me not to identify with one or more particular family members. Perhaps memories of my own place in my family constellation were being revived. At any rate, I found that I had to make a deliberate effort to keep my own feelings out of the situation.

This phenomenon may be present in any counseling relationship, I realize, and most of us have been trained to deal with it. Yet for me the condition was closer to the surface when faced with an entire family than with one individual.

wwwwwwwwwwwwww *By R. Mathis, a trainee of A. Bodin*

As a psychology intern, it was my good fortune to be involved in consultation sessions about family therapy and intervention. This series of informal and formal presentations provided one of the more stimulating aspects of the total training year.

One of the most informative techniques utilized by Dr. Bodin was the use of hypothesis while watching a family being interviewed by different therapists on video-tape. The interns were asked to form hypotheses for future treatment, a prognosis, and how to begin therapy. The process of active attention to cues provided by Dr. Bodin and the video-tape was an extremely helpful technique for teaching family therapy procedures.

Another intriguing training device was a role-playing demonstration using a family case provided by the interns. In this event, Dr. Bodin called for the principal therapist to act out the role of the strongest and weakest members of the family constellation. This approach forced a variety of views of the family dynamics and provided an active teaching process as opposed to the more traditional lecture/case-presentation approach.

428

Perhaps the least helpful activity provided for the family therapy series was the suggested bibliographies and reading lists. After moving out of the graduate school environment, one of the needs for young interns is to be able to tie readings to experiences. Suggested book lists or studies that are not discussed in relation to experiences and present case involvements lose much of their appeal.

I greatly appreciate the opportunity to comment about Dr. Bodin's *active* teaching approach to family therapy.

ⱮⱮⱮⱮⱮⱮⱮⱮⱮⱮⱮⱮⱮⱮⱮ *By C. Skinner, a trainee of A. Bodin*

There was virtually nothing in Arthur Bodin's Mental Research Institute survey course in family theory and therapy which I have not subsequently found useful. One thing, however, which I had hoped to find there and did not find was a comprehensive outline of family theory today — an organized and logical presentation of who thinks what and how these various views mesh or clash. I had been reading greedily and was glutted with half-digested concepts and New Vocabulary catchwords. Now I wanted a cohesive arrangement of pigeonholes. Dr. Bodin's predilection, however, appeared to be a tantalizing family therapy smorgasbord, spiced with characteristic anecdotes about the work of various leaders in the field. I had fun, but did not emerge with the global grasp of theories and trends I had hoped to achieve (in six sessions).

What I did emerge with, however, was the extremely valuable experience of observing Dr. Bodin in action with a family, and of pulling apart with him afterward what had gone on and comparing his perceptions of the family dynamics with ours. And it was a joy to find him willing to discuss freely with us what he *thought* had led him to follow one tack and not another, where he was trying to go, and whether he or we thought he got there. I particularly remember one brilliant session in which his pursuit of a daughter's grief over the loss of her dog and her anger at her mother for having disposed of him led Dr. Bodin (and

429

them) back to the daughter's similar feelings at the death of her father eight years before — a crucial and hitherto unresolved, although buried, source of trouble between them. In this one session I learned things about family systems and ways of making contact with them that I think I could have apprehended only through this kind of direct observation and discussion. These parts of the sessions were for me the heart of the course, and that aspect which I found most helpful to my effort to bridge the gulf between family theory and its applications in work with families.

wwwwwwwwwwwwww *By E. Leiter, a trainee of H. Mendelsohn*

I found supervision on the whole a very positive experience. This is proven by the fact that I made a special request to continue working with you next year.

It wasn't any specific bit of advice or technique that mattered most, but rather a kind of acceptance of me as a therapist and as a person. What I needed was support, to make me feel more secure as a therapist. Most of the difficulties I encountered were due to countertransference, in which my own problems served as blocks and prevented me from acting in ways in which intellectually I knew would prove effective. At such times the supervision served in a way as a kind of surrogate therapy that enabled me to see the problem clearly so that I could work. Sometimes I felt that this was inappropriate and that I was revealing private matters better left to therapy. On the other hand, it was I who opened it up. You never seemed to pry and always maintained a respectful distance. It was this attitude of warmth and acceptance combined with respect which helped me the most.

At times, however, I felt that the anxiety engendered in me by the family transferred through me to you; when this would occur, I felt a pull to produce something to alleviate *your* anxiety. When this happened, you were not as helpful as at other times when you were not as anxious.

430

thirteen
is everybody watching?

H. Mendelsohn and A. Ferber

For the past two years, a group of us — psychiatrists, psychologists, social workers — who supervise family therapist have met in a weekly seminar to try, through mutual observation and discussion of our work, to do better supervision.

The "supervision" we speak of is a process that guides the professional development of family therapists. The supervisor is in charge of the supervisory meetings, and refuses control over any other situation. The supervisee brings information to the supervisor about family therapies

431

he (the supervisee) is conducting. The supervisee also brings information about his development as a family therapist, and, when relevant, his general life situation.

The supervisor and supervisee compare this information with their personal models for "ideal" courses of therapy, professional development, and life situations. If the actual approximates the ideal, the supervisor delivers a blessing. If there are discrepancies between actual and ideal, a negotiation ensues wherein the supervisor tries to change the behavior of the supervisee. The supervisee's personal development as a therapist is the central concern of the process. Greater or lesser degrees of attention are paid to the therapies of families, and the personal lives of supervisees.

In the seminar, our usual procedure was to observe a member of our group conduct a supervisory hour with his supervisee behind the one-way screen. In the second hour, the post-session, the group would discuss its observations of the supervisor's work, often using role-playing, occasionally family sculptures, psychodrama, or any other experiential technique that occurred to us, to illuminate the observed process. Most of us who participated in the seminar found it an extraordinarily alive, exciting, stimulating, provocative, and educational experience. For some of us, indeed, it was the best seminar in a setting where good seminars (also using live observation, role-playing, etc.) are the rule rather than the exception.

THE SEMINAR COMPOSITION

We were a mixed group: initially six psychiatrists, five psychologists, and four social workers, with a wide disparity of backgrounds, levels of training, and therapeutic orientations. For example, of the six psychiatrists in the seminar during the first year, two had begun, and three had already completed, formal psychoanalytic training. The second year of the seminar, three of the psychiatrists had European backgrounds with substantial experience in the

432

social psychiatry programs of their native Czechoslovakia, Scotland, and Israel. This heterogeneity of background — we even had an Egyptian co-existing with two Israelis! — may have been an important factor in the rapid evolution of a task-oriented group cohesiveness.

A similar heterogeneity in personality, temperament, lifestyle, even dress and manners, may have been as important as the more explicit differences in therapeutic orientation. Our sessions were regularly enlivened by marked contrasts, clashes, and conflicts.

Ties to the institution were equally varied. Some were full-timers, some half-timers, and some one-day-a-week consultants. Two of the most active participants had no formal connection at all: they were family therapists and supervisors of family therapy in suburban family agencies who simply asked to be included in the seminar. Fortunately, there was little extrinsic pressure on anyone (to protect his job or secure "promotion") to perform well (i.e., safely).

"Ideology"

The tone, form of work, rituals, practices, even the very structure of the seminar, reflected and interpenetrated with the pervading ideology of the family studies section at Bronx State Hospital. The seminar served as a useful tool in acculturating the newcomers to the prevailing values of this subculture.

We came to believe in:

1. *Eclecticism.* There is no "one" theory of family therapy that has all the answers. This concept is *not* based on a nihilistic rejection of theory as opposed to practice, but derives instead from an appraisal of the present status of family therapy theory. Indeed, there is an enormous impetus to look for conceptualizations from many different disciplines and many different frames of reference. And as with theory, so with practice — there was encouragement to innovate, experiment, "try on" whatever techniques seemed appropriate to the specific situation. Now this eclecticism

433

isn't easy to live with — especially for the novice therapist (and therefore, his supervisor). Moreover, this absence of a codified set of rules for conducting family therapy (and for its supervision), co-existing with a spirit of skeptical iconoclasm, often encouraged the use of "wild," sometimes inappropriate maneuvers — rationalized by the philosophy that "anything goes . . . you can try anything once."

However, what *is* gained from this atmosphere of militant eclecticism is a marvelous lack of the ossification and rigidity so characteristic of training institutions, and the tremendous enrichment that comes from attending, however skeptically, to many different conceptualizations and frames of reference, and the heady freedom to innovate and experiment.

2. *Experience first . . . conceptualize later!* This slogan derives, in part, from the philosophical position just described and, more important, from the empirical fact that experiential techniques are exquisitely suited to illustrate *process* — and process is what we deal with.

We are always striving to help the novice therapist experience his "self" as part of and apart from the family system he is treating. Our goal is to maximize use of self: to develop the capacity consciously to move in and out of the family system — with active awareness of these moves. And this is best taught experientially.

The concept of system induction, for example, is certainly teachable as an intellectual idea. We find it is learned faster, better integrated, more "available" in the clinical situation, when it has been not only academically defined and demonstrated, but also actually *experienced* in the learning situation.

3. *Commitment to openness.* This is not just a philosophical *desideratum*. The work suffers when hidden conflict is not exposed and dealt with — that is, the work of family therapy, the work of supervision, the work of the seminar itself.

4. *Meticulous attention to group process.* Good family therapy (and good teaching of family therapy) demands

enormous risk-taking. The group can either provide the support to take the risk — or it can become the vehicle, *par excellence,* to avoid risk and prevent growth. Considerable vigilance is required — and rigorous commitment to a continuing scrutiny of the group's own process is a critical part of the contract.

We believe that without this vigilance, our seminar might have bogged down into a series of increasingly empty exercises. For example, there was ample opportunity to use the group to avoid risk-taking. First we observed, especially in the early stages, a reluctance to expose work, and collusive processes between the supervisor, his supervisee, *and the members of the seminar,* to go through the motions of an observed supervisory session, and continue the empty ritual into the post-session. Second, it was "safer," in the post-session, to deal with the dynamics of the family in the treatment just discussed, than to stick to the work of the seminar — examination of the supervising process. Third, the presence of visiting firemen could be used to divert and inhibit the task at hand (although it was striking to observe how much more often the visitors became induced into our on-going system).

Examination of the above phenomena and the revelation of the underlying anxieties that produced them proved remarkably liberating; more important, it allowed the work to move on.

Similarly, phenomena produced by the group-life itself — struggles around leadership, dominance, intra-group competitiveness, etc. — were not permitted to sabotage the work of the seminar, but became, instead, clinical data for us to look at, understand, and deal with — as we must do with the families we treat, the students we teach — and, alas, with our own families and social sub-systems.

And, finally, we were repeatedly impressed by the induction of the entire seminar into the family systems under our indirect observation. Patterns of communication, affective tone, and underlying themes proved contagious and invasive. The impact of a disintegrating family on the thera-

435

pist and supervisor would be reflected in the seminar's suddenly questioning the efficacy of family therapy as a treatment modality. (As, conversely, we observe a supervisor, insecure about his competence to supervise family work, subtly cue in his supervisee to get the family to request individual therapy for its identified patient!)

Our attention to group process, it should be emphasized, was not in the form of a therapy group, or encounter group (although encounter techniques were occasionally employed). There was relatively little navel-contemplation. Rather, we tried to use the group process as a tool to understand impasses in our work and in the attempt to find ways to overcome these impasses. A derivative, but by no means trivial, benefit to the members of the seminar was an improved alertness and sensitivity to the similar phenomena we all meet in our work as family therapists.

5. *The concept that the student therapist* (the supervisee), no matter how scant his previous training, *is responsible for the process of the family he is treating.* The supervisor is responsible for the process of the supervision he is conducting.

IDEOLOGY AND REALITY

The forms of supervision were shaped as much as possible to reflect and embody this ideology.

The supervisor was free to choose any style or format of supervision, and to negotiate the terms of the contract individually with his supervisee. At one end of the spectrum, some supervisors chose the conventional format of a discussion of the supervisee's report of a session. At the other extreme, some supervisors chose to "sit in" at the family therapy session, functioning as a co-therapist or live consultant. In between, some supervisors observed the work as non-overt participants, from behind a one-way screen or through playbacks of audio- and/or video-tapes.

The contract between supervisor and supervisee was entirely voluntary — indeed, the supervisee was not even assigned a family for treatment (and supervision); it was his responsibility to "find" a family and begin treatment. The alacrity (or lack of alacrity) with which the supervisee begins treating a family becomes a useful focus in the negotiation of the initial contract between supervisee and supervisor

The supervisor did not report on the supervisee's work — no grades, no reports to "superiors," no evaluation filed in a dossier. This is not to say there was *no* evaluation. On the contrary, we believe that, ideally, a constant process of explicit mutual evaluation should take place all the time — that such explicit evaluation helps provide important data around which the contract between the supervisor and the supervisee can be regularly renegotiated and the supervision improved.

But life is rarely ideal. From time to time we observed work in a situation where the family studies section's control over the process was limited by the pressures of an impinging system. For example, a school of social work insisted upon formal evaluation of its students placed with us in training. Or, occasionally, a supervisor occupied a staff position with administrative authority over his supervisee. (The most striking example of this occurs among the psychology interns. They are routinely supervised by the man who makes hiring decisions for the institutional jobs most of these same interns are seeking!)

Although these are typical practices in many agencies and institutions, we repeatedly witnessed how such intrusions prevented the openness and trust we consider an absolute pre-condition for effective supervision. We found the work improved when the supervisor at least made explicit the bind in which the supervisee was thus placed — and attempted to explore with the supervisee ways out of the bind.

In addition to these obviously flagrant contradictions between the practice and the preaching, similar phenomena — on a much more subtle level — required serious attention for the supervision to move well.

437

In our observation of some fifty supervisory hours, we were struck by the repetitive occurrence of certain problems that seemed to confront, with almost monotonous regularity, both the experienced and novice supervisor.

Control. Failure of the supervisor to establish and maintain control of the process in the supervisory session was the most common pitfall in the supervisions we observed. This failure always placed the supervision in serious risk of becoming merely a pleasant rite, with, at best, both parties basking in pseudo-mutual warmth, secure from any danger of new growth, or, at worst, destroying by an insidious contagion the therapies under supervision.

We do not know whether the almost universality of this issue in the supervisions we observed is simply a phenomenon of our competitive culture which contaminates almost all relationships with problems of dominance-submission, or whether it was the threatening material (always involved in family therapy) which created something akin to psychoanalytic "resistance."

Whatever the origins of the problem, it is clear that control of the process is necessary to deal with *all* the relevant phenomena to achieve the goals of the supervision. Control requires of the supervisor his conscious and constant attention to every aspect of presented behavior, including such often neglected data as kinesics, leakage phenomena, communication patterns, etc. Although there was as much variation in style and technique for maintaining control as there was in the actual personalities of the supervisors, all effective supervisors were clearly always "in charge."

Contract. The optional contract varied with the specific grouping. Each dyad is different, and the maximum contribution a supervisor may make to the growth of his supervisee varies with who his supervisee is, and where he's at, in time. However, certain crucial issues of *contract* must be clear:

1. The mutual obligations — and the limits to these

obligations. (A specific example: The supervisee is responsible for the therapy he is conducting; the supervisor, for the supervising process.)

2. The supervisor/supervisee relationship is a valid focus of observation. For example, in a discussion of "problems," supervisors described various supervisees as "dependent," "competitive," "reluctant," "anxious," "over-ambitious," "intrusive," etc. Although these labels may be accurate clinical descriptions, we believe it is more useful to look at the entire *relationship,* rather than at the intra-psychic structure of the supervisee. Such examination is not only more illuminating, but also more effective in short-circuiting the development of a pathological dyad.

3. The degree of the supervisor's participant observation. Does the supervisee present, at one extreme, a loose rendering of his therapy session for comments? Or is the supervisor allowed to "sit in" on the therapy session as occasional live consultant? If the latter, what rules are established to maintain the therapist's control of the therapy?

Induction and Replication. One of the most dramatic and heuristically useful ways to teach the therapist the nature (and power) of the family system under treatment is to demonstrate the almost inevitable induction (at least transiently) by the family system of the supervisor-supervisee system.

Such phenomena, when exploited for training purposes, are rich opportunities to clarify the system under observation and, more important, to develop the student's capacity to experience himself both in and out of the system.

It goes without saying, of course, that such induction phenomena can be kept merely occasional and transient only through careful attention to the process; without such attention the supervision itself may be doomed to repeat the same treadmill ballet with which the family is stuck: additional dancers, but the same choreography. Even worse

439

— we have observed (fortunately, only rarely) the induction of a family system by a pathogenic supervisor-supervisee system.

Outside Systems. These may impinge on the supervisory relationship in covertly destructive ways. We see this most commonly and most glaringly when the supervisor has administrative power over the supervisee in another context. Unfortunately, there often is realistically no way out of such system-binds: However, a sensitive supervisor can expose the existence of the bind; focus an exploration of the potential consequences to the supervision; and cooperatively search with the supervisee for solutions to the problems posed. This discussion itself, honestly pursued, can help develop the very openness and trust — the existence of which the impinging system threatened to subvert.

Problems of Co-therapy. The advantages of a co-therapist, particularly for the novice therapist, have been advocated so clearly and so frequently they need no repetition here. However, co-therapy teams are particularly vulnerable to induction and we now recommend *against* the casual formation of a co-therapy team *unless the partners are prepared for a serious commitment to work on their own relationship.* Otherwise, they are "set-ups" for system induction, and the supervision — if it is to go anywhere at all — must deal relentlessly with this process.

Finally, but most important: the *sine qua non* of good supervision is the establishment of conditions that make for openness and trust. It is incumbent on the supervisor to use every available indicator to monitor the relationship for this quality. (Skillful reading of kinesics can be especially useful.) It then becomes the supervisor's responsibility to search out any influence (whether an objective phenomenon like the pressure of an impinging system or a subjective distortion in the mind of the supervisee like the projected expectation of perfect work), and to deal with it.

Equally important, the supervisor must be rigorously self-observant. Just as the supervisor's openness provides a model for the student, and sets the tone for the relationship,

440

conversely, subtle cues, especially non-verbal, from the supervisor can also cut off openness and signal to the supervisee that the material is too charged for this supervisor to hear and respond to.

It will be noted that we do not address ourselves to the question of the boundary between supervision and therapy of the supervisee. Although this was a frequently debated issue in our seminar, we believe that it is essentially a false issue — that many supervisors are, in fact, counter-phobic in their avoidance of appearing to "do therapy" with their supervisees.

We believe that:

Family therapy, because of its immediacy and aliveness, much more than individual therapy, elicits therapist responses which relate to the therapist's own family of origin or family of procreation. We do *not* view this as "unanalyzed counter-transference phenomena." Rather, we see this as an inevitable and natural process and one which the therapist will be encountering throughout his professional lifetime. The supervisor's task is not to help the therapist "solve" his family problems, but to teach him to be aware of, and to cope with, the secret presence of his own family in the treatment room.

In the relationship between supervisor and supervisee, issues of dependence/autonomy, submission/dominance, distance/intimacy may arise. These are relevant data to be examined, and indeed are really issues of contract. Not dealing with them can cause supervisions to founder; dealing openly with them may resolve secret but paralyzing impasses both in the supervision and in the treatment.

THE SEMINAR AS A TEACHING DEVICE

The main usefulness of this kind of seminar is that it speeds the "seasoning" of the novice supervisor. It makes available to him the combined experiences of all his

441

colleagues in the seminar, thus providing at least a nodding acquaintance with different problems in supervision that could otherwise be acquired only over an enormously long period of time. In the process, the supervisor gains significantly in self-confidence. We found the sharing of experience supportive in the best sense of that word. Moreover, the repetitive observation of collusive alliances between family members, supervisee, and supervisor, to avoid exposure and maintain existing equilibria, helps sharpen the alertness to (and ability to interrupt) similar phenomena in his own work. Finally, the openness of the discussions within the seminar — especially the *responsibility* to attend to and comment on the group process — provides a model for the supervisor's behavior with the supervisee.

There remain, however, a number of as yet unresolved issues.

The observation of *one* supervisory session, providing a cross-section of the process, rather than its observation over an extended period of time, generates pressure to produce some degree of movement within each observed session. In our post-session discussions, there was often a significant split among members of the seminar with the psychoanalysts, in particular, most consistently urging a less ambitious goal for each session. It may well be that devoting every third or fourth hour to the same supervision (i.e., a continuous case) might help resolve this issue and demonstrate some of the process that develops only over time.

There is no question that being observed introduces new phenomena into the system under observation. We have taken that as a *given,* and have functioned on the assumption that the artificial stress of such observation will highlight what happens in the system under other, more natural, stresses.

During the early months of the seminar, we had the supervisee sit in on the post-session that immediately followed the observed supervision of his work. We felt, at that time, that this practice was in keeping with our philosophy of promoting maximum openness. As the seminar evolved, however, we came to feel that this practice could not be useful to the supervisee, and it markedly inhibited our own discussion of the process. The supervisee was an outsider coming into a seminar in which the evolution of a group process had made possible a degree of openness for which the supervisee was neither prepared by experience nor supported by a group of his own peers. Free discussion proved either "traumatic" to the supervisee or interfered with the supervisor's freedom to choose the maximally effective timing of his own interventions in relation to the process.

A brief word about an interesting variation of our usual format follows. A meeting was divided into three parts:

Part 1: The student therapist conducted a family therapy session before the one-way screen. Behind the screen, our seminar observed the therapy. *But the supervisor on that case was not included.* We saw the actual live material; he had to depend only on the data reported to him.

Part 2: The student therapist and the supervisor conducted their usual supervisory hour before the one-way screen. The student therapist reported on the session he had just conducted, which the seminar had witnessed. Behind the screen, the members of the seminar watched the inevitably distorted description of the therapy session they had just observed.

Part 3: The post-session. Now the supervisory process was discussed.

We experimented with this variation only in the last few meetings of our seminar, and it is therefore too soon to assess the usefulness of this format as a teaching device. Certainly it demonstrated the expected limitations of basing supervision only on the data reported by the therapist. We have not had adequate discussions, however, on the philosophical issues implied by this innovation. There are some, for example, who might argue that it is the supervisee's

443

perception of the experience that is the proper subject of the supervision rather than what actually happened. Even discounting that issue (most family therapists are interested in system and process, not merely mental representations of the phenomena), there still remains for the supervisor the question of how best to deal with the subjective distortions of the student therapist.

When the scientific community began systematically to observe ongoing psychotherapies, it became obvious that most therapists weren't doing what they thought they were doing. For the first time, the possibility arose of describing accurately what happens in psychotherapy.

We are now convinced that the process of supervision can similarly benefit from "everybody watching."

fourteen

study your own family

P. Guerin and T. Fogarty

Once upon a time, an all-together-now asked two lone wolves if they would put together a series of "we" statements in the form of a chapter for the all-together-now's book. In the spirit of camaraderie and friendship the two lone wolves tried. But try as they might they just could not make "we" statements. It was almost as if it were against their "religion." As a result, the chapter to follow is divided into two sections, one by each of the authors.

P.G.

The inevitable has come to pass. Family therapists, having established a beach-head in psychological circles, are now turning their attention to working on their own families. But what does "working" on one's own family mean and what place does it have in training family therapists? What it means depends to a great extent on how the trainee and supervisor view family therapy.

To some therapists family therapy is a technique to be tried when all else fails or when individual therapy is not feasible. Others see "family" as a new approach to emotional problems. To them psychological problems are a product of dysfunctional relationships. Each of the dyadic relationships in the family is interconnected, forming a relationship system. How this relationship system works is of primary importance. "Why" explanations, though plausible, are of secondary importance. Those who see "family" in this way make working on one's own family an important part of their personal and professional life.

Murray Bowen has been a major proponent of this view, and has stressed the importance of the trainee's working on his own family. In practice he has carried this to the extent of presenting the "work" he has done on his own family at a workshop presentation and later in print (1971).

While under Bowen's supervision as a psychiatric resident at Georgetown, I began "working" on my own family. For the past three years I have continued this work and at present see it as a lifetime project. Now, in my position as a "family" supervisor, I liberally use examples from this work to seed the idea with trainees.

Stories about one's own family have a certain shock value and are usually listened to intently. The various ways the message behind these stories is heard, however, are always of interest to me. It is often heard as "go visit your grandmother," or "go back home and tell the ol' lady off," or "go back home and make everybody happy." In supervision I usually field such responses by agreeing that it can be fun to see grandma, triumphant to tell the ol' lady off, or gratifying to promote togetherness, but that I don't see any of them as accomplishing anything in themselves. At any rate, none of these are what I mean by working on one's own family. The best way to define what I mean is by describing what I do in the context of my own family. When a problem arises in my family, I try to examine my own behavior (i.e., how I am thinking, feeling, and operating). For instance, if my wife appears depressed or one of my daughters becomes whiny and irritable, I will look to my behavior in my relationship with my wife, the troubled child, each of the other children, my parents, etc. The purpose of this is based on the idea that if my wife's depression or my child's behavior is an expression of a family problem, I have a responsibility for my part in the process. I believe that the only one I can change is myself, and therefore if I hope to exact change in the family process there must be a change on my part. I remember an instance during this past year in which I was aware of being moderately depressed and somewhat irritable. At dinner I noticed that my oldest daughter was engaged in one of her sporadic bouts of thumb-sucking. I dropped some sardonic comment. My daughter replied, "Daddy, if you don't stop picking at me, I'm going to suck my thumb for the rest of my life." We all laughed. After dinner in the relative isolation of my office, I was able to figure out the following seemingly connected series of events. Early in the week the emotional tone in the extended family had been especially tight. In response to this extended family difficulty, my wife predictably pulled back, establishing distance between herself and other family members. Sensing this pulling back, I, according to form, began crowding in on her by repetitive questioning and expert but unsolicited supervision on household projects. This method of crowding usually results in increased distance on the part of my wife, and I begin taking this distance personally — thereby further intensifying the situation. When things get to this point between my wife

447

and myself, our oldest daughter's feeling barometer picks up the rising level of tension. As her own anxiety level rises in response to this, she begins making frequent mistakes or appearing confused and helpless. Watching this, I will become irritable and begin to press her.

If sufficient pressure is applied, pacification by oral gratification becomes apparent. All of these observations may or may not be true, but using them as a basis for a hypothesis on how the present situation evolved, I could then begin an attempt to change my own part in the process. Actually my daughter's comment on the possible perpetuation of her thumb-sucking had succeeded in decreasing some of the emotional intensity. This decrease had enabled me to begin thinking about the situation. Once I attempted to bring about some change in my part of this process, I would then be able to validate or invalidate part or even all of my hypothesis.

The plan of action I decided upon called for me to cease questioning or commenting on either my wife's or my daughter's behavior. In place of this I would make comments in my wife's presence like, "It sure is peaceful to live with someone who doesn't burden me with personal thoughts and feelings," or "I can't stand people who are always talking about their troubles." Immediately after a comment like this I would make a quick exit, instead of waiting for or even expecting a response from my wife.

Where my daughter's performance was concerned, instead of a barrage of irritable corrections, I would say, "Can you do that wrong once more, honey? I think it's good for kids to practice doing things wrong," or "After you have finished practicing I want you to spend the next half hour sucking your thumb." I would then leave the room.

Moves such as these served several purposes. I was able to check my anxiety and decrease the crowding of my wife and daughter, while still letting them know that I was aware of what was going on. Handling things in this way made it possible for me to view their behavior as less of a personal affront. Given enough room, my wife was able to

448

move toward me and open up the issues which were bothering her. Once the anxiety level of the whole family had decreased, we were then able to deal with the problems in the extended family in a more meaningful and successful way.

Obviously the outcome of this story was satisfactory or I wouldn't have used it as an example. But more important to me than the success of this individual operation was the fact that I had learned something. One of the recurring, automatic behavior programs in my family had been spelled out and an attempt had been made to change it.

The trainee's response to "hero" stories such as these is often,* "Sounds interesting, but how does one go about it?" The first step is to obtain a minimal groundwork of theoretical ideas. The best published source of these at present is Bowen's article on "The Use of Family Theory in Clinical Practice" (1966). The next step is to take out a pencil and a large piece of paper and draw out a schematic diagram of your own three-generational family relationship system. This schematic diagram is called a genogram. I shall attempt to illustrate by using my own family system. (See Figure 1.)

The genogram provides a guide for following the action. It's like the program at a football game or perhaps even more like the coach's blackboard at half time. It names and numbers each of the family members and their relationships to one another. You start the genogram with the central and primary relationship in the nuclear family — that between the spouses. Squares are drawn to represent men, circles to represent women, with no offense intended to the men. You then insert the ages of the individuals inside their respective square or circle. On the line connecting the square and circle you place the date of marriage. I am thirty-three, my wife is thirty, and we were married in 1963. (See Figure 1A, page 459.) Next comes the completion of the nuclear family by adding the children. My wife and I

---

*In my experience, fifty percent of trainees express interest. Of this fifty percent only one-half actually do anything with the idea.

have three girls ages six, four, and one. (See Figure 1B, page 459.)

At this point the functioning of the nuclear family can be considered. The presence or absence of work productivity, socialization, isolation, emotional, and physical symptoms are reviewed. Then the state of the various relationships is scanned, with an eye toward how emotional issues are handled. The relationships that appear to work well and those with the most difficulty are pinpointed. An attempt is made to define the shifting patterns of alliance and how they operate. The effect the functioning level of one family member appears to have on the functioning level of other family members is defined. These matters having been considered, you expand the genogram to include the extended family — each spouse's family of origin. (See Figure 1C.)

My wife's side of the extended family consists of her mother, age sixty, and two younger siblings. Both siblings are married, one living in New York City, the other in Washington, D.C. Her brother has two daughters. My wife's father died in December, 1969. In constructing a genogram, the dates of important events such as deaths, births, marriages, retirements, etc., are always worth investigating. Events such as these have a profound emotional impact on families. Like adolescence and old age, they are normative crises. If the family relationship system is flexible and open, there are open lines of communication. Through these lines emotional issues get dealt with, rather than closed off and buried. As a result, the impact of such events on the family system will be absorbed and dissipated.

If the opposite is true and family behavior patterns are more fixed, channels of communication get closed off and feeling-laden issues are buried. Apprehension over controlling one's own feelings or dealing with the emotional response of others prevents the open airing of issues such as the death of a family member. In this type of "closed-system" situation, emotional or physical symptoms will often appear in one or more family members. For example, a local school psychologist referred a family to me, in which the twelve-year-old son

450

was symptomatic. His performance in school had dropped far below his potential and he appeared clinically depressed.

During the past year the boy's need for glasses had been discovered. The fact that this would prevent his following his father's career was considered an important etiologic factor. Filling in the genogram, the fact of the maternal grandfather's death fourteen months prior to the family's initial visit was uncovered. Grandfather was a prominent and successful man. He took a great deal of interest in his family, especially his daughter and his grandson.

As such, he was an important functioning part of this family. His untimely death had been a shock. The family, however, quickly accepted it as one of the tragedies of life. They had remained brave and stoic throughout the funeral ritual, shedding only the respectable amount of tears. His death left a large empty space in the family. The boy and his mother frequently thought of him. These thoughts inevitably provoked a lot of feelings. But mother wouldn't talk about it, "because it's morbid." The son wouldn't talk about his thoughts and feelings, "because it would upset mother." As a result, mother would find convenient times when no one was around to cry and get it over with, rather than burdening anyone with her troubles. Her son found himself unable to concentrate, having difficulty sleeping, and without the energy needed to get involved with his heretofore favorite projects. He would find himself thinking of grandfather, wishing he could talk to him again, wishing he had had a chance to tell him some things before he had died. True to the image of the "brave soldier," he kept these thoughts and feelings to himself. The opening up of the issue of grandfather's death in the family session led to the discussion of these thoughts and feelings and the effect of keeping them closed off. I instructed the mother and son to work consciously on keeping the issue open by purposely discussing grandfather's death, when these thoughts and feelings would arise. This enabled them to deal with the feelings. As a result, the son's depression lifted and his school performance rose sharply.

To return to my own genogram, both of my parents are living and age sixty-three. I have one sister, who is married. My sister and her husband have one daughter. My parents and my sister both live in Fairfield, Conn., within five minutes' traveling time of each other. (See Figure 1D.)

The physical location of the various parts of the family system is another area to investigate. In some families a cohesiveness appears evident. When this is present, you will find multiple members of a family all living within walking distance of one another. There is frequent visiting back and forth. In other families, there is an explosive quality. When this is present, you will find family members spread to all corners of the globe. The frequency of contact is minimal at best. It often happens that a person from an explosive family will marry someone from a cohesive family, and become absorbed into the cohesive family structure of the spouse. In my family this doesn't appear to be the case, as strong elements of cohesion are present in both parts of the extended family.

The issue of physical proximity and distance within the family has another facet. People tend to deal with emotional conflict by either becoming over-distant or over-involved with the problem. For instance, one person may respond to family problems by telephoning one or more family members daily. On the other hand, another person may move three thousand miles away and reduce contact with family members to a minimum. In order to deal with emotional conflict, a certain degree of physical distance seems necessary. Moving one's self outside of the range of the family's emotional bombardment is necessary to facilitate a relatively objective view of what is going on.

I now live within fifty miles of my extended family. Up until two years ago, I lived three hundred miles away, so the tension input from my extended family was much less intense than at present. It took much less energy on my part to deal with the relationship problems as they arose. On trips to visit the extended family I would often get caught up in the conflictual part of the family emotional process. I could feel myself tightening up inside and the ability to observe and think about what was going on would become markedly impaired. It would take up to a week following my return from the visit before I could begin to think again. Since moving to within fifty miles of my extended family, the emotional input has greatly increased, as has the amount of energy necessary to keep myself loose emotionally. On one occasion during this past year, I found myself caught up in attempting to deal with a conflictual process in my extended family. I made several attempts at thinking it out but drew a blank. The absence of a flow of ideas about a particular problem is a good index of the degree to which one is emotionally caught up in a feeling process.

While struggling with this, a professional trip to Boston happened along. On the day of my departure I made another attempt at sorting out the difficulty by visiting my parents. The visit was at best unproductive. It was not until I had been in Boston for twenty-four hours that a flow of ideas about the situation began. As a result, I was able to sort out my part in the process. On my return trip, I made a re-entry into my extended family. This time I was emotionally loose and had a plan of action. I was able to reverse my part in the process and as a result, the conflict was eventually resolved.

Instances like this point to the importance of physical distance. On the other hand, people tend to equate maturity with an avoidance of contact with extended family members, particularly parents. Being three thousand miles away and not having had contact with one's parents for years is seen as independence. In my experience, rather than independence, it represents a reactive distance to unresolved conflict in an extremely important relationship. Planned distance to enable thought and planning for re-entry is essential. Reactive distance leaves the problem unresolved and attempts to close off the feelings connected to the conflictual relationship. Unfortunately, these closed feelings will out, most often in a camouflaged form in one's nuclear family.

The names and numbers, physical location, and frequency of contact of family members have been filled in on the genograph. Important happenings such as deaths have been investigated. The next step is to define the triangular sets within the relationship system of the family.

The emotional process in the family system appears to move in such a way that interlocking triangular building blocks are formed. The concept of the triangle is one of the primary ones in family systems thinking. It is based on the idea that the emotional process between two people is unstable and thus moves to stabilize itself by triangling in a third person or object. This triangulation may take place by the active movement of one or both parties to triangle a third or by the third party's being caught up by the anxiety in the tottering dyad and being pulled into the emotional process as a stabilizer.

In any people triangle, there are three points (representing the individuals) and three legs (representing the relationships). The process works so that at any given time, two points and the leg connecting them are cozy and pulled together. Simultaneously, the other two legs are distant and the point connecting them is in the odd-man-out position. For instance, referring back to my genogram, let's look at the triangle concerning my mother, my sister, and myself.

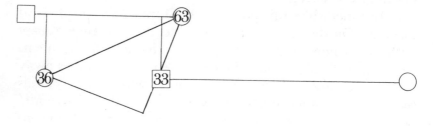

Figure 2

My mother and sister are together and my mother begins to talk about her displeasure with me. The emotional process between my mother and myself is being run at my sister. If my sister reacts to this communication by agreeing

454

with mother, she and mother form the cozy or pulled-together leg of the triangle, and I am in the odd-man-out position. On the other hand, if my sister reacts to mother's communication by defending me, she makes the leg of the triangle between us the cozy one and mother is in the out position. My sister might further solidify the pulling together by telephoning me to complain about mother. And so the process goes on. . . .

The dysfunctional or undesirable aspect of this process is that it prevents the emotional process between two people from ever being worked out. In this way, personal, one-to-one, open relationships, in which there is a mutual sharing of personal thoughts and feelings, cannot develop. Detriangulation of oneself and the development of a one-to-one personal relationship with each family member are the pot of gold at the end of the rainbow in the project of working on one's own family. In order to accomplish this, it is therefore necessary to do the work of spelling out the triangles that exist in one's family. The process of detriangulating one's self is complex. Basically, it entails a definition of the process and a plan of action whereby self ceases to participate in it. For example, in the triangle just discussed, if we flip that around so that mother is communicating to me her displeasure with my sister, I can attempt to detriangle myself in the following way. If I do not react on a feeling level to my mother's communication, I can take her hypothesis, "Your sister has faults," and run it into the ground by finding so many things wrong with my sister that mother, in a predictable fashion, will begin to defend her. In addition, I can phone my sister and indicate to her that she should find a better way to relate to mother. By this series of moves, I have given them back to one another to work out their problem. Maybe they will or maybe they won't. But I have fulfilled my responsibility by not participating in a triangulation of the conflict.

Realizing that the number of triangles multiplies with the number of people, it is easy to appreciate the complexity of the family process. Faced with this real complexity, one can only begin to spell out the triangles and deal with them as they become active. In the beginning, it is especially wise to try to pick out a few of the more dormant triangles and try your hand at those. That is preferable to waiting for one to become active and hit you over the head. In this regard, I found it was initially much easier to work on my relationships with my wife's half of the extended family. This was the area in which I was first successful. These successes spurred me on to the greater challenge of my own nuclear family and my half of the extended family.

The most difficult work for me has been in attempting to establish a one-to-one personal relationship with each of my parents. The trainees I have supervised who have tried this project also found this to be so. When an attempt is made to exact a change in a relationship with one parent, there is usually a pulling together of both parents into a position of "*we*-ness." Parents are experts at the lateral pass. For instance, if I open up a conflictual issue with my mother, she will invariably pass the ball laterally to my father with a, "What do you think about that?" This is usually followed by a statement like "We've always thought . . ." Therefore it is impossible to accomplish any work on a one-to-one relationship while both parents are physically present. In attempting to do this work, arrange to have a time and place where it is possible to be alone together.

Despite this difficulty, working on my own family has enabled me to see my parents as real people. At this point I don't believe I over-value or under-value either of them. Although on the one hand I am perhaps more aware of their shortcomings, I believe that each one of them is more knowable to me now and that I am closer to each of them than at any other time in my life. One thing is certain; I don't view them as the malignant cause of my shortcomings.

There are many reasons for sharing this work with trainees. First of all, it demonstrates to the trainees that you really mean what you say, and furthermore that you do what you say. You don't propose that others — patients and trainees — work on their families while you do something

456

else, or nothing at all. It also demonstrates your willingness to be open about yourself, and personalizes the work. In turn, it makes clear to the trainee that you are interested in his own family as well as those families he is seeing professionally. In addition, the presentation to the trainee of your work on your own family gives him a frame of reference from which he can launch his own work.

Of the twenty-five percent of trainees who, in my experience, take on the project of working on their own family, all have found it to be helpful personally and professionally. The part they find most difficult is thinking out a plan of action and doing something different once the process has been spelled out. Doing something to change your behavior in the context of your relationships with spouse, children, parents, etc., is the route to differentiation of self from other. It is this planning and doing which is the most difficult emotionally and separates the successes from the failures.

Another important aspect of the work a trainee does on his own family is the relationship between the trainee and his family supervisor. This is dealt with extensively in Part II of this chapter.

〜〜〜〜〜〜〜〜〜〜〜〜〜〜〜〜〜〜〜〜〜〜〜〜〜〜〜 *References*

1. Eastern Pennsylvania Psychiatric Institute Conference on the Family, March 1967.
2. BOWEN, M. (1971), Toward the differentiation of a self in one's own family. In *Family Interaction,* ed. J. Framo. New York: Springer.
3. ——— (1966), The use of family theory in clinical practice. *Comprehensive Psychiat.,* 7:5 (Oct.).

457

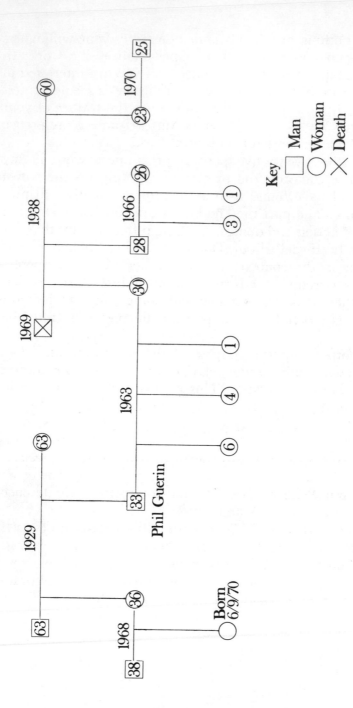

Key

□	Man
○	Woman
✕	Death

Phil Guerin

Born 6/9/70

Figure 1

458

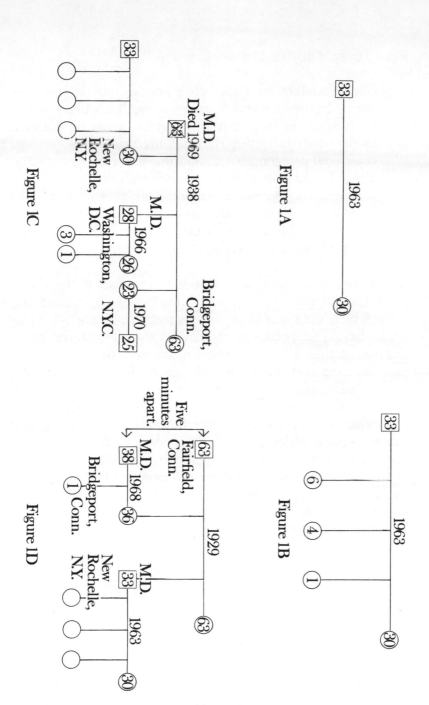

Figure 1A

Figure 1B

Figure 1C

Figure 1D

459

George walked into the office and we introduced ourselves. In direct response to questions, he told me about his position in the training program, what he planned to do when he finished, what his orientation toward emotional problems was, and some other pertinent data. Then I told him about my own training, experience, practice, etc. Again, in response to questions, he told me that he was married, had one son, and a little about his parents. Then, I sat back and asked what he would like to do with the rest of the hour.

It would be hard to tell, out of context, if the above paragraph described either a training hour or a "treatment" hour. Much the same thing occurs in both. There is a focus on gathering of pertinent data, and then a gradual clarification of the "I" position of the trainee. Initially his "I" position is spread out to include his profession, his family, and his particular position in time. From the start, the context of supervision is set to include the total self of the supervisee — profession, inner self, family, viewpoint, and future. This is followed by the supervisor's doing precisely the same thing. I tell people of my own family, orientation, training, viewpoints, practice — a necessarily general but inclusive definition of me and my context. This is designed to set the scene. It will hopefully lead to each of us seeing himself as a part of a continuum, and to the development of a personal relationship.

George starts to tell me about families. I sigh with relief. At least he is seeing some families. In the worst of supervision, the trainee lapses into individual dynamic thinking and ponders about seeing a family some time in the future. The future is now. It is difficult to follow George because he keeps giving me historical data full of holes, liberally laced with gratuitous explanations and interpretations about what is going

460

on inside these people he is talking about. I long to have them there so that I can ask them what they are thinking and feeling. But I persist, trying to show interest. I find myself really wishing that he would talk about his own family.

When I was in supervision, I would either try to impress the "big man" with how much I knew or look to him for wise answers. I would be generally relieved when the whole thing was done with. I assume he was too. My supervisors would refer to me as if I were an impersonal machine, and I don't really believe they knew what they were talking about. Heaven forbid that I should ever get to know them. Supervision, like all human contact, tends to start with two people talking about a third — the patient. This is to be expected and endured. Fools rush in where wise men fear to tread. Distance between self and other is narrowed gradually. There is a routine, a ritual, a format which leads into the possibility of a relationship going further. It is not so troublesome that this ritual exists, but that it so often gets stuck there. To unstick, the supervisor must be alert, like a halfback going around end, for an opening.

George is telling me about a family. The husband lives alternately with his wife and a mistress. George thinks the husband is a homosexual and is full of explanations about the man. I notice that George seems to document every viewpoint by "I feel this and I feel that." I wonder what a homosexual is. It seems to me that this family is in a triangle. I try to explain this to George. He looks confused. I search for a piece of paper and draw a diagram of a triangle. Then I illustrate it with examples from my own family. "It's like this, George. If my wife is doing something with my son that I believe is absolutely wrong, then I have a tendency to jump in and give her the truth, which only I possess. If I jump in, then she and I get into a fight and while we argue, son goes out the back door on his way. My wife

461

retreats to her room and I sit down and ponder how I am going to straighten out all the other members of my family. The result of my jumping in is to increase the emotional intensity of anger, prevent discussion, allow my son to parlay the triangle, and simply to repeat things that haven't worked in the past and won't work in the future." As I talk, I can see ol' George's eyes light up a bit; he even begins to chuckle. I wonder if he has had some of the same experiences. This is what you call an opening.

In the process of supervision of families, more often than not, I find golden opportunities for the development of a struggle. My own experience in my family and in my practice has convinced me that this kind of a development is useless and often destructive. I try hard to listen to what the other fellow has to say; then I try to get my ideas across. I try to take an "I" position. With George, he saw homosexuality and I saw a triangle. I generally start with some kind of an abstract explanation of what a triangle is and this, as often as not, simply does not work. Yet, it forms a baseline. Then I draw pictures and try to demonstrate it visually. This helps. It always helps. Seeing something will sooner or later help to clarify an idea. Then I move it into the concrete and the personal. It was concrete because I gave an example of a specific situation in a specific family. It was personal because it referred to myself and my own family. The results are almost inevitable. They are not inevitable (nor should they be) in terms of agreement. They are inevitable in terms of the beginning of openness. We now have the beginning of a context wherein George can take a stand and I can too. We can be honest with each other. Furthermore, the first teaching experience of families, "What is a triangle?," has been put out on the table. It has been put there in a personal way. I did it first with my own family. I ain't caught a fish yet but I can see them biting. What's more, they don't even know they're biting. Now I'm starting to get into business.

462

The next meeting, George doesn't show up. He is attending some important meeting on the "Importance of transference-counter-transference in the development of the female carrot" at the New York Psychoanalytic Association. Without further comment, this is a most discouraging development. But I persevere. After all, they pay me, and the other parts of the job ain't so bad. There are some people there that I actually enjoy. The next week, George is back. He tells me about the meeting and I'm sure glad he went to it. What the hell? George deserves such a fate. I think he is hopeless. Something wakes me from my sleep. George is talking about his family. How about that? He found a triangle. He knows they exist. This is a phenomenal development in view of the fact that every family has about five million of them. George is alive. The trouble is that George doesn't even know if he is alive. But hope springs eternal within the human breast. George found a triangle. We are back in business. George starts to talk about himself and his wife. It seems that he has a mother-in-law that he has no trouble with. The only trouble is that he can't stand her and that he stays away from her. Of course, this isn't a real problem. He has taken care of this in his analysis. He can explain it now. It's just that he hasn't spoken to her in ten years. Of course, someone might consider it a problem because, every time the subject comes up, he and his wife fight. Well, they really don't fight, they just don't talk to each other for one week.

The teaching of family therapy or family theory is a most discouraging prospect. It is like swimming against the tide. Yet there is an audience, a group of people who really want to know. George jumped out toward it and then took a massive retreat. Yet, the next time he jumped he landed smack in the middle of his own family triangle. Now I know that he is gettable, he is reachable. Now he has to live with it. He can no longer run. He has a triangle in his own family.

If what I have to say is really useful, then I should be able to document it. The context has been set. The continuum has been set. The rewards of good deeds earlier done may now be reaped. We have taken the pains to set the context in a continuum wherein his family, profession, and other interests now meet with my family, profession, and interests. He doesn't move in a straight line, but what does? He has opened his mind so that he can see. That is all I ask. There is something personal for him to deal with in his own family. Now he can begin to see what I mean. My family is my system. That is where my most intense involvement lies. I care more about my family than any person that I supervise. I will tell George that. He'd better understand it. I think that now he can understand it. He begins to find out that he must really deal with his mother-in-law. Staying away from her is no solution. He is beginning to find out that distance is a useful tool to "think," but that distance never solves problems. Explanations are great until one has a problem in one's own family. Then, one wants results. But, "What is the price?"

George tells me about something that he tried. He asked his mother-in-law over. She came. His wife loved it, but after her mother left, told him that he did it to embarrass her. He felt resentful. He likened it to a family that he was seeing. He could understand that this man might not be a homosexual, but that he might feel neglected and seek consolation outside the family. I stayed quiet. This guy was thinking. I didn't want to impose my thoughts on someone who was thinking. I would like him to continue. He has a question. What is this thing we do here? He has a psychoanalyst. He takes his personal problems there. I am supposed to be teaching him. What am I doing? I hear this as an equalizing statement. He no longer looks up to me. He is ready to deal with me. Now I can confront him. "What do you want?" I ask. "Spell it out." He is on the spot. By now he likes it, but he also is seeing that it exacts an emotional price from him. Tough. I should charge him.

There is no question but that supervision and teaching of the family are a very difficult job. Too many take it as something interesting or entertaining. The basic notions of triangles, fusion, distance, etc., are so different from ordinary dynamic psychology. The best and perhaps only way to really understand these ideas is to try them out in one's own family. The trainee can be encouraged to do this by having him view it as an innocent experiment. If one can predict to him what will happen when he tries it, then he is impressed and fascinated. This may disturb him if he is used to taking emotional problems to his analyst. This also sets up another potential triangle between the supervisor, the supervisee, and the analyst. It offers a concrete example of what a triangle is. It offers an opportunity to see self as a part of a continuum which spreads through the family, the analysis, and the teaching. In this sense, there is no difference between treatment, teaching, living in one's own family, or one's professional life. Any supervision that limits itself to the trainee and the family he is seeing is practically worthless. It becomes but an intellectual exercise. Supervision should cease as such. The whole family of the supervisee should be involved just as in "treatment" or having a family picnic. This would eliminate much of the artificial flavor. A professional who comes to me with a family problem invariably learns more about family therapy than any pure supervision experience can produce by itself.

George brings a family in for me to interview. He is obviously impressed by the interview. He discusses the family and what he sees me doing. Then he compares me to another family therapist and says that I am really not so different. Toward the end of the hour, he raises an issue. Something about his family is bugging him. He has been getting letters from his mother which indicate that things are not going well in the extended family. One of the reasons he moved to New York was to get away from them. He had thought that the problem was solved. Now he is concerned and wondering if this is so. He can feel the emotional pull from the extended family. Mother tells him that he doesn't care.

The particular details of George's difficulty with his extended family do not particularly matter. What is clear is that he does have to work on his parents. Growing up, he was triangled into his parents. He was overly close to his mother and distant from his father. The third leg of the triangle was the distance between father and mother. When George married, he moved away from mother and created a pull in that overly close leg of the triangle. Now he was hearing rumblings and repercussions from the extended family. This was a golden opportunity for him to do something. It would have to be something different since he would not want to duplicate the previous dysfunctional triangle. He wrote them a letter. As usual, it was addressed to both. Despite this, the content of the letter was directed to his mother. She answered the letter. When he replied, he opened by directing the content to his father. He asked specific questions about his father's business that his father alone could answer. Toward the end of the letter, he dropped a "reverse fusion" on his mother, who had told him that he didn't care. She fused with him. She acted as though she could read his mind and his motivations. She acted as if she was inside his head. She acted like a psychiatrist. The reversal is just like the old statue-of-liberty play in football. He wrote that he had been getting the impression lately that she was cool to him and that she really was ignoring and not caring about him. George had much difficulty understanding precisely why he even wrote this letter.

George came to the next visit fairly glum. Nothing was going right. His wife read the letter before he sent it. She felt that he was being unnecessarily cruel to his mother, just as he was to her at times. Father had written a long reply which didn't seem to amount to much, except that he hadn't replied before. Father included a message which said that his mother wanted George to call her. George was discouraged. Fortunately, he had a session with his analyst that afternoon and would be able to cathect his discomfort.

George was beginning to learn. Now he could appreciate that there is such a thing as an emotional system. As soon as he changed, everybody in the system told him to get back in his place. His father tried to move away into his distant position and get his mother to deal with George again. Mother got hurt and pulled into herself. Even his wife fused into telling him his motivation was cruelty. George was also beginning to learn that change is difficult, more difficult than sitting in a chair reciting problems to harmless others. It meant action, movement. It often meant doing things which would create discomfort in others and doubt, confusion, and unrest in self. It meant that writing a letter to father could change the position of mother and wife. He could now begin to see the interconnections between members of the family system. He said: "My God, I married someone just like my mother."

George and I finished out the rest of the year, fritzing around between the families he was seeing and his own family. It never really became work on his family because he never even seriously thought of bringing his wife in. He fritzed around at the periphery. Yet he did learn something. One year later, I ran into George again. He hadn't seen a family in that whole year. He was still interested in systems and somehow thought that he could eventually use this in his work in public health.

fifteen
the therapist's family, friends, and colleagues

A. Ferber and C. Whitaker

Carl Whitaker asked Andy Ferber to "do a tape" for distribution in a series that Whitaker had recorded. The following is an edited transcript of this conversation. It occurred at noon, on March 25, 1970, in Whitaker's room at the Fairmont Hotel in San Francisco. We consumed a bottle of wine during the conversation. Both of us were attending the American Orthopsychiatric Convention, without our families. There was no formal preparation for the conversation.

CW: Andy suggested that we talk about the immediate contexts in which one tries to practice family therapy.

AF: How do you find a place where you can survive?

CW: What can you do about the place you're in so that you can develop family therapy in it without getting your throat cut?

AF: Well, that's a little fancy; I figure we're talking more to rookies than we are to old pros. I've seen a lot of the best guys in the business get squashed in trying to change a place. I think for the beginning it's better to tell people to seek the kind of place where they can survive before we get into that fancy stuff of changing your own system. The family therapist does not do the family therapy. He is a node in a network. The minimum effective unit for doing family therapy is a network that consists of the therapist, some of his intimate family and friends, and some kind of colleagial support. I figure that the most important supportive context is the family that will let you do it.

THE THERAPIST'S FAMILY

CW: Your own family you're talking about?

AF: Yes, your own family. That's what I want to get clear, not the treatment patient family, but the therapist and his family.

CW: Tell me some more about that because I don't really know what you're talking about.

AF: A lot of husbands and wives of therapists are mad at them. The problems that "one-to-one" therapists get into is that their wives or husbands get jealous of what is going on in the office that they're excluded from. In family therapy, the problem is different. You, the therapist, get much more stirred up by what you are doing, and you bring home a lot more of your own upset than you do when you are doing individual therapy. Almost all the family therapists that I know are bringing their wives in and telling them about the work — and the wives are getting interested. They ask their wives' advice. When you are doing individual therapy, you can imagine that you know everything, but when you are doing family therapy, your limitations get clearer, so you have to ask people. For instance, what do wives do when they are menstruating . . . or they have a kid and it stays up all night . . . whose side should I be on in this? Immediately the wives get brought in. At a more primitive level, you go home and you are upset; you have been inducted into this family in the office, they have you caught into something. When you get dumped on by some system or person that has more power than you, you go home and you dump on somebody that's got a little less. And so, very often you have to have your wife available to detoxify you when you come home down in the depths or up in the air. If she's not there, you're in trouble. You need her. Your own family becomes much more your own therapist in family therapy than is the case in individual therapy.

CW: So you are beginning to get upset about your relationships within your own family and when this happens, you begin to see in your own family what you saw in the office family.

AF: That comes next, that's a different process. I'm talking about a very primitive kind of contagion now. You get messed up in your work, you come home messed up, and you have to rely on your natural family to straighten you out.

CW: Now I think that's really the responsibility of the cuddle group, the professionals that you work with, and I hear you saying that isn't enough. That may be a well-taken point.

AF: Well most guys that I know, myself included, do our practice in the evening or on Saturdays and are out to make as much money as we can in the money-

470

making time. We go right home from the office. We don't go cuddle with a cuddle group. There is a kind of latency in this; it's not until you get the kids to bed that you start to find out how upset you are. You're getting ready to go to bed with your wife, and you find that you don't feel close or tender — you have to get to where you are still stuck.

CW: Why are you not ready for intimacy?

AF: It's usually because you're still stuck in the family in the office that you can't stick yourself into your wife. At this point either she's going to get angry and say, "You don't love me anymore." You say, "Yes I do," and there is trouble. Or else she's going to say, "Here I am and you're hung up and I don't know where it's at; it's not my fault, so maybe I can help you." That's seeing in your own family what you saw in the office. As soon as you start to do family therapy, you also begin to realize that you have a rather limited and idiosyncratic model for "family" that you happen to live by. And isn't it funny that people are doing it *that way* and here you're doing it *this way*?

CW: Especially if *that way* turns out to be ahead of where you are.

AF: It often looks that way. So then you go home, and if you've got a kind of stuckness in your own family, you are a little afraid to try to pull and experiment. You sit there full of resentment, because all of a sudden you've got a goal about where you might be, and you realize that you're in a family that you can't move with.

CW: That's if you're afraid to share it.

AF: Yes, you have to experiment with your own family. Try to start to change the family that you live with along the lines of some of the things that you preach to the families you work with. Sometimes it works, and a lot of times it makes trouble.

CW: This is back to the old business that we talked about

471

several times, of the doctor/patient relationship that goes on bilaterally between most couples. It goes on not only in the terms of one-to-one, but also in terms of family modeling.

AF: It's a little different. It's not that you are treating each other. That was the first piece, the contagion. This is having an open enough family system to change your blueprints, your plans for your family, when you see something new and interesting.

CW: It's almost as if you are saying that every family therapist ought to have some family therapy for him and his own family.

AF: I wonder about that sometimes. A lot of my colleagues and myself have had this, often bootlegging it from friends, like Jane and I have from you and Muriel. When I first got into family therapy, six years ago, Jane was outside of it. She said, "Family therapy would have been fine for my parents, but I prefer individual therapy for myself." It's changed. The other day we had a hassle and she said, "If we don't settle this one we are going to see a family therapist." I said, "Oh no, we'll settle it."

CW: Well we have done the other thing, which is increasingly bringing Muriel into my work with families. We work with couples and groups, and therapist and spouse marathons, where she functions as a co-therapist with me. This gives her a feel for what I'm involved with, and gives me an opportunity to get past some of my guilt feelings about not being as open with her as I can be with patients.

AF: That's tricky. Do you find yourself being more relaxed and more open with people who are labeled patients?

CW: Even more mature, which is just devastating.

AF: I guess I've got a different kind of expectation than you do. I figure that I'm going to be more mature with my patients. My own family is the place where I'm the biggest baby.

472

CW: The way that most therapists have solved this problem has been to start educating their wives about what they're doing, playing some tapes of sessions, bringing their wives into supervisory sessions at various times, getting treated, etc.

AF: I'm trying to shape our training so that we trust each other enough to tell each other about our own families. Every trainee has to do it, a project on either the family that they live in or the family they came from, and then present it to the seminar group.

CW: And you're not having the wives in on this story?

AF: We haven't done that yet. That might be a good idea.

CW: It's scary. The whole thing is so scary because once you begin to drop the fences, you don't know what's going to happen.

AF: You're right! I'm not sure that most marriages that I know could take this kind of joint training.

CW: No, I would think it would be very risky. But these people who are trying to become family therapists, or to get more adequate at it, are certainly going to have to struggle with their own families. It's not just wife, it's also kids.

AF: You know more about that than I do. My kids are only six and three. Until now I've gotten more help and benefit for my kids. I see myself being nicer to the kids in families I'm treating than to my own. Then I try and carry the nicer way home. When I feel I'm failing in my work, sometimes I take it out on my son. Josh and Elizabeth haven't given me much direct backtalk yet; they are a little too young.

   I've seen several family therapists get divorced in the course of becoming a family therapist. They realize that life could be better; then they try to change it; and the spouse stands pat.

CW: Well, that's a scary thing. I haven't seen that. My thought about it is that it may relate to the individual therapy that one or the other gets. If they believe in family therapy they ought to take their wives and do something about it.

AF: They all tried. In the first situation, his analyst became the family therapist. The spouse felt that his analyst was on his side. The second couple went to a family therapist for maybe six months or a year. Then they went back into individual therapy, and whomever you want to blame, the fact is they are now getting divorced. The third couple are still in family therapy. Even though they're separated, they're in family therapy together. They're enjoying their family therapy, but they feel at the moment they're going on separate tracks.

CW: I have several families like that. It's very interesting. One second marriage for the man in which he and his second wife are going through with the divorce, both of them clear that they can't really be people and married until they get divorced. They are assuming they're going to then get re-married. I guess what I felt we left incomplete on this was if you get in a hangup like this and it doesn't resolve itself in a month or two in your own family, what would we suggest that people do? You sort of said go see a family therapist.

AF: Try the rest of your support network first — ask close friends. Say, "We feel we have this hangup. You probably noticed, but were too polite to mention it to us." "You want to risk telling us a little bit about it?" If that kind of polite opening up doesn't help some, I guess then I'd suggest going to find a family therapist whom you can trust. If you do too much family therapy on your friends, at least in this day and age, you lose friends.

CW: I'm very skittish about the use of friendship in this support system that you're talking about. But that may be because I'm a generation older. I'd be much more apt to make a formal move, or try to spell it out between us.

474

AF: I'm not sure that's true. I think you'd use a friend first. Think about your work in Atlanta, how many times you went to that group of intimate friends.

CW: I'm sure that must be true. That's what I meant by the cuddle group.

AF: I'm not sure what the switch point is, but my rule for friends is as long as it can be reciprocal, it's ok. Don't ask them to do anything for you that you wouldn't want to do for them.

CW: I'm sure that's very true, that the whole process of social therapy or whatever you want to call it has to be reciprocal in order to be valid.

AF: With a formal therapist it's cash for treatment, whereas with friends it's love for love.

CW: That's right, it's a different world.

AF: I feel ready to go to the colleagues.

CW: Okay.

THE COLLEAGUES

AF: Going very quickly through big contexts . . . there's a world revolution in social forms going on — the young *vs.* old polarity is part of it. This is clear in this country. It's all over the mental health professions, too. Everyplace you go, you'll find a split within staffs, between those who are more fraternally person-to-person centered, have looser and more open systems, and think more of sharing experiences and taking chances, and those who think more in terms of traditional doctor/patient models, privacy, closed information, and straight hierarchical power systems. I think family therapy and family therapists largely adhere to the new social forms, and anyplace which is compatible or congenial to that kind of a subculture will be one in which a family therapist has a half chance of prospering.

CW: That's a very good point!

AF: Contrarywise, in a place that's run on hierarchical

475

bureaucratic lines, where the information goes up and the orders come down, you're going to have trouble. Some of the basic assumptions of family therapy are: look what's going on in your context, and describe accurately what's happening. You know, it's perceived as rude — worse than that, as rebellious behavior — in the kind of standard bureaucratic set up. Time and again family therapists get killed in such setups. The worst kind of setup is one where the actual power structure is a hierarchical one, and there's a piped-in ideology of democratic nonsense, like "We're all friends here, it's a nice place, you can say anything." Actually it's information up, orders down, and cloak and dagger stuff. For that matter in any context which isn't candid, you're in trouble as a family therapist. You're whole scene is a "Let's show each other our work, sit in, consult with each other, there are no secrets." To the extent that the place you live in and work in deals in secrecy and closed doors and gossip and hidden rooms, you're in trouble. The nature of your work is either going to transform that social system, or make them so nervous that they're going to have to kill you.

CW: So it's either they're going to have to change to be more open, or they're going to kill you because you are open.

AF: Right. The third alternative is get yourself an independent base of support, by which I mean money, and build a castle. But it's really hard living in an armed castle in a hostile country. You don't realize how high your defense budget is.

CW: Very nice, very nice! You're saying that you not only need a cuddle group, you also need a power structure support, an official pattern of safety, a permissive context. A place that says, "It's all right, I like what you guys are doing" — and really means it. Then you know what you're doing doesn't challenge how

476

they operate, or they are willing to modify their operation to include some of your operations.

AF: That takes time. If they're going to move, I'd say in terms of the time scale, if you feel that somehow they're for you, but they don't understand you and they're willing to learn something from you, then you should be willing to give an organization between two and three years to really catch on. If they haven't made significant change by that point, they're just sweet-talking you. But to expect it much before then is to press faster than ingrained social patterns change. At least that's the way I read it as I go around.

CW: Let's talk about the face-to-face group then. The consultant, the co-therapist, the other family therapists that you work with day after day after day. Some of these guys have a problem planning work. The questions I get asked! "What do I do, when I don't have a colleague; I'm doing this all by myself in private practice, or in a community clinic where nobody else believes in families?"

AF: Pick a person you really like a lot, and at the same time whom you don't feel is slavishly dependent upon your good opinion. Then start doing co-therapy with him. I find that the best support is a co-therapist whom I really like, and who will talk back when he or she thinks that I'm out on a limb. And you build your colleague network by doing it with lots of other people, and having them do it with each other.

CW: Yep, yep. Boy I sure believe in that. I don't really think you have to like the other co-therapist. I think you have to respect him, you have to see him as a real person. I don't think he has to be an intimate.

AF: By intimate, you mean somebody you socialize with outside of the work?

CW: Yes, or somebody whom you feel personally related to. I think you can be professionally related on a solid level without having to be personally related.

477

AF: I find for co-therapy to work with me, the operating rule has got to be that the co-therapist and I have to be able to talk about and negotiate anything that comes up in the course of the relationship. It always seems to get into such unpleasant matters as who is being competitive with whom, whether the co-therapist and I are sexually attracted to each other, and Christ how do you solve that one?

CW: And who's going to steal the patient?

AF: You have to be able to make it absolutely clear with each other where you stand, including that we're very close in here but we don't want to socialize on the outside, and we won't push an intimacy that we don't have.

CW: We used to say that the only co-therapist you can get is somebody for whom you're willing to be patient and therapist. I've gotten past that. I don't think that's necessary. I think it's great, you know, if you have it.

AF: Another thing that helps in building a face-to-face support network is to show each other your work.

CW: Yep.

AF: If you start reporting to each other about it, it gets into competitive bullshit. A way of keeping it honest, in whatever you're face-to-face work group is, is to have a rule that at least once each year everybody's got to show their work to each other. Real honest-to-goodness work. Video-tape, one-way screen, or something. We have to learn how to be helpfully critical to each other. Keep your group open enough so that people can say when they don't feel the help is being quite so helpful. The way to keep your group open is to stay with the work, and to realize that there are no right answers at this point of time. Everybody is doing the best he can, and it's more important to try and be accurate in *describing* to each other. What you see is the overbearing therapeutic thing. They start doing therapy on each other, which is an under-

478

handed way of saying, "You ought to stop what you're doing and start doing something else."

CW: Great, great. Well I sure agree with that. If the two therapists can be very different in their way of operation, and if they respect each other, they can do co-therapy together with the family, and still be what they are.

sixteen

vvvvvvvvvvvvvvvvvvvvvvvvvvvvvvvvvvvvvvvvvvvvvvvvvvvvvvvvvvvvvvv

a conversation about
co-therapy

A. Napier and C. Whitaker

AN: Let's begin by saying what we mean by co-therapy. By the way, why don't I begin as an interviewer in this section?

CW: OK. I think of co-therapy (some people prefer the term multiple therapy; anyway, two therapists working with a family) as more like the easel on which we do the painting, a structural part of it.

AN: Good, because I can't imagine the kind of therapy you do taking place without a co-therapist, and I can't imagine anyone really learning your style without working in the same room with you. Which reminds me: I think you ought to say pretty clearly what you are up to when you go into therapy, because I think it's *very* different from the way many therapists see what they are doing. In their paper, Ferber and Beels accept John Bell's definition of the family therapist as somebody who tries to make the family a more perfectly functioning group. They qualify it, but I think your approach is very different, your set.

CW: I think we ought to start out with that. Is the purpose of the family therapist to increase the adequacy of the family, modify the symptoms, increase coping capacity, help them learn how to communicate with each other, all these ways of talking about what I would call family counseling, at the risk of being insulting, or is it to promote growth in the family?

AN: I assume you are up to the latter.

CW: Right. And I think of it as very different.

AN: Growth sounds mystical to me when I think about it. Could you define it?

CW: The growth of the family, as it is with the individual, is a process of breaking out of those things that stalemate the freedom to change, and the freedom to be more spontaneous, more creative, more *emergent*. And this would involve an increasing sense of unity in the family, freedom to be *with* each other; and an increasing individuation, so that each member of the family is increasingly free to be himself, and increasingly free to belong to the family. I think these are synchronous and grow concurrently. Also, this must include an increasing freedom to be part of triangles, to team, to form other unions within the family — sub-unions. For the men to form a kind of group, for father-daughter to have an as-if affair, as well as mother-son, without guilt and without attack from the other part of the marriage.

AN: That sounds like a kind of "smooth function" in a way, but one that is slippery, flexible, unconscious,

481

and enjoyable. Would you say growth is when the unconscious process can dominate and the family enjoy it?

CW: Well, it should result in that. If they grow, they should be less and less constrained by custom, by family codes, by communication patterns, by societal mores, by the whole business of the culture-bound, time-bound, space-bound, historically-bound. To me the whole business of growth means increasing unification. Maturity is the competence to be unitary.

AN: Define again, would you: unitary?

CW: Let me say it in terms of *me*. Part of growth is a unitary individuation: *all* of me is headed in whatever direction I'm headed in. The lack of growth is when I fight myself, and psychotherapy is an effort to get over my blocks, so that wherever I'm headed, all of me is headed there.

AN: A total turn-on.

CW: Right. And this should be true of the family too. It should be possible to help them break out of their cancellation of each other, their neutralization of each other, their mystification of issues, *à la* Laing. Or what we call "dedication to chaos." To me that's a beautiful description of the non-growth setting: The family has an agreement that whenever anything happens, somebody will stop it. This happens in so many professional settings, too; all you have to do is start something, and there will be all sorts of people ready to stop it. And in the family this sort of process can be really destructive, when the only unification comes from everybody denying himself. This is what makes them into an ego mass — a mass of goo. And nobody has an ego, including the family.

AN: So one of the prime jobs is to get something to "happen" in the family that comes out of their own guts, that breaks the log jam?

CW: Yes. Now the difference between these two approaches to therapy. You can treat a neurotic by

482

manipulation, technically — by conditioning therapy, by hypnosis. And you can modify a family so that it's "doing better" by manipulation, by communication training. But I think we're talking about a different level of involvement and change when we discuss growth. Here the therapist has to *model* by his own growing, and force the family into putting enough of their guts into this thing so that they break out of their defensive coping patterns that have had them paralyzed.

AN: So we are talking about two differences between yours and a good many psychotherapies: a different end-point for the family, hopefully making them an open, more *unstable* system in that they are *spontaneously* changing; and a different level of involvement of the therapist. He is deeply involved in the therapeutic process on a personal level. I think you *are* involved with these families — I remember your really furious attack on one father. I'm sure it changed the direction of that man's life. And later with the same family, I remember being envious of your tenderness with the oldest daughter.

CW: I certainly felt really turned-on both times. I didn't expect to be, but suddenly there I was. That's where the co-therapist is so important. Without a co-therapist, I wouldn't have dared that kind of involvement.

AN: But you can be very evasive too. You move in and out of being involved very quickly at times. And at times you seem really playful with a family's distress, but in a way that usually comes off as loving. Like in rapid succession you'll give a couple ten alternatives to their present fight; ways they might vary it. It comes on as a kind of good-natured teasing. Teasing isn't really the right word.

CW: You know the story of the scarecrow? The traveler went by a field on his way south. He saw a scarecrow out in a field and stopped to talk to it. "Don't you get lonely being out here in the field all the time?" he asked. "No, not really," said the scarecrow. "I enjoy scaring the crows." So they talked a while and the traveler went on. On the way back in spring he stopped again. This time the crows were nesting in the scarecrow's hair, and he had become a philosopher — I'm convinced that a lot of what I do that turns out well is because I can enjoy my own sadism.

AN: That is what is missing in most of the writing about family therapy. Nobody talks about enjoyment, either by the therapist or the family. Most people concentrate on making the family a "perfectly functioning group."

CW: Well, I certainly don't think the function of family therapy is to produce a well-functioning family. Like a well-functioning person to me is an automaton. And a well-functioning family is one that fits into this crazy world. Hell, you fit into this crazy world and you're obviously crazy. But one of the things that comes out of growth I think is the thing we had with this family recently where everybody in the family, one after the other, were into their craziness all in one interview.

AN: That's a distinctive part of your approach to therapy. You're after getting into the fantastic element of experience.

CW: That's right. As long as you stay with rational adjustment, you are not in the world of maximum growth. The most powerful growth comes out of the irrational part of the self. An experience of your own craziness, an experience of your own turned-on-ness, so that you happen to yourself, you don't *do* things; you're *being* what you are, the family is *being* what it is. It's not striving to be, it's not "doing better."

AN: Not prestructured. How about "prefabricated living?"

CW: Yes. To better that sort of thing is for the birds.

484

While we're talking about general things, let me add this: I don't think psychotherapy is all enjoyment and emotional involvement, obviously. One of the things I like most about family therapy is its professional, work-oriented slant. And it is open — without the connotations of a *tête-à-tête*. Now — there is a big job to be done, and to do it right I need lots of power. Unless I feel I have that power with a family, I don't even begin.

AN: You demand — nicely, but rather firmly — that therapy start with a certain structure; and that usually means the whole family be present, perhaps even the grandparents. If there are exceptions, they don't occur until after you have decided to allow them.

CW: Yes. At least initially I insist on making decisions about structure. I want the whole family there because they are all involved; and I don't hesitate about bringing in a co-therapist. I just do it. In deciding on structure, I take a straightforward, paternal role.

AN: But as I see it, you aren't directive once they have accepted your structure. You leave the initiative and the "direction" therapy takes up to them. The extent to which you can sit back and wait for the family to take the initiative is impressive. I think of it as a demand on your part that the family struggle with being creative — and the crux of that question being whether or not they have the impulse.

CW: Part of having power with a family is realizing that real power comes only if it is given freely by the people involved. Giving the family the initiative is a way of saying that I respect their right to take their lives where they want them, and that I respect their effort to grow.

AN: In return they must trust you with some of their struggle.

CW: It isn't all altruism, either. Like everybody else, I

485

have tried from time to time to supply the motivation for patients, and you just get your fingers burned. At any rate, I am very careful to avoid taking over the basic initiative in the therapy. The primary responsibility is the family's. That doesn't mean I have to be passive, of course.

AN: One can always tell jokes to liven up the hour if the family won't do anything.

CW: Or let them sweat with the responsibility.

AN: Let me tell the reader something about the training program at Wisconsin. (*aside*) My vantage point is that of a recent trainee in the department of psychiatry at the University of Wisconsin who now teaches part-time there in addition to consulting and private practice.

The typical training-year group includes ten to twelve psychiatry residents and four or five psychology fellows (interns and post-doctoral fellows), though the number of residents is being expanded. The first-year resident is introduced to family therapy during a six-month rotation on the university hospital's in-patient psychiatry wards. This service is organized on a total milieu involvement, and a good many couples and families are hospitalized together for brief periods. In addition, brief family therapy is a part of the treatment of most hospitalized individuals. The first-year resident finds himself confronted with many very disturbed families, and the press to learn to deal with them is intense. Carl Whitaker consults frequently on these wards; his method is to see a family with the resident and his team, to launch into the middle of the family dynamics; he concludes with a discussion involving the family, the team, the group of observers from the ward, and other trainees. He demonstrates his style of working with the family, makes recommendations for continuing treatment, and discusses issues and philosophy in family therapy. These consulta-

486

tions are scheduled weekly and there is usually a waiting list of residents who want consultations. There is no regular family therapy seminar for first-year residents, probably a mistake since they are under pressure to learn to deal with families at this time.

Carl also teaches a weekly seminar in family therapy that is open to anyone who wants to attend, but is part of the regular program for second-year residents and psychology fellows. The seminar is fluid, constantly changing. One week two trainees may bring in a family they have been working with and Whitaker may jump in very actively in several roles. He explores what has been going on or not going on in the therapy to date, pushing the family and co-therapists to share feelings about each other that may be threatening. He may work intensively on the family's problems, pushing much more intrusively than he could if he were the continuing therapist. Finally, he makes recommendations for continuing treatment, often bringing the group that has been observing into the room for this discussion.

At times Whitaker teaches didactically, in a free-wheeling, from-the-hip manner, responding to whatever comes up. It may be administrative problems with families, questions about his way of approaching individual therapy, theoretical questions about family dynamics. Sometimes Carl demonstrates with a family from his private practice, or he interviews families he has terminated with as follow-up. There is no systematic review of literature, though references are handed out periodically and occasionally discussed on demand. The seminar is usually lively and fast-moving, sometimes argumentative; sometimes, however, it comes to impasse if the group will not take the initiative.

There is no organized activity in family therapy for third-year residents, or for psychology fellows who have attended the second-year seminar. Trainees who are most identified with family therapy usually ask to see families with Carl as co-therapist, and anybody who is really interested gets to do some work with him. There is usually a group of four or five trainees, sometimes fewer, who meet informally, and who work regularly with Whitaker. It is very much an apprentice system in which favored apprentices get the best training. I feel that most of the best learning comes in this intensive co-work; it is not "sitting in" and observing, but active participation, though Carl is almost always clearly the dominant therapist.

Whitaker is also available for consultation on cases trainees at any level are having problems with. He will talk about the case, but prefers to consult with the family present.

Family therapy training at Wisconsin has been very much a one-man school; the fact of a talented, strong personality at the center of a program has advantages and disadvantages. The advantages are in the chance to learn a distinctive approach at close range, and to learn from a warm, available, very powerful teacher. The disadvantages have largely to do with dependence: Many trainees try to imitate Carl's style, though most find that pretty hollow after a while and give it up; there is probably too much dependence on Carl's availability in a crisis; and too many people compare themselves unfavorably to Whitaker. One counter-trend against dependency on the teacher is the extensive use of co-therapy among trainees. Almost all trainees in this setting who are learning family therapy work together, and there is a great deal of discussion of shared cases. Increasingly the video-tape is being used by co-therapy teams to provide feedback on their performance. And older trainees often are asked to consult on beginning trainees' cases. The therapist's feelings of inferiority and bewilderment in the face of demanding families are most likely to emerge in these trainee co-therapy relationships, as are competitive feelings. The young therapist practices and tests his individuality most intensely in these peer treatment teams. Social networks in the department often overlap working partnerships — friendships frequently grow out of co-therapy relationships, though sometimes people give up working together once they have become friends.

Whitaker's approach to therapy is a personal one; it equates being a therapist with pursuit of personal growth. It is anti-system and anti-technique, pro-creative. A good many trainees complain that Carl is cryptic, unpredictable, and that his approach to therapy is, like art, not really "learnable." They agitate for more structure, more rational analysis, more presentation of technique. They cry that they are fascinated by family therapy but not learning it. These are legitimate complaints; not all psychotherapy is serendipity. To meet these objections staff is being increased and more didactic presentation is planned.

CW: We worked out several functions of the co-therapy arrangement. It obviously is part of *treatment,* and I think a very important part. It is part of *training,* as when I take a resident or fellow on as a co-therapist. I also use it as a *demonstration model* when I see a family in a new setting.

AN: It can be part of *consultation,* in which the consultant takes part in the on-going therapeutic process. He is related not only to the family, but to the family's usual therapist, and to the relationship between the two.

CW: The consultation can be used many different ways. In Atlanta we often had a consultant in on the second interview to help with diagnosis. Here I often get asked to help with structuring the beginning of therapy — who should be there, how often, etc. Or

489

when things go haywire I get called in to help *re*structure the situation. There is the impasse consult, when things have reached an impasse in the therapy, and the consultant helps break them out of repetitive patterns. Or the catalyst consult, where he simply helps to accelerate the process.

AN: You often get asked to consult when the trainee sees the couple with one or both sets of parents.

CW: Yes. Let me add something to that. I often suggest beginning with a conference including the extended family, or at least bringing them in early in therapy. I consider that conference a sort of "family reunion" not a session in which to do therapy with the parents or really even accomplish anything on an overt level. I think a lot is accomplished implicitly, though.

AN: I guess one thing that gets conveyed is the message that we aren't trying to break the family apart, and that we welcome the larger family group's endorsement of the couple's effort toward growth.

CW: It also helps me understand the couple. You don't really know somebody until you know their parents. Often it is easier to sense the magnitude of an individual's struggle and the growth they have already done if you know a little about the patterns they have lived with. But I think the most important thing that happens is a shift in the couple's perceptions of their own parents. Looking at their parents through the eyes of the therapy context, each partner may do some internal "sorting out." They may see some of the changes their parents have made, some of their growth in the years since the images of these parents were internalized. That is, they may have been seeing their parents as they were twenty or thirty years ago when they were children. And suddenly they catch themselves up short with the realization that the parents have changed. If you don't get the parents involved in the therapy, those images may remain unchanged, or may change much more slowly.

490

Obviously one needs a co-therapist to take on such complexity. We were talking about other uses of co-therapy too. A major aspect of co-therapy is the potential it offers the two therapists to advance their own personal growth. It offers a chance to fight out differences, to struggle with being separate from the other, as well as together. The struggles we go through — being together and deferring to each other, coming through with each other, being leader and follower — all these things are part of our struggle to grow, and they serve as *models* for the patients. This model is a vital element in therapy.

AN: An intriguing aspect of co-therapy is that the two therapists form a bilateral participant/observer. One holds back and observes while the other participates on an emotional level — gets involved. I like the analogy of tennis; one plays up front at the net while the other falls back and takes the long shots. And then they reverse.

CW: In his study of Malone and me, Scheflen (1966) showed that one of us would be therapist for six minutes, then he'd back out and the other one would be the therapist. The patients see that there are two people there, but the therapist is the *twosome*. We had that portrayed beautifully recently when you were absent and we wasted a whole hour because the therapist, the twosome, wasn't there. It was as if I was a friend of theirs and we were talking about a psychotherapy that had been taking place.

AN: Or the case where the family makes slips and calls one of us by the other's name. One girl dreamed about you but called you my name.

CW: I want to take up my belief that one teacher (in the case of supervision) or one therapist is idiosyncratic. I had a psychopath once who said, "Well, I can see you, but I could never handle two people at once. That's just like having the whole *world* in here." And I think that's what it amounts to. As soon as there are two therapists, it then becomes a cultural thing. It amalgamates the one-to-one intimacy and the social adaptability.

AN: It becomes less of a guilty, anti-social collusion if another person is in on it.

CW: Yes. And also I think very important in multiple therapy is the tendency for the two therapists to reactivate the oedipal struggle much more powerfully than one therapist could. There are three therapists: you, me, and us. And that combination suggests the oedipal triangle.

AN: We talked earlier of the two therapists as parent models; one more intrusive, one more receptive.

CW: And I think the symbolic aspects of co-therapy used in training are important. The parent-child symbolism. The identification of the teacher with the trainee, the trainee with the teacher, and the whole experiment of the triangle. The co-therapist works in the oedipal setting too and he has to do something about his own jealousy, envy, the generation gap. And we struggle not only negatively, but positively. We each get a kick out of belonging to the other's generation, and in the sense in which we work together this is a powerful gain.

AN: One of the big gains in working in co-therapy is *mobility*. And one of the things I appreciate most is that the trainee gets mobility in and out of responsibility. I can move in and confront a powerful family much more readily if I have some backstop.

CW: Multiple therapy also prevents the therapist from getting emotionally trapped in a family and going stir-crazy, like the wife at home alone all day with five kids.

AN: An aspect of co-therapy that I think is very significant is the mobility it gives you in moving in and out of a feeling involvement. One of the therapists can become very powerfully involved affectively, while the other stays back and keeps the super-ego role, or the rational role. One can let go with a creative fantasy involvement if he leans on the other's support. These fluctuations should probably be reciprocal and fluid without one person's getting locked into a stereotyped role.

CW: The situation usually prevents that — it's open enough so that any pattern gets noticed and pointed out. But in addition to providing flexibility in therapy, the co-therapy relationship can also lend a healthy stability. The patient calls and wants an emergency appointment, or there is a struggle over structure or the problem of ending. These administration problems are handled by the *twosome* of the therapists just by the necessity of talking it over. And I think they are handled much more competently that way.

AN: Not just administrative problems — it helps to talk about everything.

CW: Right. It makes the two therapists *put things into words* and cross-check with each other. One of the real problems in the one-to-one setting is that the therapist talks to himself. In co-therapy I talk to another person. That was one of the things Scheflen discovered in studying me, and Malone said it seemed to him that we often did what we *said* we did, much more than the individual therapists. And I'm pretty sure that has to do with talking to each other about a joint experience that we somehow have to put into "public" language. Not only do the therapists tend to talk to each other about what they do, but they "metacommunicate" much more easily about the transactions between therapist and family. That is, with the co-therapist present, a reference point exists that triangulates or loosens up the lock-in between family and therapist and makes it easier to talk about.

AN: And the two points of view of the experience give us a "stereoscopic view" of the family, a third dimension of depth. I guess that kind of multiple image models for the patient a pluralistic view of his own universe. I want to mention another thing I get out of the teaming process. I feel that sitting beside you in the therapy hour gives me access to a whole range of your kinesthetic cues that I would miss if I were listening to a tape, or sitting on the other side of the mirror, or even sitting on the other side of the room. I particularly benefit from your relaxed posture, your calm manner and other cues that let me know you aren't as uptight with the family situation as I might be as a greenhorn. And I find similar kinds of things true in work with other therapists. It is always striking to react to a family in one way and to suddenly sense that the therapist sitting nearby feels very differently, reacts very differently — he is tense, or bored, or irritated, and you sense it immediately. It makes me respond much less rigidly since I realize more of the multiplicity of ways it is possible to respond.

CW: I agree. Let me say that the more experienced therapist can also get something from this non-verbal sharing process. I benefit from your excitement about the family — it helps me avoid being a mechanical whore in a situation where I'm too comfortable. I think it is important to underline the importance of the therapists sitting together. It coordinates the therapy process, because the family hasn't got to shift their line of view when the other therapist says something. It also outlines the fact that the therapists are separate from the family, like the enemies of the family status quo that they *really are*.

AN: And it makes the therapists' model much more clear and visible when they sit together. I wonder if it also makes the two therapists less competitive?

CW: Probably. It certainly helps them be more "in tune" with each other. There is another area where the co-therapy contributes a great deal, and that is with the problem of acting out. Barbara Betz said, "The dynamics of therapy are in the *person* of the therapist," and that statement has meant a lot to me. If you assume, as I do, that all acting out in therapy is for the benefit of the therapist, and that it has to do with the therapist's own involvement, then the co-therapist makes it much less likely that this kind of avoidance of anxiety by taking it outside the therapy will take place. The co-therapist will spot the other's fixation on one issue or one person. He will expose a covert romance so that the patient doesn't have to go out and be promiscuous to be able to talk about sex with the therapist. But not only can the co-therapist interrupt a negative process, he can also accelerate intimacy between any individual and the other therapist, or between the family and the therapist. Like the other day when you told the wife who was locked up in this instant transference with me that she could be open about her affection for me. That sort of thing I call "cross-ruffing," in which one therapist augments the person of the other and the involvement of the other with the family. He can help the other have an *open* romance with someone or an open fight.

AN: Yeah, and I think it is very powerful when one therapist sticks his neck out and the other therapist backs him up. It can't be an artificial response or it will sound hollow.

CW: You did that the other day. You said, "I saw it exactly the same way." And the way you said it left a significant silence in the room — if two of us felt it, it must be so.

AN: The co-therapist then — let me see if I can summarize this — acts as a triangulating agent between the other therapist and the family. He can monitor and break up certain kinds of patterns that look destructive or he can — which is probably more important — increase the involvement between the other therapist and the family. He can do it im-

495

plicitly, by being a reassuring presence, or actively by encouraging the family or a person in it to come toward the therapist, or by encouraging or endorsing the therapist's move toward the family.

CW: Co-therapy also makes ending so much easier. Nobody writes about ending, I suspect because everybody feels guilty about it. And because it is painful. But ending is much less painful when you have a co-therapist, a family of your own, as it were, to relate to. And the patients can feel less guilty about leaving, knowing the therapist has his own relationship to support him. They don't feel such an enormous debt to the therapist.

AN: I think it is particularly good for the young therapist, also, when the therapy fails to get anywhere, or the outcome is tragic. The co-therapist can make the difference between its being a bitter, dead-end experience that turns you off to a whole area or problem or a growth-producing episode. A resident and I failed recently with a very sick family and we really needed each other in working through that involvement.

CW: We've been talking about the advantages to the trainee. We should be more specific about the training situation. What did we come up with as assets for the trainee in working in co-therapy with a more experienced therapist?

CO-THERAPY AND THE TRAINEE

1. For the trainee, co-therapy provides a foxhole or roost from which to watch the melee. He can feel the bullets whiz by, sense the old soldier's gait, his stance, feel the pressure on him. He can watch, take notes, masturbate, and occasionally take a step outside. It is a graduated stress, one which the trainee can escalate and de-escalate at will, in and out of the family, in and out of responsibility.

2. The post is an ideal clinical research method. When

496

scared, or bored, the trainee can take more notes. Not only does he learn dynamics, but he learns dynamics that have probably eluded the old master. Combat is a good analogy because of the stress, but the apprentice to the artist or craftsman is probably better.

3. The trainee gets a lot from the supervisor. One of the best things is that the supervisor is dethroned. He stammers at times. His patients quit therapy at times. He doesn't always understand. He isn't always loving. What a relief to both that he is a human being.

4. Not only that, but if they are to make the co-therapy work, both parties have to respect and like each other as persons. The trainee can't always be pretending that he is fighting with his father, though he will do some of that, and the supervisor has to get over his dependence on his status. The latter has to rescind the pseudo-superiority of role, though hopefully he has an actual superiority of expertise.

5. The supervisor can provide the trainee with a rare and powerful opportunity to be creative, to try out maneuvers and explosions and forays with the assurance of skillful support when he inevitably gets into trouble.

6. The trainee has access to the supervisor's feeling life, instead of just his thoughts about something. He sees his involvement with the treatment process and therapy is less likely to seem like a chess game.

7. Feed-back is in the air. Supervisor criticizes the trainee on the spot, when it is alive for both. Trainee critiques supervisor, oh so rare. What a relief for both that can be — and helpful to the supervisor. This real-time feed-back is not painful or destructive, because it has a function. Both are jointly treating the family and feed-back is an essential component of their work together.

8. The family will likely critique the co-therapists by risking an attack on one, carefully reserving the other to maintain stability of the therapy. Without the pairing, this feed-back would be less likely.

9. Co-therapy enthrones the family as it dethrones the supervisor. The family owns itself and the therapists are less

likely to get caught up in its struggles outside the therapy hours.

10. Administration of a case is taught in the process of treatment as it is negotiated between the therapists.

11. Process is kept in focus, rather than the painful rumination on abstract theoretical issues common to much supervision.

12. In general, therapy is taught as a personal experience, not a function or technique.

AN: It sounds as if co-therapy is a panacea. At least we have been fairly effusive about it. We should talk about pitfalls, dangers, difficulties. Co-therapy can be a hell of a mess.

CW: It certainly can. Co-therapy is a lot like marriage, especially since it implies a binding contract to stick together to treat a family. That "binding" obligation can bring out a lot of stress in the relationship between the co-therapists. If I'm right in my belief that the real therapist is the twosome, then that relationship is crucial to the outcome of the therapy.

AN: Why don't we resort to our list again, to simplify matters?

PITFALLS AND POTENTIALS

A. Choice of Teammate. The greatest single mistake is in casual, careless choice of teammate. You should probably choose someone:

1. whom you personally respect (personhood);

2. who attracts, interests you;

3. who is complementary in some respect (personality, role experience, etc.).

B. Beginning.

1. You need to get married before you have children. It obviously helps to have a good relationship before you begin seeing a family. If it is an expedient marriage (assigned supervisee or other imperative such as only one

498

other co-therapist available) then expect some storminess before things get worked out; or a polite, low-key operation.

2. A typical initial difficulty is the mother-in-law problem. One therapist begins first with a couple or family, gets into difficulty, and brings in a co-therapist. The relationship with the first therapist — even after a few interviews — is sufficiently involved so that the new therapist feels like an intrusive mother-in-law.

    a. The new therapist can get more involved by seeing the family alone for a few interviews.

    b. If the relationship between the first therapist and the family is of long duration, the second therapist can only be a consultant between first therapist and family, though this can be a very valuable contribution.

3. Problems of beginning are often complicated by one therapist's involvement with only part of the family. Obviously the best beginning is a first interview with the whole family and both therapists present.

    a. If one of the marriage partners has been seen individually, even for a few interviews, the other should be seen individually, preferably by the in-coming co-therapist, for an equal "access" to the therapeutic team.

    b. It is very difficult for someone who has worked with one individual in a family for any length of time to be successful in therapy with the whole family. Certainly, he will need a co-therapist who can relate to the whole system. The therapist who moves from individual therapy to involvement with the whole family should plan for a period of "mourning" the passing of the individual relationship. Both he and the patient will need to work through their sense of loss of the one-to-one intimacy. A consolation is that even greater intimacy is possible in the larger group, though it must be shared.

C. Working It Out.

1. Many co-therapists remain just two separate individuals working together without a real marriage. They don't develop a teamed effort, an intuitive rhythm of

working, each moving in and out of the family. To be really effective the co-therapists must develop an involvement with each other and their work must have many of the attributes of a good marriage: the right to be an individual and separate, the freedom to be together, with an unconscious, reciprocal rhythm in which the two function like one person; a basically loving relationship in which both people are struggling actively to grow. No small order, that.

2. Paradoxically, teaming grows out of willingness to let the other "do his thing." Individuality has to come first. Either therapist should feel free to be comfortably "out of it" when the other is productively engaged with the family.

    a. Like a good parent, ask yourself: "Does he love the children?" If the answer is yes, then let the co-therapist proceed.

    b. Support if you can even if you don't understand fully what he is up to.

    c. Learn to be comfortable with being alone when you are.

3. Many co-therapy relationships falter because one or both are afraid to fight in front of the family. If you feel the co-therapist is being destructive, or if he doesn't allow you the freedom you allow him, raise hell with him right then and there.

    a. The most important element in therapy is the model the therapists present. An intense fight between the therapists can be enormously beneficial for the family. It teaches them how to fight, and it allows them to be free of the guilt of being the only people in the world with problems.

    b. The alternative to fighting out differences is a pseudo-mutuality between the therapists, hardly therapeutic since the family easily picks it up. The temptation is for the family then to act out the therapists' aggression.

4. Incessant competition between the therapists is very

500

damaging to the therapy. Each is determined to be dominant.

a. It appears that each wants the favor of the family, wants to be adequate in their eyes.

b. Actually, the battle is often for the other therapist's approval — for permission to be "lead dog."

c. Either therapist should be willing for the other to be dominant for a while. A convenient pattern is to let the one who takes the initiative first pursue it until things seem to have run their course. He will usually welcome help in a few minutes.

d. Even though one therapist may be more experienced or more expert, the other of course has equal rights to be himself in the hour. If one therapist feels persistently "crowded" in the therapy, he should probably fight it out.

5. A common mistake is that one or both can't ask for help from the therapist. A façade of pseudo-adequacy keeps the partners from sharing confusions, fears, discouragement about the therapy process. Ideally, each should be willing to be patient or therapist to the other co-therapist.

6. Role fixation in the co-therapy relationship (teacher and student, psychiatrist and social worker, etc.) is a waste of everybody's energy. Furthermore, it models another separation for the family.

D. Approach to the Family.

1. Assuming teamship, even a good team can err badly in their stance *vis-à-vis* the family. One of the very worst errors is to set up a "we-it" relationship with the family.

a. The team treats the family like an object and tries to manipulate the individuals. This implicitly hostile attitude can take many forms, from "teaching communication" to trying to engineer structural changes in the family.

b. Manipulativeness can be rooted in a decent motive — the feeling that one is responsible for "doing something."

501

c. A gingerly respect for the family's initiative is healthier than feeling constantly responsible.

d. Assume that the family, if allowed, will provide its own impetus for growth and will intuitively provide the basic organization for that growth.

e. Trying to structure the sessions in advance or by a "system" deprives the family of its growth integrity.

2. Another damaging pattern is a team *vs.* family approach in which the therapists constantly pressure the family and thus induce them to balk.

3. *Folie à deux.* Most mistakes in co-therapy occur because neither therapist "notices" a pattern. Both may have the same transference (not counter) to the family. They fail to evaluate their sessions, their direction, the quality of the interaction between therapists and the family. Things get worse and worse until a crisis forces them to look.

a. The team needs to be able to go in and out of the family and in and out of the therapy effort itself.

b. When the team cannot get distance on the situation, they should ask for a consultant, even if one of the therapists is a supervisor.

E. Help! At the risk of repetition, there are numerous points when it is helpful to bring in a consultant:

1. At the beginning of the therapy, to aid in diagnosis, and to assist in structuring the process (who should be there, how often, etc.).

2. When things are going fairly well, but slowly and without much feeling (catalytic consult).

3. When things are at an impasse in the therapy effort. The family isn't getting better, or is getting worse. Repeated consults may be necessary to move things substantially. Sometimes the consult can be in the context of a marathon session.

4. When the therapeutic marriage is on the rocks. When the two therapists can't resolve their fight, they should get help with it. The working-out should be done with the family present.

502

5. When the therapy must be restructured, the children have stopped coming, or will be brought into treatment.
6. When the grandparent generation is brought in. This is a valuable addition to therapy, but it requires an outsider who can relate evenly to the whole system. A team of four is not a luxury in the face of such complexity — if they can really work as a team.
7. In fact, frequent consultation is an easy way to begin.

CW: One thing we didn't talk about is the therapeutic fringe benefits for the two co-therapists in doing co-therapy — like Bill Lewis's saying to the family recently, "Listen, he comes on tough, but he's a cream puff underneath." It's one thing for Bill to tell me that, but when he says it in front of the family, it gets into new levels of my perceptions of myself.

AN: Co-therapy also gives the therapists a good excuse to share that kind of perception about each other. Difficult to do it without the family.

CW: Yes. On another time Bill got so uptight about my always being late that he was going to quit the whole therapy, back out. And I got very hurt, panicky, very upset that he might leave. All of a sudden we had a new kind of relationship because he said, "I'm going to file for divorce." So I got a chance to tell him how much our marriage means, and he worked through that. He beat me for being late, and I finally said, "I'll try to change, but I really don't think my pathology in being late is any worse than your pathology in always having to be on time. But I'll try to adapt mine." He laughed at that point, but two weeks later he came back and said, "I've been thinking about that and I think you're right, and I think it helped me." Now we don't fight about it — though it's still a problem at times. It's just a "fact" we have to contend with. There are always things like this to fight about in any therapy, and it can be therapeutic for the two therapists to open up about them.

503

AN: We were just talking about the difference between psychotherapy and supervision. Can you expand that?

CW: OK. Many people struggle with the question of whether or not you can be personal and "therapeutic" in the supervisory hour, or whether you should limit the interchange between supervisor and supervisee. I think you can be just as personal, just as attacking or as tender in a supervision hour as in a therapy hour — *if* it's related to the function you're talking about.

AN: If it's something that gets in the way of treating the patient . . .

CW: Or of relating to the supervisor, or to the supervisee. I don't think there is any limit to how personal you can get, as long as it's tied to the therapy supervision. It really might be called, in some cases, task-oriented psychotherapy, or action-oriented group therapy, or reality therapy. A lot of things can go on in the supervision that are therapeutic, though I think it would be a mistake to call it therapy. Therapy defines a contractual arrangement in which one person defers his total participation so that the other one can increase his sense of non-responsibility and his freedom to capitulate completely to the other person in an artificial situation that won't destroy his individuality.

AN: So in either case you have a set of priorities that give a structure to what you do.

CW: But neither structure — supervision or therapy — should keep you from being personal.

AN: What about the case in which the trainee has really major problems in the therapy and they begin to make him a "patient" in supervision?

CW: Well, the only way then is probably to get involved in the therapy directly. I would rather do that anyway. I'm not interested in being a supervisor at a distance. I would rather come in as a consultant, a

504

co-therapist, or even a non-participant observer — just come in and watch and leave.

AN: But you wouldn't limit how personal you got in supervision out of fear that it might lead to intensive psychotherapy?

CW: No. I would just not let it get to that — I'd say we have a mandate to treat the patient and learn about therapy, and if it leads to the supervisee's trying to become a patient, I'd cut it off. That's my responsibility, of course, not his. If you restrict supervision to the place that it's not functional, which is what you'd have to do if you stopped short of a really significant involvement, then you are making it into a supervision game. Besides, I don't like the term supervision — consultation is better. And you know another thing we left out — multiple therapy allows the young therapist to leave the patient or family in the office.

AN: I can definitely agree that the young therapist inevitably takes the patient home with him.

CW: And if you are part of the therapeutic team, then you leave the interview there. It makes it existential.

AN: The responsible party is the co-therapy relationship and it is temporarily on vacation.

CW: And you do avoid the explicit decision-making when the co-therapist is absent.

AN: Another thing it does for the young therapist is help him with the whole area of failure — we mentioned that briefly.

CW: Yeah, oh boy. I'm in one now where the therapist had had to struggle with three or four suicide attempts by the patient. I came in as consultant and have stayed on as co-therapist. The suicidal threat has disappeared — and I think in part because it can't be used aggressively any more. It isn't against him, it's against them, and split in half. It's also true that the fact that *he* didn't care was a "sin," while the fact that *they* don't care is just a fact. It's a powerful thing to watch.

AN: There is also the instance in which a team works hard with a family and fails. Without the chance to share the failure, one person might just turn off entirely to family therapy.

CW: I suppose it works the other way too. If you treat a family alone and they get better, you come out of it with a delusion of grandeur, whereas if you see them with a co-therapist it's just a job well done. Makes the whole thing professional.

AN: Well, I think you do lose a kind of excitement that goes with seeing people alone, albeit maybe a fantasy excitement.

CW: That's a good question, really. Whether we lose a secret titillation of our grandiosity, or whether it's something we're using the patient for, like the mother who uses the child for a lapel button. My feeling is that the kind of joy I have in multiple therapy is something I search for and don't find in solo therapy. Early in my experience I got kind of a joy from individual therapy, but I think it was probably from a sense of power and manipulativeness. Later, I think it's a sense of manipulativeness and distancing. Solo work has a kind of supercilious undercurrent that I'm suspicious of, whereas in multiple therapy it's really a warm joy at the personal freedom to be involved.

seventeen

~~~~~~

making it

L. Greenhill

Family therapy training can be started early in medical training, and will work even in the hectic pace of a pediatric internship. Many of the conflicts and changes a first-year psychiatric resident goes through are intensified if training begins during internship. The following describes my experience with five families, referred for treatment of an acting-out child, the techniques and problems of live supervision, and the reactions of the families as seen in taped follow-up interviews.

507

In this highly personal account of my training in family therapy I hope to show that a beginner, strapped for time because of internship duties, can still become truly involved in and manage the treatment of troubled families.

During my pediatric internship, I had the unusual opportunity of receiving weekly supervision in family therapy. I soon discovered that pediatrics and family therapy training mixed well because both emphasized the entire family's health; both fields demanded long-term, active involvement by the physician. As an intern on the ward, I learned pediatrics by taking an active role in patient care. Similarly, first-hand, responsible psychiatric contact with disturbed families taught me more than theoretical texts, seminars, or demonstrations by other therapists could have. I came to feel that I had something to do with the outcome of the case, and thus worked harder to grasp the family as a system could within.

Learning to deal with families grew out of deeply personal changes in my attitude about my role as a doctor, difficulties with supervision, and feelings about the families themselves. I had to become aware of my own discomfort around troubled families, my prejudices against them, and my acting-out in the role of the therapist. Doing family therapy with the supervisor in the room was also difficult. Live supervision brought out such supervisor-supervisee issues as dependency, competition, and dealing with anger in front of patients.

I began with a rather simple, unstated, unformulated treatment approach. I planned to point out scientifically to each family their characteristic "destructive" patterns of interaction, while staying out of the conflict myself. Somehow, I believed that my precise insights would magically motivate a family to change. Later, follow-up studies were done on four of the five families. From these sessions, I learned that I had helped, in some cases, by improving the families' ability to talk to one another, not giving out "insights" from "on high." Hindsight also revealed that I had helped communications only where I had become

508

deeply immersed in the family system, occasionally even by taking on a surrogate family role.

GETTING STARTED

Getting started meant getting supervision, selecting patients, scheduling meetings, and making a therapeutic contract. Lewis Fraad, M.D., director of Pediatric Training, encouraged me, gave me free time, and provided patients from the pediatric clinics. For supervision, I contacted Andrew Ferber, M.D., director of the Einstein Bronx State Family Study Section, with whom I had done research as a medical student. I eventually lined up five families, and scheduled meetings for twice a month.

Recruiting families from pediatric clinics was not difficult. Many schools refer families to the clinic because the children behave badly in class. I found four families by school referral and the fifth family came themselves after their adolescent made a suicide gesture. Although Ferber suggested I pick only families where the parents were present and there was no trace of psychosis, I ignored his choice in three of the families. Later on I realized that I had chosen and was most successful with upwardly mobile middle-class families, who exhibited predictable behavior, and remained intact in crises. They were families like mine.

Scheduling meetings for five families became a real headache. No regular time could be set for appointments because of a constantly changing intern rotation. Cancellations were frequent because nights on duty were unpredictably busy or slow. Later I realized how missed meetings served to help me avoid difficult family interaction.

I made a therapeutic contract with each family. We usually agreed to work together to help the child. Covertly, I decided that I would work to help the whole family. As the family became involved with me and seemed committed to therapy, I would risk talking about treating the whole group.

509

Medicine, Family Therapy, and Me: Some Conflicts

Conflicts between the two fields eventually arose. During internship, my primary goal and allegiance had to go to my six to twenty ward patients. The every-other-night-on schedule left few nights or weekends free. I eventually learned to ask another intern to "cover" my patients while I saw families or obtained supervision.

Other conflicts were more subtle. I had to overcome a negative attitude toward families in trouble. I unquestionably condemned, ridiculed, or rejected clinic families who violated the middle-class ideal of what parents or children should be like. Families plagued by accidents, battered children, and overdoses of medication were not only negligent but "stupid" or "bad" or "hopeless." Another type of "bad" family doubted my medical omniscience, questioned my decisions, pestered me with questions, made my work harder, or put me on the spot. I remembered a two-year-old child with urticaria who continuously paced in circles, calling for her mother; her separation-anxiety drove the parent to sign her out in the middle of a complex workup for collagen disease, going against "my orders." From an intern's viewpoint, she and her mother were "unmanageable" (didn't obey the doctor). Yet she was a superb patient for a family approach to psychosomatic disease. I condemned another family who had allegedly battered their child to death and were reluctant to talk about their "accident." Of course, the parents were morally and legally in trouble, but should not have been refused all help. I discovered how many such prejudices I held when I began doing family therapy. Bodin (1969) comments on the many counter-transference problems or "parataxic distortions" beginning family therapists have as they either become critical of a family or take sides unconsciously.

Taking emotional risks became another difficult task in learning family therapy. My medical school experience taught me that the physician often shows great strength in the face of overwhelming difficulties by denying feelings.

510

After all, I denied my own anger, resentment, and depression over an every-other-night work schedule. I then could turn to the family, encourage and support denial, strengthen defenses against overwhelming feelings, and help them, for example, mourn the death of a child.

Medical responsibilities could often protect me from involvement in the morass of family emotions. I was taught to help a family with their mourning, but could I sit with them all night when so many other duties called? An overpowering number of medical tasks dictated that all situations be met with strictly limited acute intervention. The skills required in chart writing, lab test arangements, diagnosis, rounds, blood drawing, and IV pushes came first in making me feel that I was doing a good job as an interne. My philosophy of patient care was based on the management of routine responsibilities and acute emergencies, while isolating feelings from situations that involved me. Sitting behind a pediatric clinic desk in a white coat, I wanted to deal with " 'real' life-or-death emergencies," not get involved in complex unresolvable family attitudes toward illness, marital conflicts, or me.

Supervision: Whom IS This Therapy For?

I had to learn an entirely new approach to being supervised. As an intern, I had "presented" cases to ward attendings, ritualistically and formally delivering the standard grand rounds presentation, replete with facts and historical data. Such formal presentations didn't work in family supervision. Often Ferber would interrupt my family histories and ask how this or that family member had reacted when hot issues had come up. He hounded me for minute-by-minute accounts of behavior in the sessions, and wasn't interested in the families' detailed account of their past. He suggested that I bring in the families so he might teach me to work directly with my observations of family behavior rather than their reports. We would interview the families together and he would supervise directly.

Before we saw the families together, we discussed our roles *vis-à-vis* one another as co-therapists. He suggested three possible approaches. Ferber might do an "evaluative exhortatory" family interview, and I would watch. Secondly, he could be "extraneously non-participant," only asking a question here and there, while I ran the session. Finally, he suggested I run a regular interview and he could later move in, partially as a peer consultant and also as a consultant to both the family and me. I chose the last approach, hoping that we would appear as practiced co-therapists to the family.

At first, I didn't understand the process of "live supervision." I had never done psychotherapy before, much less run a family group with a supervisor in the room. How could I learn from Ferber if I did the therapy? Like many beginners, I thought that one learned the method and role model by passively watching the supervisor at work. I wanted external support and direction from a supervisor, not occasional remarks while I was doing the therapy. I feared that Ferber's interventions would be restricted to devastating criticisms. The imagined threat of continuous criticism made me self-conscious, inhibited, and detached. Would the family continue to work for me in unsupervised sessions, if I "looked bad" in the joint sessions with Ferber? As an intern, I wanted to appear the confident healer. Miyoshi and Liebman (1969) have noted the beginner's concern with the proper medical "image" projected to the family.

Although I was afraid of Ferber, I was more afraid of exposing my own feelings. It was difficult to share instantaneous reactions, "improper thoughts" (I'm afraid of you when you talk that way) with the family, or even alone with the supervisor. My medical model and my personality dictated that the patients should be supported from the doctor's denial of suffering. I should remain neutral in arguments, suppress angry feelings, and leave all the dangerous, risky work up to Ferber. Like other new therapists, my own restraint probably served the families' need to keep away from conflict.

As I tried to remain calm and neutral, I found my

512

feelings emerge. Somehow when I said, "Don't you see that your wife is crying?" my tone and gesture would communicate, "You callous bastard, no wonder everyone in the family thinks you're the bad one." I acted out in other areas as well. Following a difficult family session, I came late or canceled the next session because of an emergency (I usually had fallen behind in my internship duties and had not planned well for the meeting).

My guarded and confused feelings made the planning of therapeutic tactics more difficult. My initial approach was to control the family, to have them "perform" for the supervisor, to lead them through conflictual areas. Well, this just didn't work. Often they rapidly slipped out of my control and took over, losing me in their maze of typical defenses, detours, false fights, phony issues. I recall discussing report cards when the family was defending against discussing the anxiety-laden issue of the mother's possible surgical hospitalization. When I began to flounder, I would wait silently for Dr. Ferber to bail me out. It was difficult to ask Ferber for help or support in front of the family. An intern just does not discuss the pros and cons of therapeutic alternatives before his patients. Co-therapy with Ferber suffered because of this block in our communications.

During the second year, when I was a psychiatric resident, both Ferber and I dealt with the issue of dependency conflicts in our supervisory relationship. We joined a continuous case seminar on "How to Supervise Family Therapy." The other supervisors watched and analyzed our work as co-therapists with Family 1 in front of a one-way screen. They pointed out that I had magnified Ferber into an omniscient, god-like figure. Ferber, of course, wanted me to look good before the other teachers and be a credit to him. But I imagined that he demanded impossible levels of insight and empathy. Unable to match up to these expectations, I became angry. I took his instructions as "pushing" and often had a "put-down," humiliated posture. In some ways, Ferber and I seemed to be re-enacting the mutual derogatory system of Family 1. It was the members of

Family 1 who eventually told us how nervous, quiet, and downcast I became when working with Ferber in front of the one-way screen.

Opening up this problem in front of the family was a real breakthrough in therapy. I stepped back, stopped identifying so completely with the supervisor, developed my own therapeutic role, and learned about myself as a member of a therapeutic team. Rubinstein (1964) notes how the resident reveals his maturation when he reaches the point where he can openly discuss counter-transference feelings. Open discussion is also good training for the family. Family 1 saw how their therapists had been able to handle problems of self-esteem without succumbing to mutual derogation tactics.

My medical training made the open discussion of supervisor-supervisee conflict difficult and embarrassing. Yet, somehow, I survived and Family 1 remained in therapy. In fact, their frequent reference to this discussion made me realize that airing of any conflict in a therapeutic group, even between therapists, can be essential to treatment success.

LEARNING TECHNIQUE

For the most part, learning technique meant studying the families' communications with them. We got the family involved by working as their communications experts. Everyone was encouraged to talk more openly. Rhetorical statements such as, "I don't know why he does this," were turned into real questions the family worked on. The tendency to talk to the therapist rather than to each other was stopped. Family members were continuously instructed to confront each other and talk without flying into rages.

I learned that the session moved more smoothly if I continuously fed back my observations of non-verbal behavior. In Family 4, for example, we proved that M had been intimidated by the entire family by pointing out his cowering posture and his hesitance to speak.

Communications training could help families verbalize

or recognize non-verbal cues. If repeated gestures (covering mouth, withdrawing from discussion, looking down) seemed to instruct another member to "stop talking," we made this instruction explicit. We pointedly said, "See how he is covering his mouth and looking down, as if he didn't want us to talk about this topic." Also people were made to talk while tuning out certain paraverbal communication. We instructed in Family 4 to speak without pointing, leaning forward, snarling, or using threatening tones of voice, behaviors which stifled interchange on the topic. We used polling to liven up a group repressed by one member. Whenever someone said, "The rest of the family agrees with me on this," we instructed the person to poll the other members to hear what they really thought, which often turned out to be quite different than expected.

When all else failed in opening up communications, Dr. Ferber set up role-playing. He would instruct the children to reproduce an argument of the parents. On other occasions, he would take on the role of one of the family members, adopting, for example, the father's tone of voice, posture, and mood. He would then communicate directly, saying "Don't you [wife] see how hurt I am when you do that?" It was amazing how the family would begin conversing with Ferber but address their replies directly to the imitated family member. Ferber's role-playing was quite provocative, for he openly expressed their covertly angry and critical feelings toward each other or toward me.

In addition to training family members in the art of communication, we strove to give the family insight into their system of interaction. Our techniques clearly delineated leaders, sides, and allies. Once, throwing keys at a sleeping family member actually revealed that the quiet mother, rather than the articulate father, was in control of both the meeting and the family. It was she who noted the deviant behavior. Roles were also clearly shown by arranging the seating to match the sides taken on a particular issue. In Family 4, we arranged the pro- and anti-mother forces on opposite sides of the therapists and produced a real con-

515

frontation between the mother and the proband. Occasionally seating rearrangement eliminated buffers who served to stop communication. By removing the youngest son from the mother's side in Family 1, everyone learned how she used the boy both to block communication with her husband and taunt him with the child's closeness to her. Parents were instructed to watch their children interact; occasionally the children would revealingly pantomime the parents. Children were asked to help by pointing out the parents' non-verbal behavior whenever they saw it. In Family 3, the children learned to remind their mother of her snarling, attacking, pointing, provocative posture. Occasionally, the family really needed a tape-recorder to view their own behavior, and the mother of Family 4 recalls how the replays had helped her.

Tapes not only were used to give the family insight into their own behavior, but also to instruct the therapists in technique. Impressions which had been lost in the rapidly changing events of the interview returned in the context of the actual interaction. New issues were heard with each replay, for certain neutral family behavior was revealed to be a diversion from hot topics which had been passed by all too quickly.

Tapes made me aware of my own feelings during the session. If I lost control of the meeting, or if highly charged emotional issues came up, my voice changed. Beginning with warmth, support, and interest, my voice became filled with guardedness, coldness, anger, and condescension. The tapes taught me to listen to my own voice and focus on my own emotional reactions during the whirlwind of family therapeutic process, and avoid spending all my time making speculative interpretations. Being more of a warm, sympathetic listener and less the expert always in control was a much more practical and appropriate goal for me.

WHAT VALUE HAS THIS TRAINING, ANYWAY?

At the end of two years, we sat down to review the

516

training experience. What had happened to the families? I was a first-year resident, and deeply interested in the positive or negative effect of my work. Had I achieved my goal, changing family interaction through insight? "Improvement" rates from family therapy vary between seventy-five percent (multiple-impact therapists helped fifteen out of twenty families), (see MacGregor, 1964), and ninety percent (crisis intervention, Langley, 1968). Yet therapeutic methods and outcomes described were different and not comparable.

We decided to use follow-up interviews to evaluate therapeutic outcome. We wanted the family to describe their own experience in therapy as openly and frankly as possible. I would especially listen for their comments about me, about my relationship to my supervisor, and their feelings about being used in a training situation. Finally, both Ferber and I wondered if the treatments had helped the families.

We designed the interview to produce maximum openness and interaction from the family. The follow-up session was structured with a set of simple short questions and a tape-recorder running for about thirty minutes. Fulweiler (1967) notes that the family is implicitly commanded to talk or to work harder if the therapist is absent from the room but watching (one-way screen or tape-recorder). I would stay out of the room so the families could freely bring up their feelings toward me. I realized how important such feelings were, and how I had hesitated to deal with them during the early phase of my training. In those early planning phases, neither Ferber nor I realized that the tape-recorder and the empty room would elicit some of the hottest interaction we had seen during the therapy.

The mechanics of getting the family in and starting the follow-up interview consisted of a phone call or calls, the explanation of purpose, and the selection of someone in the family to ask the questions. Four out of five families eventually appeared. I explained to them that I needed their impressions and comments on their treatment to help other patients. Furthermore I told them I had thought about them

517

often and wanted to see them again to see how things were going. I realized later how important in therapy it had been to indicate these warm personal feelings.

Choosing the family interrogator was done by hunch. I discovered there was always a local therapist in the family who had taken on the role of go-between. This person had been spokesman, argument settler, and negotiator in some of the earlier sessions. The interrogator asked each of the family members the following questions:

1. How did the problem change after seeing the doctor?
2. How is the problem now?
3. What did you think of the treatment?
4. Did the treatments help you?

DESCRIPTION OF THE FAMILIES, THERAPIES, AND THE OUTCOMES

Listed below are brief synopses of each family's presentation and course of therapy. I have paid particular attention to their comments about therapy during the follow-up visit.

Family 1. Family 1 is a black West Indian family consisting of the father (aged thirty-five), the mother (thirty), and four sons aged fourteen, twelve, ten, and eight. The ten-year-old boy had become a behavioral problem in school after older brothers had rejoined the family, depriving him of the position as eldest. Before, these older brothers had lived with a maternal grandmother in the West Indies.

Issues apart from separation and sibling rivalry emerged immediately. The parents' relationship was often mutually derogatory, mistrustful, and competitive. While the wife was the disciplinarian and planned most of the family activities, the husband asserted his own identity as the "bad guy" in the group by derogating her efforts. He was cold, mistrusting, and had a precarious, easily injured self-esteem, and great pride. Every weekend he went to parties and social gatherings without his wife, staying out the entire night. While the wife tearfully presented her stories

518

of abuse and neglect, the husband would react by looking at the ceiling, by making callous remarks, or by generally acting the role of the "bastard."

The father had a responsible position, was college-educated, and had typical middle-class aspirations. The wife worked as a counter woman in a laundry.

My original contract was to help the family with the ten-year-old. I clearly defined the school misbehavior as a family responsibility. As the boy stopped acting up, the contract was changed. I openly stated that the couple should begin working on their marital relationship. The family remained in therapy for the next twenty-three months with Dr. Ferber acting as supervisor.

The father had often been more successful than other family members at recruiting and organizing discussions. I gave him the job of interrogator during the follow-up interview.

Initially no one could agree on the real problem that originally had brought the family to therapy. Both the proband and his older brother felt the school misbehavior was the major difficulty, while the rest of the family worried about the parental fighting. In any case, all felt there had been an improvement in both areas.

All thought the treatments had helped by improving communications between family members. Real changes had occurred; open discussion between the parents enabled them to "try harder" and shorten arguments. The father's night out remained a problem, and he was confronted with it on the follow-up tape, yet neither side became explosively angry. The mother found the weekly opportunity for the family to talk extremely important. Even the husband felt his wife nagged him less after going to the sessions. The boys assured the parents that they now knew one another well enough to win The Newlywed Game. The boys saw the therapist as someone they could talk to, then "saw what was wrong and told you how to fix it." They felt that I had become part of the family.

On reviewing the case, I felt that the mutual derogation

system of the couple still remained, but the family had drawn closer by talking to one another. The father had become more trusting and more in control of the family, and his self-esteem did not seem to be so involved in feuds with his wife. The wife, who had developed a strongly positive transference for me and had tried to set up a triangle between her husband, herself, and me, had become slightly more independent and self-reliant. The marriage had reached a slightly new equilibrium, between two more independent people.

Family 2. Family 2 was a Puerto Rican family consisting of a forty-five-year-old father, a forty-year-old mother, and their adopted Puerto Rican son. Both parents worked and had strong middle-class aspirations. The fifteen-year-old had a seizure disorder and one hospitalization for a paranoid schizophrenic break. Provoked and teased in class, he had fractured another student's skull and had been suspended. The parents worried that the boy would be unable to finish high school.

I picked up the case in the neurology clinic, where I began treatment by controlling the seizure disorders and giving medication to reduce the anxiety. I contracted with the family to treat the epilepsy and teach both parents how to deal more effectively with their son. Family therapy was thus arranged. In addition to his twice-a-month family session, the boy began to call me at home between sessions to talk. The entire family has remained in therapy for over twenty-three months with Dr. Ferber supervising my work for only four sessions.

I soon discovered that both parents tolerated the boy's autistic behavior at home, supported his dependency needs, and resisted his efforts to get a job. Furthermore the boy and the mother operated to shut out and denigrate the father. The patient would hold his mother's hand, pat her back, kiss her, copy her posture. But he would get noticeably upset if his father touched him, pulling away in disgust. Both parents laughed when he performed this behavior.

The family interrelationships improved. I supported the

520

boy's move toward independence and his family gradually gave him responsibility. In the therapy sessions, he gradually began to accept his father and became less dependent on his mother. He achieved considerable stability by developing an obsessive interest in coin collecting, spending most of his free time on this hobby. He had also began passing his courses in high school, and obtained a job as a messenger boy.

I chose a half-sibling of the patient's to run the follow-up session. He spoke excellent English and had used his language abilities to help the family in their dealings with city agencies.

The parents saw the main problem for treatment as the boy's withdrawal, autistic behavior, anti-social outbursts, anger toward the father, and lack of interest in school or work. The patient continued to see the problem medically, and was glad he had no more epileptic seizures.

All family members stated that there had been improvement. Two years later, the family found the boy friendlier, working, going to school, and not fighting with his father. However, they still worried about the boy's slight unco-operativeness at home and the possibility that he would relapse after I stopped therapy.

Family therapy had helped. The entire group no longer had such great investment keeping the boy dependent. Yet no insight had occurred. No one understood that the family had turned away from the destructive triangle of boy-mother-father which had served to isolate the two parents and denigrate the father. I had changed the system by supporting the boy's independence, both in therapy sessions and encouraging his calls to me at home. I had helped by becoming involved as a father surrogate in the family system and taking pressure off the father.

Family 3. Family 3 consisted of a forty-five-year-old black postal worker, his thirty-five-year-old wife, and two daughters, aged thirteen and eight. I first saw them following the admission of their older daughter to the general pediatric ward in a coma. Her parents, whom she described

521

as "rigid," had bawled her out for disobeying them by talking to boys in the park. Subsequently, she took an overdose of anti-histamines to make herself sick, but not to kill herself.

In the hospital the mother and daughter asked me to help them discuss the situation with the father. They anticipated an enormous angry explosion when the father discovered his daughter had taken an overdose. They wanted protection. I contracted to talk to the family for two or three sessions to work out the problem of the overdose, and then refer them to an outside clinic and therapist. Dr. Ferber did no active supervision on the case.

During the family interview, conflicts over parental control emerged as the major problem. When asked about their concerns about their daughter, they spontaneously said they were afraid the patient would make a mistake with boys and ruin her life. Both parents became angry and defensive and told me I had the wrong ideas about dating. It became clear that the argument prior to the suicide gesture had been ostensibly about boys, but also about control.

When I told the father of the overdose he took it as a challenge to his authority. He was amazed that "his daughter would do such a thing" and then said, "You know I am not angry. I am just glad the little twirp didn't kill herself." The father's tone of voice and gestures expressed anger that the girl had humiliated him. The mother and daughter huddled in a corner, crying. I pointed out his non-verbal angry gestures and told him even I was afraid of his potentially violent anger. He simply laughed at my observation.

After three discussions, the family was referred to an appropriate out-patient clinic. When the clinic therapist had asked about the mother's own dating experiences, she became quite upset and refused to return for the next appointment.

Their lack of cooperation continued, for I had trouble bringing the family back for follow-up. Eventually the mother and daughter came in for an interview. Since the mother had formerly acted as a go-between in the father-daughter confrontation, I gave her the questions to ask.

The taped interview itself was quite short, both mother and daughter answering the questions briefly and somewhat uncooperatively. What did appear on the tape indicated that the therapy had been neither helpful nor relevant. Both denied that there had been any problems initially and that the overdose was only "an impulsive mishappening." The crisis had shown both parents that their daughter was "capable of such a thing." Now, over one year later there had been no more crises because the daughter now "obeys her parents completely." The girl herself felt that the treatments had failed to change feelings and hadn't helped the family to discuss hot issues openly.

Both also felt that I had misunderstood the situation because I was white. Thus, I had failed to understand that it is improper for a black girl to date until she is fifteen. Furthermore I wouldn't know that blacks (who have suffered so much) would never commit suicide. The mother was also amused over the fact that I had been frightened of the father, "a non-violent man."

I found it difficult to get involved with this family because I was white and because neither the family nor I wanted to discuss the color problem, their anger, and their insecurity about parental control. I learned that it would have been better to talk about my negative, critical reaction to their authoritarian stand and to their color. Open discussion of my counter-transference might have been more successful in keeping the family in therapy.

Family 4. Family 4 consisted of a thirty-five-year-old white, Catholic, separated housewife, her three boys, aged fifteen (P), twelve (M), and eight (R), and two daughters aged ten (Ma), and four (G). M had been referred from school because of an immature, stubborn, whining manner, frequent fighting, and an explosive uncontrollable temper.

Like the first family, I arranged to help the boy with his school misbehavior. Later on it became clear that I was really working on improving the mother's relationship with the children.

Dr. Ferber, who supervised almost every session, focused on the mother. She was a chronically depressed, bitter, resentful woman who saw all her troubles in terms of her children's misbehavior. She had apparently picked out M as the scapegoat because he most resembled her own violent, alcoholic husband.

Dr. Ferber attempted many maneuvers to break through the system of electing M scapegoat. He supported M and didn't let him play scapegoat (giggling while the mother lectured him). He stopped the mother when she began her endless listings of M's misbehavior. He divided the family into pro-mother and anti-mother forces, and asked the kids to openly describe the mother's non-verbal provocative gestures. M himself began to realize that "I act dumb because she [the mother] tells me I'm dumb." Ferber insisted on making the mother listen to her own voice on tape-recordings, and pointed out how provocative she was.

After several sessions she became contrite, depressed, and withdrawn, and complained that family therapy was not helping her. Even with considerable support, she could not continue, and the family dropped out after twelve sessions.

I gave P, the oldest boy in the family, the role of questioner in the follow-up session. P had acted originally as the enforcer in the family, punishing M for misbehavior. Yet he was the most verbal and most mature of all the children and occasionally served as a go-between in the pro- and anti-mother battles. He was an excellent questioner.

Like the first family, Family 4 had difficulty during follow-up in deciding what the original problem had been. The mother felt that she pushed too hard, demanded too much of M and became too easily angered when he resisted her. However, the rest of the family saw the major problem as a scapegoating of M, especially by P. P had since dropped out of school and begun to spend most of his time away from home. The rest of the family saw P's absence as the main reason M was no longer being scapegoated.

The family system continued to operate. R now was being picked on as M had been, and throughout the tape R is unmercifully teased by all. They continued to need a constant scapegoat, and now R had moved into the slot. P had put so much distance between himself and the mother that M was now the oldest "father substitute," and R his closest rival.

Yet both the mother and M felt the treatment had been successful. M had enjoyed the therapy, for it allowed everyone to "get things off their chest." He openly described how the family had worked to scapegoat him earlier. The mother felt that family therapy had been valuable in demonstrating the negative effect her voice and manner could have upon her children. Several months after stopping therapy, she recorded her voice on a home tape-recorder, and found improvement.

More than any other family, Family 4 was able to use communicative training. They learned to put non-verbal behavior into talk and to take risks in expressing feelings.

Family 5. Family 5 was a large Cuban family consisting of a forty-five-year-old father who worked as a superintendent; his attractive thirty-five-year-old wife, two sons, aged ten and two; two daughters, aged twelve and nine; and the patient, an eight-year-old girl. She had been referred to me as an interesting case "for a future psychiatrist" because of a past history of head banging, thumb sucking, autistic speech, and masturbation in school. Her bizarre behavior had erupted briefly when a sister had undergone heart surgery. Now, though asymptomatic, she was completely uncooperative at home, frequently disobeying and fighting with the mother.

I contracted to help the family understand and work with the girl's behavior problem. I made the stipulation that all members had to be present initially. Dr. Ferber did no active supervision with this family.

Allowing the otherwise restless children to make drawings while I talked to the parents proved to be the key technique of therapy in Family 5. As Kwiatkowska (1967) notes, "family art evaluation provides . . . a rapid but revealing glimpse of the psychological functioning of a family unit." I asked them to draw pictures of each other and the parents. Their excellent portraits revealed important issues, such as the father's cold, distant attitude, the problems of masculine identification for the oldest boy, sibling rivalry, and how each of the siblings saw the patient as extremely disturbed and infantile.

I discussed the artwork openly with the entire family, and saw the drawings come to life. In contrast to the past history, the patient appeared intelligent, communicative, responsive, and non-psychotic but scapegoated by other family members as the "crazy one." The mother was very sensitive and temperamental, over-protective of her daughters (fearing sexual attacks on them as they left the house), and subject to wild, uncontrollable outbursts of rage. The father was cold, withdrawn, uncooperative, and belittled his wife's hysterical nature in front of the children. The two parents never appeared in the same picture and were never drawn smiling. I rapidly learned that most family members regarded the parental conflict as the major family problem.

Couple therapy was impossible in this family for the father refused to cooperate, not showing up after the first meeting. I explained that both parents were absolutely essential to any therapy. When he had missed four visits I terminated my contract with the family, gave them my phone number and told them I would see them as soon as the father was interested in joining. They never called back.

Family 5 was very difficult for me to work with. The extremely active children in noisy drawing sessions, the hysterical mother, and the constant battles in mixed English and Spanish were confusing. I found myself sitting behind the desk with a white coat, a distant position I took with no other family. The counter-transference anxiety, which made me physically draw away from the family, could have been used therapeutically to help the family. I also had begun

526

to feel that no progress in therapy was possible as long as I had to agree to leave the father out and continue seeing the scapegoated child as the patient.

Family 5 could not be found for follow-up interview.

Discussion. In discussing the impressions of the follow-up interviews, I would like to point out some recurring features which turned up on follow-up that helped me to redefine my position as a therapist at the end of two years of training. New therapeutic approaches that I was unaware of in early training evolved out of my experiences. Different families seem to require different therapies, as Lyman Wynne (1965) points out. Finally I began to understand the difficulty in evaluating outcomes in family therapy.

The stability of the family system is the critical recurrent factor in family therapy. No matter how intensive my attack, their pattern of interaction remained inviolate. When I tried to change Family 3's attitudes toward sex and parental control, they blocked, became defensive, and stopped working in therapy. Even with over a hundred sessions with Family 1, the pattern of mutual derogation between the parents remained a primary method for interaction. Family 4 was the most brilliant example of the family system stability. The scapegoat role necessary for the mother's functioning simply switched from one male to the other as the children grew up.

Thus, I had to reject my original goal of making a major change in the family system of interaction. Crisis, often the outcome of some destructive family system, often resolved with no apparent change in the system. Even with reported improvement, mutual derogation continued in Family 1, some covert parental support of the boy's autism remained in Family 2, and scapegoating lingered on in Family 4.

The families themselves saw benefit from therapy when they had learned to talk with one another more openly. All three families with reported improvement noted that there had been family communication and closeness. Specifically, open discussion of formerly unspoken but shared behavior

527

had been added to their communications. The boys in Family 1 were no longer frightened to confront their father with his night out. Every family member could see and talk about the scapegoating and the mother's destructive carping in Family 4. Follow-up interviews pointed out that improved communications was a valuable goal of family therapy. Perhaps an interaction system will eventually change, but only after the family can get over hurdles in talking to one another.

I discovered that I often kept my goals secret from the family. I "seduced" the family into therapy in almost all cases, contracting with them to treat the "identified patient." My work with Family 3 was the only time that I put all my cards on the table. In the crisis-intervention nature of my work with this one family, I immediately redefined the overdose as a family problem, which may have played on their guilt, made them defensive, and blocked therapy. Having more time with the other cases, I had followed my inclination to gradually widen the treatment perspective to include all members. I learned to wait before questioning the family myth that painted all interactional problems as the result of one bad apple, the identified patient. The families' frequent inability during the follow-up interview to define their original problem may be a result of the differences between their stated and my covert contract.

I soon discovered that I could not use an identical approach in each one of the families. In the early days in training, I believed that every family problem could be treated the same way. I would observe the family and simply explain how the identified patient's pathology was a result of their destructive family interaction patterns. Once they understood the complex dynamics of their problem, I hoped that the family would correct these pathological patterns by themselves. Family therapy has to be more flexible and subtle, for each of my families was different and demanded different techniques. Conjoint family interviews plus some individual supportive therapy was the primary method of treatment of the schizophrenic boy in Family 2. Exploratory

528

therapy focusing on immediate interfamilial interaction proved workable with the mother in Family 4, but deep psychodynamic issues weren't dealt with. Simple family counseling was used with Families 3 and 4. Advice was given, tasks at home suggested, but no attempts were made to promote insight. A combination of couple therapy and family counseling was most useful in Family 2.

The tape-recorder was immensely useful. Not only the mother in Family 3 was helped, but I learned from listening to replays. My voice took on self-confidence and warmth as training progressed. Furthermore, the follow-up sessions, designed around the running tape-recorder in an empty room, promoted intense family interaction.

The follow-up interviews underlined and brought home essential features of learning family therapy. For therapy to work, I had to be involved in the family system, sometimes as a surrogate family member, and feel responsible for the eventual outcome of the treatment. Then the family could gradually assume some of the responsibility for its treatment. Finally I had to let go and sit back while the family took its own direction.

My training in family therapy helped me "break through" to close work with families. Getting immersed in a family meant dealing with my own counter-transference feelings of disdain toward families in trouble and of anger at family defenses. Getting so close to patients meant giving up an image of the distant uninvolved healer-on-high. Live supervision made it difficult to hide behind any medical shield. Open discussion of anger and dependency problems between Ferber and me in front of the patient did not tarnish my image, as I had feared, but actually taught the family how to deal with its own feelings. Concentrating my efforts on training families to communicate more effectively actually made me communicate more clearly and get in touch with my own feelings.

SUMMARY

Five families, referred for treatment of an acting-out

529

child, were seen on a twice-a-month basis for varying lengths of time during my internship year in pediatrics. Follow-up interviews were taken two years after the beginning of training with four of the five families.

Careful analyses of these four families revealed that although little change had occurred in characteristic programs of family interaction for the two-year observation period, communications had improved. Three families seen for over ten visits reported that family therapy had helped by increasing familial closeness through talking. Each of these treatments meant a direct involvement and commitment from me. The only family that seemed to benefit from "insight," Family 4, reported that replays from the tape-recorder had helped them. Family 3, where my counter-transference problems had been severe, was seen for three visits and reported little help from family therapy.

Learning family therapy was difficult for me as an intern, for I had to renounce my own ideas of the physician as the uninvolved, emotionally safe healer. I had to become immersed in conflicts with family members, with my supervisor, and with myself. It was necessary for me to take responsibility for the treatment in the beginning. Responsibility increased my involvement until I often felt like a member of the family, as I did with Families 1 and 2. I gradually learned to allow the families to take over their own treatment. My own background was important, for I found that I work best with upwardly mobile middle-class families. For me, learning family therapy was experiential rather than theoretical, a personal synthesis forged from careful observations of minute-to-minute reactions of the family and myself. Internship is not too early a place for the potential psychiatrist to learn to make such observations.

~~~~~~ *References*

1. BEELS, C. and FERBER, A. (1969), Family therapy: a view. *Fam. Proc.,* 8: 280-318.

2. BODIN, A. (1969), Family training literature: a brief guide. *Fam. Proc.*, 8:272-279.
3. FERBER, A. and MENDELSOHN, M. (1969), Training for family therapy. *Fam. Proc.*, 8:25-32.
4. HALEY, J. (1969), An editor's farewell. *Fam. Proc.*, 8:149-158.
5. ———, HOFFMAN, I., and FULWEILER, C. (1967), No man's land. In *Techniques of Family Therapy*, eds. J. Haley and L. Hoffman. New York: Basic Books.
6. KWIATKOWSKA, H. (1967), The use of families' art productions for psychiatric evaluation. *Bull. of Art Therapy*, 69.
7. LANGLEY, D., PITTMAN, F., MACHOTKA, P., and FLAMENHEET, K. (1968), Family crisis therapy: results and implications. *Fam. Proc.*, 7:145-158.
8. MACGREGOR, R., RITCHIE, A., SERRANO, A., SCHUSTER, R., MCDONALD, E., and GOOLISHIAN, H. (1964), Results. In *Multiple Impact Therapy with Families*, 212-246. New York: McGraw-Hill.
9. MIYOSHI, B. and LIEBMAN, R. (1969), Training residents in family therapy. *Fam. Proc.*, 8:97-105.
10. RUBINSTEIN, D. (1964), Family therapy. In *Teaching of Psychotherapy*, ed. Intern. Psychiat. Clinics, 1:431-442. Boston: Little, Brown.
11. TISCHLER, G. (1968), The beginning resident and supervision. *Arch. Gen. Psych.*, 19:418.
12. WYNNE, L. (1965), Some indications and contraindications for exploratory family therapy. In *Intensive Family Therapy*, eds. I. Boszormenyi-Nagy and J. Framo. New York: Harper and Row.

section four
Strings in the Bow

introduction

A. Napier

Rather naïvely, Margaret and I enrolled our three-year-old Sarah in a Montessori nursery school for a week. Sarah came home twice complaining, "Mommie, that school is for older children." So Margaret went and observed and discovered that they were teaching the children the one correct way to stack blocks, and even the correct way to wash your hands, each finger individually. So, being fond of young children, we took her out.

Assume, if you will, that family therapy is on its way

toward being outmoded. It is becoming respectable, and departments of this and that are looking for people experienced in seeing families "intensively." The system, the body politic, can develop antibodies that permit it to live with this new virus comfortably, provided the virus is not too virulent. But assume also, if you will, that family therapists are foxy and cunning, and habitually rebellious, and are at work developing mutants, new strains.

The Victims

Early, very early, it was a vague, alien force: "I fall unexpectedly, my eyes I cannot trust, and voices speak to me words and thoughts unmentionable. I am swayed, I am prey to an evil force that makes me act against my will. I am a stranger to myself, and my family and friends edge away from me." According to man's own custom, he may have blamed a person, a god, a totem for his affliction; and he sought help from an appointed person, probably as mystified as he, who could have used a variety of techniques to appease, supplicate, bribe, punish, and so forth, the evil influence. Sometimes, in what Sir James Frazer has termed "sympathetic magic," the medicine man would take the role of the sufferer, acting out the process of falling ill, coming near insanity or death, then slowly recovering, a kind of desperate modeling, a competition with the evil presence for influence over the sick one. It was assumed that one could influence by being part of, like, similar to.

The development of scientific thought after the Renaissance must have been an enormous relief. The idea that mysterious forces could have some tangible and manipulable reality, albeit miscroscopic and somewhere behind the familiar walls of the sensible world, was hopeful. The scientist, for his access to this world through his intellect and his symbol-tools, was endowed with some of the magical quality of the medicine man, the oracle, and soothsayer.

The relief must have been so great, however, that there was a great temptation to use the physical model, particu-

536

larly in psychiatry, to the exclusion of other angles of view of the patient. Ronald Laing, in *Politics of the Family,* poignantly describes the misuse of the physical disease model in the Kraepelin era. A boy, unreasonably angry with his father, "falls ill," is sent to be "cured," and progressively declines, a tragic victim of dementia praecox. Laing lays bare the missed truth — the family struggle that was subsumed and captured under the physical disease threat. But the new science was used to maintain the old structure: there is a villain, external and foreign, and invasive, penetrating, debilitating: "I am a stranger to myself, diseased, brought down early, and my family and my friends edge away from me."

The idea of a psychological force couched in other than superstitious, animistic terms, did not begin with Freud, but it almost came to blossom there. Freud seized upon the sins of the fathers, traced the foreign influence of parents towering over the children, preying upon them. When he learned that parents had not really seduced their children, that there was not literally a physical trauma, he faltered, then searched elsewhere. Freud's physicalistic bias may have prevented him from seeing the subtleties of psychological power in the family struggle. Some now tend to see the oedipal conflict, for example, as a family drama whose lines are implicit, mutual, with a structure that is only partially visible — murmured subtly, but a presence nonetheless. Freud largely abandoned the family, though his successors took it up again, and he proceeded to become a systems theorist. But the system was internal, and it had its old structure of the villain, the intruding, penetrating, debilitating wish: "Out of nowhere comes this power, alien and invasive, and I am a stranger to myself, a killer, an overwhelming child, and my family and friends edge away from me." The patient and his doctor were creatures of social Darwinism, of the age of individualism, where independence was god and thus oneself the ultimate enemy, the unpredictable element that could fail and throw one into treacherous arms — family, friends, community. Perhaps faith in reason

537

and science gave sustenance to the solitude of the psychoanalytic ideal.

Later, things become even less clear. There was an era
in which mother was firmly established as villain, schizo-
phrenogenic and otherwise. It was easy to extend this
accusation to the relationship, the symbiotic bond between
mother and child. The ideas of intrapersonal dynamics were
extended to interpersonal dynamics, and one could search
for patterns: mother and daughter are colluding against
father and other daughter, and the daughters are plotting
together too. Gradually the idea of the family system
emerged as the superordinate villain. For some, the historical
family of childhood remained the focus, while for others the
past was rejected altogether and immediate communications
processes assumed an appealing clarity. The development of
systems theory out of the demands of coordinating massive
technological projects (and organizations) provided a neutral
model for looking at the family. The growth of behavioral
theory, and its notions that behavior persists because it is
reinforced, helped ease the "patient" out of the role of helpless victim.

We are losing villains and victims. The situation — the
ethos, the gestalt, the process — is more often the object of
our interest. It is a pretty unsophisticated therapist who
looks for fault in a family's dilemma or who admits such as
a search. And it's probably progress that the theory of rela-
tivity has its analog in human struggles, but it does mean
the loss of a certain moral passion. A lack of villains is
reassuring, but bland — without a cohesive center, a fibrous
strand of values which says: "Here I am, integral, whole,
and living; you intrude upon me and I will battle you for
myself." For the psychotherapist who is maximally involved
in the potentials for being human, groping for the larger
scope of the human dilemma does not mean giving up the
subjectivity of being a person.

We suspect the primitive mythology holds, but the
voices we increasingly hear are those of the family: "We
fall unexpectedly, our eyes we cannot trust, and our voices

speak to each other words and thoughts unmentionable in our earlier, happier days. We are strangers to each other, and our family and friends edge away from us." And we suspect other villains: the multiple stresses coming out of our past across the generations; the infected and beautiful river that is our source; the pressures of this anonymous and brutalizing world that isolate families and leave husbands and wives with such enormous stresses that they attack and flee from each other in panic, separating generations; the pressures that make us form armed and murderous groups against one another. The society is the superordinate villain of the day.

AND PARTIAL VICTIMS

What may save the family therapist finally from being objective about the families he works with is his vulnerability. If the primitive cry against the villain still exists, and if we still do not have sure remedies, at least we have the structure, the ritual, of helping. The ritual is the same, though our tools are finer. And the therapist practices a kind of sympathetic magic; he is culpable, implicated, involved in the very process that he is trying to influence. Deny it or not, he is involved, and not in the play-acting manner of the primitive medicine man practicing sympathetic magic. He provides a context for families in their attempts to grow, but he is part of the society and its stress, and not only in his attempt to be therapeutic but in his living he is subject to other, larger, contexts.

The family therapist is vulnerable to his own systems, to the societies and sub-societies that support him. If he is like most of us, he comes from a disturbed family, which is probably redundant in this society, and though he may have had individual therapy himself, he probably hasn't been a patient in family therapy. He may have resolved some of his family conflicts in his mind, but in the interpersonal reality they may still exist. When he encounters a family that hits a certain resonance, he begins to realize that those latent conflicts are not so latent. The work as a family therapist involves him in a very powerful, sometimes threatening, way. And it isn't just his historical family that becomes complicated in his work; the therapist's immediate family conflicts invade the way he sees the patient family. If he has a strained relationship with his wife, the patient-wife will feel it.

The influence is not simply negative, of course, and it is not one-way. The therapist misses his own family when he is at work, and his warmth and involvement with them are often available for the client family. He can feel the client family's distress because he and his have in some measure been there, and whatever relief or openness or movement he has achieved in his own family is at the heart of his worth to this new family. Not only does he bring a rich immersion in his own immediate family to the treatment situation, but he takes something back to them. He takes the distress and upset of working with families, and often is caught up in a sad and tense musing as he sits at the dinner table, emerging from the day. But he brings home a sense of opening possibilities, new structures, and alternatives, as well. He unwittingly becomes a therapist in his own family — usually distressing to the family, but growthful if his attitude is loving and not just another weapon. So it is a carrying and trading, an ebb and flow of influence that is cumulative and shaping.

Part of the stress has to do with the crucible in which families scramble today. There is no doubt: the single nuclear family is in trouble, almost everywhere. Its major burden is its rootlessness, its aloneness with its tasks. Parents are somewhere else; the business you can't trust; the neighbors you never see; and friends are a help, when you see them, but never enough. Sometimes, late at night, the parent wakes up and on a sea of silence hears the ship creak, feels it drift, fragile and solitary, with its cargo of lives. Anyone who works with families is in the middle of stress — and vulnerable.

The family therapist is vulnerable on other counts. His craft is new, its tools relatively experimental, improvised.

540

There are no technical schools, and no clear-cut manuals. There is a widespread uneasiness among enthusiasts and beginners and even old professionals about "what to do." But there is also a dedication to creativity, a savoring of the newness, that makes us suspicious of such leanings, suspicious of orthodoxy. The better question is probably "What do *you* do?" Increasingly people are exchanging video-tapes and watching each other work, and this openness may be breeding a healthy tolerance for diversity. There is, nevertheless, the uncertainty, brother to the exhilaration, of being in frontier territory.

Like any business, psychotherapy is dependent upon the consensus of the community, professional and citizen, for its survival. In these times of crisis there are plenty of customers, and they are usually readily convinced of the worth of family therapy. But the professional community is usually suspicious, and often hostile. This is a serious problem, since family therapy is not a cottage industry and needs colleague support. Families are so collusive, so subtly powerful, that teamwork, and support for teamwork, seem essential. An analysis of difficulties that family therapists encounter in established systems would require more effort and space than we have at this point. But we stand forewarned of our vulnerability in the professional community, for we as therapists are something like villains — foreign, invasive forces. It is not simply that others are threatened and made anxious by family therapy (for they certainly are, and probably ruminate about their own fantasies of their inadequacy *vis-à-vis* this new thing); we are more like any revolutionary group struggling over power. Family therapists question procedures and systems that employ large numbers of people and control massive budgets. If we were not in some trouble with the prevailing system we would not be creative, but if we entertained seriously the fantasy of overthrowing the system we would be childish. Like a religion we may have to work by proselytizing, particularly among the young, and that is best done by visibly having a good time at doing a good job. Meanwhile, some of the strengths of family

541

therapy — its effectiveness, its acceptability to the customers, its appeal to trainees, its aliveness and instability and power and openness — make it a threat, and the therapist a risk, among colleagues.

There is, then, a network of support and vulnerability. The therapist's personal life, his quest for growth, his involvement with his own family, provide a context for the work itself — caring about and struggling with the family must have its roots in one's intimate family. If that struggle fails, the work of family therapy must suffer, and our experience is that many family therapists who get divorced give up the work. The therapist's coming out of a nurturing, intimate family provides a nurturing context for the growth of client families. There is an intermediary system of colleagues that buffers and insulates the therapist as he moves between his family and the client's, and this support system is vital. It provides the essential strength to be professional.

The family therapist would probably be too vulnerable if it were not for two mitigating factors. The therapist can, when his family is in trouble, go for family therapy. Increasingly, he will probably do so. The other hopeful is the co-therapy relationship. Co-therapy, which most of us feel is usually essential to good family therapy, provides a kind of professional teaming which may give us an exit from the isolation of the traditional work-set in this society. It may be the most effective way of inducing strangers to family therapy to trying it, and it provides a sharing, feedback system that permits constant improvement of the process. The co-therapy relationship also is a first step in developing genuinely supportive colleague relationships that might expand to include larger systems.

This section deals with variants, offshoots, and similar living irregularities in the image that is developing of family therapy. They are perhaps the growing edge in the area of structure and approach (some creative artists can take any traditional format and be creative in it). We end looking toward the future, toward the inventiveness that will be necessary in the years to come.

542

It would be interesting to try to cast for some of the titles that will be emerging as the society changes: "Psychotherapy of the Small Commune;" "Family Therapy of the Three-Divorce Network;" "Group Therapy of the Unmarried Married;" "Twelve-Therapist Intervention in the Corporate Crisis;" "The Use of Public Television in Modeling New Alternatives to Family Living Styles;" "Crisis Intervention in Large-Group Conflicts;" "Treatment of the Double Marriage;" "The Development of the Problems-Negotiation Center;" "Feedback, Incorporated;" "Teaching Conflict Resolution in Marriage by Tape Cassette;" and so forth.

eighteen

how to succeed in family therapy

J. Ranz and A. Ferber

HELLO

The Farrells reached our doorstep by a somewhat circuitous route. Their nine-year-old daughter, Mary, had been suffering from a chronic debilitating illness almost since birth, requiring frequent medical checkups at a nearby hospital. During one visit Mrs. Farrell described her home situation to Mary's social worker. She and her husband had recently undertaken to raise three nephews (aged eleven, ten, and six) who had been orphaned four months before by the death of their father. Their mother died a year previous to

544

the father's death. Three other children of this marriage went to live with the mother's sister on Long Island. The Farrells, who had raised three extremely well-behaved children, were unprepared for the sudden onslaught of three active young boys. The oldest boy, Kevin Boyle, was a constant troublemaker, and the Farrells were having little success in controlling him.

The social worker sensed that the Farrells would be receptive to family therapy, since it might help them cope more effectively with their difficult situation. The financial hurdle, however, appeared to be insurmountable. Mr. Farrell was a hard-working small businessman, but there were eight people living in his household, and he also partially supported a son going to a nearby private college. Because of its large size, the family was eligible for Medicaid, and Mrs. Farrell was told to look into whether their insurance would cover family therapy. She did, and it did, and the first major hurdle was surmounted.

Mrs. Farrell called Dr. Ferber in November, 1969. She asked if he would see them to help them cope with Kevin. He asked if they had any other children, and she explained that there were Kevin's two younger brothers, Timmy and Joseph, and the Farrells' own daughter, Mary. They would bring the boys, but preferred to leave Mary at home. "Why?" Her brother Henry had died just six months ago, a victim of cystic fibrosis at age fifteen. Mary, also suffering from cystic fibrosis, had been extremely close to Henry. She was very sensitive and they did not want to upset her unnecessarily. Besides, she was a very well-behaved young girl, and presented no problems at home. Dr. Ferber explained that he liked to see everyone living at home at least once and that Mary, in particular, needed to be there if he were to get a clear picture of the family. Mrs. Farrell agreed reluctantly. She asked if he wanted to see her mother and aunt, both widowed, since the two women also lived with the family. "Yes, indeed, bring them along." Dr. Ferber also told Mrs. Farrell that he would arrange for a colleague, Dr. Ranz, to join him in the sessions. "Why?" Dr. Ferber said he generally worked with a co-therapist, and with a family of eight, covering three generations, he needed all the help he could get.

IT'S GOOD TO SEE YOU

When we walked into the conference room to meet the family for the first time, we shook hands with each person in turn, and noted the rather graphic seating arrangement:

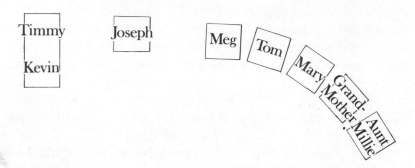

There was a tight semicircle made by the adults, with Mary firmly enmeshed within. We saw the two older boys forming their own group, with Joseph trying, rather ineffectually, to bridge the gap. We asked the parents to open out their circle to include the boys. This was attempted half-heartedly, and a distinct gap still remained. The boys refused to move even halfway, and preferred to stay on the couch when invited to move closer to the rest of the group.

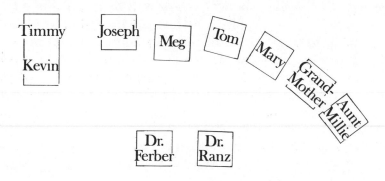

546

How Are You?

We acquainted ourselves with the complex makeup of the family and charted the family tree on the blackboard (see Figure 1). Mr. and Mrs. Farrell were about fifty, Irish Catholic, living in Newtown, which was a small suburban community in Westchester County. The maternal grandmother had been briefly hospitalized in a state mental hospital during the past year because of senility. She and her sister currently occupied their own section of the Farrell's medium-sized house. The two widows generally ate with the family and often cared for the children when both parents were out.

The Farrells had had three natural-born children. Only one was still alive. Their first-born, Ann, died at three of cystic fibrosis. Terrance, aged twenty-one, was healthy, and attending a Catholic college within a twenty-minute drive of his parents' home. He visited frequently on weekends, and attended about half of our family sessions. The third child, Henry, had died recently. Mary was an adopted child, although this fact was never acknowledged in her presence during the sessions.

Each Person Makes a List

As soon as we had finished gathering this information, the parents made a concerted effort to thrust Kevin at us as their "problem" and as their sole reason for being there. They told us he repeatedly disobeyed them, and often started fights at home and at school. Kevin sat, disgruntled, on the edge of the couch as far from the others as he could be, and intermittently engaged in distracting laughter and whispered with Timmy.

At the end of the first session we gave everyone the following "homework": Each family member was to compose a list detailing what he liked about the family, and also what he would like to have changed; no person was to consult with anyone else about the lists until they came in the following week.

547

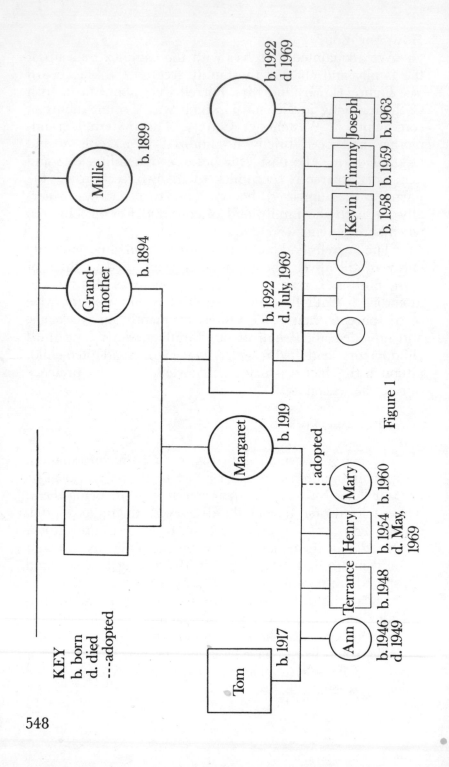

Figure 1

548

KEY
b. born
d. died
---adopted

Standard Operating Procedures

Some of the rules we set forth in that first session are part of our standard operating procedures. We asked that all persons living at home be brought into contact with the therapeutic process, at least peripherally. We directly required that people talk to (not at or about) each other, emphasizing that adults should talk *to* children. To facilitate re-examination of sessions and to allow sick or otherwise absent members to keep up, we tape-recorded all sessions. Finally, we made it clear that while we would take responsibility for controlling the structure of the meetings, the family had the responsibility for initiating what was to be discussed.

Problems and Situations

When the family returned with their lists for the second session, we quickly learned that most members of the family wished to see less strife and do more things together. There was a striking absence of references to sickness and death, which suggested considerable denial in a family that had very recently experienced three deaths, and had a chronically ill child. We agreed with the family that strife was a *problem* stemming from the stresses inherent in trying to bring together two families with such different life-styles. We said we would work with them on this problem, if they so wished. We redefined Kevin's behavior, not as a problem in itself, but as a part of a larger problem . . . the family's apparent need for a scapegoat. Specifically, then, we could help them deal with Kevin's behavior, but *only* if they agreed to work on it as part of the struggle to help change a pattern that required a scapegoat. The family skeptically accepted our quaint description of their "bad-boy" problem. We suggested to them that the absence of references to sickness and death pointed to incompleted mourning. The feelings and thoughts each person had about the deaths he had recently experienced, and Mary's ongoing illness, were

549

not being shared. The family was treating this as a situation to be endured. They did not label the incompleted mourning as a problem. Finally, we agreed with the family that Joseph's being temporarily on crutches (he was suffering from Legg-Perthes disease, a chronic but not progressive bone disease of childhood) was a situation that did not need to be treated as a problem in family therapy.

By the end of that second session we had outlined a working plan acceptable to both therapists and family. We had set out three major goals, each stemming from an identified problem:

1. Controlling strife by better uniting the two families;
2. freeing the mourning process from its struck track;
3. unscapegoating Kevin.

GHOSTS

At our third meeting we began to work on the mourning process. We encouraged each member of the family to bring forth personal memories of Henry and of the boys' parents, asking the listeners in turn to empathize and comment.* The boys idealized their former home in Connecticut. They made numerous comments about how much they disliked Newtown, the school, their friends, etc., and how much better Connecticut had been. Indeed, the boys had been asking to return to Connecticut for a visit (they had not done so since their father's death), and although the Farrells had agreed to do this, no definite plans had been made. We encouraged the entire family to make the excursion as soon as possible, and to report back to us what the experience was like.

During the following week the trip was made. This made a tremendous impact on everyone. Kevin and Timmy enjoyed themselves immensely, collecting souvenirs which they displayed to us. Joseph was not so comfortable there;

---

*We are following Operational Mourning models described by Eric Lindemann and Norman Paul.[10, 12]

550

he remembered few people and felt that Newtown was his real home. Joseph had been living with the Farrells about six months longer than his two older brothers. Kevin and Timmy reacted to Joseph's statements by calling him a "traitor," and not talking to him for the rest of the session. Mary, quite upset, said she felt things had been better before the boys came to live with them and she wished they weren't there. Mrs. Farrell recalled with some bitterness that her dead brother, the boys' father, had been such a well-behaved youngster, and that she felt his later drinking problem must have been caused by troubles with his wife. Mr. Boyle died of a bleeding ulcer, aggravated by heavy drinking in the years prior to his death.

In the fourth session there was some talk about Henry, the dead son.

Meg: *(talking about caring for Henry in the few months prior to his death)* "He was so good, he never complained of all the suffering . . ." *(stops, becomes tearful)*

Ranz: "Go on . . ."

Meg: "I can't, I can't talk about this with all these people here."

Tom: *(gets up and whispers in Dr. Ranz's ear)* "Mary — it's fatal. . . ." *(few moments of awkward silence)*

Timmy: *(makes funny face at Joseph, who giggles)*

Kevin: *(runs towards microphone to tap on it)*

Tom: "Get away from there!"

Ranz: *(to Mary, who is silent and very pale)* "Would you tell us your last memories of Henry?"

Mary: *(very tearful — throws arms around Terrance, sobs)*

Meg: "She always gets . . ."

Ranz: *(motions for Meg to stop)* . . . *(to Mary)* "Do you want to talk?"

Mary: *(nods head yes — then begins slowly)* "We used to play chess together. He would let me beat him . . . *(pause)* When I saw him in the casket

I thought his lips moved. I wish he were still alive, I want him back."

After these few sessions, we felt that the mourning for the boys' parents had progressed well, particularly aided by the planned trip to Connecticut. Mourning for Henry, however, did not proceed quite so well. Following the above discussion, the family resisted further discussion of this topic. Looking back at this, we feel we colluded with the family's resistance to break open their particular pandora's box — Mary's precarious medical condition. Any attempts to further the group's mourning for Henry resulted in the inevitable comparisons between Mary and Henry. A successful resolution of this problem was not achieved during our sessions with the family.

BLACK SHEEP, SCAPEGOATS, AND LITTLE LAMBS

During the fifth session, an attempt was made to scapegoat Kevin. Kevin got very annoyed at Timmy for interrupting a story he was telling and complained that Timmy always did that to start fights and to get Kevin in trouble. Mrs. Farrell acknowledged that that used to happen when the boys lived with their parents, but believed that Kevin was no longer being blamed for every fight. Still, she said, he never stops complaining. We remarked that Kevin complained so much because he was carrying the burden of all the children. Meg admitted she felt that Timmy was a nervous and fearful child who never revealed his fears to them. We pointed out that Timmy could not complain because it would be out of character. He had a role to play as problematic as Kevin's role of a scapegoat. He played the part of the ever-cheerful, mealy-mouthed milk-toast, expressing what he believed adults wanted to hear. For Timmy to do otherwise would have been too frightening. It would have been courting parental disapproval, and a possible loss of love.

We commented that each member of the family played

a role. Mary was always the shy, well-behaved child, inhibited and clingy. Joseph was regressed and constantly seeking physical comfort. Meg was the traffic cop, frantically harassing everyone to "be good," while ignoring the issue raised, and Tom the disapprover who would withdraw and glower menacingly from a corner. The Farrells recognized that these roles were, at best, "parodies" of good behavior and began to see that the others were nearly as troubled as Kevin though less outspoken. The Farrells asked how they could help the children express what was on their minds. We said that direct questioning and encouragement (as we did with Mary) would help somewhat, but that it would be asking too much of the children to give up their distorted conceptions of "good" behavior just by talking about it. We suggested an experiment during sessions. The children would not have to worry about behaving well. They could speak up when they liked, and move about the room freely. They were invited to bring in material (such as toys, games, books) to play with during the session so that they might be less bored. We explained that children often express themselves more openly by their actions than by words.

As expected, the children proved to be quite eloquent in their activity. During the next (sixth) session, Joseph roamed about from one person to another, sitting on any available lap. Mary's movements were more patterned — she would go from Mother to Father to Terrance, and always ended up sitting in the protection of one of the three. Kevin repeatedly set up walls about him — with chairs, the blackboard, other people. Timmy chattered endlessly. The parents acted as if most of this activity simply wasn't happening, seemingly taking care not to attend to any child any more than the others. Indeed, the only consistent response the parents gave was to reprimand someone (more often Kevin than the others) for some behavior they felt they couldn't ignore. We suggested that much of the children's behavior appeared to be attention- and attachment-seeking in nature. Tom and Meg were advised to encourage the children to come to them for physical comforting. Meg responded positively with "That's the first concrete suggestion I've heard."

Kevin was skillful at subverting attempts to "unscapegoat" him. He quickly grasped that we wanted to break through the family's natural tendency to hide behind a façade of "polite" talk and behavior. He came prepared each week with provocative tidbits that always succeeded in arousing the rest of the family. He was following our direction, yet remained the troublemaker. He was having his cake and allowing it to be smashed in his face. In the seventh session we asked the family to help Kevin by ignoring his provocative behavior when possible, and by attending to and encouraging his constructive behavior. This suggestion resulted in a warm and productive encounter at home in which Tom helped Kevin with his homework. Kevin's work improved and Tom reported pleasure over being able to deal with Kevin in a non-combative manner. We made a point to encourage continuation of this kind of encounter, which was a good example of meaningfully changed behavior originated by the family. (Maxim: When you see something you like, applaud like mad!)

IGNORE THE STRESS AND STONE THE SCAPEGOAT

Meg was not at the eighth session because she wasn't feeling well. Tom and Terrance had a discussion about Terrance's social life and, much to their surprise, found they were able to have a mutually satisfying talk — something they did not do often. An unstated implication was that Meg was so puritanical that Terrance could not discuss his dates with her without feeling he was acting sinfully. Meg was still absent the following week. Tom explained that she was sick and in the hospital for tests. Further questioning during the session revealed little information, and none of the children appeared particularly concerned or upset over her illness. After that session, Tom told us in private, that Meg had chronic gynecological difficulties and was in the hospital, where hysterectomy had been contemplated, but then deferred.

554

Meg returned the following week. Though nobody would admit to being concerned about her health, (just as nobody ever discussed sickness or death in this family), a smoldering feud between Timmy and Kevin flared up to crisis proportions and became the focus of the tenth session. Timmy complained that Kevin encouraged some of his friends to harass and "rough him up" after school. Kevin denied the accusation, saying he was trying to stop them from bothering Timmy. Tempers were such that even when separated by the length of the conference room, a word or a cross-eyed look between the two of them could precipitate a physical attack.

A Paradoxical Instruction

The boys were separated, not allowed to look at each other, and told not to interrupt each other until the other indicated he was finished talking. Kevin was able to follow this direction, but Timmy could not or would not. Several times he interrupted while Kevin was talking. After several such interruptions, Kevin stood up at his place, staring menacingly at Timmy. Tom yelled at Kevin to sit down, ignoring Timmy's provocative interruptions. During the eleventh session, Timmy and Kevin continued to provoke each other. We suggested a one-week trial separation. The boys were not to talk to or deal with each other in any way at home or in school. When they returned the following week, both boys wanted the separation to end. They missed each other's company, support, and protection.

The Lid Comes Off

The change in the relationship between Timmy and Kevin seemed to "free" the other children and a torrent of troubled thoughts and forbidden activity was unleashed. In the thirteenth session Kevin and Mary were reprimanded for looking at pictures that Tom felt they shouldn't see. Kevin felt he received the brunt of the criticism and com-

555

plained that Mary was favored by the parents over the other children. He further claimed that Mary played this advantage by provoking fights to elicit sympathy from her parents. Mary, tearful and angry, yelled that it wasn't true. Timmy told her to shut up, in a menacing manner. To this Tom erupted: "I won't have them talk that way to my child."

Tom's outburst struck a chord within Mary. She started crying and then surprised everyone by her next comment. She said she felt her parents fought too often and with too much vehemence, and that when they did so she was terrified one or the other might leave. Obviously shaken by Mary's feeling, the parents admitted they infrequently threatened each other in such a manner in the heat of their arguments, but both hastened to reassure Mary that she was in no danger of being abandoned by either. During the fourteenth session, Timmy reported a nightmare: He was in a swimming pool, surrounded by bodies of dead parents; the therapists were also swimming in the pool. The Farrells were standing around the edge of the pool, and Timmy was screaming for them to pull him out. Everyone talked about the dream, and the consensus was that it indicated movement toward the Farrells. At the very end of that session, Joseph spontaneously burst forth with his own complaint — he felt no one ever paid attention to him. He said he had gotten more attention when he was wearing his crutches, and now that he didn't need them nobody seemed to care for him anymore.

During this difficult period the Farrells listened without criticizing, gave reassurance when possible to Mary, held and hugged Joseph and Timmy when they looked upset. They were particularly bothered by Kevin's accusation that they played favorites with the children.

Tom: "We treat all the children the same. They're all tied; we have no favorites."

Ferber: "But the boys are tied for last."

Tom: *(furiously)* "I won't stand for that. You have no reason to speak that way to me."

This confrontation unnerved Meg. She pleaded for a quieter atmosphere.

Meg: "We've tried to adjust to the boys but we just can't do it. We're too set in our ways. We can't bend. The boys will have to adjust to us."

Kevin: "Well, I didn't want to live with you people. I want to go to Connecticut."

Tom, much calmer, told Kevin that he wasn't going to Connecticut. He revealed that the Farrells had taken the three Boyle boys since they were the most active of the six orphaned children. None of the other relatives felt they could handle the boys. The Farrells had known it would be rough, and they would not let trouble defeat them. In short, Tom's message was that they were now a family; he wasn't going to ship them off just because he was angry with them.

GRADUATION

During the next week Meg called to tell us they had been upset by recent meetings, and did not want to continue therapy. After some persuasion, she agreed to come to a session alone with Tom. At the meeting (the sixteenth session) they told us, "We feel you gang up on us. . . . You make us feel guilty for everything. You never support us." We said we felt we were now ready to support them as they now were in a position to discipline the boys without the boys worrying that their behavior might precipitate abandonment.

They returned the following week with the whole family. We supported the parents' move to assert positive control of the family, only amending their demand, "You should do this. . . ." to "I want you to do this. . . ." Not surprisingly, the boys objected. Timmy wrote "strike" on their blackboard and then led the other children in a march around the room protesting "unfairness" by parents and therapists. The children were angry. They now directed

557

their anger where it belonged — at the adults — while simultaneously maintaining a sense of humor that revealed the warm feelings and renewed confidence they felt toward their parents.

The following session, the eighteenth, opened with the announcement that the family had decided they didn't have to come anymore. We re-examined our goals as stated at the outset: 1. solidify the family; 2. help the mourning process; and 3. unscapegoat Kevin, and decided that significant progress had been made toward all three goals. As Kevin was eager to point out, there was much left to be done, but he agreed with the others that the remainder could be worked on by the family alone. An extemporaneous graduation ceremony ended our last session with the Farrells.

"FAMILY" AND "THERAPY" ARE BEHAVIORAL SYSTEMS

Carl Whitaker has said that the therapist is responsible for the therapy, and the family is responsible for their lives. We try to understand that epigram here.

We recognize that many things happened during our sessions that we allude to only in passing, if at all. In our short professional lives families seem to have stayed pretty much the same, and while the treatment of their problems has changed a little, the explanations and justifications therapists give have varied widely and weirdly. We have tried to be interesting and true to our experience in our explanations. The cost is a lack of theoretical closure and frequent inconsistencies.

BEHAVIORAL SYSTEMS ARE COMPOSED OF BEHAVIORS, NOT PERSONS

Families and family therapies may be viewed as behavioral systems. A behavioral system is composed of behaviors, not persons. Of course, the behaving is being done by people. These people think, feel, and remember, and although we cannot observe these phenomena directly,

558

we know they are important in understanding people. Here, though, we have set ourselves the task of explaining what happened during our contact with the Farrells, and we believe we can do this without describing the subjective experience of each of the family members, nor by concerning ourselves with their total involvement outside the system under observation. To describe this system, we focus on behaviors, their patterns of occurrences, and integrative relationships.

THE FAMILY SYSTEM IS CONTRASTED

The Farrells came, in effect, asking us to study their *family system*. This immediately created a new system, which we call the *therapy system*. These two systems are quite distinct. The family system's *duration* is continuous. After expected (e.g., birth of a child) and unexpected (e.g. early death of a spouse, divorce) crises and transitions, a gradual change into the next generation occurs. The therapy system lasts minimally for one brief meeting, modally twenty to fifty meetings in a year, and maximally several years of once a month to several times a week brief meetings.

The *membership* of American family systems consists of clusters of mother, father, and/or children with varying ties to lateral clusters of brothers and sisters and cousins, and lineal clusters of parents and uncles and aunts. The membership of a therapy system consists of the therapists and whatever members of the family they select to see. The behaviors of the family system occur in a very complicated site called the household as well as several other *locations,* often widely separated in space. The variety of *behaviors* is large and includes a ritual of daily activities from risings, greetings, feedings, and matings, to elaborate procurement and preparation of goods and services for one another, etc. The behaviors in the therapy system occur typically in a single cramped office and mostly consist of various sitting postures, movements, and a great deal of conversation.

The behaviors are integrated and organized by patterns

559

at many levels. Researchers have described the most micro-scopic patterns of family behaviors as well as behaviors of families occurring over several generations. Mothers and infants move in rapid, rhythmic synchrony that can be demonstrated with slow-motion film analyses.[16] Three meals a day appear. Bills are paid monthly. Thanksgiving happens yearly. The clan appears once in each person's lifetime for his funeral. In the family therapy system, regular cycles of microbehaviors have been found by Condon[5] while repetitive and alternating patterns of postures, gestures, and topics have been demonstrated by Scheflen,[15] and Beels and Ferber.[2]

The *plans* for the family system can be abstracted and are called child-rearing, provisioning, maintaining a degree of closeness to each other, etc. Therapy system plans will be described later. The *leadership* of the family system is most commonly in the hands of the parents. The leadership of the therapy system, if it is to do its job, is in the hands of the therapist. The family system has a continuing set goal — the maintenance of a pattern of relationships. The therapy system has a finite set goal: the termination of relationships between therapist and family members (see page 571).

THE FAMILY SYSTEM IS INTEGRATED WITH THE THERAPY SYSTEM

There are some behaviors that appear both within the family therapy system and the family system. The family re-enacts its face-to-face systems of relationship and com-munication in therapy. These include the patterns of posture, voice, gesture, language, ways of representing information, developing plans, expressing feelings, scorning, supporting, etc. The therapists request that the family bring to the therapy session some of their plans for, and rules about, their actual behavior outside the therapy system. Therapists try to bring these plans into awareness, and make explicit the maps of certain parts of the family's life. The therapist's aim is to appraise and alter the face-to-face relationship

560

systems of the family, and the plans and rules by which the family members conduct their lives.*

Four Models for the Therapist

We present four models of well-known events to illustrate varying ways of looking at the relationship between the family system and the therapy system.

Mediator. A mediator's job in negotiating a new contract between management and labor resembles a therapist *vis-à-vis* a conflict of interest within a family system. The mediator attempts to create a situation where the two parties may resolve, under his auspices and supervision, previously unsolvable conflicts of interest. His only powers are his good offices, persuasion, and the parties' wish to reach an amicable solution. It is often clear in such disputes that the mediator's function is to suggest compromises. Then neither side need admit to a victory or defeat, since the adversary did not initiate the new move.

Diplomat. A diplomatic model features family members as coming from different nations with different languages, customs, and rules of behavior. The therapist first must act as a translator, to be sure everyone understands one another. Furthermore, he must help each see the problems from the viewpoint of the others, so that meaningful discussion can take place. His most difficult task, perhaps, is to help develop

---

*We hope it is clear that with a different family, we would have had a different therapy system, hence a different therapy (e.g., with families other than the Farrells, there may be more attention paid to the marriage, relations between adults and their parents, dreams and fantasies, sexual difficulties, etc.). Furthermore, therapy systems can endure for longer or shorter times than did ours with the Farrells. Longer therapies sometimes, but not always, become more complex. The communicative structure of the relationships among the family members is radically altered, and the attachment between the therapists and the family members becomes more personal and messy. In psychoanalytic parlance, these developments are called cultivating and analyzing a transference neurosis. An example of such a case is "Changing Family Behavior Patterns" by Ferber and Beels.[6]

561

areas of mutual trust, to allow the opposing parties to adjust to one another without resorting to warfare or bloodshed.

Director. The therapy system is like a play, wherein the therapist assumes the prerogatives of director and eventually co-author. The family appears and is asked to stage whatever aspects of their lives that they wish to seek some help with. The therapists must structure their meeting so that the family is able to reproduce the drama of their lives in the therapist's office.* As time goes on, they gradually rewrite the script of their familiar dramas and, hopefully, leave when it has been adjusted to their satisfaction. This model highlights the family system as a stereotyped, painful trap which requires an outsider to lead it somewhere new.

Lone Ranger. As to the relative importance of the therapy system to the family system, here are an analogy and a quote from *War and Peace.*

We see the family as a ship on a long voyage. The therapists fly in by helicopter, somewhere in mid-voyage, conduct an inspection of some or much of the ship, peruse the charts of the waters ahead, the plans for the navigation, and the ship's log. They suggest some changes in the course of the voyage, perhaps fix some machinery gone awry, often clarify the relationships among the crew members, and attempt some small changes in their relationships. Then they board their helicopter, usually leaving a wireless address, and fly off while the ship continues on its way. We recommend Tolstoy's General Kutuzov[17] as a model to the family therapist:

> He will not devise or undertake anything, but he will hear everything, remember everything, and put everything in its place. He will not hinder anything useful nor allow anything harmful. He understands that there is something stronger and more important than his own will — the inevitable course of events, and he can see

---

*The authors have been much influenced by Luigi Pirandello, Harold Pinter, T. S. Eliot, and Peter Brook.

them and grasp their significance, and seeing their significance can refrain from meddling and renounce his personal wish directed to something else.

GOALS

The therapist's first job is to create and maintain a new system of relationships. We believe that all good therapists are in control of the process that unfolds during the therapy session (although of course such control may be exerted quite subtly).[1, 7, 18] While the culture encourages people to expect the therapist to direct the therapy and to be in charge of their meetings, a new set of ground rules must be established in each therapy contract and a dominance battle must be fought for the right to set the rules. Among the more common rules that therapists propose are those that state that both therapists and family members should appear at set times, remain in the room for the length of the meeting, and, when there, talk to each other. During the meeting there should be no serious physical violence, no sexual intercourse, and the therapist and family should pay somewhat serious attention to the work at hand. Patients are expected to pay their fees or some equivalent thereof. Once the general rules are accepted and the therapist's control is acknowledged, at least for the moment, the therapist sets about prescribing a secondary set of rules that facilitate the development of the work of the therapy. These rules include: people are to say whatever is on their minds; one is to listen to what the other person is saying; children may be allowed to be on less than best behavior and to play with toys and crayons, etc.

In our favorite working posture we tell family members, "You have become stuck in solving your problems, and that is why you are here. It is the *process* of problem-solving rather than the particular solutions to problems that we can help you with. Please begin talking and working with each other at whatever point you have reached in the resolution of your difficulties. We shall observe you. When and if you

563

get bogged down in your negotiations, we will try and help you proceed from there." We then face them toward each other, pointedly remove ourselves from the center of the communication position, and urge them to go at each other and attempt to resolve their difficulties. The adherence to these rules by the therapists and by the family members creates the new system of relationships.

Maintaining this new system is, unfortunately, more difficult than creating it. If the therapist runs interesting, lively, and friendly meetings, maintains a helpful context, and helps solve some of the customer's problems, he has a good chance of maintaining the therapy system. A helpful context requires that the therapist refuse to allow fighting for the sake of fighting, and steadfastly maintain that everything done in the meeting be for the eventual betterment of the membership. This may require fancy footwork by the therapists, e.g., relabeling vicious attacks as misguided efforts at problem-solving, as when Kevin's "complaining" was interpreted as a burden he carried. The therapists also continually feed warm smiles, approving headnods, benign interest, flirtatious gestures and postures, approving appraisals of the family's performance, etc., into the therapy system. This keeps a friendly and interested interpersonal climate in the room.[14] It is also the therapist's obligation to ask interesting questions, lead and pace the discussions and presentations of material, and generally conduct the meeting as an interesting human event.* If the patients try to make the meeting an unfriendly encounter or a drag, the therapists do what they can to counteract that, and as a last resort tell the patients that unless they stop doing that, they will all have to go home. The pay-off is the solution of the customers' problems. *It is the production of new behavior by the family that is the* raison d'être *of the family therapy system.*

---

*Many therapists introduce media of various sorts into the therapy. See Chapters Eight and Nine.

564

The second major therapy goal is to represent and change aspects of the family system. We regard it as axiomatic that when a family enters family therapy they do so because at some level they perceive that something is wrong with the family's typical system of relatedness, and they are thus open to changing this system. The first step in this process is to present the family system, especially in its troublesome aspects. This is done in a rather straightforward way, by asking the family to "do their thing" in the presence of the therapists. Some of the tasks we have just described do this. We expect family members to re-enact their difficulties during the the therapy session. The implicit understanding is that family members may relinquish some responsibility and be less guarded since the therapist is there to pick up the pieces.

While the family is performing, the therapists participate in the system so as to gain an appreciation of how it operates, and in particular, what needs to be changed.

THERAPISTS CONTROL THE THERAPY — FAMILY CONTROLS THEIR LIVES

As a rule of thumb, we would recommend that therapists never fight a battle unless it is absolutely necessary. One way of doing this is to insist generally that you are in charge of the process within the office, and the family is in control of their lives.* Thus, anything that happens on the outside is not your responsibility — therefore you cannot be held accountable for it. However, there comes a time in some therapies when the therapists find they must announce that unless the family changes a specific type of behavior that is occurring outside the room, the therapy will have to stop.

When new behavior occurs, families will try to re-

---

*This clearly resembles the psychoanalytic caveats of 1. be abstinent; and 2. interpret the transference.

establish their accustomed ways. The nominal head of the household will often act as if the changes are a threat to his dominance and end up doing battle with the therapists for control of the therapy system. Thus Tom, seemingly following our suggestions that the family open each meeting with what was on their minds, would often tell the boys, "Tell the doctors what you did this week." Thus, he grabbed the chance to define what was to happen next and shifted the emphasis from where the people in the room were at that moment to "what the bad boys did on the outside during the week." It is one of the therapist's most taxing tasks to watch for these attempts to restore the prior family equilibrium and to firmly continue to direct the therapy system to whatever new behavior evolves.

WHAT TO CHANGE: GOALS FOR THE FAMILY

Situations and Problems. Families come to therapists with a complicated pattern of lives that we may call their *situations.* They choose to label some aspects of their situations as problems. They generally believe that these problems create living situations that call for redress or change. A great deal of the therapy time is spent in negotiating labels. Some situations that the family has labeled problematic the therapists seek to unlabel. They would prefer that the family live with these rather than worry and fight about changing them. The therapists may seek to label other situations as problems and urge the family to try to alter these situations. We discussed the specific negotiations with the Farrells on page 549.

How Families Decide What They Wish to Change. We cannot discuss this exhaustively in this chapter. What families label as problems and what they consider potentially remediable by family therapy are questions best answered by examining the value system of the culture from which the family comes. Therapists and families sharing class and culture may have similar assumptions about what are problems and what are their solutions. Therapists and families

566

from different ethnic and social class backgrounds may have different expectations as to what the problems are and what can be done about them. It is a good idea to try to deal with the problems that the *family* labels as problems, or when this is impossible to make it very clear how you get from their definition of the problem to your own definition of the problem.

How Therapists Decide What They Wish to Change. Not infrequently the changes therapists attempt to impose on families derive not directly from what the family presents as a problem, but rather from certain (often unacknowledged) values therapists believe represent "the good family life." For example, therapists tend to believe that consistency is a value if it doesn't stultify creativeness; that overly rigid families would be better loosened up (and vice versa); that people should work hard; have fun; enjoy sex; and obey most of the Ten Commandments. We recognize that some therapists may argue with one or another assumption. In fact, any and all of these mentioned values are subject to change when and if we see things by a different light.

Our ideals of family structure influenced the goals for the Farrells in many ways. We describe several below.

ATTACHMENT

There is an acceptable range of attachment between intimates. When this bonding becomes too close, it restricts the partners from taking different postures within the relationship. Mary's bond to her adoptive parents seemed too close to us, and we worked at placing more distance between them. If the bonding is too distant, then no meaningful relatedness is possible. Kevin and Timmy seemed too distant from Tom and Meg, and we worked to decrease this distance.[4] It seemed that people must effectively mourn for lost family members, for if they don't they will not be free to relate fully to living family members. Our work toward completion of mourning embodied this concept.

567

Power and Responsibility

Parents do have more power and responsibility than children. Everyone should know and be able to discuss who has what power and who has which responsibility. The person with the responsibility for doing a job should usually have the power to decide if the performance is adequate, and to modify the performance if it is not. Tom and Meg had an arrangement for disciplining the children that was less than optimally effective, and put a hard strain on Meg. She was responsible for most of the discipline, yet Tom, in fact, had much of the power needed to implement Meg's decisions. The boys had long ago learned that they could depend on Tom to "soften" Meg's decisions (though not to change them). We urged Tom and Meg to clarify their power relationships, and, in particular, for Tom to assume more of the direct responsibility for disciplining the children.

Communication

We tried to enforce two rules about communication. The first is that anything that people do with one another may be accurately labeled and talked about. The second rule is that talk and communication about behavior should be consistent with behavior. This means we are against lying, hypocrisy, and "double-binding." A good example occurred when we supported the confrontation over the actual playing of favorites and the myth that "all children are treated equal" in the Farrell family.

Blaming

We believe that most family troubles are problems in the social system of that family and its transactions with other social systems. We take a strong stand against the blame game. The blame game is the cultural tradition which holds that when some*thing* is wrong, some*one* must be at fault.

We observed that the Farrell adults and Boyle boys were too distant from each other, and suggested that the adults begin to improve this by making the first move toward the children. The Farrells took this to mean we were blaming them for the problem. We said that no one was to blame. We had pressured them to make the first move simply because they were in a better position to do so.

It takes a good deal more work to counteract a family's tendency repeatedly to blame one member whenever stress occurs anywhere in the system. We helped the Farrells in this regard by labeling this problem "scapegoting" for them, and then directing them to discover that other family members' concerns were being submerged in the general rush to "dump" on Kevin. But a "fixed" system of this kind is not so easily replaced: we have already seen how the family resorted repeatedly to scapegoating whenever the going got rough.

The problem is *how* the social system can be changed, not *whose fault* it is. Finding a villain to blame and punish for the problem usually avoids any change in the social system that generates the problem.

This is only a partial and rather abstract list of ideals that we, the therapists, hold for the families we work with. We mentioned them because we think they are important for understanding the process of therapy. We think that negotiations involving therapists' ideals, therapists' actual behavior, families' ideals, and families' actual behaviors, eventually lead therapist and family into the courses of action that hopefully will alter the family situation.

TASKS

People Obey Instructions. Once goals have been set, and the proper moment arrives to intervene, what then? By task, we mean those behaviors that the therapists explicitly or implicitly, verbally or nonverbally, instruct family members to perform. The assumption is that through the performance of the behaviors which the therapist

569

prescribes and proscribes, the family system will change.

For instance: when the Farrell family seated itself in two distinct "camps," an opportunity presented itself to use this seating arrangement as a problem to be worked on. We might comment on the seating arrangement, with minimal elaboration, and then drop back to see what, if anything, the family chooses to do with the comment. The comment is intended to help the family "see" the existence of a problem, and to give them further impetus to do something about it. This is a good tactic when the therapist feels it is inadvisable to move in too fast; the comment implies that something should be done about this without forcing anyone's hand. A similar, if less timid, tactic is to provide an interpretation: for example, the therapist might say, "I wonder if this seating arrangement suggests that everyone is afraid to make the first move toward the others?" This move goes further than a mere comment, it suggests a possible motivation lurking under the surface of the difficulty. Telling people why they do things is a time-honored practice in psychotherapy. It is often effective precisely because it works at several levels:

1. A problem is brought to the family's attention.
2. An unstated injunction is established by the therapist that tends to make the patient think twice about doing that again (at least in front of the therapist).
3. Hidden somewhere in the interpretation is a possible suggestion, as with our suggestion to the Farrells, "Move toward each other."
4. People generally feel more in control of themselves when they think they understand why they are doing things.

Or, one may come out from behind the bushes and prescribe a task. The Farrell family was actually asked to move their chairs toward each other after the seating pattern was mentioned. The point of this task is quite straightforward: getting the family to move toward each other

570

physically. This forces the family members to relate to each other in a new and unaccustomed manner which, under therapeutic guidance, will hopefully allow them to *experience* the better results of such new relatedness.*

People Change Themselves, and People Imitate Leaders. Two other mechanisms lead the family toward new behavior. The situation itself demands change as the therapy situation is considered a place where people are expected to change their lives for the better. The other source of family change is its imitation of the therapists. In almost all primate groups a great deal of the behavior can be characterized as the membership imitating the leadership. We suspect that much of the change in family therapy systems stems from people imitating their therapists. We will say no more of these two modes of change in this chapter.

Plans of Tasks Reach Toward Goals. Some of the tasks we gave the Farrell family helped move them toward the three goals we set. We designed a plan consisting of several tasks that successively moved the therapy system toward some new state. This is a developmental process. Each task is dependent upon the state of the system at that moment, and thus a second task can neither be designed nor proposed until the reaction of the system to the first task has been ascertained.

SET GOALS: FINITE AND CONTINUING

Set Goals Lead to the Deactivation of a Behavioral

---

*Most readers should be familiar with the long-raging battle as to whether behavioral changes produced by direct instructions are more superficial (or less long-standing) than changes induced by "insight" or some other indirect instruction. We would again like to emphasize the strength of the experiential approach which is often ignored : once a family has accomplished a change in relatedness, and assuming it is a healthy change for that family, the various members will begin to *experience* themselves and their relationships to other family members in a new light, and presumably will feel better about this new way of relatedness. We cannot imagine any better way to produce lasting change in any people or systems.

System. Many human activities are enactments in complicated goal-directed and error-corrected plans. We continue to enact these goal-directed activities until we achieve the set goal, become temporarily exhausted, or change the set goal.

We wish to distinguish between two categories of set goals: *finite set goals,* e.g., an orgasm, winning a game, the completion of an annual report, the completion of mourning; and *continuing set goals,* e.g., proximity between a mother and a child; being within a territory (such as a house); maintenance of a superordinate-subordinate relationship in a social structure.

Changing the usual relational distance, bringing the Farrells and Boyle boys closer together, is our example of a continuing set goal. Finite and continuing set goals require different strategies from the therapist. If the goal in therapy is helping family members move toward unconsummated finite set goals, then the strategy is to move toward that goal with all deliberate speed. If the goal is changing continuing set goals, moving off dead-center and playful exploration of alternate possibilities are the order of the day.

Complete Mourning (Goal I): Tasks Toward a Finite Set Goal. In our first meeting, people spoke of the deaths of the boys' mother and father, fifteen-year-old Henry, and the long-dead daughter, Ann, in a fashion that suggested incompleted mourning. The family's tense, hushed, reverential, and awkward discussion of their dead people made us feel that this situation was not a dead issue. The next task was to negotiate an agreement with the family that this was something to work on. After we agreed to the general task of continuing the mourning for these several deaths, many specific tasks remained. We encouraged detailed recollections of the dead. We steered conversations to the dead, and urged people to push their memories until they were not only choked up with tears, but were crying unashamedly and openly. Tears and a warm, sad, resigned feeling satisfied us. If things remained tense, angry, withdrawn, and depressed, it signaled incompleted work, so we would press on and urge the family to recollect and talk some more. The trip to Connecticut was a key task in this sequence. If mourning is the task, it is often good to urge people to return to the graves of dead relatives, to visit living persons who knew the deceased, talk extensively with them about the deceased, to reflect upon photograph albums, records, and other mementos of the deceased, and in general to bring back and work through as many memories of the dead person as possible.

To move a family toward a finite set goal requires that the therapist has at least a rudimentary knowledge of: what that goal is and which behaviors are steps toward reaching it, as well as which behaviors are merely side tracks or running away from the goal. It is only with fairly sure knowledge that the therapist can urge family members to. do things that are often painful, uncomfortable, and feel "unnatural." When people complain that they are not being spontaneous or sincere, the therapist may tell them that if they could do these things spontaneously, they would not need his help.

Decrease the Relational Distance Between the Farrells and the Boyles (Goal II): A Continuing Set Goal. Changing a continuing set goal requires a different strategy than changing a finite set goal. The hope is that the new set goal will be more satisfactory to the family members than the prior one. However, under force of habit, or whatever one calls the conservative tendencies in social systems, there is a continual short-run pressure to return to the prior state of the continuing set goal. It is not as simple as changing the setting of a thermostat.[9]

In the very first session, we noted the large distance between the Farrells and the Boyles and we asked them to move closer. They half-heartedly complied. Yet they mentioned the desire for a closer social distance between the two families. There was not much problem in negotiating this as an area to work on. There was a constant instruction from us to them to talk to each other rather than about each other to us. This had to be repeated frequently, especially when a difficult situation arose and either the boys or the parents would try to complain to us about the other. We noticed that the boys, especially Timmy and then Kevin, sat on our laps a lot. When we first saw them with Terrance, it became clear to us that they preferred his lap to Tom's and Meg's, and snuggled up to him a great deal. Joseph occasionally went to Tom and Meg for physical contact. We urged both the boys and the parents that whenever either of them perceived the boys to be upset or lonely, either party should initiate a hugging, approaching kind of contact. Furthermore, we told the parents that instead of backing off and sitting in a rejecting posture when they wished to control the boys, they should move toward them and even physically hold them when attempting to discipline or instruct them. We told Tom and Meg not to reject the boys when the boys rejected them. We urged them to make an explicit commitment to the Boyle children, and instructed the Farrells to make it clear that the relationship was permanent. The boys had no place else to go, and whether they liked it or not they were with the Farrells. They could not provoke complete rejection. We could then tell the boys that since this was a permanent rather than a transient relationship, they might as well make the best of it. We told the parents to be firm and guiltless in their discipline of the boys, since they were committed to care for them. They certainly had the prerogative of running the family in the fashion they chose. They did not have to do everything for the boys' benefit. We taught a new style of negotiating. Since the parents had the final say, why not solicit the boys' opinion before making decisions?

When Meg attempted to terminate therapy over the phone at about the sixteenth session, we refused and insisted on getting together and talking about it. Tom and Meg said we were blaming them for the family's difficulties by saying it was all their fault; they felt guilty. We said we liked them and suggested that if their feelings were hurt by us, they should tell us. We would try to accommodate to their complaint. We said they, not we, were in charge of the family. If they did not like our suggestions, they could tell us and

574

need not run away from us. We consider this situation parallel to the boys' running away in lieu of complaining to Tom and Meg. The successful renegotiation of the therapy contract between therapists and parents, with the clarification of responsibility, was followed by a similar process between parents and children within the family. The preceding episode is an example of what has been called induction of the therapist into a pattern of the family system.[11] It resembles the development of transference in individual therapy, and is handled in a similar way: by making an interpretation to the patient that indicates you are not what he is expecting you to be.

Families in treatment are often caught in power problems: power is either abused, absent, abdicated, or the object of endless struggle. Family members readily regard the family therapists as potentially ideal models for the appropriate use of power. It is extremely important, therefore, for family therapists to become and remain aware of themselves (in effect if not in intention) as very influential executive power figures in the family therapy arena.

Small moves by therapists can seem gargantuan to family members. Thus it is even more important for therapists to exercise obvious restraint when intervening in families, to solicit comments and criticisms from family members about the therapists, and to remain open for the renegotiation of any and all deals in which they become involved. There is always the danger that therapists may fall into patterns of interacting that replicate and intensify the family's dysfunctional interactions; this is especially the case in the handling of power.

The therapist must know which behaviors of the family members are enactments of the relationship system that maintains the old continuing set goals, and which behaviors indicate an enactment of the new continuing set goals. There is a continuous interweaving of noticing and then forbidding or not reinforcing the old set goal, pushing any or several of the members toward enactments of the new continuing set goal, and then reinforcing with praise, approval, etc., any

575

performance of the relationship system as it oscillates around its new continuing set goal. Major impetus should be toward doing something different. It is not necessary beforehand to know exactly what the new continuing set goal should be. Families usually can be trusted to pick a new goal that suits them once they stop seeking an old one that does not.

BEHAVIORAL PROGRAMS

In the performance of their daily activities and in the pursuit of the individual or family set goals, families use sequences of behaviors that are culturally patterned and clearly recognizable. These have been described in several places and most clearly conceptualized by Scheflen[13] and Harris.[8] In a prior paper,[6] we pointed out how some of these organizations of behaviors can become cyclical dead ends. The task may be to change an unsatisfactory behavioral program which is getting in the way of reaching either finite set goals, or maintaining satisfactory continuing set goals. The particular dysfunctional behavioral program we discuss in this paper is a scapegoat system.

Unscapegoat Kevin (Goal III): Tasks Toward Changing a Family Behavior Program. The changing of the scapegoat pattern that featured Kevin as the bad boy was a very complex goal. While the family presented him as the problem, they did not present the scapegoat alignment that included him as a problem. We requested homework lists which required everyone to both make complaints and assign praise to various sections of the family's functioning. This gave everyone a new role in the therapy system (evaluator of the family) in addition to the one they had in the scapegoat system. We next had to label accurately the remainder of the scapegoat system, and then convince the family that everyone's behavior was interdependent, automatic, and less than optimally useful. This involved making clear how Timmy's goodness was as strange as Kevin's badness. Mary's fearful clinginess, Joseph's lap-searching, Meg's frantic and overwhelmed disciplinary efforts, and Tom's

576

fierce withdrawal were sequentially and simultaneously illuminated as parts of the same picture. By the time of Meg's illness, the members acknowledged that all these behaviors could be simultaneously produced by stressing the family system, and that no one member was necessarily the instigator of the pattern. We told Kevin to be helpful. This involved asking Kevin to do things that were clearly good and then rewarding these. We started this by praising his active and eager participation in the sessions, and then asked the parents to find things for Kevin to do at home. A more difficult task was persuading the family to reward his good behavior and ignore his bad behavior. This acknowledges that once a person (Kevin) is part of a dysfunctional system (scapegoating), he will always play his part even when the others stop playing theirs (persecutor, protector, etc.). It takes all members of the system some time to change the program. If only one person changes, the rest of the family will usually pull him back. If a person changes, it is important to shift the focus to those members of the system that haven't moved, all the while encouraging those who have changed already to hold their new place.

By the eleventh session the focus was off Kevin as the only bad boy, but still was on Kevin and Timmy as the fighting duo. The paradoxical task that was prescribed was that Kevin and Timmy should not talk to each other for an entire week. This not only revealed their strong need to be with each other, but also led to smoking out both the favoritism of Mary vis-à-vis the boys, and Tom's secret role as enforcer. This allowed us to tell Tom that the boys were perhaps in part fighting each other because they dared not accuse him of favoritism, especially since he was so fierce when accused. When Meg was sick and in the hospital, no one spoke of it and everybody fell back into the scapegoat system. We concentrated on having them talk about Meg and how they were managing without her, and passed off as a matter of expectable course that they might fall back on an old, albeit useless pattern at such a time.

The message here is: talk about the stress, not about

the old pattern after it is clearly understood and labeled by all as dysfunctional. We took the position that the scapegoat system was no one's fault, but rather a pattern they were trapped in. We taught them a new pattern in which to negotiate grievances, and some new ways to share concerns. We faced Kevin and Tom toward each other and asked Tom to solicit Kevin's opinion, then discuss matters with him, and finally make a binding decision. We urged the parents not to feel guilty about running the family in a fashion that pleased them even if the children grumbled. We coached people in practicing new patterns, and then dropped back when they seemed to be doing well.

RANZ RETURNS AND THE CHAPTER ENDS

One year later, Dr. Ranz paid a follow-up visit to the Farrell home.

"I was greeted at the door warmly by everyone except Kevin. I found him watching television; he was in a bad mood. Tom came in to say he had the idea Kevin thought that they had called me and were planning to bring him back to therapy. Kevin acknowledged he had that idea, and seemed to accept my assurance that I had initiated the contact.

"We discussed the preceding year. Terrance was away in basic training, having joined the service following graduation from college. Everyone had had a relatively healthy year. Kevin and Timmy had gone to camp during the summer, had enjoyed it, and planned to return with Joseph the next summer. Tom's older brother, who had been quite ill for some time, had died during the fall, but not before paying a visit to his own parents' graves in Ireland. Tom spoke warmly of his departed brother.

"All family members seemed to be more at ease with their memories of deceased relatives. They talked freely of Henry and of the boys' parents, were openly tearful, and showed me many pictures. They also brought out a lovely essay about Henry, written by his girlfriend and dedicated to the Farrells after his death. The boys were able to bring forth memories of their parents freely, and without too much bitterness. Clearly, the mourning process we had helped to start had progressed well in our absence.

"The relational distance between the boys and the adults had maintained the closeness achieved during our sessions. There were no longer behavioral signs of two "warring" camps, and I observed genuinely warmer interaction among family members.

"The most difficult problem, the scapegoat system, was still very severe. The Farrells placed heavy emphasis on Kevin's continued disobedience, while Kevin obediently played his role by sullen behavior and by setting up walls (as before, but noticeably less pervasively). Meg acknowledged they were so disturbed by his misbehavior they had tried to send him to other relatives, but no one would take him. I suggested the following task: Kevin was to choose *one* aspect of his life that represented a present struggle with his parents, and suggest his own resolution. If they felt it appropriate, they would agree to try his solution. Every month a new contract was to be negotiated. Kevin suggested he be allowed to supervise bedtime for the other children when the Farrells were out for an evening. They said he just wanted to have control over the others. He said, no, they would determine what time the children were to go to bed, he would only insure they actually went to bed at those times. Meg responded, 'That seems like a reasonable job for a twelve-year-old — let's try it.'

"I was impressed by the quickness with which both Kevin and the Farrells grasped the purpose of the task and their readiness to make the effort necessary to negotiate the new contract. The family had retained or could rapidly relearn some of what they had more slowly and painfully learned during their earlier contact with us.

"Satisfied that the Farrell ship was headed once again on approximately the right course, I boarded my helicopter and departed."

Just before publication we learned that the Farrells had moved toward their own resolution of their scapegoat system — Kevin was sent to live at a private school for the duration of the school year. He had spent the previous summer at this school, and enjoyed himself immensely. Perhaps this plan was undertaken because Kevin wanted to go there, rather than because the Farrells wanted to get rid of him. At any rate, both the Farrells and Kevin report that they are happy with this arrangement.

References

1. BEELS, C. and FERBER, A. (1962), Family therapy: a view. *Fam. Proc.*, 8:280-332.
2. BEELS, C. and FERBER, J. Unpublished research on the semiotics of a family therapy interview.
3. (See Chapter 8, this work.)
4. BOWLBY, J. (1969), *Attachment and Loss*, vol. I. New York: Basic Books.
5. CONDON, W. and OGSTON, W. (1967), A segmentation of behavior. *J. Psychiat. Res.*, 5:221-235.
6. FERBER, A. and BEELS, C. (1970), Changing family behavior programs. *Intern. Psychiat. Clinics*, 7:27-54.
7. HALEY, J. (1963), *Strategies of Psychotherapy*. New York: Grune & Stratton.
8. HARRIS, M. (1964), *The Nature of Cultural Things*. New York: Random House.
9. HOFFMAN, L. (1971), Deviation — amplifying process in natural groups. In *Changing Families*, ed. J. Haley. New York: Grune & Stratton.
10. LINDEMANN, E. (1944), Symptomatology and management of acute grief. *Amer. J. of Psychiat.*, 101:141-148.
11. MINUCHIN, S., MONTALVO, B., GUERNEY, B., ROSMAN,

B., and SCHUMER, F. (1967), *Families of the Slums.* New York: Basic Books.

12. PAUL, N. and GROSSER, G. (1965), Operational mourning — its role in conjoint family therapy. *Comm. Ment. Health J.* 1:339-345.

13. SCHEFLEN, A. (1969), Behavioral programs in human communication. In *General Systems Theory and Psychiatry*, eds. Gray, W., Duhl, F., and Rizzo, N. New York: Little, Brown.

14. ——— (1965), Quasi-courtship behavior in psychotherapy. *Psychiatry: J. for the Study of Interpersonal Processes,* 28:245-257.

15. ——— (1966), Stream and structure of communicational behavior. *Behavioral Science Monograph I.* Philadelphia: Eastern Philadelphia Psychiatric Institute Press.

16. STERN, D. (1971), A Microanalysis of mother-infant interactional behavior regulating social contact between a mother and her $3\frac{1}{2}$-month-old twins. *J. of Amer. Acad. of Child Psychiatry.* 10:3, 501-517.

17. TOLSTOY, L. (1938), *War and Peace,* 198. New York: Heritage Press.

18. ZUK, G. (1966), The go-between process. *Fam. Proc.,* 5:162-178.

581

nineteen

crisis intervention

R. Rabkin

In conditions of acute crisis it's, to all intents and purposes, impossible to use analysis.

Sigmund Freud, 1937

Psychoanalysis is a therapy for the healthy, not a solution for the sick.

Philip Rieff, 1956

I have previously presented the argument that social psychiatry, within which I would place crisis intervention, is not a modification or a new addition to individual psychiatry or organic psychiatry, but a distinct and separate approach to problems of human adaptation (Rabkin, 1970). Therefore, I would argue, the student of crisis intervention requires knowledge of a completely different set of theoretical proposals in the metapsychological areas of structure, dynamics, economics, diagnoses, and so forth. This is not the place to present this theoretical background, and as I do for students of crisis intervention, it seems appropriate first to merely hint about the fact that such material exists, and that there is a view of the world of psychological events completely different from the indoctrination that the students have probably had to this point. It is helpful in training to supply a reading list and perhaps some Xeroxed or mimeographed papers. Such materials should be tailored to the students' level, but uniformly consider environmental and social conditions. I myself have used Horace Miner's "Body Ritual Among the Nacirema" (1956) as a kind of light and humorous introduction to the intellectual position of social psychiatry. This paper, which is widely available as a reprint, is about a mythical tribe "that came from the West" and their peculiar rituals; "Nacirema" is American spelled backwards. (The paper never divulges this and is straight-faced in its tone to the end.) This is a nice little joke that tends to get people thinking about our social systems. Other readings could include Goffman (1961) and Jules Henry (1963). Unfortunately, none of this material will be read initially or be seen as helpful until there is a growth crisis in the life of the student, which the instructor should immediately but gently attempt to bring into being.

I hand out this sort of material initially, and also a description of the forthcoming learning experience, mostly because students expect it, not because they will find it helpful at this point. I think this is particularly true of the more educated student, some of whom collect bibliographies and feel more comfortable with something in their hand with writing on it. It gives them the lay of the land. Now the object is to entice them into it.

I proceed into an apprenticeship relationship almost immediately. A student is attached to a therapeutic team and allowed to "watch" from behind a one-way mirror and then to "participate"* as he becomes more and more confident that he has something to offer. The "medical model" is most appropriate at this point. As those of you who are doctors will remember, once you entered the hospital, you did not have the luxury of being a "student." There was work to do. It was "watch one, do one, teach one." At this stage, if the student cannot contribute during a session, he must stay out of the way. There should be no engagement in theoretical issues and no time taken for intellectual help. However, if the student looks shocked, as if he is going to faint at the sight of blood, he should be given some sympathy. If the student feels something grossly wrong is going on, he should be immediately invited to do it better, or correct whatever mistakes he thinks are occurring.

Here we meet the first technical problem. The student is probably very good at hopelessness or destructive criticism. By that I mean it is perfectly possible for a new student to come out with this sort of helpful advice: "That woman is castrating." If there is a telephone from one side of the mirror to the other, the student may call in and say to the therapist the same remark or, perhaps declare that someone is schizophrenic. This type of observation will occur over and over again with students unless something is done. It is the equivalent of an interpretation in psychoanalytic theory (of course delivered totally incorrectly). What the student must be told at this point is, "Yes, but to what task does that lead? Should I just tell the woman that she is castrating? Should I tell her husband, or what? Call the police?"

This point must be very well-understood by the student. In crisis intervention, it is not appropriate to "interpret the

---

*It is my opinion that no one can just observe a session in progress if he is known to be so doing and is part of the network of the therapeutic team. As the slogan goes, "If you are not part of the solution, you are part of the problem."

584

negative" as it is sometimes in individual therapy. One must be prepared to repair it, to teach, to point out the tasks for the patients that are corrective. Thus, in the case of the so-called castrating female, to merely interpret the negative to such a woman does not suggest in which way she should change, what the consequences are, or how one goes about that. This is not the place for me to discuss in detail how to deal with women who don't understand men (and vice versa). But I am identifying the very first process that takes place with a student who has joined a team doing crisis intervention.

I think it is important to indicate that in the model I'm proposing, many students spend their first year or two doing very little but watching experts. These students are usually young and inexperienced, and it is perfectly appropriate for them to do nothing because they are not yet in a position to be helpful. They do not have a backlog of informed experience themselves in their own lives, and they have not seen sufficient problems in other people's lives to be helpful. They must also spend some time examining how to assume the role of therapist. When I mention a year or two, I am trying to be as honest as I can. With very experienced people you might expect about three months of inactivity. However, it is vital to allow the inexperienced student to spend that year or two producing very little. What you then have in the second and third year is a decent, valuable therapist. If the student begins to pretend to more skill than he has because of pressure from the social system, he will start to get into a lot of trouble. It is one thing to take an individual patient who has relatively little wrong with him and have him meet three times a week with a student who is pretending to be a therapist, and another thing to do this with life-and-death issues — let us say, recent incest. In the meantime, until the student learns something, if he feels particularly guilty about just observing he can be very helpful running certain errands and doing leg-work in between sessions. The leg-work, which usually involves background studies of the situation, can be

585

fascinating and exciting to the student and is not in any way demeaning. Students are capable of being motivated to write very informative essays about the circumstances surrounding certain crises that delight them. It goes without saying that a three- to five-year commitment is a good idea if you intend to reap the benefit of your training.

There is a type of student who is so highly indoctrinated in other approaches that it is necessary to let him fail and get into a much more serious personal crisis. One comes across old retainers at psychiatric clinics shifting toward the crisis intervention model who have to be allowed to try their usual methods before being able to interest them in learning the new. For instance, they may attempt to take a traditional psychiatric history on a lower-class, disorganized family in which the children are running all around, destroying the furnishings, and so forth. This can be a brutal experience for the therapist and first aid has to be available for him as well as the family.

Some students will be attracted to crisis intervention basically because of their rejection of all psychiatric treatment and acceptance of so-called political or social action roles. These students must be confronted immediately, but to do so it is necessary to know something about the "radicalization" of youth today. This type of student can usually be spotted by what he is reading or what he has read in the past. For the most part, they have read no psychiatry whatsoever. They have read almost no Freud and practically none of the newer, more exciting psychiatric material such as Laing and even Erikson. I found in the past that one agrees to disagree with these students. I remember two such students who left after two sessions.

I would like to caution anyone teaching crisis intervention to avoid an exclusively academic seminar situation where no actual crisis intervention work is done. In most instances, this format is set up when an organization is trying to pre-empt for its own purposes a "new and interesting" point of view. At one such place, I was told that I was most welcome (it was taken for granted that I would give a

586

seminar) because the aides were restless and it was nice to give them something special. This approach is particularly true of large civil service organizations like state hospitals, universities, and welfare departments. It is accompanied by a self-righteousness which makes it difficult to refuse the request for education which, after all, is seen as a non-controversial positive value. Unfortunately it is difficult or impossible to change from a part-time entertainer to a serious consultant. When the latter role prevails, the institution becomes the patient because it must change radically; in the former, the teacher becomes the tool of the institution. I do not mean to imply that it is in the nature of seminars that its leaders must be such a tool, but rather that it is in the nature of our current organizations which request seminars. Incidentally, the outcome of such seminars will almost invariably be character assassination. Whichever way you approach an organization, its members will self-righteously declare you mentally ill in some form or other if you challenge their prevailing philosophy. For those of you reading these remarks who are novices, this "paranoia" can be well documented. I think of the obituary for Don D. Jackson in *Family Process* (1970), and the fact that the members of the crisis intervention team in Colorado left town the day the project ended, as well as the fact that the 1968 Ortho-Psychiatry Workshop on crisis intervention was almost exclusively devoted to dealing with the response of other systems to crisis intervention. Crisis intervention is dissent. Dissent is personally hazardous and conceptually difficult. There is no hope of teaching crisis intervention unless it is possible for people to see a competent crisis intervention team *at work*. Anyone venturing into this area via seminars should have knowledge of degradation ceremonies (see Garfinkle, 1956), and have his retreat well planned.

This means that crisis intervention can probably be taught only by example. The usual supervisory method in which the student and teacher meet once a week and student works with the family has been criticized elsewhere by me

587

(Rabkin, 1970). I would just like to add that in natural groups and in life-and-death situations, this approach is too dangerous. Consider a similar medical example: one would not allow a student to take out an appendix and then come a week later and discuss it with a teacher. In fact, the surgical training model is precisely the model that I am advocating here. There must be an active and competent "surgical team" to which students can be appended in minor but helpful roles. This does not mean that some time should not be devoted to discussing things with the students. I think an hour set aside a week is both insufficient and deceptive. It is much better to get opportunities to discuss what has just gone on with students and for this purpose, as well as for many others, an after-session is a good idea. If there are Dictaphones available, it's a good idea to dictate a note about what went on.

The point I am making about the surgical training model seems self-evident to me. However, it says quite a lot about the average training program. And in this regard, I would like to tell two stories. The first brief vignette occurred on the West Coast. I was at a conference sitting next to a particularly competent therapist. A young man got up and announced that he trained a hundred and fifty people a year in family therapy. My neighbor gasped; as if under pressure, he turned to me and said, "I've been trying to train three people for two years!" At the same conference Frank Pittman and I were being subtly mocked by a young man who asked us questions the equivalent of which was "Tell us the secret of crisis intervention, oh Great Masters." Frank said that he would tell the young man in question of his discovery of "wet cocker-spaniel therapy." He described a family crisis situation in which the index patient was a woman who had become catatonic. His team went to the house one day in a pouring rain when this woman, suspecting or perhaps actually catching her husband at some infidelity, became catatonic again. Rather than the usual procedure of admitting her to the hospital, they proceeded to go to work and Frank challenged her symptomatology by saying that he was cold and wet. It was a bad day and what he really wanted was a cup of coffee. He asked her to make one. She collapsed on the floor, and, as he and his co-therapist were trying to get her to make a cup of coffee for them, there was a scratching noise on the back door. Frank opened it, and a wet cocker spaniel puppy came running in, saw his mistress on the floor, and jumped right on her chest and began to lick her face. She got up with a disgusted groan, and proceeded to make coffee.

These apparently contradictory stories — one which suggests there is no secret and the other which suggests there must be intensive training to learn that fact — are not as paradoxical as they seem. There is no secret to keeping people out of hospitals. (We have been admitting them in droves for the wrong reasons and keeping them too long.) But skill at crisis resolution takes much time and hard work to acquire.

Crisis intervention then, is often incompatible with, or subversive to the goals of many institutions which ask that it be taught. I want to underline this point: crisis intervention is indeed subversive, and students must be cautious in other courses about its application in other contexts. Most students will be getting heavy doses of unscholarly and ideological Freud, and they must be advised not to challenge their other teachers. I have frequently had to make this point in the following way. When one discusses psychoanalysis *with an analyst,* one is not discussing an intellectual or scientific point of view. One is discussing fifty thousand dollars a year.

At this point I would like to say something about the content of a course in crisis intervention.

FOXES AND HEDGEHOGS

Individual therapy always starts from general principles and derives specific examples and solutions. It is deductive. Let us take an example. If the question were, for instance, to choose men for duty in the Arctic, what an individual therapist would have to know is the general principles governing the problem — in this case he would probably think in terms of "maturity." This was certainly the case in the Armed Forces where we screened candidates for work with atom bombs, commando duty, or submarine duty, all of which can be stressful assignments. Men would be interviewed and ranked according to this general principle: the most "mature" men were sought. In contrast, crisis intervention, and social psychiatry, take a completely different point of view. Regarding the question of choosing men for Arctic duty, a social psychiatrist might recommend that these men be chosen by someone who is familiar with that specific critical situation. One chooses people who can cope with that particular problem, not those who conform to some more general and possibly irrelevant criterion such as maturity. In fact, it might be that people judged "mature" would not do too well in the loneliness of Arctic duty.

To apply what I'm saying to the teaching of crisis intervention or therapy in general, it means that from an individual psychiatric point of view one teaches general principles, such as those of dream interpretation. When one teaches crisis intervention, one teaches specifics — such as the best way to deal with nightmares in Latin families when they are experienced by adolescent girls. Obviously, the techniques for teaching the latter must be different than the former. To use another example, it is comparable to the difference between field biology and botany. The botanist knows general principles and teaches about photosynthesis and such, while the field biologist knows the names of many plants and how they grow, where they grow, and, more germane to our example, how to survive in the wild. Thus, crisis intervention requires very specific knowledge of the details of the terrain, so to speak. It is necessary to know whom to call for what sort of problems, how to negotiate with various systems such as schools and hospitals, how to find runaway children, where to get a therapeutic abortion,

590

and even what sort of cases you're familiar with and know how to handle, and what sort of cases ought to be referred to someone else who's more familiar with the problem. Behind this apparently innocuous analogy between botany and field biology lies a very serious schism in science that can be found in many of its branches. It started out as a controversy between biologists and physicists in terms of which of their fields was the queen of the sciences. In biology the split occurs between field biology and ecology on one side and botany, anatomy, and physiology on the other. Ecology has been referred to as a "subversive science," just as I've been referring to crisis intervention as a subversive therapy.

Archilochus, an early Greek poet who was a soldier, has left us with an intriguing fragment which reads "the fox knows many things, and the hedgehog one big thing." The schism I have referred to has since been described as the difference between the hedgehog and the fox. Among the mental health disciplines, social psychiatry and crisis intervention are foxes. There it is necessary to know many things. Practitioners of individual psychiatry and psychoanalysis are the hedgehogs. They know one big thing, such as the oedipus complex. This, of course, is a little extreme, but there is really a fundamental difference in cognitive style between the two types of therapists.

The best way, as I've said, to teach people to become crisis intervention therapists is to have them work along with a competent team. A good eighty percent of the work is simple go-between (Zuk) or brokerage work ("lawyer's tricks"), which requires a great deal of knowledge of whom to call, when to call, what to say, and things like that. This is particularly so if one remains problem-oriented. The remaining twenty percent of the work is much more complicated and, as one can gather from what I've already said, cannot be summarized in terms of general principles. However, even that in a sense is a general principle (or a general principle about general principles).

Another specific problem in the training of crisis intervention therapists involves getting rid of their previous indoctrination about psychiatric illnesses. I think that this point can be stated as follows: one has to convince the student that everybody comes by his problems honestly. It becomes possible to understand that certain very mystifying phenomena occur, and one can see the processes by which the mystification occurs. But this is somewhat difficult for someone who is heavily imbued with the "mysteries of the human mind." Schizophrenia is not understandable; it is mystifying. However, a family being fed up with an individual and bringing him to the hospital for admission with the consent of the individual himself (at least with his cooperation) where he is interviewed by a first-year resident who declares him "schizophrenic" as the rationale for admission, is very understandable. Here is the way Levine (1969) has put it. He suggests that there are five postulates:

Postulate 1. Every problem is a problem in a setting or in a situation; some factor in the situation in which the problem manifests itself either causes, triggers, exacerbates, or maintains the problem.

Postulate 2. A problem is in a situation because of some element in the social setting which blocks effective problem-solving behavior on the part of those charged with carrying out the functions and achieving the goals of the setting.

Postulate 3. Help, to be effective, has to be located strategically to the manifestation of the problem, preferably in the very situation in which the problem manifests itself.

Postulate 4. The goals or the values of the helping agent or the helping service must be consistent with the goals or the values in the setting in which the problem is manifested.

Postulate 5. The form of help should have potential for being established on a systemic basis using the natural resources of the setting, or through introducing resources which can become institutionalized as part of the setting.

With these postulates in mind, most of the problems that a crisis intervention team is likely to see are understandable. The opposite of a mystified view is "problem orientation." What we deal with are therefore not any of the mystifying categories such as mental illness, hallucinations, and so forth, but rather, specific, soluble problems that people have with each other and with environmental systems.

I'm reminded of the experience I had as a student when the police brought into the psychiatric admitting office of Bellvue Hospital a young man in his twenties tied up in clothesline from head to foot. I was hanging around the admitting office in the late evening and a young woman resident was on duty. She inquired of the man what his problem was and he said instead, "Will you look outside and see if there's a full moon?" I would have done it except that there was no window available. Could he tell me why he wanted to know? He said that he had turned into a werewolf. I asked him what he meant by that and he said, "Well, it's quite obvious." He held out his tied hand and said, "The back of my hand gets furry and I get brown fur all over me, and my teeth grow into fangs and I do strange things." The female resident indignantly turned to the police and said, "This man is drunk; untie him." They objected somewhat strenuously but finally gave in and he acted perfectly all right. She sent him to the alcoholic ward, which was right next to the psychiatric admitting office at that time. About ten minutes later, there was a screaming in the background which we slowly began to realize was coming from the alcoholic ward. The phone rang, and someone from the alcoholic ward was talking, hysterically, about a werewolf. We ran down the hall as aides began to appear running in the opposite direction. Entering the dark ward, we stood at the door blinking and looking down a long hallway which had low beds along the side in which the alcoholics slept. Many of these were turned over, and there were men rolling on the floor waving their arms and screaming. Down at the far end of the corridor was a group of about ten alcoholics struggling with a brown, fuzzy, animal-like object, which was bouncing up and down! Now I admit it was late at night, but we couldn't make the vision go away. There was a werewolf! With terror, we approached this monster. I still remember it; my heart beating fast as I ran down the hall in the direction of the werewolf, somewhat pleased that I had the courage to do so. (Of course, I didn't have a family then, and didn't much care about what the werewolf did to me.)

By now the reader may be convinced that I have lost my senses in telling this story. However, I wish to tell at this point a companion story before the end of the werewolf story. A colleague of mine ran a ward for the organic investigation of schizophrenia, and after some difficulty found some catatonic patients. The story I wish to tell is about just one of *these* "werewolves" — a young man who during the day was indeed catatonic. My friend was an excellent diagnostician, and this man fit all the criteria for catatonia and was quite good as a catatonic patient just as my friend was quite good as a . . . well there is no word for the person who plays the other role opposite the catatonic. At the time, quite by coincidence, a young girl came to see me who got a job at night on this very same ward. She was very concerned that she was a hopeless schizophrenic. In those days it took a lot of time to convince people that the category was meaningless. I think what finally did the trick was when she found out what was going on during the day on that ward. You see, she was quite bored on the night shift (the midnight-to-eight shift) and found a very good companion who played excellent chess. This companion was that very same catatonic man.

Of course there was no werewolf, just as there was no catatonic. When we got down the ward, we found that the young man in question had dashed before us down the ward yelling and screaming and turning over the beds. The alcoholics had done what they usually do with excitable alcoholics — they had thrown a brown fuzzy blanket over him and hemmed him in. He was surrounded by them and was standing his full height with the blanket over his head,

594

down to about his waist and was naturally even more agitated, bouncing up and down.

There is a mystifying brown blanket over many of our patients. I try to teach that as the basic point; the rest is merely commentary.

A COMMENTARY

One of the principles that I teach is that emotional states are merely labels that we apply to certain transactions, systems, or shared behaviors. It would follow, then, that if you can change these things (which to me amount to the environment or one might say the social environment of the person) then you can change the emotional states of people. I go about teaching this in the following way. I teach students to help collect those people who have been implicated in the situation; put the system into action; stay quiet (preferably in the beginning, behind a one-way mirror); and just observe the system in action. I teach them that it is perfectly all right to do this for twenty minutes if they have nothing to say and there is no violence going on, particularly if things are going well or at least seem to be moving in a healthy direction. During this time, I teach them to look to see patterns, not to listen to the story. If anyone turns in my direction and wants to tell me what's happening, I stop him and say: tell *them* what you see, don't tell me. Most people cannot play-act; they will bring you a real sample, somewhat abbreviated, and somewhat cleaned up, of the troubling behavior that actually goes on. Then we begin to see patterns. People will cycle through something — let's say everybody bickers and picks on one of the children — and then there's a stopping point. They then start over again and there's another stopping point. Now I teach the students to label this, to point it out to the family any way they can, which can include recording it, drawing pictures of it on a blackboard, or any other way, and then attempting to challenge it, attempting to do the opposite if they can't think of anything else. If people are fighting, let them be friendly. You then must switch from

595

the very inactive role to a very active and very directive role similar to that of the director in a movie. If you can get, even in the laboratory situation of the office, a social system, a transaction, a set of shared behavior, that is different from the one the people are complaining about, they should experience a kind of emotional relief; the task then becomes following Levine's Postulate 5 (the form of help should have potential for being established on a systemic basis using the natural resources of the setting).

I've obviously oversimplified many aspects of what I teach, but this chapter is not meant to be about particular content, but about how the training takes place. For instance, I haven't discussed all the problems with getting a family or natural group into the office, a task of assembly, or the problems with how to launch them into action, and so forth. This, it seems to me, is what one learns from watching a competent group in action.

〰〰〰〰〰〰〰〰〰〰〰〰〰〰〰〰〰〰〰〰 *References*

GARFINKLE, H. (1956), Conditions of successful degradation ceremonies. *Amer. J. of Sociol.*, 61:420-424.

GOFFMAN, E. (1961), *Asylums.* New York: Anchor Books.

HENRY, J. (1963), *Culture Against Man.* New York: Vintage Books.

LEVINE, H. (1969). In *Community Psychology: Perspectives in Training and Research,* eds. I. Iscoe and C. Spielberger. New York: Appleton-Century-Crofts.

MINER, H. (1956), Body ritual among the Nacirema. *Amer. Anthropol.*, 58:503-507.

RABKIN, R. (1970). *Inner and Outer Space, Introduction to a Theory of Social Psychiatry.* New York: Norton.

twenty

on unbecoming family therapists

R. Fisch, P. Watzlawick,
J. Weakland and A. Bodin

> *In our day everything seems to*
> *be pregnant with its contrary.*
> Karl Marx

> *Life is a game, of which rule*
> *number one is: this is no game;*
> *this is dead serious.*
> Alan Watts

Like any other professional, the family therapist is
threatened by professional deformations, none of which is

as insidious as the gradual, almost imperceptible straying from the established doctrine. Very little has as yet been said — let alone published — about these dangers, but we believe that the sounding of a note of warning can no longer be delayed. Our task will not be an easy one, for the phenomena which we have come to identify over the course of many years are subtle and do not readily meet the eye of the critical observer. They are of a multi-faceted nature and can perhaps best be referred to collectively as the Danger of Unbecoming Book Therapists (abbreviated DOUBT), wherein "book" refers to the right theory and technique of family therapy.

By and large, these dangers stem from two different sources, one of which is located in the therapist, the other in his patients. In the give-and-take of the therapy situation, these two influences are bound to be present simultaneously and to overlap, interpenetrate, and compound each other to the point of utter frustration. We present first these two classes of DOUBT phenomena, and then show some of the many ways in which their combination can corrupt the process and outcome of any treatment.

THE THERAPIST

Talking first about the *therapist* himself, we find that he is threatened by the ever-present danger of paying more than lip service to the idea that he is not treating individuals, but human relationships and systems formed of such relationships. While no reasonable objection can be raised against a colleague's defending family therapy against the orthodox schools of intrapsychic dynamics by the expedient of frequent references to interaction, systems behavior, and systems pathology, he should nevertheless realize that there is a limit to which he should push this philosophy in his practical work.

Family therapists are an unruly crowd; the quantum jump from their original training to family therapy has proved a heady wine for some of them, who in the seclusion of their private offices are experimenting with ideas of yet another jump, this time from the orthodoxy of family therapy to treatment methods which do not even yet have a name. Revolution as an aim in itself is an ever-present danger — witness the many East Europeans who first fought the Nazis, and then after their liberation fought the Communists. It seems to us that not all of our colleagues possess the moral fibre to resist the temptation of pushing the idea of interaction to extremes, such as taking it quite seriously. Then they are eventually beset by great doubt — or rather, great DOUBT. The main part of this chapter is, therefore, devoted to pointing out where these colleagues are losing contact with the established and accepted theory of family therapy, by what arguments they try to justify their deviations, and how these arguments can best be countered.

THE PATIENT

The danger which the *patients* unwittingly bring into the therapy game has been known for some seventy years. Regrettably, we all have become complacent about this danger during the last fifteen years or so. In fact, a recent survey conducted by the New Caledonian Institute of Experimental Psychopathology* shows that references in the literature to this phenomenon have dropped from 86.2% in 1917 to a mere 2.7% in 1968 ($x^2 = 17.351, p = >.000$)! We are here, of course, referring to the patient's persistent tendency to *escape into health,* a most exasperating problem, wrecking the successful course of many a well-planned therapy. Over the decades, this phenomenon has lost none of its importance, and it is in this connection that therapists in DOUBT are very likely to display one of their simplistic and yet so subtle sophisms: reduced to its simplest terms, these colleagues argue that if a therapist accepts the patient's complaint as a reason for *starting* therapy with him, he should by the same logic accept his statement of satisfactory

---

*Personal communication.

improvement as a reason for *terminating* treatment. They further argue that there is no evidence in the literature of any crises arising in the lives of patients who stopped therapy simply because *they* felt better, no matter how their therapist felt. This second argument is especially specious, for one cannot demand the same rigorous evidence for a well-known fact of everyday experience as for a more unusual phenomenon. Indeed, the very absence of documented evidence for the danger of a patient's flight into health proves that this is something known to everybody in the field and hardly requires proof. It is almost as if somebody doubted the universally known fact that red-haired people have impulsive personalities, just because this fact has not yet been scientifically researched.

After these introductory remarks and warnings, we are now in a better position to appreciate the complications which arise as soon as the two propensities just described begin to compound each other. We shall next consider a number of particularly crucial issues, but do not claim our presentation to be exhaustive.

LENGTH OF TREATMENT

An important issue is likely to arise early, usually in the first session — at least one family member will probably ask how long they will all have to come. We, of course, believe in the paramount importance of clear, unambiguous and straightforward communication. Yet, we doubt that you the therapist should come right out and tell them, "Anything from eighteen to thirty-six months." In all likelihood, some family members would create an unpleasant scene by gasping and asking rather pointedly, "Are you kidding?" There are better, less crude ways of firmly implanting in the minds of all concerned your own certainty that family therapy is a long-term, open-ended process of restructuring personalities and changing deep-rooted patterns of communication and of family homeostasis. It is usually best to deal with this question subtly. Announce in a matter-of-fact

600

way, "I have Tuesday at three open now, so that will become our regular hour." One may then inquire about "parental models," the nature of their parents' marriage, how they were raised by their parents, etc. But perhaps the most effective way is to translate all marital or family complaints into forms of "communication difficulty." From long experience we can guarantee that with a minimum of effort you can thereby dispel any naïve notions of rapid change — so that even if rapid change were somehow to occur in the course of treatment, the family would themselves realize that they must be doing the right thing for the wrong reason, i.e. that they are merely escaping into health. By no means should the therapist encourage any discussion about concrete goals of treatment, since the family would then know when to stop treatment.

We do not exclude the possibility that circumstances beyond your control may at times force you to embark on a time-limited course of treatment. In these cases, emphasis on professional ethics will assist you to label your service as purely a stop-gap measure, something superficial and of temporary value only, and ease the family into long-term therapy as soon as circumstances will permit.

EXPERIMENTER BIAS AND ALL THAT

The only reason for mentioning these well-known facts is that therapists in DOUBT are very likely to see the length of treatment as at least a partial function of the therapist's conviction that it has to be long. They quote the work of Robert Rosenthal (1966) who showed that the performance of laboratory rats (and of human beings in rat-like situations) depends on the bias (i.e., the basic assumptions and beliefs) of the experimenter. According to his regrettable conclusions, the actual outcome of the experimenter-subject interaction reflects much more the prejudices of the former than the pathology of the latter. Quite independently from Rosenthal, very similar conclusions have recently been reached by Spiegel (1969).

601

But this is not all. Certain colleagues of ours are quietly voicing their belief that all theories of psychotherapy have limitations which are logically inherent in *their own* nature (i.e., the premises of the theory). These colleagues insinuate such limitations are typically attributed to *human* nature. One of their examples is that in terms of the postulates of psychoanalytic theory, symptom removal without insight must perforce lead to symptom substitution and exacerbation of the patient's condition — not because this is necessarily inherent in the mental makeup of human beings, but simply because the premises of the theory permit no other conclusion. For example, they cite the work of Spiegel (1967), who has claimed to have successfully removed such symptoms without symptom substitution. (No lack of data to the contrary needs to stop *us* from predicting that untoward effects will show up sooner or later, even if it takes decades.)

Therapists in DOUBT are particularly prone to make such mistakes in their thinking, and this should be a matter for grave concern. We might overlook their tendencies to erroneous methods of practice (nobody is perfect), but they do not even *think* right; that is serious. The simplicity of their views (which will unfold itself in all its complexity in the following pages) about reasonable goals of treatment, and their unwarranted optimism about the possibilities of change are likely to produce in their patients a typical Rosenthal effect and thus encourage the patients' unhealthy tendency to escape into health before their problems can be explored in depth. No time and space need be wasted to uncover the fallacy of these views. Any well-trained therapist can see it clearly. And most therapists, as well as their patients, have a fairly acceptable view about how deep-rooted the problems they are trying to change are. Yet, there are some who need help and guidance even in this area. A word about problems is therefore called for.

DIFFICULTIES, PROBLEMS, AND "PROBLEMS"

As already mentioned, a patient's wish for change is

602

usually accepted as the reason for taking him into treatment. Beyond this point of agreement, however, we again run into controversy. Engaging in what is strongly suggestive of semantic hair-splitting, some of our colleagues insist on a clear distinction between "difficulties" and "problems." According to them, there are at least three ways in which this distinction can be lost sight of: 1. when the presence of an ordinary difficulty is defined as a problem; 2. when the absence of a difficulty is defined as a problem; and 3. when the presence of a difficulty is denied altogether. Since these views are major challenges to our traditional assumptions of pathology, we want to present the reasoning behind them as objectively as possible, so that the reader can judge for himself as to how absurd they are:

1. There are countless difficulties which are part and parcel of the everyday business of living, for which no known ideal or ultimate solutions exist, and which become "problems" primarily as a result of the belief that there *should* be an ideal, ultimate solution for them. For instance, some therapists in DOUBT claim the problem is not that there *is* a generation gap (apparently there has been one for the past five thousand years), but that an increasing number of people have convinced themselves that it should be closed. Similarly, they believe that there is probably no other single book which has caused more havoc to marriages than van de Velde's classic *Ideal Marriage,* compared to which all *real* marriages are miserable failures.

2. According to these colleagues, an essentially similar situation arises when the *absence* of a problem comes to be considered a problem. Compared to 1., this is the opposite side of life's normal mixture of effort and enjoyment, pleasure and pain, in which someone so firmly holds the view that "life is real, life is earnest," that any occurrence of ease, spontaneity, and pleasure is perceived as signifying the existence of something wrong. The woman who upholds motherhood as a glorious sacrifice, the compulsive husband who lives only for work, are likely to define carefree behavior in others as "irresponsible," and therefore a "prob-

lem." In such cases, "no sweat" becomes something to sweat about even more.

3. Finally, they say that "problems" can arise out of the *denial* of *undeniable difficulties*. While alternative 1. acknowledges the existence of a difficulty, but insists that there must be a perfect solution, here we are faced with a basic contention: there is no difficulty and anybody who sees one must be bad or mad. This allegedly is done by people who refuse to see the complexity of our own highly complex and inter-dependent modern world and define this blindness as a "real," "genuine," and "honest" attitude toward life — thereby labeling those who struggle with these difficulties as uptight hypocrites or exploiters.

The specific ways in which therapists in DOUBT imagine these very ordinary and common views to lead to particular acute or even chronic "problems" will be described a little later, in connection with the goals of their treatment.

A moment's consideration will show where this kind of thinking would take us. First of all, what is the patient to think of a therapist who refuses to see a problem as a problem and calls it a difficulty for which no known solutions exist? He will either be encouraged to escape into health or else is likely to start looking for another therapist. Nothing needs to be said about alternative 2. — we are all only too familiar with the effects of such insidious re-definitions of established moral values. Only as far as alternative 3. goes, it does not have much of a chance to cause harm in an era in which encounter groups, politicians, and the military breed such a profusion of two-dimensional thinkers (or, as the French have come to call them since May and June of 1968, *terribles simplificateurs*).

WHAT? INSTEAD OF WHY?

It is not difficult to see that this approach to problems is anti-historic and simply overlooks the paramount importance of causation. Here again we run into a subtle sophism:

604

these colleagues do not question the fact that any behavior in the present is shaped and determined by experiences in the past. But they flatly deny that for the purposes of *therapy* there is essential value in discovering the relation between causative events in the past (pathogenesis) and the present condition (pathology), let alone in the need for the patient himself to grasp this connection, that is, to attain insight. They are even likely to disbelieve that any elucidation of the past has ever made the slightest difference to a patient's present condition. They are sarcastic about what they call the self-sealing argument that the absence of improvement in the present "proves" that the past has not yet been sufficiently explored and understood. To use their own reasoning: they are interested in the ways people are behaving in the here and now, instead of *why* people behave the way they behave. Basing their work, as they do, to an excessive degree on systems theory, they claim to have found clinical confirmation of von Bertalanffy's concept (1962) of equifinality, purporting that a system's behavior can be quite independent of its initial conditions and determined only by its present parameters. For them the current state of a system is its own best explanation, and they thus show a shocking disregard for insight as the *conditio sine qua non* of therapeutic change. One of their favorite comparisons is that of a man who, not knowing the game of chess, travels to a country whose language he does not understand and comes upon two people engaged in an obviously symbolic activity — they are moving figures on a board. Although he cannot ask them for the rules and the purpose of the game, a sufficiently long period of watching their behavior will enable him to deduce the lawfulness underlying their interaction. This, they stress, he manages to do without any knowledge of the past or of the inner states of the players, or of the "meaning" of their game. Of course, if he wanted, he could have fantasies about that meaning, but they would have the same significance for his understanding of this two-person system as astrology has for astronomy.

Having thus cavalierly dispensed with insight as the precondition for change, the question arises: how do therapists in DOUBT try to bring about change? The answer, blunt, simple and shocking, is: by something they call direct intervention, but we must plainly label "downright manipulation."

To Thine Own Self Be True

It is generally accepted that a therapist's attitude must be one of complete honesty, that he should always say what he believes (and even believe what he says), that his communications should be open, clear, straightforward, and guileless, and that he should share his own feelings, problems, and anxieties with his patients. This is particularly true of family therapists, and it is refreshing to notice the growing trend toward using the sessions for an exploration of their *own* hang-ups, and of experimenting with additional techniques of honesty and spontaneity, such as nude sessions (barring, of course, any expression of sexuality). The effect on their patients must be immeasurable.

In stark contrast to all that, certain colleagues of ours seem almost proud to play chameleons; they employ something akin to judo techniques, using the nature and direction of a human system's pathology to bring about its own downfall. Thus, instead of disarming their patients with the counterthrust of their sincerity, they are likely to yield and in yielding, to manipulate. Like their hypothetical chess observer, they study the rules of a human system's game, asking themselves: "*What* are these people doing to each other?" not "*Why* are they doing it?," and then do not shy away from even the most questionable direct interventions into the system's behavior. These colleagues are thus not true to their own selves, although it cannot perhaps be denied that in an odd way they are true to the *patients'* selves — very much like a good hypnotist who utilizes whatever the subject himself brings into the session by way of expectations, superstitions, fears, and resistances, rather than monotonously applying the one method which is most congenial to *himself*.

There exists, indeed, a large bag of tricks from which manipulative therapists can draw. They can meet the need of patients who believe in the magical by offering a magical rationale for improvement; they can oblige those who come into therapy in order to defeat the expert, by insisting that real improvement is impossible; they may heap responsibility on the incarnate caretaker until he demands to be taken care of himself for a change; they provide subtle challenge to those who challenge openly; they outdo the confirmed pessimist by sadly commenting on the unrealistic optimism of his views; and to the woman endangered by her own long-standing game of suicidal threats against her family, they may even offer helpful suggestions for a pretty funeral. It must be noted that despite their apparent "flexibility," in all these manipulations, in their frequent use of multiple therapists and assignments of so-called "homework" to patients, these therapists in DOUBT keep harping on a theme of influencing behavior by employing *paradox*, instead of being rigidly honest and straightforward whatever the costs. Nowhere does this slippery attitude become more manifest than in their outlook on the goals of therapy.

GOALS

While different schools of therapy set themselves different goals, a few common traits can be discerned. Most of us would agree that the outcome of treatment should be in the direction of what has variously been termed genital organization, individuation, heightened sensitivity, self-actualization, improved communication, or merely a positive attitude toward life. In this area we need not fear disagreement from our patients, even though in their lay language they may use more primitive terms. Thus, when asked what they expect from therapy, they may explain that they do not get enough out of life, that they would like to be happier,

607

or especially that in their family they do not communicate. Although expressed in an unsophisticated way, these definitions are useful: they are broad enough to be all-inclusive, they permit an open-ended course of treatment and therefore leave room for spontaneous change, and they take into account the complexity of human beings, with their reasons behind reasons behind reasons. Are we not all familiar with the patient who only wants to stop biting his nails, but is unwilling to consider his deep-seated oral aggressive impulses? Or the parents who complain about the misbehavior of a child, but are blind to the subtle breakdowns of their communication and have difficulty learning how to communicate clearly and openly about all subjects, including their own sexual fantasies? *We* are familiar with all this — but not those in DOUBT.

They contend that when therapists regard problems as complex, firmly entrenched, reflecting limited patient or family resources, and requiring extensive or intensive change, treatment is likely to be complex, profound, severely restricted by limited patient resources, long in duration, and uncertain in outcome. Using the Rosenthal effect positively, they contend that change can be effected most easily and rapidly if the goal of treatment is reasonably small and refers to a clearly stated and well delimited area of a human system's behavior. They have to admit that this approach seems insensitive to the big, deep, and basic problems which some patients want to talk about, but which are so broad and vague that they perpetuate themselves by this very fact. Indeed, so our colleagues speculate, more often than not a patient's problem lies in the fact that he *says* he has a problem.

The setting of reasonable, reachable goals — stated as concretely and specifically as possible — thus becomes one of their most important steps, to be taken at the very beginning of treatment. Our colleagues claim that in this task many of Alfred Adler's postulates about life styles and goals (Adler, 1928, 1956) are of immediate relevance to their

608

approach. They also believe they have shown that these goals can be reached in ten sessions or less with a wide variety of patients, and that once a patient has experienced a small change in the seemingly monolithic structure of his "real" problem, this experience of change then generates further, self-induced changes in other areas of his life.

Obviously, very little needs to be said to counter these assumptions and claims. As pointed out in earlier sections, they are anti-historic and anti-causal, but now we see that they also disregard a patient's manifestations of his intrapsychic and unconscious dynamics, as well as the deepest levels of family pathology.

Having disregarded these cornerstones of psychotherapeutic theory, our colleagues feel free to view even the long-standing nature of symptoms, not as chronicity in the usual sense of a basic structural defect in an individual or a family, but as the result of poor handling of everyday difficulties. Again, we shall let their simplistic views speak for themselves:

"Everyday difficulties" are considered those arising most commonly during the normal transitional stages in the careers of individuals and families, when shifts in family functioning and redefinitions of relationships become necessary. These transitions occur most often at certain specific points in time, e.g., from courtship to marriage, from the partial commitment to marriage to a fuller commitment at the arrival of the first child, from autonomy over the children to the surrender of part of that autonomy on the child's entrance into school, and even more so as the child becomes involved with peers in the adolescent period, from a child-oriented marital relationship back to a two-party system when the children leave home, from the work-scheduled marital arrangement itself to retirement or to widowhood and its single life (or from marriage to divorce), etc. At any one of these junctures a mishandling of the necessary adjustments is possible, and likely to perpetuate and exacerbate itself.

609

They argue that the way people perpetuate their problems by trying to resolve them in inappropriate, if time-honored, ways is the most important single vicious cycle that they have been able to observe in their work. This pattern can perhaps best be described as the presence of positive instead of negative feed-back loops. For instance, the typical rebellious teenager, when faced with parental discipline, will increase his rebelliousness, which in turn is likely to increase repressive action by his parents, which in turn makes the teenager more rebellious, etc. A similar pattern is often at work between a depressed patient and his family — the more they try to cheer him and make him see the positive sides of life, the more the patient is likely to get depressed. In all of these cases the action which is meant to *alleviate* the behavior of the other party in actual fact *aggravates* it, but this fact usually remains outside the awareness of everybody involved, and thus the "remedies" they apply are likely to be worse than the "disease." They behave very much like two sailors hanging out from either side of a sailboat in order to keep it from heeling over. The more one sailor leans overboard, the more the other will be forced to lean out himself, while the boat actually would be quite steady if it were not for their acrobatic efforts at "steadying" it.

In this anti-historic, anti-causal view, then, problems are seen as always existing in the here and now, to have their own lawfulness and to perpetuate themselves by their own momentum, so to speak. Poor handling of any everyday problem will tend to lead to more of the same, and this process will inexorably place ever-narrowing constraints on, and produce increasing blindness for, the alternative solutions which are potentially available at all times. People in such a situation are caught in a Game Without End (Watzlawick, 1967), a system governed by increasingly rigid rules but without rules for the change of its rules. Indeed, the inability of human systems to generate from within themselves these meta-rules is, for our colleagues at least, the

610

only useful criterion of pathology. This brings us back to the kind of therapy they practice and advocate.

THERAPEUTIC INTERVENTIONS

If pressed for an answer as to how they expect to bring about change, having discarded most principles of psychotherapy and, in particular, of family therapy, therapists in DOUBT are likely to claim that a Game Without End can be broken up only by the introduction of new rules into the system. They are, therefore, particularly interested in studying how systems occasionally reorganize themselves as the result of an almost fortuitous outside event. For example:

On her first day of nursery school attendance a girl of four threw such a tantrum as her mother was preparing to leave that the mother was forced to stay with her for the whole school session. The same happened on the next and all following days, and the situation turned into a severe strain on the mother's (and the teacher's) emotions and time. After about two months and before the school psychologist had a chance to take care of the case, the mother was one morning prevented from taking the child to school. The father drove her over, left her, and went on to work. The girl cried a little, but quickly calmed down and never made a scene again, although the mother resumed taking her to school the following morning. Of course, it could be argued that this was not a case of "real" pathology, but be this as it may, there can be little doubt that the case would have taken a very different course had it been given the label of "school phobia" and treated routinely, exploring the symbiotic relation between mother and child, the marital problem of the parents, and the family's modes of communication, etc. — perhaps even a chance to discover "minimal brain dysfunction" was missed.

Another example of a spontaneous remission that our colleagues claim proves their assumption that a system is its own best explanation and that change can occur quite in-

611

dependently from the historic evolution and the deeper meaning of a symptom is the following:

An unmarried, middle-aged man, suffering from an agoraphobia, had reached the point where his anxiety-free territory had become so small that even the most routine aspects of his daily life could no longer be carried out. He eventually decided to commit suicide by driving to a mountain top, about fifty miles from his home, convinced that after a drive of just a few blocks a heart attack would put him out of his misery. To his amazement and utter elation, he not only arrived safely at his destination, but for the first time in many years found himself completely free from anxiety and has remained so for the last five years.

What our colleagues regard as most noteworthy about this example is the strong paradoxical element of this spontaneous remission which reminds one of the Zen tenet according to which enlightenment comes only after the seeker has given up any hope of reaching it.

At this point, we hope the reader will be sufficiently warned as to the nature and insidiousness of DOUBT. The contagion of DOUBTers can best be controlled by early recognition and prevention of its spread. Toward that end, we will now describe in more concrete detail the handling of two cases by therapists woefully infected with DOUBT. Read, and let the reader beware! The grim and appalling evidence speaks for itself:

The mother of a fifteen-year-old boy called to seek help. She mentioned on the phone that the boy was overly defiant and hostile to her, but even more so to her husband and, in general, difficult to control, not helping with chores around the house, etc. She implied that her husband's passivity and obtuseness contributed greatly to the alienation between him and the boy. Despite the fact that the therapist could easily recognize the situation as basically a marital one, he naïvely asked the mother to come in alone! In the initial session she described the problem with the son in greater detail, but included a great deal of not very veiled dissatisfaction with the husband: his lack of leadership in the home,

612

his limited efforts at increasing the family income, and his aloofness toward her. She could sympathize with the boy for his anger and alienation, yet she herself was frustrated by the boy in her attempts to gain his cooperation at home. Book therapists will immediately recognize that the marital conflict was most important; that obviously the son was playing out the mother's hostility toward her husband and that the husband's passivity with the child served as a retaliation against his wife. The husband should have been called in and this central pathology explored. But what did our "DOUBTer" do? He gave priority to the mother's frustration with the *son*. To test out her readiness to deal more harshly with the son, he told her a joke — that "mental illness is inherited; you can get it from your children." She laughed quite openly at this and began to reveal punitive fantasies she had toward the son. She explained that she had felt quite angry, but had dealt with him too leniently for fear of alienating him and thereby losing *all* parental control.

What follows is hard to believe. The therapist suggested that she depart from honest, straightforward, direct discipline and use subterfuge, double-dealing, and sabotage! Specifically, she was instructed to complain to her son about her husband (in the second session the husband, in the wife's presence, was instructed to criticize any advice or recommendation that the mother made to the son). She was also asked not to cajole or threaten her son; all wishes for correct behavior were to be made as quiet, simple requests, with the reminder that, "I can't make you do that, but I wish it." If the son did not comply, the mother was then to use unobtrusive sabotage — to put lots of salt in his chocolate pudding, or sand in his bed, or "misplace" a treasured possession of his, etc. If any complaint were raised by the son, she was instructed to play dumb and helpless and apologize profusely for her "absent-mindedness."

In the second session, the one also attended by the husband, he was filled in as to the wife's instructions and he was asked to help her by devising other means of sabotage since his experience as a boy and man could add useful hints to the mother's implementation of this program. In front of the husband she was re-instructed to make the relationship between son and father quite difficult by complaining about her husband, and the husband was told that this was necessary since any ultimate improvement of the father-son relationship could be meaningful only if it were not made easy, especially not by the mother, and that her attempts to keep father and son apart would actually constitute a help in the long run.

We think the reader can see enough of the duplicity, insensitivity, and gimmick employed in this case. It is inconsequential that the son became more tractable at home, that the husband became more openly assertive with his wife, and that she was making efforts to supplement the family income through part-time work. *Results* are not the most important thing, and should always be treated as secondary to understanding, deeper experiences, heightened sensitivity, and awareness.

Now, should the reader have assumed that such DOUBTing is limited to marital and child behavior problems, consider the following case:

A woman in her fifties came in for help because her twenty-five-year-old chronic schizophrenic son seemed on the verge of another psychotic break. Since the age of fifteen, when he had been diagnosed as schizophrenic, he had spent the majority of his time in mental hospitals and had been in almost continuous treatment with a succession of psychotherapists. The son was asked to come in with her on the second visit, and he displayed the mannerisms and speech characteristics of schizophrenia. The therapist was naïve and callous enough to tell him to stop talking "crazy" if he wanted to be understood — and the unfortunate patient complied. He then described some power struggles he got into with his parents, especially his mother. These struggles usually centered on how much money he was to receive and when. Essentially he felt that he was entitled to more allowance and on a much more definite basis. The mother felt that his questionable mental state made it unfeasible to just hand over money which he might squander, and she felt it more appropriate to dole out money on a week-by-week basis, never indicating in advance how much it might be. It appeared to the therapist that her major criterion for doling out money was the son's psychotic behavior, but her reluctance to come across inclined the son to utilize even more psychotic behavior. The therapist then instructed the son to *deliberately* utilize his psychotic behavior, explaining that since the son felt helpless to contend with his parents' intransigent refusals to comply with his monetary wishes, he had every right to defend himself by threatening to cause an even greater expenditure on their part by his having to go to a mental hospital again. The therapist suggested that this threat could best be conveyed by turning on the psychotic behavior. He made a few comments on what this behavior should look and sound like, comments which were mostly along the lines of what the patient was doing anyway.

This kind of case and its handling is most disturbing: there was no regard for the sensitivity of the schizophrenic son, no attempt made to translate the richness of his metaphoric speech, no exploration of the mother's dependency-overprotectiveness. There was little attempt to get the father in (one telephone call had been placed to him and he refused to come in to see yet another of the son's many therapists, saying that he had "had it"). No explorations were made into any of the many, many possible areas of the family dynamics. These were all ignored by the DOUBT therapist, who proceeded to make only the most crass and superficial interventions. Again, the fact that the mother no longer felt intimidated by the son's psychotic behavior, that she decided to avoid the constant struggle over money and simply arrange that a larger amount be paid on a definite basis, or the fact that the son saved this money until he purchased a car, which in turn gave him greater independence from the mother who had acted as his constant chauffeur — none of this is significant in the face of the therapist's depriving the family of the rich and rewarding experience of exploring,

615

investigating, discussing, and understanding the depths of their family dynamics and its probable rottenness, which should, of course, have received the highest priority, regardless of the time and anguish that this would have entailed.

FINAL WARNINGS

Whenever the reader who wishes to remain a book therapist is approached by a therapist who talks about specific goals of therapy, of strategies and tactics of therapy, of frank manipulation, of shortening therapy time, of dealing with family problems by seeing only one member of the family, and who concerns himself with concrete results, that reader should be most on guard. He is very probably dealing with a DOUBT therapist. Yet some of them can be quite convincing, influential, and even worse. Some therapists in DOUBT get so carried away with their fantasies that they begin to view problems of behavior in the wider social world — in schools, business organizations, social agencies, even politics and government — in a similar simplistic fashion. One shudders to think where *this* might lead. It is therefore especially important to scotch this trend before its infection spreads. To this end, we offer a few helpful methods for discrediting and dismissing the DOUBTers' arguments and statements, to save oneself and the public from total contamination:

1. Remind yourself and him that what he is saying is not really new or different — that it is something rather traditional, only phrased in new words. Cite supporting and authoritative references.

2. Tell him that you have already tried what he has been talking about and that while it was of mild interest, it was not really effective and you discarded it long ago.

3. Tell him that while what he says is intriguing, it really requires a charismatic (or some other deviant, perhaps psychopathic) character to do it effectively, or to *want* to do it at all, and that this obviously excludes you since you are normal.

616

4. After he has gotten through fully explaining the rationale for his innovations, insist that he is leaving out the one fundamental basis for his assumption and imply that if he were to state it, it would simply be a book assumption already in use.

5. As a last resort, nod approvingly throughout his explanation and finish it by ignoring the chronic cases and saying quite cheerfully that indeed you have long been convinced of the important place that "crisis intervention" plays in the armamentarium of treatment as a stop-gap until real therapy can tackle the basic, underlying problems.

Good luck!

ᴡᴡᴡᴡᴡᴡᴡᴡᴡᴡᴡᴡᴡᴡᴡᴡᴡᴡᴡᴡᴡᴡᴡᴡᴡᴡᴡᴡᴡᴡᴡᴡᴡᴡᴡᴡ *References*

ADLER, A. (1928), *Uber den nervösen Charakter,* 4th ed. Munich: Bergmann.

——— (1956), *The Individual Psychology of Alfred Adler.* New York: Basic Books.

ROSENTHAL, R. (1966), *Experimenter Effects in Behavioral Research.* New York: Appleton-Century-Crofts.

SPIEGEL, H. (1967), Is symptom removal dangerous? *Amer. J. Psychiat.,* 123: 1279-1283.

——— (1969), The "ripple effect" following adjunct hypnosis in analytical psychotherapy. *Amer. J. of Psychiat.,* 126: 91-96.

VON BERTALANFFY, L. (1962), General systems theory: a critical review. *General Systems Yearbook,* 7: 1-20.

WATZLAWICK, P., BEAVIN, J., and JACKSON, D. (1967), *Pragmatics of Human Communication.* New York: Norton.

twenty-one

multiple family therapy

H. P. Laqueur

This chapter is the result of several conversations between me and Andy Ferber. It also contains contributions made by Madeleine Zunitch, M.S.R.N., who has worked with me since 1955, and Carl Wells, Ph.D., and Arlene Klesa, B.S.R.N., who have been closely associated with me since 1960 and 1953, respectively.

The four of us, and many others who came in for shorter periods, were responsible for involving some psychiatrists, psychologists, social workers, psychiatric nurses and other professionals and laymen in dealing with more than nine hundred families over the last seventeen years, first in New York (at Creedmoor State Hospital and several clinics and doctors' offices), and now for the last two years in Vermont, where video-tape and film added significantly to our work and research.

After Andy Ferber read our first rough draft, he decided that we were too academic and pontifical in our writing and stated that we talk much better than we write. He also said that some of my illustrations would tell more than many fifty-dollar words. I therefore submit the questions he asked with our recorded verbal answers, and believe that out of this, plus a list of our former publications, an impression can be obtained of how we go about our "thing."

1. What are you doing?

We bring four or five families together who each have been referred to us through my doctor's office, or our community mental health clinic, or the hospital.

We explain to them that we intend to handle their problems jointly, but with the understanding that each family should feel free to do one of three things after the first session: 1. come back for more talking; 2. stay away and try somewhere else; 3. come back and just listen, but feel free to bring only as much of their own "problem" to the forum as they feel safe to do.

Our emphasis is not on sudden mental disrobing and self-exhibition, but rather on gradual participation to the extent that one can bear the risk of being reached with expressions of bewilderment or perhaps even criticism.

2a. How do your sessions begin?

I guess we begin by this statement to the families in a first session: "We don't know who in each family is the sickest one. We don't take it for granted that the patient who was referred to us of necessity is also the person in the family who needs help most. In fact, we prefer to think that the relationships between the person who came to us and those around him are seriously disturbed — so we should like to help correct these relationships and all of you here function better. This should then enable each of you to get along better with each other and have a feeling that life is worth-while."

2b. *How are new families introduced?*

New families are introduced by their names and then subsequently one of the older families will say, "You are new here — we were once at that point — we know how difficult this can be — but maybe it can help if you just briefly tell us why you came?" "Yes, that's the idea — just give us headlines!" Or someone else or the therapist may say, "This usually comforts the newcomers who learn that others have felt pain and embarrassment, too."

2c. *Why do you mix families from varied socio-economic layers and different educational backgrounds together?*

We mix them together because nothing is as sterile as five Catholic lawyers and their families. They never talk about anything but superficialities. The more random the better. The daughter of a taxidriver and the son of a professor can cause their parents much more efficiently to talk about parent-child relations than pre-programmed people of similar backgrounds.

3a. *When do you feel you interfere too much?*

We feel that we are interfering too much when our patients or families withdraw and become timid or super-ficially intellectual in their responses.

620

3b. When do you feel you interfere too little?

We feel we interfere too little when meetings deteriorate into simply chit-chat or hostile focusing on *issues* rather than *attitudes*.

3c. When do you feel that you do things just right?

When a session moves rapidly from one emotional problem to the next with clear indication of mutual learning and involvement within a family and between "old-timers" and "newcomer" families.

4. What makes you think that what you do is different from the work of therapists with single families?

My patients and families have occasion to compare themselves in actuality with others in similar situations, and they can see how they can produce better or poorer attitudes in others by repeated inefficient behavior, brought to the situation from much earlier acquired patterns.

5a. If you find a family dropping out, do you go after them either by letter, home visit, telephone? how do you determine what is the reason for their absence?

We are very flexible — we usually phone, write, or I have one of my teammates (social worker, nurse, psychologist, local aide in a community center) follow-up by visit or other contacts. There may be genuine reasons, like change in work-hours, so that our liberal policy of being available evenings, Saturdays, or Sundays may not help. If we feel that discontinuing attendance is due to actual "resistance" or to mistakes made by us or other families, we may follow a brief course of individual or single family contacts until the mutual confidence between the absentee and the rest of the group is restored.

5b. How are families finally separated, graduated, or excommunicated from the group?

If a family does not drop out in the first five sessions, they usually (with very rare exceptions, e.g., when they move to a far-away town) stay together, becoming more and more expert at handling problems of "newcomers" while still growing — more slowly — to understand their own hangups and erroneous attitudes. It is then up to the therapist to decide — after twelve months, as we had to do in our government research groups — or after eighteen and more months in ordinary family therapy groups (which seem more beneficial) — that a family now should try things on their own and come back only if they really cannot. Excommunication has not happened in my experiences. Some people may have felt "out of favor" with the majority in their group — but this became rather a stimulus than a hindrance.

6. How do you lead your group?

Andy Ferber likes our metaphor that the therapist should act like the conductor of an orchestra. That means he must know his score, he must know where he is going with these families, and he must have a short-term and a long-term plan for the interaction that he means to produce. Of course, if he just sits in the group and smiles passively and lets everybody do as they darn well please, then nobody gets much out of it. If he aggressively intervenes and closes out people who give him momentary discomfort, he may discourage those who may have had something to say but don't dare provoke his anger. Ferber felt that the "conductor" must be on the podium but should respect the "soloist" and not interrupt without necessity. We feel that the "conductor" must bring up the shy and fearful and hold back the loud, ruminating, redundant monologues or two-way interaction that sometimes develop in a repetitive

622

manner. Between the two extremes of passive and over-bearing attitudes lies the art of skillful therapy, which is sensitive to the needs of the majority in the group.

All of us have written papers theorizing about process, skill and feed-back. These have stimulated discussion and the feed-back of these discussions has stimulated new theories. We are a long way from really understanding the multiple family therapy process, the phases from reaching relief *via* resistance to final improvement, but we can see this, after experiences with nearly nine hundred families, as a thing that happens over and over again. People are at first wary and anxious, and wondering why the heck they should exchange their worries and problems with other families; then they find that at *least* one family gives them support, so that the pain of exposure to anxiety-provoking situations decreases. Then, however, as people come to grips with what they think is bothering them, things get tougher and people have to accept the truth that they may be causing a good many of their own troubles. It is much more comforting to ascribe symptoms to medical or biological causes than personal attitudes and behavior which must be modified. Only if one has the courage to go through perhaps twenty or more agonizing sessions can real solutions be eventually found, and this takes place in the third phase. Talking about process, we don't even know whether behavior change should precede or follow change in insight. In most instances, I believe that insight comes later. Better mutual attitudes come first. It is very important that the feed-back into the family system of experiences of other families takes place continually, and that more advanced families help more regressed ones. However, sometimes surprising things happen when a new family with very severe symptoms all of a sudden sets out to "cure" everybody else's troubles.

Also, parents see nothing wrong in asking their adolescent children to disrobe mentally in the group because they are supposedly patients. At the same time the parents will fight the therapist tooth and nail if they are asked to disclose their own true feelings. I have made drawings illustrating this unfair situation and perhaps this shows better than words how discriminating this demand is.

7. Can you give us some examples of interaction?

1. Sharon told about her dissatisfaction with her husband, who would not even let her call an alcoholic friend and assist him to a bus and to his home. The husband immediately accused her of infidelity. Mary, who has been unfaithful to her husband many times, got scared, put her fingers in her mouth, and bit her nails. Mary's husband, a scoundrel, looked at her and said, "You see? You are being unfaithful and I let you do as you please. Maybe I should be like the other husband." Mary's mother said, "If I didn't check on both of you, you would play the field." The immediate effect of Sharon's remark was lively interaction in Mary's family, so the therapist asked, "How did you come to the hospital?" Mary said, "My husband said, 'If you don't like things as they are, kill yourself.' " He answered, "I didn't think she would do it. She came at me with a knife and said she would kill me in my sleep, and to show her I had no fear I purposely went to sleep and she did not. So I thought that because she would not kill me, she would not try it with herself." The therapist replied, "I believe suicide is still somewhat easier than homicide for some people." The whole group laughed. Mary's husband said, "I thought that if somebody admits intentions to kill himself, then he will never do it." Mary and Sharon answered in unison, "Don't bank on it." The group was now deeply concerned, and began to discuss serious feelings of loneliness and suicidal depression occurring in several members.

2. A taxidriver said about his nineteen-year-old daughter, a patient in the hospital, "I don't want her to come in later than ten o'clock in the evening. I see enough in my work to know what dangers a girl can run into in a city." "You are just trying to keep me to yourself, Daddy,"

624

said the daughter. "I cannot stand to be checked on all the time." Father and mother, to the girl, replied, "We only want what is good for you." "And I will never let you be alone except with a good person because I know what can happen to you," added the father. Jim (a schizophrenic seventeen-year-old son in another family) commented, "These people can argue till doomsday, but they will always be arguing about the same things. Why doesn't her dad see that he has a thing going for her that he will not admit to himself." Now several families chimed in and realized that the father's intense quarreling was a reaction-formation to feelings for her which were illicit because of their incestuous nature. Through the process of indirect interpretation it became possible for others and then for the father himself to accept the existence of this difficulty and, therefore, gradually effect a pattern change. He may eventually be less hostile and aggressive when she goes out on dates. This result could not have been achieved without the presence of the other families because of the father's extreme defensiveness in direct head-on confrontation.

3. "I can't stand it when you always nag me," said a daughter to a mother. The father felt that the mother, indeed, went a bit far with her criticism, so the mother, who in this family occupied the *"control tower,"* vehemently attacked her husband. Two other mothers chimed in, "Your daughter does give you a hard time, but I wonder whether you see that she only substitutes for your husband who does not dare speak up to you." Two more husbands said, "Yes, Dennis, try to be more of a man." The controlling mother broke out in tears, "Nobody has any feelings for me. I have to do it all alone." Several families rallied to her support, "Why do you always have to fight for what you want?" "Nobody listens to me any more when I'm sweet. I have to yell to be heard." Several families began to review their own mutual attitudes and particular behaviors, and a simple belligerent remark from a daughter became an opportunity to re-evaluate their attitudes and positions.

8.   *How do you put your groups together?*

In the beginning, we put groups together randomly. Posters in all the nurses' stations on thirty-three wards advised personnel and patients that we had family therapy meetings on Sundays. Patients told their relatives, "If you want to understand what is troubling me, you better come to Dr. Laqueur's Sunday meetings."

Soon our meetings became too large and had to be split into sub-groups led by Drs. Stark, Phillips, Deane, and others. This development is different from what we did in New York, where all the patients were originally all on one ward and their parents were seen automatically together by the doctors during visiting hours.

In the ward therapeutic community, it was natural and logical that parents and children were seen together in large Sunday meetings, and that the families who had already received care and treatment helped the new arrivals. In Vermont, there was no such thing as family therapy meetings before my arrival in 1968. Families were occasionally seen, but only incidentally for crisis intervention. Today, recent admissions are encouraged to seek family therapy in addition to other treatments that the hospital provides, and after the patients are released, the contact with families in such Sunday meetings is maintained. But we do not yet have very good prolonged contact with families, except with those groups where video-tape or filming is used at regular intervals. This system needs improving through contact with the regional after-care clinics.

One area in which the new family therapy staff of the Vermont State Hospital needs to work is contact with the families of long-term patients. Here, the different physicians in the Vermont State Hospital will have to be asked to be helpful.

9a.   *What are workers in MFT being trained for?*

Training therapists to do multiple family therapy

626

requires first a clear understanding of the specific responsibilities that go with this type of treatment.

The individual therapist sees himself responsible for the *care* and *treatment* of a sick *person*; his responsibility for that person's nuclear family and network of friends, acquaintances, and persons related to his employment or field of study is felt to be secondary.

The family therapist is often consulted by a *family*, not just a primary single patient. He may view his task as first having to help the family to operate better with each other within the family, and second to improve their social, biological, psychological, and ecological relationships with the surrounding world. He may, therefore, sometimes view the family's needs as a whole group as having higher priority (or falling into a different category) than the needs of any individual person.

A person engaging in multiple family therapy sees his responsibility primarily as an intermediary between *surrounding society* and *poorly functioning families* (and/or a *network* of people), with a high-priority responsibility to make sick families relate better both in intra- and inter-familial relationships.

The individual patient may of course be seen and helped by the family therapist, but the perspective of his function within his family and societal supra-systems retains the value of a primary focus. Therefore family therapy does not strive to resolve *individual pathology,* but concentrates instead on disturbed relationships, and inter-group interfaces.

The famous saying, "The patient always comes first," may be a dangerous ethical trap. It is an open question how much a person is being helped when we make him see his own interests as supreme and those of everyone else as secondary. Surely, to give a sick person more self-confidence, better self-acceptance, and liking for himself is important — but the danger of overdoing things and letting a person become disproportionately preoccupied with himself is a danger inherent in prolonged individual psychotherapy.

9b. *What else are people being trained for?*

I think if five families went on a trip across the country with tents and camping facilities in a large bus, they would come to know more about each other, both in a pleasant as well as in a negative sense, than if they traveled in five individual cars. In fact, I don't know of any five families who ever made a trip jointly in five individual cars. One or two families perhaps might have, but not more. I think this is the tradition that man's home, and this includes the family car, is his castle, and that in the privacy of his home, he conducts himself differently with his family than he does in the presence of others. We hear a great deal about American families being democratic families, in which certain matters are decided by voice vote or majority. We hear that wives assume that they have equal rights and an equal vote with their husbands, and children think that they should be consulted about plans and decisions. I am not certain that this is entirely correct. In many families we find authoritarian fathers or mothers, grandparents, or maiden aunts who "rule the roost" in anything but a democratic way. Therefore, such a family, if exposed to another family, or more than one, in a community vehicle, spending time together day and night, would more likely detect many areas of personal friction. Nobody likes to have pointed out to himself how arbitrary, unfeeling, and thoughtless he is.

Children today expect to have the right to complain to each other and their friends about parental attitudes. They take it less for granted that parents have and should have authority to make decisions, and they call some of these decisions irrelevant and out of place. Let us imagine five normal families on a bus trip where children band together to tell their parents that they are out of touch with the times and that they don't know their arms from their elbows.

This is about the condition we find at the beginning of a session with this difference only: we so far have done multiple family therapy only with *problem* families. We really don't know how families without a problem label would behave in this closeness of communication.

The therapist needs skilled perception to know how to deal with such stresses.

10. *How do you deal with the continually absent members of the family? Is the importance of such absence discussed by the group and what is done?*

Yes, we often think that an absent member from the family session may very well be the most important person in the home setting. This was the reason I was somewhat skeptical about some family therapy groups set up in the daytime. Mothers and daughters were having therapy, but providers rarely could be present, and if they were, the women tore into them and made them look like black sheep. I feel that it must be pointed out to the families that each member, even a small infant, provides important cues to behavior. I think people should be encouraged to bring all family members, and this is the reason why we prefer to work on evenings and on weekends when providers can be present without loss of job income. I know that this is hard on the staff, but, after all, we are here to serve our families and our off-duty time can be adjusted administratively while theirs cannot. It is also possible that the most important member of the family might be a lame grandmother or mother-in-law in a wheelchair at home who cannot come to the meetings. This may be discovered by an early home visit, which we personally encourage our staff to make, and also it can be discussed when looking between the lines to answers about questions as to who runs the family and makes the rules. If this information is not obtained, completely erroneous conclusions about the family processes may be drawn. I feel that it is even important to know who sleeps in what bed and at what time of the day; how the family rooms are arranged; whether they have meals together or everybody raids the refrigerator and cooks for himself at different times; whether there is one or more television sets, etc. We once had a schizophrenic patient, twenty-one years of age, who had grade "A" marks in school and college. Suddenly, at twenty-one, he fell in love, and collapsed in a catatonic state. He was a well-dressed man of generally fine, intelligent, well-dressed, middle-class parents. He was the only child, and a home visit by one of our student nurses showed us that the parents had an elaborate living and dining room in their suburban house, but had only one large bedroom. They had slept together in a large bed all their life and the son slept on a couch at the foot of the parental bed. Neither they nor he had had one moment of privacy in their lives. Things like this must be seen to be understood. They do not come out in ordinary conversations. Therefore, in my book, the absent member and the home situation are tied together as the most important clues to the meaning of relationships and disturbances.

11. Without going into too much depth about the use of video-tape, tell more about its use for training of therapists and playback to the families: how, when, and where is it used?

Video-tape is used on three levels: 1. to make tapes for training of therapists and observers; 2. to provide edited material of dramatic impact to play back to families to show them what they do to each other; and 3. to make tapes of high quality that can be kinescoped and, together with 16mm. films, produce educational material like the film that we had on exhibit at the A.P.A. in San Francisco and the A.M.A. in Chicago.

Trainees vary in their amount of resistance to verbal supervision, but it is a cinch to get points across to them when they see themselves concurrently with the supervisor on video-tape. All the non-verbal stuff they are doing becomes immediately meaningful. (We have picked up Andy Ferber's suggestion to pay special attention to the way people meet, recognize, and greet each other. These shots done in repeated series can be highly meaningful.) We gen-

630

erally use two cameras with zoom lenses, set up so that each camera sees half of the group, which is seated in an ellipse. The monitors of Camera I and Camera II are checked by a person with experience in this field, who then judges what is more important and places, with the help of a split-screen device, those images on the tape that should be more important during the review of the hour. With the help of earphones and throat microphones, the director and cameraman can communicate, and in addition to this, when I observe a group, I can talk to the individual cameraman and suggest that they should focus on something I see but that they may not have in their field. For instance, when they become fascinated with an interchange between two persons close to each other, I may direct one of the cameras to the opposite side of the room where a little aside between two other people, a joke or a fearful expression, may change the mood of the room through gestures, change of position, twiddling of fingers, or shoveling of feet. The total impact of non-verbal communications on the over-all mood in the room cannot be underestimated. Long dialogues between people are discouraged by therapists anyhow, unless they are very emotional, and therapists will tend to bring more people in to widen a one-to-one exchange, but with video observations this may not always be necessary, because at a certain point one can stop the session and say, "Let's all look at the last ten minutes and see what has happened here," and many people will suddenly become aware of their actions as they could not be before video-tape recording. To me, video-tape is the most important breakthrough for psychiatry, like the microscope was for bacteriology, because it enables us for the first time, under economically feasible conditions, to fully record and retain interaction and study it with those involved for as many times as it is profitable to produce more insight. Some trainees can't stand looking at a whole session at once. I can understand this, and accept their preference for showing a video-tape with as many stops and interruptions as they wish to make in order to discuss what they have seen. With the families, we do the pre-editing, and show them what we think is therapeutically significant, because a few tries have shown that families get awfully tired of watching seventy-five minutes of tape without interruption, no matter how significant it would be.

12. Metacommunication

If I am above you in an administrative, military, or authorized, regulated hierarchical relationship, I have the right to demand that you should answer me directly and openly, while you do not have the right to ask of me that I should tell you all that I know. The person on the higher step on the ladder has the right to privacy and secrecy that the person below him cannot claim. Persons in authority control property, communications, access to publicity media, while persons at the bottom of the ladder have no right to free information about all matters, and cannot reach the general public with the same ease as the higher-ups. Parents reserve for themselves the right to be secretive, yet they demand complete openness and honesty of their children, and call them liars if they answer evasively or distort the facts.

The demand of the young generation that authority and underdog share feelings openly with each other is understandable. It creates problems, because if the person in the superior position has access to information that the lower ranks do not share, he may rightfully be worried about things while the young ones aren't. It is not without reason that Henry IV in his monologue said, when he watched his peacefully sleeping soldiers before the battle, "Heavy rests the crowned head." The right to privacy and secrecy, the communication of information only to those who "need to know," has its place in a proprietary society, but of course it can be *evil* when states and authorities resort to secret political tactics that offend the average citizen. This may be one of the reasons why we have such a broad political discussion between the students on college campuses and the government. Young people are asked to serve and risk their lives for their country, the government of which does not

632

always tell them why their sacrifice is necessary. We should understand why young people like to know what they have to die for rather than being sent as common fodder into battles, the significance of which they do not understand.

On a small scale, we find this debate between generations in family therapy. "Don't smoke grass; it is illegal," says papa. The youngster says, "Grass is not as harmful by a long shot as all the booze you drink, Dad." Here we see a true therapeutic problem.

13. *My definition of multiple family therapy, greyhound bus and lifeboat models*

Multiple family therapy is a *tool to teach individual families* a great deal about their behavior by *setting up mirrors* (in reality and subsequently on film and on videotape) in which they can *compare the things they are doing to each other*. Thus a patient after a session expressed what he saw as *bringing several families together*.

At a recent meeting in Boston, about three out of every ten family therapists told me that they were now using this technique, which seven years ago was reported by us for the first time at the APA in St. Louis, Missouri. Murray Bowen said that he can get a great deal done working with one family while others are watching.

This is our Greyhound bus model. We did this in New York with groups of up to seventeen families at one time (starting as early as 1951). During the first half of the session a therapist (and sometimes one "fellow patient") conducted an interview. Then the families took turns being "on the hot seat," and being permitted a "press conference," with the other families acting as interviewers during a forty-five-minute question-and-answer period. This therapy, in which new families gradually replaced the old, continued for eight and a half years. Very high levels of freedom of communication and sophistication were reached.

In 1951, we began with a Sunday afternoon group of seventeen families who all had in common a "primary patient" (who might be an adolescent, a father, or mother, or even a grandparent) who was on the "insulin ward" and on biological treatment; we kept this going till 1960. We had to add a second Sunday-morning group of eighteen families, because all our male and female insulin patients wanted to have "their" families involved in this procedure. The ward became a forum where all matters pertaining to mental illness and its social, psychological, and biological consequences (and interfaces between patient, society, family, therapeutic institution, and intervening teams) could be ventilated and elucidated.

As we went to a larger and more modern building and became a research ward involved in the care of one hundred families simultaneously, and sometimes of two hundred patients and families on "aftercare," we came to understand the need for smaller groups, and decided on patterns of five (four to six) families for each session, who would be placed together randomly in each session, and who had to learn to keep "their" patient well and out of the hospital once he was placed on "convalescent care" in the community. We have followed this pattern since 1960, when I transferred to Vermont, thus treating a total of about nine hundred families either with multiple family therapy in small groups or with family systems analysis of the type described earlier for the period from 1951 to 1960.

Whether one uses the smaller *lifeboat-community* type of multiple family therapy technique, or the larger *making a long trip together on a Greyhound bus* type of *family systems approach* is a matter of taste and opportunity for each therapist.

14. Can you compare successful and unsuccessful co-therapy operations?

Unsuccessful: 1. Your empathy goes to another person than does mine in a conflict, and you try to undo what I am doing.
2. You intellectualize about facts and issues

while I am trying to make the group aware of feelings and attitudes.

I point out to a person that he (or she) looks hurt — you deny it and say this is their "normal way" of looking. You and I are interchangeable — we both can commit the same error in different settings with different co-therapists.

Some therapists are so good at their craft that they feel they do not need co-therapists. Others feel that too much goes on in a group of people of families to catch all the cues (many of which are non-verbal "asides" or "unconscious responses"). A helpful co-therapist can — without hurting the process embarked upon — say, "Peter, I guess you did not react to what went on — you missed over there with Joe . . . should we not give him a chance to say what he feels?"; or he might even openly (but without hostility) disagree with something that is being done. A rude or negatively interfering therapist is not always an absolute disaster for a group, since he provides for new ways of dealing with conflict. A New York therapist and friend of mine works with married couples' groups — seventeen months, once-a-week, four couples for an hour and a half, and now recently also with family therapy with families with "battered child" problems. She thinks it is easier for such families to work while other families are present and have similar problems. She and her co-therapist like to sit next to each other and to talk openly about concurrences or disagreements about warring partners in the group. Sometimes, both she and the doctor support one partner, sometimes they express understanding for the viewpoint of the opposite sides. Both try to stay away from *issues* (and therefore do not believe in court trial "phantasies" as expressed in the paper in Masserman's *Current Psychiatric Therapies,* Vol. IX (1964)) and concentrate on feelings and attitudes. They sit next to each other and communicate by a slight touch of the hand. I have preferred, whenever possible, to sit opposite my co-therapist in the circle (as I did with Miriam Agreski, Hollis Siser, Lillian Sarno, and Madeleine Zunitch) for visual signals, although lately (with Bill Deane, Al Steady, and Jim Rice) we sometimes sit next to each other, although I feel less comfortable that way.

This New York therapist thinks that two women who like each other can work well as co-therapists together — but with married couples she likes a male therapist to help her create the image of a well-working *couple* as therapist team.

I think it is essential that the two therapists should agree about philosophy and technique. If they differ, this spells trouble for the group, who may finally decide that they are not here to help the therapists overcome their differences.

When I told my New York friend how much my groups learn about their non-verbal behavior from videotape, she felt that this was very helpful, particularly with split-screen and zoom lenses, and expert camera operators. But she pointed out that a group can learn to observe and point out to individuals (who are in the habit of saying, "Who, me?") that they look sulky or sarcastic or seductive or any other feeling — love that they may mean to disguise. It may be a good device for therapists to train group members to watch for and remark on many non-verbal signals and elicit reactions in this way.

twenty-two

network therapy

R. Speck and C. Attneave

In network therapy we assemble together all members of the kinship system, all friends and neighbors of the family, and, in fact, everyone who is of significance to the nuclear family that offers the presenting problem. In our experience, the typical middle-class urban family has the potential to assemble about forty persons for network meetings. These meetings are held in the home. Gathering the network together in one place at one time releases potent therapeutic potentials.

The assembly of the tribe in a crisis situation probably

637

had its origins in prehistoric man. Tribal meetings for healing purposes are well known in many widely varying cultures. Network therapy organizes this force in a systematic way.

When a therapy network is assembled, they meet with a team of network intervenors. It is doubtful if this type of therapy should routinely be undertaken by one person working entirely alone. The first strategy, then, is the selection of a team. Preferably they should be not fewer than two or three people who know each other well enough to have considerable trust in one another, and who have familiarity with each other's styles of relating and general behavior. Division of roles and skills is important, but not pre-ordained. A particularly happy combination is for one person to be skilled in large group situations, and able to command easily the flow of attention and energy of a network, as well as know when and how to turn it loose on itself.

The role of the leader is somewhat like that of a good discussion leader or a good theatrical director (particularly if he or she knows the Stanislavsky techniques). A sense of timing, an empathy with emotional highlights, a sense of group moods and undercurrents, and some charismatic presence are all part of the equipment that is desirable. Along with the ability to dominate, the leader must have the confidence that comes with considerable experience in handling situations and knowing human beings under stress. Equally important is the ability to efface oneself, to delegate emphatically and pointedly, and to diffuse responsibility rather than collect it for oneself. This last set of characteristics is particularly essential and often overlooked. One neophyte group commented that in their "networks" they did all the talking. By comparison, those organized by experienced teams appear deceptively to run themselves after getting started. In fact, in several instances the team has been known to leave at about eleven o'clock, and be told the next day, "We didn't even notice you'd gone until after twelve — and we kept right on talking until about one-thirty."

The other team members should also have something

of the same characteristics, and contribute special skills. If the network includes a wide range of generations, it is often helpful to have one youth and one grandparent type on the team so that mingling, and facilitating participation by many of the network, is easier to elicit and support. Also, the suppression of manic, overanxious, or inopportune comments is easier if the network member is matched in appropriate fashion and status by a team member. There are always divisions of the total network into committees, buzz sessions, or free-floating conversation. Team members can effectively help focus these small groups, with which they should blend easily.

If there are three or more team members, one will usually be selected as a scapegoat, and be telephoned or villified whenever the network or any part of it is angry at the leader or frustrated by its own impotence. This role might as well be anticipated, even though one cannot always predict before the first meeting whom the network will elect for this sacrificial position.

An important skill that needs to be present within the team is some familiarity with non-verbal encounter techniques and their impact on groups and individuals. The emphasis on the scientific, cybernated world has overlooked the importance of feelings and emotions to the extent that most rituals are omitted, or ridiculed, even while the youth of the land cry out for meaning and for some way of learning how to "feel." The non-verbal reactions of the group are not only extremely sensitive cues and clues for the intervention team, but by playing upon them and building a non-verbal network experience, a ritual function takes place. The release of tension from jumping, shouting, or screaming — the calming of a group swaying, the solidarity that comes from huddling, hand-clasping, all of these tie the network together in a way that merely meeting and talking cannot do. One often notes that if a pattern of non-verbal openers has been utilized in the first meeting, the network members feel uneasy if it is omitted at the next meeting. That newcomers or latecomers are most easily welded into the social setting via these techniques is almost self-evident if one observes the number of informal non-verbal rituals that are part of common courtesy such as offering chairs, moving over, touching, exchanging meaningful looks, etc.

Scattered in the crowd, the intervention team can respond to the leader's directions spontaneously and dramatically, catalyzing the contagion and drawing everyone into participation. If the dignified "doctor" is willing to take off his shoes and sit on the floor, or look at the ceiling and let out a rebel yell or a war-whoop, or close his eyes and sway, with the whole group looking on, then it becomes safe for the housewives and husbands, the kids and the parents, the relatives and the neighbors to do it, too.

Quick verbal and non-verbal exchanges of information are also facilitated by a team that is used to working together. The leader may need to know a piece of information, a relationship, a development of insight or resistance in some sub-section of the network. When space and organization permit, small conferences make this flow easy. The leader can also utilize the team to verify impressions, check strategy, switch roles, and just let off steam. When conditions are too crowded or the session activities do not permit personal conferences, postural and body communications are important, and the ability to break in, or to toss the ball quickly and deftly about the team, becomes more important. Network sessions last three or four hours, and leadership is strenuous. To keep optimally fresh, some spelling off, as well as a change of pace, is desirable.

It sometimes seems as though this teamwork by the professional intervenors is also fundamental as a modeling for the network. This is easily realized if one observes the activists, but the more passive members also learn that it is safe to fumble, to stick one's neck out, and to trust.

In one first network session involving a teenage drug user and his friends and family, the youth group was most reluctant to discuss openly their use and experience with various drugs, as well as their ideas about it, until the matched youth member of the team spoke up frankly about his own curiosity and experience. In challenging a peer, they found that the older generation was both interested and attentive to their views. Once the stereotyped defenses were down, the older members of the network were amazed to find themselves feeling defensive about diet pills and tranquilizers. This opening up was facilitated when the team member in their group insisted that the discussion was relevant and necessary. The leader was able to capitalize on the commonality demonstrated, instead of the confusion in role reversals, and to shift the pressures away from stereotypes about drug addictions and onto the more pertinent relationships involved. Team-member support allowed the leader to capitalize on the mirror-imaging between the generations — a task which would have been otherwise much more difficult.

GOALS OF THE INTERVENTION TEAM

Naturally the personality, physique, and "aura" of each individual denotes some of the limits of his or her role on the team. The common goal of the team is something else, and whatever the ingredients, the team must be committed to it, regardless of the division of labor.

The goal that overarches all network intervention is to stimulate, reflect, and focus the potentials within the network to solve one another's problems. By strengthening bonds, loosening binds, opening new channels, facilitating new perceptions, activating latent strengths, and helping to damp out, ventilate, or exercise pathology, the social network is enabled to become the life-sustaining community within the social matrix of each individual. This does not happen if the intervenors act like therapists toward the patients, since implicit in the therapeutic contract is delegation of responsibility for healing to the therapist, even though eventually most therapies provide a terminal phase where responsibility for self is returned to the patient or family.

The intervention team must be on guard at every turn to deflect such attempts and to keep the responsibility within the network itself. This means being able to live with one's own curiosity when the network activists gain enough confidence to take over. It means real, not pseudo, confidence in network members who know the problems and the landmarks and terrain of the distressed person's life space. They must be free to do the thinking and acting that will evolve more practical and efficient solutions than the professional could. It means the willingness of team members to be available to consult without being drawn in, and it means having sufficient clinical experience and intuition to be able to make quick and decisive judgments. Above all, it implies a shared working philosophy of faith in human beings, and a satisfaction in seeing them rise to occasions, rather than a faith in a professional mystique and a need to be central and depended upon.

If this goal and faith are part of the team's fibre, they are communicated to the network in a positive and safe manner. Even suicidal and homicidal gestures can usually be controlled and handled by the network. The professional judgment that evaluates quickly both the gesture and the network strengths is important. It takes a good deal of acumen to know when it is safe to say, "Leave him out in the rain; when he gets wet he will come in and he ought to find you drinking coffee in the kitchen, not hanging out the window whining."

We have found that in every network there are members whom we call *activists*. Network activists perceive the need for someone to take over temporarily, and they require support from the team in stepping into the breech. It takes guts on the part of a network committee of activists to sit with parents around the clock while they let their boy learn what it is like to earn his own living. It takes compassion to invite a defensive, embattled couple to dinner, a card party, or a style show and make them comfortable among guests and strangers. It takes reserves of patience to find job after job for an inept and unwilling depressed person, and to help him succeed almost in spite of himself until he finds out that he can amount to something in somebody's eyes. Moreover,

642

it takes considerable courage for most professionals to turn these responsibilities over to someone else who hasn't anything but his humanity, concern, and horse sense to guide him through the traps professionals know so well.

An experienced team knows that if they wanted to, they could take any network and shift over to individual and family therapy and be busy for the rest of their professional careers. For it is not only the index patient's distress that is dealt with; many other families and individuals in the network bring their distress to the surface, and the network deals with it. The network team, working through the activists, enables the network to begin the important human task of solving one another's problems. The ambivalence of one set of parents is resolved when they find a role dealing with parallel problems down the block. One man's need for manual labor is matched by someone else's inside track into a hideaway that is available. This is the way that society has always functioned best — whether in extended families, small communities, clans, communes, or fraternal organizations. And it is this potential within any group of forty or more people related by common concern for one another that is to be unchained by the network effect. *There is no other single goal — not cure, not treatment, but to enable people to cope and to share their strengths in coping and also in reaping enjoyments and pleasures that restore their potentials and set them up to handle the inevitable next crises of living.*

When these goals are clear, the skills needed by the team are relatively simple to define: the ability to relate to people, to sense group and sub-group moods and strengths, and to facilitate, focus, and reflect back confidence. The particular disciplines and techniques are raw materials, not prerequisites. The intervention team will blend them with experience, and use any and all when appropriate.

SEQUENCES AND PATTERNS

With experience, too, comes the sense of order to the

643

events that transpire, and a pattern falls into place. This makes it easier to work with the numbers of people involved and their sub-groupings. It makes sense of the highs and lows of the ploys and counterploys, and of the permutations behind the seemingly infinite changes each network brings to the organizational possibilities of human social relationships.

Not all of these patterns have yet been identified and explored. It is part of the fascination of network study and intervention that there are unmapped vistas, and mountains to be climbed before new ones are glimpsed. The sequences and patterning sketched here may after some years seem like the early maps of the new world that show California as an island, and connect the Great Lakes to the Western seas. Had the earlier explorers waited for the surveyors, and perhaps later the aerial photographers, before opening trade routes and establishing outposts, the wilderness would remain and the cities of Europe and the coastal plain would be even more crowded and explosive than they are now.

The assembly, or pre-network, phase has already been described. The opening session is usually considered one of a series, although on two occasions a single network meeting has been held and subsequent follow-up indicated that the network effect had productive effects (in one case persisting for well over a year). Theoretically the one-session intervention might be the ideal, but it is doubtful that it will be very often approximated when a network has to be assembled and created around the distress of an individual and his family. The experience of many religious groups who rely on the network effect of a conversion experience like a revival meeting suggests that even though this is a potent force, it has to be renewed periodically or the group falls back into fragmentation. Other groups provide for renewal at a lesser peak through family reunions, seasonal festivals, life-cycle celebrations of birth, marriage, and passage from one stage of the life cycle to the next, including death. Network intervenors need to be cognizant of this, and if possible, direct the energy of the network toward some such self-

644

recharging cycle of its own, within whatever context seems appropriate to the group.

The principal reasons for continuing meetings beyond the "tossing of the first rock into the pool" is the need for practice, learning, and insight to develop, since one trial learning is usually not very permanent or predictable. The reinforcement that comes with shared coping experiences tends to make the network a stabilized social unit that can continue to function without professional coaching. A series of six meetings seems to be satisfying to all concerned and practical, although sometimes three or four are adequate. The first session is usually one that ends on a high pitch of excitement and discovery of each other within the group. The reality of the fact that the professionals are not going to take over at some point or another is not always clear to the network at this time, and in fact the illusion of professional protection and sanction may be very important at this point to free the members of the network to explore one another more spontaneously. Hope and communication are both characteristic of this phase.

The strategy for the first session is plotted by the team on the basis of acquaintance with the problem gathered in the pre-network discussions with the family about its distress. The leader will count on quick feedback from team members of sub-groupings and moods as the network gathers. Individual team members arriving early and watching the host family and others can quickly sort out the alignments and the feelings as well as the relationships from the kinesics, the voices, and the clusterings.

New team members often ask, "What do I do?" The answer is simple: Set the example of friendly interest, open communication, and unobtrusive returns of the ball whenever anyone moves to put the professional in charge. If asked, identify yourself by name, and if pressed, by occupation or professional role. If not asked, let people assume you are another member of the network, because for the next few weeks that is what you will become. Use whatever social skills seem appropriate, establishing human contact with as many people as possible, but also do a lot of listening and observing. Locate the refreshments, the bathrooms, the cloak rooms, the kitchen, the back door, the fans, the extra chairs, the ash trays, the telephone and its extensions. Help move furniture if necessary. Get to know the people and the environment thoroughly and as quickly as possible. If there are pets, identify them and their names and dispositions. Likewise, the children. Above all, don't get caught with the team standing grouped together staring at the people like zoological specimens. Never seem to be talking at length about any interest that cannot be shared with part of the network. This is not only rude, it's destructive of morale.

Be prepared for many anxieties and much fear at the first session. Very few people will have any idea why they are there, and there will be many who are apprehensive about the distress of the family who invited them, about the risks they may be taking themselves, and about much that they have read and heard and misinterpreted about the whole profession of psychotherapy. In fact, those who have had experience in marathons or group or individual therapy may be even more wary than the completely naïve. This anxiety has its function, since, as the session relieves it, the relaxation and confidence are potent reinforcement for continuing with the network intervention model. However, the clinical skill and ability to relieve false fears and to focus feelings realistically can be important at this stage.

Once the group has gathered, the leader takes charge. He needs to introduce himself with an outline of the problem and the network methodology. This is a brief sales pitch, and like many similar openings, has impact beyond the cognitive level. Information may not be retained so much as a sense of purpose and direction.

Almost immediately after this introduction, the leader introduces encounter-sensitivity techniques. This rapidly inducts the network into what we have called a group high, where enthusiasm, activism, and polarization can break down ordinary social barriers and defenses that isolate each network member prior to the assembly. A fight for control is often noted here as the distressed person, his family, or a network member attempts not to participate. The team scattered through the group stimulates, initiates and infectiously pulls the fringers into the group. During this prelude the leader often establishes control not merely of the network, but through it, of the dissidents and distressed persons in a highly significant fashion. These non-verbal periods need not be long: three, five, ten minutes at most. But they do seem to be the first big splash into the pool that begins the realignment of network bonds and binds.

These non-verbal rituals should end with the group's feeling solidified, in contact with one another, and quiet. At this point, the leader quickly forms a structure for dialogue and discussion.

In conducting a new session the leader's sense of timing is crucial, including his ability to shift the tempo, and adapt the rate of change, introduce themes, and provide the staccato and legato punctuation that builds to crescendos of maximum impact.

In introducing dialogue, the leader shifts the members' positions to form an appropriate grouping. The physical arrangements depend on the setting, which is usually the living room and dining room of ordinary homes. Frequently, people are seated on the floor as well as on chairs, sofas, and stairways. One format that is adaptable to many such settings is the use of concentric circles.

An inner circle of six to ten people is rapidly designated, and asked to sit on the floor in the center. These are the more outgoing, often younger, members whose talk will stir up ripples and begin to polarize the group. Sometimes an outer group is designated because the older, less immediately involved, group has naturally seated themselves on the comfortable peripheral furniture. At times there is a middle group interposed by the apparent vagaries of seating and furniture arrangement. This middle group may serve as a buffer or mediator between the inner and outer groups, which will soon be polarized by the task assignments of the conductor.

647

The leader not only selects the most communicative group first, but also arranges to polarize issues by dividing along generational lines, or in some other way dramatizing the tensions and differences that exist. He sets a topic for discussion and controls the outside group to prevent interruptions. This keeps the discussion focused, with everyone promised, and later given, their turn for similarly interruption-free expression.

Often a fairly neutral, but subtly loaded question is good for a kick-off. Like, "What do you think of John?" or "How many of you have used drugs?" or "What do you think is the basic problem in this family?" No one is allowed to escape from commentary, but no one is embarrassed. Skill at giving the sanction for open expression is of paramount importance and both leader and team need to be alert to protect individuals even while encouraging openness.

The purpose of the multiple circles is to produce more intense inter-action in smaller sub-groups of six to ten persons. The forty-plus group of the assembled network is too large a group for free group discussion. Also, the advantages of multiple polarizations (within each sub-group) allow the development and syntheses of various dialectics. It is important to elicit competitive polarities with diverse opinions, and to resolve some of these. The wide range of topics discussed helps the network begin to select and focus on the major issues to be dealt with to resolve the predicament in a nuclear family. Each sub-group is given its turn to interact, with the other sub-groups instructed to not interrupt, and to listen. Later each will have a chance to criticize what has been said by the other sub-groups. An empty chair in the inner circle is an excellent device to use when there is pressure to be heard by peripheral members. If the group is large and active, two empty spaces may be placed in the inner circle. Anyone not in the focal group may take the empty chair as a signal for a chance to speak. Having spoken, he is then obliged to return to the outer group and give way to someone else. Other devices of this nature are within the repertoire of every group leader or skilled teacher who uses discussion techniques. The important thing is to get the group talking to one another rather than holding a dialogue with the professionals or rehashing old arguments among themselves.

As the discussion gets several ideas going, and some confrontations emerge, the focal group is shifted off the center stage and another group is brought forward before premature resolutions are frozen into the system. At first it appears that very little is being settled. This phase is a kind of brainstorming. The leader and team are setting the ground rules for widespread participation and much airing of opinions, suggestions, and ideas. The objective is to get out in the open misinformation that the group can correct as well as information that the group can validate.

An important rule is no polite secrets. Indeed, the professional network intervenor not only does not promise confidentiality, but he establishes the precedent that there will be none. The team helps see to it that this is carried out. At first, the reverse of the usual professional ethics seems to shock everyone. Soon the network members demonstrate their relief at being able to speak openly about things they already had observed, but couldn't deal with. "We knew you and John disagreed, but you would never let us help you understand before. . . . " "I was embarrassed after that night you drank too much at my house because you never gave me a chance to say I felt the same way. . . ." "I was angry because you didn't let me know about Aunt Minnie's funeral for three months, so I didn't think you cared. . . ."

It is quite usual for people to think that their secret fears, foibles, and worries are hidden when they are patently obvious. It is also true that often people know only half-truths about one another, when the whole picture makes far better sense. But most heartening of all is the way in which people can not only "take it" when truths and secrets are shared, but also how within a social network the resources for supportive acceptance appear, along with a common-sense, hard-headed approach to the things that need to be changed.

The sequence of polarizing, shifting and refocusing, with everybody listening is timed to end again with a restatement of a specific problem. At the end of the session buzz groups, or a free-floating refreshment and visiting period is in order. Before breaking up, the leader designates the next time to meet and sets the assignment of a specific task-oriented topic with this in mind. This is usually enough to get everyone talking and as soon as that is assured, the team exits with minimal attention to goodbyes, beyond the bare amenities, until the next meeting.

Initiating the Network Process

Consider a case in its initial phases, where decisions as to the strategy to be employed have not yet been made. A nuclear family consisting of a mother and father in their late forties, a twenty-five-year-old daughter and an eighteen-year-old-son came to the clinic for help following Jim's acute psychotic episode, during which he thought his mind was being tape-recorded and his thoughts played over the local radio stations. He also thought that the telephone system in the house was monitored by outside wires, and enlisted the aid of his parents in tracing the wiring throughout the house in a frantic effort to cut off this source of outside interference. It was fascinating to learn that the sister worked at a local radio station taping spot announcements and advertisements, and resisted the initial efforts to involve her in any family conferences.

At the first session with the whole family, an attempt was made by the intervention team to find out just what kind of help the family was looking for. Among the possibilities were hospitalization for the son, psychotherapy for the whole family conjointly, and the assembly of their loosely knit social network with an attempt at network intervention by our team. A potential goal in the minds of the team was the mobilization of a peer-supporting network that might enable Jim to move out of the house and find employment and social relationships more appropriate for his age

650

and status. The family was opposed to hospitalization, and at first resisted family therapy by using the sister's work as an excuse for all being unable to attend. They were intrigued by, but even more frightened at, the thought of network intervention, insisting that it would be impossible to assemble the forty persons we gave as the minimum number necessary. Jim began to assert himself at this point, and expressed reluctance to include his friends and peers in the same network as the parents' peers and kin.

What we are trying to communicate by this anecdote is that the resistance to any form of therapy or intervention rests on the lack of familiarity with it. One is unable to conceptualize the processes and change modalities about to be unleashed. Human beings universally resist change, and those in distress are usually most defensive in the face of a choice about whether to introduce a new element or not. If they have never heard of network intervention, the vast majority of people will want to proceed cautiously.

In fact, both the team intervenors and the patient's nuclear family nexus prefer as simple an intervention as is feasible. However, where the simple measures such as counseling, individual psychotherapy, group therapy, and family therapy have also been rejected, and where they seem inadequate to solve the family's predicaments, the potential network intervenor has to expand his own horizons and begin formulating strategies around a new theoretical base. This is essential to get himself into a network set. Once he is able to do this it is not extraordinarily difficult to guide the family into thinking about themselves and their problems in network terms. We believe that this line of thinking does not involve any difficult problem, but we underline the seemingly obvious fact that *unless one thinks in a new frame of reference,* the likelihood of the intervenor's being overwhelmed by the difficulties he perceives often prevents him from doing the obvious.

The family in question, even before actually completing their own network assembly, discussed the idea with many others. A new family called the clinic and startled the intake worker by saying, "We have a son with a problem just like Jim's, and the Jenkinses have told us about how you assemble networks to help solve it. Do you think you could do one for us?"

THE ASSEMBLY PROCESS: ADVANTAGES OF RAPID ASSEMBLY

Once again it might be well to examine the predicament, the distress, and the forces suggesting the appropriateness of network intervention. In this case a forty-two-year-old mother had four children under school age. The oldest, a girl, was not presented as having any problems. The next, a three-year-old boy, was dramatically frightening everyone: mother, siblings, baby sitters, neighbors, and kin, by grabbing knives and threatening to kill them. He appeared to be trying to avenge his father's murder, which all the children and the mother witnessed. The killing was an aftermath of a neighborhood quarrel, when a neighbor's older son (under the influence of drugs) invaded the home and stabbed the father in the presence of his family, who were watching a TV program.

The third sibling was severely damaged from birth defects affecting his central nervous system and was quite hyperactive. The last sibling, born after the father's death, was mongoloid and was in need of corrective plastic surgery.

Although the mother was not overtly depressed, she was drained of energy coping with the four small children. She had moved from her previous home because of the overwhelming associations of loss and terror. She had lost contact with many of her old friends, and had no extended kin since she grew up in foster homes. However, there were some foster sisters as potential network participants.

The usual rationales for intervention in a case of this sort involve the treatment of the mourning and loss problems of mother and child(ren), and also the search for social agencies to relieve the mother of some of the more pressing and energy-draining responsibilities in the care of defective children. One might suggest that by relieving the mother of

652

her burdens, one simply assumes them or hands them on to professionals, if one follows the sick-and-needy person model. However, a rapid assembly of the interested and able friends, neighbors, relatives, and, if indicated, agency personnel, the foster families of the past, and perhaps the church-related persons of the present, could gather a large enough group to stimulate considerable change. Presented with the predicaments, and given the responsibility to jointly participate in their solution, both mother and network members, under the stimulus of the network effect, may generate some innovative and creative solutions, support the control needed for the abreacting boy, and help the mother not only mourn but find and form new relationships. All this could be accomplished in a much more efficient and self-perpetuating fashion than the conventional assumption of professional responsibility and patient dependence.

SLOWER ASSEMBLY: ADVANTAGES AND DISADVANTAGES

Most reports of the assembly and creation of networks for therapeutic intervention deal with cases in crisis where rapid decisive action is almost without option. We recently had experience with the assembly and creation of a loosely knit social network around a nuclear family with a son who had an acute psychotic episode and was on the verge of hospitalization because of delusional ideas, erratic behavior, and family turmoil. Unique features in the network pre-assembly phase included reluctance of the family to do anything about their predicament but call and talk to the social worker for hours. They refused to relinquish control over their own situation, yet they kept asking for help. They asserted this control after accepting (hesitantly) the idea of network assembly by disregarding the instructions merely to call and invite all the people they and their son knew for a meeting at a given time and place. Instead they made a series of visits. They spent a couple of hours with each of about ten such friends telling them about the network idea and discussing their own problems. Only after several weeks of this did they get into gear and begin phoning and settling specifics of time and place.

This slow-paced use of five or six weeks to mobilize the network is unique in our experience in the assembly and creation of networks, and suggests the following hypothetical formulations:

1. Slow assembly, controlled by the rate of dissemination of information which feels most comfortable to the patient's immediate family, sets the network-effect phenomenon into operation before the large assembly. Much of the network interventive action has already occurred before the larger meeting. Assembly in this case could confirm and validate actions and perceptions already shared, and could facilitate more energy displaced in the directions already set in motion. The first actual meeting of the network might resemble a second- or third-stage meeting of a more rapidly assembled network.

2. Some danger of stasis might occur because the family has already selected out its own system from the available social matrix. In our experience the rapid assembly and creation of the network in a chaotic crisis situation seem to have the advantage of multiple foci which could be relatively easily rocked or shaken loose by various strategies in order to introduce new structures and form new relationships. The rapid assembly of social networks, within ten days or two weeks of being consulted about a crisis situation, makes up the largest number of our interventions. It is our clinical impression that more significant changes in occupation, in role performance, and in network relationships (vincula) occurred when crisis situations forced the rapid assembly of the network. However, we have not yet seen enough slow assembly cases to be sure of those speculations.

3. One related type of impasse is the danger of polarization if the immediate family controls the slower process of assembly. If the bonds of the group are knotted and tied, it is sometimes difficult for the intervenors to untangle and realign the group members. It may be that good fortune plus technique are needed to remove the constraints of the

654

central members of the group and produce the network effect. The potential violence unleashed if this procedure is successful may spill over to involve police action or other disagreeable effects.

This risk is probably particularly true if the polarization occurs around two or more groups (called clusters), whose members are closely tied to each other within the network. The intervenors are then set up for a large-scale re enactment of the classical situation when a well-meaning mediator attempts to reconcile a battling couple and gets clobbered by both of them.

4. On the positive side, however, the slow assembly process, if contact is maintained with the distressed group, allows the intervenors access to more information than is usually available when rapid assembly is utilized. In this particular case the son with the schizophrenic label revealed that he and his friends had been using a variety of drugs, including marijuana, hashish, barbiturates, amphetamines, and possibly mescaline, and LSD. Because of one of the author's experience on the psychedelic drug scene with similar cases, it gave him strong clinical hunches that the psychotic process would not be as ingrained as in cases where the use of drugs occurred in the absence of peer relationships, or in cases where drug use had not been a part of the clinical picture.

By having this information in advance, it is possible to set goals for the network assembly that include other less "loaded" areas of concern, which may enable the polarized factions to find common elements around which to re-form. These include appropriate employment for the son, who graduated from high school six months ago and is not presently motivated for either work or further education, and possibly moving the youth out of his home into a semi-structured or somewhat loosely peer-supervised living arrangement — a pad in the center of the city, for instance.

At this point in time there is simply not enough experience to provide the criteria for selecting appropriate cases for slow assembly versus rapid assembly of the network. Nor is there evidence to decisively rule either process in or out as a method of choice.

INVOCATION OF EXISTING NETWORKS

The utilization of an existing group which possesses the membership variety characteristic of a social network and invoking it rather than creating a new social structure via the assembly method is not as common. It seems applicable where minority group members depend upon tribal assemblies, or where the nuclear nexus in distress centers much of its life around some such organization as a parish, a cousin's club, a block organization, or the like. If this group provides the heterogeneity of most rapidly assembled networks, much the same processes can occur. If, however, it has factions, some of the dangers of selectivity of polarized sub-groups and stasis, as considered in relation to the slow assembly process, may occur. In either case, the usual convocation of such a group can add impetus to the network effect if properly amalgamated with the tasks of solving the distressed nexus predicament.

The technical differences often are problems of how to arrange for invoking the network. It is usually not enough for the intervenors and the nuclear family or distressed individual to agree upon the idea. One or more members of the intervention team should preferably already be known, by reputation if not personally, to be an informal center of influence or authority figure in a group to be invoked. If it is a rather formal group, at some point the priest, medicine man, club president, or other role-assigned figure will need to be consulted.

Once introduced, the intervention team needs to demonstrate a lack of desire to take over the group or to reform it, as well as mild positive empathy for its avowed goals and activities. The idea that the nexus in distress is in some way caught in a bind which prevents full utilization of the supports offered by the group calls forth some expres-

656

sion of need from the leaders for a revitalizing process of the whole group. From this point on the intervenor is on familiar ground, using his discretion in communicating confidence in the network effect's multiple impact without promising miracles.

Another difference in technique is probably the fact that some of the rituals familiar to the group have potential affect-laden charges that can be utilized in place of innovative non-verbal techniques to loosen binds, form bonds, and to stimulate growth of new vincula. Non-use of a ritual response when it is expected is also effective in developing new perceptions and awareness.

PEER NETWORKS: SPECIAL CASES

Peer networks are powerful social agencies in the contemporary culture. They seem to be an age-graded stratification phenomenon, with varying degrees of limits; probably a maximum of about a fifteen-year span is typical for older people and a narrower range for youth.

One needs first of all to recognize that they exist and are as potent a force as the multigenerational networks if they can be properly invoked to assemble. They have varying degrees of tightness, from a loose network to highly structured groups. When the generally loose-knit associations are assembled the process is much like that of the creation of a network for a family, but the actual creation of a network of peers from scratch has not been seen as feasible. Rather it seems more effective to take advantage of the natural groupings that abound.

Two natural sources of peer networks are adolescents and work associations. An example of a hippie/peer social network and its interventions was seen in the course of a long-term observation in a pad. A group of college students who had formerly been part of a fraternity formed the plexus of the network. A formal fraternity group had been broken up because of the group use of drugs, and this nucleus rented a large old Victorian home and set up a

657

commune living arrangement. Although several dropped out of college, most of them eventually graduated.

The intervenor gained access to the peer group through the development of a therapeutic relationship with one of its members when he panicked after prolonged use of LSD and other psychedelic drugs plus amphetamines. When he described his living arrangements, he was asked if we could meet with all the persons who customarily assembled in his pad, and the result was our seeing from six to twenty of his peers on typical weekly visits.

Over the course of a year we got acquainted with about a hundred youths at this pad, many of whom comprised peripheral members of the peer system of the original nexus. Some of these peripheral members were connecting links with drug-dealing networks. Others were pad crashers who were freaked out or runaways looking for a place to hide. At different times the peer network provided for one or more young persons in acute "schizophrenic crisis," who were allowed the isolation and security they needed, a chance to talk about their panic, and generally secure sub-cultural approval for the "trip" they were on in their personal distress. Network intervention in this instance was a matter of utilizing the natural setting as innovatively as the youth who had created the life-style in the first place.

By contrast, interventions with work associates as a peer network seem stiff and formal. On one occasion, the authors, together with Mrs. Jean Barr, were invited by a professional group of about one hundred and fifty persons to do a network intervention on the vincula and structure of their organization. This group seemed to have a number of problems, among them an affective tone of depression ascribed to uncertainties about the usefulness of the organization. There was also an unperceived exclusion of new members and a general fearfulness about the general political climate expressed in much small talk about the manipulations of city and county governments and the availability of funds.

The disruption of the usual seating structure, business

agenda and task orientation of the group's annual meeting loosened the habitual bonds rather quickly. Some non-verbal group process techniques furthered the evocation of more fundamental relationships stripped of formal role restrictions. The use of freely formed sub-groups who were then directed to develop a polarized dialogue, and the heightening and relaxing of tensions to prevent clear-cut crystallization, were carried out by the team during the course of a whole day during which not more than ten people dropped out or were replaced by late comers. The network session itself ended on a good high note, and the intervenors left the group with a feeling that the goals of involving the newer and younger members and revitalizing the relationships at many levels had been well-initiated.

As in the case of invoking existing networks, the invocation of professional associations, unions, service clubs, and other formal peer group networks needs to be done at the invitation of someone in executive authority. Interestingly enough, the organization itself, as well as an individual or a small group within the peer group, may be the social unit in distress, and may request help with its own predicaments. An outside intervention team is probably best utilized for this type of "therapeutic" activity, since any member of the group who could set off the network effect would probably be quickly organized into the hierarchy of the group structure or ejected by counter pressures from the threatened establishment in its resistance to change.

THE NETWORK EFFECT

Early in our experiences with various kinds of networks, we became aware of a phenomenon that seems appropriately called *the network effect*. Originally it was noted that a new process had been set in motion which had little to do with the intentions of the network intervenor. It was a bonus that in some ways made the network therapy seem more fun and more interesting, but it seemed tangential to the goal-directed tasks of therapy. Later reflection and discussion have raised some theoretical questions which strongly suggest that perhaps this network effect accounts for much of the impact of the various types of network intervention, and is an essential characteristic of social behavior in a basic and fundamental way.

This process is difficult and elusive when one tries to describe it, because it is largely non-verbal and unconscious. It might be more easily recognized removed from the therapeutic setting and examined in social settings, where it occurs spontaneously. For instance, in Preservation Hall in New Orleans, old black men from the early Dixieland era improvise and invent jazz nightly. The audience of habituées and tourists begins the evening relatively unrelated to one another, at separate tables and in couples or small groups. Under the mystical, religious, tribal, hypnotic, musical spell they become closely knit together. They sit tightly pressed. The small group boundaries dissolve. They clap, sway, beat out rhythms, and move their bodies in a united complex response. The group mood is a euphoric "high" and the conventional binds dissolve. New relationships melt away the conventional barriers of status, generation, territory, and sex. Young white women, lower-class black men, old-maid spinsters, and hippie youths recognize a mutuality and express it in gesture, contact, and verbal expression. This lasts until the musicians give out and the people leaving form some new bonds. They leave in groups they might not have ever contemplated before they came. For those brief hours they have become involved with one another and with humanity in general in new ways, with new feelings, new relationships, new bonds. However briefly, they have been a part of a social network, and they have felt its effect.

Other examples are rampant in the contemporary and historical scene. Religious revival meetings, tribal healing ceremonies, and alumni association "big game" celebrations are institutionalized examples of this process at work. Newer phenomena such as the Woodstock Festival, peace marches, civil rights activities, and revolutionary militant group meetings are contemporary examples. Although neither

660

might like to admit it, some hope of expressing this process unites the Lions Club in its group-singing climax to its regular meeting, and the Beatles with their tribal photos as a trademark on their record albums. The network effect is a "turn on" phenomenon of group interaction. Once people have made this initial change, they can never step into the same river of human relationships again.

Sometimes they try, and they indulge in all the defensive counter-maneuvers used to repress or neutralize any other strong affective experience. This produces its own resonance, and can produce counterwaves of new network effects if many people are involved. Utilizing and harnessing the network effect and steering it as it begins to move about a group is one of the essential strategies of network intervention technique. The evocation of the effect is probably one of the common strategies to the variety of interventions involving networks, and the different foci used may help evolve a typology or classification that will make discussions more meaningful.

Perhaps a metaphor will help at this point: If the water in a deep pool represents the gelatinous binding and bonding between people, the widening ripples following the fall of a large rock are the visible network effects changing the apparently solid surface and stirring the whole mass into new relationships. Counter-ripples collide as the waves reach boundaries or are drawn into eddies that pre-existed, setting up theoretically never-ending patterns. More complex patterns can be achieved quickly by skipping the rocks off the surface, or by sending a boat across or by opening a new channel. But unless something persistently stimulates the water, either by changing the boundaries or organizing new splashes, the pattern eventually subsides again, leaving the surface calm, but the specific relationships realigned.

In our clinical experience we have discovered the equivalent of all of these phenomena, and are considering the variable desirability of permanent and transient changes that can be effected. For instance: in the case of one young schizophrenic girl who was symbiotically bound to her

661

mother, activation of several network members broke through the usually reticent relationships enough for them to find her an apartment, physically move her into it, and support her through the initial phases of disorientation as the symbiotic bonds gave way to more personal ego boundaries. The ripple effects were observed as the ring-leader of this group, who had been unemployed for several months spending his time writing poetry, began to look for a job. In a matter of weeks the associated efforts had transformed him from a sloppy-looking, bitter, depressed and angry young man into a clean-cut business executive type with medium-long hair (no value judgment intended). Another member who had participated in breaking the index girl's symbiotic binds, temporarily separated from her husband, saying that she had finally found the strength to stand up to him and renegotiate the relationship. The example could be spun out to illustrate the reactions that affected employment, marital, personal, and interactional patterns in the lives of at least a dozen members of the social network over the next six or eight weeks.

It would seem that the network effect begins once members realize that they are now part of a special human cluster (group). Therapeutic intervention labels this a network and works within the newly formed associative groupings — tightening vincula (bonds), stimulating nexi (closeness), and coalescing clusters (loosening bonds that keep groups separate and functioning independently of one another and of the network). The use of this vocabulary illustrates how the professional is not immune to a strong drive observed in most groups to try to develop rules that regularize and give the new associative bonds some permanence to the network effect experience.

The members at first experience a new feeling of freedom. There are fewer rules, at least fewer formalized ones, in the new context. The network intervenors try to keep this openness, this sense of new options alive so that the network members learn for themselves how to be innovative and creative. Learning is rapid as they discard regulations which do not work or which are limiting, and begin to cherish a certain looseness of regulations which potentiates freedom. This sense of freedom, validated through shared intimate experience, is a "high," a euphoric experience which energizes the group with confidence so that they can begin to tackle their everyday problems. Partially their success is due to the fact that their problems have been redefined, by the new group culture, which strips off old labels, collapses old roles, and punctures old bags that are difficult to get out of. This last allusion is particularly apt, since the contemporary rediscovery and reapplication of this network effect in a therapeutic context belong as much to the hippies and young radicals of today as to the professionals. A never-ending parade of examples of re-invented social values and cultural forms, as well as new realities, confronts anyone who looks for it in the contemporary scene.

When we began to conceptualize in this way we began to get rid of the "sick" model for many patients, and this felt good. We also began to get rid of the "healer" model for the therapist, and this leaves one uneasy — particularly in figuring out how to collect fees for an as yet undefined service, to a new population, in intuitively defined ways. Tradition tells society what is acceptable to the majority of the group by defining what is sick. When called upon, therapists take the sick person and tell him he must become like the majority, for which the system will reward him. What hasn't always been realized in using this model is that this system needs a certain number of persons to scapegoat — to define as sick — in order to define itself. Thus if one person gets over his needs for being scapegoated he has to be replaced by someone else. An alternative left for a patient is to find that being sick is more fun, and remain chronically ill. In either case, therapists are apt to find themselves in the middle of a cybernated pegboard game in which if you press one peg sometimes two or three more pop out. Most of the time only one pops out — but only occasionally and apparently by chance do no pop-ups occur.

The network effect can scramble the cybernated peg-board, open up new feed-back connections, make everybody both an experimenter and a validator of new options. Suddenly the only acceptable and needed epithets are WOW! FANTASTIC! RIGHT ON! and *no one is sick*.

In Conclusion: Some Thoughts about Human Social Systems

In our world today, some workers in the social sciences have to become organized in their thinking about behavior and the modification of behavior in large human groups. In the McLuhan world of instant tribalization, each of us is influenced by mass behaviors — from protests to festivals. We are involved positively or negatively in the characteristics of what Abbie Hoffman has called the Woodstock Nation, or what Roszak has called the counter-culture. This has some implications of a polarization of mankind into youth and adults which may be due to a fragmentation of social networks that in the past held generations together with a sense of unity in time and space.

Youths fear the destructive potentials of the cybernated technocratic world, which they feel will lead to the imminent destruction of both man and nature. Adults, on the other hand, feel that we have an affluent and manageable system which can be exploited further to bring health, happiness, and security to the "motivated." Like it or not this is the predicament facing mankind today. Therapists need to be willing to begin to experiment and study those human group phenomena at levels which have been thought of as political during the past couple of centuries. Unless we do this, it is questionable how relevant therapy, or indeed the social sciences in general, are going to be. The culture is changing so rapidly that the old methods of intervention with individuals, families, and groups are not meeting the requirements of the situation.

Rapid social change creates identity confusion in both the adult generation and in youth. Prescribed models for

664

behavior no longer function effectively and results of actions cannot be anticipated with confidence. This is readily seen in the way youths have established radical changes in dress codes and opened up to public view many relationships that were cloaked in Victorian mystery. They have also shaken up the adults as they have demonstrated their social and political skills in large assemblies, and as they have openly challenged institutions disliked by the over-thirty generation who felt change could occur only slowly. Granting that there are many variables contributing to effectiveness, and that youths are not always successful in avoiding violence or achieving change, there is still ample evidence that they have established some forms and uses of social relationships.

Such social mutations create new tensions and precipitate distress which should not be interpreted as a new guise for old pathologies. Clinically adolescents seen today are not the same as the youth of the past two or three generations. They appear depressed and hopeless, but they admit it rather than blame themselves. They see the world situation as hopeless and they are hungry — but for dialogue, not therapy. They are suffering from real distress of the soul, and so are their parents, teachers, and peers. Intuitively they sense something more than they can express about this change.

If the psychotherapist is to maintain relationships with human beings in this predicament, if he is to be able to be of any value to relieve distress, he has to innovate.

It seems to us that the utilization of the network effect has much promise as a constructive innovation. It provides a chance for the healing of torn bonds and the gentle freeing of binds. Network intervention may be able to evoke the potential capacity of people to creatively and cooperatively solve their own problems as an antidote to the aura of depersonalized loneliness of post-industrial society.

twenty-three

~~~~~~

critique of a sacred cow

A. Scheflen and A. Ferber

Family therapists, in keeping with the values of middle-class Western culture, tend to regard the nuclear family as an inevitable and rather sacred institution. Middle-class American agencies tend to impose this social structure on people of other classes and cultures as a matter of policy. Family therapists tend to maintain the cohesion of isolated nuclear families as a matter of implicit strategy.

But the nuclear family is *not* a universal or "biological" adaptive social unit. It is a rather recent outgrowth of the industrial, urban city. In modern times, the nuclear family has tended to become isolated from the extended family and often from the larger social organization in general. When this happens, the nuclear family becomes a non-viable and maybe a pathogenic social unit — unless, for instance, economic and other circumstances are ideal.

We hope to encourage family therapists to reevaluate their position. Is it wise for them to try to maintain isolated nuclear families? We believe it is undesirable to stigmatize extended family ties as pathological. It is important to relieve families that are blaming themselves, other members of their family, and their therapists when they find that the maintenance of their nuclear unit is in difficulty. They are blaming themselves for failing to adapt to an adverse social structure.

We want very much to convince our fellow mental health professionals of our viewpoint. We want to enlist their aid in changing public policies, so as not to continue to impose nuclear family organization on people.

A Brief History of Family Forms and Their Development

Men and apes live in social groups with a relatively high constancy of membership and differentiation of role relationships within the group by age, sex, and dominance hierarchy.[1, 8] Contemporary man is the only higher primate who lives in social groups where major decisions about the behavior of himself and his intimates are made by members of the species who do not know him, and with whom he has no personal contact. We think this causes trouble. It is our contention that we remain biologically adapted to life in a face-to-face social group composed of five to a hundred individuals. In a face-to-face group, negotiations about power, sex, food, cuddling, etc., are rapid, responsive to changes in the system, and exceedingly familiar. Early man may not have liked where he stood with his brethren, but he knew exactly where he stood, and with whom. We have no clear idea about how differentiated nuclear family struc-

667

tures were in these bands of hunters and gatherers. Evidence from the rapidly disappearing contemporary cultures with hunting and gathering technology indicates a variety of forms, all of which show less differentiation of the nuclear family than contemporary industrial societies.

A dramatic change in social organization occurred during the Neolithic Revolution. Agriculture developed, animals were domesticated, and the population exploded. Larger social units started to appear. Military conquests — as opposed to skirmishes between bands of hunters — became possible. These larger social units were ruled by a pharaoh, king, or other hierarch. At this stage, much economic and social power remained in the family and face-to-face group. But considerable military, political, and economic power came to be located in impersonal and distant hierarchic structures. The family form characteristic of this stage of organization was an extended family with many sub-households of both same- and other-generation kin living within easy walking distance. The major axis of power was hierarchical, usually father-son, or less commonly, uncle-nephew.

The second and later, transition is from an extended family organization to an isolated nuclear family. According to Sjoberg,[22] nuclear family households began to appear in the urban centers of Europe in the fifteenth century. Nuclear family units had been present as a sub-unit of family groupings. These groups, consisting of fifteen to seventy-five relatives, resided under a common roof, and continue to exist to this day throughout the world outside the urban centers of Europe and the United States.

Several other social developments appeared in urban Europe at that same time. Romantic love originated in central Europe and gradually spread among the upper classes.[15] Protestantism appeared, featuring a sort of two-person relation between the individual and God. One could speculate that these cultural developments had a feature in common. There seemed cultural "mutation" toward the adoption of a smaller social unit — a unit that was basically dyadic.

668

At this period, greater attention was first paid to those we now call the mentally ill. Thousands of witches were burned. In Paris, eccentrics were institutionalized for the first time, and institutionalized psychosis thus appeared.[10] The demise of the extended family brought unmarried family members to public notice and made them public charges. This change brought a greater incidence of visible psychosis and deviancy.

The nuclear family was greatly increased by its use as a production unit, in a cottage, during industrial development. A new bourgeoisie emerged throughout Europe. To date, the isolated nuclear family remains a middle-class phenomenon, particularly in industrial America.

At first, the separate nuclear family domiciles of a clan were located close to each other. Some extended family organization was preserved, and much control was maintained over sub-units. In the eighteenth century, however, extensive migration occurred. Many nuclear family units moved to other continents. The ties of the extended family were weakened, but it still remained a common practice for the members of a family to re-establish their connections in the new world. Migrants also tended to form enclaves with close ties between kinship families of a larger clan in an ethnically homogeneous locale. The nuclear family units of such a grouping tended to live in the same block of a neighborhood, for instance, and they obtained and held housing nearby as their relatives were gradually brought from Europe. These practices are still carried out by Puerto Ricans, southern Italians, and other ethnic groups. Some peoples, Eastern European Jews, for instance, still retain the extended family cohesion by institutionalizing it in a family business.*

---

*It strikes me that what we now call "the generation gap" has been around for a while. The separation of the nuclear family from its extended family roots created a generation gap, but the distance was formalized by the establishment of a new home. And this kind of separation may have been necessary if families were to change to meet changing times. As Margaret Mead has pointed out, the mobile

The high status of the nuclear family tends to be a class matter in urban America. White Anglo-Saxon Protestants tend to live in and advocate nuclear family relationships. The W.A.S.P. tradition has long featured the ability to be mobile without ties to the extended family, though most cultures of Europe have been strongly oriented to extended family attachments. In America the people of these cultures tend to accept or aspire to isolated nuclear family units when they become acculturated and socially upwardly mobile. American Italians, American Irish, and American Eastern European Jews tend to disguise their extended family ties if they are aspiring to middle-class acceptance. But people who resist middle-class movement and mainstream acculturation still maintain extended family arrangements when they can. Well-known examples are the working-class Italians and Central Europeans, the Puerto Ricans, and the non-mainstream black Americans.

On the other hand, the mobile business and intellectual élite of the twentieth century increasingly divorce themselves from the extended family. They become proud of their ability to move to a distant city and establish a nuclear domicile with little dependence on their relatives. Since the 1940's, the Americanized version of psychodynamic thought has made a positive value of upward mobility. It has become regarded as pathological or immature to maintain ties to parents and relatives.[24]

WHY IS IT STILL HAPPENING?

Industrialization, centralization of power and informa-

---

nuclear family is an ideal unit for accommodation to rapid change. What we may be witnessing now is an acceleration of the change process, so that the split occurs *within* nuclear family units. The young don't wait to leave and set up their own homes before they rebel and strike out in new directions. Furthermore, they put a lot of pressure on the old folks to change too — or at least to confront their children's new world politics. — Napier.

tion, urbanization, and rapid rates of social change increase the number of isolated nuclear families.

Especially in the last fifty years, large numbers of persons are moving into cities from farms and towns. They are met by housing and work arrangements that favor isolated rather than extended family living. The first generation of migrants usually manages to cling together, and retain a social structure and identity more allied to the farm and the old country than to the new city. But they urge their children to become different from themselves. If the children succeed in becoming different from their parents, they become isolated. If they do not become different from their parents, they are often scorned as social failures. By the third generation, most upwardly mobile immigrants are acculturated to the urban, relatively isolated, nuclear family.

Policies formed in large, formal social organizations, in both socialist and capitalist countries, are responsible for maintaining isolated nuclear families. Armies, businesses, political and professional bureaucracies are all selfish enemies of ties to both community and extended family. These institutions are structured to maintain themselves, and are relatively impervious to feed-back from kin. Individuals are encouraged to move up or down socially without bringing their kinfolk with them. When nuclear families are moved geographically, it becomes difficult to sustain organizations with kin and community. Reward is for maximal production within the organization and minimal attention to social responsibilities outside the organization.

Profit-oriented systems probably tend to glorify the isolated nuclear family because it keeps the economy hot. Isolated nuclear family arrangements favor wasteful duplication of consumer hard goods such as cars, bathrooms, cooking facilities, houses, etc. This style of living also leads to excessive wastage and under-utilization of soft goods such as clothing and food.*

---

*The bureaucracies — military, industrial, political, and professional — that break the extended family and community roots of families can seem to serve as a kind of substitute family. They have fringe benefits,

If a nuclear family unit becomes isolated from its extended family, certain services may thereby be lost to its members. The sharing of economic burdens, help with house repairs and household tasks, and intervention in nuclear family troubles are well-known examples. Unless the nuclear family unit is wealthy enough to purchase such services or able to replace the nuclear family relationships with a network of close friends, this loss is not replaced.

Ordinarily these two ideal conditions do not obtain for the isolated nuclear family. Few families are wealthy enough to hire all of the services of an extended family. Consequently, the life style of the business élite is not economically feasible for most middle-class aspirants who try to ape it. Thus, the isolated nuclear family is likely to have three characteristic problems:

1. *The tasks now assigned to the nuclear family are too much for two parents to handle.*

The adults of a family must first of all make a living. This task is difficult enough these days. Often the father must have two or three jobs, or put in long hours, and the mother as well may have to work to keep up with the

---

and an aura of "We'll take care of you." But these organizations are under tremendous stress themselves, and the veneer of maternalism is very thin. When stress rises in the organization, the families feel it — witness reports of a soaring divorce rate in the space-flight communities when budget cutbacks began occurring. What seemed appealing to the family that joined the company — a substitute family without any of the emotional encumbrances — now turns on them. There is no real security here. What families seem to need is a kind of support network that is *noncontingent* — where you can oversleep or fail to meet your quota and they will still keep you. If young families don't want to struggle with their extended families (and I assume that middle-class families wouldn't permit businesses, etc., to break them up if they didn't want some separation from extended kin), they have to look elsewhere for support, and increasingly they seem to be forming peer-level systems, communes and cooperatives. — Napier.

standards of middle-class life. The values of the middle-class outlook demand continuous self-improvement and advancing status. So both parents may have to continue their educations, learn new skills, read trade journals, magazines, and books of the month. In addition, the ethos demands a well-rounded social life, so they must go to parties, benefits, scout and parent-teacher meetings. They must also participate in community and national affairs. And, somehow, they have to have recreational pursuits to keep in shape and hobbies to prepare for retirement.

The middle-class aspirant must be active and devoted when he is at home with his family. In marriage there is to be courtship, romantic love, orgasmic sexuality, and companionship. And one must keep the shop in order. The car, television, roof, heating system, and so on, must be maintained. Last but not least, the children are to be fed and cleaned, trained, educated, played with, and taken to educational and recreational affairs.

Marital partners are routinely unable to carry this load of activities. They nearly always try to explain their failure by blaming themselves or each other. Some of us divorce our wives, or have been divorced by them, with the hope that a partner can be found who can keep up with all these demands.

Frequently, the middle-class family seeks psychotherapy because of these failures. But the psychotherapist is a member of the present set-up, and cannot meet the demands either. In his work on the intrapsychic reasons for failure, he adds still more ideals for the individual to meet. The sense of shame or disillusionment is increased by seeing or reading about the happy, middle-class family depicted on television, in magazine articles, or at P.T.A. meetings.

We can generalize that the myths of a people are always maintained by pretending that others achieve the ideal.* It is thought unwise to let peons in on the realities, for maybe they would stop trying.

*Birdwhistell,[6] for one, described middle-class myths about the American family and gave them a perspective.

673

The isolated nuclear plan of living is also a hardship for the unmarried, divorced, widowed, and unmarriageable people who used to find residence, companionship, and usefulness in the extended family. These people are pushed into isolation by the coupling of their relatives. They are thus condemned to social isolation if they lack social skills, or to institutionalization as public charges if they are unable to live alone. These unmarried relatives are also lost to the nuclear family as a source of much-needed help with child care and other family tasks. Currently, these individuals are a disproportionate share of the customers of caretaking institutions.[9] Unmarried relatives could again become a source of much-needed help, and be cared for themselves while doing so.

2.   *The isolated nuclear family is not an adequate social unit for human satisfaction or child rearing even if its maintenance tasks can be carried out.*

The parents of some nuclear families do manage to keep up with their routine maintenance tasks. They employ services to carry out some of them, and they curtail others. But the nuclear family is too small a social unit in another sense. Alone, it cannot provide sufficient social experience for its members. According to our present concepts of child development, the mother must maintain personal contact with the infant to prevent the impairment of socialization. In addition, we believe the infant must later develop personal bonds with both parents. Still later, a child must interact with a number of older people in order to enrich his experience and make sufficient identification. At all ages, it is helpful to have more than one adult to turn to. Adults, too, require a number of bonds in order to provide important satisfactions such as nurturance, companionship, and professional relationships. There are not enough members in a nuclear family to provide this variety of bonds and experiences. This may not be as important if the members of the family have access to people outside the nuclear

674

family. However, the nuclear family limits access to others.

A variety of explanations is provided by family members who impose such limitations. The marital partners are often afraid of infidelity if they permit each other and themselves contact with adults outside the family. It is one thing to encourage a wife to seek parental satisfactions from a father-in-law, but quite another to allow one's boss or older neighbor to provide these. Many husbands seek mistresses who are nurturing and maternal, in spite of the myth that they are unfaithful in search of sexuality. On the other hand, a bind occurs if marital partners take over the parental functions for each other; the sexuality of the marital relation may be decreased.

The parents of an isolated nuclear family may find it difficult to allow outsiders to aid in maintaining their sexuality. In the extended family, the brothers and the father of a wife often tease her about sexuality. They touch her and flirt with her. To some extent these functions are taken over in middle-class society by colleagues and friends of the husband. Husbands are similarly stimulated sexually by the wives of their friends and women colleagues. While relatives are often trusted with such functions, neighbors and business colleagues are not. Thus these sexualizing activities are often curtailed by members of the isolated nuclear family.

Restrictions are often placed upon the contacts children make with outsiders. Neighbors may be members of a different religion or social class, reinforcing the fear that the child will be introduced to unacceptable ideals if he has contacts outside the home. Often the parents, socially isolated themselves, require a close interdependence with their children to keep them close at hand. In the city, parents fear that their children will be run over or beaten up if they cross the streets to another household.

Taboos against contact with non-relatives impose a serious pathological situation on the children and women of certain cultures. Puerto Rican Spanish women, for instance, do not ordinarily have social contact with non-relatives, so they become socially isolated when their husbands migrate.

They stay home alone, feel estranged in a new country, and sometimes become paranoid.[3] In our studies of families in the urban ghetto,* one of our Puerto Rican women subjects did not go out of the house or have a Puerto Rican visitor for six weeks. Her children did not leave the apartment except for the noon hour when the parish priest supervised their play in the church courtyard. Both parents were afraid of muggings and sexual assault even in the halls of the apartment house.

If the family is isolated, it tends to break down into separate and sometimes antagonistic dyads. Sometimes the parents join together and exclude the children. Such a dyad tends to become regressive.[21] Sometimes the mother forms an excluding relation with one or more of her children. The father, thereby excluded, may form a closed relationship with a favorite daughter or someone outside the family. His withdrawal from the marriage further ties the mother and the other children together. Eventually, the household consists of two or three closed relationships alienated from each other in addition to one or more totally isolated members.

Such small, closed groups tend to cause internal disorganization, and to cause close sub-group formations and/or isolation of one or more members. Psychiatrically hospitalized patients usually come from the most isolated families of a social or ethnic group.[9] [11] There is more or less agreement among psychiatric theorists that a mother-child symbiosis leads to psychopathology. In our opinion, these structural arrangements discussed above are pathogenic.

When the members of a family do not have access to outsiders, the nuclear family becomes a total institution.[12] This is often the case when a nuclear family group migrates from an extended family to an environment of relative strangers. Possibly this situation is even more restrictive in the case of ethnic groups whose people traditionally live in

---

*We place video cameras in the home and observe family behavior around the clock for weeks.

predominantly extended family arrangements, since such people are ill-prepared for life outside their extended family. An isolated nuclear family may also be cut off from the interventions which relatives traditionally make. If there is trouble in a household, relatives do not have to be consulted or asked to help (provided they are sufficiently close to know there is trouble). They come and force an intervention. They place sanctions on a parent who is not doing his job, or they help him. They intervene in a marital battle or they force a reconciliation at times of separation. Interventions like this may be unwelcome, but they are often necessary to maintain the functions of the family.

It is easier to prevent friends and neighbors from intervening. They can call upon a taboo against interfering in the affairs of another family. The parents of a household often go to great ends to maintain a public image of family efficiency, closeness, and harmony, and they train their children to do so. Adults who are socially active often avoid speaking about family problems at social gatherings — they will talk about business matters to their friends and neighbors but will not reveal failures in their roles as parents or difficulties in their family life. They do not seek advice in these matters. Concealments of this nature are very successful and give the illusion that other families are more successful in handling their problems. This further fosters greater secretiveness and isolation.*

The isolation of a nuclear family seems to induce vicious cycles that result in social isolation. Thus, certain conditions in society as a whole tend to make the nuclear family a pathogenic unit.

---

*This is an insidious process. The more isolated families become from each other, the harder it is for them to "confess" their sense of isolation and inadequacy to other families. They get no sense of a shared dilemma, no sense of stroking and help. The marital partners blame themselves first for their feelings of panic and inferiority, but soon they turn and attack each other, like rats in the classical shock-box. The stress is turned inward on other family members, and before long the family begins to break apart. — Napier.

3. *The isolated nuclear family is an ecologically unfortunate social form.*

Geographically mobile nuclear families contribute to the approaching ecological catastrophe in several ways.

These families probably have third and fourth children to keep the mother company in her increasingly isolated middle years, thus adding to a swelling population. Nuclear families consume more space, housing, automobiles, and other hard and soft goods than a larger household unit would use. This contributes to the depletion of resources and pollution of the eco-system. This high consumption may also be a result of the substitution of material things for personal relations as life's satisfactions.

Frequent changes of geographic location and close ties to large organizations prevent members of these families from becoming involved in community affairs. They often do not know their communities and their neighbors well enough to become effective and responsible citizens. This lack of power has allowed producer interests such as real-estate developers, highway construction men, and large property holders to exert local influence in a fashion that is further detrimental to the quality of life.

OFFICIAL SANCTIONS OF THE ISOLATED NUCLEAR FAMILY

Unfortunately, mental health and welfare professionals help maintain this situation. Most believe in the nuclear family. Most are members of the mainstream of middle-class culture, or aspirants to status. Accordingly, they may fail to question the basic premises of their way of life. In talking to them about the matter, we find an implicit myth that the isolated nuclear family is a biologically necessary structure as old as man. They associate dependence on the extended family with schizophrenia, immaturity, passive dependency, and an unresolved oedipus complex. They are proud of having left their parents and relatives. They view this as a matter of self-actualization and maturity for which they

678

take personal credit. They do not view separation from the extended family as something trained into them with other aspirations of middle-class mobility.*

The high evaluation of the nuclear family is often part of the ethnocentricity of middle-class theorists. Psychodynamicists sometimes view extended family cultures as somehow primitive. As a consequence "success" and the "cure" of mental illness are to be achieved by separation from the extended family. In this effort a "mothers-are-villains" tactic has become a mainstay of psychotherapy, and in general separation from the extended family is encouraged.†

So far, the mental health and welfare professionals have not taken a stand against the destruction of neighborhoods in urban renewal. They do not recognize that extended family arrangements, and network relationships which can supplement or replace these, are also destroyed. The importance of this dislocation has not been recognized by middle-class people, one-sidedly focused on the value of the nuclear family.

Welfare workers, social workers, and family therapists alike tend to sustain marriages and nuclear families. In our observations of family therapy, we have noticed that the ultimate strategy usually aims at increasing the stability of

---

*Furthermore, once a nuclear family unit has evolved a life-style that they feel is an "improvement" over their families of origin, whether gained through treatment or other ways, they may feel forced to remain isolated from them in order to protect this change, to avoid a kind of regression. Treatment of extended family networks would avoid this enforced separation. I feel that growth is a continuous process, and that it takes support from others to maintain. If the therapist is to avoid creating perpetual patients, he needs to build in support for continuing growth in extra-professional groups — extended family or peer support systems. — Napier.

†McBride[17] claims that people need more bond-servicing and stroking, not more alleged insight into what seems to be wrong with them and their present efforts. Maybe this is why the new encounter approaches and other group get-togethers which feature face-to-face and tactile contact are becoming so popular.

the nuclear family. Middle-class humanitarians and professionals act paradoxically about family cohesion. They foster the integrity of the nuclear family, which is often pathogenic or unsuccessful, while ignoring or even being hostile to the continuity of the extended family. Thus, attempts at maintaining social order are focused at only one level of social organization. Yet the maintenance of a system requires dynamic equilibrium at all levels of organization. We would hardly expect that the patient would be saved by a physician who restored the chemical equilibrium of cells while he severed the connections between organs.

All in all we are suggesting that the psychodynamicist and the middle-class welfare worker are unwittingly bringing hardship on a number of people whom they are trying to help. The problem is that they have generalized a middle-class ideal and conceived of it as a norm. Middle-class American myths about the nuclear family applied to public policies of welfare and treatment may aid in bringing down the very system these policies are intended to sustain.

WHAT CAN MIDDLE-CLASS MENTAL HEALTH PROFESSIONALS DO?

Not much. We have always provided a paid, and sometimes enduring, friendship for our customers. This has usually been useful, though sometimes we have done many useless or evil things.

Psychodynamic individual therapists tell individuals what to do to maximize the patients' own gains in their intimate and extended family networks. However, these therapists usually accept as immutable reality all social structures that the patient brings to therapy, other than the relations between himself and other individual nuclear family members.

Family therapists sometimes tell nuclear families what to do about their lives outside the nuclear family, but rarely do it for them. These therapists prefer to find "reasons"

680

within the nuclear family to explain its problems, and to write off as unchangeable (by the therapist) outside conditions.

In our society where obligatory kin ties are trivial, those with the greatest social facility create kin and friendship networks that work for them. The less socially apt become increasingly isolated and seek help from therapists or "helping" bureaucracies. Recent innovations in "therapy" have attempted to activate latent kin and friendship networks and/or use a team to do the work of an extended family network for a nuclear family.[3, 19, 23] All the aforementioned therapies are laudatory social bandages. They will bring some measure of peace, pleasure, and harmony into the lives of a few of the casualties of our social system.

Until some of the following policies of the society are changed, however, we can expect an increasing flow of troubled, isolated nuclear families and alienated individuals. These policies:

1. Reward devotion to large, formal institutions and penalize involvement in family and community;
2. Reward individual achievement and social mobility and punish devotion and social commitment to friends and family;
3. Subsidize housing that accommodates only nuclear families and destroys neighborhoods;
4. Subsidize institutions that promise to care for and rehabilitate the disabled or deviant, without doing either as effectively as a subsidy to a family might;
5. Tax all arrangements other than isolated nuclear families at much higher rates;
6. Bind decision-makers to put profit and increasing production and consumption of goods as the primary guidelines for choices.

We must change these policies!

1. ALTMAN, S. (1966), *Social Communication Among Primates.* Chicago: Univ. of Chicago Press.
2. ARIES, P. (1962), *Centuries of Childhood.* New York: Knopf.
3. AUERSWALD, E. (1968), Interdisciplinary versus ecological approach. *Fam. Proc.,* 7: 202-215.
4. BALES, R. and PARSONS, T. (1955), *Family Socialization and Interaction Process.* Glencoe, Ill.: Free Press.
5. BELL, N. and VOGEL, E. (1960), *A Modern Introduction to the Family.* New York: Free Press.
6. BIRDWHISTELL, R. (1966), The American family: some perspectives. *Psychiatry,* 29: 203-212.
7. CHRISTENSEN, H., ed. (1964), *Handbook of Marriage and the Family.* Chicago: Rand McNally.
8. DEVORE, I. (1965), *Primate Behavior: Field Studies of Monkeys and Apes.* New York: Holt, Rinehart and Winston.
9. FERBER, A., KLIGLER, D., ZWERLING, I., and MENDELSOHN, M. (1967), Current family structure: psychiatric emergencies and patient fate. *Arch. Gen. Psychiat.,* 16: 659-667.
10. FOUCAULT, M. (1965), *Madness and Civilization — A History of Insanity in the Age of Reason.* New York: Pantheon Books.
11. FRIEDMAN, A. *et al.* (1965), *Psychotherapy for the Whole Family.* New York: Springer.
12. GOFFMAN, E. (1961), *Asylums.* New York: Anchor Books.
13. GOODE, W. (1964), *The Family.* New Jersey: Prentice-Hall.
14. ——— (1963), *World Revolution and Family Problems.* London: Collier-Macmillan Ltd.
15. HUNT, M. (1959), *The Natural History of Love.* New York: Knopf.

16. KIRKPATRICK, C. (1963), *The Family as Process and Institution*. New York: Ronald Press.
17. McBRIDE, G. (1970), Personal communication.
18. MURDOCK, G. (1949), *Social Structure*. New York: Free Press.
19. RABKIN, R. See Chapter 19, this work.
20. RUSSELL, B. (1929), *Marriage and Morals*. New York: Liveright.
21. SCHEFLEN, A. (1960), Regressive one-to-one relationships. *Psychiat. Quart.*, 34:692-709.
22. SJOBERG, G. (1960), *The Industrial City, Past and Present*. New York: Free Press.
23. SPECK, R. (1969), Network therapy — a developing process. *Fam. Proc.*, 8:182-191.
24. SUSSMAN, M. (1968), *Sourcebook in Marriage and the Family*, 3rd ed., 72-95. Boston: Houghton-Mifflin.

twenty-four

families, change, and the
ecological perspective

E. Auerswald

I have been asked by those compiling this book to write a chapter on how to work with families as a change agent who uses the epistemological* base of ecology. Since one of the keynotes of the ecologist is concern with the *context* in which a phenomenon occurs, that is, broadening the field of inquiry first before narrowing the field by looking into the problem "in depth," I shall follow that sequence.

I had better begin by defining ecology, since it is a word

*In this paper, I am using the term epistemology to denote how a person or a group of persons processes information.

which was virtually unknown to most people until a couple of years ago when it suddenly burst into the limelight, and most of those who use it have not bothered to seek out its definition. They have, therefore, defined it according to their own associations, and some have defined it very narrowly indeed. Some seem to use it as a synonym for conservation, and others, the "cleanliness is next to Godliness" crowd, seem to use it to denote environmental cleanliness and aesthetic quality. Some confine its use to the study of bounded segments of the universe called eco-systems.

Yet the definition of this word, or of whatever word we choose to carry the particular denotations and connotations I have in mind, is, in my view, extraordinarily important, since the rise in usage of the word signals a revolutionary shift in the search of our species for knowledge that will contribute to its survival. Until recently, we have developed our body of knowledge, our science, on the assumption that if we can learn how to keep *individual* humans alive and healthy for longer and longer time spans, we would, in the process, insure the survival of that collection of individuals we call mankind. We have been telling ourselves that we are pretty good at this. After all, look how much longer people in some parts of the globe are now staying alive than they did in the past. But we are now discovering that our assumption is incorrect. We are discovering that simply prolonging the life and well-being of *individuals* will *not* ensure the survival of our *species*. And a by-product of this discovery is the further recognition that we are also not doing as good a job with individual survival as we thought we were, since it has become apparent that we are destroying some groups of individuals in the process of enhancing the lives of others.

Such a discovery is surely revolutionary, since it tells us that the *way* we have been thinking about man's existence is not only limited in scope, but, more fundamentally, it is *wrong*. It tells us that the epistemology of our science — at least that of our life science — has put us on a track of linear thinking that goes over a cliff.

There are very visible symptoms of this. Our cities,

constructed in a manner which reflects the old style of thought, are dying; the human support systems we call services are becoming ineffective and, worse, sometimes collectively destructive; our country is protecting our anachronistic life-style by carrying on an anachronistic war in Indochina which is incredible in its death-dealing absurdity; we are stockpiling nuclear weapons; we are ruining our physical environment. We seem hell-bent on a course of self-destruction. Yet our society, including our leaders, seems incapable of thinking of ways to change course.

What is called for is a whole new epistemology, and, in my view, the beginning organization of such a new epistemology lies in the definition of this troublesome word — ecology. Therefore, I do *not* believe that, because the meaning of the word has become so distorted in popular usage, we should abandon it for another. Doing so would avoid a dialectic that is crucial. We had better make an issue out of its definition, because we are at a point where the game we are playing is for keeps. We could be dealing our last hand.

Ecology has been defined broadly by many as the science of survival. I believe we could further define it as the study of beginnings and endings in the dynamic and changing balance of the universe. For the life sciences, then, a derivative definition might be the study of life and death in time and space. Throughout this chapter, I will be using this latter definition.

In my attempt to get us on common ground by first seeking a definition, I have implied what, by itself, is a rather pessimistic view of the chances of our species to survive. It appears pessimistic because it would seem from what I have said so far that we are in such an early phase in the development of a new way even to *think* about human problems that we will probably share the fate of the dinosaurs before we solve the problem. This has occurred because I am restricted here to words on a page, which dictates that I communicate in a linear way. I must make points in paragraphs, one after another.

The truth is, in my opinion, that we are far from lost.

686

Although a new ecological epistemology and a body of resulting theory have not been clearly stated in one place where each of us can go to be programed, they are, nevertheless, already with us, implied in a large body of theory and information which has been taking shape over the past forty years or so. Some examples of new sciences that, in my view, have relevance to an ecological epistemology are communications theory, general systems theory, cybernetics and information theory, and many others, including some for which descriptive words have yet to take shape, such as the study of territoriality, or the study of interface phenomena. Not only have we gone a long way toward the development of theory, but, thanks in a large extent to some of that very theory, we also now have the tools to work with; the technology, the hardware.

We are thus prepared to enter a whole new age which offers the exciting possibility that many of the problems that have plagued mankind for millennia can be solved. One would expect that those who have grasped these issues would be filled with hope and excitement. Instead, they are filled with pessimism and despair. Why? Because, without the support of those in positions of power, they cannot get on with the task. Instead of acquiring support, they have found themselves under attack. They have become enmeshed in a battle in which they have been unwillingly politicized, forced into arenas of conflict over political and economic ideologies.

There is a growing group of such people, coming from a large number of sociocultural and educational backgrounds, who have become convinced that political process will not produce change in the society of mankind with the rapidity necessary to prevent ecological disaster. They are attempting to escape from the trap of politicization. As ecologists, this group is convinced, furthermore, that understanding of current human problems and effective remedial action is not possible within the linear framework of any single discipline. They are currently beginning to refer to themselves as "post-disciplinary" and "post-political." In thought and action, they target on the current phenomenon

687

of rapid social change in the hope that means can be found to change social attitudes and thinking styles in those whose awareness of man's contributions to his own destruction is lacking. This line of thought has led this group into the contemplation and use of strategies and tactics for change which are based on the creation of information environments. Media ecology is a growing field, especially since closed-circuit and cable television feed-back networks have appeared on the scene with the promise that they will provide one means among others of creating change in the life view of individuals and groups. In essence, this group aims at *creating* ecologists, or at least people who think in terms of the universal ecological balance.

It is, of course, no accident that this group of middle-aged scientists finds its allies among the young. A large and growing percentage of the youth of the world have grown up in information environments created by the technological explosion. Since World War II, information input to which children are subject has been accelerating at an incredible rate, and the breadth of the field producing the messages which comprise that input has been expanding with astounding rapidity. My six-year-old son knows more about space than I do. Furthermore, he is aware of the dilemma created for his "elders" of eighteen by the prospect of being drafted and subsequently killed in an anachronistic war. I am awed by the degree to which he seems to understand the context of this issue. I have not taught him the issues involved. He has learned them in an environment in which the information is consistently present. He and my eight-year-old daughter think like ecologists. Although *I* may have contributed to *their* thinking style, I have not contributed to the same style which clearly exists in their friends, whose fathers are seldom available because they work twelve hours a day in some corporate skyscraper organization based in New York City, while their families live in suburbia. The information leading to the life view and the thought style of these youngsters enters their orbit daily through the communications media.

688

Shands[12, 13] has suggested that the process which has produced startling differences in the structure of life view, in value assignments, and in thinking styles between the pre-electronic and the electronic generations can be considered a social mutation analogous to a genetic mutation on the biological level. Indeed, if I read him correctly, he is not at all sure that one need even consider this comparison in terms of analogy, since it is likely that social and biological change will turn out to be the same process, differing only as to the vehicle carrying the messages (i.e., an RNA molecule or radio waves).[13] Be that as it may, it is apparent that many of our youth, to a growing extent, are a new breed of cat. They have seen the world from the moon. They live on spaceship earth. They are generically concerned with life and death in time and space. They are, I believe, ecologists — a few knowledgeable, most not. Although their youthful pretentions and assumptions of omniscience continue, as always, to annoy their elders, it cannot be denied that they are different. They are, I also believe, the advance guard of the generations that, if given the chance, will determine the destiny of mankind.

The poverty of our spoken and written language and the ossification of our society spring into bold relief when we recognize that we have generally been reduced to labeling these people "radicals." We use a political term to describe a group who are in ideation less primarily concerned with political ideology than they are with species survival. In his monograph "On Social Time," Gioscia[6] suggests what is to me an appropriate and more differentiated alternative. The rate of change in social systems varies markedly from system to system. Within a given social system, an individual man functions most efficiently as a sub-system when his operations, including his social behavior and thinking, are synchronous with the operations of that system. Gioscia labels the alternative state to that of synchrony as a state of achrony, and further differentiates achrony as follows: if change occurs in an individual, as sub-system, at a slower rate than in a social system he inhabits, he falls behind.

689

Supra-system and sub-system no longer are in a state of synchrony; the individual, using Gioscia's terms, is, in relation to the larger system, in a state of "anachrony." (He becomes an "anachronism.") If the individual, as sub-system, changes at a faster rate than the system he inhabits, he is, in relation to it, "ahead" of it, or in a state of "metachrony." Gioscia rounds out his space-time paradigm by defining "epichrony" as a state in which one escapes "above" time into transcendental thinking, and "catachrony" as a state in which one is weighed down by time, trapped "beneath" time and unable to cope with it. Within this paradigm it is obviously nonsensical to label all people who are meta-chronic in relation to a particular social system with a term such as "radical" that has become heavily weighted with political connotations. I submit that this is what we have done with our youth, who, to a large extent, have bought our label.

I find Shands' notion of social mutation and Gioscia's space-time paradigm extraordinarily useful in understanding a great deal of what is happening in our society today. Since we are herein concerned with families, if we wander from the social macrocosm through the looking-glass (the one-way mirror) into the microcosm of family, what, in this context, do we see?

First let's look at the so-called "middle-class" family. Intergenerational conflict in families has, of course, always existed, but the view through the mirror nowadays reveals more and more often a vignette characteristic of our day. A long-haired, bell-bottomed youngster or two or more, from the electronic generation, are sitting in a room with their parents. The parents, products of a pre-electronic world, grew up during, or in families formed in, the great depression of the 1930's. They learned a life-view leading to a life-style essentially predicated on the thesis that success in life is measured by the level of one's achievement on a vertical economic scale, or possibly one's intellectual achievement in a given professional discipline, although that achievement is also very often tied to economic status as well.

690

They define *survival* in economic status terms, and they believe in the American dream of freedom to escape from the restrictions of one economic or intellectual class by moving into another "higher" on the scale. They have integrated a set of values which includes the notion that one must protect that brand of freedom at all costs, even if it is necessary to go to war and kill other human beings to do so. Within that framework, they are usually friendly, compassionate, loving, concerned human beings in relation to those who share the framework. They are linear thinkers.

Growing numbers of their children, however, are products of the post-World War II electronic age as described above. They define survival in terms of the information environments in which *they* have grown. Most of the time, they have not experienced serious economic deprivation. The threats to their survival which stand out are war itself, of any kind, and other ecological disasters. They are ecologists. The two groups operate with a different epistemology based on different assumptions. They screen incoming information through different cognitive templates.

The content of the intrafamilial conflicts created by this situation depends to some extent on the societal expectations of each of the sexes as reflected in the attitude of the parental generations. Boys as prospective fathers, husbands, and breadwinners are expected to follow a plan designed to equip them for these roles. Boys of the electronic generation frequently will not accept their parents' plan. One boy put it this way in an exchange with his father: "Dad, you live in the halls of the Empire State Building. You spend your life climbing stairs. I don't want to live there. I want to live in the countryside, and make it beautiful. You can live your way, but let me live mine." His father's response was characteristic: "So go live there. But what's your plan? I don't really care if you don't go to college this year, but what about next year? If you don't fit in, you'll never be a success." The boy replied: "Oh, forget it! You just don't dig me at all." This exchange occurred after a series of prototypical clashes about the style of the boy's dress, the length of his hair, his seeming unconcern with planning his life and with money, and his antiwar politics.

Within Gioscia's paradigm, that boy, who did not share his father's early life experience and who thus sees only a caricature of his father's world, views his father as behind the times, an anachronism. The father does not understand and cannot integrate the boy's life view because it has emerged in a budding social system that is discontinuous with his own. He cannot view his son as avant-garde, or, in Gioscia's terms, metachronic. He judges the boy's behavior only according to his own life view. He winds up seeing him as lazy, rebellious, irresponsible, and sooner or later, sick. He is dismayed that his son has turned out to be a "radical."

Like all people, this father needs to feel that his life energies have been expended in meaningful ways in order to maintain his self-esteem. The constant subtle implication in the way the boy communicates with him that he is an anachronism who is, furthermore, rather stupid, is extraordinarily threatening. It is as if the boy implies in his every statement that his father has wasted his life, albeit unknowingly. Furthermore, most messages that flow between father and son pass in the night. Even when the words used are common to both, messages coming from either party often emanate from a context not shared by the other. The points at which father and son can touch each other through verbal and much of nonverbal communication become fewer as each tries again to touch and fails. The two become as strangers. The now famous statement by a "hard-hat" father on television that he would kill his boy rather than see him destroy the American flag, which he uses to symbolize his way of life, is more understandable in this context, and the despair of many sons, who have come to the conclusion that their fathers will never understand them, seems reasonable. Boy and father are attempting to communicate out of irreconcilable contexts. Almost every exchange creates conflict, and the mutual sense of closeness and affection they may once have shared survives only in memory.

692

There is violence at this interface, the collective expression of which has been appearing in places where affluent youth plant bombs in their fathers' edifices. They do not wish to kill the father of remembered years. They are determined, however, to destroy the social system that seems to make him an enemy. How awful it is to encounter the notion that to grow up one must accept the idea that one's once loving father is really a "pig," or, conversely, that giving a son his adulthood means allowing him to be a "radical extremist" who will, if he can, tear down his parents' world. It's much easier to decide the culprit is really the police, or the Weathermen, or the weak college presidents, or the Communists, or drugs, etc., etc. The neatest trick of all is to relegate all of this to the combined arenas of politics and medicine and to decide that all "radicals" are "sick." A saddening observation is that while youth attacks the structural symbols, their elders, responding, attack them.

Since we are concerned with whole families, let's look very briefly at other family members. Conflicts between girls of the electronic generations and their pre-electronic parents seem, in my experience, somewhat less sharply drawn probably because the socio-familial expectations are different for them. Similar communications breakdowns occur, however, usually in the areas of sexual and/or political beliefs. Fathers, as always, are less competitive with their daughters, and usually quicker to forgive than they are with their sons. But a daughter's rejection of daddy's values is sometimes more of an insult to his male narcissism than a son's. Father's anger may be more acutely intense, but he is more likely to relegate his daughter to the category of "lost woman" than he is to see her as a threat to his own integrity.

Mothers in these families vary immensely in their ability to span the troubled interface between children and fathers. However, they seem on the average a bit more able than fathers to integrate the life view of their electronic children, probably because our society does not as often expect them to be arbiters of social issues. But even if such is

693

the case, mother is often trapped between the kids and daddy, who confront her with the question, "Whose side are you on?" The roles of "understanding mother" and "faithful wife" have become increasingly difficult to maintain at one and the same time. Mother is often seen attempting unsuccessfully to reconcile the irreconcilable life views of the warring elements of her shattered family without really understanding either, and without the knowledge that they are, in the end, incompatible. This results in a state of affairs which, for some women, can be extraordinarily confusing and disorganizing. It is not uncommon for these families to seek help because mother is "cracking up." Other mothers, fearful that they will jeopardize the remaining years of their marriage, painfully choose to join the father, often accompanying their choice with an effort to help their children establish their own "autonomy" quickly and get out of the house.

The tragic outcome of these events which I have obviously generalized is that a growing generation of children, having caught but a glimpse of the future society, are left hanging developmentally in mid-air, without the supports they so badly need during their transition into adulthood. They can neither go back to a peaceful family scene, nor see clearly the fabric of the social scene into which they are moving. It is no wonder under these circumstances that a Woodstock happening can occur; that they experiment with new social systems to replace the family system as we have known it; that, since they have been labeled radicals and thus politicized, they participate collectively in revolutionary political activities that often seem stereotyped; and that, as Gioscia puts it, they choose a group of drugs which have as one of their major effects the obliteration of the sense of time and the heightening of momentary perceptual experience. No one has provided them acceptable alternatives. They are attempting to "go it alone" through trial and error in an essentially hostile or, at best, unresponsive adult environment. That a few of them have concluded that they must blow up the symbols of that environment should come as no surprise.

Within the context described above, let us take a look at so-called "lower-class" families. First of all, many lower-class families live with a style which is essentially middle-class regardless of the added difficulties produced by a low income. In many of these families the same picture described above applies. But that segment of poor families who have lived under poverty conditions over many generations and whose family life-style has been determined by the need to find bread for today and pleasure in the moment, with the result that their capacities to plan have been blunted over the years,[2] comprise a group which does not seem to be responding in the same fashion. When I look at these families, I get a sense of double vision. On first glance, I see the following: as a result of the civil rights movement and the growth of militant anti-poverty groups, most of them seem now to be focused on efforts to join the pre-electronic middle-class. They are developing their capacities to plan and their youth are more prone to be involved in militant groups whose revolutionary goals are focused on getting a slice of the pie. Conflict within these families does not seem to be as clearly a result of social mutation as it is the result of hesitancy on the part of more conservative or fearful parents to assume the militant position of their youngsters.

There are some common perceptions in the life view of the children of the chronically poor and those of the middle-class. While the children of the chronically poor are, by general life-style focused on getting bread for today and finding some fun in the moment, the children of the more affluent have chosen the same focus as a result of the conditions previously described. Both groups are actively concerned with survival in the face of perceived oppression to a degree unparalleled in the history of the United States, at least. Within Gioscia's paradigm, however, most of the children of the very poor seem anachronistic with relation to the middle-class electronic generation. They are still after

695

a higher rung on the ladder, while the electronic kids want to throw out the ladder. As time goes on, this suggests that this group may feel themselves isolated not only from the middle-class establishment, but from the electronic middle-class youth as well. The break-up of the uneasy alliance between electronic youth and disadvantaged youth can already be seen in our urban communities and on our troubled campuses.

Thus, following through with my first glance, the hope that chronically poor families will be strengthened as a socializing force seems unlikely to be realized, since if, as a group, chronically poor families do reach a point where they begin to operate as planning groups, they will be ready to join the society of middle-class families at just about the point in time when those families are disintegrating.

But, if I take a second look at the world of the poor, there is a hopeful trend developing which may undo this irony. I have written elsewhere[1, 2, 3] about the degree to which chronically poor and socially dependent families become trapped in a web of helpers, each operating out of organized helping systems constructed like windowless sky-scrapers on an empty terrain, and how the *combined* efforts of several such helping systems, operating to a large extent incommunicado one to another, can, and often do, harm such families. Although some of the leaders in the revolution of the poor have been co-opted by the linear thinking and the language of pre-electronic industrialized society, and continue to plan and promote programs based on the assumption of linear cause/effect relationships (e.g., "drug programs" for the "drug problem"), others have not. Those who have not been co-opted are usually those who themselves grew up as members of the isolated group of the chronically poor, who began their development from a position in which they were unfettered by the programming imposed on those of us who grew up in the industrialized, vertical, "skyscraper" society. When this group entered into the arena of social action, it became necessary for them to confront the complex web of social systems that had created

696

and were perpetuating the state of poverty. They became planners, and the very complexity of their task demanded a departure from linear thinking. They became, in this process, social ecologists. Their plans, like the plans of the most differentiated members of our middle-class youth, are not linear and programmatic.

What I am leading up to is that we have three groups among us: a segment of middle-class youth; a segment of the chronically poor who are mostly members of minority groups, largely black; and a group of ecologists within the older generation of scientists, who are joining in an effort to preserve our species. This coalition is, in a sense, attempting to become the "therapist" of mankind. From thence comes the quality of "a movement," or, if you will, "*the* movement." The movement (change) sought is a worldwide acceptance of the ecological way of thinking, of the new epistemology.

From a broad view of the social context within which we are currently operating, let us now look at the somewhat lesser arena of how those life-support systems we call services are delivered. Our service systems have always been constructed in ways that are based on linear cause/effect type of thinking. If we look ecologically at New York City, for example, and momentarily screen out of our vision all but the service systems, what do we see? For the most part, we see vertically organized bureaucratic pyramids standing on the city terrain like windowless skyscrapers with guards at their doors to assure that no one gets in except those who will accept help in a manner that is defined by the system inside. (In psychiatric clinics and social agencies we call the guards "intake policies.") Each, however, operates differently and each is considered a program to deal with a specific piece of human need. Inside are workers who operate according to a prescribed linear progression. Doctors, for example, follow a standardized linear procedure: get the presenting symptoms; take a history of the development of those symptoms; do a physical exam for signs of illness; get what laboratory tests are needed; make a diagnosis; treat the

697

illness diagnosed; follow-up the treatment. If the illness is one with a biological etiology, and a way of treating it is known, the person, who in that setting is no longer a person but rather a patient who belongs to a particular doctor, will get help. But woe betide the person whose symptoms result from conditions originating outside the skin, or as a result of complex life situations beyond the purview or competence of the specialist he consults.

One man I know developed headaches during a protracted fight with his wife over the ADC welfare check. Since it was sent in his wife's name, he wanted her to cash it and give the money to him to dispense so that he could visibly maintain his position as head of the household in the eyes of his children. His headaches were diagnosed by an internist, playing his linear game, as "atypical migraine." When treatment for migraine didn't work, he was sent to a psychiatrist. His son, in the meantime, as a result of the family turmoil, behaved in ways which got him scapegoated at school. He also wound up in a psychiatrist's office. The father was defined as an "obsessive-compulsive character with psychosomatic headaches." The boy became a "behavior disorder," and his removal from his family to residential treatment was recommended. Breakup of the family was prevented only because the family found some helpers who defined calls for help as ecological phenomena, and worked accordingly. It had not occurred to the helpers who thought in linear ways that a department of welfare practice which routinely allocates checks to mothers could have any relevance to the problem. That the boy was responding to family problems was understood, but the assumption was that since he was being made sick by his family, he should be out of it. Once the family problem was defined as an ecological phenomenon, four hours of work eliminated the headache and got the boy back in the groove in school.

It is not my intention to present a successful case history with this abbreviated story. I have discussed the same family elsewhere.[3] The point I wish to make is that, in order to accomplish the outcome, it was necessary that the situation be confronted by a delivery system made up of people with a mix of skills who were not locked in time and space into an appointment system in an office or into a vertical organizational and departmental system that limited the field in which they could think and act. The system that responded was a mobile team that defined the calls for help emanating from the family as ecological phenomena and proceeded in a problem-solving operation that, in the language used above, was post-disciplinary. They automatically considered the service systems themselves as ecological systems which, in this instance, were more harmful than helpful. Examples of the structure and operations of systems working this way are becoming more abundant in the literature, primarily the literature of community-based helping systems. Three excellent papers, one by Hoffman and Long,[8] one by Hoffman and Hetrick,[9] and one by Brickman,[5] come to mind.

Narrowing our sights once again, let us look very briefly at the "field" of family therapy, which in my view is currently in a state of turmoil which parallels the state of all disciplines or "fields" of knowledge, resulting from the contextual events I have tried to describe above. From the epistemological point of view, those who are interested in families of whatever configuration and in techniques of producing useful change in distressed families fall into three groups: those whose way of thinking about problems follows traditional linear epistemology; those who developed with or switched to the ecological epistemology; and those who are in transition from the former to the latter.

All three groups utilize the information that has been accumulated about how families function and how they get in trouble. All three groups "see" families. When a member of any one of the three groups enters a room to talk with a family for the first time, he will often seek much the same information and seem to behave in very similar ways. What is not visible to the observer, especially over the span of only a few such interviews, is that the information extracted is

699

being ordered differently according to the epistemological base in use by the interviewer. Interview techniques, therefore, overlap greatly, even while the conceptual contexts used by family interviewers may be totally discontinuous. This phenomenon, I believe, has been the source of much confusion among the nuclear group who have been promoting work with families. It has not really become an issue in the dialectic among family therapists to date. As a group, and I include myself in the group, we have been attempting to treat therapy as a new modality of treatment. The whole notion of modalities arose within the linear epistemology which is now being challenged. Instead of confronting the epistemological issue, we have instead looked for a common ground of experience upon which we could, by spotting differences and similarities among us, construct a theory of family therapy. We have done what we have always done; we narrowed our search by looking *into* what we are up to instead of first broadening our field by looking at the *context* in which we are doing it. As a result, we have been for awhile enamored of contrasts in our therapeutic styles, techniques, and personal theories. But, because of the contextual — especially the epistemological — issues we did not confront, we were never able to find an external boundary that would allow us to feel comfortable in our "field." I submit that we must deal with the context, or we shall continue to founder.

Finally, we can narrow our sights to the issue of technique about which I was asked to write this chapter. Most of the techniques of work with family systems *per se* about which many others have written eloquently in this book and elsewhere will be used by helpers who think and work ecologically at various points in time during work with any given family. They will be brought into the larger context at points in time when they are useful in accomplishing a particular task. Families will continue to be seen in offices during appointments, for example, when work of this kind has been shown to be clearly necessary to alleviate the distress signaled by a call for help, but only when the need

700

for such work has been clearly established during the exploration of all facets of the ecological context out of which the call arose. Other techniques, including work with individuals, will also be used from time to time in the same context. A growing set of additionally useful techniques is being developed in other arenas where the operational goal of producing change in human systems exists. Techniques of advocacy, legal maneuvering, group confrontations, and the whole technology of expanding information environments, for example, are germane to the task of the change agent concerned with families.

New techniques must and will evolve. For example, we ought to be able to construct environments using our new technology, especially media technology, that would success-fully provide for the fathers from the linear-thinking skyscraper society the integrated experiential input they need to understand the social mutation that has produced their sons and thus to reunite this alienated pair.

The work of Ross Speck[14, 15, 16] and others with networks or "tribes" is an example of an exciting new technique which is based in the ecological epistemology, and Laing's work[10, 11] with so-called "schizophrenics" is right on target.

Beyond this I have very little to say about specific tech-niques of producing change that has not been said by others elsewhere, with the possible exception of a way to structure an arena of information exchange and planning for problem-solving which I have been using for several years. I shall call it the *intersystems conference*.

The technique consists of a gathering held at the most convenient site of all members of a family who have issued a call for help, including available "extended family," pertinent friends, and representatives of each system in the family's community having an interest in the family or its members, such as teachers, welfare workers, clergymen, law enforcement officers, etc.

When all are assembled, a survey is first done as of how those present "see" the family and its "problem(s);" what they have been trying to do "for" them; and how they have

701

been trying to do it. Then an exploratory interview is done with the family and a consensus reached as to what the intrafamilial needs are. Then the thinking of the intrafamilial group is compared with that of the extrafamilial group of "helpers," discrepancies noted, and an effort made to resolve them. A plan is then constructed based on a consensus of all present as to what could resolve the defined problem(s). The plan is broken down into tasks, and the specific tasks assigned to those present most able to deliver them. Then a "chairman" of the task force is elected to act as *ad hoc* administrator in the implementation of the plan. Subsequent gatherings are held as needed for reassessment or adjustment of the plan or for information-sharing — especially when new people enter the original group as replacements or because new tasks have arisen in the process of carrying out the original ones. Several results accrue with this technique.

By exploring problem areas with the family in the presence and with the participation of representatives of all systems with an interest, common information as to the family's needs is shared by all. Useless dialogue between various people and systems resulting from discrepancies created by different vantage points is avoided.

Tasks spill out very clearly during the exploratory process and the matching of tasks and appropriate agency or person occurs almost automatically. The tendency of people in several helping arenas to assume total responsibility for meeting all the needs of a given family, even though unequipped to do so, is circumvented.

The nature of some tasks that show up as clearly desirable in the overall plan upon which consensus is reached frequently deviates in some way from what has been done to date, or from the accepted format of practice in the system within which the task assignee works. When the latter happens, the worker, who returns to his own system, must begin a dialogue there in an effort to get around attitudes, rules, and procedures that impede his effectiveness in performing the assigned task. Often such impediments are well

702

known to him and other workers in his agency, whose previous attempts to change them have ended in frustration. He now, however, goes back to his system with a task defined by others in the community. The definition of his task is no longer his own. He cannot, therefore, be challenged as easily by others in his agency since it no longer represents purely his own opinion. If he is not allowed by the system to carry out the task, and if the same task appears in enough situations in which several workers from the same organizational system are involved, pressure for changes in attitudes, policies, and procedures will build up within the system. The necessary changes will already be defined by the nature of the task. Sometimes this pressure is sufficient to produce the needed change. At the very least, it contributes another vector in the effort now growing to change the structure and operations of helping systems of all kinds to make them more responsive to the needs of those they serve.

By the election of a "chairman," an *ad hoc* administrative structure is created to administer the conduct of the plan for help agreed upon. Emphasis from that point on can be on coordinated action. There is no place in this arrangement to pass the buck.

A range of information is introduced to all present which does not allow for simple linear cause/effect type of thinking. Those present are forced to think about the issues raised in ways that are more in tune with what I have called the ecological epistemology.

As for training — "becoming a family therapist" — the best way I know to expose interested people to situations in which they will begin to think as ecologists is to throw them into an urban ghetto with the task of figuring out what to do for families in distress, while simultaneously creating an information environment for them which contains what we know about individuals and about families and other social systems, and including a view of general systems theory, cybernetics, information theory, cultural anthropology, kinesics, general ecology including social ecology, chronetics, human territoriality, and any other body of information

703

germane to the tasks they encounter, including knowledge in the use of hardware. They will, under these circumstances, either find ways of helping families, using an ecological epistemology, or they will disorganize and opt out. To avoid the latter outcome, selection of trainees from the groups I mentioned previously, who come with the ecological way of thinking built in, will prevent many headaches.

The use of video-tape feed-back is extremely useful, because it exposes the complexity of the field it plays back and allows for manipulations of information in time in ways that combat linear simplicity. Although I have not seen it done, I believe that a very useful training (and research) experience could be provided by giving a trainee portable video-tape equipment with the task of documenting the ecology of a call for help.

And as for research, suffice it to say that the vistas opened to view by the new epistemology are staggering.

In conclusion, let me make explicit the bias which comes out loud and clear in this chapter. Yes, I do believe that we all must learn to think like ecologists. My belief is born of the conviction that U Thant is probably correct when he estimates that we have at most ten years before the point of no return in our headlong rush toward extinction will be reached. If there is the slightest chance that he *is* correct, and if we cannot manage to get the parents of our day to understand the cry of their children, it is just possible that our interest in families may become, not just academic, but horribly irrelevant. While none of us has the power to change the thinking style of the world, we can by our own thinking and our everyday operations promote and contribute to such crucial change. For the sake of our children, I believe we must do so, so that they may have children, too.

〰〰〰〰〰〰〰〰〰〰〰〰〰〰〰〰〰〰〰〰〰〰〰 *References*

1. AUERSWALD, E. and NOTKIN, H. (1969), Psychosocial

services in a comprehensive health program — an ecological view. Unpublished manuscript presented at Amer. Public Health Assn. Meetings.

2. AUERSWALD, E. (1968), Interdisciplinary versus ecological approach. *Fam. Proc.*, 7:202-215.

3. —————— (1968), Changing concepts and changing models of residential treatment. In *Adolescence: Psychosocial Perspectives,* eds. G. Caplan and S. Lebovici. New York: Basic Books.

4. —————— (1968), Cognitive development and psychopathology in the urban environment. In *Children Against School: Education of the Delinquent, Disturbed, Disrupted,* ed. P. Graubard. Chicago: Jollett.

5. BRICKMAN, H. (1970), Mental health and social change. *Amer. J. of Psychiat.*, 127:413-419.

6. GIOSCIA, V. (1970), On social time. In *The Future of Time,* eds. H. Yaker, F. Cheek, and H. Osmond. New York: Doubleday.

7. —————— (In Press), *Varieties of Temporal Experience, Vol. I, TimeForm,* New York: Gordon and Breach.

8. HOFFMAN, L. and LONG, L. (1969), A systems dilemma. *Fam. Proc.,* 8:211-234.

9. HOFFMAN, L. and HETRICK, E. The Broome Street network. Unpublished manuscript.

10. LAING, R. (1970), *Knots.* New York: Pantheon.

11. —————— (1969), *Politics of the Family.* New York: Pantheon.

12. SHANDS, H., Communication and community. Unpublished manuscript.

13. —————— (1969), Integration, discipline, and the concept of shape. *Annals of the N.Y. Academy of Sciences,* 164:578-589.

14. SPECK, R. (In Press), Networks. *Angaea — An Inter. J. of Social Change.*

15. —————— (1967), Psychotherapy of the social network of a schizophrenia family. *Fam. Proc.,* 6:208-214.

16. —————— and RUEVENI, U. (1969), Network therapy: a developing concept. *Fam. Proc.* 8:182-191.

appendix
films about family therapy

T<small>ROUBLE IN THE</small> F<small>AMILY</small>

NET Film Service, U.S.A., 1965, 90 minutes, sound, black and white 16mm. motion picture.

Presents subjects from a middle-class New England family with emotional problems not unlike those of many families across the country. Bobby, their 15-year-old son, though bright and capable, was not doing well in school, and the family, under the advisement of a school guidance counselor, decided to enter family therapy. Through extensive

706

use of the one-way mirror technique, the candid reactions of the family were recorded. Scenes from nine of the thirteen actual therapy sessions are included in this film. Dr. Norman L. Paul attempts to discover the roots of this family's emotional problems and their lack of communication. As background for the therapy sessions, Dr. Nathan W. Ackerman, clinical professor of psychiatry at Columbia University, discusses the technique of family therapy with producer Harold Mayer.

For borrow or sale from: Indiana University, Audio-Visual Center, Bloomington, Indiana 47405.

THE ENEMY IN MYSELF

Excerpts from three family interviews by Dr. Nathan Ackerman over an eighteen-month period; initial and follow-up interviews after treatment by another therapist. Family includes mother, father, and two boys.

Available on rental ($25.00) from the Family Institute, 149 East 78th St., New York, N.Y. 10021.

IN AND OUT OF PSYCHOSIS

Excerpts from three family interviews by Dr. Nathan Ackerman over an eighteen-month period; initial and follow-up interviews after treatment by another therapist. Family includes, mother, father, daughter, and grandmother (briefly).

Available on rental ($25.00) from the Family Institute, 149 East 78th St., New York, N.Y. 10021.

HILLCREST FAMILY SERIES

A series of eight films — four family interviews with same family by (1) Nathan Ackerman, (2) Murray Bowen, (3) Don Jackson, and (4) Carl Whitaker; and four brief talks following each of the interviews by the above therapists. Family includes mother, father, two sons, and two daughters.

707

n be rented or bought from the Psychological Cinema
, Pennsylvania State University, University Park,
ania, 16802 for about $75.00 rental or $1895.00 sale.

A FAMILY THERAPY WITH FOLLOW-UP

Gerald Zuk, Ph.D., commenting on his handling of an
interview. The first reel (from the eighth interview with the
family) reveals elements of pathogenic relating in the family
and shows steps taken by the therapist to oppose it. Reel II
is a follow-up four months later discussing the outcome of
the therapy. Family includes mother, father, and two adolescent daughters.

Film currently available from Eastern Pennsylvania
Psychiatric Institute (EPPI), Henry Avenue and Abbottsford
Road, Philadelphia, Pa., 19129. No price has yet been set.

TWO COUPLES — TWO SESSIONS EACH

Complete one hour sound color films of the third and
fourth interviews with two couples who continue in therapy.
The couples are young, lower middle-class, anxious, and fun.
Therapist is Andrew Ferber, M.D.

The films were paid for by Hoffman LaRoche incor-
porated. They may be rented from The Family Studies
Section, Bronx State Hospital, 1500 Waters Place, Bronx,
New York 10461.

Further video-tapes and films in this series may become
available in the near future.

index

709

710

712

produce new behavior in family system, 564

training, 241

Go-between, 190

Goffman, E. (ref.), 351, 354, 364

Gordon, A., trainee report, 417

Grandparents, presence in family interview, 490

Greenhill, L.

"Making It," 507–531

relationship to book network, 20

Grolnick, Lawrence, relationship to book network, 29

Group

formation in network therapy, 644–646

high in network therapy, 646

membership in multiple family therapy, 620

process as teaching material, 246

in supervisor's seminar, 435

relation to individual, 206

Growth of family, 481

Guerin, P.

as supervisor of Spikes, J., 407–414

as supervisor of Ziegler, P., 414–416

autobiography, 100–106

lone wolf position, 397

relationship to book network, 31

report of patient, 67–69

"Study Your Own Family," 445–458

Haley, J., 41

autobiography, 113–122

"Beginning and Experienced Family Therapists," 155–167

relationship to book network, 32

systems purist, 187–188, 190–192

Hall, E. T., 357, 360, 366

Harris, Gentry, comments, 214–219

Health, flight into, 599

Hearing in communication arts, 360

Herman, Adele, relationship to book network, 35

Hierarchies and information, 632

Hierarchy, decline in current families, 41

vs. open system, 475–476

Hill, Rod, relationship to book network, 29

Hippie networks, 657

History

in family therapy, 159

of seminar development, 240–241

Home visits in multiple family therapy, 629

Homicidal gestures in network therapy, 642

Hopelessness, as a standard student posture, 584

Hospitalization, inadvisability of, 589

"How to Go Beyond the Use of Language," 272–317

"How to Succeed in Family Therapy," 544–581

Human distress, 536

explanatory models, 536

family as villain model, 538

intrapsychic model, 537

physical disease model, 536

systems model, 538

Human species, survival of, 685

Humor in family therapy, 290

Hypnosis of children by parents in normal development, 294

Identified patient, 157–159

Identity shaping

function of supervisory groups, 236

in supervision, 460–466

Idiot-expert format, 148

Impersonality of Albert Einstein College of Medicine, Psychiatric Department, 240

Incestuous longings in multiple family therapy, 625

Independence in training, 267

Individual

ideology of, 685

orientation, social Darwinism, 42

relation to group, 206

Individuation within family, 482

Indoctrination in family therapy training, 399

Induction

demonstrated in supervision, 439

of supervision into therapist-family patterns, 439

715

717

719

722

724